THE SPACES IN BETWEEN

THE SPACES IN BETWEEN

INDIGENOUS SOVEREIGNTY WITHIN THE CANADIAN STATE

TIM SCHOULS

UNIVERSITY OF TORONTO PRESS
Toronto Buffalo London

© University of Toronto Press 2024
Toronto Buffalo London
utorontopress.com

ISBN 978-1-4875-8741-3 (cloth)
ISBN 978-1-4875-8740-6 (paper)
ISBN 978-1-4875-8742-0 (EPUB)
ISBN 978-1-4875-8743-7 (PDF)

All rights reserved. The use of any part of this publication reproduced, transmitted in any form or by any means, electronic, mechanical, photocopying, recording, or otherwise, or stored in a retrieval system, without prior written consent of the publisher – or in the case of photocopying, a licence from Access Copyright, the Canadian Copyright Licensing Agency – is an infringement of the copyright law.

Library and Archives Canada Cataloguing in Publication

Title: The spaces in between : Indigenous sovereignty within the Canadian state / Tim Schouls.
Names: Schouls, Timothy A., author.
Description: Includes bibliographical references and index.
Identifiers: Canadiana (print) 20230510175 | Canadiana (ebook) 2023051040X | ISBN 9781487587406 (softcover) | ISBN 9781487587413 (hardcover) | ISBN 9781487587420 (EPUB) | ISBN 9781487587437 (PDF)
Subjects: LCSH: Indigenous peoples – Legal status, laws, etc. – Canada. | LCSH: Sovereignty. | LCSH: Self-determination, National. | LCSH: Indigenous peoples – Canada – Politics and government. | LCSH: Indigenous peoples – Canada – Government relations.
Classification: LCC KIB1832 .S36 2024 | LCC KF8210.S4 S36 2024 kfmod | DDC 323.1197/071 – dc23

Cover design: Christian Fuenfhausen
Cover image: Cover art © Mulidzas-Curtis Wilson, www.curtiswilson.ca

We welcome comments and suggestions regarding any aspect of our publications – please feel free to contact us at news@utorontopress.com or visit us at utorontopress.com.

Every effort has been made to contact copyright holders; in the event of an error or omission, please notify the publisher.

We wish to acknowledge the land on which the University of Toronto Press operates. This land is the traditional territory of the Wendat, the Anishnaabeg, the Haudenosaunee, the Métis, and the Mississaugas of the Credit First Nation.

University of Toronto Press acknowledges the financial support of the Government of Canada and the Ontario Arts Council, an agency of the Government of Ontario, for its publishing activities.

Brief Contents

Cover Artist's Statement by Mulidzas-Curtis Wilson xv

Acknowledgements xvii

Introduction: Claiming the Spaces In Between 1

1 Contending Sovereignties: Prospects for Coexistence 26

2 Identity Politics: Citizenship and Belonging 57

3 Policy: From Political Sovereignty to Colonial Subjects 97

4 Policy: Signs of a Postcolonial Reality? 137

5 The Courts: Colonialism's Constraints and Sovereignty's Opportunities 180

6 Treaties Old: Sharing Lands and Resources 224

7 Treaties New: Landed Citizenship 252

8 Self-Government: Incremental Sovereignty 291

9 Partnerships: Shared Ventures, Shared Sovereignty 327

Conclusion: Occupying the Spaces In Between 369

References 373

Index 397

Contents

Cover Artist's Statement by Mulidzas-Curtis Wilson xv

Acknowledgements xvii

Introduction: Claiming the Spaces In Between 1

Learning Objectives

Rekindling Sovereignty, the Wet'suwet'en Way

Choice of Terminology

Key Themes

SOVEREIGNTY, SELF-DETERMINATION, AND SELF-GOVERNMENT

COLONIALISM

THE SPACES IN BETWEEN

Objectives for This Book

Discussion Questions

Notes

1 Contending Sovereignties: Prospects for Coexistence 26

Learning Objectives

The Federation of Sovereign Indigenous Nations and the Chiefs of Ontario

Sovereignty in Principle: Indigenous Leaders Speak

PRE-CONTACT STANDING

PRIOR OCCUPANCY

INTERNATIONAL LAW

IS SOVEREIGNTY AN INHERENTLY WESTERN CONCEPT?

Sovereignty in Practice: Four Models

DELEGATED MODEL (MUNICIPALITY)

INHERENT MODEL (THIRD ORDER OF GOVERNMENT)

AUTONOMOUS MODEL (TREATY FEDERALISM)

INDEPENDENT MODEL (INDIGENOUS RESURGENCE)

Crossing the Divide: Building Indigenous Sovereignty Incrementally

Conclusion

Discussion Questions

Suggested Readings
Notes

2 Identity Politics: Citizenship and Belonging 57
Learning Objectives
The Membership Codes of Sandy Lake First Nation, the NunatuKavut Inuit of Labrador, and Alberta Métis Settlements
Who Are the Indigenous Peoples of Canada?
ABORIGINAL PEOPLES
INDIANS
MÉTIS
INUIT
Membership and Citizenship: Emerging Indigenous Control
The Indian Register and the Complications Created by Bill C-31
WHO QUALIFIES AS INDIAN?
BILL C-31 (1985)
PROBLEMS CREATED BY BILL C-31
Who Can Call Themselves Indigenous? The Case of Joseph Boyden
Incremental Sovereignty Illustrated: The Qalipu Mi'kmaq First Nation
Conclusion
Discussion Questions
Suggested Readings
Notes

3 Policy: From Political Sovereignty to Colonial Subjects 97
Learning Objectives
A Remarkable Speech to the United Nations General Assembly
Indigenous Nations: Pre-contact Sovereigns
Indigenous Sovereignty Constrained: The Early Pre-Confederation Era
THE DOCTRINE OF DISCOVERY AND *TERRA NULLIUS*
THE ROYAL PROCLAMATION OF 1763 AND THE TREATY OF NIAGARA OF 1764
Indigenous Sovereignty Denied: Later Pre-Confederation and Post-Confederation Policy
THE *INDIAN ACT*
THE RESERVE SYSTEM
IMPOSED SYSTEM OF BAND GOVERNANCE
RESIDENTIAL SCHOOLS
Indian Act Amendments
The Gendered Dynamics of Colonialism

Conclusion
Discussion Questions
Suggested Readings
Notes

4 Policy: Signs of a Postcolonial Reality? 137
Learning Objectives
Sovereignty Re-emerging: Post-1969 Indigenous Ambitions
Post–World War II Indigenous Activism
The 1969 White Paper and the 1970 Citizens Plus Response
The 1973 *Calder* Decision and the Launch of the Comprehensive and Specific Claims Process
CALDER DECISION (1973)
COMPREHENSIVE CLAIMS
SPECIFIC CLAIMS
CRITICISMS
POSITIVE DEVELOPMENTS
Section 35 of the *Constitution Act, 1982*
The 1995 Inherent Right to Self-Government Policy
The 2005 Kelowna Accord
The Justin Trudeau Liberal Government's 2015–21 Policy "Reset"
Conclusion
Discussion Questions
Suggested Readings
Notes

5 The Courts: Colonialism's Constraints and Sovereignty's Opportunities 180
Learning Objectives
Case Study: Landmark Ruling Affirms Tŝilhqot'in Nation Holds Aboriginal Title
The Supreme Court of Canada Speaks
Aboriginal Rights
R. v. SPARROW (1990)
R. v. VAN DER PEET (1996)
R. v. GLADSTONE (1996)
R. v. PAMAJEWON (1996)
R. v. POWLEY (2003)
IMPLICATIONS AND ANALYSIS
Aboriginal Title
ST. CATHERINE'S MILLING AND LUMBER CO. v. THE QUEEN (1888)

CALDER ET AL. v. THE ATTORNEY GENERAL OF BRITISH COLUMBIA (1973)
GUERIN v. THE QUEEN (1984)
DELGAMUUKW v. BRITISH COLUMBIA (1997)
TSILHQOT'IN v. BRITISH COLUMBIA (2014)
IMPLICATIONS AND ANALYSIS
Aboriginal Treaty Rights
WHITE AND BOB (1965), *SIMON* (1985), *AND SIOUI* (1990)
R. v. MARSHALL (1999)
R. v. MARSHALL; R. v. BERNARD (2005)
IMPLICATIONS AND ANALYSIS
Duty to Consult and Accommodate
HAIDA NATION v. BRITISH COLUMBIA (2004)
TAKU RIVER TLINGIT FIRST NATION v. BRITISH COLUMBIA (2004)
MIKISEW CREE FIRST NATION v. CANADA (MINISTER OF CANADIAN HERITAGE) (2005)
REQUIRED STEPS IN THE DUTY TO CONSULT
CHIPPEWAS OF THE THAMES FIRST NATION v. ENBRIDGE PIPELINES INC. (2017)
CLYDE RIVER (HAMLET) v. PETROLEUM GEO-SERVICES INC. (2017)
IMPLICATIONS AND ANALYSIS
Sovereignty's Opportunities
Conclusion
Discussion Questions
Suggested Readings
Notes

6 Treaties Old: Sharing Lands and Resources 224
Learning Objectives
Case Study: Treaties Absent, 1921–73
Treaty Peoples and Treaty Nations: Differing Perspectives
The Numbered Treaties
TREATY 1 (1871)
TREATY 4 (1874)
CONFLICTING VERSIONS AND INTENTIONS
Historical Treaties and Options for Indigenous Sovereignty
THE COURTS AND TREATY RIGHTS
SPECIFIC CLAIMS POLICY
THE TREATY LAND ENTITLEMENT PROCESS
Conclusion

Discussion Questions
Suggested Readings
Notes

7 Treaties New: Landed Citizenship 252
Learning Objectives
Into the Contemporary Era
THE COMPREHENSIVE CLAIMS PROCESS
THE BRITISH COLUMBIA TREATY PROCESS
CONFLICTING OBJECTIVES
Modern Treaties as a Means to Canadian State Control
EXTINGUISHED, MODIFIED, OR NON-ASSERTED RIGHTS
LAND
RESOURCES
CASH
SELF-GOVERNMENT
Modern Treaties as a Means to Restored Indigenous Sovereignty
CONSTITUTIONAL PROTECTION
RECOGNITION OF ABORIGINAL TITLE
ACCESS TO RESOURCES
ENHANCED POLITICAL POWER
ONGOING CHALLENGES
Case Study: Two Modern Treaties in Action
THE *NUNAVUT LAND CLAIMS AGREEMENT*
THE ALGONQUINS OF ONTARIO AGREEMENT-IN-PRINCIPLE
IMPLICATIONS AND ANALYSIS
Conclusion
Discussion Questions
Suggested Readings
Notes

8 Self-Government: Incremental Sovereignty 291
Learning Objectives
Band Governance
THE SQUAMISH NATION (BC)
Legislated Self-Government Agreements
THE SIOUX VALLEY DAKOTA NATION (MANITOBA)
THE MÉTIS NATION OF ALBERTA

Treaty Self-Government Agreements
THE KLUANE FIRST NATION (YUKON)
Sovereigntist Positions
THE MOHAWK OF KAHNAWÀ:KE (QUEBEC)
The Priority of Treaty Federalism?
The Gendered Dynamics of Power
Conclusion
Discussion Questions
Suggested Readings
Notes

9 Partnerships: Shared Ventures, Shared Sovereignty 327
Learning Objectives
Setting the Stage: The Truth and Reconciliation Commission's Calls to Action #43 and #45
Resolving Claims, Restoring Resources: Incremental Treaty Agreements
Consulting Indigenous Stakeholders: Accommodating Indigenous Interests
UNDRIP AND THE PRINCIPLE OF "FREE, PRIOR, AND INFORMED CONSENT"
CONSENT AND PRIVATE CONSULTATION PRACTICES
IMPACT AND BENEFIT AGREEMENTS
CRITICISMS AND CONFLICTS
BENEFITS
VOISEY'S BAY
EAST WEST TIE TRANSMISSION LINE
VANCOUVER INTERNATIONAL AIRPORT
TRANS MOUNTAIN PIPELINE
Indigenous Nations and Joint Economic Initiatives
THE MEMBERTOU FIRST NATION (CAPE BRETON, NOVA SCOTIA)
THE MUSKEG LAKE CREE NATION (SASKATCHEWAN)
THE OSOYOOS INDIAN BAND (BRITISH COLUMBIA)
Co-management Initiatives
LAND USE PLANNING AND PARKS
Haida Gwaii
Tahltan Nation
Mi'kmaq of Nova Scotia
Dehcho First Nations
NATIONAL INDIGENOUS GUARDIAN NETWORK
WILDLIFE MANAGEMENT, FISHERIES, AND COASTAL CONSERVATION
Haudenosaunee

Nunavut Wildlife Management Board
Nisga'a
Pacific North Coast of British Columbia
IMPLICATIONS AND ANALYSIS
Conclusion
Discussion Questions
Suggested Readings
Notes

Conclusion: Occupying the Spaces In Between 369

References 373
Index 397

Cover Artist's Statement

THE CANADIAN NATIVE FLAG

Throughout my life, I have come to learn all the different relationships, interactions, hardships, and struggles that First Nations people have faced in this country. This history goes back to time immemorial, and there have been many negative impacts on both sides. I am a person who always tries to see the glass half full, and even with all the difficult situations we have faced, I still love the country I live in and am proud to call myself a Canadian … and First Nations Canadian. I wanted to create a design that represents both my cultural heritage and the country in which I live.

The design within the maple leaf is a head of a killer whale in the shape of an oval. The killer whale head is surrounded by some traditional designs called split "U" shapes.

The two designs on the red side bands are K'utala-Salmon. Salmon seemed the perfect way to convey the importance of family, friendships, and strength in numbers. There are as many types of people living here in Canada as there are types of salmon. I would like to see us coming together in the future, not only my First Nations people, but all of Canada.

Salmon are known for dependability and renewal. Kwakwaka'wakw people think of them as a provider and a symbol of fertility and good health. The salmon is the source of life for our people, and we depend on the salmon as our main food source in the past, present, and hopefully the future.

Mulidzas-Curtis Wilson,
www.curtiswilson.ca

Acknowledgements

This book grew organically out of a university course I crafted in response to a lifetime of research, writing, teaching, and conversations on Indigenous issues in Canada. While I may have been the one to animate this project, a chorus of voices accompanied me along the way, lending to me their knowledge, perspectives, critique, and gentle but insistent corrections. As such, the imprint of many hands can be found within its pages and for that I am truly grateful.

Core support for this project came to me from encounters over many hours with students, elders, and faculty members who seek community within the inspirational setting of Capilano University's Kéxwusm-áyakn Student Centre. It was here that I derived much insight, critical perspectives, and support from elders such as Latash and Ernie George, faculty colleagues such as David Kirk and Clay Little, and from the many Indigenous students arriving from points all across this beautiful land now called Canada and who chose, for a time, to call Capilano their university home. Inspiration also came to me by way of the many Indigenous persons who so generously gave of their time to share their ideas and experiences in my classes. In particular I wish to thank Kory Wilson, Jody Wilson-Raybould, Syexwáliya Ann Whonnock, Leah George, Glen Coulthard, Ernie George, Valerie Cross, and Bruce McIvor.

To Capilano University I extend heartfelt thanks for providing me with the supportive academic environment I needed to develop my initially tentative ideas into what eventually became the core of this book. This book would simply never have gotten off the ground had it not been for the sabbatical oasis given to me by my university through the 2017–8 academic year. The strength of what was eventually to become my successful bid for a sabbatical was lent substantive weight by crucial letters of endorsement provided by then dean of the Faculty of Arts and Sciences, Julia Denholm, and colleagues Ed Lavalle and David Kirk. Thank you to all involved in Capilano University's sabbatical adjudication process for believing in this project.

Having trusted colleagues who provide a context for probing academic engagement, a rigorous exchange of ideas, and gentle offerings of encouragement, is essential to the venture of research and writing. On this score, I am the recipient of an abundance of riches. In the School of Social Sciences, I wish to thank in particular, Cheryl Schreader, Charles Greenberg, Gillian Crowther, Maureen Bracewell, Bob Muckle, Rita Isola, Graham Cook, Nigel Amon, Robert Campbell, Sean Ashley, and Sandra Cooper. Thanks for always being in my corner, offering words of encouragement, tips on strategy, and also when needed, aid in attending to wounds. To my colleagues in political science, I owe a special debt of gratitude. To those since retired, such as Paul Tennant, Ed Lavalle, Cam Sylvester, and David Winchester, thank you for setting me on my way. For those still with me or more newly acquired, such as Hamish Telford, Ramjee Parajulee, David Matijasevich, and Michael Laurence, thank you for steadfast companionship offered in our quest to render the political world intelligible to both ourselves and our students. I reserve a special word of thanks to my dear colleague Paul Mier, a companion in all things political and life. Thank you for being such a good friend to me in the deepest sense of the word.

To the four anonymous reviewers who worked so hard to make my initial manuscript into something worthy of entering the public domain, I extend a heartfelt thank you. Your incisive comments and criticism showed me where, and in what ways, I could add much needed texture, nuance, sophistication, and depth to the analysis. Thank you also to Mat Buntin, Marilyn McCormack, Stephen Jones, Rebecca Duce, Janice Evans, Leanne Rancourt, and all those at the University of Toronto Press for seeing this project through the production process to completion. Your generous extension of encouragement, editorial advice, and good cheer were resources that I confidently and repeatedly came to rely on.

To my family who love and support me in so many ways, including when writing a book, I say: I could not have done it without you. Thank you to my parents, Peter and Jeanette, and to my sisters and their spouses, Lynn and Marc, and Michelle and Tim for regularly reminding me that it is time for a walk, or dinner, or a holiday, together. Thanks also to my children and their partners, Emma (and Andrew), Darren (and Sandra), and Adrian (and Daniella), who fill my heart with joy. To be in your company is to experience the very best that life has to offer. To Emma and Andrew, I am additionally grateful for bringing the beauty of children back into my life. To Zoey and Griffin, I say thank you for helping me rediscover how to play.

Finally, my greatest debt and heartfelt thanks goes to my life partner, Rita. You have stood by me and loved me through every opportunity as well as every challenge and hardship presented by this adventure called life. With gratitude, it is to you that I dedicate this work.

INTRODUCTION

Claiming the Spaces In Between

LEARNING OBJECTIVES

1. To explain why sovereignty matters to Indigenous peoples.
2. To distinguish between self-determination, self-government, and sovereignty and to explain how each informs the rights of Indigenous peoples.
3. To assess whether Canada is moving into a postcolonial period in its relations with Indigenous peoples.
4. To identify in what ways Indigenous rights serve to challenge the legitimacy of the Canadian state.

Indigenous peoples have long struggled to define their political status in relation to the Canadian state. Over the course of this difficult journey, Indigenous peoples have consistently striven to establish their rights as distinct political communities entitled to decide their own destiny free from external political interference. Views concerning the success of Indigenous efforts are naturally varied. Some are convinced that Canada is increasingly coming to terms with its colonial past and is making significant progress on Indigenous issues. For example, the proposition that Indigenous peoples have a right to self-determination is now broadly accepted among the global community of states, including Canada. It is this right to self-determination that informs the

46 articles of the **United Nations Declaration on the Rights of Indigenous Peoples**, which Canada fully endorsed in 2010. Prime Minister Justin Trudeau subsequently promised in 2015 that the Canadian state would conduct relations with Indigenous communities on a nation-to-nation basis and that it would establish a reconciliation framework premised on the recognition of Indigenous rights and full implementation of the articles in the UN's Declaration.[1] Further developments have since followed, including a pledge to implement all 94 of the **Truth and Reconciliation Commission's Calls to Action**, a promise to establish a new fiscal relationship with Indigenous nations, and a commitment to an effective and meaningful national action plan in response to the 231 Calls to Justice contained within the **Final Report of the National Inquiry into Missing and Murdered Indigenous Women and Girls.**[2] Taken together, these initiatives suggest to some that Canada is now "moving into a postcolonial period" (Wilson-Raybould 2019, 17).[3]

From the perspective of others, however, prospects for the fulfillment of the Indigenous right to self-determination are regarded far more skeptically. They point to ongoing conditions that perpetuate illegitimate Canadian state control over the identities, political standing, ancestral lands, and life prospects of Indigenous peoples. This experience of control is informed by what Jody Wilson-Raybould identifies as "a longstanding pattern in Canadian history of denying Indigenous peoples and their rights" (Wilson-Raybould 2019, 170). Among the experiences of denial that she identifies as particularly damaging are "the passage and imposition of the ***Indian Act***, the establishment of residential schools, efforts to eradicate Indigenous cultures and languages, the alienation of Indigenous peoples from their homelands and territories, and the lack of implementation of the treaties, or the failure to complete them altogether" (Wilson-Raybould 2019, 170). So, while Canada may well be on the cusp of a postcolonial period, an unsettling parallel reality must also be confronted. The impacts of Canada's colonial history run incredibly deep, and according to some are still perpetuated in multiple forms of violence against Indigenous peoples that cause them real damage into the present day.

It should therefore come as no surprise that when Canada celebrated its 150th birthday on July 1, 2017, Indigenous peoples' responses were rather mixed. Canada's achievements were celebrated, much stock being put in the 1867 ***Act of Confederation***, Canada's commitment to multiculturalism and to its protection of a robust set of individual rights, Canada's provision of good jobs and excellent health care to the vast majority of its citizens, and Canada's role in the world as a promoter of global peace. But for many Indigenous people Canada's 150th anniversary did not carry the same celebratory tone. Six Indigenous scholars shared their views of Canada at 150 in the *University Affairs Newsletter* of June 7, 2017 (MacDonald 2017).[4] They said that for them and their people, Canada represents 150 years of oppression. What is worth celebrating, therefore, is not Canada's accomplishments but rather Indigenous peoples' "history of resistance, resilience, resurgence, and restoration." The six scholars conclude that if Canada is to be a country worthy of celebrating, Indigenous and non-Indigenous Canadians must resolve to work together to fix "what was broken." For them, national reconciliation is the framework that ought to guide Canada's commemoration, a reconciliation that includes a commitment to "a renewal of our treaty relationship, a recognition of Indigenous sovereignty and self-determination, and a renewed nation-to-nation relationship" (MacDonald 2017). If the prognosis of these six Indigenous scholars is accurate, then it would seem that the vital work of decolonizing relations between Canada and Indigenous peoples is far more complex and challenging than many might have first thought.

In this book I rely heavily on the concept **sovereignty** and the metaphor of the **spaces in between** to describe various features of the Indigenous decolonization project in Canada. It is important, therefore, to define both from the outset, although I will return to each repeatedly, defining their meaning further as we encounter different manifestations of each throughout the various chapters of this book. Suffice it to say for now that when I refer to "sovereignty," I take it to mean to have ultimate authority and final decision-making power over a specific population and territory (Frideres 2020, 204; Nadasdy 2017, 11–12, 38–45). A sovereign people are those who are self-defining in all matters essential to their way of life, including belief systems, social organization, cultural expression, political decisions, relationship to territories, and development of resources (Simpson 2014, 10, 141; McNeil 2016, 100). Furthermore, and importantly for my purposes, sovereignty carries with it the expectation that those who enjoy it do so because they are recognized to be autonomous political actors to whom a duty of non-interference is owed. That is, a sovereign people are those who exercise political authority and decision-making power over a specific population and territory to the exclusion of all others.

Sovereignty, based on this definition, is the political context in which many Indigenous peoples claim to have an ongoing right to live. Indigenous peoples regularly point out that their nations were sovereign in the pre-colonial period. Moreover, the fact that French, British, and later Canadian governmental authorities simply assumed that they had the right to assert sovereignty over Indigenous nations and their territories did not somehow thereby magically wipe Indigenous sovereignty out. Many Indigenous peoples say that all this assertion did was impose a form of illegitimate foreign rule upon Indigenous peoples. No one disputes the fact that the imposition of colonial rule has served to curtail, constrain, regulate, and appropriate Indigenous sovereignty. But what many Indigenous peoples generally do not accept is the proposition that their sovereignty was thereby extinguished (Green 2014a, 5; RCAP 1996c, 202). Indeed, it is not unusual to encounter Indigenous people today who say that their sovereignty remains intact, it is real, and, in the words of Audra Simpson, "should be upheld and understood robustly" (Simpson 2011, 211).

It therefore makes perfect sense that this concept of sovereignty would also often be deployed in connection to the political aspirations of Indigenous peoples in the contemporary era.[5] As Joanne Barker observes, it is a term around which many Indigenous peoples have mobilized efforts "to reverse ongoing experiences of colonialism as well as to signify local efforts at the reclamation of specific territories, resources, governments, and cultural knowledge and practices" (Barker 2005, 1; see also Nadasdy 2017, 48–87).[6] Demonstrating precisely how so and in what ways this concept has served as a political tool for Indigenous people to open up space for their own emancipation in their relations with the Canadian government is a central objective of this book.

I shall also regularly invoke the metaphor of "the spaces in between" to describe various features of the Indigenous emancipation project within Canada. The contention of this book will be that while Canada maintains its position of dominance with respect to the exercise of state sovereignty, Indigenous nations have nevertheless managed to carve out and reclaim areas of significant political power from the Canadian state as their own. By means of strategically acquired legal concessions, often at the level of the Supreme Court of Canada, hard-fought political negotiations, and sometimes through simple declarations of intent, Indigenous nations have managed to compel the Canadian state to roll back its extension of jurisdiction over them, and in doing so have enhanced their prospects for political sovereignty within Canada. As such, they have increasingly come to occupy what I will metaphorically refer to as "the spaces in between" – that is, spaces for the expression of Indigenous sovereignty within the framework of Canadian sovereignty. It is to this dynamic of Indigenous resistance to colonialism and associated paths toward more edifying Indigenous–Canadian state relations that this book will constantly return. To get us thinking about what is at stake in using the language of sovereignty and "the spaces in between" to both confront and eliminate sources of Indigenous colonial oppression, consider the following story.

REKINDLING SOVEREIGNTY, THE WET'SUWET'EN WAY

A $6.2 billion Coastal Gaslink pipeline project, proposed in 2012 and approved by the Government of British Columbia in October 2018, is scheduled to run for approximately 670 kilometres across BC from Dawson Creek to Kitimat, the site of LNG Canada's massive liquid natural gas export facility now under construction. Its planned path is through the Wet'suwet'en peoples' traditional territory, which brought on an intractable dispute.

Provincial approval for the pipeline was contingent, in part, on LNG Canada and Coastal GasLink successfully negotiating impact and benefits agreements with the 20 plus First Nations affected by the development. Typically, such agreements provide guarantees of construction jobs to local First Nations in the short term and assurances that a share of the millions of dollars generated by the project will be transferred to the First Nations in the longer term. By the end of 2018, impact and benefits agreements had been successfully negotiated and signed with the elected band councils of all First Nations along the pipeline route, including the six band councils that make up the Wet'suwet'en Nation.

At the same time, however, since 2010, members of the Unist'ot'en clan of the Wet'suwet'en Nation have occupied a camp dedicated to defending the land against the construction of pipelines through the nation's 22,000 square kilometres of traditional territory.[7] They say that pipelines will endanger the natural environment and its resources and unduly restrict members' access to their ancestral lands (Saltman 2019, A8). The problem from the perspective of many of the Unist'ot'en clan members (and others within the nation) is that while TransCanada was able to secure agreements with the elected band councils of all 20 First Nations along the route, including the six Wet'suwet'en band councils, it had failed to consult and to secure agreement from the nation's hereditary chiefs.[8] They hold that as creatures of the federal *Indian Act,* the jurisdiction of the band councils extend to the borders of the nation's reserve lands but no further. They also point out that under traditional Wet'suwet'en law, it is the pre-existing hereditary system that is the legitimate source of sovereign authority over all political, social, and economic activity that occurs on the 22,000 square kilometres of the Wet'suwet'en Nation's traditional territories. Consequently, it is the hereditary system and not the band council that is entitled to exercise decision-making authority over all matters that have an impact beyond reserve borders, including pipelines. These critics insist that neither elected band council nor Canadian governmental authority has jurisdiction over the traditional Wet'suwet'en territories for they have not been granted such political power under Wet'suwet'en traditional laws (Smart 2019b, A5; Penner 2019, A6).

The position of the Wet'suwet'en band councillors, however, is quite different. They argue that their authority operates independently from that of the hereditary chiefs. Councillors concede that their political authority is delegated to them by the federal government (an unhappy circumstance of colonialism), but they are nevertheless elected bodies and as such may act on behalf of their members. It is their responsibility to consider all options designed to enhance the social and economic well-being of the Wet'suwet'en people, and in the view of the band councils, the promised impact and benefit agreement goes some considerable distance in accomplishing precisely such objectives. The band councillors argue that they signed the deal because the agreement provides immediate opportunities for employment and future prospects for "better education, elder care, and services for their members" (Smart 2019b, A5).[9]

Thus, we have a fundamental internal dispute over the status and legitimate deployment of Indigenous political decision-making power. Between the positions of the Wet'suwet'en elected band council and hereditary chiefs there appears to be no clear point of convergence. On the one hand, the operation of band council delegated authority, mobilized to meet immediate community needs; on the other hand, the operation of the pre-existing hereditary systems of governance, mobilized to protect the integrity of Wet'suwet'en ancestral lands beyond reserve boundaries.

The intractable nature of this dispute erupted dramatically in early 2019 and again in early 2020, capturing the attention of Canadians across the country. In late 2018 the Gidimt'en clan of the Wet'suwet'en Nation set up a second checkpoint near the Unist'ot'en Camp on the Morice River Forest Service Road to deter workers from reaching the Coastal GasLink pipeline project construction site. Three weeks later, a court order injunction was served, the RCMP moved in, and 14 people were arrested and removed from the site. While support for the position of the Wet'suwet'en hereditary chiefs quickly mobilized across the country, a major confrontation was averted in this case because the hereditary chiefs agreed to abide by the injunction in exchange for a guarantee that no other persons would be arrested and that the Unist'ot'en Camp would be allowed to remain in place.

The same could not be said, however, for what happened in early 2020. On December 31, 2019, the BC Supreme Court granted Coastal GasLink an expanded injunction against any further efforts to block construction of the pipeline. The Wet'suwet'en hereditary chiefs responded in early January 2020 by issuing the company with an eviction notice. Subsequent attempts by the Government of BC to de-escalate the conflict failed.[10] Shortly thereafter, the RCMP began enforcing the injunction by arresting and removing people who had built a new encampment and who had felled trees to block the service road leading to the pipeline worksite. This time, however, those who supported the position of the hereditary chiefs across the country were quick to mobilize into action. Within days, "solidarity" protests erupted in the streets of numerous Canadian cities, while rail blockades in Quebec, Ontario, Manitoba, Alberta, and BC ground rail traffic across the country to a virtual standstill.[11] Throughout this quickly escalating and now national crisis the position of the hereditary chiefs remained resolute: They would entertain no meetings with federal or provincial ministers until such time as the RCMP and the pipeline workforce had left Wet'suwet'en territories.

Facing mounting and seemingly intractable public pressure, the RCMP and pipeline workforce decided to retreat, paving the way for talks between Canada, BC, and the Wet'suwet'en hereditary chiefs. Subsequent negotiations led to a memorandum of understanding (MOU) between the three parties, signed on May 14, 2020, setting out broad terms for the recognition and subsequent negotiation of Wet'suwet'en rights and title. Interestingly, the MOU was completely silent on the matter of the Coastal GasLink pipeline itself. The MOU declared that "Canada and BC recognize that Wet'suwet'en rights and title are held by the Wet'suwet'en Houses under their system of governance." It then set out timelines over a 12-month negotiation period to restore Wet'suwet'en jurisdiction (either exclusive or shared with Canada or BC) over such areas as child and family wellness, water, wildlife, fish, land use planning, resources, revenue sharing, and "such other areas as the Wet'suwet'en propose" (Government of Canada 2020b).

Important to notice is that the now longstanding dispute between the hereditary chiefs and elected band councils was not repaired by the negotiation strategy used to achieve the MOU. In a joint statement released by five of the six Wet'suwet'en bands, councillors declared that while they supported the goal of expediting negotiations on Wet'suwet'en rights and title, they could not endorse the MOU on the grounds that they "had been cut out of the negotiation process and kept in the dark about the contents until the last minute" (Palmer 2020, A16; see also Carrigg 2020, A10). According to the elected leadership, because the hereditary chiefs had failed to craft the MOU in consultation with all Wet'suwet'en people, including the elected chiefs and councils, they had neglected their responsibilities as set out in traditional Wet'suwet'en law.

Taken together, the series of events set in motion by the Coastal GasLink dispute have proven to be extremely challenging for the Wet'suwet'en Nation. It has not helped their situation that these events were played out under the intense scrutiny of national and international media attention. From the vantage point of Indigenous sovereignty, however, the Coastal GasLink dispute has drawn into particularly sharp focus the following essential point: If their governing structures are to be seen as legitimate by the Wet'suwet'en people themselves, it is they who must find a way to both confront and, if possible, reconcile the roles of the colonially imposed band councils with that of the traditional hereditary governance system. Ultimately, this is an internal political matter for the Wet'suwet'en people themselves to sort out. It is not for Canada or BC to decide who is to be their negotiating partner based on criteria of political expediency and preferred policy outcomes: band councils in the case of pipelines, and hereditary chiefs in the case of broader matters such as rights and title. Instead, respect for Wet'suwet'en political sovereignty involves Canada and BC taking appropriate distance from the Wet'suwet'en people while they deal with the difficult task of crafting their preferred governance model in keeping with their own customs and traditions. Simply put, sovereignty means that the Wet'suwet'en people must take the lead in their own political reconstruction process. And as it turns out, without diminishing the intractable difficulties associated with the pipeline dispute itself, the MOU did take one significant step in the direction of Canada recognizing Wet'suwet'en sovereignty.

It is abundantly clear that there was considerable opposition expressed by the Wet'suwet'en band councils to what they took to be the exclusionary process that led to the ratifying of the MOU. But at the same time, it is worth noting that the language of the MOU also seems to provide the Wet'suwet'en Nation with an important opening for the exercise of their own political sovereignty. As a first step, the MOU stipulates that Aboriginal title will be implemented and political jurisdiction transferred only when there is "clarity on the Wet'suwet'en governance structures, systems, and laws," a process that the MOU further notes requires the participation of all and which ultimately is subject to ratification "by the Wet'suwet'en people." The MOU then goes on to say that once an agreement on a "Wet'suwet'en Nation Reunification Strategy" has been reached, the Wet'suwet'en people will then be ready to take the next step in their nation-rebuilding project – namely, implementation of their Aboriginal rights and title according to a schedule agreed to by the Wet'suwet'en, Canada, and BC, each "under their respective system of governance" (Government of Canada 2020b).

Taken together, then, the MOU does seem to offer considerable reassurance that in the important debate about the role of the hereditary chiefs and the *Indian Act* band councils in the governance of their nation, it is the Wet'suwet'en people themselves who must make all the final decisions. The intractability of the dispute, however, ought not to be minimized. By December 2021 (two years after Wet'suwet'en opposition to the pipeline generated solidarity protests across the country), the Wet'suwet'en people remained divided, the protest (or land defence) camps were still in place, and arrests continued. Indeed, by August 30, 2023, pipeline installation along the 670-kilometre route, including through Wet'suwet'en traditional territory, was 97 per cent complete.

I tell this story because it demonstrates particularly vividly the challenges associated with addressing conflicts over Indigenous sovereignty within Canada. At their heart lies the struggle to reconcile the longstanding and repeated Indigenous assertions to sovereignty over their peoples and territories with the sovereignty to which Canada presumes it is also entitled. But as we also see, this struggle to reconcile competing sovereignties is further complicated by the fact that many Indigenous peoples do not operate as sovereign entities at all but rather are governed by and operate within the constraints of Canadian state instruments such as the *Indian Act*. Therefore, not only must the competing claims to sovereignty between Indigenous nations and the Canadian state be reconciled, but so too must the competing sources of alleged legitimate political power within Indigenous nations.

Clearly, the nature of the political relationship between Indigenous nations and the Canadian state is complex, comprising many layers. Throughout this book, however, I will keep the notion of Indigenous sovereignty at the centre of my analysis. I do so because I want to call into question the assumption that Canada is justified in asserting its sovereignty over Indigenous peoples and their territories. In essence, employing Indigenous sovereignty as our focal point will invite us to examine the credentials of the Canadian state itself. I believe that Indigenous nations should not have to be forced to assert their sovereignty against a Canadian state that had no right to appropriate it in the first place. Therefore, it is my contention that where the Canadian state continues to assert such control, to that degree the Canadian state exercises its political power illegitimately. Or, as put by Eva Mackey, "if Indigenous sovereignty continues to be dismissed … there can be no ground for better relationships between Indigenous peoples and other citizens in settler nations" (Mackey 2016, 16). This book constitutes an exploratory examination of what those better relationships might look like using the idea of Indigenous sovereignty as its point of orientation. The question for me, therefore, is not how Indigenous sovereignty might be reconciled with Canadian sovereignty (as if it were pre-existing), but rather, how ought Canada's presumed sovereignty be reconciled with that of Indigenous peoples, a sovereignty that both pre-existed Canada and remains in existence to this day (Nadasdy 2017, 59; Asch 2014, 32)?

CHOICE OF TERMINOLOGY

Prior to European contact, concepts such as "**Indigenous**," "**Aboriginal**," or "**Indian**" simply did not exist. As Kevin Bruyneel points out, it is only in the setting of European-based conquest, colonization, and settlement in North America that such concepts acquired meaning (Bruyneel 2007, ix). These concepts arose in response to the tendency of European settler societies to contrast what they took to be the shared identities of peoples such as the Mi'kmaq, Algonquin, Anishinaabe, Assiniboine, Siksika, and hundreds of other tribal groups and nations with their own. Consequently, terms such as "Indigenous," "Aboriginal," and "Indian," must be understood as the product of co-constitutive relationships with terms such as "colonizer," "settler," and "Canadian" (Bruyneel 2007, ix). Each set constitutes a generalization that signifies something important about the shared experiences that serve to differentiate the one grouping from the other. As Joyce Green explains, on the Indigenous side of the relationship, that shared experience is generally marked by "colonization, racism, loss of territory and resources and political and legal subordination" (Green 2014a, 2).

When confronted with the challenge of having to make a choice about which concepts to employ, I will proceed as follows. Throughout this book, I have chosen to use the term "Indigenous," as it is the one favoured by the United Nations Declaration on the Rights of Indigenous Peoples and is also the one preferred by many Indigenous peoples (see Wilson-Raybould 2019, 225–6). In general, the term "Indigenous" is now widely used in the international community to refer to peoples who have a shared historical experience of occupying lands prior to those lands being seized by a colonial power and who have since been subjected to the forces of colonization by larger or more dominant settler populations. Typically, the experience shared by all Indigenous peoples across the world is that they have been or continue to be subjected to colonial rule. In addition, Indigenous peoples usually consider themselves to be distinct from the surrounding settler populations and, in most cases, are determined to preserve and develop their distinct identities as autonomous and self-sustaining societies into the future (Cobo 1983, paragraph 379).[12] By virtue of their shared experience of colonization, both past and present, Indigenous peoples are also often regarded as uniquely entitled to make claims against the colonial state now occupying their traditional territories, claims that typically come in the form of rights to self-determination, land title, and different forms of restitution. I will also use the plural term "peoples" to indicate that there are many distinct Indigenous populations, each with their own identity, culture, language, relationship to ancestral lands, and traditions. And, finally, to avoid collectivizing distinct populations and distinct experiences, I will use the names of specific Indigenous nations wherever and whenever possible.

While "Indigenous" is the more internationally recognized term to refer to the descendants of the first occupants of a country, I will also make occasional use of such terms as "Aboriginal," "First Nations," "Native," or "Indian." In each case, my reliance on the term will be dictated by the circumstances or context in which it is used. For example, certain authors choose to refer to Indigenous peoples as "Native" or as "Aboriginal," and so when consulting or citing their work I will refer to Indigenous peoples as the authors themselves do. In other settings, use of the terms "Aboriginal," or "Indian" will be necessary. Most notably, "Indians," and the categories of "status" and "non-status" must be used when discussing a legal document such as the *Indian Act*. However, in most other settings, the term "Indian" will be avoided because it was imposed on Indigenous peoples by agents of the Canadian state. In addition, when referring to the ***Constitution Act, 1982*** and subsequent Canadian court decisions on the meaning of constitutionally protected Aboriginal and treaty rights, the term "Aboriginal" must be used as this is in keeping with the language of both the Constitution's Section 35 and the court system's jurisprudence. Indeed, the Canadian Constitution makes no mention of Indigenous peoples at all. Instead, it lends recognition exclusively to "Aboriginal peoples" who are, in turn, divided into three groupings: **Indians** (now commonly referred to as First Nations), **Inuit**, and **Métis**. Consequently, it is to the Aboriginal (rather than Indigenous) peoples of Canada that the Aboriginal and treaty rights recognized and affirmed under Section 35 belong.[13]

Indigenous peoples also regularly refer to themselves as "**nations**," and so I shall do the same. At the same time, however, it is important to keep in mind that Indigenous peoples use the term "nation" in a variety of ways. As explained by the Royal Commission on Aboriginal Peoples (RCAP), some use the term to refer to a broad group of Indigenous people "whose members have a shared sense of national identity based on a common heritage, situation and outlook, including such elements as history, language, culture, spirituality, ancestry, and homeland" (RCAP 1996c, 157). When used in this broad sense, an "Indigenous nation" would likely be made up of a number of local communities living on distinct traditional territories. But in other settings, the term "nation" is used fairly narrowly to refer to "a single local community of Indian people living on its own territorial base, often a reserve, governed by the *Indian Act*." (RCAP 1996c, 157). RCAP observes that while many Indigenous people use the term "nation" to refer to themselves in this narrower sense, many others prefer the broader usage because they consider it to be both more inclusive and more consistent with their history, traditions, and identity (RCAP 1996c, 157).

The important question for the purposes of this book is whether the principal unit of sovereignty can be the local Indigenous community or whether it ought to be the Indigenous nation taken as a whole. My approach will follow the lead of such Indigenous scholars and activists as Joyce Green and Jody Wilson-Raybould. Both accept the proposition that, in principle, there is nothing to prohibit either local Indigenous communities or broader Indigenous nations acting as sovereign political units in their relations with the Canadian state. In practice, however, most local Indigenous communities (i.e., former ***Indian Act* bands**) will simply lack the institutional capacity to assume responsibility for the full range of policy areas that could legitimately fall under the authority of Indigenous governments. In such cases, suggests Wilson-Raybould, the process of Indigenous nation rebuilding is an exercise that must "occur at a level also beyond the band – typically as an aggregation of bands at the tribal level" (Wilson-Raybould 2019, 36).[14] What both say must be avoided at all costs are inclinations to rely on *Indian Act* bands and reserve governance as the model for moving forward. Joyce Green explains that as creatures of the federal government, *Indian Act* bands are by their very nature limited "to self-administration of the regulatory and policy framework of the colonial state" (Green 2014b, 29; Green 2020, 248). Jody Wilson-Raybould adds that *Indian Act* band councils are an impoverished form of self-government because they are "based on models developed by the federal government to deliver its programs and services" (Wilson-Raybould 2019, 141).[15]

The task at hand, therefore, is to rebuild Indigenous models of governance that are capable of "making laws, resolving disputes, and generating the means to pursue a collective vision" (Wilson-Raybould 2019, 141). In some instances, local Indigenous communities may well be capable of spearheading such a rebuild while in others, the broader Indigenous nation will be the more appropriate unit. The essential point from Green's and Wilson-Raybould's perspective is that the unit chosen must be one that is the creation of Indigenous nations themselves and not the Canadian state (Wilson-Raybould 2019, 35–6). It must also be a unit that is sufficiently muscular to sustain and advance "countervailing claims to land, resources, political capacity and sovereignty" (Green 2014b, 30). In short, whether large or small, the Indigenous unit must be sufficiently robust to be able to lead in the process of its own decolonization in relation to the Canadian state.

Finally, the very awkward nomenclature "**non-Indigenous**" also enters regularly into the book's narrative. I use it to refer to Canadian citizens who are not Indigenous. It is generally not advisable to characterize a group of people through repeated reference to attributes they do not possess. Such use is both incredibly vague and can carry with it negative connotations. That said, the category of Canadian citizens, excluding Indigenous peoples, is far too diverse to be captured by a single term. I could characterize non-Indigenous peoples as "Canadians." But Indigenous people are also citizens of Canada (though sometimes reluctantly), so to offset Indigenous peoples from the rest of "Canadians" is not really accurate either. One thing that can be said with certainty, however, is that most Canadians are not Indigenous, and thus their identification with the Canadian state is not fraught with the kinds of challenges, disappointments, marginalization, and explicit denial of rights that feature prominently in the experiences of Indigenous peoples. For the purposes of this book, I have not found a more sophisticated and nuanced substitute for the term "non-Indigenous." I therefore use it simply to indicate that there is a class of Canadian citizen for whom the experience of being "Indigenous" to this land does not apply. These Canadian citizens share a different fate in that their ancestry originates in places other than Canada.

KEY THEMES

SOVEREIGNTY, SELF-DETERMINATION, AND SELF-GOVERNMENT

In this book I rely on a set of terms that serve as the political foundation upon which the Indigenous emancipation project within Canada is being built. These terms are "sovereignty," "self-determination," and "self-government." While these terms have distinct meanings, they are also inextricably linked, and when applied to Indigenous peoples they are extremely useful in clarifying the nature of their political struggle to redefine their relationship with the Canadian state. For most Indigenous peoples, these terms serve to establish the requisite starting point as well as range of present and future possibilities for the fulfillment of their rights within Canada. What follows defines each of these terms.

First to sovereignty, which I take to be the appropriate starting point for conceptualizing Indigenous–Canadian state relations. Earlier I established that sovereignty refers to the capacity of a political community to make autonomous decisions about the direction of its collective life on its own lands, free of external interference (Little Bear 2013, 6, 7). According to this definition, a sovereign people are those who have the power to define themselves in relation to each other, to their lands, and to other sovereign peoples. For Indigenous peoples, the assertion to sovereignty constitutes an important strategy to regain control over their own lives and lands because of the internal and external implications associated with its practice. Internal sovereignty refers to the authority a political community exercises over its people and its territory. External sovereignty refers to the authority that a political community exercises in its relationships to other sovereign political actors (McNeil 2016, 101; see also Asch 2014, 101–3). With respect to both its internal and external attributes, autonomy is the defining feature. A sovereign political community is one that can define its own identity free of external impositions or constraints (internal), and it is one that is able to establish and maintain relations with other sovereign political communities on terms of its own choosing (external). Sovereign political communities, in other words, tend to regard one another as political equals and, as such, are generally inclined to order their relations with one another based on cooperation and consent rather than on coercion (Panagos 2016, 61).

When applied to Indigenous peoples, I take sovereignty to mean that they are justified in asserting autonomy from the Canadian state in the sense that they need not submit to its authority outside of their consent. As pre-contact sovereign nations, Indigenous peoples claim they retain the right to self-determination over their peoples, territories, cultures, and languages in keeping with their own laws and traditions. And as pre-contact sovereign nations, they also claim that they retain the right to establish political relationships with the Canadian state on their own terms, whether that be through alliances, treaties, constitutional recognition and protection, or any other legal and political arrangement of their choosing (McNeil 2018, 293–7). In the chapters to follow I will argue that Indigenous sovereignty ought to be recognized and respected by Canada in these two senses. In short, it is sovereignty that ought to serve as the organizing principle for the structuring of relations between Indigenous nations and the Canadian state, now and into the future (Nadasdy 2017, 38; Asch 2014, 126).

Self-determination can be understood as the most foundational of Indigenous rights and also as the principal means by which Indigenous sovereignty is realized in practice. Simply put, Indigenous sovereignty is expressed through self-determination. Within international law and legal practice, self-determination has been established as the minimum standard "necessary for the dignity, survival, and well-being of Indigenous peoples throughout the world" (Assembly of First Nations [AFN] 2019, 2). According to the United Nations Declaration on the Rights of Indigenous Peoples (UNDRIP), these minimum standards include the right "to freely determine their political status and freely pursue their economic, social and cultural development" (Article 3). Article 4 confirms Indigenous peoples' "right to autonomy or self-government in matters relating to their internal or local affairs," while Article 5 validates their right "to maintain and strengthen their distinct political, legal, economic, social and cultural institutions." Article 26 further affirms that Indigenous peoples have "the right to lands, territories and resources that they have traditionally owned, occupied or otherwise used and acquired" and it instructs states to grant "legal recognition and protection to these lands, territories and resources." Taken together, the various components of the right to self-determination as set out by UNDRIP equip Indigenous peoples with a powerful normative and legal tool to call into question the legitimacy of the terms under which they have been drawn into the fabric of the Canadian constitutional order (Papillon 2014, 10). In short, the right to self-determination validates and protects Indigenous peoples' capacity to define themselves; to govern their peoples, lands, and resources; to satisfy their needs; and to live their ways of life free from external constraints or interference.

Self-determination can take many forms, including the practice of **self-government**. As put by RCAP, self-government must be understood as flowing from the principle of self-determination as it constitutes one practical way in which the principle can be put into effect (RCAP 1996c, 108–9). Simply put, if the right to self-determination refers to the capacity of Indigenous peoples to make choices about their lives, self-government refers to one possible outcome of such choices being made (RCAP 1996c, 174–5). For practical purposes, then, I take the term "self-government" to mean the ability to resolve disputes, make laws and policy, and more generally pursue collective goals for the development of a people (Frideres 2020, 198). Two further implications follow from this definition. First, to be self-governing, Indigenous peoples must be able to design their own institutions of governance according to their own priorities, including their constitutions, laws, and political decision-making processes. And second, Indigenous peoples must possess governance systems that are sufficiently powerful to be able to make the kinds of collective decisions that they determine to be relevant and central to their lives. As described by RCAP, this decision-making authority must embrace two distinct but related goals: Indigenous peoples must be able to exercise greater authority over their traditional territories and its inhabitants, and Indigenous peoples must be able to exercise "greater control over matters that affect the particular Aboriginal nation in question: its culture, identity, and human well-being" (RCAP 1996c, 140).

In keeping with the principle of self-determination, Indigenous peoples also tend to reinforce their right to self-government by using the language of "**inherency**." The right is described as originating from their occupation and jurisdiction over their peoples, lands, and resources prior to European contact. It is inherent because the right originates with Indigenous peoples in their capacity as sovereign nations prior to European colonization and the imposition of European and then Canadian law upon them. Furthermore, many Indigenous people assert that their **inherent right to self-government** not only survived colonization but remains intact today. Indeed, far from being surrendered or lost, Indigenous peoples regularly point to the existence of the historical treaties and alliances with the French, British, and later Canadian states as evidence that their right to self-government was both recognized and affirmed by colonial powers. In the contemporary context, what the inherent right translates into is a requirement that the Canadian state support Indigenous peoples' right "to govern themselves under institutions of their own choice and design." Because the inherent right does not depend on the Canadian state for its existence, "no one can give them this right, they say, and no one can take it away" (RCAP 1996c, 139; see also Nadasdy 2017, 59).

To sum up, while Indigenous peoples use a variety of terms to characterize their political aspirations, they are generally united in their declaration that they have a right to self-determination based on their status as pre-colonial sovereign peoples. Furthermore, this right to self-determination is said to authorize them to make their own independent decisions about their internal governmental arrangements and the character of the relations they wish to take up with the Canadian state. Recognition and affirmation by the Canadian state of Indigenous peoples' standing as pre-existing political sovereigns, in other words, is regularly asserted as the foundation upon which Indigenous nations ought to be rebuilt.

COLONIALISM

As mentioned, the background conditions against which Indigenous peoples assert sovereignty are the debilitating impositions of **colonialism**. In general, colonialism is best understood as a system of foreign governance imposed on a population and territory by an external political force. In the Canadian case, what was once a system of external colonial imposition on Indigenous peoples by the imperialistic French and British later became a system of internal colonial control imposed by the Canadian settler state. Unlike what occurred in South Asia and much of Africa, for example, French and British settlers in Canada did not eventually return to their lands of origin (though often only after a protracted period of resistance by the colonized), but rather decided to stay on permanently. It was their intent to gradually displace Indigenous peoples from their lands and to absorb Indigenous societies into their own (Mackey 2016, 4; Simpson 2011, 205). This process of settler colonialism and internal colonization of Indigenous populations, therefore, can best be characterized as "a system of control, domination, and even elimination of original inhabitants by a settler state that asserts sovereignty, in the sense of supreme authority to rule, over an entire population" (Grant 2018, 112).[16] Numerous commentators also argue that this process of colonization is ongoing. Hayden King, for one, characterizes settler colonialism "as a structural and permanent phenomenon, as opposed to an event or an era" (King 2018, 113; see also Simpson 2017).

After an initial post-contact period of rough nation-to-nation reciprocity secured through agreements like military alliances and commerce and friendship treaties, Indigenous peoples have had to endure a centuries-long sustained attack on their sovereignty, territories, and identity by the French, British, and subsequently Canada. In fact, the Canadian state and European powers before it put the concept of sovereignty to work to justify their dispossession and marginalization of Indigenous peoples. The infamous "Doctrine of Discovery" is one particularly glaring example. Derived from a series of Papal Bulls originating in the fifteenth century, the Doctrine of Discovery justified colonial suppression of Indigenous sovereignty on the purported grounds of European racial superiority. Based on a unilateral declaration that Indigenous peoples were inferior by virtue of being uncivilized heathens, colonial powers simply accepted the proposition that Indigenous peoples were not nations and therefore did not possess the political sophistication necessary to exercise sovereignty in ways that were recognizable or consistent with European practices. Consequently, the British (and later) Canadian state felt perfectly justified in treating Indigenous peoples as their subjects to be governed as they saw fit. Indigenous rights were subsequently denied on explicitly ethnocentric and racist grounds. Colonial powers believed that only they possessed the requisite attributes necessary to act as political sovereigns – a superior religion, economic system, property rights regime, and set of governmental and legal structures among them.

What followed was an intense and protracted period of "Indian" policy designed with the specific intent of assimilating Indigenous peoples into the purportedly more civilized and progressive Canadian society. An additional motivation for assimilation was to remove and relocate Indigenous peoples from their ancestral lands to establish "vacant" land for the settlement of European immigrants who were coming in waves to the new country now called Canada. The *Indian Act*, the band governance system, reserves, and residential schools all sought to integrate Indigenous peoples into Canada on an individual level, "preferably by entry into the working-class level of society" (Townshend 2015, 36). Taken together, "Indian" policy was a deliberately integrated system, its various components designed to assess, manage, and control Indigenous life at every turn.

Canadian state efforts to manage and control Indigenous life are particularly well illustrated by the decisively gendered nature of settler colonialism. Joyce Green observes that because colonialism has been gendered, "its effects are experienced differently by men and women," and almost always to women's detriment (Green 2020, 244). Following Green, Leanne Simpson explains how the internalization of colonial **patriarchal structures** within Indigenous communities led to a situation where women often did not and still do not have the same level of power or access to resources as their male counterparts. She points out, for example, that Indigenous women were specifically targeted by patriarchal assumptions about "correct" gender roles, which dictated that women must be domesticated while men seek gainful employment. These colonial intentions were then codified into policy through the *Indian Act*. The 1876 version of the *Indian Act* decreed women could not possess land or marital property nor were they allowed to exercise political power within their communities as they were prohibited from running for chief or council and voting in band elections (Simpson 2017, 104, 105). Remarkably, these highly discriminatory measures remained in place until 1951 when a number of the most egregious provisions of the *Indian Act* were removed on the grounds that they simply could not be justified against any reasonable standard of human rights. Yet other discriminatory provisions of the *Indian Act* remained firmly in place until relatively recently. Between 1876 and 1985, for example, Indian women who married a non-Indian man lost their Indian status, while Indian men were able to confer status upon their non-Indian wives. Rauna Kuokkanen points out that the consequences of this policy were particularly devastating for women. As she explains: "for Indian women, 'marrying out' literally meant a reality of exile from their communities, and hence from their rights and ties to their families, cultures, and identities" (Kuokkanen 2012, 233). The cumulative effect of these and numerous other discriminatory policies leads Leanne Simpson to conclude that Indigenous women, who once were "autonomous, influential, and economically and politically powerful" within their nations, were transformed into becoming "dependent, subservient, second-class citizens confined to the domestic sphere in colonial society" (Simpson 2017, 109–10).

This "Indian" policy turned out to be not only a colossal failure but it also constituted a fundamental abrogation of what most now accept as Indigenous human rights. Indigenous identity was denied, cultures undermined, religious practices outlawed, and ancestral lands, resources, and political power stolen. And Indigenous peoples suffer to this day because of it. For example, with respect to indicators such as poverty, unemployment, housing and homelessness, health, life expectancy, and education, Indigenous peoples generally fall well below the Canadian national average (AFN 2019, 4–10; Courchene 2018, 17–42; Wilson-Raybould 2019, 34). Rates of suicide, alcohol and drug abuse, and incarceration also far exceed numbers found among the general Canadian population. The result is that many Indigenous people are driven to become welfare recipients, finding themselves reliant on resources and programming delivered by the Canadian state. In short, Indigenous ways of life have been subjected to a sustained, centuries-long attack, all in clear violation of what we now know to be their fundamental right to self-determination. According to Joyce Green, it is these devastating state practices of colonialism that frame the conditions in which Indigenous assertions to sovereignty are now being advanced against Canada (Green 2014b, 23).

Given the stakes involved, it should come as no surprise that despite having violated Indigenous rights at every turn, the Canadian state is nevertheless inclined to want to maintain its tight grip on power both as a matter of political and economic interest as well as out of concern for its own survival. Gary Wilson, Christopher Alcantara, and Thierry Rodon demonstrate in a recent study, for example, that the entire institutional configuration of the Canadian state is designed to "continue to privilege and protect state sovereignty over Indigenous sovereignty." As they put it, "Canadian institutions such as the courts and judicial system, the House of Commons and Cabinet, the party system, and the constitutional order in general recognize the primacy of state sovereignty despite efforts to show that Indigenous legal orders continue to exist and should be held as co-equal to Canadian ones" (Wilson, Alcantara, and Rodon 2020, 25). In their regular confrontations with the Canadian state, therefore, it is no exaggeration to say that what many Indigenous peoples seek to do is fundamentally realign the political structures and institutional logic of the Canadian federation itself.

THE SPACES IN BETWEEN

It is against this coercive and destructive dynamic of colonialism that we witness the rise of Indigenous political activism, motivated by the Indigenous right to self-determination and against the assertion to absolute sovereignty by the Canadian state. The core message can be distilled to one essential theme: Indigenous peoples argue that they are entitled to an identity as sovereigns with authority over their own lives, a political standing that they call on the Canadian state to both recognize and respect.[17] And the message seems to be resonating, at least to a degree. A core objective of this book is to show where the tight political grip that the Canadian state has held over Indigenous peoples is loosening and has been loosening at a steady rate for several decades. As we shall see, repeated and persistent acts "of resistance, resilience, resurgence, and restoration," particularly since the 1970s, are gradually leading to corrections (though often limited ones) in some of the power imbalances that exist between Indigenous nations and the Canadian state (MacDonald 2017). In John Borrows's estimation, the cumulative effects of these actions are that "Crown sovereignty is beginning to be constrained in Canada" (Borrows 2017a, 28). In sum, Indigenous peoples have not disappeared in the manner that the Canadian state might once have wished.

But the problem, of course, is that the setting within which Indigenous peoples seek to defend and advance their right to self-determination is within, or in the context of being surrounded by, the Canadian political system. Indigenous sovereignty, in other words, is inescapably contained within and constrained by Canadian sovereignty. And in response, Indigenous peoples have taken an offensive position. They seek to push back the boundaries of the Canadian state wherever those boundaries are experienced as incursions into Indigenous peoples' right to be self-defining. I believe it is this act of pushback across multiple fronts that has created the territorial and jurisdictional spaces Indigenous peoples have come to reoccupy, spaces that were once theirs and, most importantly, are still theirs today as a matter of right. What we see, in other words, is the (re)activation of an Indigenous refusal to accept the assertion to absolute sovereignty by the Canadian state.[18]

I have adopted and adapted the political notion of "the spaces in between" from the work of Audra Simpson and Kevin Bruyneel who refer to the same dynamic of (re)activation as "nested sovereignty" and "the third space of sovereignty," respectively.[19] According to Simpson, "nested sovereignty" is the condition of Indigenous political orders being embedded within but nevertheless straining against settler governance. While the condition of Indigenous sovereignty being "nested" within Canada is a result of Indigenous dispossession (one sovereign proliferates at the other's expense), Simpson nevertheless points out that Indigenous peoples regularly deploy their own sovereignty in ways that challenge the boundaries and lawfulness of the Canadian state. Insofar as these challenges have proven successful, to that degree Simpson says "Indigenous sovereignties and Indigenous political orders prevail within and apart from settler governance" (Simpson 2014, 10–12, 115–16). It is in these acts of successful redeployment of Indigenous sovereignty within the boundaries of Canadian sovereignty that I witness Indigenous peoples occupying what I shall identify in forthcoming chapters as "the spaces in between."

Bruyneel characterizes the Indigenous struggle for liberation in the American context in language that closely resembles that of Simpson's. Using a boundary-focused approach, Bruyneel argues that from the perspective of many Americans, the Indigenous claim to sovereignty is unclear "because it is not easily located inside or outside the United States." From the standpoint of mainstream America, however, the options available are quite clear: either Indigenous peoples are part of the United States, in which case they are not sovereign, or, if sovereign, "they cannot be part of and thus make demands on the United States" (Bruyneel 2007, xiii).

Bruyneel counters that to present Indigenous political status in a way that classifies it as either "in" or "out" of the United States is far too simplistic because it fails to take into account the corrosive effects that the imposition of American colonial rule has had on Indigenous peoples. Indigenous peoples were once sovereign, but because of "centuries of neglect and outright abuse" at the hands of European colonizers and American settlers, the Indigenous capacity to express their sovereignty has been severely restricted (Bruyneel 2007, xv). Consequently, when Indigenous peoples now fight for their liberation and sovereignty, they are forced to do so within the very "political system that set Indigenous people so far back in the first place" (Bruyneel 2007, xv). Bruyneel characterizes this struggle as one over boundaries. In their resistance to colonial rule, Indigenous peoples have no choice but to work "on, across, and against the boundaries of American political life" (Bruyneel 2007, xvi). Bruyneel's work is then devoted to identifying those places within America where Indigenous resistance has resulted in Indigenous groups both securing and expanding opportunities for sovereign tribal expression. He refers to these places as "a third space for sovereignty" because they exist "neither simply inside or outside the American political system," but rather are supplemental to it (Bruyneel 2007, xvii). These are spaces, in other words, that transgress colonial impositions and challenge colonial rule, and in the process of doing so they carve out locations within American politics for the fuller expression of Indigenous agency and autonomy (Bruyneel 2007, 1).

Following Bruyneel (though with a slight adaptation in language), I too find the term "the spaces in between" to be a powerful metaphor to explain the position that many Indigenous nations now occupy within Canada because of their resistance to colonial rule. Their efforts to carve out and (re)occupy "spaces in between" the exercise of sovereignty by the Canadian state has contributed substantially to Indigenous autonomy and well-being. But at the same time, the process of deconstructing and dismantling colonial structures is an ongoing one, often fiercely fought and far from over. It is also a frustrating process because change is slow and at best incrementally acquired. As such, my repeated use of the metaphor "the spaces in between" is also meant to be provocative. There is more space to be (re)acquired in the Indigenous quest to push back against the stifling incursion of Canadian boundaries into their lives. It is my intent to show, by means of examples across a range of jurisdictions, where and how expanded space for the expression of Indigenous autonomy is being reacquired. In short, what these various declarations of Indigenous sovereignty serve most fundamentally to do is challenge the legitimacy of the Canadian political order and Indigenous peoples' presumed place within it (Green 2020, 248). This book seeks to substantiate and lend normative support to this process.

The seven topics chosen for political analysis in this book demonstrate various features of this Indigenous project of resistance to colonialism and quest for greater autonomy in Indigenous–Canadian state relations. From the large and highly complex field of Indigenous studies, this book deals specifically with (1) the question of political power and how it has been understood and strategically employed to advance the project of Indigenous self-determination; (2) Indigenous identity and citizenship, both with respect to who is entitled to define it and under what conditions; (3) Canadian Indigenous policy, with a view to identifying how, at times, it has gravitated toward partial recognition of Indigenous sovereignty but more typically has worked to facilitate the assimilation of Indigenous peoples into the Canadian political order; (4) Indigenous rights as defined by Canadian courts and the degree to which those definitions have both enhanced and constricted legal space for the expression of Indigenous sovereignty; (5) treaties and the degree to which they protect and advance Indigenous prospects for greater well-being and political autonomy; (6) self-government and the question of political jurisdiction, particularly with respect to emerging models and the degree to which each provides opportunity for Indigenous nations to exercise sovereignty over their peoples, resources, and territories; and (7) partnerships, examined across a range of sectors, as illustrations of emerging commitments to shared sovereignty between Indigenous and non-Indigenous peoples. It is to the beginnings, the developments, and more recently to the actual experiences of Indigenous peoples exercising their political sovereignty within and against the boundaries of the Canadian state that this book devotes its attention.

OBJECTIVES FOR THIS BOOK

Turning briefly to the objectives of this book, I have two. First, it is intended to serve as a primer into a range of topics that are of central concern to the conduct of political relations between Indigenous peoples and the Canadian state. The book intends to show readers why identity politics, policy, law, treaties, self-government, and partnerships are central to those relations and how each might be approached to acquire a deeper understanding of what is at stake for both Indigenous peoples and Canada in the resolution of these matters.

Second, the book is designed to contribute to the debate on Indigenous sovereignty and by doing so is explicitly normative in its intent. The book is motivated by my desire to identify prospects and possibilities for the enhanced exercise of Indigenous sovereignty within Canada. As such, the book devotes considerable attention to the important matter of reconciliation, an imperative that in my view must go beyond formal apologies of damage done, as offered by the federal government in 2008, to also address structural imbalances in political power. If Indigenous peoples are to be reconciled with the Canadian state, such reconciliation calls for the recognition and empowerment of Indigenous political institutions commensurate with their right to be self-defining within Canada. It calls for a recognition and protection of the Indigenous right to occupy and control their ancestral lands and to benefit from the resources of those lands. It calls for closing the socioeconomic gap that exists between Indigenous and non-Indigenous peoples. Most fundamentally, as put by Jody Wilson-Raybould, "reconciliation means confronting and ending the legacy of colonialism in Canada and replacing it with a future built on Indigenous self-determination" (Wilson-Raybould 2019, 99).[20] Reconciliation, in other words, must be built on the foundation of Indigenous sovereignty, a foundation that in turn must motivate Canada to accept that Indigenous peoples are entitled to preserve and develop their societies, cultures, economies, and political institutions in freedom (Green 2020, 248–9). In sum, the book's broad treatment of an array of topics central to Indigenous–Canadian state relations, coupled with its commitment to frame that analysis within the imperative of Indigenous political sovereignty as a pathway to reconciliation, is intended to provide readers with a comprehensive and critically engaged perspective to understand what better relations between Indigenous peoples and the Canadian state should look like.

I also need to identify myself in relation to this work. I come to it as a non-Indigenous scholar and teacher. I cannot claim an Indigenous perspective, nor do I have intimate knowledge or experiences of Indigenous culture or of the injustices Indigenous peoples have suffered. I am also fully aware that I live and work on the unceded traditional territories of the Coast Salish peoples, including in my case (as a resident of Vancouver) the Squamish, Musqueam, Sechelt, Tsleil-Waututh, and Lil'wat nations. I recognize that I reside on these lands without having secured either prior permission or an invitation from the local Indigenous nations and therefore am implicated in the very colonial dynamic that I seek to challenge and undermine throughout this book.

But at the same time, the perspective I bring to this work is one informed by a deep commitment to decolonization. In this sense, my analysis is not "objective." My credentials for writing in this area come from a long commitment to doing research, teaching, and advocating in solidarity with Indigenous peoples. I have also worked as an advocate alongside Indigenous peoples in such settings as the Canadian court system, Canadian constitutional politics, and more recently as a member of my university's Indigenizing the Academy Committee. In each setting, I am motivated to research, write, teach, and advocate out of a deep concern for the rights of Indigenous peoples. I accept the proposition that Indigenous peoples are entitled to political sovereignty and I seek to educate my students to consider the merits of this fundamental claim. I seek to uncover the nature of Indigenous resistance against the forces of colonialism and then seek to identify the many important ways in which Indigenous peoples are carving out political space within the Canadian state for their own self-actualization. In addition, I ask the reader to bear in mind that this book is not primarily concerned with politics conducted internal to Indigenous communities and nations themselves. Indeed, as a non-Indigenous person, this is an area in which I lack the requisite standing to offer much by way of comment. Instead, this book is about the interface between Indigenous and non-Indigenous political worlds and how each might be reconciled to the other. As a scholar who is situated on the non-Indigenous side of the political boundary but who is deeply committed to respecting Indigenous rights, I believe that my perspective can add value to the discussion about what such reconciliation could entail. In short, as a Canadian, I wish to be part of a country that deals respectfully with the Indigenous peoples who are caught within its borders. I am in favour of any political measures that promote this most noble and essential of causes.

DISCUSSION QUESTIONS

1. Should sovereignty matter to Indigenous peoples? Why or why not?
2. Is Canada moving into a postcolonial period in its relationship with Indigenous peoples? What would lead you to suggest either yes or no?
3. Are both the Canadian state and Indigenous nations entitled to sovereignty? In what ways are these sovereignties in competition? Should Indigenous peoples be satisfied to practise their sovereignty within Canada?
4. In what ways if any, do Indigenous rights challenge the legitimacy of the Canadian state's right to exist?

NOTES

1. This pledge to fully and unequivocally endorse the United Nations Declaration on the Rights of Indigenous Peoples was made by the Government of Canada in May 2016. Endorsement has since been followed up by legislation in the form of Bill C-15, which received Royal Assent on June 21, 2021. The legislation is designed to provide a framework for the Government of Canada and Indigenous peoples to fully implement the Declaration. Among other things, the legislation requires that the laws of Canada be brought into conformity with the articles of the Declaration and that the Government of Canada, along with Indigenous peoples, develop a national action plan to achieve the Declaration's objectives.
2. See Truth and Reconciliation Commission 2015 and National Inquiry into Missing and Murdered Indigenous Women and Girls 2019. It is worth noting that the federal government intended to release a national action plan on missing and murdered Indigenous women, girls, and 2SLGBTQQIA+ people upon the one-year anniversary of the release of the Final Report (June 3, 2020). However, the COVID-19 pandemic disrupted the Liberal government's timeline, leading to a significant delay in the action plan's release.
3. Jody Wilson-Raybould notes that in the mandate letters she and others ministers received subsequent to their appointment to the Liberal cabinet in 2015, Prime Minister Justin Trudeau declared that "no relationship is more important to me and to Canada than the one with Indigenous peoples. It is time for a renewed, nation-to-nation relationship with Indigenous peoples based on recognition of rights, respect, cooperation and partnership." See Wilson-Raybould 2019, 65.
4. The six Indigenous scholars are Naiomi Metallic, assistant professor and holder of the Chancellor's Chair in Aboriginal Law and Policy, Dalhousie University, Mi'kmaq, from Listuguj Mi'gmaq First Nation, Quebec; Shirley Williams/Migizi ow-kwe, elder and professor emeritus,

Nishnaabemowin language, Indigenous studies, Trent University, Odawa-Ojibway, from Wikwemikong Unceded Indian Reserve, Manitoulin Island, Ontario; Janet Smylie, associate professor, Dalla Lana School of Public Health, University of Toronto and holder of the CIHR Applied Public Health Chair in Indigenous health knowledge and information, Métis with kin ties to Manitoba, Alberta, and Saskatchewan; Bob Kayseas, professor of business and associate vice-president, academic, First Nations University of Canada, Nahkawe (Saulteaux) from Fishing Lake First Nation, Saskatchewan; Karla Jessen Williamson, assistant professor, educational foundations, University of Saskatchewan, Inuk, from Maniitsoq, Greenland; Qwul'sih'yah'maht/ Robina Thomas, associate professor, School of Social Work, and director of Indigenous Academic and Community Engagement, University of Victoria, Coast Salish, from Lyackson First Nation, BC. See Macdonald 2017.

5 Though Joanne Barker is quick to point out that not all Indigenous peoples "share the same understanding of what sovereignty is or how it matters, nor [can] all of their concerns and labor … be reduced to sovereignty as a kind of raison d'être." Taking it one step further, Indigenous scholar Taiaiake Alfred argues that Indigenous assertions of sovereignty are entirely inappropriate because it traps Indigenous political aspirations within a European state paradigm that is completely at odds with political concepts grounded within Indigenous cultures. Faced with such critique, Barker nevertheless remarks that "following World War II, sovereignty emerged not as a new but as a particularly valued term within indigenous discourses to signify a multiplicity of legal and social rights to political, economic, and cultural self-determination." In the next chapter I will demonstrate how, and in what ways, using the concept of sovereignty can serve to bolster Indigenous political power without undermining the integrity of Indigenous cultures. See Barker 2005, 1, and Alfred 2009, 79–84.

6 Note that while sovereignty implies ownership of territory, there need not be a strict correlation drawn between the two. Sovereignty does not require land ownership in order to be present. Land stewardship is also a possibilty. The key here is that the nature of the relationship to the land be one that is decided exclusively by the Indigenous peoples involved and that this jurisdiction (whether justified through ownership or stewardship) is respected by external political actors (i.e., the Canadian state).

7 The Unist'ot'en camp is made up of a number of facilities, including a pit-house, a permaculture garden, a solar-powered mini grid, and a healing lodge. The camp also protects the sacred headwaters of Talbits Kwah (Gosnell Creek) and Wedzin Kwah (Morice River). See Temper 2018, A15.

8 TransCanada Corporation is the company behind the Coastal GasLink pipeline project. In January 2019 it announced plans to change its name to TC Energy.

9 Indigenous legal scholar Val Napoleon observes that matters are even further complicated by the fact that elected band chiefs and councillors are also members of family houses and occupy positions in the hereditary system, sometimes as hereditary chiefs. See Penner 2019, A6.

10 The Government of BC appointed former New Democrat MP Nathan Cullen as the provincial liaison to the Wet'suwet'en hereditary chiefs in the Coastal Gaslink pipeline dispute. Despite Cullen's best efforts to de-escalate the conflict, he ultimately failed to find a solution satisfactory to the Wet'suwet'en chiefs, the RCMP, Coastal Gaslink, and other parties.

11 The city of Vancouver was particularly hard hit by street protests, which disrupted traffic on an almost daily basis throughout February 2020. Access to the BC Legislature in Victoria was also blocked by protesters on February 12, 2020, the day of the Throne Speech, making it difficult for MLAs and government workers to gain access to the building. Rail blockades were set up by members of the Mohawk Nation at Tyendinaga, Ontario; members of the Gitxsan Nation at New Hazelton, BC; and members of the Neskonlith Indian Band near Kamloops, among other locations.

12 See Jose R. Martinez Cobo, Special Rapporteur of the Sub-Commission on Prevention of Discrimination and Protection of Minorities, who, in his 1986 Report on the Study of the Problem of Discrimination against Indigenous Peoples, wrote:

> Indigenous communities, peoples and nations are those which, having a historical continuity with pre-invasion and pre-colonial societies that developed on their territories, consider themselves distinct from other sectors of the societies now prevailing on those territories, or parts of them. They form at present non-dominant sectors of society and are determined to preserve, develop and transmit to future generations their ancestral territories, and their ethnic identity, as the basis of their continued existence as peoples, in accordance with their own cultural patterns, social institutions and legal system" (paragraph 379).

13 While the terms "Indigenous" and "Aboriginal" could, and often are, used interchangeably in the Canadian context, it is important to highlight that there is an important difference between them. The term "Indigenous" could apply to anyone with Indigenous status living in Canada, whether Native American, Maori, Torres Strait Islanders of Australia, and so on. However, such Indigenous peoples have no entitlement to the aboriginal and treaty rights recognized and protected under Section 35 of the *Constitution Act*. These rights are reserved exclusively to Canada's Indian, Inuit, and Métis (or Aboriginal) population.

14 The Royal Commission on Aboriginal Peoples is less flexible in its approach, insisting that the appropriate unit for Indigenous self-determination is the "nation," a term that under international law RCAP says is equivalent to that of "peoples." According to RCAP, for the purposes of effectively exercising the right to self-determination an Aboriginal nation must be "a sizable body of Aboriginal people with a shared sense of national identity that constitutes the predominant population in a certain territory or collection of territories." For RCAP, size matters because it believes that size constitutes an important measure of Indigenous capacity. By its criteria, RCAP estimates that "currently, there are between 60 and 80 historically based nations in Canada, compared with a thousand or so local communities." See RCAP 1996c, 182.

15 Wilson-Raybould further describes *Indian Act* governance as follows: "it is an impoverished notion of government where the Chief and council are, for the most part, glorified Indian Agents delivering federal programs and services on behalf of Canada, where band councils have limited recognized legal authority to enact laws or make important decisions, and where accountability is primarily to Canada and not our citizens." See Wilson-Raybould 2019, 32.

16 Joyce Green establishes a close connection between the forces of imperialism and colonialism. With respect to Canada, for example, Green explains that its formation as a country "was initiated in the predatory economic and political activity of primarily European states, leading to the imposition of political and economic relationships on those they dominated." This process of foreign imposition Green defines as imperialism. Green further explains that imperialism morphs into colonialism when the imperial state establishes permanent settlements "with people from the imperial state." The relationship established with Indigenous peoples is characterized by Green as a colonial one because "the benefits accrue to the imperialist community at the expense of the colonized." See Green 2014b, 20.

17 Where the assertion to Indigenous sovereignty is concerned, however, nothing is ever straightforward. As one of the anonymous reviewers of this book points out, while many Indigenous nations press for recognition of their pre-contact sovereignty, it is also likely the case that through the colonial period Indigenous nations were compelled to give some of their sovereignty up. The reviewer observes, for example, that some argue that both the historical and modern treaties constituted exercises in which Indigenous nations gave up land and sovereignty. The reviewer identifies the Nisga'a and Tsawwassen treaties as examples.

18 In keeping with the sentiment as I characterize it, Paul Nadasdy argues that the experience of sovereignty is "intimately tied up with the construction, reconstruction, and maintenance of boundaries." Indeed, as he describes it, "sovereignty is fundamentally an exercise in boundary making." See Nadasdy 2017, 17.

19 Gary N. Wilson, Christopher Alcantara, and Thierry Rodon refer to the same phenomenon as "nested federalism," which they characterize as a governance arrangement that carries both structural opportunities and inherent constraints for Indigenous peoples. On the one hand, nested arrangements allow Indigenous peoples "to leave the jurisdiction of the Indian Act and exercise self-government," but on the other, the fact that they are inescapably politically and geographically "nested" within existing provinces and territories means that opportunities for self-rule are limited. As they explain it, in response to Indigenous demands for regional autonomy or self-rule, Canadian political elites have participated in creating new regional governments, but they also insist that the territorial integrity of the federal unit in which that government is located not be challenged nor that the constitutional structure of the broader federal system be threatened. In short, the authors conclude that nested federal arrangements are inherently limiting because they are designed to preserve "the fundamental structure of the

system, which is premised on the notion of Canadian sovereignty divided solely between two levels of government: federal and provincial." See Wilson, Alcantara, and Rodon 2020, 3–11.

20 The call to reconciliation also stands at the centre of the Final Report of the Truth and Reconciliation Commission of Canada. While the commission makes regular reference to the importance of truth-telling and apologies as part of the process of reconciliation, it also insists that healing itself is not possible outside of building respectful and healthy relationships between Indigenous and non-Indigenous peoples going forward. According to the commission, meaningful reconciliation must include "concrete actions that demonstrate real societal change," including, among other things, "revitalization of Indigenous law and legal traditions." See Truth and Reconciliation Commission of Canada 2015, vi, 6–7, 8, 12, 16.

CHAPTER 1

Contending Sovereignties: Prospects for Coexistence

LEARNING OBJECTIVES

1 To articulate why sovereignty is the primary principle upon which the justification for Indigenous rights rests.
2 To explain why justifications for Indigenous sovereignty must include references to their status as independent nations in the pre-European contact era.
3 To identify four models or approaches to Indigenous self-determination, including the challenges that each pose to the configuration of Canadian federalism.
4 To explain why the *Indian Act* band council system is an objectionable form of self-government from the point of view of Indigenous sovereignty.
5 To articulate in what ways Indigenous peoples are increasingly coming to occupy spaces in between the exercise of Canadian sovereignty to express their own nationhood.

Given the diversity of Indigenous political perspectives, there is no one single view about what Indigenous **sovereignty** ought to mean for the relationship between Indigenous peoples and the Canadian state. As we shall see throughout this book, the precise meaning of sovereignty can and does take on a number of forms. However, while positions vary, Indigenous leaders and scholars generally hold the view that as former political sovereigns, Indigenous nations remain entitled to exercise their right to self-determination in ways consistent with their own aspirations. That is, each nation remains entitled to set its own course, at its own pace, consistent with its own objectives for self-determination, now and into the future. As Jody Wilson-Raybould explains, the essential point from the perspective of sovereignty is that the important work of rebuilding Indigenous nations must be led by Indigenous peoples themselves: "No Crown government – or anyone else – can lead or do this work" (Wilson-Raybould 2019, 103). Sovereignty, in other words, means that Indigenous peoples are owed a duty of non-interference by the Canadian state as they engage in the internal process of reconstituting themselves as peoples and nations, as they rebuild their capacity for self-governance, and as they work out more equitable terms for the kinds of relations they wish to take up with Canadian governments. This chapter begins by identifying how the various features of this Indigenous assertion to sovereignty are justified at the level of principle.

With the different understandings of sovereignty clarified at the level of principle, I can then take the next step in the chapter's argument. Here I consider what sovereignty, as expressed through the Indigenous right to self-determination, can mean in practice. I will consider four models, each distinct from and in some respects exclusive to the others. I then offer an assessment of the merits and utility of these models, urging consideration of an alternative approach, one that I believe is both fully responsive to the Indigenous assertion to sovereignty within Canada while also avoiding the temptation to trade in the language of normative absolutes. This approach is principled, pragmatic, flexible, and process driven. It supports the proposition that Indigenous peoples are entitled to sovereignty but argues that what sovereignty entails can be expressed differently, across a range of options. What is essential in all cases of sovereignty's expression, in other words, is that it provide for the fullest expression of Indigenous identity and self-determination possible, in keeping with the aspirations of Indigenous peoples themselves. To get a sense of how Indigenous peoples assert their claim to sovereignty within Canada, the chapter starts with two brief case studies.

THE FEDERATION OF SOVEREIGN INDIGENOUS NATIONS AND THE CHIEFS OF ONTARIO

Indigenous leaders and organizations regularly use the language of sovereignty to articulate their visions for a decolonized future within Canada. Understanding what Indigenous leaders and organizations mean by sovereignty, therefore, is central to understanding the nature of their quest to free their peoples from all forms of colonial control. According to Paul Nadasdy, the importance of Indigenous sovereignty is considerable because it "serves as the conceptual precondition" for the Indigenous right to self-determination and self-government as well as "for Indigenous-state relations more generally" (Nadasdy 2017, 52). In their wide consultation with Indigenous scholars and activists as editors of a book on philosophy and Aboriginal rights, Sandra Tomsons and Lorraine Mayer are drawn to the same conclusion. They write, "if some Indigenous contributors [to the book] are correct, sovereignty is the right upon which all of the others rest – it is their source and justification" (Tomsons and Mayer 2013, xxxii). So, what is the Indigenous assertion to sovereignty all about? What does it entail, and how ought it to be understood? Consider what each of the Federation of Sovereign Indigenous Nations and Chiefs of Ontario have to say.

The Federation of Sovereign Indigenous Nations (FSIN) is an organization representing the interests of 74 First Nations in Saskatchewan. The FSIN defines its mandate as primarily devoted to advocating "for the protection and enforcement of Treaty rights and responsibilities, based on the FSIN's Treaty Implementation Principles." These treaty principles, in turn, situate the ideal of sovereignty at the centre of their design. For example, the FSIN traces the origin of First Nations to Mother Earth, the source of all their relationships to the "land, all forms of life, and our sovereignty." This original relationship to the land, coupled with the fact that First Nations "occupied North America as sovereign nations long before other people came to our shores" is then used to justify the ongoing existence of an Indigenous right to self-determination. The FSIN insists that the First Nations of Saskatchewan never surrendered nor were deprived of their sovereignty through military conquest – indeed, they say quite the opposite occurred. According the FSIN, the **Royal Proclamation of 1763** affirmed Indigenous sovereignty, thereby setting up a legal and political process for First Nations "to enter into Treaty and other political accords with other Nations." In essence, as the FSIN sees it, treaties served as conduits for First Nations and the Crown to affirm one another as sovereigns. The political implications that follow from this recognition are tremendously important for both the past and the present. As put by the FSIN, First Nations have always made their "own laws, institutions, and jurisdiction which reflects [their] culture, values, and jurisdiction," and as political sovereigns they remain no less entitled to do so today. In short, treaties are said to have validated the political power of Indigenous nations, including their inherent right to self-determination. It is for this reason that the FSIN concludes: "Our sovereignty defines our nationhood and this will continue forever" (Federation of Sovereign Indigenous Nations 2007).

The Chiefs of Ontario, an advocacy forum for 133 First Nations in Ontario, expresses the Indigenous entitlement to sovereignty in similar terms. In their document *Understanding First Nations Sovereignty*, they too link the source of their inherent right to self-determination to their status as (former) sovereign nations. For the Chiefs, the right to self-determination carries with it "jurisdiction (the right, power, and authority) to administer and operate our own political, legal, economic, social, and cultural systems." Especially important is the land and Indigenous peoples' relationship to it. They state that "the land is the founding source of our identity and culture," and as such, they carry "great responsibilities to protect and preserve the land." Treaties also feature prominently in the Chiefs' understanding of sovereignty. They claim that recognition of their sovereign nationhood was secured through treaties, which further established how the treaty partners would coexist. As sovereign nations that "never surrendered our rights or title in right of the Crown or the successor state of Canada," treaties put them in a working arrangement with "the successor state of Canada … on the basis of a government-to-government relationship" (Chiefs of Ontario n.d.).

SOVEREIGNTY IN PRINCIPLE: INDIGENOUS LEADERS SPEAK

Noticeably absent in the two above declarations of sovereignty is any reference to state-like systems of organized power. Generally speaking, Indigenous peoples do not harness Western notions of state power to the political ambitions of their nations nor do they adopt Western state models as those best equipped to advance Indigenous interests.[1] Indigenous scholar Bonita Lawrence points out that "for Indigenous peoples … nationhood was (and is) not a matter of size or of maintaining a formal government structure or a coercive state apparatus" (Lawrence 2012, 28). What Indigenous peoples do insist on, however, is their ongoing right to exercise control over their peoples, resources, lands, and relations with the Canadian state in ways that reflect their own understandings of themselves as nations. It is sovereignty in the form of peoples making political decisions for themselves, free from external control, that seems to be what is at issue for most Indigenous peoples, not the acquisition of independent statehood (Webber 2016, 81).

Indigenous leaders generally speak of sovereignty in quite different terms, and they also tend to justify its applicability to their political circumstances by means of a distinct set of criteria. They regularly point to a notion of sovereignty that originates within the people who make up Indigenous nations rather than with the attributes of a nation (or state) itself. For example, Leroy Little Bear suggests that for Indigenous peoples, sovereignty is really all about distinct peoples occupying particular territories and making their own decisions. As he puts it: "When we look at the notion of sovereignty from an Aboriginal perspective … it really is about independence. It is about the group, tribe, First Nation, whatever we call it, making up its own mind" (Little Bear 2013, 7). Indigenous sovereignty, in other words, is construed as the ability to give expression to the Indigenous "self" as distinct peoples with distinct identities that separate them from others. It is a sovereignty that, as John Grant puts it, "comes from below rather than from above like state sovereignty" (Grant 2018, 141).

The problem that follows, of course, is that Indigenous peoples have no choice but to give expression to their sovereign selves within a setting of colonial domination. Consequently, Indigenous leaders are compelled to adopt arguments that not only serve to establish the credentials of their assertion to sovereignty, but which, at the same time, seek to discredit the assertion of Canadian state sovereignty over their peoples (Macdonald, F. 2014, 615). They must, in other words, carve out space for the expression of Indigenous sovereignty within the Canadian state, an exercise that Audra Simpson describes as one that regularly puts both orders in "terrific tension" with one another (Simpson 2014, 10). The kinds of arguments that Indigenous leaders advance to present their case for sovereignty come in the following forms: (1) the pre-contact standing of Indigenous political systems; (2) the rights that flow from Indigenous prior occupancy; and (3) the rights that are established in international law. Each argument serves in some sense as a form of political resistance against Canadian state domination.

PRE-CONTACT STANDING

First, Indigenous leaders point out that **pre-contact** Indigenous nations were clearly sovereign in the sense that they exercised exclusive political authority over their citizens, lands, and resources, though, of course, this authority was often exercised in ways very different from that of European states. Each Indigenous nation had its own unique political system, domestic law, and protocols regulating relations with other nations – the practices of the Mi'kmaq, Iroquois, Blackfoot Confederacy, and Inuit, to name just a few examples, differing as much from one another as they did from their European counterparts.[2] In each case, Indigenous governments fulfilled key political tasks typically associated with sovereignty: they maintained order, resolved conflicts, regulated geographical boundaries, cared for the land and its resources, decided citizenship, and generally represented the interests of their citizens, all in keeping with the distinct values and beliefs central to the life of each nation (Belanger 2018, 295–6; see also Simpson 2017, 3). Consequently, as Roger Townshend points out, "it would be arrogant and ethnocentric to recognize only a European model of political organization as capable of possessing sovereignty" (Townshend 2015, 36).

It is also clear that when Europeans first arrived on North American shores, they understood that what they encountered were highly sophisticated Indigenous confederacies. Consequently, not only were Europeans dependent upon Indigenous peoples for their very survival, but they were also compelled to engage with Indigenous leaders in acts of political diplomacy to gain access to the plentiful resources that had drawn them to the continent in the first place. By necessity, Europeans conducted their early political relations with Indigenous nations as independent foreign sovereigns. As the weaker partner, Europeans realized that if they were to thrive in North America, they simply had to conform to Indigenous peoples' diplomatic expectations of them. The diplomatic result typically generated treaties, designed to create and maintain cooperative relations between European and Indigenous foreign partners based on an ethic of mutual respect and consent.

The Royal Proclamation of 1763, in turn, lent formal legal recognition to the treaty process that both preceded and followed it. By means of its provisions, the British Crown guaranteed that there would be no settlement on Indigenous lands without Indigenous consent. In return, Indigenous peoples were promised that they would not be "molested or disturbed" in the territories remaining under their jurisdiction. They would continue, in other words, to operate as sovereigns on their territories, much as they had done before, but with the added benefit that treaty partners would support one another in times of need or crisis (Asch 2014, 96–7, 101; see also Ladner 2018, 260).

As described by Leanne Simpson, "we signed early treaties as international diplomatic agreements with the Crown to protect the land and to ensure our sovereignty, nationhood, and way of life" (Simpson 2017, 5; see also 9). Gina Starblanket further argues that treaties played the dual role of establishing formal relationships while at the same time guaranteeing that Indigenous nations would not be incorporated into the settler-colonial state (Starblanket 2019a, 20).

PRIOR OCCUPANCY

Second, Indigenous leaders argue that their assertion to sovereignty is supported by the fact that their peoples were the **first occupants** of North America. As we shall see later in this book, the Supreme Court of Canada has made the reality of original presence or **prior occupancy** one of the central pillars upon which it has built its entire doctrine of Aboriginal rights (McNeil 2007, 6–7). In its words, Aboriginal rights exist "because of one simple fact: when Europeans arrived in North America, aboriginal peoples were already here, living in communities on the land, and participating in distinctive cultures, as they had done for centuries" (*R. v. Van Der Peet* 1996, para. 30). Michael Asch refers to this justification as "temporal priority," which he describes as a principle holding "that people who were here before European settlement have rights which those who come later must recognize" (Asch 2014, 34; see also Asch 2018, 32–3). As a principle, then, the idea of "temporal priority" or original occupancy lends powerful justification to the Indigenous assertion to sovereignty, particularly as applied to Indigenous jurisdiction over their ancestral territories. There can be no doubt that when compared to Europeans, Indigenous peoples were first or prior occupants. Furthermore, Indigenous peoples had occupied their ancestral territories for generations, the land being the source of all relationships and resources essential to a meaningful and fulfilling Indigenous way of life. And Indigenous peoples continue to possess deep connections to their lands today, connections that have formed and been nurtured over the course of centuries. On these historical grounds alone, Indigenous leaders say that compared to settlers, Indigenous peoples have a much stronger claim on the land.

When historical arguments are combined with those informed by identity, the Indigenous position only strengthens. Indigenous leaders regularly refer to the land as integral to their peoples' sense of identity, often in profoundly spiritual ways. They speak of the responsibilities placed on their peoples by the Creator to care for the land and for the plants and animals with whom they share the territory that has been entrusted to them. As put by Laurelyn Whitt, "for many Indigenous peoples land is constitutive of culture and identity. Far from being 'disassociated' with the land, traditional Indigenous forms of governance hold themselves accountable above all for protecting the land and resources that constitute them as distinct peoples and towards which they have crucial role responsibilities" (Whitt 2013, 189; see also McGregor 2020, 189–90 and Starblanket 2020, 24). A restoration of Indigenous sovereignty, therefore, is a political necessity because it is inextricably linked to the central Indigenous task to care for creation. Conversely, as Deborah McGregor explains, to be denied sovereignty is to be prevented "from exercising their duties and responsibilities to all their relations," which also effectively means that

Indigenous peoples are denied the right to security of their distinctive collective identities (McGregor 2020, 191).

INTERNATIONAL LAW

Third, Indigenous leaders also regularly deploy the language of **international law** to substantiate their claims to sovereignty. Rauna Kuokkanen explains that "Indigenous rights advocates have been instrumental in redefining the concept of self-determination and advancing collective rights in international law." She says that what Indigenous leaders have managed to do is secure a place for Indigenous human rights within "the third-generation human rights, centring on collective rights and, in particular, the right to self-determination" (Kuokkanen 2012, 227). When framed as a human right, the collective right to self-determination is most fundamentally about the equal right of all peoples to live free from discrimination and to remain distinct peoples, firmly in control of the circumstances in which they live. Michael Asch points to the 1960 United Nations Declaration on Decolonization, reaffirmed in identical language in the 2007 UNDRIP, to illustrate what this fundamental human right involves: "All peoples have the right to self-determination; by virtue of that right they freely determine their political status and freely pursue their economic, social, and cultural development" (Asch 2014, 60, 65).

The fact that the Indigenous right to self-determination has been denied and that they have become internally colonized peoples is, therefore, a profound injustice by the standards of international law (Grammond 2009, 32). International law also outlines what is required by way of reparation. Short of their consent, sovereignty could not (and still cannot) be acquired by colonial powers over Indigenous peoples by means of occupation. Instead, as argued by Asch, "the right to political self-determination of colonized peoples remains" (Asch 2014, 60). Consequently, the nature of the political remedy required is clear: as put by the Assembly of First Nations, Indigenous nations are entitled to have their sovereignty restored. In its words: "The Canadian government has at no point been able to provide proof that First Nations have expressly and of their own free will renounced their sovereign attributes. Our position is that Indigenous Peoples have never renounced their international juridical status as Nations or Peoples" (AFN 2018a, 1).[3] In essence, according to the standards of international law, Indigenous peoples retain both their right to be internally self-defining and their right to exist in a nation-to-nation relationship of political equivalency with the Canadian state. The Indigenous assertion to sovereignty, in other words, requires of the Canadian state that it withdraw the illegitimate extension of its sovereign power over Indigenous peoples.

IS SOVEREIGNTY AN INHERENTLY WESTERN CONCEPT?

There are some scholars, however, who argue that sovereignty ought not to be pressed into the service of Indigenous emancipation given the concept's European origins. Within mainstream political science, for example, there is a presumption that when someone raises the issue of sovereignty, what is actually being referred to is the phenomenon of "state sovereignty" (Bruyneel 2007, 23). Taiaiake Alfred is one such Indigenous scholar who warns Indigenous leaders not to confuse Indigenous nationhood with state sovereignty because he believes it is not "the appropriate model for indigenous government" (Alfred 2009, 79). The problem, as Alfred sees it, is that the concept draws on European notions of a unitary state where sovereignty is typically expressed through an absolute political authority that has little, if any, legal constraints imposed on its use of political power (RCAP 1996c, 111; see also Ladner 2017, 169). To adopt such a state model is dangerous, says Alfred, because traditional Indigenous notions of nationhood draw from very different meanings and perspectives about the nature of law, governance, and culture (Barker 2005, 19). As he puts it, "traditional indigenous nationhood stands in sharp contrast to the dominant understanding of 'the state': there is no absolute authority, no coercive enforcement of decisions, no hierarchy, and no ruling entity" (Alfred 2009, 80).

Alfred therefore concludes that authentic expressions of Indigenous nationhood must reject European state models of sovereignty that perpetuate hierarchical notions of governmental power and exploitive domination of territory. Instead, they ought to take their point of orientation from Indigenous philosophies that respect "the understanding of power in indigenous cultures" (Alfred 2009, 80). When Indigenous leaders choose traditional approaches to Indigenous governance, Alfred believes they must also reject the terms and conditions of colonial rule. It is important to Alfred, in other words, that Indigenous leaders strive to undermine "the intellectual credibility of state sovereignty as the only legitimate form of political organization" (Alfred 2009, 87). Because the concept is not embedded in Indigenous philosophies, Alfred concludes that "sovereignty can never be part of the language of liberation" (Alfred 2009, 78).

There is much to appreciate in Alfred's compelling critique of sovereignty's Western, colonial origins. But despite problems of the kind that Alfred identifies, there are scholars who nevertheless hold onto the view that the concept can and should be adapted for use in the Indigenous struggle against colonial domination (Nadasdy 2017, 46–52 76–7; see also Mackey 2016, 15–16; Simpson 2014, 105; and Bruyneel 2007, 224–5). Indeed, as Paul Nadasdy points out, even Alfred himself seems to provide an opening in his own analysis for the possibility of sovereignty's rehabilitation. As Nadasdy explains, while at times Alfred seems "to reject sovereignty altogether, at other times he argues instead that indigenous peoples must reject not the term itself but only the Euro-American *meanings* assigned to it" (Nadasdy 2017, 47). In effect, what Alfred seems most concerned about is that the notion of sovereignty be severed from its Western legal roots. If transformed in ways "that respects the understanding of power in indigenous cultures" then he too seems willing to accept the proposition that sovereignty can become part of the language of Indigenous liberation (Alfred 1999, 54; see also Alfred 2005, 42; 2009, 80).

I conclude, therefore, that for the notion of sovereignty to be useful to the struggles of Indigenous peoples, it must resonate with their cultural experiences and political ambitions. But what does that mean exactly? For the purposes of this book, I believe that sovereignty can resonate with Indigenous experiences if taken to mean two things.

First, sovereignty must be de-linked from its "statist pattern" (Alfred 2009, 80; Ladner 2017, 164). We need to avoid definitions that dictate that sovereignty is a political attribute exclusively reserved for independent states. Instead, I apply the notion of sovereignty to political communities that have (or are entitled to have) the ability to make their own decisions about the direction of the collective life on territories that they regard as their own (Bruyneel 2007, 23; Little Bear 2013, 6–7). When understood in this way, the concept can be readily applied to the historical and current struggles by Indigenous nations for liberation from the legal and political constraints imposed on them by the Canadian state.

Second, the notion of sovereignty must have cultural relevance for the Indigenous nations that choose to use it. For example, in its examination of Indigenous approaches to sovereignty during its public hearing phase, the Royal Commission on Aboriginal Peoples observed that witnesses did not refer to sovereignty in terms that would authorize their right to establish all-powerful governments over their peoples or territories. Instead, when witnesses spoke of sovereignty they did so with respect to the practice of political responsibility. As explained by RCAP: "for many Aboriginal peoples [sovereignty] means that the people take care of themselves and the lands for which they are responsible. It means using political power to express the people's will" (RCAP 1996c, 112). Based on these observations, RCAP concludes that far from accepting Eurocentric notions of sovereignty, Indigenous peoples tend to present very different understandings. Their approach to sovereignty is informed by deep commitments to the practice of taking responsibility for the land, maintaining balanced relationships, and preserving a measure of community autonomy from one another (RCAP 1996c, 111–12; see also Little Bear 2013, 6–7 and Ladner 2005, 939–40).

Based on evidence presented by RCAP and others, it seems reasonable to conclude that the notion of sovereignty can be, and in many instances has been, brought into conformity with Indigenous political visions and cultural understandings of themselves and their place in the world (Nadasdy 2017, 77–81). Indeed, on this matter RCAP is very clear: the concept is being used by Indigenous peoples to support and enhance the development of their cultural and political identities (RCAP 1996c, 108–15). Therefore, I conclude that insofar as the language of sovereignty is being used to mobilize and consolidate such Indigenous visions for themselves in relation to the Canadian state, to that degree sovereignty can also serve as an important tool for Indigenous decolonization.

But finally, we might ask, why expend so much effort to rehabilitate a concept whose roots lie so deep within the soil of "European languages and political thought" (RCAP 1996a, 111)? Why not heed Alfred's warning and simply abandon the notion of sovereignty in favour of a more relevant, Indigenous-informed alternative? Here I follow Nadasdy's lead by arguing that sovereignty is an indispensable political tool because of the powerful legitimating role it can play in the lives of Indigenous peoples (Nadasdy 2017, 51, 76–7). Sovereignty implies the presence of government, which is precisely what Indigenous peoples need in order to give full expression to their right to self-determination. Sovereignty also attributes to Indigenous nations a political status that refutes "the dominant notion that indigenous peoples were merely one among many 'minority groups' under the administration of state social service and welfare programs" (Barker 2005, 18). In short, sovereignty is important because through it Indigenous peoples are entitled to claim "concrete rights to self-government, territorial integrity, and cultural autonomy under international customary law" (Barker 2005, 18; see also Nadasdy 2017, 84). Sovereignty advances the powerful notion that Indigenous peoples are entitled to take up government-to-government relationships with the states in which they are found.

What conclusions can be drawn from the preceding analysis? What does the language of sovereignty actually tell us about what Indigenous peoples seek in their quest for justice and reconciliation? I offer three observations.

First, many Indigenous peoples in Canada hold the position that their nations retain sovereignty as a matter of principle, but their ability to practise their sovereignty has been severely diminished by the historical and political relationship of dispossession imposed on them by the Canadian state. Consequently, the language of Indigenous sovereignty often serves as a form of political resistance against Canadian state domination. Through it, Indigenous peoples seek to disentangle themselves and their communities from the monopoly of power imposed on them by the Canadian state (Ladner 2005, 924; Green 2009, 42).

Second, many Indigenous peoples believe that the Canadian state's assertion to sovereignty can only apply to settlers and not to themselves. Indigenous peoples did not consent to submit themselves to the sovereignty of the Canadian state. Therefore, in as much as the Canadian state does exercise sovereignty over land and resources in the country now called Canada, this right comes to Canada as a product of treaty arrangements in which Indigenous nations agreed to release and, in some situations, share its jurisdiction. In a hierarchy of descending sovereignties, in other words, it is the sovereignty of Indigenous nations that ought to be given priority over that of the Canadian state, and not the other way around.[4]

And third, as sovereign nations, Indigenous peoples may choose how to govern themselves. They are in a legal position to exercise control over any area of jurisdiction that follows from their sovereign right to be self-defining. And this means it is up to Indigenous nations, not the Canadian state, to decide what constitutes the appropriate reach of their own powers of self-government.

SOVEREIGNTY IN PRACTICE: FOUR MODELS

As we have seen, many Indigenous peoples in Canada maintain that they possess political sovereignty, a position that comes to them because of their status as free-standing, independent nations prior to contact, their prior occupancy on the land, and their ongoing right to self-determination under international law. The question of interest for us now turns to practical matters. What might Indigenous sovereignty, as practised in Canada, look like? What follows describes four prevalent models or approaches found within Canadian political discourse, all of which compete for public attention. Each is, in some sense, deficient by the standards of the others. All are informed by contending visions about how Indigenous sovereignty is to be understood and brought into both a workable and fair arrangement with the sovereignty of the Canadian state.

The first model (**municipality**) advances a vision that ignores Indigenous sovereignty altogether, opting instead for a form of self-administration in which power is delegated to Indigenous nations from the federal government. In this model, state sovereignty is taken to be divided solely and exhaustively between federal and provincial governments, and this is as it should be. The second model (**third order of government**) advances a vision that would see Indigenous sovereignty drawn into the fabric of the Canadian state, taking its place within a reconfigured federalism as a third order of government alongside that of the federal and provincial orders. Here Indigenous sovereignty is taken to complete Canada according to a design that ensures the sovereignty of the Canadian state remains essentially uninterrupted and intact. The third model (**treaty federalism**) advances a vision that would see Indigenous sovereignty exercised alongside that of the Canadian state according to protocols in which each takes the other to be an independent political actor. Here Indigenous sovereignty is taken to be equivalent to that of Canadian sovereignty, which means that the nature of their joint occupation of the land now called Canada must be defined through treaties. The fourth model, or more accurately approach (**Indigenous resurgence**), advances a vision that would see Indigenous sovereignty exercised entirely independently of and without any reference to the Canadian state. Here Indigenous sovereignty is taken to authorize Indigenous peoples to revitalize their traditional legal orders and governance systems immediately and under their own authority, preferably under conditions that involve a wholesale repudiation of what are seen as the irredeemably colonialist ambitions of the Canadian state.

DELEGATED MODEL (MUNICIPALITY)

The first approach comes in the form of a **delegated model**, which, strictly speaking, means that supreme political authority or sovereignty remains in the hands of the Canadian state. Few if any Indigenous peoples regard this approach as acceptable when pitched as a long-term strategy for Indigenous re-empowerment because it constitutes an ongoing denial of Indigenous sovereignty.

The best illustration of the delegated model in action comes to us through the *Indian Act* band council system. Importantly, there is a huge difference between the structure of the Indigenous nations that occupied territories and exercised jurisdiction across North America prior to and upon the arrival of Europeans and the Indigenous nations of Canada today. The process of colonization has had devastating impacts on what used to be large and influential Indigenous nations, "causing many of them to be fragmented into smaller units" (McNeil 2007, 4). It was the establishment of Indian reserves and the imposition of the corresponding band council system through the *Indian Act* that are responsible for the creation of these tiny Indian bands, most of which are now referred to as "First Nations." It is important to remember, says Bonita Lawrence, that these bands are only "small subsets of pre-existing nations." She points out that "instead of acknowledging the existence of fifty-odd Indigenous nations across the land, Canada recognizes over six hundred tiny subgroups of these nations as Indian bands," which are scattered across more than 2,200 reserves across the country (Lawrence 2012, 5; see also Wilson-Raybould 2019, 47). According to Lawrence, this scattering exercise was by design.

When formerly large Indigenous nations are fragmented into tiny Indian bands, they are much easier to control. Under these circumstances, for example, it was much easier to impose a delegated model of Indigenous governance that was designed to promote Indigenous assimilation into the fabric of the Canadian state (Ladner 2006, 6).

How is the delegated band council system structured? Under the band council model, the federal government derives its power from the Canadian Constitution, and band councils derive their power from the federal government. The primary instrument for federal control over "Indians and lands reserved for Indians" is the ***Indian Act***, a federal statute first passed in 1876 (*Constitution Act, 1867*, Section 91(24)). The *Indian Act* defines both the scope and limitations of band council governmental power. The Act defines the basis for membership in Indian bands and the procedures for election to its governments; it lays out what are best construed as the largely administrative powers of those governments; it defines the relationship of band members and their reserve lands to provincial governments; and it "establishes a regime for the management of reserve lands and the economic activity of those who belong to bands" (Cassidy and Bish 1989, 40; see also Abele and Prince 2006, 572–4; and Wilson-Raybould 2019, 21–2, 66, 103).

It should be noted at this point, though, that band councils today generally exercise a greater degree of discretionary political decision-making power than was permitted in their original design. Indeed, federal, provincial, and territorial governments have long engaged in active campaigns to delegate some of their political authority to encourage Indigenous nations to exercise greater power over the design and delivery of some local services. Policy areas that have been targeted for particular attention include education, family and child welfare, social development, housing, language, and culture (Papillon 2014, 117). Enabling legislation is then passed by either one or both levels of government (depending on which level of government has "delegated" its authority to the Indigenous nation), which authorizes the Indigenous nation to assume jurisdiction over the local service just negotiated. Power is thereby expanded through a process of gradual augmentation.

At the end of the day, however, there is no sidestepping the fact that the powers Indian bands exercise are conferred on them by the Canadian state and are generally limited to specifically local or sectoral matters. Consequently, Indian bands may well exercise a degree of power over a local service of importance to them, but they do so only at the pleasure of the authorizing government. In addition, the limited power that Indian bands do have is subject to all kinds of constraints. For example, they can have their by-laws overturned by the federal minister responsible; a sizable proportion of most band revenue comes from the federal government, often with strings attached; and the federal government is always in a position to either unilaterally change or cancel band-delivered programs (Wilson-Raybould 2019, 32, 103; see also Flanagan 2019, 19–28). In short, Indigenous governments are ultimately accountable for the exercise of their political power to federal authorities rather than their own citizens. It is on the basis of grounds such as these that Kiera Ladner concludes "fundamentally, band councils are colonial institutions" (Ladner 2006, 8; see also Green 2020, 248). The delegated model simply offers Indigenous nations no formal recognition as sovereign political actors.

However, as a matter of practice, I believe that this "delegated" approach can be construed as lending some recognition to Indigenous sovereignty if understood in a very specific way. For those Indigenous nations who wish to resume "the exercise of their inherent authority in a gradual manner," the delegated approach can be seen as one way in which Canadian governments can give back to those nations the power that was theirs all along, beginning with those high-priority policy areas that Indigenous peoples identify themselves (RCAP 1996c, 143). As argued by Kevin Bruyneel, delegation (or "devolution," as he calls it) in such circumstances can be seen as "a matter of the federal government's 'giving back' rather than just 'giving' powers to tribes." The act of delegating powers, in other words, is not, nor should it be seen as, "a creation or gift of the United States" (or in the Canadian setting, a creation or gift of Canada) (Bruyneel 2007, 175). Instead, it is important to remember that at the time of European contact, Indigenous peoples were sovereign, and although colonial rule curtailed and tightly regulated that sovereignty, it has never been extinguished (RCAP 1996c, 202). Consequently, what Indigenous peoples now seek are opportunities to restore that sovereignty by means of any number of political strategies available to them.

One such strategy can come in the form of the delegated model, but I hasten to add only if it provides a foundation upon which to build an expanded scope for autonomous Indigenous decision making (Abele and Prince 2006, 573). For example, if a degree of local Indigenous autonomy can be acquired through a delegation of state powers to such sectoral areas as education, family and child welfare, social development, housing, language, and culture, the subsequent experience of local capacity building that results can, in turn, be dedicated to further efforts at achieving local control over other high-priority policy areas like lands and resources. Leroy Little Bear further adds that simply taking over a program from the Canadian government is not being sovereign. However, if that program is rearranged and brought into conformity with the cultural needs of an Indigenous nation, this would constitute fundamental change of a kind that he believes is consistent with the practice of sovereignty (Little Bear 2013, 8–9). The cumulative effect over time is an enhanced capacity for self-determination. Put differently, while the delegated model is often taken to authorize no more than a form of local self-administration, it can also, under the right conditions, be used to lend support to Indigenous efforts at rebuilding their own sovereignty. Just how this is possible is a topic that I will take up later in the book.

INHERENT MODEL (THIRD ORDER OF GOVERNMENT)

The second model develops an approach that would see Indigenous sovereignty drawn into the fabric of Canada, taking its place within a reconfigured federalism as a third order of government. Here Indigenous sovereignty is taken to complete Canada when aligned alongside that of the federal and provincial governments (Poelzer and Coates 2015, 224).

This approach begins from the premise that Indigenous sovereignty is **inherent** to Indigenous peoples because of their status as independent, self-governing nations well before Canada was established (Frideres 2020, 205). While the inherent rights of Indigenous peoples have long been denied by the Canadian state, it is the contention of those who espouse this model that Section 35 of the Canadian Constitution was designed specifically "to address and overcome this denial" (Wilson-Raybould 2019, 11). Introduced in 1982, Section 35 is taken to provide explicit recognition and protection to Indigenous rights, including treaty rights, and, while not explicitly stated, to self-government rights as well (RCAP 1996c, 166, 202). As the inherent right to self-government is now said to be entrenched within the Canadian Constitution, it naturally follows that this recognition also provides the basis for Indigenous peoples to assert that their relations with Canadian governments must be conducted on the premise that both are sovereign political actors. Indigenous rights are no longer to be denied, assimilation and marginalization is to be relegated to the colonial past, and Indigenous peoples will henceforth conduct their relations with Canada as political equals (Grant 2018, 124). In short, behind the inherent model stands a particular view of the place Indigenous peoples ought to occupy in their relationships to the Canadian state: it must be a partnership based on mutual respect, cooperation, and the sharing or merging of sovereignties.

Importantly, however, because recognition and protection for Indigenous rights is now established within the Canadian Constitution, this means that Indigenous peoples are also required to submit to its authority. The character of this submission is illustrated by the kind of political power to which Indigenous governments are said to be constitutionally entitled. Most spokespersons take the position that Indigenous governments are entitled to exercise distinct jurisdictional authority within the framework of Canadian federalism. Most typically, this new arrangement is described as one in which Indigenous governments function as one of three distinct orders alongside that of the federal and provincial governments (RCAP 1996c, 166). The task at hand, therefore, is to negotiate a new division of powers between federal, provincial, and Indigenous governments such that each has access to the bundle of powers for which they are particularly well suited and uniquely qualified. In the case of Indigenous nations, these powers must be such that they have primary (though not necessarily exclusive) authority over their own citizens and territories except insofar as those powers may be subject to other provisions found within the *Constitution Act, 1982*, including the ***Charter of Rights and Freedoms***. The general sentiment expressed is that Indigenous nations must be able to exercise their right to self-determination within a system of cooperative federalism where power is shared between the three orders in their joint jurisdiction of the entire country (Abele and Prince 2006, 576–9; RCAP 1996c, 112; Wilson-Raybould 2019, 8, 50, 57, 59). Put otherwise, when situated within this model Indigenous peoples do not challenge Canadian sovereignty so much as take their place within it. They consent to join Canada as full and equal (third order) governments in an integrated federal system.

Just how Indigenous sovereignty could be accommodated within the framework of Canadian federalism has been the subject of much study. One of the most robust models ever put forward is to be found within the final report of the 1996 Royal Commission on Aboriginal Peoples.

Appointed by the Conservative government of Brian Mulroney in 1991, RCAP was mandated to investigate and recommend ways of improving life conditions across all sectors for Indigenous peoples in Canada.[5] RCAP operated from 1991 to 1996, generating countless pages of transcript hearings, commissioning a wide-ranging set of research papers, and publishing a five-volume report containing 440 recommendations.

At the level of principle, RCAP championed a nation-to-nation (or what I will refer to in the next section as "treaty federalism") model that would have Indigenous nations operating alongside the Canadian state as autonomous political actors bound together through commitments to mutual recognition, respect, and cooperation.[6] RCAP employed the historic "Two-Row Wampum" as expressive of this vision. The term originates from an early seventeenth-century wampum belt that represents an agreement between the Dutch and Haudenosaune in which two parallel lines symbolize the partners' intent to navigate the same river in peaceful coexistence but to remain in separate vessels, honouring a duty of non-interference with respect to each other. Essential to this image is that while territory and resources may be shared (both travel the same river), the navigation and internal conduct of relations within each ship are to remain entirely separate. According to this vision, Indigenous nations are to retain complete sovereignty in their bilateral relations with the Canadian state.

At the level of practice, however, RCAP opted for political arrangements that essentially integrated Indigenous nations into the Canadian state as third order governments. On the one hand, therefore, RCAP argued that the Indigenous right to self-determination grants Indigenous peoples' governmental powers that can promote "a high degree of sovereignty," but on the other hand, it declared that those powers must be exercised "within Canada" (RCAP 1996c, 172). A recalibrated Canadian federalism, therefore, became RCAP's preferred solution. As put by RCAP, federalism is the best way forward because it provides "the basis for recognizing Aboriginal governments as one of three distinct orders of government in Canada." The hallmark of Canadian federalism, it said, is a commitment to shared sovereignty, which means that, in the "three-cornered relations" that link Indigenous, federal, and provincial governments, all three "are sovereign within their respective spheres and hold their powers by virtue of their constitutional status rather than by delegation" (RCAP 1996c, 240).

In terms of actual design, RCAP recommended the following regarding how Indigenous sovereignty should operate within Canada: Indigenous nations would have "an *actual* right to exercise jurisdiction over certain core subject matters … of vital concern to the life and welfare of the community" as well as "a *potential* right to deal with a range of matters that lie beyond the core area and extend to the outer periphery of potential Aboriginal jurisdiction" (RCAP 1993, 38). The criteria for determining the difference between *core* and *peripheral* authority as well as areas that lie outside Indigenous jurisdiction relate to what RCAP termed "Indigenous identity and interest." Core areas refer to those law-making responsibilities in which Indigenous nations should have jurisdiction if they are to be self-defining. These areas would include citizenship; lands and resources; social, educational, and health services;

economic development; language and culture; and various aspects of the criminal justice system (RCAP 1996a, 221–2). Peripheral areas refer to those law-making responsibilities in which Indigenous nations may have an interest but that also have "a major impact on adjacent jurisdictions or attract transcendent federal or provincial concern" (RCAP 1996a, 223–4). These areas (among them criminal justice) require a substantial degree of coordination between Indigenous, federal, and provincial governments, so RCAP concluded that Indigenous governments must not legislate in these areas "until agreements had been concluded with federal and provincial governments" (RCAP 1996a, 224). Areas that lie outside Indigenous jurisdiction, according to RCAP, include national defence, international trade, banking and currency, bankruptcy and insolvency, navigation and shipping, postal service, and so on (RCAP 1996a, 222–3). These are areas in which the federal government currently possesses jurisdiction, and RCAP was of the view that these matters are best handled at the national level.

While many spokespersons support the proposition that Indigenous sovereignty can and should be expressed within the framework of Canadian federalism, Martin Papillon explains that this approach does have its limits. Within this model, Indigenous sovereignty is required to operate within the already established boundaries of the Canadian state. Consequently, "even if Aboriginal governments are recognized as predating the Canadian federation, they are ultimately still operating within a constitutional structure defined without their consent or involvement" (Papillon 2014, 119; see also Grant 2018, 124–6; Tully 2008, 285–7). They may well acquire an equitable place in a reconstituted Canadian federalism, in other words, but they do so at the cost of having to submit themselves to the ultimate sovereignty of a Canadian state in which they remain relatively small political players.

And even securing an equitable place within a reconstituted Canadian federalism is open to question. RCAP's model is purportedly built on the foundation of the Indigenous inherent right to self-determination. Yet in the next breath RCAP insists that the substantive meaning of that right must be subject to the outcome of negotiations with the federal and provincial governments. One could then justifiably ask whether the right is inherent at all. How can the right be inherent if RCAP (and others) insist that its expression must be contingent on securing the agreement of Canadian governments (Murphy 2005, 12; Starblanket 2019a, 19)? In short, while the inherent model certainly authorizes enhanced Indigenous political autonomy, it does so within a framework that refuses to question the credentials of the Canadian federal constitutional order and Indigenous peoples' subservient place within it (Wilson, Alcantara, and Rodon 2020, 6). Kiera Ladner therefore concludes that this model offers Indigenous peoples little more than a position of "negotiated inferiority" within Canada (Ladner 2018, 247; Asch 2014, 106).

AUTONOMOUS MODEL (TREATY FEDERALISM)

The third approach comes in the form of an **autonomous model**, which presumes that Indigenous sovereignty coexists alongside that of the Canadian state. According to this approach, Indigenous sovereignty is a political entitlement that flows independently from Indigenous nationhood, not the Canadian state, and justifies maximizing Indigenous separation from Canadian political oversight (Starblanket 2019a, 19). Far from operating as a third order of government within a reconstituted Canadian federalism, in other words, this approach would have Indigenous governments restored to a position of political autonomy "*outside* the institutions of Canadian federalism" (Papillon 2014, 119). As Indigenous sovereignty is said to be equivalent to Canadian sovereignty, a decolonized future must include political arrangements in which the constitutional orders of each operate distinct from and alongside that of the other. Frances Abele and Michael Prince describe the essential difference between the inherent and autonomous models as follows: "instead of joining the Canadian confederation, sovereign Aboriginal authorities establish a relationship with the confederation, defined by treaty" (Abele and Prince 2006, 579).

Within this model, it is historical relations that serve as the normative prototype for future engagement. Spokespersons observe that Indigenous nations were initially treated by European powers as sovereign, demonstrated by the fact that early relations between Europeans and Indigenous nations were formalized through diplomatic treaties and alliances to which both offered their consent. It is this model of "treaty federalism" that is put forward as the foundation upon which contemporary partnerships between Indigenous nations and the Canadian state ought to be rebuilt (Papillon 2014, 119; 2020, 221; Ladner 2003, 47). The model suggests, in the first place, that the Indigenous right to self-determination, including governance, originates from outside of the Canadian state, and in the second place, that Indigenous peoples were and still are self-determining nations "with their own distinct legal and political orders" (Papillon 2020, 221). Indigenous nations, in other words, stand ready to resume their place as treaty partners in bilateral relations with the Canadian state. For example, as John Borrows demonstrates at length, many Indigenous constitutions remain alive and well and so need not be created so much as rearticulated and then brought into formal political relationships with Canada's Constitution (Borrows 2010). According to this perspective, then, political liberation entails a high degree of political disentanglement and separation from Canada. As put by James Tully, "Indigenous peoples can be free and self-determining only when they govern themselves by their own constitutions, and these are equal in international status to Western constitutions" (Tully 2008, 286). What this model calls for, in other words, is a radical realignment of the way in which Indigenous and Canadian sovereignty is both conceptualized and organized.

While there is no single Indigenous perspective that captures the essence of the treaty federalism model in its entirety, there are several Indigenous scholars who have described or developed significant components of it. James (Sákéj) Youngblood Henderson and Kiera Ladner are two such leading scholars who provide sophisticated and eloquent accounts about why they believe this model is essential to a revitalized Indigenous relationship with Canada.

Henderson begins his analysis by demonstrating that the origins of treaty federalism have long roots extending through time to the first treaties that were negotiated with Britain (and subsequently Canada). According to him, these treaties served to "conciliate pre-existing Aboriginal sovereignty with assumed Crown sovereignty," and as such are "derived from the mutual consent of the First Nations sovereign and the British sovereign, both of whom were and remain independent of one another" (Henderson 2008, 20). Henderson insists that at no point did treaties serve to divest Indigenous nations of their inherent sovereignty. Instead, he says, the indispensable purpose of the treaties was to maintain "Aboriginal sovereignty and governance over their shared territory and peoples" (Henderson 2008, 21).

Ladner echoes Henderson's position on the original meaning and intent of treaties. She argues that the early treaties signed with the British constituted legal agreements between sovereign nations to share land and resources but on the premise that both would offer the other recognition of nationhood and would commit themselves "to a continuous nation-to-nation relationship" (Ladner 2005, 944). From here, Ladner takes the argument one step further. She says it was certainly the case that treaties signalled British recognition and affirmation of the Indigenous right "to self-government and a continuation of sovereignty." But no less importantly from the Indigenous side, treaties "also recognized and affirmed a right to self-government and sovereignty for the settler society within indigenous nations" (Ladner 2005, 944). What Ladner points out, in other words, is that it was sovereign Indigenous nations who agreed to carve out some space for the expression of British political autonomy within Indigenous traditional territories and not the other way around. Indeed, it could not have been otherwise because Indigenous nations were on the land first. Both Ladner and Henderson therefore conclude that sovereignty resided with Indigenous peoples then, and sovereignty resides with Indigenous peoples now. Says Henderson, "the imperial treaties extended Aboriginal governance, they did not reduce it" (Henderson 2008, 21). Consequently, the Canadian state is not now, nor has it ever been, in a position to grant Indigenous peoples the right to self-determination nor, for that matter, to take the right away.

It is this vision of treaty federalism that Ladner and Henderson offer as the antidote to colonialism. Under a treaty system, says Ladner, "Canada would have to come to the realization that it is just one of many nations with which power and resources must be shared" (Ladner 2003, 56; see also Henderson 2008, 20). As Ladner sees it, treaty federalism establishes an Indigenous "parallel constitutional order," one that exists alongside and enjoys status equal to that of the Canadian federal order. Martin Papillon refers to this arrangement as a "double federation," a state of affairs in which one layer is built upon the other in a descending order of priority (Papillon 2020, 222). First priority goes to treaty federalism. This layer specifies how lands, resources, and political power are to be distributed and shared between Indigenous nations and the Canadian state. Next in priority comes Canadian federalism. Within this domestic constitutional order, Canada has chosen to govern itself through the 1867 constitutional division of powers between federal and provincial governments (Ladner 2003, 57). Naturally, it is to be expected that as treaty partners Indigenous nations and the Canadian state will be bound up together in all kinds of political and economic alliances (layer one). But importantly, where internal domestic affairs are concerned, the model dictates that the treaty partners are to leave one another alone (layer two). In

Ladner's words, each should be able "to chart its own course forward and decide how it is to govern itself and relate to other nations" (Ladner 2003, 56). It is this original condition of Indigenous–Canadian bilateral interdependency and domestic autonomy that colonialism is said to have undermined and that the treaty federalism model aims to restore.

In summary, a treaty federalism model that would see Indigenous nations govern themselves alongside the Canadian state carries with it several essential attributes. First, the Indigenous right to self-determination is inherent to Indigenous nations themselves – they are the self-authorizing source of their own political power as informed by their own traditions, cultures, and values. Second, there are no areas of responsibility in which Indigenous governments cannot claim, at least in principle, a right to govern themselves. These areas include ancestral lands, resources, financing, citizenship, and any matter pertaining to the political, economic, social, and cultural well-being of Indigenous citizens. And third, as put by Joyce Green, there are good grounds to question the proposition "that Canada is the necessary framework for the exercise of Indigenous self-determination." As she sees it, the "settler" requires "unsettling," which may well require that the political relationship be flipped the other way around. In Green's words, "Canada, a settler state initiated by colonialism, needs to be legitimated as a post-colonial state by Indigenous reconciliation, political protocols, treaties, Indigenization of state institutions, and right relationships enacted into the future" (Green 2020, 249). For starters, this means that the power of Indigenous governments must not to be interfered with, altered, or constrained by Canadian governments outside of Indigenous approval. In short, Indigenous governments ought to exist alongside rather than within Canadian federalism.

INDEPENDENT MODEL (INDIGENOUS RESURGENCE)

The fourth and final model (or, more appropriately, approach) comes to us from a group of Indigenous scholars who seek to animate Indigenous self-determination from the vantage point of **resurgence**. While motivated by a variety of concerns and perspectives, these scholars are bound together by a shared concern to advance two very practical and radical ambitions.[7] In the first place, they urge Indigenous peoples to turn away from the Canadian state by refusing to take up its offers of recognition through rights-based approaches to Indigenous politics, especially when those offers are cast in the form of third orders of government or enhanced municipality status. Such overtures are identified by them as nothing more than small modifications to a settler-colonial dynamic in which the Canadian state persists in its unified, consistent, and deliberate ambition to dispossess Indigenous peoples of their lands, resources, political power, and very identity. In the second place and by way of remedy, these scholars contend that Indigenous peoples must turn inward by focusing exclusively on themselves, exercising powers of self-determination to rehabilitate their nations and cultures free from the coercive influences of colonial impositions of power. Such acts are said to be an authentic source of Indigenous revitalization because they place the resurgence of traditional Indigenous "life-ways," including spirituality, governance, languages, social and economic practices, and ecological relationships, at their normative centre (Starblanket and Long 2020, 10). There can be no restoration of Indigenous authenticity, in other words, outside of refusals "to consent to the apparatuses of the state" (Simpson 2016, 328). Indigenous peoples simply must seek self-recognition and self-actualization outside the boundaries of the Canadian colonial system if their true Indigeneity is to be restored.

When applied to the political realm, Indigenous resurgence scholars argue that colonialism can only be defeated when Indigenous peoples first articulate and then bring their nations into conformity with their own distinct approaches to governance. They must not strive to bring their nations into alignment with the standards of the colonial state by seeking validation from it, nor allow their political structures to be assimilated into its colonial legal and political frameworks. In short, resurgence scholars encourage maximum separation from the Canadian state, both politically and culturally. For them, Indigenous and Western pathways represent two fundamentally distinct, and more importantly oppositional, value systems (Alfred 2009, 25). If Indigenous peoples are to survive as Indigenous peoples, they must reconstruct their political identities in ways that repudiate Western liberal and capitalist options, and which at the same time lead them to reclaim and embrace their much more authentic Indigenous ones, options they say are still readily available to them because they remain within the custodial care of their elders, among others (Simpson 2017; Starblanket and Long 2020, 1).

Glen Coulthard is an Indigenous resurgence scholar who provides a particularly incisive critique of Indigenous political strategies that seek, as a first priority, recognition for the Indigenous right to self-determination from the Canadian state. He is especially suspicious of official Canadian state forms of recognition granted to Indigenous peoples by way of rights, treaties, and governments (Simpson 2017, 176). According to him, the state may well have turned over some land, money, and political power to Indigenous nations, but not in a manner that fundamentally transcends the configurations of colonial power that are the sources of Indigenous subjection in the first place (Coulthard 2014, 3). Indeed, Coulthard argues "that instead of ushering in an era of peaceful coexistence grounded on the ideal of *reciprocity* or *mutual* recognition, the politics of recognition" only serves to reinforce the imposed structures of the colonial system (Coulthard 2014, 3). Why is this? Coulthard offers the following by way of explanation.

Coulthard contends that Canada acquired its land and resources through deliberate theft from Indigenous peoples. In the guise of addressing this colonial theft, Canada now chooses to recognize Indigenous peoples' rights by granting specific concessions to them by way of land claims and self-government agreements. Yet, for Coulthard, the fulcrum of power has remained fundamentally unchanged. As he sees it, the recognition offered to Indigenous peoples is, in fact, an asymmetrical exchange because, throughout all negotiations and subsequent agreements, the Canadian state maintains its monopoly on power, massaging outcomes for its own benefit (Elliott 2018, 65–6). Without a doubt, Indigenous peoples have captured additional land, resources, and political jurisdiction as a product of these negotiations. But Coulthard's point is that the recognition granted Indigenous peoples offers limited freedoms because it is informed by liberal ideals that box Indigenous peoples into predetermined categories with limited cultural rights and partial concessions via self-government and land claims packages. Indigenous peoples are thereby placed at a profound disadvantage (Coulthard 2014, 35). As Coulthard puts it, Indigenous peoples are enticed "to *identify*, either implicitly or explicitly, with the profoundly *asymmetrical* and *nonreciprocal* forms of recognition either imposed on or granted to them by the settler state and society" (Coulthard 2014, 25). And what is the result? Coulthard argues that Canada thereby successfully absorbs Indigenous peoples into its liberal democratic framework, and by extension the colonial system remains very much intact (Simpson 2017, 176).

This built-in limitation inherent to the liberal politics of recognition compels Coulthard to urge Indigenous leaders to go deeper in their analysis of the wrongs perpetrated against their peoples. Indigenous peoples must not rely on the goodwill of the Canadian state by asking politely for forms of recognition that, even if "granted," will in no way "significantly modify, let alone transcend, the breadth of power at play in colonial relationships" (Coulthard 2014, 31). Instead, he urges adoption of a two-pronged strategy that he calls a "resurgent politics of recognition." First, Indigenous peoples must strive to fundamentally break "with the background structures of colonial power," which includes explicitly calling "into question the dominating nature of capitalist social relations and the state form" as an appropriate approach to Indigenous governance (Coulthard 2014, 39, 24, 35). And second, Indigenous peoples must develop a "decolonial praxis" that involves "some form of critical individual and collective *self*-recognition" informed by "the understanding that our cultural practices have much to offer regarding the establishment of relationships within and between peoples and the natural world built on principles of reciprocity and respectful coexistence" (Coulthard 2014, 48). Without conflict and struggle of this sort, Coulthard fears that the terms of Indigenous recognition will remain in the hands of the Canadian state "to bestow on their inferiors in ways that they deem appropriate" (Coulthard, 2014, 39). In short, Coulthard urges the maximum Indigenous exit from the Canadian state that is possible. Indeed, for him, Indigenous survival depends on it.

Coulthard looks to traditional Indigenous cultural values as a critical resource for informing Indigenous emancipation. Audra Simpson and Leanne Betasamsosake Simpson take us some distance in understanding what this emancipation project could look like in practice. Like Coulthard, both advocate for a politics of Indigenous independence, described as commitments to develop distinct expressions of life, including institutions of governance, without need for validation by the Canadian state. Audra Simpson expresses this imperative of independence as a stance of "refusal." In the interest of preserving their own sovereignty, Indigenous peoples simply must refuse all action that would have them move "into settler citizenship and the promise of whiteness" (Simpson 2016, 328). Leanne Simpson expresses the same sentiment, arguing that Indigenous peoples must resist the temptation to participate in colonial structures and processes, devoting themselves instead to stepping out of those structures and processes as their first act of resistance. For her, "retreat" is the first tenet in Indigenous recovery. Colonial structures associated with "the dispossessive forces of capitalism, heteropatriarchy, and white supremacy" simply cannot serve "as an organizing platform and mechanism for dismantling the systems of colonial domination" (Simpson 2017, 33, 34, 176).

If the first tenet of Indigenous emancipation is to refuse Canadian state offers of recognition, Leanne Simpson's second tenet is grounded within Indigenous (in her case, Nishnaabeg) ways of knowing and being informed by what she identifies as place-based practices and relationships (Simpson 2017, 182). The key for Simpson is that Indigenous peoples must come to know and express "who we are," a process that requires hard work in "revitalizing our intellectual practices and our relationship to the land" (Simpson 2017, 67). Simpson tells us that the sources of Indigenous emancipation are already present within the pathways of knowing and being that have long informed and given life to Indigenous nations over the course of centuries. All that needs doing, she says (though she recognizes that the task will be hard), is to reawaken these "socially inherent capacities for agency and change" and have them serve as the source of "grounded normativity" for both present and future Indigenous practices (Simpson 2017, 24, 30; Elliott 2018, 68). As described earlier, essential areas targeted for reawakening include relationships to land, culture, and community as well as traditional practices associated with governance and economic activity.

Naturally, what this process of reawakening or "resurgence" requires will vary from nation to nation since the Indigenous experience is heterogeneous, marked by great variety in "local contexts, histories, cultures, human agency and imagination" (Elliott 2018, 69). Simpson, therefore, is quick to point out that experiences of "resurgence" will differ depending on the particular circumstances of the Indigenous nation involved. Despite expected variety in resurgence journeys, however, Simpson is convinced that all must feature one shared element as integral to their processes: each nation must strive to recover and rebuild their identities internally and self-referentially, outside the systems designed to uphold the power of the colonial state (Simpson 2017, 6). In the case of her own nation, Simpson encourages her people to embark on what she calls a "flight path out of settler colonialism" by "building an Nishnaabeg presence, an Nishnaabeg present, that embodies and operationalizes the very best of our nation because that is what we have always done" (Simpson 2017, 17, 6, 162).[8] For Simpson, centring on the sources of their own Indigeneity in this way is where the building blocks are to be found to begin to live in a radically altered, dismantled colonial present (Simpson 2017, 20, 49, 175).

At one point, Leanne Simpson asks the question: "Why, then, do we continually seek recognition from Canada when we know it never ends well?" (Simpson 2017, 181). Critics of Indigenous resurgence scholars offer a twofold response. In the first place they reply by saying that they understand the motivation for the question given the repeated "terrible experiences of our people within Confederation at the hands of the colonial governments" (Wilson-Raybould 2019, 59). It therefore makes perfect sense that replacing the politics of "recognition" with the politics of "self-recognition" would contribute to a high degree of personal and community satisfaction. But, in the second place, argues Paul Nadasdy, the matter simply cannot end there. Indigenous peoples may wish it otherwise, but they are now inescapably surrounded by and embedded within the Canadian state. Consequently, if they are to gain a measure of control over their own lives, some form of negotiation and agreement with the Canadian state would appear to be a political necessity (Nadasdy 2017, 14–15).

Of course, what Indigenous peoples do not need is validation from the Canadian state as a precondition of resuscitating their culturally distinct ways of life and their traditional institutions of governance. But what they do need is adequate political space to give expression to those distinct ways of life once resuscitated, and for this the Canadian state must agree to get out of the way. And it is precisely at this point that I suggest the language of sovereignty can make a powerful contribution (Nadasdy 2017, 15, 17). Sovereignty discourse and Indigenous advocacy efforts have expanded Canadian state understandings and subsequent offers of recognition about the nature and scope of the Indigenous right to self-determination. For example, it is now commonplace to hear Canadian governments at all levels speak of Indigenous peoples as nations with rights to territory and to political jurisdiction over their peoples, lands, and resources. These achievements, however partial and incomplete, are nevertheless the product of negotiations and agreements in which the Canadian state has conferred recognition upon Indigenous peoples that approximates, at least in some sense, the ways in which Indigenous peoples themselves wish to be seen. For this reason, I would argue that the politics of recognition can, and indeed must, serve as a facilitative adjunct to Indigenous efforts at launching what Simpson refers to as "flights paths" in their own resurgence.

One further point ensues. Perhaps the power of the Indigenous resurgence movement's compulsion to "turn away" from the Canadian state lies not so much in its rejection of the idea of Canada per se, but rather in its rejection of the settler-colonial version of Canada. Leanne Simpson argues that "there is virtually no room for white people in resurgence" because it is they who must "get out of the way" if proper respect is to be shown for "Indigenous self-determination and nationhood" (Simpson 2017, 228, 237). But getting out of the way is not the same as being told to disappear. As Michael Elliott explains, "despite possible first impressions, resurgence does not advocate the permanent or absolute cessation of discursive engagement with settler society" (Elliott 2018, 62). What it does advocate is for non-Indigenous peoples to examine the legitimacy of their own state structures with a view to shifting them to "radically different grounds" (Elliott 2018, 62). Along with resurgence, in other words, comes an invitation to reconciliation. The caveat, however, is that the nature of this reconciliation must be informed by a deep structural critique of the processes and institutions that sanctioned the immoral assertion of power by the Canadian state over Indigenous peoples in the first place. Reconciliation is a possibility but the criteria for its success are both rigorous and highly demanding. To qualify as "co-protagonists" in the decolonization exercise, non-Indigenous peoples must first be willing to undermine "the intellectual and moral foundations" of the entire settler-colonial order (Elliott 2018, 71). What follows next is that non-Indigenous peoples must be willing to accept the invitation to embrace the alternative political and social realities presented to them by their

Indigenous neighbours and then must seek to bring their lives into conformity with them. For resurgence scholars, a renewed dialogue based on such genuine respect and reciprocity demands nothing less.

As for moving forward in practical terms, resurgence scholars insist that as a first step, if Indigenous nations go to the Canadian state and ask that their sovereignty be recognized, they are not acting as sovereigns at all (Palmater 2015, 242). Instead, what Indigenous nations must do is simply assert their sovereignty, act on it, and expect that it will be recognized and respected. As described by Simpson, the task at hand is for Indigenous peoples to rebuild their nations on their own terms, revitalizing and enacting their own laws, living according to their own cultures and traditions, regenerating their own land tenure systems, and reauthorizing the sources of their own traditional governance structures, all without waiting for Canadian state permission (Simpson 2017, 238; see also Papillon 2020, 230–1). In short, in order to live sovereignty, Indigenous peoples must assert sovereignty, which means most fundamentally that they must extract themselves from the constraints of the Canadian state. They must, in other words, challenge the sovereignty that the Canadian state misappropriated from Indigenous nations by simply taking that sovereignty back.

Concerning practical strategy, it is also worth pointing out that the positions of resurgence scholars and treaty federalists are not necessarily at odds with one another.[9] No doubt, treaty federalists would not support the positions of those proponents of Indigenous resurgence who urge that Indigenous revitalization must include a wholesale rejection of the Canadian state. What treaty federalists would support, however, are Indigenous resurgence efforts to rebuild their own constitutional orders, governing capacities, laws, and distinct ways of life. Indeed, it is precisely such political capacities that Indigenous peoples will need to rebuild if they are to operate effectively in their renewed nation-to-nation engagement with the Canadian state. From the perspective of treaty federalists, then, *internal* Indigenous community revitalization efforts can be seen as the necessary political foundation upon which renewed *external* Indigenous–Canadian state relations ought to be built. To that end, treaty federalists are likely to be supportive of the resurgence movement's efforts to bolster Indigenous pathways of living and of being separate from the Canadian state despite the fact that they are more inclined than resurgence scholars to look favourably upon interacting with Canada through political negotiations and treaties.[10]

In sum, the Indigenous resurgence project can be said to contain two fundamental objectives. First, it encourages Indigenous peoples to take up an opposition position in their relations to the Canadian state. Indigenous rehabilitation is seen to be a possibility if and only if Indigenous peoples repudiate all forms of colonial brutalization perpetrated by the Canadian state upon their peoples. And second, Indigenous peoples must turn inward if they are to find authentic sources for their own individual and community revitalization. Liberal white Canadians have little to nothing to offer in this respect because they have more often than not been a source of "dispossession, capitalism, white supremacy, and heteropatriarchy" (Simpson 2017, 228). What Indigenous peoples must do instead is act with Indigenous presence, and for this all they need do is consult the already existing Indigenous realities present within their own cultures, languages, and social and political systems.

CROSSING THE DIVIDE: BUILDING INDIGENOUS SOVEREIGNTY INCREMENTALLY

It is time to take stock of the ground we have covered thus far to prepare ourselves for the last step in this chapter's argument. Each of the four models described above structure political relations between Indigenous and non-Indigenous peoples very differently, and as a result each constitutes a distinct approach available to Indigenous nations as they seek to decolonize their political institutions from Canadian state paternalism. The first delegated approach constitutes a form of integration into the Canadian state but is also marked by the expression of Indigenous resistance to the forces of assimilation by means of assertions to sector-specific jurisdictional autonomy. The second inherent approach also represents a form of political integration, but this time based on a constitutional division of powers in which Indigenous nations are recognized as autonomous political actors in a system of cooperative Canadian federalism. The third autonomous approach allows for independent Indigenous statehood as a theoretical possibility, but certainly settles for nothing less than a separate and autonomous form of Indigenous nationhood existing alongside a much more structurally diverse Canada. The fourth independent approach is the most explicitly radical because it constitutes an outright rejection of the Canadian state as the institutional space within which Indigenous peoples ought to settle. Instead, it urges Indigenous "resurgence," understood as demonstrations of sovereignty in which Indigenous peoples simply live "as they have always done" without reference to or concern for the Canadian state and its expectations for Indigenous peoples (Simpson 2017, 247). In sum, each represents a different view about what Indigenous sovereignty ought to entail for the relationship between Indigenous peoples and Canada. But each also takes the presence of sovereignty for granted, asking only how that sovereignty ought to be conceptualized, where it ought to be located, and how it ought to be distributed. Forthcoming chapters will demonstrate that there is no one single Indigenous viewpoint on this matter.

I should say from the outset that I do not advocate for one or another of these approaches as inherently superior from the vantage point of either principle or practice. Indeed, I do not believe that it is my place to judge. What I shall demonstrate throughout this book is that Indigenous peoples and their supporters tend to take different positions on the merits of each approach depending on the political context and their political priorities. What is imperative in my view, however, is that in all cases the Canadian state should be required to roll back its jurisdiction over Indigenous nations so that they have the freedom to either modify or fundamentally transform their relations with Canada as they themselves see fit. Mandatory in this dynamic, in other words, is that Indigenous sovereignty, linked as it is to the right to self-determination (including the right to self-government), lead to increased control by Indigenous peoples over their own affairs. It ought to be up to Indigenous peoples to take the lead in defining their myriad relationships to the Canadian state, not the other way around. In short, I take sovereignty quite simply to mean that Indigenous peoples are entitled to freedom from colonial domination. It is this conception of sovereignty that I intend to defend.

It is also my view that Indigenous leaders employ the discourse of sovereignty as an effective tool to carve out a multitude of "spaces in between" the exercise of Canadian sovereignty for elements of their own nationhood to re-emerge. As we shall see in forthcoming chapters, Indigenous "spaces" are emerging all over the Canadian political landscape as a result of the sheer perseverance and determined hard work of Indigenous peoples (and increasingly their non-Indigenous supporters). Over the course of Canadian history, Indigenous peoples have been unrelenting in their quest to challenge the colonial imposition of state power upon them. James Tully describes this dynamic as follows: "Indigenous peoples struggle *for* their freedom as peoples in resisting the colonial systems as a whole … [and] they exercise their freedom *of* manoeuvre within the system … with the aim of modifying the system in the short term and transforming it from within in the long term" (Tully 2008, 265, 276).

It is this simultaneous Indigenous struggle of resistance *against* and *within* the Canadian political system that will be the focus of my attention throughout this book. Both struggles represent Indigenous assertions to sovereignty that refuse to be silenced. Both struggles are dedicated to increasing autonomy for Indigenous nations within and sometimes against the Canadian political order. The Indigenous resurgence approach is generally the most demanding because it insists that the right to sovereignty entitles Indigenous peoples to maximize that "space" by fully disengaging from the Canadian state. The treaty federalism model is more conciliatory in tone because it looks favourably upon the prospect of political agreements with Canada, but it does so on one condition: those agreements must be animated by a commitment on the part of both partners to give each other equivalent political "space" to function as full sovereigns in the relations they take up with one another. The third order of government model, in comparison, accepts the proposition that the inherent right to self-determination exists within Canada, and as such its proponents are generally content to carve out "space" for the expression of Indigenous sovereignty within the currently existing (though expanded) constitutional and federal order (Wilson-Raybould 2019, 59). And the delegated model, while the least desired in terms of "space" offered, is the point from which most Indigenous nations begin and from which most launch their quest for enhanced political power and the reacquisition of sovereign status.

What can also be said with certainty is that until relatively recently, the scope for the expression of Indigenous sovereignty has been profoundly diminished by the policies of the Canadian state – indeed, almost to the point of extinction. Consequently, I think it is fair to say that almost all efforts aimed at increasing autonomy for Indigenous peoples, whether modest or more far-reaching in scope, will have some positive effect on creating new spaces in between the exercise of Canadian sovereignty for Indigenous self-expression. The question is whether Indigenous efforts that call into question the legitimacy of the sovereign order of the Canadian state as it now stands can also serve to lay the groundwork for the modification and potential transformation of the larger Canadian state system. Based on the evidence to date, forthcoming chapters will show that there is room for both optimism and pessimism.

So where does this leave us? On some level I believe we need to accept a rather unsatisfying state of affairs – there simply is no instant solution on offer that will restore to Indigenous peoples a level of sovereignty within Canada that is consistent with their right to self-determination. As James Frideres observes, "it has taken hundreds of years of colonial domination to produce what we now have, and so there is no reason to suggest that change will happen overnight" (Frideres 2016, 218). Change is happening, to be sure, but it is also painfully slow and, as Patricia Monture-Angus indicated some decades ago, "will come in small steps" (Monture-Angus 1999, 35; see also Wilson, Alcantara, and Rodon, 2020, 170). When we survey the political landscape, therefore, whether it be with respect to Indigenous citizenship, Canadian Indigenous policy, the jurisprudence on Aboriginal rights and title, the status of treaties and self-government agreements, and the forging of economic partnerships, we are led, inevitably, to the following conclusion: the project of rebuilding Indigenous sovereignty within the Canadian setting is still very much in a state of development and remains, as yet, far from complete.

Still, change is occurring, most notably in the half century since the withdrawal of the 1969 **White Paper on Indian Policy**. And what we see, despite frustrating delays and sometimes infuriating setbacks, is that incremental steps are being taken in the quest to rebuild Indigenous sovereignty. Indigenous peoples are negotiating and sometimes simply asserting the powers they need to develop their nations and enhance the well-being of their peoples. We see this in areas as varied as education, health care, child welfare, housing, community infrastructure, resource management, economic development, job creation, and taxation, to name just a few examples. In all cases and across all issues, the goal of Indigenous peoples is to reacquire or "take back" their inherent powers to be able to once again make decisions free from external interference by the Canadian state. And the cumulative effect is that Indigenous nations are gradually emerging from under the heavy yoke of colonial rule. Each time a settlement is successfully negotiated between an Indigenous nation and the Canadian state, another step is taken in the direction of enhanced Indigenous autonomy. Indigenous nations are working within and sometimes against the Canadian political system to express and enhance their inherent right to self-determination. What I believe we are witnessing, in other words, is the incremental reacquisition and the gradual restoration of Indigenous sovereignty. Indigenous peoples will settle for nothing less. Where precisely this is occurring, and in what forms, are topics I take up in the rest of the book.

CONCLUSION

We began this chapter by reviewing how the Federation of Sovereign Indigenous Nations and the Chiefs of Ontario describe what a robust form of Indigenous sovereignty ought to entail. While each version is not identical, the ingredients they put forward as expressive of sovereignty are remarkably similar. Each declares that Indigenous nations possess inherent rights to self-determination and therefore are entitled to govern according to their own laws, values, and traditions in keeping with the responsibilities and obligations bestowed on them by the Creator. Both also declare that because Indigenous nations possess equality of political status with the Canadian state under international law, the preferable route for formalizing their nation-to-nation relationships is through treaties. Treaties are said to both dignify and elevate the agreed upon terms of coexistence between Indigenous nations and the Canadian state because they begin from the premise that both are sovereigns.

However, while treaty federalism may well serve as the ideal for some Indigenous organizations and activists, it is not where most Indigenous nations find themselves in their relationship to the Canadian state today. Instead, the Indigenous journey in Canada is better characterized as one in which Indigenous peoples are taking incremental steps toward political practices that reflect some form of restored sovereignty. The steps taken are often small (though sometimes larger) and invariably fall into spaces that Indigenous peoples have managed to carve out for themselves in between the exercise of Canadian sovereignty.

At the same time, Indigenous peoples continue to encounter resistance in response to their ambitions for enhanced sovereignty. Consequently, the process of decolonizing the relationship between Indigenous peoples and the Canadian state is likely to be a long one. Reconciliation of an order consistent with the fulfillment of Indigenous rights is not just around the corner. Instead, the Indigenous effort to (re)acquire sovereignty is better regarded as a process comprising a series of steps in which each step serves as the foundation for taking the next. In short, Indigenous sovereignty is a political condition that currently exists in a partially realized form, but it is also an aspirational objective that is still very much in the process of becoming.

DISCUSSION QUESTIONS

1 What criteria do Indigenous peoples use to justify their standing as sovereigns? Can these criteria withstand critical scrutiny?
2 What is the nature of the difference between third order and treaty federalism approaches to Indigenous self-determination? Is one to be preferred over the other from the perspective of both principle and practice?
3 Why do some Indigenous scholars insist that Indigenous peoples can only achieve true freedom when they disentangle and then radically separate their nations from the Canadian state?
4 Can Indigenous sovereignty be expressed in a meaningful way if it can only be done in spaces that exist in between the exercise of Canadian sovereignty? Or are such spaces, by definition, too restrictive?

SUGGESTED READINGS

Abele, Frances, and Michael J. Prince. 2006. "Four Pathways to Aboriginal Self-Government in Canada." *American Review of Canadian Studies* 36 (4).

Alfred, Taiaiake. 2009. *Peace, Power, Righteousness: An Indigenous Manifesto*, 2nd ed. Toronto: Oxford University Press.

Bruyneel, Kevin. 2007. *The Third Space of Sovereignty: The Postcolonial Politics of US–Indigenous Relations.* Minneapolis: University of Minnesota Press.

Coulthard, Glen Sean. 2014. *Red Skin, White Masks: Rejecting the Colonial Politics of Recognition.* Minneapolis: University of Minnesota Press.

Elliott, Michael. 2018. "Indigenous Resurgence: The Drive for Renewed Engagement and Reciprocity in the Turn away from the State." *Canadian Journal of Political Science* 51 (1).

Grant, John. 2018. "The Crown and the Aboriginal: Imaginaries of Sovereignty and Control." In *Lived Fictions: Unity and Exclusion in Canadian Politics.* Vancouver: UBC Press.

Green, Joyce. 2020. "Enacting Reconciliation." In *Visions of the Heart: Issues Involving Indigenous Peoples in Canada*, edited by Gina Starblanket and David Long. Toronto: Oxford University Press.

Henderson, James (Sákéj) Youngblood. 2008. "Treaty Governance." In *Aboriginal Self-Government in Canada*, 3rd ed., edited by Yale D. Belanger. Saskatoon: Purich Publishing.

King, Hayden, and Shiri Pasternack. 2018. *Canada's Emerging Indigenous Rights Framework: A Critical Analysis.* Toronto: Yellowhead Institute.

Ladner, Kiera. 2018. "Proceed with Caution: Reflections on Resurgence." In *Resurgence and Reconciliation: Indigenous–Settler Relations and Earth Teachings*, edited by Michael Asch, John Borrows, and James Tully. Toronto: University of Toronto Press.

Little Bear, Leroy. 2013. "An Elder Explains Indigenous Philosophy and Indigenous Sovereignty." In *Philosophy and Aboriginal Rights: Critical Dialogues*, edited by Sandra Tomsons and Lorraine Mayer. Toronto: Oxford University Press.

McNeil, Kent. 2018. "Indigenous and Crown Sovereignty in Canada." In *Resurgence and Reconciliation: Indigenous–Settler Relations and Earth Teachings*, edited by Michael Asch, John Borrows, and James Tully. Toronto: University of Toronto Press.

Nadasdy, Paul. 2017. *Sovereignty's Entailments: First Nation State Formation in the Yukon.* Toronto: University of Toronto Press.

Papillon, Martin. 2014. "The Rise (and Fall?) of Aboriginal Self-Government." In *Canadian Politics*, 6th ed., edited by James Bickerton and Alain-G. Gagnon. Toronto: University of Toronto Press.

———. 2020. "The Two Faces of Treaty Federalism." In *Canadian Politics*, 7th ed., edited by James Bickerton and Alain-G. Gagnon. Toronto: University of Toronto Press.

Simpson, Audra. 2014. *Mohawk Interruptus (Political Life across the Borders of Settler States).* Durham: Duke University Press.

Simpson, Leanne Betasamosake. 2017. *As We Have Always Done: Indigenous Freedom Through Radical Resistance.* Minneapolis: University of Minnesota Press.
Starblanket, Gina. 2019. "Constitutionalizing (In)justice: Treaty Interpretation and the Containment of Indigenous Governance." *Constitutional Forum* 28 (2).
———. 2020. "Crises of Relationship: The Role of Treaties in Contemporary Indigenous–Settler Relations." In *Visions of the Heart: Issues Involving Indigenous Peoples in Canada*, edited by Gina Starblanket and David Long. Toronto: Oxford University Press.
Tully, James. 2008. "The Struggles of Indigenous Peoples for and of Freedom." In *Public Philosophy in a New Key. Volume 1: Democracy and Civic Freedom.* Cambridge: Cambridge University Press.
Webber, Jeremy. 2016. "We Are Still in the Age of Encounter: Section 35 and a Canada Beyond Sovereignty." In *From Recognition to Reconciliation: Essays on the Constitutional Entrenchment of Aboriginal and Treaty Rights*, edited by Patrick Macklem and Douglas Sanderson. Toronto: University of Toronto Press.
Wilson, Gary N., Christopher Alcantara, and Thierry Rodon. 2020. *Nested Federalism and Inuit Governance in the Canadian Arctic.* Vancouver: UBC Press.
Wilson-Raybould, Jody. 2019. *From Where I Stand: Rebuilding Indigenous Nations for a Stronger Canada.* Vancouver: Purich Books.

NOTES

1 It is worth noting, along with Paul Nadasdy, however, that Indigenous nations do have to adopt some of the features of states to "function in a universe of states and state-like political entities." For example, "the new First Nations that have emerged from the modern treaty-making process are composed of citizens, and their governments exercise significant – if limited – jurisdiction over clearly defined territories and peoples." Nadasdy concludes that when taken together, these attributes are fundamentally state-like in their design. See Nadasdy 2017, 7.

2 For a rich description of the political systems named as well as the political systems of several other Indigenous nations, see RCAP 1996b, 43–97; Borrows 2010, 59–106; Helin 2006, 65–86; and Miller 2004, 52–65.

3 One further point ensues. As Rauna Kuokkanen explains, Indigenous peoples have good political reasons for going to international forums such as the United Nations to petition for the protection of their rights. By doing so, they signal their "preference for employing international human rights instruments rather than the human rights mechanisms of nation-states, and in this way, avoid subordination to the state and to its national legislation." See Kuokkanen 2012, 244.

4 On the question of the legitimacy of the Canadian state's claim to sovereignty, see Asch, 2014, 11, 32. He speculates that if Indigenous peoples did indeed enjoy sovereignty prior to contact

with European powers, then it is not Indigenous sovereignty that needs to be reconciled with Canadian sovereignty. Rather, what is at issue ought to be formulated in exactly the opposite way: it is Canadian sovereignty that needs to find a way to coexist with the prior and ongoing existence of Indigenous sovereignty. See also Nadasdy, 2017, 59; and McNeil 2018, 302–5.

5 The following three paragraphs draw substantially from my summary of key RCAP recommendations as found in Schouls 2003, 126, 127.

6 In making this distinction between RCAP's approach to the inherent right to self-determination from the point of view of both principle and practice, I follow the lead of Abele and Prince 2006, 588.

7 The Indigenous scholars who I identify as part of the resurgence movement include Taiaiake Alfred, Glen Coulthard, Audra Simpson, Leanne Betasamosake Simpson, and Jeff Corntassel.

8 Operationalizing the very best of the Nishnaabeg nation includes deep engagement with all the Nishnaabeg practices and ethical processes that Simpson identifies as central to Nishnaabeg identity. These include "story or theory, language learning, ceremony, hunting, fishing, ricing, sugar making, medicine making, politics, and governance." See Simpson 2017, 19.

9 I thank one of the anonymous reviewers of this book for identifying this natural point of alignment between the positions of resurgence scholars and treaty federalists.

10 Thanks to the above identified anonymous reviewer for providing me with the inspiration for this sentence.

CHAPTER 2

Identity Politics: Citizenship and Belonging

LEARNING OBJECTIVES

1 To explain why Indigenous control of their own citizenship is a central component of their right to self-determination.
2 To distinguish among the constitutional categories of Indian, Inuit, and Métis.
3 To outline in what ways the *Indian Act* has fundamentally disrupted traditional Indigenous notions of citizenship and the Indigenous ability to define their own identity.
4 To identify the ways in which the Section 10 amendments to the *Indian Act* put First Nations in a stronger position to control their own membership codes.
5 To describe the ways in which the *Indian Act* discriminated against Indigenous women and to evaluate whether Bill C-31 and subsequent federal legislation (Bill C-3 and Bill S-3) effectively remedied that sex-based discrimination.
6 To explain the challenges associated with establishing oneself as Indigenous.

This chapter examines how Indigenous peoples have been identified by both the Canadian state and Indigenous nations. Identity is an extremely important matter for Indigenous peoples, in large part because the Canadian state has worked so persistently to eradicate that identity as part of its larger colonial project to assimilate Indigenous peoples. The legacy of this colonial effort continues to be experienced intensely into the present and generates significant tensions between Indigenous and non-Indigenous peoples as well as between Indigenous individuals (especially women) and their nations. Central questions here concern the development of appropriate criteria for deciding who should be included for membership within Indigenous nations and who should not, and what counts as an authentic expression of Indigenous identity.[1] Indigenous identity and how it is constructed, maintained, presented, controlled, and passed on is a complex matter and one that constitutes the central concern of this chapter. The complexity of Indigenous identity is especially compounded by numerous challenges associated with gender, and to that end this chapter will also draw upon the important work of Indigenous feminist activists and scholars.

As peoples who possess the international human right to self-determination, Indigenous nations already have the inherent right to freely determine the criteria of their own membership. In this sense, Indigenous peoples are not unique. They share with all peoples of the world the universal right to choose the terms of their own membership.[2] The problem for Indigenous peoples lies in the fact that their inherent jurisdiction over citizenship as set out in international human rights law has been stripped from them by the Canadian state. This reality is illustrated in particularly stark terms by the illegitimate imposition of the identity categories of the ***Indian Act***'s Indian registration, band, and band membership systems, all of which have worked to undermine Indigenous approaches to citizenship and belonging (Frideres 2020, 26–7). Furthermore, while all Indigenous peoples have suffered as a result of these identity impositions, a disproportionate burden of this suffering has been borne by Indigenous women and children. In response, as peoples with rights under international law, the Indigenous position can be distilled to two propositions: first, they simply must have jurisdiction over the terms of their own membership (including gender equality) if their capacity to be self-defining as distinct peoples is to be restored (Green 2009, 41; Simpson 2014, 178). And second, the Canadian state simply must learn to exercise self-restraint by practising a duty of non-interference where Indigenous identity and citizenship is concerned (Palmater 2011, 55).

The chapter begins with a discussion of First Nations, Inuit, and Métis identity. It asks the question, "Who are the Indigenous peoples of Canada?," doing so with reference to the Canadian Constitution's Section 35 categorization of Aboriginal peoples as Indian, Inuit, and Métis. The chapter then takes up the topic of the *Indian Act* registry and the associated problems that occur when living under the constraints of a legal classification that is both state imposed and has been state regulated to meet both patriarchal and colonial objectives. Most seriously, those constraints have discriminated in the past on the basis of sex, and more pertinently for the present, continue to discriminate on the basis of race. It is against the complex background of legal criteria such as these that the chapter examines the degree to which Indigenous peoples are now in control of the membership of their own nations. As this chapter demonstrates, while the *Indian Act* and the associated legal categories of "status Indian" versus "non-status Indian" continue to significantly complicate and confuse the issue for First Nations, Métis, and to a limited extent Inuit, Indigenous nations are nevertheless making substantial progress in re-establishing their right to control and define their own membership codes. A key concern commonly expressed here is the need to dismantle the identity categories of colonization by removing the distinction between having Indian status and being a member of a nation. Ultimately, the objective is to have the state-imposed and patriarchally informed terminology of "bands," "Indians," and "band members" replaced by more equitable Indigenous conceptions of identity, citizenship, and belonging (Wilson-Raybould 2019, 117). On this score, while considerable challenges remain, I argue that Indigenous nations are enjoying some degree of success. To get a sense of how this struggle for membership control is being realized by Indigenous peoples, the chapter starts with three brief case studies.

Before proceeding, however, one caveat is in order. As this book is concerned (in part) with understanding the political identity of Indigenous peoples within Canada, it makes good sense to place a chapter about the nature and circumstances surrounding the formation of that identity early in its pages. As the preceding indicates, however, despite ongoing Indigenous resistance, Indigenous identity today has unfortunately been deeply implicated within and profoundly distorted by the historical forces of colonialism. Consequently, it is my view that contemporary (often emancipatory) expressions of Indigenous identity cannot be properly understood apart from those colonial forces that have sought to usurp and replace them, the *Indian Act* being chief among them. To that end, readers may wish to consult my extensive treatment of the *Indian Act* found in the next chapter together with their consideration of the material in this chapter. Chapter 3 provides an overview of the legal and political forces that sought to render Indigenous notions of identity intelligible within the British and later Canadian colonial framework, and as such it provides important legal and political context.[3]

THE MEMBERSHIP CODES OF SANDY LAKE FIRST NATION, THE NUNATUKAVUT INUIT OF LABRADOR, AND ALBERTA MÉTIS SETTLEMENTS

For Indigenous peoples, the issue of self-determination as it relates to membership in their nations significantly impacts their identity and sense of well-being. Membership within a nation provides Indigenous peoples with a community, a setting within which to work out and give expression to their identity, and an opportunity to enjoy the material resources, services, programs, and benefits that come to the nation and the members within it. Membership serves to unite persons who share a common ancestry, culture, history, and way of life. It also grants individuals the right to participate in the political decisions of their nation and the opportunity to reside on and enjoy use of the nation's ancestral lands. From the perspective of community identity, integrity, and ongoing development, therefore, it stands to reason that Indigenous nations would claim the right to control the rules for community membership. Their right to self-determination and their capacity for self-definition depends on it. To this end, many Indigenous nations across Canada have crafted their own membership codes.

The Sandy Lake First Nation is a community made up of 2,500 persons and is located 1,000 kilometres northwest of Thunder Bay, Ontario. It maintains an affiliation with 29 other Indian bands scattered across Ontario's north who are linked together through historic ties as members of the Nishnawbe Aski Nation, a signatory to Treaty 5 (Goar 2009). The Sandy Lake First Nation declares in its preamble that its membership code "is based on the Sovereignty and inherent right of the Sandy Lake First Nation given to us by God the Creator" (Sandy Lake First Nation 2015, 1). In addition to accepting all persons who were members prior to the nation assuming "control of its membership pursuant to section 10 of the *Indian Act*," the Sandy Lake First Nation's code states that "a person is entitled to have his or her name entered in the band list ... if he or she is of Indian descent, is not a member of another band, and is the natural child of two band members, of one band member and a non-Indian, an adopted child of a band member, or is the spouse of a band member" (Sandy Lake First Nation 2015, 2). Chief and council are authorized to take responsibility for all matters relating to band membership, including making "decisions on all applications for membership within three months of receiving them" (Sandy Lake First Nation 2015, 4). Appeals are to be reviewed by a special appeals committee, made up of five members, "appointed by a Band Council resolution from the five geographical areas of the community." The committee is to make a recommendation to chief and council, whose decision in turn, once rendered, is "final and conclusive" (Sandy Lake First Nation 2015, 5).

The NunatuKavut people are of mixed Inuit and European heritage, number approximately 6,000 persons, and reside in 23 communities scattered across central and southern Labrador. The elected NunatuKavut Community Council includes a president, vice-president, 11 councillors representing the six regions of NunatuKavut territory, two elders, and one youth councillor. Of its five departments, the Social Sector Department is in charge of its membership registry. The NunatuKavut membership code is relatively short, contained in just two pages of the NunatuKavut Nation's Constitution. Membership is open to persons of "Native ancestry" who are originally from Labrador. The NunatuKavut Nation offers three classes of membership, all of which are lifelong. Each class corresponds to different criteria and carries with it different rights and privileges. They are in order of descending robustness: full member – resident, full member – non-resident, and alliance member.

To qualify as a full member in either the resident or non-resident category, a person must be "of Inuit descent who is a member of the historic Inuit community of South/Central Labrador and who is accepted by the modern Inuit community represented by NunatuKavut." An alliance member must either be able to demonstrate that they have "lived in NunatuKavut area for a minimum of seven years" or that "one parent or grandparent was aboriginal and was primarily resident for a minimum of seven years in one of the designated communities" of the nation (NunatuKavut Nation 2015a). While alliance members and non-resident full members have rights to some specific program and service areas as defined by council, they do not share with full resident members harvesting, voting, representational, or other rights. Membership across all three categories carries with it an obligation to advance the objectives and interests of NunatuKavut and "to observe all the applicable by-laws and policies" (NunatuKavut Nation 2015a). While the NunatuKavut Constitution makes no specific provision for the appeal of membership application decisions, its governance policies set out a procedure for a membership committee of three persons (non-council members) to assist the membership clerk to make membership decisions in unclear cases (NunatuKavut Nation 2015b).

The Métis membership process of the eight Métis Settlements of Alberta provides yet one more example of efforts by Indigenous nations to secure greater control over their citizenship criteria. Alberta is the only Canadian province to recognize a Métis land base within its borders. The eight settlements are located in the east-central and northern areas of the province, comprising 512,121 hectares (or 1.25 million acres). As of 2016, there were approximately 5,000 residents on the eight settlements. Each settlement has a government made up of five locally elected members who form a council and who exercise law-making and other regulatory powers, including consideration of applications for membership, as set out in the Government of Alberta's *Métis Settlement Act*. Individuals wishing to become a member of one of the Métis Settlements must apply to its council and in the application demonstrate that they have Canadian Aboriginal ancestry, identify with Métis history and culture, are at least 18 years old, and have been a member of a Métis Settlement or have lived in Alberta for the past five years (Province of Alberta 2000, 46–7). The settlement council must consider the application within 90 days of the application being received, sending the applicant notification of its decision within 45 days (Province of Alberta 2000, 47, 48). Approval will be granted subject to the applicant meeting all criteria on the membership application to the satisfaction of the council. The applicant must also demonstrate that they "will have suitable living accommodation in the settlement area" and are "committed to living in the settlement area and preserving a peaceful community" (Province of Alberta 2000, 48, 49). Council decisions can be appealed to a seven-member tribunal that, if the parties to the dispute agree to in advance, can settle the matter conclusively.

With some variations in emphasis, the three membership codes described are essentially the same with respect to four core elements that must be met to qualify for membership. Individuals must self-identify as an Indigenous person (whether First Nations, Inuit, or Métis), they must have an ancestral connection to the Indigenous nation in which they seek membership, they must demonstrate a commitment to the way of life advanced by the nation, and they must secure community acceptance. Self-identification and ancestral connections, in other words, must also be complemented by a genuine willingness on the part of prospective members to participate in the nation's culture, practices, and traditions or, more broadly, its way of life.

Community acceptance is built on the expectation that individual applicants take their Indigenous identity seriously and that they want to work out the expression of that identity within the context of the Indigenous community they seek to join.

All three membership codes are also informed by either explicit or implicit references to Indigenous sovereignty. In the three cases described, Indigenous sovereignty is constrained because the membership codes are validated as authoritative either through a federal or provincial statute.[4] But at the same time, each code also reflects governing arrangements that are a product of choices made by the Indigenous nation itself. In each case, for example, the Indigenous nation employs criteria for membership that reflect community priorities and traditions. The codes also provide for checks and balances by including appeal procedures that safeguard individual rights and interests. In as much as these elements are independently derived and applied, the Indigenous quest to be in political control over its own membership is being advanced. But as I shall also demonstrate, the heavy weight of the *Indian Act*'s legal imposition of the category "Indian" still puts significant constraints on the ability of Indigenous nations to exercise sovereignty in this area. For Indigenous women in particular, the imposition of those legal categories has significantly diminished their political power, community status, and material resources. Consequently, with respect to the question of identity and membership, the Indigenous right to self-determination can at best be described as only partially fulfilled. While the right may be inherent, the respect granted to that right by the Canadian state is developing but not yet complete.

WHO ARE THE INDIGENOUS PEOPLES OF CANADA?

The Indigenous peoples of Canada are an extremely diverse group, made up of many nations (Tsawwassen, Siksika, Dene, Mohawk, Mi'kmaq) with distinct histories, cultural traditions, and ways of life. What binds the Indigenous peoples of Canada (and indeed the world) together is the fact that their peoples and nations both predate the presence of colonial societies and that they identify themselves to be separate from the colonial society that now occupies and regularly dominates them on their ancestral territories. As explained by José R. Martinez Cobo, Indigenous peoples not only share a common experience of colonial oppression, but also a common commitment to survive as distinct peoples. In his words, they "are determined to preserve, develop, and transmit to future generations, their ancestral territories, and their ethnic identity, as the basis of their continued existence as peoples, in accordance with their own cultural patterns, social institutions, and legal systems" (Cobo 1983, para. 379). The Indigenous assertion to sovereignty is animated by this most fundamental of ambitions. Without the political security that sovereignty provides, Indigenous peoples will simply be unable to enjoy their basic human right to self-determination and thus their entitlement to determine their own destinies and maintain their standing as distinct peoples.

ABORIGINAL PEOPLES

While the concepts of "Indigenous" and "Aboriginal" are often used interchangeably, it is only the latter who are granted formal legal and constitutional recognition in the Canadian context. Canada accords no such recognition on Canadian soil to the rights of Indigenous peoples such as the Cherokee of the United States, the Náhuatl of Mexico, the Ashaninka of Peru, or the Maori of New Zealand, to name just a few examples. As the concept "Aboriginal" is the one accepted in Canadian constitutional law and, for the purposes of this section, contemporary Canadian census research, it is this concept that I shall use in the pages to follow. Doing so gives us access to statistical research that seeks to identify a number of the key characteristics that distinguish various categories of Indigenous peoples in Canada from one another as well as from their non-Indigenous counterparts.

The ***Constitution Act, 1982*** identifies the "aboriginal peoples of Canada" to include the "Indian, Inuit, and Métis peoples of Canada" (Section 35(2)). By means of this constitutional declaration, Canada establishes that "aboriginal peoples" exist as a distinct legal category of peoples within Canada and that each is in some fundamental sense separate and distinct from one another. The *Constitution Act, 1982* also declares that the "existing aboriginal and treaty rights of the aboriginal peoples of Canada are hereby recognized and affirmed" (Section 35(1)). This provision establishes that part of what it means to be "aboriginal" in Canada is to have distinct, constitutionally protected "aboriginal rights." While there is an ongoing debate about what the substance of those "aboriginal rights" amounts to, each of Indians (or First Nations), Inuit, and Métis have made it abundantly clear that it must include a restoration of their right to self-determination, a basic human right that belongs to all the peoples of the world and that was illegitimately stripped from them through violent encounters with colonialism (Green 2014a, 1).

Aboriginal persons are individuals who can trace their ancestry back to before European settlement occurred in the territory now known as Canada. The Canadian census distinguishes between persons possessing Aboriginal ancestry and those possessing Aboriginal identity. In the 2016 Census, Statistics Canada identified 2,130,520 persons as claiming Aboriginal ancestry while 1,673,785 persons claimed to be Aboriginal based on their identity. For the former, their Aboriginal ancestry likely has a negligible impact on their identity, while for the latter their Aboriginal ancestry plays a pivotal role in how they define themselves – that is, they perceive themselves to be in some fundamental sense an "Aboriginal" person. The "ancestry" category makes up 5.9 per cent of the Canadian population while the "identity" category constitutes 4.9 per cent (Statistics Canada 2017, 1). Of those who reported an Aboriginal identity, 58.4 per cent were First Nations, 35.1 per cent were Métis, and 3.9 per cent were Inuit (Statistics Canada 2017, 2).

Aboriginal peoples reside all across Canada, though not uniformly so. More than half of the First Nations' population is concentrated in the western provinces while almost one-quarter live in Ontario. Of the Métis population, 80.3 per cent are found in Ontario and the western provinces, with Ontario accounting for one-fifth of the national total. Three-quarters (72.8 per cent) of Inuit live in Inuit Nunangat, a territory stretching from the westernmost Arctic to the eastern shores of Newfoundland and Labrador. Of those, the majority (63.7 per cent) live in Nunavut

(Statistics Canada 2017, 3, 4, 6, 8). Statistics Canada documents that over half of the First Nations population (55.8 per cent) live off reserve, while nearly two-thirds of Métis (62.6 per cent) live in a metropolitan area (Statistics Canada 2017, 3, 5). In total, over half (51.8 per cent) of Aboriginal people in Canada live in a metropolitan area of at least 30,000 people, with the cities of Winnipeg, Edmonton, Vancouver, and Toronto leading the way (Statistics Canada 2017, 9). Indigenous people constitute a majority of the population only in Nunavut and the Northwest Territories.

Statistics Canada also reports that "Aboriginal languages – grouped into 12 language families – have been central to the history of First Nations people, Métis, and Inuit in Canada and continue to play a vital role to this day" (Statistics Canada 2017, 10). More than 70 distinct Aboriginal languages were reported in the 2016 Census, of which at least 30 had 500 speakers or more. At the same time, the number of Aboriginal people "who could speak an Aboriginal language was higher than the number with an Aboriginal mother tongue" (Statistics Canada 2017, 10). This fact leads Statistics Canada to conclude that many Aboriginal persons are learning an Aboriginal language as a second language.

A further noteworthy statistic is the phenomenal rate of growth among Canada's Aboriginal population. Statistics Canada documents that since 2006 "the Aboriginal population has grown by 42.5% – more than four times the growth rate of the non-Aboriginal population over the same period." Moreover, this trend is almost certain to continue. Based on population projections in the next two decades, Canada's "Aboriginal population is likely to exceed 2.5 million persons" (Statistics Canada 2017, 1). This growth is attributed to two main factors: "the first is natural growth, which includes increased life expectancy and relatively high fertility rates," and the second is due to changes in self-reported identification. Statistics Canada points out that more and more people "are newly identifying as Aboriginal on the census – a continuation of a trend over time" (Statistics Canada 2017, 1). The Aboriginal population is also young, the average age in 2016 being 32.1 years, almost a decade younger than the 40.9 average age of the non-Aboriginal population (Statistics Canada 2017, 2).

INDIANS

Of the threefold legal classification of Indigenous peoples in Canada – Indians (or First Nations), Métis, and Inuit – it is only First Nations people who are categorized as either status or non-status Indians, the former again being divided into those living on or off reserve. Status Indians are those who meet the definition of "Indian" as set out in the *Indian Act* and who are also treaty or non-treaty "Indians." The *Indian Act*'s system of deciding who is eligible for status is largely determined by whether a person's parents have status. While the rules have changed considerably over the years, children born after April 17, 1985, must have two status parents to pass that full status onto their own children. If one of the two parents of a child is not a full status Indian, then that child cannot pass on full status to their children if those children, in turn, are born of a relationship with a non-Indian person. For the purposes of the *Indian Act*, those children effectively become "non-status" or non-Indians. This process and accompanying eligibility criteria are colloquially known as the two-generation cut-off rule.[5] The First Nations population numbered 977,230 people in 2016, a total that includes both those who are registered (or have status) and are treaty Indians under the *Indian Act*, and those who are not registered (or non-status) (Statistics Canada 2017, 1). Of that number, 744,855 (or 76.2 per cent) were registered while 232,375 (23.8 per cent) were not (Statistics Canada 2017, 3). Unlike status Indians, non-status Indians are not on the Indian Register kept by the Government of Canada. This means that even though non-status Indians may well regard their Aboriginal ancestry to be integral to their identity, they are not subject to the terms of nor are they entitled to the benefits made available to status Indians under the *Indian Act*.[6]

It is also important to emphasize that the legal categories of "status" and "non-status" Indian were created by the Canadian state for its own administrative convenience. They do not necessarily represent how First Nations peoples identify themselves, and for many they are, at best, inappropriate. Indeed, in almost all cases, the legal classification as "Indian," whether "status" or "non-status," was imposed on First Nations people without their consent. The category of "non-status" Indian is particularly problematic. It conveys the impression that those individuals are somehow not worthy of recognition as "aboriginal peoples" and that they should not be entitled to the same "aboriginal rights" as their "status" Indian counterparts. In addition to legal standing under the *Indian Act*, most registered or status individuals (though not all, depending on band membership criteria) are members of one of more than 600 First Nations or Indian bands in Canada.[7]

MÉTIS

The Métis population numbered 587,545 people in 2016, registering the largest increase among the three Aboriginal groups since 2006, up 51.2 per cent (Statistics Canada 2017, 1). The term "Métis" refers to people who are of mixed First Nations/Inuit and European ancestry. Many of those who qualify as Métis are those who are the product of families created through intermarriages resulting from the fur trade.[8] The Métis provided a leadership role in the development of western Canada, involving themselves in the facilitation and development of trade and transportation routes as well as local self-governance. The term "Métis" also refers to the descendants of the original Red River region of the Métis Nation in Manitoba. This community is popularly known for its participation in the Northwest Rebellion of the late 1800s, led by Louis Riel and Gabriel Dumont, a rebellion that sought to secure Métis land title and rights in advance of the purchase and transfer of Rupert's Land from the Hudson's Bay Company to Canada. The Métis were initially successful, as they were able to set up a provisional government that negotiated terms for the creation of the province of Manitoba in 1870. However, a petition sent to Ottawa to protect Métis land rights in advance of the creation of the provinces of Saskatchewan and Alberta led to an unsatisfactory response when measured against Métis aspirations at the time. A rebellion ensued, lasting two months, culminating in a trial in which Riel was accused of treason and subsequently executed on November 16, 1885.

Over time, the Métis have developed into politically distinct peoples and communities right across Canada with their own unique identities, cultures, ambitions, histories, and political objectives (Belanger 2018, 150–74). As peoples, they regularly frame their ambition to live as distinct peoples in the language of an inherent basic human right to self-determination within Canada. Although the Métis are excluded from the *Indian Act* (just like non-status Indians), they are legally regarded as Aboriginal peoples with a corresponding set of Aboriginal rights, including harvesting rights, land rights, and limited rights to self-government. For example, the Alberta government has accepted a Métis right to self-government by means of eight Métis Settlements, each of which exercises power over certain areas of jurisdiction. Not everyone with mixed First Nations and European ancestry can claim to be Métis and a beneficiary of Métis rights, however. The 2003 *Powley* case at the Supreme Court of Canada established that to qualify as Métis, an individual must self-identify as a Métis, must have an ancestral connection to a historic Métis community, and must be accepted by a Métis community as one of their own (*R. v. Powley* 2003, paras. 30–3). In short, the Métis are neither First Nations nor Inuit. They are distinct peoples marked by their commitment to live together, sharing a way of life that is rooted in traditions that are unique, most typically drawn from both European and Indigenous sources.[9]

INUIT

The Inuit population numbered 65,025 in 2016, an increase of 29.1 per cent from the 2006 Census (Statistics Canada 2017, 1). They reside in the far north, mostly above the tree line on land comprising the northern shores of Canada and the islands of the Arctic Archipelago (Grammond 2009, 82). Historically, the Inuit were largely nomadic, hunting and fishing according to the cycle of the seasons. The Inuit are distinct from First Nations and Métis by virtue of their deep connections to northern lands, the source of their unique identities, cultures, economies, language, and history.

A 1939 Supreme Court ruling established that the Inuit fell within the meaning of "Indian" under Section 91(24) of the *Constitution Act, 1867*. While this ruling did not require that the *Indian Act* apply to the Inuit (i.e., there is no registration scheme for Inuit as there is for Indians), it did instruct the federal government to take responsibility for them by providing programs and services like health and education.[10] By the 1950s and 1960s the Inuit began to settle in (or were forcibly relocated to) 50 permanent communities. This measure caused significant disruption to their traditional way of life, resulting in large-scale Inuit dependence on the federal government for income and social assistance. Yet the Inuit retained many of their distinct cultural practices, including a close relationship to the land and its animals as well as to their language, Inuktitut. The Inuit have also been active in pursuing land claims agreements. Their objective has been self-determination. They wish to control the terms of their own economic development and consolidate a hold on lands and political jurisdiction consistent with their right to be self-defining. The agreements since negotiated now cover much of northeastern Canada and include the Nunavik, Nunatsiavut, Nunavut, and Inuvialuit regions (Courchene 2018, 221–32).

The Supreme Court of Canada decision in *Daniels v. Canada* (2016) adds an important layer of complexity to the question concerning what it means to be "Aboriginal" in Canada today. In this decision, the Supreme Court ruled that Métis and non-status Indians qualify as "Indians" under Section 91(24) of the *Constitution Act, 1867*. Consequently, the Supreme Court established that the federal government has a fiduciary responsibility for these individuals, thus ending the longstanding jurisdictional dispute about their constitutional standing within Canada in which neither the federal nor provincial governments claimed responsibility for these peoples. While the Supreme Court refused to set out what this fiduciary responsibility amounts to in the case of non-status Indians and the Métis, it did instruct the federal government that it must negotiate with each in good faith on all matters determined to be in their interest. The potential implications of the *Daniels* decision are considerable. As "Indians" for the purposes of the *Indian Act*, each of non-status Indians, Métis, and Inuit are now eligible for the material benefits associated with federal programs designed to meet the unique fiduciary obligations (however defined) that the federal government owes to each group. At the same time, however, it is worth bearing in mind the virtual certainty that the beneficiaries of the *Daniels* decision will decrease considerably in numbers over the years to come. The federal restrictions imposed on who can transfer Indian status to their children under the rules of Bill C-31 have decisively seen to that.

MEMBERSHIP AND CITIZENSHIP: EMERGING INDIGENOUS CONTROL

One of the most elemental features of political sovereignty is the ability of a people to define and control the terms of their own membership or citizenship. This ability is one of the most fundamental rights of any government, Indigenous governments included (Kuokkanen 2012, 227–31). Indigenous peoples simply must be able to define and control the terms of their own citizenship, including its corresponding rights and duties, if they are to be able to create communities in keeping with their own values and priorities.[11] Recognition of the Indigenous inherent right to exercise jurisdiction over their own citizenship consistent with international human rights law is offered by the UNDRIP where it declares in Article 33(1) that "Indigenous peoples have the right to determine their own identity or membership in accordance with their customs and traditions." Building on the foundation provided by this right, the Declaration then draws out its practical implications by stating in subsection (2) that "Indigenous peoples have the right to determine the structures and to select the membership of their institutions in accordance with their own procedures" (Green 2014b, 33). Yet the position of the Canadian government has consistently been that it alone has the authority to define and apply the terms of citizenship in Canada, preferring instead to use the term "membership" when it comes to belonging to an Indigenous nation. According to this view, while Indigenous peoples are "citizens" of Canada, they are "members" of their nations. The first is presumed to serve as a precondition for the latter.

In the pre- and early contact period, citizenship in Indigenous nations and membership within the social and cultural milieu of an Indigenous way of life were one and the same thing. Status on both counts could come to an individual in a variety of ways. Most directly, citizenship was a right acquired by being born to a parent who already was an accepted member of the Indigenous nation (Cassidy and Bish 1989, 54). The systems associated with incorporation were diverse, including clan systems, matrilineal (mother-based) and patrilineal (father-based) kinship systems, and hereditary systems, all of which included provisions for marriages and adoptions. During this period the acquisition of citizenship was flexible, as it could be acquired through several routes, including birth, marriage, adoption, and residency (Government of Canada 2019, 1). As the Joint Technical Working Group of the Assembly of First Nations and Indigenous and Northern Affairs Canada puts it, "citizenship recognition was based on self-identification and gender-neutral kinship and community ties" (Joint Technical Working Group 2008, 4). In whatever way determined, during this period Indigenous nations were in full control of their own citizenship, exercising the right to set boundaries and to establish the criteria concerning who its members were and were not (Frideres 2020, 26).

But much has changed over time. Since at least 1867, the Canadian government's regulation of Indigenous identity by means of the *Indian Act* has significantly complicated the matter of Indigenous citizenship, particularly for First Nations.[12] As a first step, *Indian Act* rules dictated that large Indigenous nations were to be divided into many smaller bands.[13] Pamela Palmater explains that the Canadian government's motivation for pursuing this policy was clear: "it was much easier for colonial governments to manage Indian affairs in individual, fragmented communities, than to deal with larger, more powerful nations" (Palmater 2011, 144).

State control through the fragmentation of once great Indigenous nations was further facilitated by the imposition of internal divisions on individuals within their bands. For instance, for many Indigenous people today, their identity as "Indigenous" is decided for them by whether they fall under such *Indian Act* categories as "status Indian" and "band member." The *Indian Act* further sets out how individuals qualify for registration as an Indian, it dictates eligibility rules for band membership, and it determines that Indian bands are to be placed on a particular piece of land or lands called reserves. It is also status Indians, in their capacity as band members, who fall under the political jurisdiction of the *Indian Act*–manufactured chief and council system. Taken together, membership (as distinct from citizenship) is now most typically associated with an individual who belongs to a particular band "as opposed to cultural and political affiliations with a particular Indigenous nation" (Palmater 2011, 144; see also Green 2009, 40). And as Palmater further points out, "many Indigenous individuals now speak of themselves as status and non-status Indians as opposed to Mi'kmaq or Maliseet peoples," to name but two examples (Palmater 2011, 144). Why do they do so? In large part out of necessity because of the incentives built into those identity categories by the Canadian state. For example, an individual must be a status Indian to qualify for certain federal government programs and services, and an individual must be a band member to live with their families on reserve. And, adding yet one more layer of complexity, under the new 1985 rules of the *Indian Act*, it is now entirely possible to be a status Indian but not a band member.

But, as many are quick to point out, these *Indian Act* categories have nothing to do with the political composition of Indigenous nations as they once were. Whether an individual is a status or non-status Indian, a band member or non-band member, would seem to be utterly irrelevant from the perspective of whether that individual is entitled to qualify as Indigenous or is eligible for citizenship within an Indigenous nation. It will come as no surprise, therefore, to learn that Indigenous leaders have been hard at work in their quest to regain control over the rules for their own citizenship. The challenge is enormous because the standard for success in this quest is an extremely demanding one. As explained by Jody Wilson-Raybould, "long-term solutions do not lie in further tinkering with the Indian Act." She then adds, "the real and ultimate solution to addressing ongoing discrimination in the Indian Act lies with full recognition of First Nations jurisdiction over our own citizenship" (Wilson-Raybould 2019, 117). To accomplish this objective, Indigenous leaders insist that their peoples must seek out ways to restore notions of Indigenous citizenship that are in keeping with their self-identity as peoples and that reflect their customs and traditions as nations. As they see it, this is essential to Indigenous self-determination and, by extension, to their sovereignty.

In 1985 the scales were tipped more favourably in the direction of respect for Indigenous sovereignty. **Bill C-31** was introduced in the Parliament of Canada. The Bill was drafted specifically to address the stifling conditions of federal government control over Indigenous identity and citizenship.[14] In essence, Bill C-31 had three objectives: first, remove more than 100 years of gender discrimination from the eligibility criteria for those entitled to register as Indians under the *Indian Act*; second, restore Indian status to those who had been enfranchised against their will due to discriminatory provisions within the Act; and third, recognize the right of Indian bands to control their own membership codes. Important to note is that the federal government continues to have control over who can be registered as an Indian under the *Indian Act* and what rights and benefits are attached to that registration. I will deal with the tangle of issues set in motion by the removal of sex and other forms of discrimination from the *Indian Act* in the next section. Here I address the opportunities and challenges presented by the *Indian Act* amendment that put Indian bands in a position to take charge of their own membership codes. It is my view that by means of this amendment an incremental step was taken in the direction of returning to Indigenous peoples their right to control their own citizenship, and that by doing so Bill C-31 also restored a measure of their political sovereignty.

Before 1985, band membership usually went hand in hand with Indian registration. To be a member of an Indian band, an individual also had to be registered as an Indian under the *Indian Act*. After the 1985 Bill C-31 amendments, however, bands could choose to determine their own membership criteria. As a result, depending on those criteria, it became possible for individuals to have Indian status under the *Indian Act* but not necessarily be members of bands. Conversely, individuals could also be members of bands without necessarily being a status Indian under the *Indian Act*. These two categories are now conceptually distinct and for practical purposes are separated from one another. The motivation for this separation was quite simple. All "status" Indians would continue to fall under the jurisdiction of the federal government, but the question concerning band membership was left to bands themselves. Henceforth, this was a matter for Indian bands to decide.

The road to Indigenous control over their own membership criteria, however, was still subject to a number of federally imposed requirements and constraints. According to the amended *Indian Act*, if bands wished to acquire control over their membership eligibility rules, they had to meet several conditions. **Section 10** of the *Indian Act* stipulates that "a band may assume control over its own membership" if it meets three democratic requirements: (1) a majority of the band's electors must give its consent to the band's control of its own membership; (2) the membership rules must include a mechanism for reviewing decisions on membership; and (3) the rules must not deprive persons of membership who previously had the right to have their name entered on the band list (*Indian Act*, Section 10(1), (2), (3), (4)). The clearest step taken in the direction of enhanced Indigenous power, however, was secured through the following provisions. Once a band assumes control of its membership list, it has full power to decide who is to be added or deleted from the list "subject to the membership rules established by the band." For both clarity and good measure, the *Indian Act* further stipulates that from the date that a band assumes control of its membership, the federal government "shall have no further responsibility with respect to that Band List" (*Indian Act*, Section 10(8), (9), (10)). In other words, it is to be the band membership code as defined by the band itself, rather than by the *Indian Act*, that will henceforth set the rules for deciding who may be a band member. It is this feature of Bill C-31 in particular that I would argue restored to Indigenous nations an important element of their original sovereignty.

Many First Nations have moved forward to provide a basis for citizenship within their own nations by drafting membership codes. Of the over 600 recognized First Nations in Canada, 229 now determine their own membership under Section 10 of the *Indian Act*, while an additional 38 control membership through self-government legislation (INAC 2015b).[15] For those First Nations that to date have opted not to acquire control over their membership rules under Section 10 (about 57 per cent), their lists continue to fall under the jurisdiction of the Indian Register under **Section 11** of the *Indian Act.*[16] As of June 28, 1987, and thereafter, those First Nations that chose to leave their membership lists under the purview of the Department of Indigenous and Northern Affairs (INAC) were required to accept the condition that all persons with Indian status would also be entitled to band membership (*Indian Act*, Section 11(2), (3)). INAC maintains the membership lists for these First Nations. At any time, however, a First Nation may choose to take control of their membership code, but doing so requires that the First Nation protect the rights of all individuals already registered and added to the band list to retain their membership within the nation (*Indian Act*, Section 10(4), (5)).

First Nations that opt to create their own membership codes often establish eligibility rules that reflect their own cultures and customs.[17] As we saw with our case studies of the Sandy Lake First Nation, NunatuKavut Inuit, and Alberta Métis Settlements, some combination of (1) individual identification with the Indigenous nation, (2) a connection to the community through ancestry, and (3) community acceptance feature heavily in the criteria they employ. Some nations emphasize ancestry and family connection to traditional lands as central to their code, while others focus on the importance of being nominated by community members and a demonstrated willingness to protect and promote the way of life central to the community (Lawrence 2004, 68). Where blood quantum is used to verify ancestry, it is usually set at 25 or 50 per cent. As for the ancestry criteria, Pamela Palmater identifies four general approaches that are in use: those that rely on a one-parent descent rule (38 per cent); those that rely on a two-parent descent rule (28 per cent); those that rely on a blood quantum rule (13 per cent); and those that rely on rules based on Sections 6(1) and 6(2) of the *Indian Act* (21 per cent) (Palmater 2011, 151–2).[18] With respect to the last category, those same Section 6(1) and 6(2) *Indian Act* rules apply by default to those First Nations that have chosen not to develop their own membership codes.

There can be no question that the Indigenous right to determine their own membership codes is an important step toward restored sovereignty. Whatever the criteria developed, the authority to establish and apply membership criteria now rests with those Indigenous nations that choose to exercise it. Indigenous nations are now in control of deciding who may live on reserves or traditional territories, who may participate in local elections and referendums, who may share in community assets, who may benefit from community programs and opportunities for employment, and who may live within and develop the culture of the nation. Furthermore, once membership codes are established, the federal government may neither interfere with its composition nor exercise any power over maintaining the list. From the vantage point of citizenship and belonging, membership and the capacity to control it is central to Indigenous peoples' right to be self-defining. It is Indigenous peoples themselves who ought to be in the position to decide who its members are and thus who is entitled to identify with and partake in the specific cultural practices and traditions of a given Indigenous nation.

But membership also remains a politically contentious and highly sensitive matter. There is the issue, for example, of ongoing federal government control given it still decides what procedures First Nations must follow to generate what it deems to be an "acceptable" membership code (see rules above). On these grounds, it could be argued that the self-determination offered by way of membership control is really only a half-measure. Full sovereignty, based on the universal right of all peoples to define their own membership, should include complete authority to decide who belongs and who does not belong without any Canadian governmental regulations, restrictions, or interference (AFN, 2012a, 5). By way of a start, Jody Wilson-Raybould urges Indigenous nations to conceive of their own citizenship outside of the stifling categories of the *Indian Act.* It would be far better in her view, and also far more in keeping with the Indigenous right to self-determination, to discuss citizenship "within the broad context of Nation building" as informed by "our own laws, customs, and traditions" (Wilson-Raybould 2019, 116, 117). Such codes could include, among other things, demonstrated relationships through kinship ties (though not mediated by blood quantum),[19] commitment to the well-being and development of the nation, acceptance on the part of members of the Indigenous society, and respect for and willingness to live under and submit to the laws, customs, and traditions of the nation (Palmater 2011, 208).

But membership remains politically contentious for another important reason. Indigenous feminists argue that exercises in Indigenous "decolonization, healing, sovereignty, and nation-building" that do not address "the dire conditions in which many Native women find themselves" (including poverty and violence) can be no exercise in nation-building at all (Anderson 2010, 85). According to this perspective, prospects for healthier Indigenous nations depend on Indigenous leadership confronting the undeniable collusion that exists between the forces of colonialism and patriarchy. Shari Huhndorf and Cheryl Suzack point out, for example, that for many Indigenous women, their marginalization "is compounded by the fact that a critical component of colonialism throughout the Americas involved the imposition of Western gender roles and patriarchal social structures" (Huhndorf and Suzack 2010, 2). The result for Indigenous women has been irretrievable loss, whether in the form of identity, "power, status, or material circumstances" (Huhndorf and Suzack 2010, 3; see also Green 2017b, 4–7). Exercises in Indigenous nation-building, therefore, must place the feminist ambition to secure civil rights for Indigenous women (including the right to citizenship and belonging within their communities) at the forefront of their emancipatory agendas. Indeed, to do otherwise, say Indigenous feminists, is to run the danger of leaving the patriarchal gender hierarchies that perpetuate Indigenous women's oppression very much intact.

These feminist observations lead us to the matter of the *Indian Act* itself and the considerable harm it has inflicted upon Indigenous identity and traditional Indigenous mechanisms for deciding citizenship. Outlining features of this problem is what I will take up in the remainder of this chapter. For while it is the case that many Indigenous nations now exercise primary jurisdiction over citizenship, they do so against the backdrop of colonial patriarchal influences and coercive governance practices that have deeply penetrated their nations and, by extension, profoundly disrupted their capacity to design membership codes in keeping with their communal aspirations.[20] To see how this is so we must return to the *Indian Act*, and more particularly to Bill C-31 and the legacy of legal amendments set off by its structural deficiencies. In addition to establishing the right of First Nations to control their own membership codes, Bill-31 also sought to remove a number of (especially gender-based) discriminatory provisions from the *Indian Act*. Gender neutrality is an essential feature of any law purporting to be based in equality. But what the Bill C-31 revisions did to address these discriminatory provisions was to set off a whole chain of related events that made the prospects for Indigenous control over their own membership that much more difficult. Subsequent attempts to eliminate these problems by way of Bill C-3 (2011) and Bill S-3 (2017) have been only partially successful. Paraphrasing Audra Simpson, certain forms of rights (namely, the right to self-identify as a status Indian) inevitably "carry with them the residue of state imposition" (Simpson 2014, 190). In the remainder of this chapter, I will explain in what ways.

THE INDIAN REGISTER AND THE COMPLICATIONS CREATED BY BILL C-31

From the perspective of sovereignty, political communities ought to have the right to define who their members are according to criteria of their own design. In the case of Indigenous nations, however, this right was undermined by the Canadian government when it introduced the *Indian Act* in 1876. Without any consultation or agreement from Indigenous nations, the federal and provincial governments divided state sovereignty over all areas of jurisdiction between themselves as set out in **Sections 91 and 92** of the ***Constitution Act, 1867***. Section 91(24) gave the federal government power to legislate with respect to all matters concerning "Indians and lands reserved for Indians," including authority to radically transform the individual identities of Indigenous persons into a Euro-Canadian image. The policy goal of the *Indian Act*, therefore, was animated by two essential objectives. First, by way of a long-term objective, its intent was to assimilate Indigenous peoples into the Euro-Canadian mainstream. But second, and more immediately, it intended to "protect" Indians from Euro-Canadians until such time as they were deemed to be sufficiently prepared to be absorbed into the purportedly superior Euro-Canadian way of life. To this end, the *Indian Act* established the legal means for the Canadian government to coerce Indigenous peoples into abandoning central features of their distinct ways of life, including their traditional gender roles, cultural identities, and political structures (Eberts 2014, 148).

The legacy of this long-term assimilationist project, carried out over the course of more than 100 years, has been both confusing and devastating from the vantage point of Indigenous control of Indigenous identity (Wilson-Raybould 2019, 114). As Pamela Palmater observes, "federal control over Indianness and membership has become the primary filter through which government, society, and even some Aboriginal groups have come to view Aboriginal peoples" (Palmater 2011, 39). The problem with this, as Joyce Green sees it, is that "terms like *Indian* or *native* are macro-categories created by the colonial imagination without references to actual communities or nations of Aboriginal people" (Green 2009, 40). The effects of these categories on the life prospects of individual Indigenous peoples, and especially Indigenous women, have been profound. As Palmater explains, to qualify for access to Indigenous rights, it is not enough that an individual be able to demonstrate that they are Mi'kmaq, for example, but they must also be able to "meet Canada's definition of an Indian which Canada alone controls" (Palmater 2011, 39). Of course, Indigenous understandings of their own identity have persisted over time despite the coercive impact of the *Indian Act*, and as demonstrated above Indigenous peoples now exercise some sovereignty in defining their own membership rules. My point is simply to draw attention to the fact that the *Indian Act*'s obsessive concern with "Indian" identity has had a deep impact on the practical circumstances of Indigenous peoples' lives. It is those with Indian status, for example, who have privileged access to real material benefits like health care, education, and in many cases the right to enjoy the cultural security and sense of belonging that goes with living on reserves (though the 2016 *Daniels* decision has now compelled the federal government to re-evaluate the restricted scope of its Section 91(24) responsibilities) (Brodsky 2014, 101, 118; Eberts 2014, 149).

WHO QUALIFIES AS INDIAN?

The *Indian Act* of 1876 was a product of the consolidation of several pre-Confederation pieces of legislation, including the ***Gradual Civilization***

Act of 1857 and the ***Gradual Enfranchisement Act*** of 1869.[21] While the *Indian Act* has been subjected to numerous amendments over the years, today it more or less still retains its original form. The Act was designed to govern all matters pertaining to Indian life, including Indian status, the structure of Indian bands, and Indian reserves. The Act was also a product of Canadian Confederation itself. Essentially, the federal government wanted to unite all Indigenous nations under one policy and regulate all Indigenous people under one law. Under the Act, all "Indians" were to be treated uniformly and controlled to achieve the same end – gradual civilization for the purpose of assimilation into the Euro-Canadian way of life. To this end, the Act established a paternalistic regime of federal governmental control over all aspects of Indigenous life. For example, the Act outlawed traditional Indigenous political, social, cultural, and religious institutions and replaced them with Western-style institutions like male-elected and male-run band councils, Christian churches, wage labour practices, and residential schools (Eberts 2014, 148). The Act also defined who qualified as an Indian by way of assigning Indian status.[22] In law, an Indian (or status Indian) is quite simply anyone who is registered or is entitled to be registered as an Indian (*Indian Act*, Section 6(1)(a); see also Giokas and Groves 2002, 50). Indigenous persons who meet these oddly circular criteria are registered as such under the Act and their names are placed in the Indian Register – a central registry established in 1951 and maintained by the federal government (Vowel 2016, 27–8; Courchene 2018, 58–61; Frideres 2020, 31). As already discussed, a 1985 amendment to the Act separated Indian status from band membership. Bands can now develop their own membership codes. However, this amendment did not put bands in the position to decide who gains or loses Indian status. It is still the federal government who controls the Indian registry and defines who is entitled to be an Indian.

It is the *Indian Act*'s dual policy focus on paternalism and assimilation that led to the crafting of highly ethnocentric and sexist rules concerning who qualified as an Indian. Jody Wilson-Raybould observes that initially "the definition of 'Indian' was quite broad and more reflective of how we saw ourselves." For example, early definitions of who qualified as an Indian "included any person either of Indian birth or blood, reputed to belong to a particular group of Indians, married to an Indian, or adopted into an Indian family" (Wilson-Raybould 2019, 114). However, in the interest of assimilation, it did not take long for the definition to become much more circumscribed (Eberts 2014, 148). Most significantly for our purposes, 1869 Eurocentric patrilineal rules (male lineage) were imposed on all Indigenous nations to determine who could inherit Indian status. It was Indian women and their children who were specifically singled out for loss of status based on Victorian notions about gender in which it was simply assumed that women were the responsibility of men who were expected to serve as their protectors and as the family "breadwinners" (Simpson 2017, 104; see also Brodsky 2014, 104–5; Eberts 2014, 149, 151).

The initial Act of 1876, therefore, established that to qualify for registration, an individual must be a male person of Indian blood who belonged to an Indian band, any child of such a person, and any woman married to such a person (Courchene 2018, 61; Grant 2018, 114; Kuokkanen 2012, 233; Palmater

2011, 41–2; Simpson 2017, 104). Conversely, an Indian woman who married a non-Indian man (or non-status man) lost her legal status as an Indian and all the rights associated with that status (e.g., the right to live on her reserve, share in band assets, and own or inherit property on reserve).[23] The children of such a union similarly acquired no legal rights as an Indian. By virtue of marrying a non-Indian man, both wife and children were considered, for all practical purposes, to have been assimilated. In legal terms, an Indian woman's status was entirely determined by the status of her husband. In short, as summarized by Leanne Simpson, "gender and sexuality were crucial areas in which officials evaluated Indigenous nations and intervened when Indigenous practices contravened assimilatory policies" (Simpson 2017, 104). Colonial powers were determined to impose "Western gender roles and patriarchal social structures" on Indigenous peoples on the grounds that doing so would contribute to their betterment (Huhndorf and Suzack 2010, 2; see also Brodsky 2014, 104–6; Eberts 2014, 151–5).

From 1876 onward, successive amendments to the Act only served to further entrench these gender-based eligibility criteria (*Indian Act*, Section 12(1)(b)). Descent, and more particularly descent through the male line, remained the main criteria for passing on Indian status. There would be no substantive change to these sexist provisions until revised *Indian Act* rules were implemented in 1985 and subsequently amended again at the instruction of the Canadian courts in 2011 and 2017. Needless to say, this gender-based discrimination had catastrophic effects on the lives of many Indigenous women and, by extension, their families and their peoples. Not only was the size of the Indigenous population considerably reduced, but by "marrying out," Indigenous women and their descendants were also effectively exiled from their communities, thus depriving them of their identities, cultures, languages, property, treaty rights, and in many cases their often considerable political influence and power (Kuokkanen 2012, 233; Courchene 2018, 61; Eberts 2014, 152; Green 2017a, 177). It is not surprising, therefore, that Indigenous feminists have long insisted that the liberation of Indigenous women must be seen as a necessary and vital component of the broader Indigenous self-determination movement (Huhndorf and Suzack 2010, 5; Kuokkanen 2014, 126–7).

In addition, the *Indian Act* established a mechanism for enfranchisement. On the condition that Indians sever all ties to their Indigenous nations, they could take up the rights and responsibilities of full Canadian citizenship (Courchene 2018, 60). To encourage assimilation, for example, Indians were told that they could vote only if they "enfranchised." But to vote, Indians would have to give up their Indian status. In addition, because Indian status was passed through the male line, any Indian who did enfranchise automatically transferred that standing to his wife and children. Not surprisingly, Indians were not eager to enfranchise on these or any other terms, and so for a time the federal government engaged in a policy of non-voluntary enfranchisement. Individual Indians who became lawyers, doctors, Christian clergy, or university graduates were automatically enfranchised (Frideres 2020, 29; Vowel 2016, 28). The same occurred to those Indians who had served in the armed forces or those Indian women who married non-status men. Such individuals were deemed to be sufficiently "civilized" (or in the case of Indian women, sufficiently cared for by their non-Indian husbands) to no longer be in need of the artificial "crutch" of Indian status to safeguard their well-being. While the policy of enfranchisement was developed on the purportedly benevolent grounds of inviting Indians into full membership in the Canadian family, its actual ambition was far more sinister. As explained by Chelsea Vowel: "Enfranchisement was a concrete way to assimilate Indigenous people out of legislative existence, extinguish their rights, and solidify colonial control over lands and resources" (Vowel 2016, 28). The policy of enfranchisement was rolled back in small steps over time but was not fully struck from the books until the *Indian Act* amendments of 1985.

BILL C-31 (1985)

In 1985, Bill C-31 was passed largely in response to the lobbying efforts of Indigenous women undertaken in the 1970s and 1980s (Brodsky 2014, 107; Eberts 2014, 155). These women operated in a political climate informed by the civil rights movement, which both inspired and lent support to their ambitions to challenge the entrenched hierarchies of male power prevalent within Indigenous organizations and band councils and was in turn reinforced in federal legislation, including the *Indian Act*.[24] The target of their political activism was to challenge what they identified as "the collusion between colonialism and patriarchy," a condition they claimed had rendered Indigenous women politically powerless, socially marginalized, and subject to all manner of sexual violence (Brodsky 2014, 104; Green 2017b, 9–12; Huhndorf and Suzack 2010, 1). In response, Indigenous feminist activists spearheaded a series of strategically targeted political campaigns throughout the 1970s and 1980s to confront what they identified as the "systematic disempowerment of Indigenous women in all of its dimensions" (Huhndorf and Suzack 2010, 5). What they demanded were political and legal remedies that would, among other things, restore Indigenous women to equal status and membership within their Indigenous communities, mitigate those conditions that contributed to their experiences of violence and poverty, and offer protection to their rights to full participation in Indigenous governance (Green 2017b, 12–17; Huhndorf and Suzack 2010, 6).

It is in this broader context of Indigenous feminist activism that Indigenous women such as Jeanette Lavell, Yvonne Bedard, and Sandra Lovelace challenged the *Indian Act* in both Canadian and international courts. They did so on the grounds that its provisions stripping women and their children of their Indian status and prohibiting them from living on reserves was discriminatory (Brodsky 2014, 107; Eberts 2014, 153). While all cases were rejected by the Supreme Court of Canada on the grounds that "as all Indian women were treated equally by the Indian Act (that is, all were subject to the same discriminatory provisions), there was no inequality in the application of the law," the same outcome was not the case at the international level (Green 2017a, 183; see also Kuokkanen 2012, 234; Eberts 2014, 153–4).

In the 1981 case of Sandra Lovelace, the United Nations Human Rights Committee determined that Canada was not living up to its obligations under the **United Nations International Covenant on Civil and Political Rights**. Lovelace, a Maliseet woman who had lost her Indian status through a marriage that later ended, was denied the right to return to live on her reserve. Yet Article 27 of the UN International Covenant guarantees that persons belonging to minorities may enjoy their own culture and language in their community with other community members, a right of access that the UN Human Rights Committee determined Lovelace was clearly being denied (Eberts 2014, 155; Kuokkanen 2012, 234; Frideres 2020, 33). This UN Human Rights Committee declaration (and the considerable embarrassment it caused Canada), coupled with the adoption of the ***Charter of Rights and Freedoms*** in 1982, paved the way for Canada to enact major *Indian Act* revisions. Bill C-31 received Royal Assent on June 28, 1985. Its provisions were crafted to bring the *Indian Act* into conformity with the gender equality guarantees of the *Charter* (Sections 15 and 28) and to end the century-old policy of enfranchisement. In addition, as discussed earlier, the Bill validated the Indigenous right to set the criteria for their own membership.

In addressing one set of problems, however, Bill C-31 precipitated a whole series of others, most of which have proven intractable and beyond the ability of either the federal government or Indigenous nations to fully resolve. The Bill did not fully eliminate gender discrimination; it established the "two-generation cut-off rule," which denied some with reinstated status the right to pass that status onto their children; and it failed to provide adequate material resources for the many newly reinstated status Indians to return to their nations of origin. Before examining the nature of these problems, however, it is important that we examine the features of Bill C-31 itself, a task that I take up next.

Under the new rules of the *Indian Act*, Indian status is now passed on through descent alone, without any reference to gender. Consequently, female Indians and their children are now said to have the same right to status as their male counterparts. No one, for example, can gain or lose status through marriage. All that a person needs now to be eligible for status is that one parent has or had (if deceased) status. These are the new *Indian Act* rules going forward, but what did Bill C-31 offer by way of redressing the injustices of the past? All Indian women and men who had lost their status prior to 1985, either because they "married out" in the case of women or because they were enfranchised, were given the opportunity to apply to have their status and the status of their children reinstated. The policy of enfranchisement was also abolished. Consequently, under the terms of the new rules, if a person is born with or acquires status (e.g., through adoption), that status now remains in the possession of that person for life. It cannot be rejected, given up, or taken away. Also worth noting is that non-Indian women can no longer acquire status through marriage to status Indian men. It is estimated that, to date, approximately 174,500 individuals were reinstated on the Indian Register as a result of the new *Indian Act* rules for registration (Government of Canada 2019, 12; see also Brodsky 2014, 107; Courchene 2018, 92, 94; Eberts 2014, 155; Frideres 2020, 32).

So how do the new descent rules work? How does an individual actually acquire Indian status? Is it enough, for example, to be born to parents where at least one of them has status? The answer to the last question is yes, but with qualifications. Bill C-31 created two types of Indians – those who have status as Section 6(1) Indians and those who have status as Section 6(2) Indians. From the perspective of rights and entitlements under the *Indian Act*, both categories are the same. Whether registered under Section 6(1) or 6(2), each individual has full status as an Indian.

Where the sections differ, however, is with respect to rules of descent, and more particularly, the ability to pass Indian status on to children. If a person with Section 6(1) Indian status and a non-status person have a child, that child will have Section 6(2) Indian status under the Act. If that Section 6(2) person, in turn, has a child with a non-status person, that child will not inherit Indian status. Put in the form of an example, if your Section 6(1) grandmother (or grandfather) marries a non-status person, your mother (or father) will be a Section 6(2) Indian, and if they then marry a non-status person, you will have no status at all.[25] The outcome is that after two generations of marriage with non-Indians, Indian status is lost. This is referred to as the "second generation cut-off rule." It should come as no surprise that these categories would carry with them the perception that to be a Section 6(1) Indian is far better than to be a Section 6(2) Indian given the latter's more restricted capacity to transmit Indian status and its corresponding rights (Brodsky 2014, 108; Eberts 2014, 155–6).

Strictly speaking, the new *Indian Act* descent rule does not employ blood quantum to decide Indian identity, but it still amounts to a racial standard because to qualify as a status Indian, a person must have at least one-quarter (25 per cent) Indian blood. Thus, ancestry continues to be the deciding factor in who qualifies as a status Indian (Vowel 2016, 29). Those registered under Section 6(1) are assumed to have two registered parents and on those grounds can pass Indian status onto their children. Those registered under Section 6(2), however, are thought to have only one registered parent and so must marry another registered Indian (either a Section 6(1) or a 6(2) Indian) if they want their children to inherit status. In essence, those individuals registered under Section 6(2) have access to fewer rights than those registered under Section 6(1) (Government of Canada 2019, 12). The key to retaining Indian legal status, therefore, is ongoing in-marriage among status 6(1) or 6(2) Indians (Brodsky 2014, 108–9; Frideres 2020, 32).

PROBLEMS CREATED BY BILL C-31

With the enactment of Bill C-31, the Canadian government declared that justice had finally been done. It had removed all discriminatory provisions from the *Indian Act*, and it had provided measures to reinstate Indian status and band membership to all those who had lost it in the past through no fault of their own. Yet three closely interrelated lines of criticism were levelled against Bill C-31 almost immediately upon its release. All three point to problems associated with the dramatic increase in the numbers of non-status Indians in Canada and the corresponding difficulties that both non-status and reinstated status Indians have had in their attempts to (re)join their Indigenous nations.

The first criticism pertains to what critics identify as the residual presence of sexism in the *Indian Act* despite marriage having been removed as a basis for the loss of Indian status by women. This problem was generated by old categories in the Act setting the terms for the reacquisition of Indian status under the new rules. Essentially, children of brothers and sisters who married non-Indians prior to 1985 received different treatment in determining their eligibility for registration. The outcome was an ongoing form of gender discrimination, a matter raised and successfully litigated through the Canadian court system by Sharon McIvor as a *Charter* challenge under the Section 15 equality rights provision.[26] In December 2010, the federal government passed Bill C-3, its response to the *McIvor* decision (Brodsky 2014, 101–4).

Essentially, the problem can be described as follows. Women who had their lost Indian status but were reinstated under Bill C-31 were given status as Section 6(1) Indians, but their children were given status as Section 6(2) Indians. These children, in turn, could only pass their status on to their children if they married a Section 6(1) or 6(2) Indian. But the same rule did not apply to men. Indian men who married non-Indians prior to 1985 passed their Indian status onto their wives. Consequently, both were Section 6(1) Indians, a status that was not taken away from the non-Indian women by the provisions of Bill C-31. The end result, therefore, was discriminatory, as the children of those marriages inherit status as Section 6(1) Indians despite the fact that their mothers were non-Indians. Unlike their Bill C-31 reinstated Section 6(2) Indian counterparts, these children could marry non-Indians and still pass on their Indian status to their children. So, as it turned out, a hierarchy of rights still existed because those who had lost their status based on gender and then subsequently regained it were still relegated to a lower legal level of Indian status security (Olthuis, Kleer, Townshend, 2012, 240–4; Courchene 2018, 92, 94; Green 2017a, 183–4; Vowel 2016, 30). In short, members of the same extended family could well find themselves registered under different categories, with preference given to those who could trace their lineage through patrilineal descent (Brodsky 2014, 109).

The federal government eventually sought to correct this feature of sex discrimination through Bill C-3, the *Gender Equity in Indian Registration Act*, which came into force on January 31, 2011. Through it, the grandchildren's mother acquires the right to register under a new Section 6(1)(c.1) instead of Section 6(2), the clause under which she was required to register as a result of Bill C-31. Her children, in turn, are now entitled to be registered as Section 6(2) Indians as opposed to having no right to register at all. The federal government estimated that because of these changes, approximately 45,000 descendants of Indian women who had been previously excluded would now be entitled to register as status Indians (Brodsky 2014, 100). By means of these amendments, therefore, the federal government believed that all gender-based discrimination within the *Indian Act* had now finally been eliminated (Vowel 2016, 31; Brodsky 2014, 111).[27] Yet, as Pamala Palmater points out, the enactment of Bill C-3 only suspends loss of status for those who are eligible under its terms by one generation. Consequently, while the gender discrimination in Bill C-31 may well have been corrected, the more egregious gender-neutral second generation cut-off rule based on one-quarter blood quantum remains untouched (Palmater 2011, 115; see also Brodsky 2014, 112).

But the story does not end here. As it turns out, Bill C-3 did not fully end gender discrimination but rather just addressed the particular circumstances raised by the Sharon McIvor case (as significant as these were). As determined by the Quebec Superior Court in its August 2015 ruling in

Descheneaux c. Canada (Procureur Général), some *Indian Act* registration provisions still constituted an unjustifiable infringement on the *Charter*'s Section 15 equality rights on the grounds that they perpetuated different treatment between Indian men and Indian women and their descendants. In particular, the court identified four situations that required legislative reform. While fairly technical, they are as follows:

- differential treatment of first cousins whose grandmother lost status due to marrying an unregistered man before April 17, 1985 (referred to as the cousins' issue);
- differential treatment of women who were born out of wedlock to registered fathers between September 4, 1951, and April 17, 1985 (referred to as the siblings issue);
- differential treatment of minor children who were born of registered parents or a registered mother, but who lost their Indian status because their mother married an unregistered man after their birth and between September 4, 1951, and April 17, 1985 (referred to as the issue of omitted minors); and
- differential treatment of children born to registered mothers who choose not to provide the name of the father for inclusion on the birth certificate (referred to as the unknown or unstated parent issue) (Office of the Parliamentary Budget Officer 2017, 3; Frideres 2020, 34).

In addition, there was the lingering matter of the arbitrary "1951 cut-off" rule. This rule stipulated that those individuals who were born before September 4, 1951, and were descendants of women who lost status for "marrying out" going back to 1869 were not eligible to acquire status for either themselves or their children. Bill C-31 had restored eligibility only to those who had lost status between the consolidation of the Indian Register in 1951 and the enactment of Bill C-31 in 1985.

Introduced in the Senate in 2016, Bill S-3 constituted the third attempt by the federal government to end gender-based discrimination in the *Indian Act*. In response to calls made both inside and outside Parliament for "6(1)(a), all the way," the Liberal government agreed to broaden Indian status eligibility to all those affected by gender-based discrimination, including those identified in the four categories described above. In a two-stage implementation process commencing on December 22, 2017 (in which the four situations identified above were addressed) and concluding on August 15, 2019 (in which the "1951 cut-off" rule was eliminated), Bill S-3 authorized generations of excluded persons to register as Indians under either the *Indian Act*'s Section 6(1) or 6(2). A government news release later estimated that between 270,000 and 450,000 individuals could apply, though by December 2020 only 10,000 had been registered (with an inventory of 12,000 more applicants still under review) (Government of Canada 2020a, 5).

To conclude, after a torturous six or seven generations' experience of living under an *Indian Act* regime that legitimized gender-based discrimination, Indigenous peoples now have some relief. In a recent statement, the Liberal government declared that patrilineal and matrilineal lines are now finally properly aligned going all the way back to 1869. Consequently, as far as the government is concerned, "all known sex-based inequities in the registration provisions have now been eliminated" (Government of Canada 2020a, 3).

In the midst of all these reform initiatives, however, what has not changed is the federal government's presumption that it continues to have the right to define who qualifies as an "Indian." But as we know, it has long been the position of Indigenous leaders that they take their inherent right to self-determination to mean that the Canadian state must abandon an *Indian Act* regime that assigns Indigenous identity through a registration system. Instead, as sovereign nations, it is they and not the Canadian state who ought to be in the position to define who they are as peoples (Frideres 2020, 36; Palmater 2015, 50–1). Yet on this score, to date, the Canadian state has been unwilling to concede to Indigenous peoples' significant jurisdictional ground.

A second, potentially more devastating criticism of Bill C-31 has been directed at its so-called "second generation cut-off rule." Under it, Indian status is lost after two continuous generations of Indians parenting with non-Indians. The policy has been targeted for criticism in part because of its built-in hierarchy of rights. As explained by Megan Furi and Jill Wherett, people registered under Section 6(2) have fewer rights than those registered under Section 6(1), because they cannot pass on status to their child unless the child's other parent is also a registered Indian (Furi and Wherrett 2003, 8; see also Government of Canada 2019, 9–10). But in addition, the likely effect of the rule over the long term will be a precipitous decline in the number of status Indians, and this despite the significant increase in status Indian numbers brought on by the huge wave of reinstatements precipitated by Bill C-31. So worrying is this trend that Chelsea Vowel concludes this rule essentially serves as a replacement for the policy of enfranchisement because it too is designed "to legislate Indians out of legal existence" (Vowel 2016, 29). This virtual guarantee of precipitous decline is borne out in the data of a population projections study undertaken by Stewart Clatworthy and Anthony Smith close on the heels of the passage of Bill C-31. They conclude that, given the high rates of intermarriage with non-Indian (or non-status) persons (62 per cent for the off-reserve population and 34 per cent for the on-reserve population), Indian status for many will be extinguished after two successive generations (or 50 years) (Clatworthy and Smith 1992, i).

The primary problem with the "second generation cut-off rule" is that it continues to equate Indigenous identity with a quantifiable and measurable indicator like a blood quantum. Indigeneity is assumed to be present if Indians have full or half or a quarter Indian blood, but after that Indigenous identity is, according to the categories of the *Indian Act*, assumed to be so "diluted" as to be either negligible or non-existent. It is as though "diluted" blood quantity is taken to be necessarily connected to corresponding decreases in ethnocultural community identification. Framed this way, the "second generation cut-off rule" could be construed as an effort on the federal government's part to protect the Indigenous collective right to cultural integrity (Government of Canada 2019, 11). Indigenous critics have been quick to point out, however, that Indigenous identity is not purely a product of ancestry alone. Other factors must also be taken into account, among them culture and language acquisition, residency within an Indigenous nation, commitment given to and offered by an Indigenous nation, and a shared sense of belonging to an Indigenous nation over time (Palmater 2015, 48). In other words, Indigenous concepts of membership are not based on rigid blood quantum requirements but rather on "culturally and politically based concepts of nationhood" (AFN 2012b, 11). In short, some Indigenous critics see the "second generation cut-off rule" as an exercise by the Canadian government in racial engineering, intended to "bleed off" Indian status and, by extension, its responsibility for Indians within a couple of generations (Lawrence 2004, 64–81; Palmater 2011, 43–54). In the words of the Assembly of First Nations, the *Indian Act*'s one-quarter blood quantum rule may well apply equally to male and female persons, but it "serves as a new way to unilaterally and arbitrarily cull the status Indian population" (AFN 2012b, 9).

The third criticism concerns the matter of prospects (or lack thereof) for reinstated status Indians to rejoin their Indigenous nations. The vast majority of Bill C-31, Bill C-3, and Bill S-3 registrants live off reserve and, as a result, it is within the ranks of the off-reserve Indian population that the greatest increase in the status Indian population has occurred. Furi and Wherrett observe, for example, that the off-reserve status Indian population more than doubled between 1981 and 1991, in large part due to reinstatement of those eligible for status under Bill C-31 (Furi and Wherrett 2003, 7–8). These numbers can only be expected to grow as those reinstated under the terms of Bill C-3 and Bill S-3 join the ranks of those newly registered under Bill C-31. Most of those eligible to register as status Indians do not expect to return to reserve communities given the reality of their long-established remote connections. But for all those reinstated women and children who have wanted to return to their nations to live, the route has not always been easy and, in many cases, has turned out to be impossible. Sometimes nations have not been a position to accommodate them, while in other cases nations have simply not wanted them back. The overriding reason for this rejection is attributed to a lack of reserve-based resources. All status Indians, whether living on or off reserve, are eligible to receive non-insured health benefits and can apply for post-secondary financial assistance. For those living on reserve, however, the federal government provides additional resources. These include "funds for housing, elementary and secondary education, health services, and social assistance" (Furi and Wherrett 2003, 12). In addition, there are the intangible benefits of personal growth and security that come with living on traditional territories and participating in the social practices, cultures, and traditions of the people who constitute your community.

After 1985, federal expenditures on reserves did increase to assist Indigenous nations with the task of integrating their reinstated returnees into their communities. At the same time, however, Indigenous leaders pointed out that the additional funds were not adequate to meet the needs of the reinstated women and children as their new demands were placed on top of already severely underfunded programs (Government of Canada 2019, 12; Vowel 2016, 32). Yale Belanger describes situations in which "local animosities developed" because lifetime reserve residents "often looked unfavourably on returning individuals, who demanded a percentage of pre-established budgets, leaving less available per person" (Belanger 2018, 139). In short, lack of resources, particularly with respect to land, housing, infrastructure, and social services, has simply made it impossible for many reinstated status Indians to return to their home nations. Many nations are quite simply in no position to provide potential new members with an adequate standard of living. The effect has been to further complicate Indigenous identity by denying access to community membership and an associated sense of security and belonging to many who seek it, thus further fragmenting Indigenous nations.[28]

To sum up, Indigenous nations see control over the terms of their own citizenship to be a central feature of the right to self-determination. Consequently, Indigenous nations have registered their objection to externally imposed definitions on their identity, whether that be in the form of Indian registration or band council membership systems. The *Indian Act* is quite simply an attack on Indigenous sovereignty, thus the often-repeated calls by Indigenous peoples over the years for its repeal.

At the same time, while it yet exists, the *Indian Act* must not be allowed to serve as a tool for gender or other forms of discrimination. The damage it has inflicted has not only undermined the Indigenous right to self-determination but also the rights of women and their descendants to self-determination within their own communities. It is in the context of such attacks on Indigenous identity that the reform movement resulting in Bill C-31, Bill C-3, and Bill S-3 must be understood. Indigenous women were quite simply fighting for their individual right to be included within the group (as fragmented as it may be). As put by Rauna Kuokkanen, "without individual self-determination, meaningful and viable collective self-determination of Indigenous peoples is simply not possible" (Kuokkanen 2012, 236–7). In short, as Indigenous women see it, by fighting for their individual survival, they also contribute to their collective survival.

From the perspective of political sovereignty, however, I wish to underscore the point that the elimination of all known gender-based inequalities within the *Indian Act* registration system constitutes but an incremental step. As important as it is that women and their descendants be made eligible for Indian status on the same basis as their male counterparts and their descendants, it is still the case that the *Indian Act* represents an oppressive tool of colonial control. Indigenous leaders tell us that the identity categories of the *Indian Act* do not reflect Indigenous cultures and traditions and, as such, they undermine the Indigenous human right to define for themselves who they are. As captured by the Assembly of First Nations, "amendments to the *Indian Act* can only change the manner in which our fundamental human rights are violated" (AFN 2012b, 8). Full restoration of Indigenous sovereignty, therefore, requires that the Canadian state get entirely out "of the 'business' of determining status under the *Indian Act*" (Government of Canada 2019, 16).

WHO CAN CALL THEMSELVES INDIGENOUS? THE CASE OF JOSEPH BOYDEN

One additional question is worthy of consideration. As we have seen, Indigenous peoples live in a colonial environment in which a welter of identity categories and hierarchies have been imposed on them by the Canadian state. But Indigenous peoples also assert their own identities, often doing so in reaction to and independently of state-imposed categories. The question we are left with, therefore, is what makes for an authentic Indigenous identity? Who qualifies as a "real" Indigenous person? Are there established criteria that an individual must meet? And who has the authority to decide? These are perplexing questions that have been seriously complicated by the imposition of the identity categories of the *Indian Act*. For those Indigenous persons living within their nations on ancestral lands, or for those who have close ties to both nation and lands, Indigenous identity is fairly straightforward – they are members of families linked to nations located on traditional territories that, when taken together, define the circumstances of their sense of self and place on the earth. But for others who lack such ties because they live in towns or cities or because they are descendants of a long chain of intermarriages with non-Indigenous persons or non-status Indians, claims to have an Indigenous identity may be more difficult to establish. Indeed, if such individuals do so, they may well be subject to challenges. It was precisely in circumstances such as these that the Indigenous credentials of novelist Joseph Boyden were subject to rigorous public scrutiny in the fall of 2016 and spring of 2017.

Joseph Boyden, a novelist with self-proclaimed Indigenous roots, has enjoyed considerable fame as a result of the commercial success of his books *Three Day Road*, *Through Black Spruce* (a Giller Prize winner), and *The Orenda* (a CBC Canada Reads winner). Shortly before December 2016, Jorge Barrera of the Aboriginal Peoples Television Network (APTN) wrote an article challenging Boyden's claim to Indigenous heritage. While over the years Boyden has claimed his family roots extend to the Métis, Mi'kmaq, Ojibway, and Nipmuc peoples, Barrera wrote that "Boyden has never publicly revealed exactly from which earth his Indigenous heritage grows" (Barrera 2016). A veritable storm of commentary on social media quickly followed. Some argue that the right to determine Indigenous identity rests with Indigenous nations. According to this view, if an individual is to be in possession of an authentic Indigenous identity, it must be nations that grant it by virtue of laying claim to the individual as one of its own. You are Indigenous, in other words, because you belong to a nation. This understanding would certainly be in keeping with the United Nations' working definition, which identifies the experience of being Indigenous with membership in communities located on traditional lands that have "unique cultures and ways of relating to people and the environment … that are distinct from the dominant societies in which they live" (United Nations 2007, 1). On this score, Boyden's credentials are rather thin. Boyden claims a connection through adoption to a Moose Cree First Nation family in the James Bay region of Mushkegowuk. He worked as a teacher in the region and was also active in getting the youth out on the land at Camp Onakawana on the Abitibi River (Talaga 2017). But the community as such has not verified him as one of their own. And as for ancestry, here too there is cause for suspicion. Boyden states he is "from a mixed-blood background of mostly Celtic heritage," with "Nipmuc roots from Dartmouth, Massachusetts, on his father's side and Ojibwe roots from Nottawasaga Bay on his mother's side" (Talaga 2017). When asked to verify these ancestral roots through documentation, however, Boyden offers no more than stories – stories that he says come to him through the generations, in the tradition of Indigenous oral histories.

At its heart, this debate about Boyden's identity concerns authenticity and who can legitimately claim to be Indigenous. This is particularly important in Boyden's case because he regularly speaks for Indigenous peoples. He writes about them in his novels, and he has won awards as an Indigenous author. Is it enough, therefore, to self-identify as Indigenous in the way Boyden does? Or must a person also be accepted by an Indigenous nation for a claim to Indigenous identity to be on firm grounds? Boyden believes he can self-identify as an Indigenous person because he has deep and meaningfully felt ancestral connections to his Indigenous ancestors. So if ancestry is not enough to verify identity, then surely all those Indigenous persons without legal status and with no direct ties to a land base or to a nation would have a difficult if not impossible burden of proof placed upon them. Overwhelmingly, such persons will not be able to meet the criteria. Boyden would seem to be one such person who falls into this camp.

Yet Boyden has expended considerable effort ever since his credentials were questioned to justify himself as an Indigenous person with a right to speak and write as such. He has worked at explaining and clarifying his Indigenous lines of ancestry. He has identified several ties he has to a variety of Indigenous homelands. He has demonstrated his devotion to Indigenous culture and his commitment to vindicate Indigenous history and advance Indigenous rights. And he has secured validation as an Indigenous person by several Indigenous leaders who have both standing and respect within the Indigenous community (Boyden 2017). But at the same time, Boyden also offers no apology for his "hybrid" identity. In the end, he says of himself, "I'm a white kid from Willowdale with native roots" (Talaga 2017). He appears content to be both non-Indigenous and Indigenous. He rejects the idea that to be human a person must have a totality identity. He also does not accept the proposition that to be a "hybrid" human being is to live in a world of irreconcilable internal contradictions. He accepts the normalcy and authenticity of being a person in which "a small part of me is Indigenous, but it is a huge part of who I am" (Tremonti 2017). In short, he does not take his position to be one that borders on "identity fraud."

Others beg to differ. Some Indigenous scholars and activists have said in response that Indigenous identity is about far more than "blood" or DNA. According to Métis writer Aaron Paquette, "it is about community. It is about who claims you" (Goetz 2016). Kim TallBear, Canada Research Chair in Indigenous studies at the University of Alberta, makes the same point. She says, "Indigenous peoples are more concerned with what connections you have to existing communities and families than what percentage native blood you have." According to her, being Indigenous is certainly "not about some long-ago ancestor that you might or might not be able to name or prove" (Goetz 2016). What makes the case of Joseph Boyden particularly troubling for some Indigenous commentators is his presumption that he has the right to speak for Indigenous peoples. According to Robert Jago, an Indigenous activist, "an ancestral connection to Indigenous people doesn't give Boyden permission to speak on their behalf. If you're a member of a community, you're a member of a polity and can represent it. If you are a member of the race alone, with no ties to a community, then you've got an interesting conversation topic at parties but that's where the representation has got to stop" (Goetz 2016). For Jago, in other words, Boyden simply does not have a legitimate claim to speak for Indigenous peoples. He has neither the requisite ties to an Indigenous nation nor is he claimed by one. On these grounds Hayden King concludes that Boyden's presentation of himself constitutes a form of "ethnic fraud," a fraud moreover that he believes does a profound disservice to those who are "legitimate" Indigenous peoples (King 2016).

Whether Boyden's defence is sufficient to establish that he has the credentials to live, speak, and write as an Indigenous person is not for me to judge, though of course the question concerning who can and who ought to be able to judge remains one of great importance. What Boyden's case does illustrate, however, is how corrosive the effects of colonial policy have been on Indigenous identity. While the *Indian Act* and other policy measures may have failed in their efforts to eradicate Indigenous identity, they have certainly left a legacy of entrenched artificial hierarchies and deep legal divisions between Indigenous peoples. In the end, therefore, should Boyden be seen as a "white" interloper or a "pretendian" who wishes to use his exceedingly thin Indigenous credentials to secure benefits (like acclaim as an Indigenous author) that would otherwise be unavailable to him? Or should Boyden be seen as an individual with Indigenous ancestry who is justified in wanting to both nurture and give expression to his Indigenous affiliations, thin as they may seem, to enrich his life?

It is certainly the case that for close to a century Canadian governmental policy established strong incentives for Indigenous peoples to suppress their Indigenous affiliations, and many did so. But times have changed, and today we see the rekindling of Indigenous pride, the re-emergence of Indigenous cultural expression, and the re-establishment of Indigenous political leadership anchored in and informed by strong claims to sovereignty. In this more positive setting of Indigenous identity affirmation, many Indigenous people are returning to (or are entering for the first time) the Indigenous community fold. It is not surprising, therefore, that the debate over what ought to be the requisite credentials for a person to be able to claim an Indigenous identity will remain complex and difficult to resolve. What is clear, however, is that the Canadian government must exercise restraint in this regard. If the assertion to Indigenous sovereignty is to be taken as seriously as it should, then this is ultimately a matter for Indigenous peoples themselves to decide. As for getting on with this task, Indigenous scholar Pamela Palmater provides a helpful starting point. She suggests that as Indigenous peoples take on more responsibility for defining the terms of their own identity, they acknowledge "the damage that has been done by the incorporation of colonial notions of Indigeneity and take positive steps to undo the harm by being more inclusive in their nation-building exercises" (Palmater 2011, 175).

INCREMENTAL SOVEREIGNTY ILLUSTRATED: THE QALIPU MI'KMAQ FIRST NATION

Since at least 1985, many Indigenous nations have asserted their fundamental human right to decide the terms of their own citizenship. Many have resisted the externally imposed *Indian Act* categories of Indian status and its corresponding criteria for community membership, opting instead to take steps to define themselves. The Canadian government has conceded to Indigenous nations the jurisdictional space that rightly belongs to them by means of the amended *Indian Act*'s Section 10 as well as through self-government agreements.[29] As noted earlier, of Canada's 618 First Nations, 229 now determine their own membership codes under Section 10 while a further 37 do so under terms set out in their self-government agreements (INAC 2015b).

By means of these initiatives, Indigenous peoples are taking incremental steps toward re-establishing sovereignty over their own citizenship. Undeniably, this process is still in its beginning stages as there are many Indigenous nations whose membership rules are still defined by the *Indian Act*. And in addition, there are those who argue that insofar as Indigenous nations acquire power over their membership rules through federal legislation, Indigenous sovereignty is, in fact, being denied. How can one infer that Indigenous sovereignty is being restored, critics ask, when the Indigenous power in question is being delegated to them by the Canadian government? I would suggest, however, that the significance of Section 10 for Indigenous sovereignty be measured in a different way. Instead of classifying Section 10 as just another example of federal delegation, it would be far better (and more accurate) in my view to regard it as a federal declaration of intent to limit the exercise of its own powers. By means of Section 10, the Canadian government has declared that it will no longer interfere with an Indigenous nation's right to determine its own membership. On this important jurisdictional matter of membership, in other words, the Canadian government has agreed to establish space in between the exercise of Canadian sovereignty for Indigenous nations to exert their own power.[30] And this is as it should be since the Indigenous inherent right to self-determination includes the human right to identify their own citizens. In what follows I present a case study to illustrate how an Indigenous nation – namely, the Qalipu Mi'kmaq First Nation of Newfoundland – has handled the challenges associated with defining citizenship. This nation has reclaimed jurisdiction over its citizenship but in doing so has also had to address the considerable challenges brought on by colonialism. The question we confront is whether the outcome is consistent with what the Qalipu Mi'kmaq would take to be the full measure of their right to be self-defining.

For the Qalipu Mi'kmaq First Nation of Newfoundland, their right to be a self-defining people was drawn into particularly sharp focus because of the circumstances that first brought the nation into existence. When Newfoundland joined Confederation in 1949, Canada and Newfoundland simply decided that no person living in Newfoundland would be considered an "Indian" as defined by the *Indian Act*. Indigenous peoples were presumed to have been enfranchised and assimilated, particularly so because prior to joining Canada, Newfoundland had never enacted legislation granting Indigenous peoples' legal recognition. This lack of recognition, compounded by a social environment pervaded by racism, meant that many Indigenous peoples had hidden their identities over the generations and had seldom spoken about their Mi'kmaq ancestry (Grammond 2009, 84). Rates of intermarriage with non-Indigenous people were also high. The legacy of this history, then, was that until recently there were many persons in Newfoundland who have Indigenous ancestry but no corresponding close ties to a Mi'kmaq nation of origin.

This policy of denying the identity of Indigenous peoples in Newfoundland was not reversed until 1984, when the Canadian government formally recognized one Mi'kmaq community on the Conne River as the Miawpukek Band (Qalipu First Nation n.d.). A 2008 agreement between the Canadian government and the Federation of Newfoundland Indians (representing Newfoundland's Mi'kmaq communities) paved the way for the creation of the Qalipu Mi'kmaq First Nation in September 2011. At the mere stroke of a pen, the Canadian government turned all non-status Indians in Newfoundland into potential status Indians. It also turned all of Newfoundland's Mi'kmaq communities into the single Qalipu First Nation, granting the nation legal standing as an Indian band under the *Indian Act* (Palmater 2011, 129). The nation agreed that it would possess no reserve lands and thus would be landless, but that its jurisdictional reach would extend across the entire island, encompassing its 66 traditional Mi'kmaq communities. Politically, the nation is governed by an elected chief and council, the latter drawn from nine electoral wards that cover the province. In addition, two vice-chiefs represent western and central Newfoundland, areas where the Mi'kmaq population is more heavily concentrated (Qalipu First Nation n.d.).

A newly constituted Indian band needs members and so, in the lead up to the order in council that established the Qalipu Mi'kmaq First Nation as an *Indian Act* band, an enrolment process was established. Applications for membership were reviewed by an enrolment committee made up of an equal number of representatives from Canada and the Federation of Newfoundland Indians (Qalipu First Nation n.d.). As set out in the 2008 agreement, the following qualifications would have to be met by each applicant to be registered as a founding member: (1) proof of Canadian Indian ancestry from a Newfoundland Mi'kmaq community prior to Confederation (1949); (2) no prior registration on the Indian Register on the date of the Qalipu First Nation Recognition Order coming into effect (September 22, 2011); (3) clear self-identification as a member of the Mi'kmaq group of Indians of Newfoundland; and (4) acceptance by the Mi'kmaq group as a legitimate community member based on a current and substantial connection (INAC 2017). Based on these relatively open and generous criteria, the nation expected to receive approximately 10,000 applications for membership (Mintz, Tossutti, and Dunn 2017, 301).

In the first stage of the enrolment process approximately 27,000 applications were received, of which 23,877 were deemed eligible for registration as founding members. Subsequent rounds in advance of the November 30, 2012, application deadline would solicit an additional 70,000 applications, bringing the total number of applicants to over 100,000. This was a staggering and completely unexpected total, equivalent to about one-fifth of the population of Newfoundland. The enrolment committee was quite simply overwhelmed by these numbers. It was also concerned that many of those applying might be rediscovering and reclaiming their Mi'kmaq status purely for personal gain. In reaction, the committee urged the Canadian government and Federation of Newfoundland Indians to rethink its enrolment strategy.

A revised enrolment policy was spelled out in the 2013 Supplemental Agreement. Under its terms, all applicants would now have to meet more rigorous criteria. In addition to the aforementioned qualifications, all applicants would also have to demonstrate that their "current and substantial" connection to the "Mi'kmaq groups of Indians of Newfoundland" went beyond close family contact to include active participation in the cultural and social life of the Qalipu Mi'kmaq First Nation. This criterion was deemed particularly pertinent for those applicants who did not live in or around one of Newfoundland's Mi'kmaq communities. Furthermore, all applications, whether already approved or still awaiting a decision, would be reviewed against these more robust standards. In the case of rejections, however, all applicants would have access to a time-limited appeal process. With these new community participation requirements in hand, the desired effect was attained. As of fall 2017, of the 100,000 people who originally applied, 18,044 were accepted for founding membership in the Qalipu First Nation while more than 68,000 applications were rejected (INAC 2017).

What conclusions can be drawn from this complex and difficult exercise by the Qalipu Mi'kmaq to establish themselves as a nation? In the first place, the legacy of Canadian colonial policy ran tremendous interference with the nation's ability to establish straightforward qualifications for membership. The identity of the Mi'kmaq of Newfoundland was severely compromised by aggressive policies of enfranchisement and assimilation, leaving many today with little more than weak ancestral connections to the Mi'kmaq of the past. Many who would like to rekindle those community connections through membership in the Qalipu First Nation, however, are effectively disqualified. They simply cannot muster the objective evidence necessary to demonstrate that they are active participants in the cultural and social life of the nation. Sadly, therefore, these people are effectively "lost" to the Qalipu First Nation because of historical circumstances and governmental policies over which the Qalipu Mi'kmaq had no control.

A second, more positive conclusion, however, follows from the Qalipu First Nation's creative approach to the fact that it is an Indigenous nation without a land base. The nation has demonstrated that an Indigenous right to control its own membership need not necessarily go together with residency on an exclusive Indigenous land base in the form of a reserve. The members of the nation are scattered in communities across the entire island of Newfoundland, yet they have devised a political governing structure by means of a wardship system that has the capacity to reach out to and provide programs and services for all its people. The Qalipu Mi'kmaq have demonstrated, in other words, that Aboriginal rights need not originate in nor depend on a designated land base. The exercise of deciding membership is ultimately about the Qalipu Mi'kmaq's right to be self-defining. It is a right concerned with identity and culture that need not be artificially contained and expressed within the limited confines of a reserve to be fully enjoyed.

And third, it would seem that the capacity to be a self-defining Indigenous nation does require strong commitments on the part of individual members to the social and cultural well-being and development of the nation. It was this capacity that was thrown into doubt when the initial solicitation of applications for membership resulted in an overwhelming 104,000 responses. Membership only has meaning when there are individuals within an already existing Indigenous nation who desire to belong to it because they are committed to working out their social and cultural identities together. It was for this reason that the Qalipu Mi'kmaq tightened their membership criteria. "The main focus of membership was meant to be people who live in or around Mi'kmaq communities," said Fred Caron, a ministerial special representative for the Department of Indigenous and Northern Affairs (*CBC News* 2017). For those individuals not living in or near a Newfoundland-based Mi'kmaq community, it would be difficult (though not impossible) to demonstrate that they have the kind of current and substantial connection to the Qalipu Mi'kmaq that is required for real commitment to the nation.[31] This does not seem to be an unreasonable conclusion to draw.

Clearly, political sovereignty, the human right to be self-defining, and Indigenous control over the terms of Indigenous membership are all intimately connected. As part of their assertion to political sovereignty, Indigenous peoples increasingly insist on the right to control their own membership. To control their own community boundaries, Indigenous nations must be able to decide who does and who does not qualify as a member. Community boundary control, in turn, is important because it supports the political objective of each Indigenous nation to preserve and protect its unique culture and identity. If Indigenous nations are to exercise their human right to be self-defining, they must have a rigorous and engaged membership committed to the survival of their people. Membership codes are singularly designed to make such survival possible. Codes are designed to protect the scarce resources still left to Indigenous nations against undeserving claimants. Codes are also designed to protect vulnerable cultures and identities against the pressures of the more powerful, surrounding non-Indigenous population. In short, codes are designed to enhance prospects for Indigenous well-being and the revitalization of Indigenous nations. Though awkward, sometimes controversial, and often fraught with difficulties brought on by over a hundred years of colonial interference, the membership code of the Qalipu Mi'kmaq is but one example of an Indigenous nation struggling to create conditions conducive to the emergence of precisely such a committed membership.

CONCLUSION

As this chapter has demonstrated, the challenges associated with Indigenous citizenship and belonging are complex and many-sided. One conclusion, however, is abundantly clear: the Canadian state's imposition of identity categories and rules for community membership on Indigenous peoples over the past century has generated deep divisions within Indigenous nations. Furthermore, recent attempts to correct those divisions, as featured, for example, in Bill C-31, have only stimulated a new set of concerns and problems.

We have also seen that for Indigenous nations, citizenship, understood as the capacity to be self-defining, is one of the most fundamental of their human rights to self-determination. Consequently, Indigenous nations do engage in practices that have them resisting externally imposed governmental definitions of Indian status and rules for community membership. They have devised membership codes based on qualifications such as ancestry, self-definition, community acceptance, and demonstration of civic commitment to the nation, qualifications, moreover, that they take to be consistent with their self-identity as peoples. The Qalipu Mi'kmaq is but one Indigenous nation actively engaged in the exercise of boundary construction and maintenance. While the criteria they have devised are seen by some as controversial, they are nevertheless very much of their own making and, as such, adequate to the task of distinguishing themselves as their own distinct nation in relation to Canada.

At the same time, many disenfranchised Indigenous persons (especially women and their children) have fought hard for their right to be (re)instated into their communities. The legitimate concerns of these individuals should not be neglected. While the Indigenous right to be self-defining must include the right to exclude, such decisions must not be taken without due consideration of their potential harmful consequences. Those individuals without status or who live off reserve and who desire to be (re)instated, for example, simply ask that due consideration be given to the fact that they have been arbitrarily separated from their kin and cultures by state-imposed legal categories that have nothing to do with their Indigenous identity.

DISCUSSION QUESTIONS

1 Do the legal categories of Indian, Inuit, and Métis accurately capture the identity of each Indigenous group? Or do these labels fundamentally misrepresent that identity?
2 In what ways has the *Indian Act* both confused and substantially undermined Indigenous people's ability to define their own identity?
3 Why has the *Indian Act* been charged as sexist? What reasons might have been offered to justify this sexism historically? Have attempts in the recent past to remedy this sexism been adequate?
4 What attributes ought a person possess to claim an Indigenous identity? Who should have the power to decide?
5 Based on the Qalipu First Nation experience, what are the essential elements that ought to go into a membership code?

SUGGESTED READINGS

Brodsky, Gwen. 2014. "McIvor v. Canada: Legislated Patriarchy Meets Aboriginal Women's Equality Rights." In *Indivisible: Indigenous Human Rights*, edited by Joyce Green. Halifax: Fernwood Publishing.

Chartrand, Paul L.A.H. 2002. *Who Are Canada's Aboriginal Peoples? Recognition, Definition, and Jurisdiction*. Saskatoon: Purich Publishing.

Eberts, Mary. 2017. "Being an Indigenous Woman Is a 'High-Risk Lifestyle.'" In *Making Space for Indigenous Feminism*, 2nd ed., edited by Joyce Green. Halifax: Fernwood Publishing.

Frideres, James S. 2020. "Who Are You?" In *Indigenous Peoples in the Twenty-First Century*, 3rd ed. Toronto: Oxford University Press.

Grammond, Sébastien. 2009. *Identity Captured by Law: Membership in Canada's Indigenous Peoples and Linguistic Minorities*. Montreal: McGill-Queen's University Press.

King, Thomas. 2012. "Too Heavy to Lift." In *The Inconvenient Indian: A Curious Account of Native People in North America*. Toronto: Doubleday Canada.

Lawrence, Bonita. 2004. *"Real" Indians and Others: Mixed-Blood Urban Native Peoples and Indigenous Nationhood*. Vancouver: UBC Press.

———. 2012. *Fractured Homeland: Federal Recognition and Algonquin Identity in Ontario*. Vancouver: UBC Press.

Palmater, Pamela D. 2011. *Beyond Blood: Rethinking Indigenous Identity*. Saskatoon: Purich Publishing.

———. 2015. "The Silent War: Government Control of Indigenous Identity." In *Indigenous Nationhood: Empowering Grassroots Citizens*. Halifax: Fernwood Publishing.

Schouls, Tim. 2003. "Approaches to Aboriginal Identity." In *Shifting Boundaries: Aboriginal Identity, Pluralist Theory, and the Politics of Self-Government*. Vancouver: UBC Press.

Simpson, Audra. 2014. *Mohawk Interruptus (Political Life Across the Borders of Settler States)*. Durham, NC: Duke University Press.

Simpson, Leanne Betasamosake. 2017. "The Sovereignty of Indigenous Peoples' Bodies." In *As We Have Always Done: Indigenous Freedom Through Radical Resistance*. Minneapolis: University of Minnesota Press.

Vowel, Chelsea. 2016. *Indigenous Writes: A Guide to First Nations, Métis & Inuit Issues in Canada*. Winnipeg: Highwater Press.

Wilson-Raybould, Jody. 2019. "First Nations Jurisdiction over Citizenship." In *From Where I Stand: Rebuilding Indigenous Nations for a Stronger Canada*. Vancouver: Purich Books.

NOTES

1 For a personal account of the difficulties presented by this myriad of identity categories, see Pam Palmater's chapter, "The Silent War – Government Control of Indigenous Identity," in Palmater, 2015, 43–51.

2 I thank one of the anonymous reviewers of this book for this important insight. As put by the reviewer: "The international human right to self-determination includes the inherent right to define one's own membership. This right is universal and not unique to Indigenous peoples. If this right were properly respected, then the illegitimacy of the *Indian Act* becomes clear."

3 In particular, I urge readers to consult the material found in Chapter 3 under the heading "Indigenous Sovereignty Denied: Later Pre-Confederation and Post-Confederation Policy." Here I discuss the features and corresponding destructive effects of key "Indian" policy initiatives as put forward in the *Indian Act*, the Indian reserve system, the imposed system of band governance, and residential schools.

4 In the case of Indian bands through Section 10 of the *Indian Act* and in the case of the Alberta Métis Settlements through Part 3 of the *Métis Settlements Act*.

5 I shall have a good deal more to say about how persons receive and then pass on Indian status later in this chapter under the heading "The Indian Register and the Complications Created by Bill C-31."

6 Benefits include services provided by the federal government on Indian reserves such as health, education, welfare, and policing, as well as federal funding for band governance, cultural initiatives, and economic development. Status Indians living on reserve are also entitled to federal and provincial tax exemptions for income earned on reserve.

7 The term "First Nations" is now generally preferred over that of "band," as used in the *Indian Act*. The term "First Nations" carries with it a meaning associated with founding peoples who, by virtue of having been on the land first, are entitled to rights of possession of traditional territories and the political and jurisdictional powers necessary to govern those territories.

8 The difficult and challenging task of deciding who is entitled to claim a Métis identity, particularly since non-status Indians are also often the children of one Indigenous and one non-Indigenous parent, just like the Métis, is a topic of extensive academic investigation. For a small sample, see Belanger 2018, 150–74; Giokas and Chartrand 2002, 83–125; Chartrand 2001, 1–47; Lawrence 2004, 82–101; Grammond 2009, 80–2; and Saunders and Dubois 2019, 3–17.

9 Edward Hedican remarks that some Métis tend to see themselves as the only true Canadians since they originated as a "people" on Canadian soil, unlike Europeans or even First Nations people, whose ancestral roots are located in other parts of the world. See Hedican 2013, 15.

10 The 2016 *Daniels v. Canada* decision by the Supreme Court of Canada similarly established that the Métis were "Indians" for the purposes of Section 91(24) of the *Constitution Act, 1867*, and thus are also a federal responsibility.

11 Sebastian Grammond also points out that Indigenous communities must be able to regulate membership for the purpose of deciding who is and who is not entitled to enjoy specific resources set aside for the exclusive enjoyment of community members. Land rights factor in here, for example, as bands must be able to allocate parcels of land for the use of their members. Similar provisions will be made with respect to who is entitled to enjoy harvesting rights. As resources are limited, they should only be used for their intended beneficiaries. It is therefore imperative that Indigenous communities be in the position to decide what criteria are to be employed for deciding who is a member and who is not. See Grammond 2009, 39–43.

12 The Métis and Inuit were not subjected to *Indian Act* registration and band membership rules, as were First Nations.

13 Palmater uses the example of her own Mi'kmaq nation. Once a single nation, the Mi'kmaq are now made up of thirteen bands in Nova Scotia, nine in New Brunswick, one in Newfoundland, two in Prince Edward Island, two in Quebec, and one in Maine. See Palmater 2011, 144.

14 Bill C-31, *An Act to Amend the Indian Act*, RSC 1985, c. 27.

15 An alternative method from the one laid out in Section 10 of the *Indian Act* is for First Nations to assume control of their membership through self-government negotiations. Indigenous and Northern Affairs indicates that the process in each case is essentially the same. The key difference is that the process of acquiring control over membership in self-government negotiations "is part of a larger set of negotiations as opposed to a stand-alone action" (INAC 2015b). I shall have a good deal more to say about this arrangement in Chapter 8.

16 See Section 11, Membership Rules for Departmental Band List, *Indian Act.*

17 For a description of the steps required to pass a membership code, see Olthuis, Kleer, Townshend 2012, 244–8.

18 The significance of Sections 6(1) and 6(2) for both Indian status and band membership will be explained in the next section of this chapter.

19 The Assembly of First Nations writes, for example, "that First Nations' concepts of belonging and citizenship centred within First Nations' legal traditions are not based on racialized (race-based) concepts of identity based on rigid blood quantum requirements but rather culturally and politically-based concepts of nationhood" (AFN 2012a, 11).

20 See Audra Simpson's perceptive formulation of this problem with respect to the Mohawk in Simpson 2014, 9–10.

21 For a short history of colonial laws that eventually led to their post-Confederation consolidation in the form of the 1876 *Indian Act*, see Belanger 2018, 121–4; Giokas and Groves 2002, 51–5; and Palmater 2011, 37–43.

22 All status Indians are given a status card by the federal government. The status card contains information about the individual's identity, it names the band to which the individual belongs, and it provides a registration number.

23 Similarly, an Indian woman marrying an Indian man from another band was required to leave her reserve community and take up residency on the reserve of her husband. She effectively became a member of her husband's band. All rights associated with residency on the reserve of her birth were taken to be relinquished.

24 For a comprehensive overview of a number of key themes tackled by Indigenous feminists in their confrontation with the patriarchal practices of the Canadian state, both in the past and present, see the collection of articles edited by Joyce Green in *Making Space for Indigenous Feminism* (Green 2017a, 2017b).

25 The rules are even more complex. The criteria for obtaining legal status go as follows: individuals who obtain status through Section 6(2) and who marry non-Indians cannot pass status onto their children. If Indians under 6(2) marry Indians under 6(1), then their children will be registered under 6(1). If Indians under 6(1) marry one another, their children will be registered under 6(1). If Indians under 6(1) marry non-Indians, their children will be registered under 6(2).

26 In June 2007, the Supreme Court of British Columbia validated Sharon McIvor's charge that Section 6 of the *Indian Act* violated the equality provisions of the *Charter of Rights and Freedoms* and that therefore the offending section must be amended. The BC Court of Appeal subsequently upheld the Supreme Court of British Columbia's decision in this matter upon appeal in 2009.

27 The Assembly of First Nations points out that while the 2011 amendments to the 1985 *Indian Act* make for a more inclusive statute, gender inequalities still persist. For example, "persons born before September 4, 1951 who trace their Indian ancestry through an Indian grandmother remain disadvantaged under the current scheme compared to those born before September 4, 1951 who trace their ancestry through an Indian Grandfather." This matter is currently being addressed through legislation (Bill S-3) before the Parliament of Canada. See AFN 2012b, 10.

28 For a description of the effects of the revised Bill C-31 rules on membership for one Indigenous nation, the Mohawk of Kahnawake, see Alfred 1995, 166–8.

29 I will examine self-government agreements and the degree to which they facilitate the exercise of Indigenous sovereignty, including control over membership/citizenship, in Chapter 8.

30 It remains the case, of course, that the federal government is at liberty to amend the *Indian Act* to further modify membership rules if it so chooses by simply passing legislation. The potential threat to Indigenous sovereignty over control over its own membership is therefore ever present. Undoubtably, there would be a political cost to the federal government by way of vigorous Indigenous protest if it chose to muscle its way back into jurisdictional space that it had earlier agreed to vacate. But the fact that the federal government can make changes to the *Indian Act* if

it wants to demonstrates that the nature of the sovereignty Indigenous nations exercise over their own membership rules is both precarious and fragile.

31 Based on the revised number of 18,044 members, the Qalipu Mi'kmaq First Nation will be the second largest First Nation by population in Canada. It is also expected that approximately 95 per cent of the members live in Newfoundland and Labrador, with the remaining 5 per cent living elsewhere in Canada. See INAC 2017.

CHAPTER 3

Policy: From Political Sovereignty to Colonial Subjects

LEARNING OBJECTIVES

1. To describe a number of pre-contact Indigenous legal orders and political systems to demonstrate that Indigenous nations were sovereign prior to the arrival of settlers.
2. To define the Doctrine of Discovery and *terra nullius* and explain how each was used by European powers to justify their assertions to sovereignty over North America.
3. To identify the ways in which the Royal Proclamation of 1763 and the Treaty of Niagara of 1764 can be mobilized to support the Indigenous assertion to sovereignty.
4. To explain why the Canadian government advanced assimilative policies on the grounds that doing so would help Indigenous peoples adapt successfully to changing times.
5. To distinguish between those features of Indian policy that sought to protect Indigenous peoples and those features that sought their assimilation and to offer an evaluation of each.

This chapter traces the history of colonial policy with particular focus on the corrosive effects that the exercise of British and subsequently Canadian political power has had on Indigenous nations. For more than 200 years the Indigenous peoples of Canada have struggled hard to retain their Indigenous identities, to hold onto or reacquire their ancestral lands, and to protect their political rights to self-determination. The chapter divides the sweep of Indigenous–settler relations into three distinct historical stages: pre-contact, very early pre-Confederation, and pre- and post-Confederation. Consideration of the distinct features of the post-1969 policy era will constitute the focus of the next chapter. I begin this chapter by characterizing the pre-contact era as one in which Indigenous nations operated in a manner consistent with contemporary notions of political sovereignty. Next, I turn to the early pre-Confederation period to illustrate the ways in which competing and contradictory colonial impulses were at work that both recognized Indigenous nations as political sovereigns in some contexts while seeking to secure Indigenous submission to the British Crown in others. The focus of our attention will be on the Doctrine of Discovery, the idea of *terra nullius*, and the Royal Proclamation of 1763 and Treaty of Niagara of 1764.

Finally, later pre- and post-Confederation policy is examined, the key theme being that Indigenous policy in this era was marked by an integrated and multilevelled ambition to protect, civilize, and assimilate Indigenous peoples into the fabric of the Canadian state and society. Furthermore, as we shall see, this assertion of power and control was often justified in explicitly paternalistic language informed by highly racist assumptions about Euro-Canadian superiority. This is the era when Indigenous peoples were subjected to profound marginalization through policy instruments designed to control every facet of their lives, among them the *Indian Act*, the reserve system, the Indian band governance system, and residential schools. Conversely, during this stage of approximately 150 years, the language of nation-to-nation equality and respect for the Indigenous right to be self-defining was conspicuously absent. The outcome was that the Indigenous way of life was profoundly damaged, resulting in "the disproportionate representation of Aboriginal people among the powerless, the socially alienated, and the incarcerated" in Canadian society (Miller 2004, 217).

I begin with a brief summary of a speech made by Liberal Prime Minister Justin Trudeau to the General Assembly of the United Nations in September 2017. In it, Trudeau expresses remorse for Canada's destructive Indigenous policies of the past and his hope that future government policy, informed by respect for Indigenous inherent rights, may provide fertile ground for genuine reconciliation. In subsequent chapters we will test the good intentions of these promises against the hard realities of Liberal policy development, particularly so in the arenas of treaty rights, self-government, and economic development.

A REMARKABLE SPEECH TO THE UNITED NATIONS GENERAL ASSEMBLY

Justin Trudeau's second speech as prime minister of Canada to the UN General Assembly in September 2017 was used to shine a light on a dark and sinister feature of Canada's life as a country – the story of

Canada's failures in its historical and present relationships with Indigenous peoples and his hopes that reconciliation might yet be possible. What made Trudeau's speech unusual was his choice to focus on a domestic issue rather than on an issue of global concern, particularly so because the issue he chose to focus on demonstrated so clearly that Canada has failed to meet basic global standards of human dignity and respect where the rights of Indigenous peoples are concerned. Trudeau's take on Canada, therefore, was that it is still very much "a work in progress" (Trudeau 2017). In this respect, Trudeau emphasized that Canada's responsibilities are no different than those of any other country in the world. It too must respond to the global challenges of inequality and lack of respect for the rights of peoples within its domestic borders. In Trudeau's words, the relationship that Indigenous peoples have endured with Canada has left them humiliated, neglected, and abused (Trudeau 2017).

Trudeau had little trouble identifying the consequences of this history of humiliation, neglect, and abuse. He pointed to a lack of safe and clean drinking water on reserves, inadequate educational opportunities, lack of decent work, and lack of safe and affordable places to live as particular areas in need of government attention. Perhaps more striking, however, was Trudeau's diagnosis of the origins of these problems. He readily acknowledged that while Canada is built on the ancestral lands of Indigenous peoples, they played no part in nor consented to Canada's formation, and this despite the existence of treaties that "had been formed to provide a foundation for proper relations" (Trudeau 2017). In short, Trudeau admitted to the world that "the failure of successive Canadian governments to respect the rights of Indigenous peoples in Canada is our great shame" (Trudeau 2017).

As for a way forward, Trudeau was circumspect, observing that any solutions must be a product of priorities that Indigenous peoples establish for themselves. What is clear, said Trudeau, is that the colonial pattern of Canadian governments presuming to know what is best for Indigenous peoples must end. In his words, it is Indigenous peoples who "have the right to define for themselves what a decent life might be" (Trudeau 2017). Trudeau then focused on partnerships and the need for true, meaningful, and lasting reconciliation guided by standards like those found in the UNDRIP, a Declaration that, Trudeau added, Canada now fully endorses.[1]

On the Canadian government's side of the relationship, Trudeau told the Assembly that he had issued a directive to his ministers instructing them to review all federal laws, policies, and operational practices to bring them into conformity with Canada's obligations to Indigenous peoples, including its international obligations under the UNDRIP. An initiative that Trudeau specifically mentioned as a signal of such good intentions was his government's recent decision to dismantle what he called "the old colonial bureaucratic structures" and replace it with two separate departments – a Department of Crown–Indigenous Relations mandated primarily to support Indigenous peoples in their efforts to "assume autonomy over their own affairs," and a Department of Indigenous Services with the responsibility to provide ongoing services to Indigenous peoples much as in the past, though with renewed focus on solving the problems of unsafe drinking water; closing the gap in education; building and refurbishing homes; investing in economic opportunities; protecting and revitalizing Métis, Inuit, and First Nations languages; and combating gender-based violence (Trudeau 2017). Trudeau stated that by means of these and other measures, it was the intention of his government to provide better opportunities, including "a real and fair chance at success" in life for all Indigenous peoples (Trudeau 2017). Incidentally, this decision to split the Department of Indigenous and Northern Affairs Canada into two was in keeping with a recommendation made by the Royal Commission on Aboriginal Peoples some 20 years earlier (RCAP 1996c, 373).

On the Indigenous side, Trudeau declared without hesitation or qualification that old and outdated colonial structures must be replaced with "something that respects the inherent right of Indigenous peoples to self-govern, and to determine their own future." What those structures ought to be, of course, is for Indigenous peoples themselves to decide, though Trudeau did surmise that for many they would be based on their "historic nations and treaties" (Trudeau 2017). In keeping with this pledge to decolonization, Trudeau declared two intentions. In the short term, Trudeau told the Assembly that his government would support Indigenous peoples as, over time, programs and services are increasingly delivered by them "as part of their move toward true self-government" (Trudeau 2017). And in the longer term, Trudeau promised that his government would work closely with Indigenous peoples "to better respond to their priorities, to better understand how they see and define self-determination, and to support their work of nation rebuilding" (Trudeau 2017). This high-sounding political rhetoric carries far-reaching commitments for systematic structural changes in Indigenous–Canadian state relations. Yet Trudeau seemed undeterred. He concluded his speech with the confident declaration that while the path proposed is uncharted, Canada "will get to a place as a country where nation-to-nation, government-to-government, and Inuit-Crown relations can be transformed ... not merely by government mandate, but in true partnership with Indigenous peoples" (Trudeau 2017).

The question we will consider moving forward is whether, and to what degree, the Government of Canada is actually building such partnerships.

INDIGENOUS NATIONS: PRE-CONTACT SOVEREIGNS

Based on the anthropological evidence, experts generally conclude that Indigenous peoples have lived in North America for at least 20,000 years (Helin 2006, 65). Many scholars trace their ancestral origins to Asia, arguing that Indigenous peoples arrived in North America from Siberia by way of the Bering Strait. Others, particularly within Indigenous circles, contest the veracity of this theory on the grounds that it is overly simplistic and highly prejudicial. They say it assumes that Indigenous peoples lacked the sophistication to navigate the oceans and thus must have arrived in North America by means of a land route such as the Bering Strait. In response, they argue that the incredible diversity and variety of pre-contact populations across North America suggest that Indigenous peoples migrated by means of many different routes, including those available to them by both land and sea (Hilleary 2017, 2). Whatever their ancestral origins, on one matter we can be certain: given the considerable length of Indigenous occupation in North America, about 95 per cent of Indigenous history has been lived out in the absence of European encounters or settlement (Miller 1989, 4).

It therefore should come as no surprise that when Europeans arrived on North American shores, they encountered Indigenous peoples with sophisticated ways of life that had been developed over the course of thousands of years. As Pamela Palmater explains, pre-contact Indigenous societies were characterized by complex relationships "with each other and the lands, waters, plants, and animals within their territories" (Palmater 2015, 1; see also RCAP 1996b, 37). Naturally, these complex relationships came in many forms. On the political side of the ledger, Palmater points out that Indigenous peoples possessed sophisticated governing structures, justice systems, economic practices, and military capabilities, all informed by "trusted laws, practices, and protocols passed down from our ancestors" (Palmater 2015, 1; see also Ladner 2006, 1, 2; Helin 2006, 66, 69). She further adds that both men and women had important social and political roles that varied from nation to nation: "While some nations were led by men, many of those leaders were appointed, counselled, and removed by women. Women were always valued as the life-givers of the Nations, but could also be hunters, warriors, political strategists, and/or negotiators as needed" (Palmater 2015, 1). Taken together, then, there can be no doubt that Indigenous peoples did operate as sovereign entities (though in different forms than European nations) in the sense that they exercised powers of self-determination over their peoples and territories. They were organized into strong political nations and confederacies and had developed highly sophisticated mechanisms for inter-nation diplomacy and trade (Miller 2004, 55). And while profoundly disrupted by the forces of colonialism, it is the position of many Indigenous leaders that these political and legal structures continue to exist into the present and as such can still serve as the foundation upon which to rebuild Indigenous nations today (Ladner 2006, 1). What follows briefly describes a number of these very diverse pre-contact Indigenous legal orders and political systems.[2]

To the east were the **Mi'kmaq** (the People of the Dawn) occupying Atlantic Canada in the provinces now known as Newfoundland and Labrador, Prince Edward Island, Nova Scotia (including Cape Breton), northern sections of New Brunswick, and the Gaspé Peninsula of southern Quebec. The Mi'kmaq were a people dependent on fishing, hunting, gathering, and trade, which supported the livelihood of communities that could range in size from 50 up to several hundred people (Miller 2004, 56). These communities were organized into seven districts (or *sakamowati*), each with its own name and governing council composed of a district captain, chief, heads of families, and elders. These councils were mandated to ensure that (among other things) each family grouping had protected access to specific agricultural and hunting grounds as well as fishing sites (Ladner 2006, 3; Borrows 2010, 61). In addition, the Mi'kmaq had a Grand Council (or *Sante Mawiomi*) made up of seven district chiefs to govern all Mi'kmaq people (RCAP 1996b, 48–9). The Grand Council's many responsibilities included playing a mediating role when the interests of the various districts clashed as well as taking up issues of general concern to the Mi'kmaq people across the entire region, including matters relating to international trade, war, and treaty-making (Miller 2004, 56; Gespe'gewa'gi Mi'gmawei Mawiomi 2016, 93). In sum, it is clear that in the pre-contact era the Mi'kmaq operated under a sophisticated multilevel system of government that exercised significant and far-reaching political and legal responsibilities over its people and territories. Indeed, after describing its many interrelated features, J.R. Miller concludes that the Mi'kmaq had created "a system of government that looked strikingly like federalism" (Miller 2004, 54).

The **Haudenosaunee** (people of the longhouse) or Iroquois, located in today's state of New York as well as southern Ontario and Quebec, were largely a sedentary people who relied on agricultural products in regions where crop resources were plentiful and easily available (RCAP 1996b, 52). In their early encounters, European settlers came to know the Haudenosaunee as the Iroquois Confederacy or Five Nations, a military power of such formidable strength that at times it threatened the very existence of the French and British colonial presence in Haudenosaunee traditional territories (Helin 2006, 70). The Five Nations that made up this remarkable Confederacy from east to west were the Mohawk, Oneida, Onondaga, Cayuga, and Seneca.[3] While the Haudenosaunee roamed widely to hunt, gather, trade, and engage in warfare, their primary reliance on agriculture meant that they tended to live in relatively large semi-permanent villages over the course of many years. As J.R. Miller points out, this fact had important implications for the style and structure of their governmental institutions (Miller 2004, 57).

As the Haudenosaunee lived together in relatively large numbers, they needed to develop governing mechanisms that could promote peaceful community relations and conditions for the collective well-being of all. To that end, each person belonged to a clan linked to an animal or bird totem as well as a nation. Miller describes a social system in which individuals from the different clans were located in each of the Haudenosaunee villages, thus serving as incentive between village groupings to avoid disagreement or war with one other (Miller 1989, 9; RCAP 1996b, 59). In addition, clan affiliation was traced through the female line and was also matrilocal, meaning that men joined the clans of the women they married (RCAP 1996b, 52). Supplementing these integrating social arrangements was the presence of a sophisticated political and legal system that facilitated the ability of these large Haudenosaunee nations to work together. Each nation occupied its own territory governed by its own council of chiefs (or *sachems*). Furthermore, in keeping with their matriarchal traditions, it was up to the clan mothers to decide who would be selected to serve as council chiefs (Miller 2004, 57). Supplementing both clans and nations was the Confederacy itself. This Confederacy met yearly in the form of a Grand Council made up of 50 chiefs (*sachems*) representing each of the five nations, the distribution of the positions determined in rough proportion to the size of each nation. The primary responsibility of the Grand Council was for external affairs, which could include such matters as trade, alliances, and warfare. A central characteristic of the Grand Council's mode of operation was that all of its decisions had to be arrived at by consensus (Miller 1989, 9; RCAP 1996b, 57).

The entirety of these complex social and political arrangements was documented within and sustained by a constitutional order referred to as the Haudenosaunee Great Law of Peace. John Borrows observes that this Great Law of Peace commands such fame that it now constitutes "one of North America's most recognizable Indigenous constitutions" (Borrows 2010, 73). Oral in its composition (by means of songs, stories, ceremony, orations, and wampum), the Great Law comprises principles, political jurisdictions, and a complex legal code intended to bind the Haudenosaunee into a Confederacy committed to peace, righteousness, health, and power both within and among its member nations (RCAP 1996b, 54–5).[4]

The **Algonquins** of northern Ontario and Quebec have lived on the lands of the extensive watershed draining into the Ottawa River for centuries. Bonita Lawrence demonstrates that despite their generally small size, they too were nations because each constituted "distinct socio-political units that occupied particular territories and maintained formal diplomatic relations with other nations" (Lawrence 2012, 27). As their livelihood depended largely on hunting, the Algonquin developed a sophisticated three-tiered approach to governing consistent with their objective to preserve the integrity of their nations by employing sound ecological practices. Lawrence describes an integrated governing system made up of family, band, and nation, each of which had distinct responsibilities depending on the time of year. During the winter months, extended family groupings retreated to their respective hunting territories over which they exercised control, practising conservation and other resource management techniques to preserve the plant and animal species upon which their survival depended. In the early spring and then again in the fall, the larger band would assemble, usually within "a specific region in the watershed," this time for the purpose of the goose hunt, fishing, and where applicable, the harvesting of rice (Lawrence 2012, 26). Politically, the task at hand during these gatherings was to ensure that resources were appropriately coordinated and allocated according to each family's need. Finally, once a year at mid-summer, bands met as a confederated nation "to address internal diplomatic relations among the bands as well as external diplomatic relations and treaty making with other nations" (Lawrence 2012, 26). Other events also occurred, including ceremonies to mark sacred events, marriages, and sharing of stories and songs, all undertaken as part of the Algonquin commitment to preserve and develop the identity of the nation. In short, the Algonquins operated in the pre-contact era as sovereign nations as they too had their own distinct political systems in keeping with their territorial realities and specific human needs.

One final example will suffice, this time from British Columbia's **northwest coast**. This was a region rich in food and natural resources and as such was able to support concentrations of population in pre-contact times greater than anywhere else in Canada (RCAP 1996b, 72). Calvin Helin characterizes this population as diverse, marked by distinct linguistic and cultural identities as well as names and territories that clearly marked one nation off from another (Helin 2006, 69). Yet despite differences, coastal nations also shared rich and elaborate elements of artistic expression and social organization. Scholars attribute these shared features, in part, to the remarkable natural wealth in the area that could sustain a substantial population base. As RCAP observes, coastal nations were typically highly structured societies, ordering their internal relations and access to territories and resources through complex political systems based on rank, status, and hierarchy (RCAP 1996b, 74; see also Wilson-Raybould 2019, 119). The governing system through which social order, harvesting rights, and territorial boundaries were maintained was known as the **Potlatch**.

Bev Sellars characterizes the Potlatch as "the basis of Aboriginal government" (Sellars 2016, 67). She explains that through it, ceremonies were conducted "that officiated and confirmed the social and political organization of each nation" (Sellars 2016, 69). While Potlatches are well known as mechanisms that were used to redistribute community wealth, they played other important social and political roles as well. For example, they served to transmit oral history and cultural teachings as well as to "validate rites of passage and movements in the social hierarchy such as a member of a noble family reaching adulthood and taking on a new name, or someone achieving a new title within the social grouping" (Miller 2004, 64). In addition, in some coastal nations Potlatches contributed to the land tenure system by identifying which chiefs had responsibility for which geographical areas within the territorial boundaries of the nation. Potlatches are also identified by Jody Wilson-Raybould as the traditional institution "where laws are made, disputes settled, people are married, and wealth is redistributed" (Wilson-Raybould 2019, 5). The Potlatch, therefore, was much more than a ceremony; it was an internal mechanism of social regulation and peaceful "political and economic exchange" (Sellars 2016, 68). It was, in short, the "system of governance among Northwest Coast peoples that existed prior to the coming of Europeans in the 1770s" (Miller 2004, 64). Indeed, so central was the Potlatch to their system of government that, as RCAP observes, "west coast peoples were willing to risk and endure imprisonment rather than give up potlatching when the practice was outlawed by an 1884 amendment to the *Indian Act*" (RCAP 1996b, 75).

What these four examples illustrate is that, prior to European contact, Indigenous nations were made up of highly sophisticated societies who lived in close relationship to their environment and who conducted their internal and external affairs according to codes of conduct that had served them well for centuries. The variety in their values and institutions also meant that in many cases, Indigenous nations were as different from one another as they were from their European counterparts. There was (and is) simply no such thing as a uniform Indigenous identity. Given their sophistication and presence of reliable cultural, economic, and political systems, I think it would also be fair to say that Indigenous nations did exercise sovereignty over their traditional lands, resources, and peoples, though naturally in ways quite different than that of the Europeans of that time. Consequently, when Europeans first encountered Indigenous nations, their tendency was to treat Indigenous peoples with both caution and respect.

It should come as no surprise, therefore, that early relationships between Indigenous peoples and European settlers were generally built upon strong partnerships and robust alliances of interdependence. As RCAP reminds us, a prevailing spirit of cooperation often informed relations involving trade, commercial partnerships, and military alliances with the French and later the British (RCAP 1996b, 38; Miller 2004, 66). Indeed, for some considerable time, Indigenous peoples possessed enough economic and military power that European settlers could do nothing other than treat Indigenous nations as their equals. Simply put, Europeans did not have the knowledge or resources to survive in North America's harsh climate. Nor could they succeed in their economic ambitions of harvesting fish, whales, or fur without significant Indigenous help (RCAP 1996b, 38; Miller 2004, 65; Frideres 2020, 9–10). Naturally, there were instances of conflict as gradual European population growth led to unsolicited incursions into Indigenous territories. Indigenous peoples were also deeply alarmed and troubled by encounters that led to the devastating ravages within their nations of European diseases to which they had no immunity. But the general tone of this early contact period was one of mutual curiosity and cautious cooperation (RCAP 1996b, 38). As put by RCAP, "for the most part, Aboriginal and non-Aboriginal people saw each other as separate, distinct, and independent. Each was in charge of its own affairs" (RCAP 1996a, 8; see also Miller 2004, 65).

INDIGENOUS SOVEREIGNTY CONSTRAINED: THE EARLY PRE-CONFEDERATION ERA

But at the same time, an analysis of the history of Indigenous policy in Canada has also got to take into account the longstanding European commitment to colonial expansion. **Colonialism** is the practice whereby a state appropriates a domain outside its borders for its own use. This act of appropriation is usually accompanied by settlement; the colony being made up of "settlers" from the colonizing country who remain under the control of the colonizing government. Running through this commitment to colonialism were European attitudes that were both complex and contradictory. In some cases, Indigenous peoples were seen to be military allies and trading partners while in others they were seen to be obstacles to colonial expansion and settlement that had to be removed or exterminated. Whether seen to be allies, partners, or impediments to colonial ambitions, however, the general European disposition toward Indigenous peoples was that their ways of life were inferior to their own (Grant 2018, 137). Consequently, when the French and then English colonial powers laid claim to Indigenous territories in this land now called Canada, they did so on the basis of a belief that a simple assertion to sovereignty was sufficient to displace Indigenous political authority and power. Increased European commercial activity, settlement, and missionary activity would soon follow (Helin 2006, 91).

When lined up against this European commitment to colonial expansion, therefore, Indigenous nations were treated as sovereigns by the French and British only for so long as it was a political and military necessity. In the early days of settlement, it was certainly the case that French and later British assertions of sovereignty were not accompanied by corresponding efforts to subject and rule over Indigenous peoples. European colonization took on a decidedly different character, however, when the French and especially the British began an aggressive campaign of settling among and establishing political control over Indigenous peoples. Their ambition was quite simply to gain control over resources, particularly Indigenous-occupied land. Especially after the War of 1812 with the United States, the British no longer needed Indigenous peoples as military allies and so "their value rapidly diminished" (Fleras and Elliott 1992, 40). The predominant assumption that the British settlers now brought to their relationship with Indigenous peoples was that they were obstacles hindering the progressive development of their new colonial society. Thus, despite Indigenous resistance, the settler society began to abrogate power for itself and to unilaterally set the terms for their relationships with Indigenous nations. Indigenous peoples could be justifiably subdued and subordinated according to the predominant beliefs of the time because they stood in the way of progress and settlement (Miller 2004, 67). And so, the colonial relationship became a dominant one in which Indigenous peoples "were unilaterally, and without their consent, subjected to the superior power and influence of the settler society" (Schouls 2003, 40).

Taken together, the early pre-Confederation policy era was one marked by a bifurcated view of Indigenous peoples. On the one hand, during the earliest days of contact, Europeans had to contend with the reality that Indigenous nations were sovereign and therefore, for the sake of their own military advantage and economic gain, must be treated accordingly. But on the other, there was a belief that Indigenous sovereignty could be legitimately constrained and superseded by French and British assertions to sovereignty on the grounds that their ways of life were both misguided and vastly inferior when held up comparatively against European civilizational standards (Townshend 2015, 7; Grant 2018, 137). This early pre-Confederation policy ambivalence is well illustrated by four policy instruments that existed side by side and in extraordinary tension with one another at that time – the Doctrine of Discovery, the concept of *terra nullius*, the Royal Proclamation of 1763, and the Treaty of Niagara of 1764. What follows examines the features of each. I do so because the spirit that animates all four had enormous implications for the substance of the Indigenous policy that was to follow, especially in the later pre- and then post-Confederation era, either by virtue of what that policy contained or by virtue of what it left out.

THE DOCTRINE OF DISCOVERY AND *TERRA NULLIUS*

The first step in establishing control after the invasion of a territory is for the colonial power to declare sovereignty over what it takes to be its newly discovered lands. But how could the French or English decree that they were sovereign and then take over lands that were already occupied, used, and controlled by Indigenous nations? International law, both then and now, is very clear on this point. As explained by Roger Townshend, the only circumstances under which a state may declare sovereignty over another territory is if its claim is "based on conquest, discovery and settlement, or treaty" (Townshend 2015, 36). Yet as scholars regularly point out, no state of war was declared against Indigenous nations and so, while hostilities between European powers and Indigenous nations were frequent, nothing like conquest in the international law sense actually occurred (see Vowel 2016, 238; Hamilton and Sinclair 1991, 134). Treaties with Indigenous nations were also frequently used but not, from the perspective of Indigenous nations, to relieve them of their sovereignty. What remains, therefore, is the Doctrine of Discovery and the notion of *terra nullius*. European powers engaged in a creative and liberal adaptation of these prevailing international norms at law to justify their claims to sovereignty over all the territories of North America as well as over its Indigenous occupants.

The basic premise of the **Doctrine of Discovery** (as established by two fifteenth-century papal bulls) was that the first Christian state to "discover" an uninhabited territory (or *terra nullius*) with no other prior claims upon it had the right to claim territorial sovereignty over it. Given its papal origins, this prerogative was reserved for Christian states alone (Courchene 2018, 43). The essential point for our purposes is that the "discovering" Christian state had first right of occupation and possession if and only if there were no previous inhabitants upon the land. If the land was inhabited, as North America clearly was, then the "discovering" state had rights that were limited to having first opportunity to trade, forge alliances, engage in missionary activity, and negotiate matters of shared occupancy and sovereignty with the "discovered" peoples (Mackey 2016, 47). So the Doctrine of Discovery did not give European powers immediate sovereignty over their newly discovered territories simply because they had planted a flag or cross in its soil. Instead, the Doctrine granted no more than a right, "as against other European nations, to negotiate with the people occupying the land, people who were recognized as having certain rights" (Mackey 2016, 47).[5] But this interpretation of the Doctrine did not suit the colonial ambitions of European powers. And so, what they did was take the Doctrine's concept of "uninhabited" (understood as "barren," "empty," or "devoid of occupants") and added a toxic element. They simply decided, without any justification, that the Doctrine's reference to "uninhabited" could be expanded to include any area devoid of "civilized society" as defined by European standards (Hamilton and Sinclair 1991, 131; RCAP 1996b, 43).

The Eurocentric adaptation, therefore, that came to inform the meaning of ***terra nullius*** gravitated from empty lands understood as "uninhabited lands" to empty lands understood as "uncultivated lands" or lands not put to civilized use according to Christian standards (RCAP 1996b, 43–4). With this shift of meaning in hand, European powers believed they now had legal justification to assert sovereignty over North America. Because Europeans identified Indigenous peoples to be nomadic, they believed that Indigenous peoples did not have property rights. They were simply seen to be in no position to claim sovereignty over territories they "roamed" as opposed to cultivated. The fact, therefore, that the lands were not being put to "civilized" use by a "civilized" people justified their appropriation by European settlers. They believed they would put the land to far better (usually agrarian) use in keeping with the standards of a "civilized" and Christian society.

It is easy to see why this concept of *terra nullius* is construed as racist by today's standards. At the time, European powers simply refused to accept the proposition that while Indigenous peoples were different, they were nevertheless entitled to full respect as political sovereigns. Instead, Europeans chose to construe Indigenous differences in religion, culture, political and social organization, and land use practices as inferior to their own. And once Indigenous peoples were relegated to the status of inferiority, acts of dispossession were easily justified. It was simply taken as a given, for example, that European powers should divest Indigenous peoples of their lands and open those lands up for settlement as settlers would put that land to far more productive use (Hedican 2013, 58; RCAP 1996b, 44). As the settlers began to dominate the future Canada, these views increasingly shaped moral and legal thought as well as the general thrust of Indigenous policy. Few contested the idea that Canada was sovereign with rights to claim jurisdictional authority over Indigenous peoples and their territories. Indeed, for the sake of their own betterment, it was simply taken as given that Indigenous peoples had passed under the civilizing authority of the Canadian state, which now had a trust responsibility to govern Indigenous peoples "as a matter of domestic policy" (Barker 2005, 13–14).

Today, moral-thinking Canadians now place high value on Indigenous cultures and societies as a straightforward matter of human dignity and rights. But it is worth remembering that the Canadian assertion to sovereignty over Indigenous nations and their territories was first advanced and then justified on the explicitly racist and ethnocentric assumption that Indigenous peoples were, as Felix Hoehn puts it, "inherently inferior to European settler states and were not worthy of the status and rights Europeans otherwise afforded to sovereign states" (Hoehn 2012, 85). What needs to be underscored, therefore, is that the foundations of Canada are built on doctrines and practices that are immoral, racist, and therefore unjust. It is for this reason that recent bodies such as the 1996 Royal Commission on Aboriginal Peoples and the 2015 Truth and Reconciliation Commission of Canada call for the repudiation and repeal of concepts like the Doctrine of Discovery and *terra nullius*. Both commissions argued that such concepts have no legitimate place in a country that wishes to build a renewed relationship of reconciliation between Indigenous and non-Indigenous peoples.[6] Simply put, they violate international human rights principles and treaties, documents that Canada has both ratified and signed.

THE ROYAL PROCLAMATION OF 1763 AND THE TREATY OF NIAGARA OF 1764

Not all European policy initiatives were crafted to justify the removal of Indigenous peoples from their lands or to deny them political autonomy. Running parallel to and in many cases acting as a constraint upon policies rooted in the Doctrine of Discovery and *terra nullius* were other policies more favourable to Indigenous aspirations. What one detects in this early pre-Confederation era, in other words, is the presence of a policy ambivalence of competing colonial impulses borne out of conditions of both political expediency and necessity. Policies that sought Indigenous subjection were also often compelled to operate alongside those that conceded to Indigenous peoples significant rights of political autonomy and territorial control. These more accommodative policy impulses took their queue from such measures as the **Royal Proclamation of 1763** and precedent-setting agreements like that secured in the **Treaty of Niagara of 1764**.

The early treaties between the European colonizers and Indigenous nations reflected a basic respect for Indigenous sovereignty, itself a product of the relatively strong position Indigenous peoples occupied in their relationships with Europeans at that time. The European powers understood that they needed good relations with Indigenous peoples if they were to have access to the resources of North America, like fish, fur, and timber. Good relations were also a prerequisite for the safety and developmental prospects of European settler colonies. In addition, as Julie Jai explains, the English and French needed Indigenous nations as military allies in their conflicts with one another. In fact, she says, because of their regularly dominant numbers and military strength, Indigenous nations sometimes found themselves in a position to dictate the terms of peace (Jai 2017, 119). As a result, European powers were compelled to pursue policies that were premised on concessions to Indigenous sovereignty. Europeans followed Indigenous diplomatic protocols in both commercial and military transactions through peace and friendship treaties, for example, "because they needed their help much more than Indigenous people needed them" (Jai 2017, 119). These early relations, therefore, were marked by a basic European respect for Indigenous rights to lands, by a commitment to relatively fair terms of trade in commercial transactions, and by "limited interference in the internal affairs of Aboriginal nations" (Hoehn 2012, 11).

The Royal Proclamation of 1763 reflected elements of this pragmatic concession to Indigenous sovereignty through its recognition and protection of some Indigenous rights. Following the defeat of New France by the British in the Seven Years War, the French territories in Canada were transferred to the British as specified in the Treaty of Paris of 1763. Issued by King George III, the Royal Proclamation of 1763 was designed to outline political and administrative arrangements devised to absorb Quebec into the British Empire, to address deteriorating relations between the British and Indigenous nations that had led to Pontiac's Rebellion in 1763, and to set out a protocol whereby the American colonies' westward expansionist desires might be both contained and regulated so as not to antagonize or further alienate Indigenous nations. In essence, Indigenous nations were becoming increasingly hostile toward the settlers of the American colonies who wanted to dispossess Indigenous peoples of their lands as they migrated ever westward (Borrows and Rotman 2003, 25).

According to the text of the Royal Proclamation, the solution to fostering better relations with Indigenous nations was to pursue an expansionist policy in North America mediated by a principle of coexistence among nations. The Royal Proclamation served notice that from here on, those Indian nations that resided within the borders of the British colonies were not to be "molested" or "disturbed" in the possession and use of their traditional territories.[7] All lands not subject to settlement by colonists would be reserved to Indigenous peoples as their hunting grounds. If, however, Indigenous nations chose to surrender any or all of their lands, the Proclamation stipulated that this could occur only by means of treaty at a public meeting presided over by duly constituted and recognized representatives of the Indigenous nations and the Crown. In keeping with their standing as nations, a protocol was established whereby Indigenous lands could only be alienated to agents of the Crown and not private individuals. The Crown, in turn, pledged to protect Indigenous nations against unscrupulous land transactions and to compensate them by means of a fair return. Once in the Crown's possession, the Crown could then choose to sell the land to settlers (Belanger 2018, 119; Courchene 2018, 47; Sellars 2016, 37–8).

In short, the Royal Proclamation's operating premise was that Indigenous-occupied land was land collectively held by Indigenous nations. They were understood to have a proprietary interest in the land, and on those grounds it could not be arbitrarily taken. The British promised to respect the Indigenous right to occupy their territories and reserved for their exclusive use all lands not purchased from them by the Crown (Hoehn 2012, 12). Furthermore, because it was understood that Indigenous lands could only be purchased by the Crown, the Proclamation also carried with it an implicit understanding that Indigenous nations were to be treated as free-standing political entities in their relations with the Crown. Taken together, then, it is not surprising that the principles and protocols established by the Royal Proclamation in 1763 would remain important to Indigenous peoples to this day. For Indigenous peoples, the Royal Proclamation represents an early constitutional guarantee on the part of the British to protect practices that, by 1763, were already well established. In their dealing with Indigenous nations, the British (and the successor Canadian state) pledged to conduct itself in a way that respected Indigenous rights to their traditional territories and their standing as autonomous political actors. As Thomas Courchene notes, "given this role as the guarantor of Indian land title, and the fact that this is embraced in section 25 of the Constitution Act, 1982, the Royal Proclamation is often viewed as the 'Indian Bill of Rights' and/or the 'Indian Magna Carta'" (Courchene 2018, 49).

At the same time, however, the language of the Royal Proclamation was also crafted to favour and reinforce Britain's colonial ambitions and as such should not be seen as offering a cohesive narrative of nation-to-nation reciprocity. There can be no doubt that the British were of the view that Indigenous peoples had been drawn into the protective orbit of the British Empire and this was as it should be. So while the Royal Proclamation clearly acknowledged a proprietary Indigenous interest in the land through its regular references to "Acquisitions," "Dominions," "Settlement," and "Protection," for example, its language also indicates that the British simply took it as given that the Indigenous right to land was to be exercised within the broader framework of British sovereignty (Borrows and Rotman 2003, 26). In short, the British fully expected that European settlement would continue to expand on territories traditionally occupied by Indigenous peoples. As explained by Yale Belanger, while "it might appear that the Royal Proclamation was solely concerned with protecting Indigenous land rights … the reasons for enacting it had more to do with establishing new, legal means to remove Indigenous peoples from lands coveted by settlers" (Belanger 2018, 119).

Upon evaluation, therefore, it is clear that the Royal Proclamation advanced a number of contradictory themes. In the first place, it recognized Indigenous nations as sovereigns with rights to their lands and with rights to live as they pleased. But in the second place, the Proclamation asserted that Indigenous peoples were to enjoy their rights as the Crown's "loving Subjects," living under the Crown's "Protection" on Indigenous lands that were nevertheless understood to be part of the Crown's "Dominions and Territories" (Borrows and Rotman 2003, 26). While these words might be taken to convey a comforting reassurance that the Crown will act as a fiduciary, protecting the Indigenous right to sovereignty and territory in the face of expanding European settlement, they can also be read as conveying more sinister intent. Consequently, in the third place, the Proclamation can also be regarded as a bald declaration of British superiority and power. By means of its provisions, it was assumed that Indigenous peoples could continue to enjoy their rights under British rule, but only if they accommodated those rights to the supreme authority of the British. The fact, for example, that the British subsequently believed that they were perfectly entitled to extinguish Indigenous title in exchange for small and often isolated Indian reserves, small annual payments, and limited hunting, fishing, and trapping rights points to a colonial dynamic in which Indigenous sovereignty was actually being constrained if not denied (Belanger 2018, 119). One can reasonably conclude, therefore, that on balance "the British were principally interested in extinguishing Aboriginal title through treaties in order to use the land for their own occupancy and profit" (Schouls 2003, 40; see also RCAP 1996b, 111–19).

The language of the Royal Proclamation of 1763 was drafted in keeping with preferences of the British, but the same cannot be said for the Treaty of Niagara of 1764. In fact, as Indigenous legal scholar John Borrows explains it, the kind of protection that Indigenous nations expected would flow from the Royal Proclamation was nowhere better represented than in the treaty negotiated between the British and Indigenous leaders at Niagara in 1764 (Borrows 1997, 161). This gathering of about 2,000 chiefs representing 22 nations, ranging from Nova Scotia to Hudson Bay and Mississippi, has been characterized as a "peace council" with the British in which Sir William Johnson served as representative for the British Crown (Hoehn 2012, 12; Courchene 2018, 50). Borrows writes that the council was convened for the specific purpose of renewing and extending the nation-to-nation relationship between settler and Indigenous peoples. Its specific intent was to reaffirm the Covenant Chain of Friendship, a multi-nation alliance that Borrows characterizes as one "in which no member gave up their sovereignty" (Borrows 1997, 161).

In addition to distributing copies of the Royal Proclamation at this "peace council," speeches were made, gifts were exchanged, and "the terms of the treaty itself were recorded through a Covenant Chain and exchange of wampum belts," all in keeping with Indigenous nations' approaches to diplomacy (Hoehn 2012, 13; Courchene 2018, 50). The **Two-Row Wampum** is described by Borrows as a belt of white wampum with two rows of purple beads symbolizing two peoples in two vessels travelling downstream, side by side, in a river. The belt represented the Indigenous understanding of what had been agreed to, namely, that all Indigenous signatories to the treaty were bound up together with the British in a relationship "founded on peace, friendship, and respect, where each nation will not interfere with the internal affairs of the other" (Borrows 1997, 164).

If the Royal Proclamation is read together with the kind of agreements reached at the Treaty of Niagara, a picture emerges of a relationship in which Indigenous participants conceded no acceptance to the proposition that British sovereignty was superior to their own. On its surface, we have seen that the language of the Proclamation does convey ideas about Crown "sovereignty" and "Dominion" over Indigenous territories. But insofar as the Royal Proclamation guided discussions at the 1764 Niagara Peace Council, Borrows believes that it did so in a way that affirmed Indigenous nations as sovereigns with the right to self-determination. As represented by the Two-Row Wampum, we encounter a treaty in which Indigenous nations and the British recognized each other as sovereigns and pledged themselves to one another in an alliance of peaceful coexistence, free and open trade, and a sharing of resources such as land, but only under terms to which both had offered their consent (Jai 2017, 121). As explained by Borrows, the Treaty of Niagara established that settler governments would not have authority over Indigenous nations and that in their political dealings with British settlers, all negotiations "would be mediated by the Imperial Crown in Britain" (Borrows 2017a, 22).[8]

In summary, the early pre-Confederation colonial policy period can be characterized by the contradictory themes of Indigenous sovereignty recognized when necessary but also constrained and limited where possible. Despite colonial ambitions to occupy and subject the vast territories of North America to its dominion, the presence of powerful Indigenous nations upon the land required that the British exercise some political constraint. In their early dealings with Indigenous nations, therefore, the British had no choice but to take up the practice of acknowledging the reality of Indigenous land tenure and respecting the ongoing interest that Indigenous peoples had in preserving and advancing their distinct ways of life (Schouls 2003, 40). Putting the insidious motivations of colonialism aside, it is largely for this reason that many Indigenous leaders now point to this early policy period of rough reciprocity and mutual cooperation as the normative prototype for Indigenous relations with the Canadian state today. The Royal Proclamation of 1763 and the Treaty of Niagara of 1764 represent powerful political approaches and legal precedents about how to deal with Indigenous nations as sovereigns, in control of their lands and resources, and entitled to live as they saw fit. It is this baseline that many Indigenous leaders now insist on as their target for the future. This early colonial history, however, and the land and power-sharing arrangements between Indigenous nations and the British that characterized it, was soon eclipsed by new assimilationist policy directions adopted by the Canadian government in the mid- to late nineteenth century (Schouls 2003, 41).

INDIGENOUS SOVEREIGNTY DENIED: LATER PRE-CONFEDERATION AND POST-CONFEDERATION POLICY

By the turn of the nineteenth century, the relationship of mutual cooperation and reciprocal interdependence between the British Crown and Indigenous nations began to fall apart. The political system galvanized by early treaties in which Indigenous and British partners tended to conduct themselves as each other's equals was slowly replaced by a system of internal colonialism in which Indigenous sovereignty was explicitly denied. During this period, British administration with respect to Indigenous peoples was influenced by two expectations. First, Indigenous peoples had been significantly decimated by the introduction of European diseases, chief among them smallpox and tuberculosis, against which they had no immunity. Many British fully expected that Indigenous peoples' days were numbered and that they would soon disappear (Frideres 2020, 12). And second, it was the view of the British that those Indigenous peoples who survived should be assimilated into what they took to be their far superior civilized European way of life. The prevailing assumption at the time was that Indigenous ways of life were both primitive and barbaric. Going forward, therefore, for those who still survived, they would be treated as British subjects (Palmater 2015, 2; Townshend 2015, 37).

Also, lurking in the background was the historical fact that the fulcrum of power had shifted in favour of the colonists. After the War of 1812 with the United States, the British colonizers no longer needed Indigenous nations as military allies nor, for that matter, as trading partners. And, as the numbers of colonists continued to increase relative to the Indigenous population (which was suffering a precipitous decline due to the effects of disease), Indigenous lands were increasingly coveted by colonists for the purpose of settlement and agriculture (Belanger 2018, 119). As the value of Indigenous peoples to British colonial interests began to decrease, so too did their respect for them. Belanger points out, for example, that the British began to distance "themselves from past treaty relationships, especially those that emphasized equality between peoples" (Belanger 2018, 120). In essence, Indigenous peoples were now seen "as obstacles to the progressive settlement of Canadian society" (Fleras and Elliott 1992, 41; see also Miller 2004, 224–5). According to British authorities and successor Canadian governments, the best way to eliminate the "Indian problem" was to pursue an aggressive policy of assimilation. Indigenous peoples were to be saved from themselves. If they were educated, trained, and Christianized or, in a word, "civilized," they would be able to take their place within the Euro-Canadian mainstream. Consequently, assimilation became the justification for ongoing British and then Canadian governmental colonialism, a dynamic in which Indigenous peoples were made the objects of penetrating and stifling governmental control.

With passage of the ***British North America (BNA) Act*** in 1867, the Canadian state was born. As I point out elsewhere, "although the act of confederation committed Canada to a regime of divided sovereignty between federal and provincial governments, no constitutionally guaranteed powers were set aside for Aboriginal peoples" (Schouls 2003, 41). Instead, responsibility for the administration of Indigenous peoples passed from British Imperial authority to the Canadian federal government. It was simply assumed at the time that because of its extensive reach across the country, the federal government (as opposed to provincial governments) was in the best position to inherit colonial responsibilities for all matters pertaining to Indigenous peoples. In the process, the right to Indigenous sovereignty was completely ignored. At no point during the *BNA Act* negotiations was consideration ever given to the possibility of sharing the sovereignty of the new Canadian state with Indigenous nations. Indeed, Indigenous nations were so marginalized from the *BNA Act* negotiation process that at no point were they even consulted for the sake of securing their input or consent.

Section 91(24) of the *BNA Act* assigned to the federal government all responsibility for "Indians and lands reserved for Indians." Numerous scholars and Indigenous leaders have argued that by means of Section 91(24) the federal government has a special fiduciary responsibility to Indigenous peoples, meaning a duty owed as the stronger partner in the relationship to act in their best interests by way of protecting Indigenous lands and Indigenous ways of life (Frideres 2020, 158–9). The federal government, on the other hand, has historically taken a different view. It took its responsibilities under Section 91(24) to mean that Indigenous peoples were its "wards" or children, whom it was obliged to protect until such time as they were ready to be incorporated as full citizens into mainstream Canadian life (Belanger 2018, 120; Frideres 2020, 13; Miller 2004, 68). Successive federal governments over the course of the next century, therefore, worked out in great detail an interlocking paternalistic policy structure that promoted both protection and assimilation and that located control over Indigenous peoples and their nations deep within the Department of Indian Affairs.[9] The logic of this policy initiative carried with it a certain compelling justification at that time: Indigenous peoples were to be provided with all the features of the Euro-Canadian way of life so that they could adapt more successfully to the inevitable changing times. The consequences of assimilative policies, however, as we now know, were catastrophic. The imposition of assimilative policies as contained within the *Indian Act* and as presented by the reserve system, band governance structures, and residential schools caused a "host of social pathologies, confusion, and dysfunction" that continue to afflict Indigenous peoples to this day (Helin 2006, 88).

THE *INDIAN ACT*

The main vehicle through which the federal government exercised its authority under Section 91(24) was the ***Indian Act***. A highly invasive and paternalistic law, the first *Indian Act* was passed in 1876, consolidating all pre-existing British and Canadian law pertaining to Indian status, reserves, and bands into one statute (Belanger 2018, 122; Courchene 2018, 58). Indigenous peoples played no role in the inception and subsequent development of the *Indian Act* (Helin 2006, 93). The *Indian Act* was designed by colonial administrators to play a dual role in the lives of Indigenous peoples. First, the Act was to provide them with protection by removing them from direct contact with the Canadian population. Segregation, however, was never intended to be the permanent outcome. Instead, segregation was intended to serve as an interim step on the way to the second permanent objective, namely, assimilation. Once the educational and religious objectives of state and church were realized, Indigenous peoples would be ready for full integration into mainstream Canadian society. But in order to prepare for this great leap forward, Indigenous peoples needed the "civilizing" influences of Indian agents, school teachers, and missionaries in their lives (Helin 2006, 94; Poelzer and Coates 2015, 10). It was the *Indian Act* that became the primary tool through which this assimilative objective was to be accomplished. To this end, the *Indian Act* was designed to regulate, administer, and control virtually every aspect of Indigenous peoples lives on reserves, essentially from birth until death (Courchene 2018, 60; Grant 2018, 114, 119; RCAP 1996b, 263; Sellars 2016, 62).

It is essential that we understand the comprehensive impact that the *Indian Act* has had on the lives of Indigenous peoples. Bonita Lawrence, for one, explains that the *Indian Act* "is much more than a body of laws that for over a century has controlled every aspect of status Indian life." The *Indian Act* is also what she calls a "**conceptual framework**" that has so deeply infiltrated contemporary Indigenous life that those who live by its code now see it in some sense as natural. As she puts it, the *Indian Act* produces the "subjects it purports to control," which, therefore, indelibly orders "how Native people think of things Indian" (Lawrence 2004, 25; see also Gibbins 1997, 21). It is this all-inclusive "grammar" of the *Indian Act* that Lawrence identifies as having created particular kinds of Indigenous subjects in keeping with Canadian state priorities and which has also had the effect of essentially rendering Indigenous peoples powerless. *Indian Act* categories such as "status Indian," "reserves," and "band governance," for example, have been imposed on Indigenous nations for the purpose of drawing them into the fabric of the Canadian state and then subjecting them to Canadian control (Grant 2018, 114). And in doing so, the *Indian Act* has violated Indigenous conceptions of self, community, and the land, thereby stripping Indigenous peoples of their dignity, their self-worth, and their standing as politically autonomous nations. So, if we are to understand the full impact of the *Indian Act*, we must see it as more than a statute containing a series of regulations and amendments. It must also be seen as a colonial tool designed specifically to advance a full-frontal assault on the distinct ways of Indigenous life and all means, material and otherwise, to support and sustain those ways of life (Abele 2007, 4). What follows catalogues several examples.

According to the regulations of the *Indian Act*, there was to be a federally appointed **Indian agent** placed on every reserve. Furthermore, all matters relating to Indigenous life on reserves was placed under the direct control of the agent, all for the purpose of restricting Indigenous peoples' freedom to enhance prospects for their speedy assimilation (Gibbins 1997, 22). For instance, any money paid out by the federal government to status Indians on reserve for the purpose of education, health care, or social services, or any money generated by economic activity on reserve lands was controlled by federal authorities through the Indian agent (Sellars 2016, 73). For a time, status Indians could not sell livestock or agricultural products without the permission of the Indian agent (Poelzer and Coates 2015, 11). Status Indians also could not leave the reserve without first securing a written pass from the Indian agent, whether it be to visit extended family, hunt, fish, trap, or pursue any other activity off reserve (Miller 2004, 248). The pass system was in place from 1885 until well into the 1940s (Sellars 2016, 82). In addition to being a financial manager, the Indian agent served both to administer and enforce all *Indian Act* laws, exercising a great deal of discretionary power in the process of doing so (Sellars 2016, 74). In short, the *Indian Act* made it impossible for status Indians living on reserve to exercise independence on all matters pertaining to their social and economic development (Abele 2007, 4, 30; RCAP 1996b, 258).

As for the regulations within the *Indian Act* itself, its reach extended into every facet of Indigenous life. The *Indian Act* imposed political structures on Indigenous nations in the form of band councils and it defined who qualifies as an "Indian" with a right to Indian status and thus federal government programs. The *Indian Act* also established a mechanism for the federal government to allocate and then control Indigenous peoples' lands by way of reserves and set limitations on the rights of Indigenous peoples to practise their cultures and traditions (Miller 2004, 247; Sellars 2016, 67). In addition, a policy of "enfranchisement" was prominently featured in the *Indian Act*. This policy was designed to encourage Indigenous persons to give up their Indian status in exchange for the right to become full and equal Canadian citizens with the right to vote in Canadian elections. Prohibitions on voting and on alcohol consumption for those refusing to denounce their Indian status remained in place until the 1960s (Coates 2008, 4).

The *Indian Act* took particular aim at Indigenous peoples' political independence, making it illegal under Canadian law for Indigenous peoples to function as sovereign nations. For example, in 1927 the *Indian Act* imposed tight restrictions on status Indians by prohibiting them from hiring lawyers to assist them in pursuing legal challenges against the Canadian state (Courchene 2018, 60; Sellars 2016, 88). The Act also made it illegal for groups of three or more Indigenous persons to gather together to discuss Indigenous affairs (Helin 2006, 95; Sellars 2016, 75). As Bev Sellars explains, "the Department of Indian Affairs did not want Indians to gather and discuss issues that were important to them" (Sellars 2016, 75). Three additional examples are worthy of careful attention because they illustrate in a particularly stark fashion how the *Indian Act* was used to undermine the foundations of Indigenous political structures and social life to bring them into conformity with the objectives of the Canadian government. The first was the creation of the reserve system, the second the imposition of band councils, and the third the establishment of residential schools.

THE RESERVE SYSTEM

Most Indian bands or First Nations have **reserves**. Reserves are lands that are set aside for the exclusive occupancy, use, and benefit of a First Nation. There are about 2,300 reserves in Canada and about half of them – most of these being of extremely small size – are located in British Columbia (Vowel 2016, 260; Courchene 2018, 59).[10] As there are approximately 600 First Nations in Canada, most have more than one reserve. Most of those reserves, in turn, (approximately three-quarters) are uninhabited. In total, Indian reserves make up about 28,000 square kilometres, or 0.28 of Canada's land mass (Vowel 2016, 261). Reserves are found all over the country and vary considerably with respect to wealth and opportunity. While most are located in rural and regularly isolated areas, some are located on valuable agricultural lands or are close to urban areas containing a rich array of economic and educational opportunities.

Reserves were created through several policy instruments. Many were created by treaty, some by religious orders that set aside land for First Nations, and still others by federal government orders. In all cases, however, the purpose and rationale for the creation of reserves was the same. Reserves were to play the dual function of serving as places of refuge for Indigenous peoples in the face of the gradual expansion of an often-unscrupulous colonial society, and as training grounds for Indigenous peoples to acquire skills in agriculture and the wage-based economy and to convert to Christianity. In essence, reserves were intended to offer protection in the first step of a process designed for the eventual assimilation of Indigenous peoples (Cassidy and Bish 1989, 4–5).

In truth, however, reserves were primarily designed for the purpose of getting Indigenous peoples out of the way of an expanding Euro-Canadian society. Colonists wanted to settle on the fertile lands that Indigenous peoples occupied, and the Canadian government wanted to develop transportation routes across the country (Hamilton and Sinclair 1991, 163). The generally small size of reserves, their remote locations, and the fact that Indigenous peoples often found themselves placed on lands unsuitable for agriculture illustrate that was indeed the policy objective (Frideres 2016, 16). Thus, while Indigenous peoples regarded treaties as sacred agreements setting out protocols for the sharing of land and resources with settlers, the Canadian government saw treaties as a means to extinguish Indigenous land rights and to subject Indigenous peoples to its legislative control. Placing Indigenous peoples on reserves simply made the process of their containment and management that much easier.

While reserves constitute lands set aside for the exclusive use of Indian bands, the *Indian Act* stipulates that title to those lands resides in the Crown or with the Canadian state (*Indian Act*, Section 18; Courchene 2018, 59). This means that while Indian band members have the right to live on reserve lands, the land itself is not owned by the band or its members. Instead, reserve land is legally owned by the Crown, who supposedly holds the land and its resources in trust for the band's exclusive use and enjoyment (Abele 2007, 5). Jody Wilson-Raybould describes this situation as one in which Indigenous peoples became tenants on lands they had once controlled, "under the wardship of the Crown, with limited or no jurisdiction" (Wilson-Raybould 2019, 119). Interestingly, while Crown title is asserted, that assertion does come with a self-imposed limitation. The *Indian Act* stipulates that the Crown is to manage those lands in ways that promote the interests of the resident band members. Thus, as put by Frances Abele, "there is both the assertion of the domination of the Crown, through title and other power, and the assertion of fiduciary responsibility, in the insistence that the lands are held by the Crown for the use and benefit of the other party" (Abele 2007, 7). This fiduciary commitment to land protection can be found in *Indian Act* provisions that have guaranteed "the ongoing communal nature and ultimate inalienability of reserve lands" to name but one example (Wilson-Raybould 2019, 120). Reserve lands cannot be bought or sold by individuals but must be collectively held for the benefit and enjoyment of all band members.

In the setting of the late nineteenth and much of the twentieth century, however, the exercise of fiduciary responsibilities was more frequently overshadowed by assertions to Crown domination and control of both land management practices and economic development initiatives. The text of the *Indian Act* itself testifies to this reality. Sections 18 to 41 dealing with jurisdiction over reserve lands, and Sections 53 to 60 dealing with the management of assets generated by reserve lands placed final decision-making power in the hands of the federal minister. Here we see a clear illustration of the *Indian Act*'s paternalism at work. It was simply assumed at the time that Indigenous peoples could not be trusted to make appropriate or acceptable land use decisions. Consequently, all band decisions concerning land leases, transfers, and general land management had to receive the approval of the Department of Indian Affairs (Frideres 2020, 15). And even more egregious, as reserve lands were simply presumed to belong to the Crown, the Department was not averse to expropriating those lands for its own use or to provide leases to companies on reserves without band permission or provision of any form of compensation (Abele 2007, 14; Frideres 2020, 15; Lawrence 2004, 36).

Naturally, the paternalistic practices of the past do not translate well into the present reality, dominated as it is by commitments to Indigenous self-determination and the rigorous assertion of Indigenous rights. Interestingly, in a possible early deferential nod to residual Indigenous authority, the *Indian Act* does make provision for a delegation of economic power to Indian bands under Section 60. Under its terms, a band may request "the right to exercise such control and management over lands in the reserve occupied by that band as the Governor in Council considers desirable." The 1999 passage of the *First Nations Lands Management Act* is a clear illustration of this clause being put to work. Under its terms, an Indigenous nation can opt out of the land management provisions of the *Indian Act* and establish its own land management code. The nation is thereby authorized to make its own decisions on land management practices and reserve resources, including property rights. While title to reserve land remains in the hands of the Crown, First Nations operating under the Act no longer need to secure ministerial approval. They are effectively in a position to exercise greater control over their reserve lands and resources. Jody Wilson-Raybould notes that, to date, about 12 per cent of First Nations in Canada are signatories to this framework agreement (Wilson-Raybould 2019, 122). It is also worth noting that the practice of appropriating reserve lands for purportedly public purposes (or works) is also a practice that has fallen into disuse. Indeed, today it is more common to see Indigenous nations engaging in litigation to secure financial compensation for lands that have been long lost to their communities. Bev Sellars, for example, writes about the case of the Songhees First Nation in British Columbia who were moved from their village site to make way for the city of Victoria. They sued the federal government in the 1990s and in 2006 were awarded "$31.5 million for the wrongful appropriation of lands" (Sellars 2016, 66).

Historically speaking, however, reserves were never designed to serve as protected geographical enclaves for the expression and development of Indigenous self-determination. Put simply, they were designed to protect and then to assimilate Indigenous peoples. Far from achieving this policy objective, however, what reserve living tended to do more often than not was simply isolate and subsequently impoverish Indigenous peoples (Helin 2006, 94; Frideres 2020, 15). Reserves served to displace many Indigenous peoples from their traditional territories. They divided up both nations and their lands into smaller, more "manageable" administrative units and in doing so profoundly disrupted the political and social organization of the larger Indigenous nations that had existed for centuries. Furthermore, once displaced onto reserves, it quickly became clear that as a land base they were much too small to meet most of Indigenous peoples' basic needs. In many cases, reserves are remote and situated on marginal lands that have few if any natural resources. Most offer few job opportunities. As a result, more and more Indigenous peoples began to experience difficulties in securing an adequate standard of living for themselves or their families (Flanagan and Beauregard 2013, 3). And the problem is only compounded by the fact that the geographical isolation of many reserves means that Indigenous peoples often have difficulty participating in the larger Canadian society and economy. Taken together, the aggregate result across much of Indigenous Canada is high unemployment, regular incidents of substance and alcohol abuse, high rates of suicide, early mortality for many, and crushing poverty (Courchene 2018, 17–42).

At the same time, however, while reserves are well known for their poverty, poor health, inadequate housing, unsafe drinking water, and lack of services and employment opportunities, there are also reserves across Canada where the standard of living is similar to that of the Canadian average. Reserves such as those located at Membertou, Osoyoos, and Westbank are known for their considerable wealth as a result of their optimal geographical locations, strategic deployment of economic opportunities, and sophisticated administrative and management practices. Wherever their location and whatever their standard of living, however, reserves tend to play one common and very important positive role in the lives of Indigenous peoples: reserves are often an important source of identification for Indigenous peoples because they are usually located in their ancestral territories and spiritual homelands. The fact that reserves served to segregate Indigenous from non-Indigenous peoples despite their assimilationist intent often inadvertently assisted Indigenous peoples in maintaining their community ties and in reproducing their cultural values. Reserves, in other words, provided Indigenous peoples, both then and now, with a distinctly "Indigenous" space in which to live with their families, raise their children, and give expression to their cultures. As Chelsea Vowel explains, even though reserves constitute a tiny land base for most Indigenous communities, they nevertheless provide a setting in which traditional governance systems can continue to exist, where Indigenous cultures can be practised, where traditional country foods can be harvested, and where "relationships central to Indigenous spirituality" can be nurtured (Vowel 2016, 265–6). As put by Vowel, "above all, reserves are communities with histories, families and aspirations. They experience challenging social and economic conditions. But it is vital to recognize they also create conditions for resilience" (Vowel, 2016, 266).

IMPOSED SYSTEM OF BAND GOVERNANCE

In the pre-Confederation period, British and then Canadian authorities encountered the traditional governing structures of Indigenous nations and recognized them to be legitimate for the purposes of negotiating military and trade alliances and signing of treaties. With time, however, the Canadian government imposed its colonial will upon Indigenous tribal governments. As far as the Canadian government was concerned,

Indigenous nations would no longer be recognized at the national or tribal level. Instead, under the rules of the *Indian Act*, the former great Indigenous nations were to be divided up into small subsets and then designated as **Indian bands** (Lawrence 2012, 5). Consequently, instead of conducting political relations with the 50 to 60 originally existing Indigenous nations found across Canada, the Canadian government chose instead to deal with what are today over 600 of their subdivided units (now called First Nations) (Lawrence 2012, 5; RCAP 1996c, 181; Wilson-Raybould 2019, 47, 66).

It is Indigenous scholar Bonita Lawrence's contention that the traditional national or tribal governments were deliberately bypassed to undermine and eventually eliminate the sovereignty and political power of Indigenous nations and their confederacies (Lawrence 2004, 33; see also Ladner 2006, 6; Palmater 2015, 3). In their place Indian bands were established, their political structure and very existence cast in a "civilized" democratic mould that was intended to encourage and speed up the assimilation process (RCAP 1996b, 275; Sellars 2016, 63). As explained by Kiera Ladner, the "idea was that once enough experience had been gained, Indigenous peoples would cease being Indians under the terms of the *Indian Act* and First Nations would be granted 'self-government' by way of remodeling band councils as regular municipal governments (just like other municipalities that fall under the jurisdiction of provincial governments)" (Ladner 2006, 6). In essence, says Jody Wilson-Raybould, Indian bands were created as part of a strategy to force Indigenous peoples into submission: the smaller the political unit, the easier it was for the Canadian government to control and assimilate them (Wilson-Raybould 2019, 170–1).

The *Indian Act* established band councils as the only form of Indian government that would receive legal recognition.[11] The *Indian Act* defines a "band" as "a body of Indians," "(a) for whose use and benefit in common, lands, the legal title to which is vested in Her Majesty, have been set apart ..., (b) for whose use and benefit in common, moneys are held by Her Majesty, or (c) declared by the Governor in Council to be a band for the purposes of this Act" (*Indian Act*, Section 2).[12] The *Indian Act* also established a procedure for the election of a chief and band council every two years. By doing so, the *Indian Act* effectively signalled that the Canadian government would have nothing more to do with traditional or inherited (i.e., hereditary) Indigenous governing structures. From here on, the only Indian governments that would command its attention were to be those that were democratically structured and reflected Western political practices (Abele 2007, 6; Sellars 2016, 63).

Until the 1960s, band councils were effectively controlled by the Indian agent, who was authorized to call band council meetings and to set band council agendas. In addition, the minister responsible for Indian affairs had veto power over all band council resolutions. Chief and council were authorized to exercise a limited range of delegated powers in keeping with their status as municipalities. Powers consistent with the status of Indigenous peoples as sovereign nations were, by the provisions of the *Indian Act*, no longer within their purview. In short, *Indian Act* band council governments were designed to reflect the assimilationist objectives of the time and to bring Indigenous nations firmly under Canadian state control. Once properly "civilized" in the ways of democratic governance, it was thought that Indians could then take the next step and be fully and properly assimilated into mainstream Canadian society (Ladner 2006, 6).

The political structure and powers allocated to band councils under the *Indian Act* demonstrate the extent to which Indigenous nations, despite resistance, were compelled to capitulate to Canadian state control. With respect to their political structure, for example, band councils were required to reflect Western political practices. The *Indian Act* dictates that a band council "shall consist of one chief, and one councillor for every one hundred members of the band." The *Indian Act* further requires that "the number of councillors shall not be less than two and not more than twelve" (*Indian Act*, Section 74). Chief and council are elected by majority rule, the operative assumption being that each elector has one vote, equal in weight to the vote of all others (Abele 2007, 27–8).[13]

It is important to point out, however, that in the contemporary context it is now possible for Indigenous peoples to remove themselves from these electoral provisions of the *Indian Act* and select their political leadership through community-designed or "custom" election codes. Approximately 54 per cent of Indian bands now operate using their own leadership selection methods (Standing Senate Committee on Aboriginal Peoples 2010, 6). While the term "custom" suggests traditional methods of leadership selection (employing a hereditary chief, clan, or consensual model, for example), this is an inaccurate characterization of what actually takes place. Custom elections refer more broadly to a community-designed leadership selection scheme. According to a report of the Standing Senate Committee on Aboriginal Peoples, every custom code is different. In its words, "some make only minor modifications to the *Indian Act* electoral system, such as lengthening the terms of office, while others may provide for more significant changes. These can include blending traditional forms of governance (custom councils) with contemporary governance structures (elected chief and council)" (Standing Senate Committee on Aboriginal Peoples 2010, 10). The essential point is that unlike the *Indian Act* electoral system, custom codes are the outcome of a broad consensus arrived at by band members.

As for political powers, band councils are responsible for the governance and administration of their nation's internal affairs, including most programs and services. What they do not have is independent law-making powers. Instead, the *Indian Act* authorizes band councils to make by-laws, these being powers restricted to local matters and delegated to the nation from the Canadian government. All by-laws are further subject to the approval or disapproval of the federal minister (Helin 2006, 96; Miller 2004, 70). The *Indian Act* further restricts band council powers by requiring that all by-laws be consistent with the *Indian Act* and with any regulations made by Cabinet or the minister.

In what areas of jurisdiction may band councils exercise by-law-making powers? The list is rather restrictive and is best characterized as consistent with those exercised by municipalities. Under Section 81 of the *Indian Act*, band councils are authorized to do the following:

- provide for the health of residents;
- regulate traffic, construction, building, and commerce;
- prevent disorderly conduct and uphold law and order;

- construct roads, bridges, and other public infrastructure;
- survey, zone, and distribute reserve land;
- issue certificates of possession or certificates of occupation to band members;
- preserve, protect, and manage animals on reserve, including game;
- remove trespassers on reserve;
- control the residence of band members;
- protect the rights of spouses or common-law partners and children who reside with band members; and
- impose fines on those found guilty for breach of by-laws (*Indian Act*, Section 81; see also Abele 2007, 8–9).

While band councils can pass by-laws through a simple majority vote of council, some matters require the support of a majority of community members. These include land surrender or land designation decisions, membership and custom election codes, and alcohol by-laws (Williamson and Roberts 2004, 121).

In addition, most band councils are heavily reliant on the Canadian government for revenues required to finance implementation of their by-laws and administration of their programs and services. Consequently, as Wilson-Raybould observes, transparency and accountability concerning the choices that the political leadership makes about how to allocate and distribute those revenues "is primarily to Canada and not to our citizens" (Wilson-Raybould 2019, 32). Naturally, the political leadership on reserve is held accountable for its political, administrative, and financial decisions through the "ballot box," among other mechanisms. Wilson-Raybould states that in keeping with standards of good governance, "our citizens demand it" (Wilson-Raybould 2019, 130). But at the same time, the academic literature is well supplied with examples of instances where "ultimate power and responsibility is lodged in the Minister, not in the members of the Band or the officials they elect" (Abele 2007, 10). In circumstances as varied as elections, the coming into force of by-laws, funding agreements, and financial management, to name just four examples, the provisions of the *Indian Act* maintain an overriding ministerial authority (see Abele 2007; Wilson-Raybould 2019, 129–33; MacDonald and Levasseur 2014; Alcantara, Spicer, and Leone 2012).

What is abundantly clear from the foregoing analysis is that the *Indian Act* does not create conditions for the effective exercise of Indigenous self-government, let alone Indigenous sovereignty. For example, Kiera Ladner points out that while band councils have been delegated considerable authority over programs such as health care, education, and social services in recent years, the power of the Canadian government over Indigenous nations remains formidable. The government controls band funds, it imposes administrative and accountability requirements on band-run programs, and it employs the use of third-party management in cases of purported band fiscal mismanagement. The government can also disallow band election results and can override all band council by-laws (Ladner 2006, 12). This leads Ladner to conclude that band councils operating under the *Indian Act* have no real "decision-making ability that is not subject to the authority of the federal government" (Ladner 2006, 12; Ladner 2003, 49; see also Wilson-Raybould 2019, 141).

Not surprisingly, Indigenous peoples have resisted the *Indian Act* regime and the limitations imposed by it. But while there now exist some alternatives for Indigenous nations to opt out of the *Indian Act*, these options are still relatively new. Foremost among them are self-government agreements that Indigenous nations can secure either through federal government legislation or through modern treaty negotiations. Both options provide Indigenous peoples with the political means to step out from under the *Indian Act* regime and assume greater control and law-making power over such jurisdictional areas as social and economic development, health, social services, education, and land use planning. Other options include the *First Nations Land Management Act*, which authorizes band councils to make independent decisions about the management of their reserve lands. However, as observed by James Anaya, the former special rapporteur on the rights of Indigenous peoples, "the Indian Act remains the default and still prevalent regime among First Nations" (Anaya 2014, 13).

Despite their clear structural limitations, I believe it is nevertheless accurate to say that band councils are governments, or at least they are governments in development. Factually speaking, they do perform functions that are clearly governmental in nature, and those functions do contribute to the well-being of their Indigenous constituents. Indeed, Ladner herself points out that in many Indigenous nations band councils have now taken such firm root that they are seen by their members to be legitimate governing bodies (Ladner 2006, 8, 9).[14] Wilson-Raybould offers a similar observation when she says "we can all agree that the federally imposed Indian Act is not the answer, even though it is, as a result of the colonial legacy, necessarily a starting point for conversations in communities where the Indian Act system is, in most cases, currently the primary system of administration in place" (Wilson-Raybould 2019, 71). The question I will consider in due course is whether band councils, or other Indigenous governments created through federal or provincial statute (like Métis governments in Alberta or the Inuit-dominated territorial government in Nunavut), can serve as conduits for the expression of Indigenous sovereignty. My argument will be that while the origins of many Indigenous governments may well lie within the Canadian state, this does not preclude those same governments from drawing down and exercising some of their sovereign Indigenous powers. Just how and in what ways this can occur is a topic to be taken up in later chapters.

RESIDENTIAL SCHOOLS

Alongside the assimilative pressures of the *Indian Act*, the reserve system, and band governance structures, an additional policy instrument was introduced, this one designed specifically to cause the cultural extinction of Indigenous peoples. For about 100 years, between the early 1850s and late 1960s, the Government of Canada worked with the established Christian religious denominations (Roman Catholic, Anglican, United, and Presbyterian) to run a residential school system for Indigenous children. The residential schools were created for the purpose of separating Indigenous children from their families and communities and placing them in boarding schools, usually far from home.[15] These schools were government funded and church run, priests and nuns generally serving as both teachers in the classrooms and supervisors of dormitories and school grounds. Under the terms of the 1920 *Indian Act*, attendance at these schools was mandatory. Approximately 150,000 children attended, most living in the schools almost year-round. A total of 139 residential schools existed across Canada over the course of this 100-year period (Belanger 2018, 128; Truth and Reconciliation Commission 2015, 3).

Ostensibly, the purpose of residential schools was to educate Indigenous children, but in reality they were designed to indoctrinate children into the Euro-Canadian and Christian way of life to prepare them for assimilation into mainstream Canadian society. European and later Canadian officials were convinced that not only were the Indigenous ways of life inferior, but they were also dying out. It therefore made sense that Indigenous children be removed from their communities and dying cultures and be subject to a "civilizing" pedagogy, one that would have students graduate with the skill set necessary to take their place in the mainstream economy and society (Courchene 2018, 120; Frideres 2020, 62).

As it turned out, however, the residential schools were generally poorly equipped to teach and were often significantly underfunded (Courchene 2018, 124). As a result, the schools were often overcrowded, poorly built, and children undernourished due to the poor quality and insufficient amounts of food (Lawrence 2004, 106; Frideres 2020, 63). Teaching focused mostly on developing practical skills and acquiring Christian teachings. Boys were segregated from girls and siblings from one another (Williamson and Roberts 2004, 110; Frideres 2020, 63). Girls were educated for domestic pursuits while boys acquired skills in farming, carpentry, and other trades. Attention was also paid to providing students with basic reading, writing, and numerical skills. In addition, many schools employed a half-day class schedule, the other half of the day being dedicated to maintaining the school itself; the boys were often involved in farming and general maintenance while the girls performed domestic chores (Miller 2004, 246; MacDonald and Hudson 2012, 431). The end result was a poor education, with most students accomplishing little more than a grade five academic skill set by the time they turned 18. At this point, usually after eight or nine years of schooling, students were required to leave.

Even more egregious than a poor education, however, was the residential school mandate to eliminate all evidence of Indigenous culture from the identity of their students (Miller 2004, 246–7; Courchene 2018, 119; Frideres 2020, 63). Children were forbidden from speaking their Indigenous languages and from engaging in their customary and traditional practices (Olthuis, Kleer, Townshend 2012, 376). Their hair was cut short, they were required to wear uniforms, and their days were lived out according to strict schedules, all in keeping with Euro-Canadian traditions and practices (Belanger 2018, 128). In short, the objective was "to take the Indian out of the child," or to assimilate them. At every turn, school administrators did all they could to negate the value of Indigenous cultures. And to disobey the rules was to risk severe punishment. The cumulative outcome of both education (such as it was) and discipline was that children lost their connections to their families, nations, lands, cultures, and languages (Olthuis, Kleer, Townshend 2012, 376). In addition, as a result of their indoctrination, many students acquired a deep sense of shame in being Indigenous. Given these experiences, it is not surprising that upon leaving residential schools, many Indigenous youth would later find themselves caught between the Indigenous and Euro-Canadian cultures, "feeling as if they did not fit into either one" (Williamson and Roberts 2004, 112).

The term "cultural genocide" is often used by Indigenous peoples to describe the outcome of the life experienced by Indigenous students within the walls of residential schools (Williamson and Roberts 2004, 114, Vowel 2016, 173–4). This was a concept picked up by the Truth and Reconciliation Commission of Canada (TRC) and came to form the critical lens through which it offered its evaluation and critique of what occurred during the racist and paternalistic residential school era (TRC 2015, 1). It is worth pointing out that the word "genocide" is highly politically and legally charged and therefore ought not to be casually thrown around. Indeed, Chelsea Vowel argues that for some the use of the terms by the TRC was off-putting "because they feel it unnecessarily modifies the word *genocide,* while others insist genocide must only be used to refer to the mass killing of a specific group" (Vowel 2016, 174). Clearly, there is an important distinction to be made between the terms "genocide," which seeks to exterminate a group, and "cultural genocide," which seeks a group's assimilation but not necessarily its extermination. Along with David B. MacDonald and Graham Hudson, I believe that the residential school initiative was not designed to achieve Indigenous peoples' physical eradication. When modified by the term "cultural," however, we stand on much firmer theoretical and legal ground (MacDonald and Hudson 2012, 442–3).

There can be no doubt that the residential school system was part of an interlocking policy network that sought to turn Indigenous children into Euro-Canadians. As such, "cultural genocide" is the better and more accurate term. As put by the TRC, residential schools were all about "preventing transmission of cultural values and identity from one generation to the next," and thus were intended to contribute to ending the transmission of Indigenous social and political institutions from parents to their children (TRC, 2015, 1). Insofar as residential schools were explicitly designed to "take the Indian out of the child" (without killing the child), the use of the term "cultural genocide" seems appropriate. So, while no doubt provocative, I agree with the position taken by Chelsea Vowel when she says, "I do not feel that the intent [in using the modified term "cultural genocide"] is either to inflate the circumstances [of residential schools] or to downplay them" (Vowel 2016, 174). The term merely describes what actually happened: in residential schools, Indigenous children were forced to live, work, worship, and generally conduct themselves as Euro-Canadians.

Insofar as residential schools did promote what some refer to as a cultural genocide, it can be said with certainty that those schools violated the human rights of Indigenous children. But in addition to cultural genocide, Indigenous children suffered from other forms of human rights abuse as well. Many children were subjected to multiple forms of physical, sexual, emotional, and psychological abuse.[16] They also suffered from malnutrition and from diseases like tuberculosis. The outcome of neglect, abuse, and disease was that some schools experienced mortality rates as high as 35 to 60 per cent (Jung 2016, 365). Over the 100-plus years that residential schools were in existence, an estimated 6,000 children died (Vowel 2016, 171; Belanger 2018, 130; TRC 2015, 90–7). Many of these children were buried in unidentified or unmarked graves. The veritable outpouring of grief that occurred across the country in the summer of 2021 when 215 unmarked graves were identified at the site of the former Kamloops Residential School, quickly followed by similar findings in Cranbrook, BC, and on the territories of the Cowessess First Nation in Saskatchewan (among others), testify to the callousness and general brutality of the residential school experience.

And as for those who survived (often referred to today as "survivors"), they grew up estranged from their cultures, languages, nations, and Indigenous identities. This estrangement was only reinforced during the so-called "Sixties Scoop," a period in which many Indigenous children were fostered or adopted into non-Indigenous homes. The cumulative effect of these human rights abuses was "to cast a long shadow of despair on indigenous communities," a shadow that set in motion many of the social and economic problems that devastate Indigenous communities to this day (Frideres 2020, 64, 79). The list is one with which most Canadians are well familiar: unemployment, poverty, low self-esteem, depression, alcohol and substance abuse, domestic violence, and violent, often self-inflicted deaths (Anaya 2014, 5; MacDonald and Hudson 2012, 432). Without the experience of a nurturing family life, for example, many residential school survivors lacked the knowledge and skills to raise their own children.[17] And on the cultural side of the ledger, the casualties were no less devastating. With the loss of Indigenous languages, for example, oral traditions were also suppressed, thereby undermining "the primary vehicle for intergenerational transmission of Native values, culture, and identity" (Lawrence 2004, 106; see also Courchene 2018, 126). The destructive legacy of the residential school system, therefore, has been devastating both because of its widespread effects and because of its intergenerational reach.[18]

The injustices associated with the residential school experience were brought into particularly sharp focus in the late 1980s. Residential school survivors began to sue the Canadian government and churches for damages in court. Successful prosecutions against former residential school staff led to more police investigations and, in turn, more prosecutions (Jung 2016, 366). By the late 1990s, the Anglican, Presbyterian, and United churches had all publicly apologized for the role each had played in the residential school system. Building on this momentum, the Assembly of First Nations launched a class action suit against the Canadian government in 2005, resulting in a general solution by way of the Indian Residential Schools Settlement Agreement in 2007. The settlement agreement provided for three major forms of compensation.[19] First, all those who had been to residential schools were granted a common experience payment in the amount of $10,000 for the first year and an additional $3,000 for every year in school after that. Second, all those who could demonstrate that they had been subjected to physical or sexual abuse were awarded an additional amount, as determined by an impartial adjudicator in an independent assessment process, up to a maximum of $250,000. And third, provisions were made for the Canadian government to fund healing programs, research, and commemoration projects, all designed to assist survivors and their families to heal from the trauma generated by the unique circumstances of each person's residential school experience (Independent Assessment Oversight Committee 2021, 7; see also Frideres 2020, 71–2).[20] Following quickly on the heels of the 2007 settlement agreement was Prime Minister Stephen Harper's official and historic apology for the residential school policy, delivered in a moving ceremony in the House of Commons on June 11, 2008.[21] Importantly, the settlement agreement also called for the creation of a Truth and Reconciliation Commission. I shall address a number of its central recommendations designed specifically to promote a "healing journey of reconciliation" in my consideration of the contemporary policy environment found in the next chapter (Wilson-Raybould 2019, 51).

INDIAN ACT AMENDMENTS

While the structural features of the reserve system, band governance, and residential schools were being assembled, the entire framework of Indian policy was continuously guided by and structured in response to an ever-evolving *Indian Act*. It was the *Indian Act* that served as the primary policy instrument used by the Canadian government to advance its changing expectations and priorities for Indigenous peoples over time. The ultimate goal was always to assimilate Indigenous peoples to Euro-Canadian ways. So when it became clear to governmental officials that Indigenous peoples were holding onto their cultures with considerable commitment, the assimilationist campaign became that much more aggressive.

For example, amendments to the *Indian Act* early on banned central cultural rituals and political ceremonies. These included a ban on the northwest coast nations' Potlatch in 1884 and the Prairie nations' **Sun Dance** in 1895. Yet, as explained earlier in this chapter, the west coast Potlatch ceremony constituted the basis of Indigenous coastal governmental systems. As Calvin Helin describes it, through the Potlatch, Indigenous value systems were reinforced, political rank and authority legitimized, and "rightful possession of prestige and use of chiefly power and influence" was validated (Helin 2006, 95). Bev Sellars further explains that when the Potlatch was banned, so too was a central ceremony "that officiated and confirmed the social and political organization of each nation" (Sellars 2016, 68). The penalty for participation in either the Potlatch or Sun Dance rituals was imprisonment for a two- to six-month period. From the perspective of the Canadian government, both rituals were seen to be heathen in intent and fundamentally at odds with their assimilation efforts. Particularly offensive to government officials was the anti-capitalist redistribution of property and extensive gift-giving that were essential components of each (Miller 2004, 248, 249). Despite these legal pressures, however, Helin observes that in an effort to preserve their traditional political and religious practices, Indigenous nations continued to practise their Potlatch and Sun Dance ceremonies in secret, sometimes suffering arrest as a result (Helin 2006, 95). Undeterred, the Canadian government continued its assault. A 1914 ban was imposed on Indigenous peoples living in the Canadian west and prohibiting them from wearing their traditional regalia off reserve without the permission of the Indian agent (Sellars 2016, 70). And, as already described, a 1920 *Indian Act* amendment made residential schooling mandatory so that Indigenous children would be removed from their families and thus the source of their cultures (Lawrence 2004, 35).

In 1927 a further amendment prohibited Indigenous communities from hiring lawyers to pursue legal claims against the government. At this time, the *Indian Act* also made it illegal for Indigenous peoples to hold public meetings to discuss Indigenous affairs. By means of these initiatives, the Canadian government was clearly attempting to cut off all opportunities for Indigenous leaders to organize for political purposes or to hire professional help to assist them in their land disputes with the Canadian government. Indeed, as Sellars observes, the effect of these *Indian Act* amendments was that it "allowed the government to claim the lands without any interference or court challenges" (Sellars 2016, 88).

A significant overhaul of the *Indian Act* finally occurred in 1951. These amendments were designed to remove some of its most restrictive and offensive features. Canada simply had to take action on the Indigenous human rights front, particularly against the backdrop of World War II and its associated litany of human rights abuses. There was also the matter of Canada having signed on to the new Universal Declaration of Human Rights. If Canada were not to address its flagrant abuse of Indigenous human rights, it could justifiably expect condemnation from the international community (Metallic 2020, 425). So Canada decided to act. It was at this point, for example, that the bans against the Potlatch and Sun Dance were removed (Frideres 2020, 16; Metallic 2020, 426). Also removed was the prohibition against raising money to secure the services of lawyers to advance Indigenous claims in court, as was the ban forbidding Indigenous persons from wearing traditional clothing off reserve. Provisions for involuntary enfranchisement were also struck from the *Indian Act*, though voluntary enfranchisement was still encouraged (Miller 2004, 255). The "half-day" system at residential schools was replaced with a full day of classes, and Indigenous children were permitted to attend public schools (Sellars 2016, 96). In addition, up until 1951, only Indian men were allowed to vote in band elections, a provision that Sellars explains was particularly devastating for matrilineal cultures (Sellars 2016, 98). Consequently, in 1951, women were given the right to vote for chief and councillors in band elections.

Prohibitions on alcohol consumption and voting in federal elections were not removed until the 1960s. In 1970, after a major court decision called the *Drybones* case, status Indians were also granted the right to purchase and consume alcohol in a public place. And as for political participation, prior to 1960, status Indians would lose their status in exchange for the right to vote in federal elections.[22] It was simply assumed, politically speaking, that a person could not be both an "Indian" and a citizen of Canada, entitled to exercise political rights such as the right to vote in Canadian elections, at the same time. In essence, while "Indians" were seen to be a distinctive race, they were also deemed to be politically distinct and thus separate from Canada, a position that was not necessarily at odds with the perspectives held by many Indigenous peoples at the time. It was not until 1960 that this assumption concerning the need for a single political affiliation to be entitled to Canadian citizenship was removed from the *Indian Act*. The legacy of this contradictory approach to Canadian citizenship, however, persists into the present day. Some Indigenous people take the position that they can be both "Indians" and "Canadians," held together in a dual form of citizenship. Others adopt a more critical stance. They regard "Indigenous" and "Canadian" citizenship to be diametrically opposed given Canada's centuries-long attempts to undermine Indigenous identities, cultures, and rights. Those of this persuasion are thus convinced that to participate in Canadian elections and politics is to validate political forces that have worked to destroy Indigenous identity and the sources of their own distinctive Indigenous citizenship. As captured by Pamela Palmater: "So, if it is the case that we are sovereign nations with our inherent right to be self-governing recognized as protected, then why would we vote in another sovereign nation's election process?" To do so is to effectively vote "for who will be our next Indian agent" (Palmater 2015, 242).

What did not change with all these early *Indian Act* revisions, however, was the overall governmental policy intent to assimilate Indigenous peoples. As Sellars observes, the 1951 revisions had the overall effect of returning "Canadian Indian legislation to its original form, as set out in the 1876 Indian Act" (Sellars 2016, 95). The focus of the 1951 *Indian Act* amendments, in other words, were extremely modest in their intentions. All they were designed to do was to remove those specific measures intended to "contain" Indians on their reserves. Rather than denigrate Indigenous peoples and their cultures, the emphasis now became one of equality (Metallic 2020, 425). From 1951 forward, the focus of Indian policy would be to promote measures designed specifically to facilitate the smooth passage of Indigenous peoples into the social mainstream as contributing citizens of Canada.

THE GENDERED DYNAMICS OF COLONIALISM

The preceding clearly demonstrates the multiple ways in which Indigenous peoples have suffered under the oppressive weight of colonialism. Yet not only were the practices of colonialism normalized through the denial of Indigenous sovereignty, but so too were European-derived notions of patriarchy. Thus, while both Indigenous men and women shared experiences of severe disempowerment under the universal imposition of colonialism, women were "doubly disadvantaged" because, unlike men, they also had to contend with the coercive forces of sexism on their lives (RCAP 1996b, 300). And what did this mean exactly? For Indigenous women, colonization meant that they were subjected to patriarchal assumptions about the natural order of male-dominated political, economic, and social structures. The subsequent imposition of these "morally superior" practices upon the operation of Indigenous structures meant that women's traditional gender roles were seriously devalued and their access to political power, social status, and material resources within their nations systematically undermined. The consequences were nothing short of devastating. More so than Indigenous men, Indigenous women lost access to much of that which validates a person's sense of place in the world, including their "culture, traditional territories, identity and status, children, and culturally respected gender roles" (Green 2017a,

175; see also Wilson-Raybould 2019, 181). As further observed by RCAP, "the lingering effects of this early and sustained assault on the ability of Indian women to be recognized as 'Indian' and to live in recognized Indian communities continue to be experienced by many Indian women and their children today" (RCAP 1996b, 300).

Nowhere is the imposition of patriarchal power relations upon Indigenous peoples better illustrated than in the various historical incarnations of the *Indian Act.* Motivated by ambitions to civilize Indigenous peoples, Euro-Canadians devised rules to reorganize Indigenous societies so that Indian women came to be defined through their relations to men (Frideres 2020, 9). For example, under the *Indian Act* women were denied the right to vote or run for office in the colonially imposed band chief and council system. By means of this measure, Indigenous women were stripped of the positions of political power they had traditionally held in some Indigenous nations. As discussed in the previous chapter, women were also deprived of their Indian status if the chose to marry non-Indian men, while men were entitled to pass on Indian status to their non-Indian wives. The outcome of "marrying out" often meant that women (and their children) lost connection to their communities of origin and thus their ties to family, culture, and identity (Kuokkanen 2012, 233; Green 2017a, 175). The introduction of residential schools reconfigured Indigenous gender roles even further by imposing patriarchal expectations of behaviour on boys and girls as they moved into adulthood. By means of removing children from their homes and communities, Indigenous women (and men) were essentially denied their parenting roles "of raising and educating children and transmitting language, culture and knowledge to them" (Eberts 2017, 70). In short, as argued by several Indigenous feminists, the ravages of a patriarchally infused colonialism that sought to reconfigure Indigenous women in a Euro-Canadian image left them vulnerable and socially disadvantaged everywhere (Eberts 2017, 71; Green 2017a, 175; Anderson 2010, 81–91; Stark 2020, 70–82; Starblanket 2017, 21–41).

If the displacement of Indigenous sovereignty is indeed a result of the imposition of a patriarchally infused form of European sovereignty, as James Frideres argues, then the project of Indigenous emancipation must also include enhancing the roles, responsibilities, and well-being of Indigenous women within their nations as well as within Canadian society as a whole (Frideres 2020, 1; see also Wilson-Raybould 2019, 182–3). This is a theme regularly encountered in the writings of Indigenous scholars and activists (and their supporters), especially among women. For example, Joyce Green argues that when the critique that "challenges the legitimacy of the settler states' claim to sovereignty *at the expense of* Indigenous peoples … is gendered, and when it includes feminist analysis in its formation, it has the potential to produce models of emancipation for both men and women in Indigenous communities" (Green 2017b, 15). Shari Huhndorf and Cheryl Suzack likewise insist that "social justice, in our view, can be attained only through specific attention to gender and must be considered as an integral part of, rather than a subsidiarity to, struggles for national liberation" (Huhndorf and Suzack 2010, 3). Kim Anderson adds "that until we seriously address the political, social, and economic inequities faced by Indigenous women, we will never achieve full healing, decolonization, and healthy nation-building"

(Anderson 2010, 85). And Rauna Kuokkanen contends "that securing indigenous women's rights is inextricable from securing the rights of their peoples as a whole ... without individual self-determination, meaningful and viable collective self-determination of indigenous peoples is simply not possible" (Kuokkanen 2012, 236–7, 240). Taken together, what these commentators point to is the need for remedies that restore to Indigenous women equal status and membership within their nations, equal access to all available economic and social resources, and equal participation in the self-determination ambitions of their peoples. As astutely put by one commentator, "if the erosion of [Indigenous] sovereignty comes from disempowering women, its renewed strength will come from re-empowering them" (Elsie Redbird, as quoted in Huhndorf and Suzack 2010, 6). Decolonization, reconciliation, sovereignty, and nation-building, in other words, are possible only within a context that gives priority to the empowerment of Indigenous women.

CONCLUSION

From an Indigenous perspective, the colonial period of Canada's history was nothing short of devastating. The British and subsequent Canadian colonial powers, whether through a misguided sense of benevolence or whether out of an unadulterated sense of self-interest, thought Indigenous peoples needed civilizing. What followed was a systematic process of assimilation designed to draw Indigenous peoples into the emerging agricultural and industrial society and the market economy.

The Royal Proclamation of 1763 and Treaty of Niagara of 1764 contained an initial promise that Indigenous nations would mediate their relations with the British and later Canadian state through treaties in a nation-to-nation dynamic of political equality. But the *Indian Act* deliberately undermined this promise. It refused to recognize traditional forms of Indigenous governance, imposing instead, often through force, band councils that had limited jurisdiction and no independent or "inherent" powers. The *Indian Act* also established reserves. They were designed to isolate, protect, and control Indigenous peoples to prepare them for the larger project of assimilation. But it was also clear that reserves were intended to make Indigenous land available for occupation and use by settlers. In doing so, the *Indian Act* did much to sever the relationships Indigenous peoples had to their ancestral lands and the abundant resources of those lands. Further human rights violations were perpetrated by the *Indian Act*'s outlawing of expressions of Indigenous culture and religious ceremonies. And finally, to accelerate the process of assimilation, the Canadian government and churches combined efforts through mandatory residential schooling to strip multiple generations of Indigenous children of their Indigenous identity and community membership.

The cumulative effect of this long-term program of Canadian governmental assimilative policies has been a tragedy of epic proportions. Once sovereign, independent, and free-standing Indigenous nations were reduced to state dependency, despondency, and social fragmentation. Glaringly absent throughout this history of colonialism is the political model of relations initially agreed to and still proposed by many Indigenous leaders: one that takes its cue from the Two-Row Wampum belt where Indigenous and Canadian nations exist in a relationship of mutually agreed upon interdependence (both drawing their sustenance from the same river), but where both also agree not to interfere in the internal affairs of one another (two vessels travelling peacefully side by side).

DISCUSSION QUESTIONS

1 In what respects might the Doctrine of Discovery and the concept of *terra nullius* be construed as racist?
2 Do the Royal Proclamation of 1763 and Treaty of Niagara of 1764 substantiate an Indigenous assertion to sovereignty? If so, how can these historical agreements be made to have moral and political force in the present?
3 Why do policies that promote assimilation so often fail? Is it because they ignore the important matter of consent? Explain with reference to the *Indian Act*, the reserve system, band governance structures, and residential schools.
4 Can contemporary decolonization and reconciliation projects be successful if they do not take Indigenous feminist analysis into account? In what ways can Indigenous feminism lend critical insights to the project of Indigenous political empowerment?

SUGGESTED READINGS

Anderson, Kim. 2010. "Affirmations of an Indigenous Feminist." In *Indigenous Women and Feminism: Politics, Activism, Culture*, edited by Cheryl Suzack, Shari M. Huhndorf, Jeanne Perreault, and Jean Barman. Vancouver: UBC Press.

Borrows, John. 1997. "Wampum at Niagara: The Royal Proclamation, Canadian Legal History, and Self-Government." In *Aboriginal and Treaty Rights in Canada: Essays on Law, Equality, and Respect for Difference*, edited by Michael Asch. Vancouver: UBC Press.

———. 2016. "Aboriginal and Treaty Rights and Violence against Women." In *Freedom and Indigenous Constitutionalism*. Toronto: University of Toronto Press.

Cairns, Alan C. 2000. "Empire." In *Citizens Plus: Aboriginal Peoples and the Canadian State*. Vancouver: UBC Press.

Courchene, Thomas J. 2018. "Chapter 3: Milestones in Canada–Indigenous Relations: From Columbus to the Constitution Act, 1982." In *Indigenous Nationals, Canadian Citizens: From First Contact to Canada 150 and Beyond*. Montreal: McGill-Queen's University Press.

Gibbins, Roger. 1997. "Historical Overview and Background: Part I." In *First Nations in Canada: Perspectives on Opportunity, Empowerment, and Self-Determination*, edited by J. Rick Ponting. Toronto: McGraw-Hill Ryerson.

Green, Joyce, ed. 2017. *Making Space for Indigenous Feminism*, 2nd ed. Halifax: Fernwood Publishing.

King, Thomas. 2012. *The Inconvenient Indian: A Curious Account of Native People in North America.* Toronto: Doubleday Canada.

Miller, J.R. 2004. "Chapter 5: Left Hanging in the Middle: Assimilation." In *Lethal Legacy: Current Native Controversies in Canada.* Toronto: McClelland & Stewart.

———. 1989. *Skyscrapers Hide the Heavens: A History of Indian–White Relations in Canada.* Toronto: University of Toronto Press.

Niezen, Ronald. 2017. *Truth & Indignation: Canada's Truth and Reconciliation Commission on Indian Residential Schools.* Toronto: University of Toronto Press.

Sellars, Bev. 2016. *Price Paid: The Fight for First Nations Survival.* Vancouver: Talonbooks.

———. 2013. *They Called Me Number One: Secrets and Survival at an Indian Residential School.* Vancouver: Talonbooks.

Stark, Heidi Kiiwetinepinesiik. 2020. "Colonialism, Gender Violence, and the Making of the Canadian State." In *Visions of the Heart: Issues Involving Indigenous Peoples in Canada*, 5th ed., edited by Gina Starblanket and David Long. Toronto: Oxford University Press.

Truth and Reconciliation Commission of Canada. 2015. *Honouring the Truth, Reconciling for the Future: Summary of the Final Report of the Truth and Reconciliation Commission of Canada.* Ottawa: Truth and Reconciliation Commission of Canada.

Vowel, Chelsea. 2016. "Chapter 20: Monster: The Residential School Legacy," and "Chapter 21: Our Stolen Generations: The Sixties and Millennial Scoops." In *Indigenous Writes: A Guide to First Nations, Métis & Inuit Issues in Canada.* Winnipeg: Highwater Press.

NOTES

1 When the UNDRIP was ratified by the General Assembly in 2007, Canada, along with the United States, Australia, and New Zealand, refused to do so. When Canada eventually agreed to ratify the Declaration in 2010, it qualified its endorsement by saying that it would serve as an aspirational document only. Prime Minister Justin Trudeau has since served notice that the Declaration's standards will now serve as those to which the Government of Canada will comply.

2 What follows relies heavily on the scholarship of John Borrows (2010), Kiera Ladner (2006), J.R. Miller (2004), and the Royal Commission on Aboriginal Peoples (1996b), among others, to show that Indigenous nations did indeed possess the kinds of sophisticated political and legal structures that more than justify the credibility of their claim that Indigenous nations were once sovereign.

3 The Iroquois Confederacy expanded to six nations when they were joined by the Tuscarora people in the early 1700s who fled invasion of their traditional territories in the Thirteen Colonies to the south due to agricultural settlement. See Miller 1989, 7; Borrows 2010, 72.

4 It is also worth noting the important contribution that the Haudenosaunee Confederacy made to the design and operation of the American federation. As explained by Thomas Courchane, "the US Founding Fathers wanted the American government to be (i) democratic, (ii) a federal system, and (iii) a peaceful association of the thirteen colonies. Europe of the day did not provide models for any of these requirements. However, all three attributes were embodied and embedded in the Iroquois Confederacy and represented in the Hiawatha Belt." See Courchane 2018, 73–4. This contribution was later formally acknowledged by the US Senate in 1987.

5 Francisco de Vitoria, a sixteenth-century legal scholar, is credited with being one of the first to develop a European theory of Indigenous rights. As advisor to the Papacy, he affirmed that the Pope could grant rights to discover the New World, but upon discovery the European nation had only an exclusive right, against all other European powers, to trade with the Indigenous peoples as well as to convert them to Christianity. See Ladner 2003, 45.

6 Under its recommendation 1.16.2, the Royal Commission on Aboriginal Peoples urges federal, provincial, and territorial governments to acknowledge "a) that concepts such as terra nullius and the doctrine of discovery are factually, legally, and morally wrong; b) that such concepts no longer form part of law making or policy development by Canadian governments; c) that such concepts will not be the basis for arguments presented to the courts; and d) that all governments commit themselves to a renewal of the federation through consensual means to overcome the legacy of these concepts." See RCAP 1996b, 696. Under its Calls to Action 45.i, the Truth and Reconciliation Commission simply asks that the Government of Canada "repudiate concepts used to justify European sovereignty over Indigenous lands and peoples such as the Doctrine of Discovery and *terra nullius.*" See TRC 2015, 326.

7 The Royal Proclamation states: "And Whereas it is just and reasonable, and essential to our Interest, and the Security of our Colonies, that the several Nations or Tribes of Indians with whom We are connected, and who live under our Protection, should not be molested or disturbed in the Possession of such Parts of our Dominions and Territories as, not having been ceded to or purchased by Us, are reserved to them, or any of them, as their Hunting Grounds." As reprinted in Borrows and Rotman 2003, 26.

8 Thomas Courchene adds the additional interesting observation that because some Indigenous nations believed that the Treaty of Niagara bound them to the British as military allies, they agreed to fight with them against the Americans in the War of 1812. See Courchene 2018, 50.

9 Yale Belanger astutely observes that this time period was marked by a dramatic shift in the way colonial governments related to Indigenous peoples. Rather than negotiating with them, British and the subsequent Canadian Parliament began to legislate on behalf of them. See Belanger 2018, 120.

10 The formula for determining the size of reserves varies across the country. Treaties 1 and 2 allocated 160 acres per family of five, while Treaties 3 through 11 allocated 640 acres per family of five. In British Columbia, reserves were not established through treaty but through governmental order. Here reserves were considerably smaller, set at an average of 20 acres per family.

11 The language that follows comes directly from the *Indian Act*. It could be simplified to read that a First Nation qualifies as a band under the *Indian Act* if it (1) has a reserve; (2) has government trust funds reserved for its use; and (3) has been declared a band by the federal Cabinet. See Olthuis, Kleer, Townshend 2012, 203.

12 The federal Cabinet has created new bands from time to time. A couple of examples include the Smith's Landing First Nation, established as a band in 2000 in Alberta; O-Pipon-Na-Piwin Cree Nation, established as a band in 2006 in Manitoba; and the Qalipu Mi'kmaq First Nation, established as a band in Newfoundland and numbering more than 20,000 members. See Olthuis, Kleer, Townshend 2012, 203–4.

13 Olthuis, Kleer, and Townshend note that on some reserves, "there are strong traditions of hostility to the governing structure imposed by the *Indian Act*." These authors point to the Six Nations in Ontario as one example where they observe that many band members refuse to participate in *Indian Act* elections, preferring instead to offer their political support to the traditional Haudenosaunee Confederacy. See Olthuis, Kleer, Townshend 2012, 205.

14 It should be pointed out that Kiera Ladner does not believe that *Indian Act* band councils are legitimate Indigenous governing bodies and that those Indigenous persons who accept this proposition are mistaken. Ladner argues that only Indigenous governing structures that receive their origin in and authority from independent, free-standing Indigenous constitutional orders are entitled to the status of legitimacy. See Ladner 2006, 8–9.

15 The residential schools were often built far from Indigenous communities to discourage students from running away in an attempt to return home. However, the trauma generated by the residential school experience resulted in many children running away despite the distance from home. Of those, a significant number died due to exposure, particularly if they were running away in winter.

16 For a detailed discussion of the experiences of Indigenous children in residential schools as well as an account of the kinds of abuses they suffered, see TRC 2015. For a personal account, see Sellars 2013.

17 Indeed, it is likely that the apprehension of so many Indigenous children was a direct outcome of the compromised state in which the residential school experience had left so many families and communities.

18 Chelsea Vowel describes the impact of the residential school experience on subsequent Indigenous generations as "historic trauma transition." She explains that this "refers to the cumulative emotional and psychological wounding across generations." See Vowel 2016, 172. See also Frideres 2020, Chapter 5; TRC 2015.

19 The following summary draws heavily from Olthuis, Kleer, Townshend 2012, 375–85.

20 An independent assessment oversight committee was tasked with overseeing the financial compensation process. In its final report in 2021, the committee writes that over the life of the program, $3.23 billion was awarded to 38,276 individuals. In addition, about 7,000 claims were either rejected or withdrawn. See Independent Assessment Oversight Committee 2021, 8.

21 The apology reads in part: "Two primary objectives of the Residential Schools system were to remove and isolate children from the influence of their homes, families, traditions, and cultures, and to assimilate them into the dominant culture. These objectives were based on the assumption that Aboriginal cultures and spiritual beliefs were inferior and unequal. Indeed, some sought, as it was infamously said, 'to kill the Indian in the child.' Today, we recognize that this policy of assimilation was wrong, has caused great harm, and has no place in our country." See Parliament of Canada 2008.

22 The following analysis draws heavily from comments provided to me by one of the anonymous reviewers of this book. I thank them for these important and perceptive insights.

CHAPTER 4

Policy: Signs of a Postcolonial Reality?

LEARNING OBJECTIVES

1. To identify those factors that compelled the Canadian government to finally abandon its longstanding policy of assimilating Indigenous peoples.
2. To explain how the White Paper of 1969 is informed by a liberal theory of justice.
3. To describe how the Supreme Court of Canada's 1973 *Calder* decision both precipitated and lent support to the Government of Canada's decision to take the matter of Aboriginal title seriously.
4. To distinguish between the comprehensive and specific claims processes and describe the kinds of compensation that come to Indigenous peoples by way of each.
5. To explain why recognition of Aboriginal and treaty rights in the Canadian Constitution is so important to Indigenous peoples.
6. To assess the extent to which the 1995 inherent right to self-government policy affirms and supports the Indigenous assertion to sovereignty.
7. To evaluate whether the Justin Trudeau Liberal government's 2015 to 2021 policy reset constitutes a genuine turn toward recognition of Indigenous sovereignty.

This chapter entertains the proposition that in the modern era (post-1969), or fourth stage, the Canadian government's policy tone has begun to change. As described in the previous chapter, after a long period of existing in "separate worlds," the first two stages in the relationship between Indigenous nations and the Canadian state were marked initially by the theme of Indigenous sovereignty both recognized and constrained but later by an insistence that Indigenous peoples must submit themselves to the Canadian state and prepare themselves for assimilation into Canadian citizenship. As we shall see, in the contemporary or fourth stage, significant policy constraints continue to be imposed and thus the presence of colonial relations remains very much a concern for Indigenous peoples. But the current era is also marked by a policy narrative more responsive to Indigenous assertions to sovereignty and to their corresponding right to self-determination. In short, policy indicators suggest that the relationship may well be improving.

What is certainly clear is that Indigenous peoples will no longer allow themselves to be ignored. With remarkable consistency across Canada, Indigenous peoples regularly reject various incarnations of the Canadian state's assimilative policy campaigns. Acts of resistance and persistent challenges to Canadian policies over the years have succeeded in prying loose policy concessions that create genuine spaces in between the practice of Canadian sovereignty for Indigenous political empowerment. As noted by Indigenous scholar John Borrows, "a cause for hope is that Crown sovereignty is beginning to be constrained in Canada" (Borrows 2017a, 28). This chapter identifies and catalogues where those political opportunities exist.

In particular I will focus on the policy shifts that occurred in response to the 1982 recognition of Aboriginal and treaty rights in Section 35 of the Constitution, the Supreme Court of Canada's *Calder* decision of 1973, and the Canadian state's relatively recent acceptance of the age-old Indigenous assertion to an inherent right to self-government. Along the way we will have occasion to examine the significance of a number of policy "milestones," including the 1969 White Paper and 1970 Citizens Plus response; the launch of the comprehensive and specific claims processes; the 1995 inherent right to self-government policy; the 2005 Kelowna Accord; and the capacity of each of the 1983 Penner Committee, the 1992 Charlottetown Accord, and the 1996 Royal Commission on Aboriginal Peoples to precipitate genuine shifts in the direction of an Indigenous policy more committed to "renewal and renegotiation" (RCAP 1996b, 38–40; Metallic 2020, 424). The chapter concludes by examining the credentials of Justin Trudeau's Liberal government's recent claim (2015–21) that it intends to promote reconciliation with Indigenous peoples based on a renewed nation-to-nation, government-to-government, and Inuit–Crown relationship (Newhouse and Belanger 2020, 36). The question that I will consider is whether this declaration promising a significant Canadian governmental policy reset also carries with it an intention to place Indigenous sovereignty at the centre of a renewed relationship.

SOVEREIGNTY RE-EMERGING: POST-1969 INDIGENOUS AMBITIONS

By the early 1970s, it was becoming clear that Canadian governmental policies motivated by ambitions to segregate, educate, and assimilate Indigenous peoples had not worked. The litany of devastation found within Indigenous nations across the country testified to the bankruptcy of the Canadian government's approach. Indigenous peoples' lives were marked by disturbingly high levels of poverty, unemployment, dependency on welfare, and alcoholism, and they were showing up in distressingly high numbers in Canadian courts and the prison system. The result of policy bankruptcy, coupled with political pressure stimulated by the rise of Indigenous political activism across Canada, was a concerted effort on the part of the Canadian government to invent a new policy. After one final disastrous policy campaign in 1969 designed to promote assimilation, the search for a new policy was on and, in many ways, is still in the process of taking shape today.

In the face of policy bankruptcy, the approach to Indigenous–Canadian state relations that emerged post-1970 was one increasingly driven by the ambitions of Indigenous peoples. As Greg Poelzer and Ken Coates explain, "Aboriginal proposals have driven the debate, generating some movement and an increasing amount of critical comment" (Poelzer and Coates 2015, 23). To be sure, there is no single Indigenous perspective on what the future for Indigenous peoples in Canada ought to look like. In the words of Poelzer and Coates, "individual communities have different needs, aspirations, styles of leadership, and social conditions. They will gravitate towards one of a variety of options and will, as many have done, change their tactics over time" (Poelzer and Coates 2015, 23). Nevertheless, despite variety, Indigenous approaches are bound together by a shared concern that they recover the capacity to manage their own affairs. Earlier I described this aspiration as consistent with an Indigenous right to self-determination. What is imperative from the perspective of many Indigenous peoples, in other words, is that the policy of the Canadian state be recast on the premise that Indigenous peoples possess inherent rights to direct their own internal affairs according to their own priorities. Furthermore, in as much as the Canadian state is to be a partner in advancing Indigenous interests, Indigenous peoples also insist that it must do so by first recognizing Indigenous rights, title, and interests, and second by facilitating and guaranteeing to Indigenous nations the means and ability to live as sovereigns (Newhouse and Belanger 2020, 35; Alcantara and Spicer 2016, 186).

In response, we witness in the 1970s the gradual emergence of Canadian Indigenous policy more responsive to Indigenous ambitions. This policy shift has often been frustratingly slow and uneven in its development. But despite obstacles, its emergence has been a steady and inexorable one. Taken together, the cumulative effect of these gradual policy shifts over time has been to create greater opportunities for the rebuilding of Indigenous nations – that is, Indigenous nations have found ways to occupy significant political spaces in between the exercise of Canadian sovereignty and claim those spaces as their own.

However, the sharp turn in Indigenous policy may not have happened at all had it not been for a pivotal event that occurred in 1969. In that year the Canadian government put forward one final policy initiative designed to achieve its assimilative objective. Known as the **White Paper**, Indigenous leaders' vociferous rejection of it led to the formal end of the assimilationist policy period. The fact that Indigenous leaders were so well organized to take the White Paper policy proposal down is also worthy of attention. It is therefore to the rise of Indigenous activism in the postwar period and the rejection of the 1969 White Paper that I turn first.

POST-WORLD WAR II INDIGENOUS ACTIVISM

The relentless and regularly aggressive assimilationist policies of the Canadian government over a period of 100-plus years stimulated a deep sense of injury and injustice within Indigenous nations. Moreover, Indigenous peoples did not stand by as passive or silent recipients. Active protest and resistance against government policy was pursued by Indigenous peoples throughout the twentieth century, though it is only in the past 50 years or so that Indigenous protest has had an appreciable effect in stimulating policy change (Frideres 2020, 20). Early twentieth-century protest took many forms: refusal to cooperate with the terms of the *Indian Act*;[1] carrying on with traditional customs; forwarding petitions to the Canadian and British governments; and forming various Indigenous organizations, to name just a few (Williamson and Roberts 2004, 124). Bev Sellars recounts, for example, how the Allied Tribes of British Columbia, including her own Secwepemc Nation communities, formed in 1915 to petition for rights to their lands through treaties and to demand action on social and economic problems confronting their peoples, all to little effect given Canada's by then deep commitment to the containment and assimilation of Indigenous peoples (Sellars 2016, 78–9; see also Miller 1989, 214–20).

Other acts of resistance occurred in less "visible" ways at the community level. For example, it was not uncommon for Indigenous families to be absent when it came time to round up children to send them to far-away residential schools (Miller 2004, 251). In addition, many Indigenous peoples of the west coast continued to practise the Potlatch in secret locations despite *Indian Act* prohibitions outlawing the practice (Sellars 2016, 125–6). Also, it was common practice for Indigenous peoples to leave their reserve communities without permission, despite the requirement that they could not leave "unless they had a pass signed by the Indian agent" (Sellars 2016, 82). And Indigenous constitutional orders were also regularly upheld in which political pride of place was retained for hereditary chiefs and other traditional leaders who often operated and provided leadership alongside *Indian Act* band councils (Coates 2008, 5). J.R. Miller documents with considerable detail, for example, how each of the Mohawk of Akwesasne near Cornwall, Ontario, and the Six Nations near Brantford, Ontario, defied *Indian Act* interference with their own traditional self-governance systems by opting to retain their ancient appointive systems instead (Miller 2004, 71–7).

Miller also documents the influence that various Indigenous political organizations, particularly those formed in the first half of the twentieth century, had on "undermining the foundations of Canadian Indian policy" (Miller 2004, 254). He points to organizations formed in Ontario and the western provinces as being particularly effective in this regard, though he also observes that "the emergence of an enduring and effective national body would have to wait until the 1960s" (Miller 2004, 254). For example, nationally, the League of Indians of Canada was formed after World War I. The League of Western Indians was formed in the 1920s, and the Union of Saskatchewan Indians and Indian Association of Alberta were formed in the 1930s. The North American Indian Brotherhood was established after World War II, while the National Indian Council was constituted in 1961. All have since disbanded with other Indigenous organizations since filling their vacancies (Williamson and Roberts 2004, 124; Belanger 2018, 238–46). These organizations sought redress on matters such as the Canadian government's refusal to honour the terms of treaties, its failure to protect Indigenous hunting and fishing rights, and its disregard for negotiating treaties in advance of occupying traditional Indigenous territories (Poelzer and Coates 2015, 11) In short, Indigenous peoples protested and resisted wherever and whenever they could. The fact that they were relatively unsuccessful in dislodging the structures of assimilative policy until the late 1960s is testament to the determination and resolve of the Canadian government to see its policy through (Miller 2004, 77; see also Ponting 1997, 43–4).[2] Indeed, fearing that Indigenous protest might well prove successful, in 1927 the Canadian government outlawed the organization of Indigenous political groups, thereby effectively preventing them from lobbying for their rights. This sanction prohibiting Indigenous political organization beyond the band or tribal level remained in place until 1951 (Hedican 2013, 26; Sellars 2016, 88, 96).

Many of the policy constraints imposed on Indigenous peoples' right to organize began to be lifted by the 1960s. Indeed, the 1960s provided a rich environment for the incubation of an Indigenous movement dedicated to decolonizing Indigenous relations with the Canadian state. In the post–World War II recovery environment, global human rights talk was at a premium, as were liberation movements for nations that had been former European colonies (Papillon 2014, 116). As Miller puts it, "after all, in the midst of a war against institutionalized racism and barbarity, it was impossible not to notice that the basis of Canadian Indian policy lay in assumptions about the moral and economic inferiority of particular racial groupings" (Miller 1989, 220). Many began to see that Indigenous peoples in North and South America, including Canada, were also victims of colonialism and had been subjected to profound human rights abuses.

Accordingly, Indigenous peoples began to organize, mobilizing themselves in ways that were inspired by the American civil rights movement as well as the anti-colonial liberation movements found throughout the developing world (Miller 1989, 233). National Indigenous political organizations quickly emerged, beginning with the National Indian Council (1961–8), followed by the National Indian Brotherhood (1968–82), and then reconstituted as the Assembly of First Nations in 1982 (Belanger 2018, 247; Hedican 2013, 26). Non-status and Métis groups formed the Native

Council of Canada (since renamed the Congress of Aboriginal Peoples), while the Inuit formed the Inuit Tapirisat of Canada (since renamed the Inuit Tapiriit Kanatami). Each was, and continues to be, a high-profile national forum for the expression of Indigenous concerns and ambitions. As Martin Papillon explains, these organizations regularly serve as powerful platforms for calling into question not only colonial policies such as the *Indian Act*, but also "the very legitimacy of federal and provincial authority over their lands and communities" (Papillon 2014, 116). In other words, the antidote to federal and provincial control is invariably presented by these organizations in the language of enhanced Indigenous political autonomy.

In addition to acting through these four and many other organizations, Indigenous peoples have also resorted to acts of civil disobedience from time to time, including sit-ins and blockades. Other avenues that Indigenous peoples have employed include appealing to international agencies like the United Nations, petitioning the public directly through media outlets, and engaging in activism through the creation of specific movements. A good example of the latter is the organic Idle No More movement. Launched in 2012 by four women (three Indigenous and one non-Indigenous), the immediate focus of its ambition was to confront federal omnibus legislation (Bill C-45) that had been enacted by the Stephen Harper Conservative government and which was seen to pose a significant threat to "Indigenous conceptions of responsibility for water and the natural environment" (Newhouse and Belanger 2020, 50). Underneath, however, the Idle No More movement was about so much more. Essentially, it was a broad-based movement dedicated to providing a forum for Indigenous assertions to self-confidence and to efforts dedicated to dismantling the legacy and ongoing operation of colonial control, especially over Indigenous relationships to water and land (Palmater 2015, 76–83; Coates 2015). Acts of resistance against the Canadian state came in multiple, often festive forms, including peaceful demonstrations, "teach-ins," flash mobs, and dramatic, often spontaneous, performances of the Round Dance.[3]

In the most desperate of circumstances, Indigenous peoples have also occasionally engaged in violent confrontations with the Canadian state. Scholars who study such violent confrontations generally conclude, however, that in all but the rarest of cases, settlements favouring Indigenous interests are seldom the outcome (Morden 2013, 506). They say that the Canadian state is simply not interested in "rewarding" confrontational tactics like land occupations and road and site blockades by agreeing to resource harvesting rights or land transfers, to name but two examples. As pointed out by Michael Morden, the far more likely outcome is that either the status quo is maintained or glacially paced negotiations are undertaken, usually leading to outcomes that favour the interests of federal and provincial governments (Morden 2013, 506).[4] The protest initiatives of Teme-Augama Anishnabai (1988), the Labrador Innu (1988), the Lubicon Lake Cree (1988), the Mohawk Warrior Society of Oka (1990), the Gustafsen Lake standoff (1995), and the Mi'kmaq fishing dispute at Burnt Church (2002) are just a few examples that come readily to mind.[5]

THE 1969 WHITE PAPER AND THE 1970 CITIZENS PLUS RESPONSE

It was the introduction of the 1969 White Paper (otherwise known as the Statement of the Government of Canada on Indian Policy), however, that single-handedly ushered in a whole new phase of highly antagonistic and contentious relations between Indigenous peoples and the Canadian state.[6] The White Paper had a way of crystallizing Indigenous protest like nothing else before it because "it threatened to obliterate Indian special status and, by extension, Indian identity, in one fell swoop" (Schouls 2003, 42; see also Manuel 2015, 30). The White Paper was so provocative, say some, that it set off Indigenous nations, as well as Indigenous provincial and national organizations, "in a burst of self-defining energy across the country" (Cassidy and Bish 1989, 11). A massive mobilization effort was undertaken by Indigenous peoples across the country to get the proposed White Paper policy retracted. Arthur Manuel describes this effort as "the battle of the decade" (Manuel 2015, 30). Indigenous peoples were determined to establish once and for all that the Canadian government had no business designing a policy plan for them without their peoples taking the lead in setting the agenda.

In 1969, Prime Minister Pierre Trudeau unveiled his White Paper on Indian Policy. It was Trudeau's view that all Canadians should enjoy individual freedom and equality with each citizen having access to exactly the same set of individual rights. He was highly suspicious of special status for groups (like Quebec), believing that special rights and status granted on linguistic or cultural grounds simply promoted ethnic separatism and an entirely unnecessary and highly regrettable fragmentation of the political order. On these grounds, Trudeau was convinced that federal Indian policy was seriously flawed. In his view, stringent controls by means of the *Indian Act* and isolation by means of reserves had not promoted Indian liberation but had instead created Indian dependency on governmental assistance. Paternalistic administration and distinct legal status had denied Indians their right to individual liberty and equality, thereby causing them to be "inward" looking, or so the White Paper argued (Schouls 2002, 19; Miller 2004, 258). The White Paper essentially accused the Canadian government of driving artificial wedges between Indians and the Canadian mainstream and therefore it was largely responsible for causing Indian apathy and poverty (Government of Canada 1969, 3). From the Trudeau government's perspective at the time, Indian policy to that point had been nothing short of discriminatory because it had "kept the Indian people apart from and behind other Canadians" (Government of Canada 1969, 5; see also Newhouse and Belanger 2020, 40; Sellars 2016, 109). The fact that Indians placed so much importance on their ethnic and cultural identities was simply taken to be an understandable but negative outcome of their experience of exclusion.

By way of solution, the White Paper argued that if Indians were to enjoy their right to "full, free, and non-discriminatory participation … in Canadian society" there would have to be a fundamental policy "break with the past" (Government of Canada 1969, 5). The new policy would be based on individual equality and would encourage the full and equal participation of Indians in all aspects of Canadian society. To that end, the

White Paper proposed to dismantle all Indian status provisions. The Indian Affairs bureaucracy was to be dismantled, reserves would be converted to private property that could then be bought or sold by band members,[7] legal status for Indians would be abolished, the *Indian Act* would be repealed, and all responsibility for Indian education, health care, and social services would be transferred to the provinces. The White Paper also advanced the view that treaties provided little if any value to Indians and so proposed that a review be conducted to determine how treaties could be "equitably ended" (Government of Canada 1969, 11; see also Manuel 2015, 29–32; Miller 1989, 226–7; Miller 2004, 258; Newhouse and Belanger 2020, 40; Sellars 2016, 110; Vowel 2016, 269). In Trudeau's words, "it is inconceivable that in a given society, one section of the society would have a treaty with another section of the society. We must be equal under the laws and we must not sign treaties amongst ourselves" (as quoted in Manuel 2015, 31). In short, the White Paper proposed that all the distinctive collective rights of Indians be dismantled to pave the way for a full Indian integration into the individualistic Canadian mainstream. As summarized by J.R. Miller, "the proposed policy was the bluntest and most threatening assimilative effort the federal government had come up with yet" (Miller 2004, 258). Only once fully assimilated, it was thought, would the problems of Indians be well and truly over.

It is important to understand the philosophical context of the times in which the White Paper was introduced. The Black civil rights movement that was sweeping across the United States and had so powerfully captured public attention took direct aim at exposing the deep structural racism and discrimination experienced by Black Americans and other minority groups. The solution that many proposed was a universal extension of individual rights and opportunities to all disadvantaged minorities, without distinction, including removal of all barriers to their full economic, social, and political participation. It is not surprising, therefore, that the Canadian government's approach would be to seek to empower individual Indigenous persons by pursuing policies that would have them integrated into the Canadian social, economic, and political mainstream. After all, it was precisely this integrative approach that was being taken with respect to Black Americans, women, and other ethnic and racial minorities in the United States. In this sense, the White Paper's perspective was entirely in keeping with the philosophical assumptions of those pursuing social justice in the 1960s (Poelzer and Coates 2015, 18). Governmental policymakers were deeply committed to liberal values and as such regarded the conferral of special status on Indigenous peoples to be highly regressive and discriminatory. As put by Augie Fleras and Jean Elliott, "many of those policy-makers were convinced that conferral of formal equality and protection of individual, civil, and human rights represented a step forward for aboriginal peoples, accelerating their movement into the twentieth century" (Fleras and Elliott 1992, 43).

The Canadian government was not prepared for the strongly negative and swift reaction that greeted this proposed new liberal approach to Indian policy. Indigenous nations and associations quickly galvanized across Canada, issuing their official response to the White Paper to Cabinet a year later by way of a document called

Citizens Plus (Manuel 2015, 30, 32; Miller 1989, 230; Sellars 2016, 110). It categorically rejected the White Paper on the grounds that it threatened to destroy Indians as distinct nations. It further argued that the new policy completely ignored the concept of collective rights and the fact that Indigenous peoples place tremendous value on their nation-based identities. Indigenous identity simply "cannot be reduced to an individual or private quality as the White Paper suggested" (Schouls 2002, 20). Instead, Citizens Plus offered quite a different perspective on the nature of Indigenous identity and rights. Indigenous identity can only be developed and expressed within the communal context of Indigenous nations, and for that to occur Indigenous nations must enjoy autonomy and the corresponding capacity to be self-defining. It is this imperative that the White Paper completely failed to appreciate and as such, it was accused of engaging in "the destruction of a nation of people by legislation and cultural genocide" (Manuel 2015, 32).

Particularly galling to Indigenous leaders were the White Paper's proposals to dismantle those structural features in the relationship between the Canadian state and Indigenous nations that were central to supporting the Indigenous capacity for collective autonomy.[8] Citizens Plus advanced a fundamental challenge to the idea that the "isolation" and "discrimination" purportedly promoted by Indigenous rights and distinct status were responsible for the high levels of poverty and social dysfunction found in so many Indigenous nations. Rather, Citizens Plus argued that much of the damage had been caused by the paternalistic and grossly negligent manner in which the Canadian government had historically administered Indigenous rights. A commitment by the federal government to uphold its treaty obligations, for example, would undoubtedly have contributed to maintaining healthy, vibrant Indigenous nations. Indigenous land would have been protected; hunting, fishing, and trapping rights maintained; and health care, educational facilities, and economic development provided (Newhouse and Belanger 2020, 41; Schouls 2002, 20; Vowel 2016, 270). In short, the problem was entirely of the Canadian government's own making because it had neglected its responsibilities to protect Indigenous rights and lands, to respond adequately to Indigenous needs, and to facilitate Indigenous efforts at self-determination. So, while Indigenous leaders were in full agreement with Canadian policymakers that the Department of Indian Affairs and the *Indian Act* were in need of major overhauls, Indigenous leaders were of the view that these overhauls needed to be carried out with Indigenous participation and consent and in ways that genuinely advanced Indigenous interests and rights.

The Trudeau government withdrew the White Paper within a year (March 1971), admitting that it had failed to adequately address the problems of Indigenous peoples. Trudeau even went so far as to admit that his government's preoccupation with liberal values had contributed significantly to the policy's inappropriateness (Schouls 2002, 20; Miller 1989, 231; Metallic 2020, 427). Yet White Paper-like policy proposals and the individualistic vision upon which the policy relied are still staunchly defended today among a minority of policymakers and scholars (Manuel 2015, 35; Vowel 2016, 271–4).[9] For the most part, however, the retraction of the White Paper signalled an important turning point in the direction of Canadian Indigenous policy to one more favourably predisposed to the positions of Indigenous peoples. Indigenous activism and a vibrant Indigenous decolonizing movement that was both unified and militant had won a significant victory. Indeed, Arthur Manuel declares with somewhat guarded (and skeptical) optimism that "the effective blocking action against immediate White Paper implementation that our fathers and mothers' generation undertook at the beginning of the 1970s kept the wolf from the door. Over the following 10 years, they would win a crucial court battle on Aboriginal title and rights and launch a massive campaign to ensure our rights were enshrined in the Canadian constitution. This battle would provide us with a constitutional tool for our nation-building efforts" (Manuel 2015, 35).

As we shall see in forthcoming chapters, Manuel's tempered optimism is well placed given the reality of ongoing Canadian state interests that continue to shape, and ultimately constrain, Indigenous rights and the Indigenous capacity to exercise political sovereignty. Nevertheless, while real limitations upon Indigenous rights continue to exist, the policy ground is shifting and the Indigenous capacity to exercise sovereignty is re-emerging. Indigenous peoples continue to press their case for Aboriginal title and rights, and they are achieving results by way of court decisions, constitutional recognition, treaty rights, and governmental endorsement of the Indigenous inherent right to self-government (Metallic 2020, 427). Prospects for a return to a Two-Row Wampum relationship are not out of the question.

THE 1973 *CALDER* DECISION AND THE LAUNCH OF THE COMPREHENSIVE AND SPECIFIC CLAIMS PROCESS

Across much of Canada, Indigenous peoples signed treaties in which they agreed to release some of their territories for settlers to occupy in exchange for a package of benefits including reserves. Particularly in the Canadian north and British Columbia, however, only a handful of treaties were signed, leaving First Nations and Inuit peoples in these parts of the country without reassurances that their right to occupy their traditional territories would be protected. Add in the Métis, and what we have is an Indigenous population in Canada, about one-third of which lack a land base that is legally and politically protected for their exclusive use and occupation. This situation created the setting for the emergence of the legal term **Aboriginal title**. Aboriginal title can be defined as an Indigenous right to land ownership based on traditional occupancy and use since time immemorial.

CALDER DECISION (1973)

Since the 1970s, a steady rush of court decisions has lent justification to Indigenous arguments that they have both rights and title and that these have consistently been neglected or dismissed by Canadian governments. In 1973 the Supreme Court of Canada started down the Aboriginal rights and title path when it decided ***Calder v. Attorney General of British Columbia***. The Nisga'a Nation of northwestern British Columbia sought a court declaration that they had Aboriginal title to their traditional territories in the Nass River Valley and that this title had never been terminated. The Nisga'a crafted their legal argument on the premise that they and their ancestors had continuously occupied and used their ancestral lands from time immemorial. They were the first occupants of the land and could trace evidence of the Nisga'a having lived continuously on the land right through to the present day. Based on rights of first and continuous occupancy, therefore, the Nisga'a claimed that they had a legal and moral right to their land.

Six of the seven Supreme Court justices agreed with the Nisga'a that the concept of Aboriginal title had both free-standing legal validity and is recognized in Canadian common law (Hamilton and Sinclair 1991, 123). However, Justice Judson, speaking for three members of the Court, held that whatever Aboriginal title the Nisga'a may have had to their land had since been extinguished. According to the judge, Nisga'a title simply could not have been sustained in the face of pre-Confederation legislation dealing with Crown land as the two uses would have been incompatible. On these grounds, he argued, Nisga'a title had simply been terminated even though no direct legislative measures had been taken to do so. On the other side, Justice Hall, also speaking for three members of the Court, agreed that the Nisga'a had Aboriginal title to their land based on original occupancy and use and "that Aboriginal title could be terminated only by legislation that explicitly stated this effect in clear and plain language" (Hamilton and Sinclair 1991, 123). As no such legislation could be identified in the Nisga'a case, the evidence suggested that Nisga'a title continued to exist (Hedican 2013, 72). The seventh judge dismissed the Nisga'a's application on procedural grounds, and so the Nisga'a lost their case. Despite the loss, however, the real significance of the *Calder* decision lay in the important legal precedent that had been established. The Supreme Court ruled that Aboriginal title does not derive from British or Canadian sources like that of the Royal Proclamation of 1763. Instead, Aboriginal title originates from sources outside of it, namely, within the empirical and verifiable reality of prior Indigenous occupation and continuous use of lands (Metallic 2020, 429). Furthermore, unless there is an explicit surrender of land by means of a treaty or some other valid legal process, the Aboriginal title of Indigenous nations remains intact.

The practical implications of the Supreme Court's ruling on the standing of Aboriginal title in law were immense given that much of the north, significant portions of Quebec, and virtually all of British Columbia were not covered by treaties. The Supreme Court effectively forced the Canadian government's hand in that it now had little choice but to accept the fact that Indigenous nations had a strong legal basis in Canadian law to press their land title rights. Interestingly enough, the Canadian government had intended to introduce federal legislation establishing an Indian Claims Commission to consider and decide Indigenous land claims as early as 1965 (Miller 1989, 227). However, in the rush to introduce the very differently pitched policy of the 1969 White Paper, this intention was abandoned on the grounds that a claims commission designed to compensate Indigenous peoples for loss of lands and resources was not the best way to deal with Indigenous land grievances. The vehement Indigenous rejection of the White Paper, coupled with the substantial legal weight lent to the concept of Aboriginal title by the *Calder* decision, forced the government's hand, compelling a return to its original policy intention. In 1973, Indian Affairs Minister Jean Chrétien announced a new federal policy designed to negotiate and settle Aboriginal title claims. The government divided all outstanding grievances into two categories: **comprehensive claims**, which originate in Aboriginal title that have not been dealt with through treaty or other legal processes, and **specific claims**, which seek to address complaints arising from unfulfilled treaty obligations or reserve-based land issues (Metallic 2020, 429).

COMPREHENSIVE CLAIMS

The comprehensive land claims negotiations process was officially launched when the Office of Native Claims opened its doors in Ottawa in 1974 and invited submission of proposals. The first agreement to be reached was in 1975 with the Cree and Inuit of James Bay and northern Quebec. By the end of 2020, the Canadian government and Indigenous negotiators had signed 26 comprehensive land claims and 4 self-government agreements. Of the 26 signed agreements, 18 either include provisions related to the exercise of self-government or have accompanying self-government agreements. These 26 agreements cover approximately 40 per cent of Canada's land mass (Frideres 2020, 154). In addition, at the BC level, the British Columbia Treaty Process was established in 1993 to resolve outstanding land and resources issues in the province. As of 2020, this process has resulted in seven final agreements coming into effect (BC Treaty Commission 2020, 18).[10]

Comprehensive claims agreements focus on defining and setting out the extent of Indigenous rights to lands and resources within an Indigenous nation's traditional territories. They can also contain provisions relating to self-government (like establishing law-making authority in such areas as governance, social and economic development, education, health, culture and language, and more), cash payments and taxation, administration of justice, and membership. In all cases, agreements are instrumental in setting out clear terms for an Indigenous nation's future economic development. They also involve removing the Indigenous nation from the provisions of the *Indian Act* and, as such, can be seen as a definitive step taken in the direction of decolonization. In addition, comprehensive claim agreements are given status as constitutionally protected treaty rights under Section 35 of the ***Constitution Act, 1982***.

SPECIFIC CLAIMS

Running alongside the modern treaty-making process to settle comprehensive land claims is the specific claims process. It provides redress for historical grievances arising from unfulfilled obligations under the historic treaties or from the improper management of Indigenous lands or other assets. Most specific claims originate from two sources. First, there are those Indigenous nations that advance specific claims on the grounds that they did not acquire the total amount of reserve lands their treaty had originally promised. Second, there are those Indigenous nations that advance claims on the grounds that much of the land that had been dedicated to them as reserves was lost over time due to the land being arbitrarily seized by the Canadian government for public works; rights of way for railways, pipelines, or hydro transmission lines; or European settlement (Hamilton and Sinclair 1991, 175). Redress of specific claims usually comes in the form of transfers of provincial Crown lands to Indigenous nations and monetary payments. Monetary payments are typically offered as a form of compensation for insufficient payment for surrendered reserve lands or for "failure to pay proper interest rates on band trust funds held in Ottawa, misdirection of annuity payments, and misapplication of band revenue from lease or sale of reserve land" (Hamilton and Sinclair 1991, 176).

The specific claims negotiation process launched in 1973 quickly gained a reputation for being exceedingly slow. Consequently, in 2008 a more efficient process was established, enabling Indigenous nations to procure the services of the independent Specific Claims Tribunal. This tribunal was authorized to make binding decisions and to award financial compensation to a maximum of $150 million. Indigenous nations typically approach the tribunal for assistance if their claims have not been accepted for negotiation by the Canadian government or if their claims are not settled in a timely manner (i.e., within three years) (Frideres 2020, 157). Since 1973, the Canadian government has settled hundreds of specific claims, though it should be said that the terms agreed to are not always in keeping with the results hoped for by the negotiating Indigenous nation (Metallic 2020, 430). Nevertheless, James Anaya, the former UN special rapporteur on the rights of Indigenous peoples, did observe in a 2014 report that the treaty land entitlement mechanism, designed to settle land debts, had significantly enhanced the land base owed to many First Nations (Anaya 2014, 18).

CRITICISMS

Despite the fact that Indigenous nations have received compensation for their unfulfilled Aboriginal and treaty rights, the comprehensive and specific claims processes have nevertheless been subjected to considerable criticism over the years, some since addressed, others not. In the "not addressed" category is the fact that the comprehensive claims process is notoriously slow, taking on average 25 years for the Canadian government and an Indigenous nation to complete (Frideres 2020, 154). The interminably slow pace to the negotiations can be attributed in part to their sheer complexity. Final agreements can run on for hundreds of pages and typically are divided into many chapters covering such diverse topics as lands, forests, roads and rights of way, fisheries, wildlife and migratory birds, environmental assessment, governance, justice, fiscal relations and taxation, cultural artifacts, dispute resolution, eligibility and enrolment, and implementation. But at the same time, there are other, less justifiable, reasons to explain why the pace of negotiations is so frustratingly slow. Naiomi Walqwan Metallic, for example, explains that "as a policy of the federal government ... the process is often contingent on the attitude and political will of the government in power, and some governments have been very slow to proceed on land claims" (Metallic 2020, 430). Essentially, federal governments are known to dedicate inadequate resources to the negotiation process itself, allocating an insufficient number of days and trained negotiators to the respective treaty tables, to name just one example.

But even more egregiously, the process has also been criticized for failing to deliver results consistent with what Indigenous peoples take to be the full measure of their rights. Arthur Manuel observes, for example, that "the federal government has kept the benefits so low and they demand so much ... that negotiators know they could not get support for a deal from their own people. Therefore, the negotiations go on and on and never bear fruit" (Manuel 2017, 114). Areas that have been targeted for particular criticism are the land, resources, and self-government allocations, each of which Indigenous negotiators regularly identify as falling well short of the kind of compensation they need (and to which their peoples are entitled) if they are to rebuild strong and robust Indigenous nations.

A second area of criticism relates to finances. The financial costs of negotiations are prohibitively high, which has posed a particular burden on Indigenous nations, most of whom have access to limited financial resources. Recognizing the problem, Ottawa offered Indigenous nations loans to help finance their participation in treaty negotiations. The catch, however, was that until recently all loans had to be repaid from the cash settlement portion of the final settlement. As the costs of negotiations were often considerable and thus the loans high, the corresponding and disappointing reality was that the actual monies received in cash settlements were often far less than had originally been agreed to. Under these restrictive financial terms, therefore, it is not surprising that many Indigenous nations would simply have no appetite to engage in comprehensive claims negotiations at all. Bonita Lawrence points out the irony inherent to the design of this entire process: "In seeking title to the land, they [Indigenous nations] are forced to borrow money from the very government that appropriated their lands and resources [and thus the source of their wealth] in the first place" (Lawrence 2012, 70; see also Bellrichard 2019, 3).

Repeated petitions from Indigenous leaders that the loan program be repealed on the grounds that it was fundamentally unfair finally met with a favourable response in 2019. As part of its 2019 budget commitment, the federal government announced that it would forgive all loans granted to Indigenous nations that had taken on debt to finance their comprehensive claims negotiations. In addition, all those who had already repaid their loans would get their money back (Bellrichard 2019, 2). Repayment would proceed in five equal annual instalments beginning in April 2020. Going forward, the federal government also declared it would support all comprehensive and treaty negotiations by providing Indigenous nations with non-repayable contribution funding. The estimated total amount to be repaid or forgiven was pegged at $1.4 billion (Bellrichard 2019, 2).

The third area of criticism relates to the matter of Indigenous rights. Critics have long pointed out that, until recently, Ottawa has designed the comprehensive claims process to minimize recognition of Aboriginal rights. For example, in 1973 the federal government's position was that Indigenous nations must agree to "extinguish" all their Aboriginal and treaty rights within a settlement area in exchange for the rights and benefits provided in their final agreement. When Indigenous peoples objected to the proposition that their rights be extinguished, Ottawa adopted a new approach beginning in 1986, this time captured by the concepts "modify" and "non-assert." In the first case, Indigenous rights would no longer be extinguished but rather "modified" as set out in the terms of the treaty. In the second case, Indigenous rights would continue to exist, but would never be exercised or relied upon in the future. Instead, an Indigenous nation would confine itself to using only those rights contained within their treaty.

Indigenous leaders have regularly condemned all three approaches. They argue that they should not have to give up their Indigenous rights in exchange for the rights and benefits listed in settlement agreements. If they do so, they say that they will have effectively agreed to submit themselves to a political authority that neutralizes them as sovereign entities (Lawrence 2012, 75). Instead, argue these leaders, comprehensive claims agreements must be built on recognition of Aboriginal rights and title, not on their extinguishment or modification. In response to arguments such as these, the federal government agreed to change its position in 2017. Going forward, the Liberal government of Justin Trudeau declared that "where agreements are formed, they should be based on the recognition and implementation of rights and not on their extinguishment, modification, or surrender" (Government of Canada 2017b, 4) To that end, Trudeau instructed his then minister of Crown–Indigenous Relations (Carolyn Bennett) to work with First Nations, Inuit, and Métis to redesign the comprehensive claims and inherent rights policies (Wilson-Raybould 2019, 173).

Concerning specific claims, critics observe that the Canadian government tends to favour monetary compensation over returning traditional lands (Anaya 2014, 18). Yet for many Indigenous nations return of traditional lands is their preferred option, particularly so because land carries considerable potential for land use and resource development ventures. As for those deemed eligible, the federal government unilaterally decided that the specific claims process is to be limited to First Nations and Inuit claimants alone, "except in the Yukon and Northwest Territories where the Métis and non-status Indians are included" (Hamilton and Sinclair 1991, 124). This leaves the Métis in the rest of the country without a formal process through which to negotiate specific claims (Metallic 2020, 430). And finally, the federal government has long held the position that the historical treaties signed across Ontario and the prairies included land surrenders (despite Indigenous assertions that the treaties actually constitute land-sharing agreements). Consequently, Indigenous nations under treaty are not eligible to submit proposals for a comprehensive claim to reacquire access to their traditional unceded territories, for example. All that is open to them is the specific claims process, and then only in the event of a specific treaty right violation.

POSITIVE DEVELOPMENTS

Despite criticisms, positive developments can be identified as well. Most important is the fact that the entire comprehensive and specific claims process exists because Indigenous nations do possess Aboriginal title. The fact that both types are being negotiated indicates that Canada now accepts the fact that the charges of injustice levelled against it are justified. As captured by Hamilton and Sinclair, "there is a realization today that the honour of the Crown has been besmirched badly by the immoral and sometimes illegal actions of the federal government regarding reserve lands and band assets for over a century" (Hamilton and Sinclair 1991, 177). Good faith negotiations that seek to rectify these injustices, therefore, have the potential to restore trust and promote reconciliation between the Canadian state and Indigenous nations. There are also considerable benefits to be had as a result of successful negotiations. Clear legal title and a corresponding capacity to manage land and resources can do much to facilitate the building of an economy, social well-being, and a more promising future (Hamilton and Sinclair 1991, 177). In short, claims agreements can also be said to provide a building block for the re-emergence of Indigenous sovereignty and for a new relationship with Canada. Just how this is to be accomplished is a topic taken up in Chapter 7.

SECTION 35 OF THE *CONSTITUTION ACT, 1982*

Canada's political relationship with Indigenous peoples is mediated by a constitutional arrangement that offers significant protection to Aboriginal rights. Building on the foundation of the British Crown's Royal Proclamation of 1763, the Canadian *Constitution Act, 1982* finally entrenched Aboriginal rights into the highest law of the land in the early 1980s. These constitutional provisions offer protection to Aboriginal title based on historical occupation and use of land, to treaty rights, and to Aboriginal rights associated with practices integral to the distinctive ways of life practised by Indigenous nations (Courchene 2018, 90).

Constitutional recognition of Aboriginal rights only came about, however, as a result of widespread Indigenous protests in response to federal–provincial constitutional negotiations in 1981–2 that deliberately left the issue of Indigenous rights off the table (Frideres 2020, 17). Indigenous leaders were motivated to act because they feared that if Indigenous rights did not receive constitutional recognition or protection, it would be but an easy step for the Canadian government to violate their treaty commitments and further damage their rights, or even repeal their rights altogether (Hamilton and Sinclair 1991, 124). But on the positive side, Indigenous leaders also believed that if they could get their Indigenous rights constitutionally recognized and protected, that would go some considerable way in guaranteeing no further erosion of those rights and quite possibly also pave the way for their future growth and development. As Hamilton and Sinclair put it, with Aboriginal and treaty rights constitutionally protected, "the possibility was created to achieve proper respect for these rights in the supreme law of the land" (Hamilton and Sinclair 1991, 124).[11]

The *Constitution Act, 1982* contained two provisions of particular importance to Indigenous peoples. **Section 25** guaranteed that the *Charter of Rights and Freedoms* would "not be construed so as to abrogate or derogate from any Aboriginal, treaty, or other rights or freedoms pertaining to the Aboriginal peoples of Canada, including any rights recognized by the Royal Proclamation of 1763" and any "rights or freedoms that now exist by way of land claims agreements or may be so acquired." **Section 35** recognized and affirmed "the existing Aboriginal and treaty rights of the Aboriginal peoples of Canada," which include the "Indian, Inuit, and Métis peoples." An important matter of interpretation must be emphasized at this point. From the perspective of Indigenous leaders, it was absolutely imperative that the Aboriginal rights recognized in Sections 25 and 35 not be seen as having their origin in the Canadian Constitution.

Instead, Indigenous leaders insisted that those rights be understood as having their origins within Indigenous nations, thus placing those nations in a position of political and legal equivalency to that of the Canadian state (Manuel 2017, 98).[12] When interpreted in this way, Indigenous leaders were of the view that the standing of their peoples, both within Canadian law and Canadian politics, could be dramatically transformed (Hamilton and Sinclair 1991, 125).

Significantly however, while Section 35 recognizes and affirms the (pre)existence of Indigenous rights, it does not define them. As a result, Section 37 of the *Constitution Act, 1982* (since repealed) guaranteed that a First Ministers' Conference on Indigenous constitutional issues would be convened with Indigenous leaders representing the major First Nation, Inuit, and Métis organizations. The focal point for discussion at these conferences became the Indigenous right to self-government. Four conferences, held between 1983 and 1987, failed to achieve a constitutional amendment on this matter.[13] Contrary to Indigenous positions, several premiers insisted that the right to self-government must be clearly defined in law, subject to negotiations, and exercised as delegated powers originating from within the Canadian Constitution (Hamilton and Sinclair 1991, 126; Miller 2004, 85). Arthur Manuel (along with many others) expressed his profound disappointment in the process, concluding that once again "it was impossible to underestimate the depth and intransigence of the colonial mindset in Canada" (Manuel 2015, 7; see also Manuel 2017, 99).[14]

Given these conflicting positions, one could reasonably ask whether the recognition and protection of Aboriginal and treaty rights under Section 35 carries any real weight at all. On this score there has been much debate. There are those who are at best dubious about the kind of protection afforded by Section 35. Stó:lō writer Lee Maracle is one who argues against the merits of Section 35. She maintains that if Indigenous peoples accept the Canadian Constitution as the "Supreme Law" through which their rights are mediated, they effectively reinforce colonialism because they agree to submit themselves to the Constitution of the settler state. It would be far better, in her view, that Section 35 reflect a true nation-to-nation relationship. To meet this standard, Section 35 would have to recognize the free-standing Indigenous right to self-determination as operating outside of and parallel to the Canadian Constitution (Maracle 2003, 310; see also Papillon 2014, 119). James Tully makes virtually the same point, conceding that Section 35 does offer "degrees of recognition and accommodation to Indigenous peoples." However, he also says that because the recognition is entrenched in the Canadian Constitution, the sovereignty of the Canadian state over Indigenous peoples is not challenged but only further entrenched (Tully 2008, 269). In short, as put by Jody Wilson-Raybould, "some Indigenous leaders were not comfortable with section 35, fearing the domestication of [their Aboriginal] rights" and further subjection of Aboriginal peoples "to an absolutely sovereign Crown" (Wilson-Raybould 2019, 49).

On the other hand, Julie Jai argues that the 1982 constitutional provisions and subsequent Supreme Court of Canada decisions on Aboriginal and treaty rights (to be examined in the next chapter) have substantially increased the bargaining power of Indigenous nations (Jai 2017, 115–16). It is no longer the case, for example, that the Canadian government can deny, impair, or extinguish Aboriginal and treaty rights at will. All negotiations with Indigenous nations concerning their lands, resources, or governmental powers now begin from the indubitable fact that Indigenous rights exist in Canadian constitutional law and so must be respected.

A slightly different but closely related point is made by Indigenous legal scholar John Borrows. He describes the constitutionally protected Aboriginal and treaty rights in Section 35 as a declaration of intent on the part of the Canadian state to place limits on its assertion to sovereignty over Indigenous peoples. Where Aboriginal and treaty rights exist, the Canadian state is now obliged to exercise a duty of non-interference (Frideres 2020, 196). It is Borrows's hope, therefore, that when fully operationalized, this duty of non-interference will guarantee to Indigenous peoples the protected spaces they need to consolidate their hold on lands, resources, and political power consistent with their right to self-determination (Borrows 2017a, 28). Kiera Ladner lends her voice to this hopeful sentiment. She writes, "the new constitutional order enables Aboriginal peoples to reclaim and reassert their nationhood, sovereignty, and independence." She further adds, "the *Constitution Act, 1982* inspired Aboriginal peoples to think that change was possible and that a post-colonial future was attainable" (Ladner 2003, 52). It is also worth pointing out that Canada is the only settler state in the world to have a section within its Constitution devoted explicitly to the recognition and protection of Aboriginal rights. This leads one observer to comment that while imperfect, it nevertheless elicits envy in some circles, including among Indigenous peoples in the United States, Australia, and New Zealand.[15]

THE 1995 INHERENT RIGHT TO SELF-GOVERNMENT POLICY

The Canadian government's approach to Indigenous self-government was set out in its 1995 **Inherent Right Policy** and remains its policy approach to this day. The 1995 policy certainly constituted a significant advance on what had existed before insofar as it lent explicit recognition to the Indigenous inherent right to self-government. In its words, the "Government of Canada recognizes the inherent right of self-government as an existing right within Section 35 of the Constitution Act, 1982" (Government of Canada 1995, 1). What might account for this apparent reversal in Canadian governmental policy at the time? Kiera Ladner provides the following explanation. She says that in the aftermath of the 1969 White Paper on Indian Policy, the 1973 *Calder* decision, and the 1982 constitutional entrenchment of Aboriginal and treaty rights, "it became much easier for Aboriginal peoples to get the government to talk about self-government and the dismantling of the colonial regime" (Ladner 2003, 52). By this time, for example, the Canadian government was fully aware that the *Indian Act* had little to contribute to promote legitimate Indigenous governments as Indigenous peoples defined them. As it turns out, while talks advancing the cause of Indigenous self-government stalled at the constitutional level, such talks were decisively pushed into the foreground in other highly influential political settings.

That first significant step was taken in 1983 by the **Penner Committee**.

In its search for a policy alternative, the Canadian government appointed an all-party Special Committee of the House of Commons in 1982 to provide recommendations on the best approach to implementing Indian self-government. The special committee produced a report one year later (the **Penner Report**) that closely resembled Indigenous positions on the right to self-government at that time. Rather than delegate powers, as occurred under the *Indian Act*, the Penner Committee urged that those powers be recognized as inherent in status. Indigenous self-government, in other words, ought to be elevated above municipalities and have standing as distinct third order governments within a reconfigured Canadian federalism (Newhouse and Belanger 2020, 45). The committee also recommended that Canadian governments proceed immediately to ensuring that "the right of Indian peoples to self-government be explicitly stated and entrenched in the Constitution of Canada" and that "the federal government and Indian First Nations pursue all processes leading to the implementation of self-government, including the bilateral process" (Special Committee on Indian Self-Government 1983, 44, 46).

Despite the Penner Committee's recommendations, all formal processes aimed at providing constitutional recognition for the Indigenous right to self-government came to a decisive end in 1992 when the **Charlottetown Accord** was defeated in a national referendum. Following the Penner Committee, the Charlottetown Accord proposed that federal and provincial governments pass a constitutional amendment recognizing that the Indigenous peoples of Canada possess an inherent right to self-government. Had it been successful, the Accord would have positioned Indigenous governments alongside federal and provincial governments as one of three constitutional orders. As for a mandate, the Accord described a policy setting in which Indigenous governments would be entitled "to safeguard and develop their languages, cultures, economies, identities, institutions and traditions" and "to develop, maintain, and strengthen their relationship with their lands, waters and environment" (Government of Canada 1992, 14). If passed, it was also expected that Indigenous and Canadian leaders would fairly quickly enter into negotiations with the intention of redistributing political powers between the three constitutional orders of government in ways that were mutually satisfying to each partner.

It is against this constitutional and policy background that the 1995 Inherent Right Policy was introduced. Attempts to achieve a formal constitutional amendment recognizing the Indigenous inherent right to self-government had failed to muster sufficient support, but this did not mean that support for the proposition of self-government was lacking. Consequently, the Liberal government of Jean Chrétien simply declared that as far as it was concerned, the principle is implicitly present within the meaning of Section 35's reference to "existing Aboriginal rights" and, as such, is already constitutionalized. The task at hand, therefore, was not to engage in further constitutional wrangling, but rather to work out the terms of the Indigenous inherent right to self-government in practical and workable agreements (Government of Canada 1995, 1). The Chrétien government readily conceded that "significant differences remain among some governments and Aboriginal peoples on a definition of self-government." But, said Chrétien, it was high time to put these differences aside and focus efforts instead on building partnerships to strengthen Indigenous communities to govern themselves. Indigenous empowerment and self-reliance would, from here on in, be the Liberal government's policy objective (Government of Canada 1995, 1–2).

In setting out its policy, the Liberal government outlined two levels of Indigenous governmental powers, one largely exclusive to Indigenous nations and the other to be shared with federal and provincial governments. At the first level, the Liberal government declared that Indigenous peoples have the right to govern themselves in relation to "matters that are internal to the group, integral to its distinctive Aboriginal culture, and essential to its operation as a government or institution" (Government of Canada 1995, 5). Within this category, additional Indigenous jurisdiction would also be extended to matters relating to Indigenous peoples' special relationship with their lands and resources. At this first level, the kinds of powers Indigenous governments would exercise include control over governing structures, elections, membership, marriage, adoption and child welfare, language and religion, education, health, social services, policing, land and resources management, taxation, and housing (Government of Canada 1995, 5–6).

The second level concerns areas of jurisdiction that the Liberal government declared go beyond matters of internal concern to Indigenous nations. In these areas the government was "prepared to negotiate some measure of Aboriginal jurisdiction or authority … but primary law-making authority would remain with the federal or provincial governments, as the case may be, and their laws would prevail in the event of a conflict with Aboriginal laws" (Government of Canada 1995, 6). Examples of areas of jurisdiction falling under this second category include divorce, labour, administration of justice, penitentiaries and parole, environmental protection, management of fisheries and migratory birds, and gaming (Government of Canada 1995, 6).

In setting out its negotiating starting point, the Liberal government also unilaterally established several constraints under which the Indigenous inherent right to self-government would have to be exercised. The government declared that in all cases Indigenous self-government would have to be exercised within the Canadian Constitution and would be subject to the *Charter of Rights and Freedoms* (Government of Canada 1995, 3–4). Furthermore, certain laws of overriding federal and provincial importance, such as the Criminal Code, would prevail over all Indigenous law (Government of Canada 1995, 6). And while Indigenous political power might well be construed as a form of sovereignty, it certainly was not to be understood as sovereignty in the international sense. In keeping with the sovereign power of states, for example, Canada would retain exclusive authority in areas such as defence and external relations, management and regulation of the national economy, maintenance of national law and order, and protection of the health and safety of all Canadians (Government of Canada 1995, 7).

The 1995 Inherent Right Policy certainly received its fair share of criticism, particularly from Indigenous scholars and activists (Ladner 2003; Lawrence 2012; King and Pasternak 2018; Metallic

2020). What follows identifies three of the most important.

First, because the Liberal government simply presented its new approach as a *fait accompli*, Indigenous peoples played no role in setting out the basic principles of the policy nor in working out the potential range of their governing authority. Consequently, observed critics, far from being treated as partners in Confederation, the policy shows just how Indigenous peoples remain firmly subject to colonial control. The Liberal government declared that the basic parameters of the policy were non-negotiable and only then were Indigenous nations invited to develop their self-government models, drawing from the policy's set of pre-approved parts (Boldt 1993, 91).

Second, Indigenous scholar Bonita Lawrence observes with some consternation that the language of the Inherent Right Policy limits the exercise of Indigenous self-government to purely internal matters, and more specifically to those activities integral to distinctive Indigenous cultures. She concludes, therefore, that the policy offers little more than protection to those distinctive elements of Indigenous peoples' pre-contact culture that exist today. In her view, what is left unattended and therefore outside the scope of Indigenous jurisdiction are all those matters essential to "the existence, needs, and livelihoods of Aboriginal peoples" in the present (Lawrence 2012, 64). Territorial matters like those pertaining to land use and environmental protection as well as to hunting and fishing rights, for example, ought to fall under the exclusive jurisdiction of an Indigenous nation's legal enforcement capacity. Under the terms of the Inherent Right Policy, however, no such provisions were made.

And third, the Liberal government decided at the outset that any new forms of Indigenous self-governance would not be allowed to impinge upon or diminish the overarching law-making power of the Canadian state itself. According to the policy, all forms of Indigenous self-government could materialize only after negotiations conducted with the federal, provincial, and territorial governments. Furthermore, in many cases, the powers conferred on Indigenous governments are subject to federal or provincial paramountcy or sovereignty. By these criteria, what was on offer was not the kind of self-government that Indigenous nations claim to be their inherent right. What was being offered instead, according to Kiera Ladner, was an invitation to "self-administration" or to take up a position of "negotiated inferiority" which, by definition, she argues fails to respect "Indigenous visions of self-determination, Aboriginal governance, and sovereignty" (Ladner 2003, 53).

At the same time that the 1995 Inherent Right Policy was being developed, the five-year (1991–6) public hearing, research, and report writing phase of the **Royal Commission on Aboriginal Peoples** (RCAP) was drawing to a close. RCAP had been created in response to the 78-day standoff in 1990 between the Mohawk peoples of Kanesatake and the Canadian military over the status of lands at Oka, Quebec. The violent nature of the confrontation demonstrated yet again that longstanding tensions between Indigenous and non-Indigenous peoples needed renewed attention and decisive action. Striking a royal commission was the Brian Mulroney Conservative government's response. RCAP was instructed to investigate and recommend ways to improve all aspects of the relationship between Indigenous peoples and the Canadian state. In 1996, RCAP released a five-volume final report containing over 300 policy recommendations setting out its vision for a more mutually satisfying and respectful relationship.

Nations are privileged in RCAP's final report as the central players to a renewed relationship. According to RCAP, a renewed relationship must be built on a foundation that recognizes and empowers Indigenous peoples as nations by providing them with their own distinct and autonomous place within Canada's governing structure (Newhouse and Belanger 2020, 46). RCAP places nations at the heart of its analysis for two basic reasons: first, because they existed pre-contact and continue to exist (though in often severely diminished form); and second, because nations possess the kind of institutional capacity necessary "to preserve and transmit the core of language, beliefs, traditions, and knowledge that is uniquely Aboriginal" (RCAP 1996d, 530). RCAP therefore urges all governments in Canada to recognize that "Aboriginal peoples are nations vested with the right of self-determination as recognized and affirmed in section 35(1) of the Constitution Act, 1982" and as originally arising "from the sovereign and independent status of Aboriginal peoples and nations before and at the time of European contact and from the fact that Aboriginal peoples were in possession of their own territories, political systems, and customary laws at that time" (RCAP 1996e, 155, 158). Nations, in other words, are what bind Indigenous people together and as such should be empowered to contribute to their members' multidimensional individual and collective development.

What RCAP then proceeds to do is carefully outline a series of interlocking institutional mechanisms that, if adopted, would significantly enhance the symbolic standing and political power of Indigenous nations within Canada and, by extension, give life to their inherent rights.[16] Measures include a new Royal Proclamation and companion legislation. These would supplement the recognition extended to Indigenous peoples in the Royal Proclamation of 1763 by establishing a clear set of principles to guide not only the nation-to-nation relationship between the Canadian state and Indigenous nations, but also the modern treaty-making, treaty implementation, and treaty renewal process. In addition, the combination of an *Aboriginal Nations Recognition Act*, capacity building for self-government, new federal departments, treaty commissions, an Aboriginal Lands and Treaty Tribunal, an Aboriginal House of First Peoples, and an Aboriginal Peoples Review Commission to monitor progress were all designed to assist Indigenous peoples in the task of rebuilding and re-equipping their nations to govern. In short, RCAP pushed for an equality of governmental status that would have seen Indigenous nations exercise a considerable degree of political sovereignty within the Canadian state.

It is worth noting that just prior to the release of RCAP's final report, the Canadian government reassured Indigenous peoples that their view of self-government would be reflected in the 1995 Inherent Right Policy (Newhouse and Belanger 2020, 46–7). Yet, as Metallic points out, "the Chrétien Liberal government was less than enthusiastic about the RCAP's proposals on self government and a nation-to-nation relationship" (Metallic 2020, 435). There was certainly no language used suggesting that the Canadian government was willing to recognize Indigenous nations as political sovereigns within Canada with rights to unilaterally assert jurisdiction over matters of importance to them. While the official response to the RCAP report, ***Gathering Strength***, acknowledged that Indigenous peoples do indeed have the inherent right to self-government, it tended to frame that right in largely administrative terms. For instance, in sections devoted to the task of implementing self-government, *Gathering Strength* is singularly preoccupied with the matter of building governance capacity, particularly in the areas of administration and financial and fiscal management (Government of Canada 1997, 13, 15). Any indication that structural changes were coming on the scale recommended by RCAP were clearly not present in the government's response.

Despite criticisms levelled against all policy initiatives, a good number of self-government agreements have nevertheless been negotiated to successful conclusion in recent years. Each negotiation has been conducted under the auspices of either the Inherent Right Policy, the comprehensive land claims process, or the BC treaty process.[17] The stated motivation of both Indigenous leaders and Canadian governmental officials in all cases is to ratify agreements that provide jurisdictional clarity and autonomy for Indigenous nations and, in the process, also serve to sever Indigenous nations from the restrictive terms of the *Indian Act*. What typically happens is that Indigenous nations are invited to negotiate self-governing arrangements with federal, provincial, and territorial governments, identifying what powers they need and what services they wish to provide to enhance their capacity to be both self-defining and self-reliant. And many Indigenous nations have taken up this invitation with considerable enthusiasm. Already, Indigenous nations control over 80 per cent of Indigenous Affairs departmental program financing while many also deliver such services as education, language and culture, police services, health care and social services, housing, property rights, and adoption and child welfare (Papillon 2014, 124–7; Newhouse and Belanger 2020, 44–5).

In spite of their structural limitations, in other words, self-government agreements can and do contribute to greater Indigenous control and law-making authority over a range of jurisdictions of central importance to them. Indigenous nations are beginning to set their own political priorities, they are designing programs consistent with their own nation's objectives, and they are making significant decisions about how to govern themselves in relation to other Indigenous nations and the governments of the Canadian state. Put simply, the dominance of the Canadian government in the lives of Indigenous nations is decreasing as a result of significant structural changes in federal policy over the last several decades. Whether the Inherent Right Policy amounts to a governmental declaration of recognition of an Indigenous right to sovereignty is doubtful. But what the policy does show is that the Canadian government is willing to move over and create some spaces in between the practice of Canadian sovereignty for Indigenous self-empowerment. Framed this way, the policy can be seen as an incremental step toward justice.

THE 2005 KELOWNA ACCORD

Indigenous sovereignty, self-government, and the capacity to be self-defining mean little if not built on the foundation of healthy, well-supported (in terms of housing and employment), and well-educated Indigenous communities. Yet, as has been well documented, the general socioeconomic conditions of Indigenous peoples in the context of a highly developed country such as Canada remain distressing. Indeed, the gap between Indigenous and non-Indigenous peoples with respect to indicators like health care, housing, education, and social services is considerable, and there are few signs that the gap is closing (Milloy 2008, 11–16; Larocque and Noël 2015, 240–1). As James Anaya points out, the Canadian government has been consistently unwilling to increase funding to Indigenous peoples even though their needs are higher than the general population (Anaya 2014, 7).

While Canadian governments have been notorious for their unresponsiveness to this crisis, there has been one fairly recent notable exception. Between 2004 and 2005, a series of high-profile and widely publicized roundtable consultations and meetings were convened at the direction of then Liberal Prime Minister Paul Martin. Participants included the Government of Canada, representatives from the provinces and territories, and leaders from the five national Indigenous organizations in Canada (Alcantara and Spicer 2016, 189).[18] The meetings culminated in a series of agreements colloquially known as the **Kelowna Accord**. The Accord committed the Canadian government to spending some $5.1 billion over five years, an unprecedented amount to that point in Canadian history, with promises that a second five-year period of funding and programming would be negotiated once the Accord had expired (Poelzer and Coates 2015, x). Its main commitments were dedicated to improving the socioeconomic conditions of Indigenous peoples, with particular attention paid to education, health services, housing, and economic opportunities (Patterson 2006, 1; Alcantara and Spicer 2016, 190–1; Larocque and Noël 2015, 240). The overall objective of the Accord was to close the socioeconomic gap such that the standard of living of Indigenous peoples would be essentially the same as that of other Canadians by 2016 (Courchene 2018, 103; Frideres 2020, 19). With community capacity and poverty issues addressed, subsequent rounds of negotiations could then take on outstanding matters related to land entitlements and treaty relationships (Alcantara and Spicer 2016, 190–1). In short, the first phase was intended to provide a solid socioeconomic foundation upon which to build the structural reforms necessary to support the second.

The Kelowna Accord stands out as a particularly inspiring exercise in policymaking for a number of reasons. First was its substantial commitment to investing in Indigenous communities. The $5.1 billion commitment, with more promised to come, was one that on its surface appeared large enough to make significant headway toward improving the living conditions of Indigenous peoples across the country (Alcantara and Spicer 2016, 185).

Second was its commitment to policy partnerships. The language of the Accord was shot through with commitments declaring that Indigenous leaders and Canadian governmental officials would build Indigenous policy together. Nowhere in either the proceedings or the text is there any reference to the prospect that unilateral Canadian governmental action might be taken on any policy issue. Instead, collaboration was the operative word throughout (Alcantara and Spicer 2016, 193, 194, 197). For example, the extensive consultation phase between Indigenous leaders and Canadian governmental officials prior to the ratification of the Accord was marked by a spirit of cooperation and goodwill. In addition, the Accord itself featured built-in mechanisms for all partners to monitor progress during its implementation phase. Taken together, these measures are highly suggestive of a dynamic between Indigenous peoples and the Canadian state more in keeping with a collaborative nation-to-nation model (Alcantara and Spicer 2016, 195).

And third was its commitment to Indigenous leadership. The language of the Accord was carefully crafted to ensure that the policy priorities set out in it constituted specific responses to issues of longstanding concern to Indigenous peoples, as defined by them. Furthermore, the Canadian government took measures to ensure that its role in the delivery of policy outcomes would be a circumscribed one. To it would fall primary responsibility for providing the funding. However, the Accord's actual agreements dedicated to innovation and development in Indigenous education, health care, housing, and economic development were, in many cases, designed specifically to fall under Indigenous jurisdiction and control. In addition, all policy was designed to be consistent with the very different priorities of First Nations, Inuit, and Métis. The Accord reflected an understanding that effective Indigenous policy development cannot be motivated by a "one-size-fits-all" approach (Patterson 2006, 12–13).

Unfortunately, the Kelowna Accord did not survive in its original form for very long. The Liberal government was defeated on a motion of non-confidence in November 2005 and was subsequently replaced by a minority Conservative government in January 2006. Conservative Prime Minister Stephen Harper opted to leave the Kelowna Accord unimplemented (Alcantara and Spicer 2016, 185, 192; Larocque and Noël 2015, 239). The House of Commons later passed a private member's bill sponsored by former Prime Minister Paul Martin (supported by the Liberal, Bloc Québécois, and New Democratic Party MPs) requesting that Harper's Conservative government implement the Kelowna Accord. But since private member's bills cannot force governments to spend money, the Conservatives were within their rights to ignore the vote, which is exactly what they did (Courchene 2018, 104). The Conservatives claimed that they would seek to implement a new plan, one that over the course of the nine-year period in which the Conservatives were in power (2006–15) failed to materialize (Frideres 2020, 20). The one notable exception concerned education. In 2013 Prime Minister Harper issued a discussion paper proposing major investments in Indigenous education, a proposal that the then national chief of the Assembly of First Nations, Shawn Atleo, agreed to and which was subsequently worked into the 2014 federal budget. However, as Thomas Courchene points out, it did not take long for the deal to unravel. Despite the promising title of the proposed implementation bill (*First Nations Control of First Nations Education Act*), a good number of regional chiefs were convinced that if enacted the bill "would strip authority over education away from First Nations" (Courchene 2018, 110). Consequently, the deal fell apart, taking Shawn Atleo along with it, claiming that the failed educational initiative also constituted a vote of non-confidence in his leadership.

While in opposition, the Harper-led Conservatives charged that the Kelowna Accord was too expensive and not sufficiently well thought out to justify their support (Poelzer and Coates 2015, x; Alcantara and Spicer 2016, 192; Larocque and Noël 2015, 240). Consequently, when they took power in 2006, the Accord was shelved, at least at the national level. But as a number of scholars point out, despite the Liberal defeat, several provinces decided to take action consistent with the original intentions of the Accord on their own. They believed that the Accord simply held too much public policy potential to be summarily pushed aside (Alcantara and Spicer 2016, 192, 194; Larocque and Noël 2015, 238). Consequently, particularly in British Columbia, Manitoba, Ontario, and Quebec, monitoring and benchmark criteria were established, as were elaborate mechanisms for the participation of Indigenous peoples in each of the priority policy areas that had been identified (education, health services, housing, and economic opportunities). According to Florence Larocque and Alain Noël, however, while provincial partners generally reaffirmed their commitments to close the socioeconomic gap, the actual policy impact of those commitments "left an uneven legacy" as "they did not have a uniform effect across provinces" (Larocque and Noël 2015, 238, 244). As they explain it, the larger provinces with the most institutional and financial capacity (with the notable exception of Manitoba) were in the best position to institutionalize and subsequently fulfill their original Kelowna Accord commitments.

THE JUSTIN TRUDEAU LIBERAL GOVERNMENT'S 2015–21 POLICY "RESET"

In the election of October 19, 2015, Justin Trudeau and the Liberal Party of Canada moved from third-party status to win a majority government, and they were elected again in 2019 and 2021, though in these two elections at the more modest level of a minority government. Over the course of all three campaigns, Prime Minister Trudeau was emphatic in his declaration that "there is no relationship more important to me and to Canada than the one with Indigenous peoples" (Wilson-Raybould 2019, 44, 76; 2021, 144). In keeping with this declaration, over the course of particularly his first mandate, there was a noticeable shift in Indigenous policy tone and intent. The new anthem became one in which Indigenous peoples would no longer have to prove the existence of their rights as a precondition for their recognition. Instead, Indigenous rights would simply be recognized and implemented (Wilson-Raybould 2021, 166). With Indigenous rights simply taken as given, Trudeau believed that the proper foundation would finally be in place to build "a renewed nation-to-nation, government-to-government, and Inuit–Crown relationship" (Government of Canada 2017b). To that end, the Trudeau government committed itself to fully implement UNDRIP, to develop a transformative **Recognition and Implementation of Indigenous Rights Framework**, and to enact all 94 of the **Truth and Reconciliation Commission's Calls to Action**, including launching an inquiry into murdered and missing Indigenous women and girls in Canada. Taken together, these declarations suggested that the new Liberal government would pursue deep structural changes in its relationship with Indigenous peoples. One can well understand, therefore, as put by Arthur Manuel, that "there was something very close to elation in many sectors of Indian country" (Manuel 2017, 49). The Trudeau government's commitments raised Indigenous expectations that serious efforts would finally be undertaken to reconcile Canadian assertions to sovereignty with the ongoing existence of the Indigenous right to self-determination.

It is worth pointing out that Trudeau's promise to fully implement UNDRIP and the full slate of the TRC's Calls to Action were justifiable causes for Indigenous hope that Canada would finally get it right. This is because of the far-reaching structural changes that each of these documents identify as essential to meaningful reconciliation and a renewed relationship. Neither document tinkers at the policy edges. Instead, each, in its own way, identifies the underlying causes of colonialism and then describes ways forward built upon the legitimacy of Indigenous peoples' rights to lands, resources, and forms of social, cultural, economic, and political power commensurate with their right to be self-defining. Speaking specifically to the TRC's Calls to Action, Thomas Courchene writes that what they recommend is so pivotal to "what the future ought to entail" that they are likely to serve as a "substantive lens through which to view all future legislation pertaining to Indigenous peoples" (Courchene 2018, 114, 141). **UNDRIP's 46 Articles** are no less transformative in their implications. Therefore, as benchmarks against which the success (or failure) of present and future Indigenous policy is likely to be judged, it is important that we briefly review what each put forward as its vision for reconciliation.

In the estimation of Arthur Manuel, UNDRIP constitutes "a virtual declaration of independence for Indigenous peoples" (Manuel 2017, 53). While this may be a bit of an exaggeration, UNDRIP certainly sets out a series of mutually reinforcing rights that, if implemented, would go some considerable distance in restoring to Indigenous peoples the political power and resources they need to rebuild their nations. For instance, Article 3 states that "Indigenous peoples have the right to self-determination. By virtue of that right they freely determine their political status and freely pursue their economic, social, and cultural development." As for practising that right, Article 4 specifies that Indigenous peoples "have the right to autonomy or self-government in matters relating to their internal and local affairs, as well as the ways and means for financing their autonomous functions." The Declaration then provides further guarantees consistent with the right to self-determination, including to a nationality; to distinct political, legal, economic, social, and cultural institutions, traditions, and customs; to educational, spiritual, and religious systems; to their traditional lands, territories, and resources; and more generally to all those means necessary to live a dignified Indigenous way of life. In short, by endorsing UNDRIP, the Trudeau government effectively said that the debate concerning what Indigenous rights amount to is over. The important task now at hand is to take the rights as identified in UNDRIP and breathe life into them in ways appropriate to the Canadian context.

The 94 Calls to Action contained within the 2015 final report of the TRC also carry significant transformative potential for the relationship between Indigenous and non-Indigenous peoples.

The mandate of the TRC required that it conduct historical research and hear from witnesses about their experiences of the residential schools' policies and operations. The TRC's 94 Calls to Action, however, call for an extensive program of healing and reconciliation that go well beyond the destructive legacy of residential schools. In short, its view of the "truth" and pathways to "reconciliation" touch on virtually every aspect of Indigenous life.

The TRC's approach to reconciliation identifies "reparations" and "concrete actions that demonstrate real societal change" as vital to Indigenous peoples' future (TRC 2015, 16). Most important for our purposes, however, are those Calls to Action that touch on the broad Indigenous right to self-determination. Nowhere is the TRC's intent on this score better captured than in Call to Action 45. It reads: "We call upon the Government of Canada, on behalf of all Canadians, to jointly develop with Aboriginal peoples, a new Royal Proclamation to be issued by the Crown. The proclamation would build on the Royal Proclamation of 1763 and the Treaty of Niagara of 1764 and reaffirm the nation-to-nation relationship between Aboriginal peoples and the Crown." Among its numerous recommended elements, the TRC urges that the new proclamation "repudiate concepts used to justify European sovereignty over Indigenous lands and peoples such as the Doctrine of Discovery and *terra nullius*," "renew or establish Treaty relationships," and reconcile Aboriginal and Crown constitutional and legal orders to ensure that Aboriginal peoples are full partners in Confederation (TRC 2015, 199).

In short, as a "truth" inquiry, the TRC is both unequivocal and highly prescriptive in its message. For it, the truth is that injustices were perpetrated upon Indigenous peoples of a magnitude that, in many instances (like that of residential schools), were equivalent to cultural genocide. What is now required, therefore, are measures capable of restoring to Indigenous peoples those inherent rights and jurisdictions commensurate with their ability to live, once again, as Indigenous peoples in full dignity and with respect. The question we are left with is whether the current Canadian government's Indigenous policy demonstrates sufficient progress when held up against the TRC's and UNDRIP's comprehensive visions for reconciliation.

Upon achieving office in the fall of 2015, the Liberal government's Indigenous policy priorities were crafted to meet two fundamental objectives. The first was at the political level. Much of the discussion here has been conducted at the relatively rarefied level of first principles and in the language of need for fundamental structural change in Canadian state–Indigenous relations. The second was at the immediate and pressing needs presented by Indigenous life at the day-to-day social, economic, and cultural level. Here the Liberal government declared its intention to enhance services to Indigenous nations to assist them with the task of rebuilding internal community capacity. Much of the programming at this level has been intentionally practical, aimed at addressing the cycle of poverty, dependency, and lack of opportunity so prevalent in far too many Indigenous nations across Canada (Wilson-Raybould 2019, 196).

This two-pronged approach to Indigenous policy was reflected in the Liberal government's 2017 announcement that it would dissolve the Department of Indigenous and Northern Affairs Canada (INAC) and put two new departments in its place. The **Department of Crown–Indigenous**

Relations and Northern Affairs would be dedicated to the first objective, while the **Department of Indigenous Services** would be dedicated to the second. Interestingly, this division of INAC into two separate departments had been recommended by RCAP some 20 years before (RCAP 1996c, 373). As explained by Jody Wilson-Raybould, the split was intended to be "part of a staged and coherent plan to effectively get rid of INAC in a principled way." While the Department of Crown–Indigenous Relations would be responsible for conducting "proper nation-to-nation intergovernmental relationships," the Department of Indigenous Services would eventually fade away as Indigenous nations increasingly transitioned from the colonial *Indian Act* and reliance on Canada for services toward self-government arrangements that see them designing and delivering their own programs (Wilson-Raybould 2021, 163; 2019, 70, 137). Taken together, these two policy objectives suggested that the Liberal government was serious about its intentions to decolonize its relationship with Indigenous peoples.[19] Indeed, at the end of its first mandate in 2019, the then national chief of the Assembly of First Nations, Perry Bellegarde, concluded that the Liberals had "accomplished more for Indigenous rights than any other government in its first term" (Smart 2019a, A4).

Of course, expectations concerning what constitutes an acceptable effort at decolonization by the Liberal government may well be pitched rather low, particularly so when measured against the performance of the Harper Conservative government that came before it. With some notable exceptions, the relationship between Indigenous nations and the Harper Conservatives was often troubled and regularly acrimonious. The Harper Conservatives established a reputation for crafting Indigenous policy without Indigenous input and for imposing policy upon Indigenous peoples without providing opportunities for Indigenous review. This pattern of policy imposition and lack of consultation came to be regarded by Indigenous peoples as the norm. It was under Harper's watch, for example, that the 2012 **Idle No More** protests were launched across the country. This movement was stimulated in large part by Indigenous concerns that legislative changes made through two omnibus bills (Bill C-38 and Bill C-45) effectively smoothed the waters for governments and big business to push through major resource projects like pipelines with minimal environmental assessment and Indigenous oversight.[20] To add insult to injury, a ***First Nations Financial Transparency Act*** was also introduced, requiring all Indian bands to publicly post all annual revenues and expenditures with the threat that governmental revenues would be withheld from those bands that refused to do so. In the face of these and other measures, Idle No More became a widespread movement seen by many Indigenous and non-Indigenous peoples alike to be a champion for the environment and for Indigenous rights more generally. While the Idle No More movement was at its most intense in the fall of 2012 and spring of 2013, it did not really fade from existence until the Harper Conservatives were defeated in the federal election of 2015.

Against the backdrop of the Harper Conservatives' record, a Liberal policy "reset" more favourably predisposed to Indigenous aspirations may carry the markings of a major paradigm shift in the making. But then again, good intentions on the part of well-meaning Canadian governments have been voiced before. Their practical delivery is not so easy, particularly because policy objectives committed to Indigenous assimilation have become so deeply entrenched into the political landscape. In what follows I will address three measures pursued by the Trudeau government that achieved some prominence during the writing of this book. All speak in some way to the foundational work that has characterized the Trudeau government's approach to supporting Indigenous efforts at rebuilding their nations. They are (1) its commitment to a renewed set of principles to guide Canada's relationship with Indigenous peoples; (2) its intent to rebuild relations with Indigenous peoples based on the recognition and implementation of their rights; and (3) its resolve to develop a service delivery model that makes co-development and partnerships with Indigenous peoples a priority. I shall evaluate each initiative against the standard established for policy success in this book, namely, "Do these policy initiatives establish genuine political space for Indigenous sovereignty to coexist with Canadian sovereignty?"

First, then, is the matter of principles devised to guide Indigenous–Canadian state relations into the future. In July 2017 the Liberal government released a document outlining 10 principles that it said would now guide the Government of Canada's relationship with Indigenous Peoples (Wilson-Raybould 2021, 146).[21] In that document the Liberals pledged that going forward the government's intent would be to build its relationship with Indigenous peoples on the basis of "recognition and implementation of their right to self-determination, including the inherent right to self-government" (Government of Canada 2017b, 2).

Of course, the right to self-determination means little if not robust in its actual operation. To facilitate the rebuilding of strong Indigenous governments, therefore, the Liberal government further declared that it intended to respect and implement the pre-Confederation, historic, and modern treaties, as well as uphold Indigenous rights to lands, territories, and resources. The 10 principles then go on to provide additional reassurances. Among other things, the Liberals said that they will work with Indigenous peoples to create "space for the operation of Indigenous jurisdiction and laws"; they will negotiate treaty agreements "based on the recognition and implementation of [Indigenous] rights and not their extinguishment, modification, or surrender"; and they will establish bilateral mechanisms "for closing the socio-economic gap between First Nations and other Canadians" (Government of Canada 2017b, 3, 4; AFN and Canada 2017, 2). Taken together, the Liberals professed a firm belief in the capacity of their 10 principles to deliver reconciliation. In its words, to the degree that "they will guide the work required to fulfil the Government's commitment(s)" they will also create a cooperative environment for "strong, healthy, and sustainable Indigenous nations" to flourish as equal partners of Confederation "within a strong Canada" (Government of Canada 2017b, 1, 2).

Second, the Liberal government pledged that it would rebuild its relationship with Indigenous peoples based on a **full recognition of their rights**. The Liberals preferred language of use to capture what is required here is "equality," "cooperation," and "partnerships." For example, in the prime minister's October 2017 mandate letter to Carolyn Bennett, then minister of Crown–Indigenous Relations (since repeated in the mandate letters of 2019 and 2021), the minister was instructed to take the lead in the government's efforts to build a new relationship between Canada and Indigenous nations based on the "recognition of rights, co-operation, and partnership" (Office of the Prime Minister 2017a, 3; Manuel 2017, 49; Wilson-Raybould 2019, 65, 70; 2021, 144). The letter then provides a whole battery of instructions aimed at increasing Indigenous empowerment, including increasing the number of comprehensive modern treaties and new self-government agreements; assisting First Nations in their transition away from the *Indian Act* and toward self-government; clarifying obligations and ensuring the implementation of pre-Confederation, historic, and modern treaties and agreements; and working with the Government of Nunavut to advance further devolution of power and jurisdiction (Office of the Prime Minister 2017a, 4; see also Wilson-Raybould 2019, 135–6). The letter takes one additional step. It states that as the minister takes up her many responsibilities, the prime minister expects that she does so in ways that lead to the full implementation of the UNDRIP as well as the Calls to Action of the TRC.

On February 14, 2018, the prime minister lent further weight to the above commitments by declaring in a speech to the House of Commons that it was the government's intention to introduce, by way of legislation, what he called a **Recognition and Implementation of Indigenous Rights Framework**. As described by Jody Wilson-Raybould (then minister of Justice and attorney general of Canada), the intent of the framework was to put the discussion of Indigenous rights on entirely new ground. Through the framework, "the work of government will shift from processes primarily focused on assessing whether rights exist – which, inevitably, is adversarial and contentious – to seeking shared understandings about how the priorities and rights of Indigenous peoples may be implemented and expressed within a particular process and outcome" (Wilson-Raybould 2019, 172; see also 2021, 145). Following this announcement, the Liberal government quickly embarked on a national engagement process with Indigenous peoples across the country.[22] Ostensibly, the consultations were designed to discover what Indigenous peoples thought the framework's "shared understandings" about "processes and outcomes" should look like. The government promised to have the framework introduced to Parliament by the end of 2018 with implementation to occur before October 2019. Taken together, signals pointed to the prospect of a renewed relationship that, in the words of Wilson-Raybould, "was going to be rights-based and principled" (Wilson-Raybould 2021, 148).[23]

And third, the Liberal government declared that it intended to develop a "closing-the-gap" approach to its **delivery of services**. The 2017, 2019, and 2021 mandate letters to the minister of the new Department of Indigenous Services provide insight into the government's approach. "Partnerships" is once again a recurring theme, but this time with emphasis placed on the need to "improve delivery of services" in ways that draw Indigenous peoples into the process of identifying priorities, implementation, and measuring the effectiveness and progress of all programs (Office of the Prime Minister 2017b, 3). Service delivery areas that the letters target for particular attention include health care; child welfare; housing outcomes; community infrastructure including drinking water and the elimination of all boil water advisories; primary, secondary, and post-secondary educational opportunities; a new fiscal framework that provides sufficient and predictable funding; economic development and job creation initiatives; and community sport (Office of the Prime Minister 2017b, 4–5). Particularly noteworthy are the prime minister's instructions that his ministers take the lead in developing legislation designed to address two areas of particular vulnerability: the minister of Canadian Heritage and Multiculturalism in the area of revitalizing, strengthening, and protecting Indigenous languages (Bill C-91) and the minister of Indigenous Services in the area of returning to Indigenous nations control over child and family services (Bill C-92).[24] In both cases, the legislation was co-developed by the federal government, the Assembly of First Nations, the Inuit Tapiriit, and the Métis National Council, presumably in keeping with the Indigenous claim that their right to self-determination entitles them to full control over their own languages and family services.

September 2016 also saw the launch of the long-awaited **National Inquiry into Missing and Murdered Indigenous Women and Girls** (MMIWG). While the inquiry initially encountered a significant number of growing pains in both organizational design and retention of personnel, it eventually got on track, producing an impressive two volume final report on June 3, 2019, entitled *Reclaiming Power and Place*.[25] The inquiry was commissioned to investigate why Indigenous women and girls suffer such high rates of victimization in Canada and why they are so disproportionately overrepresented among those that go missing and are murdered. According to a report released by the Royal Canadian Mounted Police in 2014, for example, Indigenous women and girls make up just 4 per cent of the Canadian population but represent 11 per cent of all those who go missing and 16 per cent of all those who are murdered (Palmater 2015, 141; Sellars 2016, 99).

Not content to simply address the symptoms, the commissioners chose to focus their investigation on the underlying social, economic, cultural, institutional, systemic, and historical causes of violence against Indigenous women and girls (National Inquiry into MMWIG 2019, 57). They also chose to expand the parameters of their investigation to include 2SLGBTQQIA+ people (two spirit, lesbian, gay, bisexual, transgender, queer, questioning, intersex, and asexual people) on the grounds that this Indigenous population also suffers disproportionate levels of violence. The commissioners' conclusions were definitive. They found that the source of oppression is fed by a racism (animated in turn by sexism, homophobia, and transphobia) empowered by colonial structures. According to the commissioners, violence stems from colonization or colonialism and relies on a racism that dehumanizes Indigenous peoples in ways that have taken on many concrete and devastating forms. Furthermore, colonial violence is difficult to root out because it has become embedded within the structures of everyday life, informing how Canadian laws, policies, and structures, including the health and justice systems, operate. The cumulative effect of this structural or systemic assault against Indigenous women, girls, and 2SLGBTQQIA+ people is characterized by the commissioners as a genocide, a condition that it defines as not necessarily the "physical destruction of a nation or ethnic group" but as the "destruction of the essential foundations of the life of national groups" with the aim of their eventual annihilation (National Inquiry into MMWIG 2019, 51).

Just as the root causes of violence against Indigenous women, girls, and 2SLGBTQQIA+ people are far-reaching, so too are the commissioners' proposed solutions. They ground their program for transformational change in the soil of human rights, restored relationships, and in particular the Indigenous right to self-determination.

The commission identified four sets of human rights as essential to what it insists must be an intersectional approach to ending oppression and violence: the right to culture (understood as access to land, languages, cultural teachings, and to families); the right to health (understood as mental and physical well-being and safety); the right to security (understood as equitable access to basic needs including shelter and food as well as education and employment); and the right to justice (understood as improved law enforcement practices, access to restorative justice projects and revitalized Indigenous law, and rehabilitation and reintegration support) (National Inquiry into MMWIG 2019, Chapters 5, 6, 7, and 8). These four sets of human rights are also seen to be interconnected and mutually reinforcing. The commission is firm in its position that they simply must be advanced together if Indigenous women, girls, and 2SLGBTQQIA+ people are to enjoy the safety, security, and human dignity that they are entitled to as human rights holders.

As for solutions, the commission insisted that they must be Indigenous-led, particularly by those Indigenous women, girls, and 2SLGBTQQIA+ people with lived (and often trauma-informed) experience. Proposed solutions and services must also originate from within Indigenous communities and nations, in keeping with their inherent right to self-determination (National Inquiry into MMWIG 2019, 169–73). The commission offers 231 recommendations, identified as Calls to Justice. Each is designed to restore Indigenous women, girls, and 2SLGBTQQIA+ people to their rightful places of entitlement and empowerment within their communities and nations. The inquiry also insisted that its Calls to Justice must not to be seen as optional. Instead, they are to be seen as legal imperatives, "arising from international and domestic human and Indigenous rights law" and as such must be implemented if Indigenous women, girls, and 2SLGBTQQIA+ people are to live, once again, in safety with the security and dignity they deserve (National Inquiry into MMWIG 2019, 168).

At the time of writing (2022), the Liberals had been in government for just over seven years, a period of sufficient length to be able to offer some assessment of their performance on its ambitious Indigenous agenda. To what degree have their good intentions concerning first principles, a renewed relationship, and a refocused service delivery model been translated into concrete public policy action? Commentators to date have offered mixed and sometimes conflicting reviews. On the positive side, the Liberal government decided to set out a long list of commitments, some with far-reaching and transformative implications. It therefore stands to reason that translating those commitments into concrete action will take time. As put by Jody Wilson-Raybould, "Rome was not built in a day, and neither is rebuilding Indigenous nations" (Wilson-Raybould 2019, 76). To that end, the Liberal government did take some decisive steps to deliver on its promises, though not all were delivered smoothly. What follows identifies a number of examples:

- In its 2016 through 2020 budgets, substantially increased funding was dedicated to a variety of Indigenous-related services, including economic development, job creation, and health care initiatives.[26]
- In partnership with Indigenous peoples, a campaign was initiated to build and renovate schools on reserves.
- New resources were dedicated to enhancing Indigenous language retention and to revitalizing Indigenous and child and family care programs.
- Significant progress was made on housing initiatives and in providing safe drinking water on reserves.[27]
- An apology was issued to the Tŝilhqot'in for colonial atrocities perpetrated against their peoples.
- Significant resources were dedicated to support Indigenous communities in their fight against COVID-19.
- A National Council for Reconciliation was established, its mandate being to monitor governmental progress in implementing the TRC's 94 Calls to Action.[28]
- On a symbolic front, two bills were passed (Bill C-5 and Bill C-8), one creating a National Day for Truth and Reconciliation (to be held every September 30) and the other adding a line to Canada's citizenship oath acknowledging that new citizens would respect the country's treaties with Indigenous peoples as part of their larger commitment to Canada.
- Bill C-15 was passed, requiring that all Canadian law be aligned with the Indigenous rights identified in the UNDRIP. A national action plan was to be produced within two years of the legislation coming into force describing how UNDRIP's objectives will be achieved with subsequent annual reports documenting progress also required.[29]
- In the 2021 national action plan released in response to the MMIWG Inquiry's final report, the Liberal government committed itself to accelerating its work with Indigenous partners to take all concrete action necessary "to end systemic racism, sexism, and economic inequality that has perpetuated violence against Indigenous women and girls, and 2SLGBTQQIA people" (Liberal Party of Canada 2021, 56).[30]

On the important matter of substantive structural transformation and change, however, a number of commentators argue that the Liberal government has been much more talk than action (Forrest 2018). For example, Hayden King and Shiri Pasternak claim that "most of Trudeau's commitments remain unfulfilled and his cabinet routinely raises expectations in public statements while lowering them in policy documents" (King and Pasternak 2018, 6). On the TRC's Calls to Action, Arthur Manuel argues that the Liberal government has "been doing a cynical dance around the substantial elements while they pick the low-hanging fruits that fit into their programs and services dependency basket" (Manuel 2017, 272) And in her memoir published after her resignation from Trudeau's Cabinet in February 2019 and subsequent ouster from the

Liberal caucus, Jody Wilson-Raybould writes that despite promises to the contrary, the Department of Crown–Indigenous Relations continues to use the treaty and self-government negotiation processes "to try to limit, alter, and even extinguish Indigenous rights, rather than uphold and honour them" (Wilson-Raybould 2021, 47). What follows provides a number of examples, first concerning principles and rights and then matters of policy and legislation.

A centrepiece of the Liberal government's purportedly new approach to Indigenous–Crown relations was to replace the comprehensive land claims and inherent right to self-government policies with the 2018 Recognition and Implementation of Indigenous Rights Framework. A national engagement process was launched in February 2018 with the expectation that, going forward, the eventual contents of the new framework would serve as the substantive lens through which all subsequent relations between the Government of Canada and Indigenous peoples would be worked out. It did not take long, however, for the entire engagement process to fall off the rails.

The Liberal government guaranteed that the content of the framework would emerge organically through a public engagement process involving Indigenous peoples and the ministers of Crown–Indigenous Relations and Justice. It also predetermined that the five months allocated to the process would be sufficient to gather all relevant contributions (from February to June 2018). Indigenous leaders did not agree. According to the Assembly of First Nations, "the schedule that Canada set for itself to undertake meaningful engagement, produce a comprehensive and substantive vision for rights recognition, obtain feedback and produce legislation was far too compressed" (AFN 2018a, 2; see also Wilson-Raybould 2021, 172). The fact that the engagement phase was designed entirely without Indigenous input also meant that the process was seen by many to lack democratic legitimacy.

More egregious still was the proposed content of the framework itself. All parties agreed that recognition and implementation of Indigenous rights ought to form the starting point for all relations between Canada and Indigenous peoples. The Liberal government and Indigenous participants encountered obstacles, however, when it came to their use of language and respective understandings of key principles and concepts. For example, under self-determination, the Liberal government proposed that it would recognize Indigenous nations and communities as legal entitles within federal legislation. As domestic legal entities, however, Indigenous leaders worried that they could "potentially lose any force they have as nations under UNDRIP or international law" (AFN 2018a, 5).

Notably, this emphasis upon "domestic containment" seemed to characterize the entirety of the Liberal government's approach, prompting the AFN to conclude that the proposed framework had "the same problems as the current Inherent Rights Policy." Rather than simply recognizing Indigenous rights to be inherent, the AFN detected an ongoing expectation that Indigenous rights would have to be negotiated. In short, in the estimation of the AFN, the language of the framework still "assumes that sovereignty and jurisdiction are held by Canada." This omission was a serious one (AFN 2018a, 5; see also King and Pasternak 2018, 4, 6, 8). The AFN therefore chose to reject the

Recognition and Implementation of Indigenous Rights Framework. The Liberal government dropped the initiative shortly thereafter.

On the policy and service delivery front, the Liberal government has also regularly encountered criticism. Here commentators point to the disjuncture they see between declarations of good intentions and actual willingness or capacity to deliver. A disturbing lack of governmental accountability in a climate intended to promote reconciliation is also identified. For example, boil water advisories remained in over 50 Indigenous communities despite promises to remove all such advisories by March 2021; the $4.5 billion Kinder Morgan Trans Mountain Pipeline was purchased by the Liberal government without consulting affected Indigenous nations along its route (Manuel 2017, 237);[31] health care providers regularly displayed disturbing instances of racist behaviour despite promises that Indigenous health legislation would be introduced to combat discrimination against Indigenous peoples in health services; and litigation was pursued in response to a landmark judicial ruling that required the federal government to provide financial compensation to First Nations children adversely impacted by the child welfare system.

As for the transformative potential for reconciled relations as envisioned by the final reports of the Truth and Reconciliation Commission and the National Inquiry into Missing and Murdered Indigenous Women and Girls, reviews indicate that the Liberal government's performance is also mixed. On the TRC's Calls to Action, the Liberal government awards itself high marks, claiming that as of June 2021 80 per cent of those that fell under its mandate were either completed or well on their way to completion. Report cards issued by outside groups, however, are less charitable, suggesting that the Liberal government has met the requirements of somewhere between 8 and 13 of the total 94 (Tumilty 2021).

Meanwhile, the national action plan to end violence against Indigenous women, girls, and 2SLGBTQQIA+ people was released on June 3, 2021. The federal government's contribution, called the *Federal Pathway*, had many commentators expressing disappointment. The Liberal government certainly agreed with the national inquiry that new programming was desperately needed in the areas of culture, health and well-being, safety and security, and justice. On this score they were beyond reproach. But the $2.2 billion of new federal programming promised to address each of these challenges was seen to be sorely lacking. Taken together, many critics argued that the Liberal government's action plan was far too piecemeal, too lacking in specifics, and too poorly funded to actually constitute a meaningful response to the crisis (Macyshon 2021, 3; Aiello 2021, 7).

In its own defence, the Liberal government insisted that the national action plan and *Federal Pathways* were not intended to be final but rather iterative, subject to updates and course correction over time (Aiello 2021, 3). Despite these reassurances, however, the Liberal government had to deal with a severe credibility problem generated by the unique circumstances of the time. Some wondered why the Liberal government would take two years to respond to the final report of the National Inquiry on MMIWG when its capacity to mobilize resources in the face of the COVID-19 crisis took mere days. While the scale of the crisis presented by COVID was of an unprecedented magnitude, many argued that the same was true of the genocide perpetrated against Indigenous women, girls, and 2SLGBTQQIA+ people. Consequently, a "thin" Liberal plan containing broad goals but little immediate concrete action was seen by some to be simply unacceptable. The Native Women's Association of Canada, for example, a major organization representing the interests of Indigenous women across the country, chose to walk away from the process (Aiello 2021, 7).

CONCLUSION

In drawing this discussion of the history of Indigenous policy to a close, one conclusion is readily apparent: the British and then Canadian assertions to sovereignty over Indigenous peoples have been consistently challenged. While Indigenous peoples have been subjected to policy that has consistently sought to "civilize" and assimilate them, they have refused to capitulate. Indeed, their resilience and strength in the face of opposition is testament to their ongoing commitment to their right to exist as distinct peoples and in their ability to mobilize all political and legal resources at their disposal to protect their identities.

What is also clear is that the Canadian government's approach to Indigenous policy after withdrawing the 1969 White Paper on Indian Policy has been one more receptive to Indigenous rights. Unfortunately, ideological and institutional entrenchment of policy imperatives devoted to protecting the hegemony of Canadian state sovereignty remain strong and therefore difficult to dislodge. But incremental steps have been taken in the quest to carve out space within Canada for the expression of Indigenous sovereignty, although, I hasten to add, almost always because of the hard and unrelenting work undertaken by Indigenous peoples. As we have seen, the 1973 *Calder* decision, the launching of the specific and comprehensive land claims processes, the constitutional recognition and protection of Aboriginal and treaty rights, and the validation of the inherent Indigenous right to self-government all represent elements of a significant change in both the tone and direction of Indigenous policy. At the very least, the Canadian government now seems to accept the proposition that Indigenous rights originate within Indigenous nations themselves and as such are not for Canada to grant but rather for Canada to accept and honour.

As for evaluating the performance of the Justin Trudeau Liberal government, judgment is very much a matter of the perspective that one brings to the debate. I surmise that the Liberal government's policy intentions align most closely to those of the 1992 Charlottetown Accord. This Accord would have seen Indigenous governments operating within the Canadian constitutional framework as a third order of government alongside that of their federal and provincial counterparts. Within this model, Indigenous sovereignty is limited because it is constrained by the constitutional necessity of having to share state power with federal and provincial governments. Nevertheless, for some Indigenous leaders the changes proposed by this model are enough to represent what they take to be a reasonable fulfillment of their Indigenous rights.

By the criteria of others, however, particularly those who hold more radical and far-reaching ambitions, the Liberal government's approach will be seen as yet another manifestation of colonialism at work. For them, what the Liberal government's lofty promises propose to do is supress the Indigenous right to self-determination within the Canadian constitutional framework rather than grant it the political and legal standing it deserves as an independent and free-standing right existing alongside that of the Canadian state. As such, the cost of the Liberal government's "decolonization" exercise is to essentially leave Indigenous peoples in a captive colonial relationship. Treaty federalism, with its parallel constitutional orders of the Canadian state and Indigenous nations existing side by side, does not make an appearance in the Liberal government's model, or so such critics would argue (King and Pasternak 2018, 4).

DISCUSSION QUESTIONS

1 While it was clear by the 1970s that Canada's Indigenous policy dedicated to assimilation was bankrupt, why has it taken so long for a new policy, more responsive to the ambitions of Indigenous peoples, to emerge?

2 How can the White Paper of 1969 be justified on liberal grounds? Can the White Paper be criticized from the point of view of a liberal theory of justice? If so, in what ways?

3 When Section 35 of the *Constitution Act, 1982* is referred to as containing a "full box" of Aboriginal rights, what does this mean? Why is it so important that this be established as a matter of principle? What ought that "full box" of Aboriginal rights include?

4 Can it be said that the Justin Trudeau Liberal government's Indigenous policy reset of 2015–21 marked a distinct departure from the Indigenous policies of integration and containment of the past? Is Canada now truly on a path to reconciliation with Indigenous peoples?

SUGGESTED READINGS

Alcantara, Christopher, and Zachery Spicer. 2016. "A New Model for Making Aboriginal Policy? Evaluating the Kelowna Accord and the Promise of Multilevel Governance in Canada." *Canadian Public Administration* 59 (2).

Belanger, Yale D. 2018. "Chapter 9: Political Organizing in Canada." In *Ways of Knowing: An Introduction to Native Studies in Canada.* Toronto: Nelson Education.

Belanger, Yale D., and P. Whitney Lackenbauer. 2014. *Blockades or Breakthroughs? Aboriginal People Confront the Canadian State.* Montreal: McGill-Queen's University Press.

Coates, Ken. 2015. *#Idlenomore and the Remaking of Canada.* Regina, SK: University of Regina Press.

Courchene, Thomas J. 2018. "Chapter 4: A New Beginning: From the Constitution Act, 1982 to the Sesquicentennial." In *Indigenous Nationals, Canadian Citizens: From First Contact to Canada 150 and Beyond.* Montreal: McGill-Queen's University Press.

Hedican, Edward J. 2013. "Chapter 4: The Politics and Resistance and Confrontation." In *Ipperwash: The Tragic Failure of Canada's Aboriginal Policy*. Toronto: University of Toronto Press.

King, Hayden, and Shiri Pasternak. 2018. "Canada's Emerging Indigenous Rights Framework: A Critical Analysis." Yellowhead Institute. https://yellowheadinstitute.org/rightsframework.

Larocque, Florence, and Alain Noël. 2015. "Chapter 14: Kelowna's Uneven Legacy: Aboriginal Poverty and Multilevel Governance in Canada." In *Canada: The State of the Federation 2013 – Aboriginal Multilevel Governance*, edited by Martin Papillon and André Juneau. Montreal: McGill-Queen's University Press.

Manuel, Arthur. 2015. "Chapter 6: The Constitutional Express: A Grassroots Movement." In *Unsettling Canada: A National Wake-Up Call*. Toronto: Between the Lines.

———. 2017. "Chapter 1: The Second Coming," and "Chapter 27: UNDRIP and the Trudeau Betrayal." In *The Reconciliation Manifesto: Recovering the Land, Rebuilding the Economy*. Toronto: James Lorimer and Company.

Metallic, Naiomi Walqwan. 2020. "The Relationship between Canada and Indigenous Peoples: Where Are We?" in *Canadian Politics*, 7th ed., edited by James Bickerton and Alain-G. Gagnon. Toronto: University of Toronto Press.

National Inquiry into Missing and Murdered Indigenous Women and Girls. 2019. *Reclaiming Power and Place. The Final Report of the National Inquiry into Missing and Murdered Indigenous Women and Girls*. https://www.mmiwg-ffada.ca/final-report.

Newhouse, David, and Yale Belanger. 2020. "The 'Canada Problem' in Indigenous Politics." In *Visions of the Heart: Issues Involving Indigenous Peoples in Canada*, 5th ed., edited by Gina Starblanket and David Long. Toronto: Oxford University Press.

Weaver, Sally M. 1981. *Making Canadian Indian Policy: The Hidden Agenda 1968–1970*. Toronto: University of Toronto Press.

Wilson-Raybould, Jody. 2019. *From Where I Stand: Rebuilding Indigenous Nations for a Stronger Canada*. Vancouver: Purich Books.

———. 2021. "Chapter Six: Justice." In *Indian in the Cabinet: Speaking Truth to Power*. Toronto: HarperCollins Publishers.

NOTES

1 Bev Sellars recounts that such acts of defiance against *Indian Act* regulations often came at a considerable cost to Indigenous peoples. She writes: "Once the Indian Act was legislated, we Aboriginal people did not throw up our hands and say, 'Well, that's the law. We have to obey it.' Aboriginal people were constantly trying to get around or disregard the racist legislation and many spent time in jail for not accepting 'the law.'" See Sellars 2016, 61–2.

2 J.R. Miller adds that Indigenous peoples were deterred from asserting themselves politically due to additional challenges they had to confront such as crushing conditions of poverty and "widespread disease and death that resulted in a declining Aboriginal population throughout Canada until approximately 1930" (Miller 2004, 78).

3 As explained by Ken Coates, the Round Dance is a traditional cultural practice found within prairie Indigenous nations that serves multiple purposes, including dealing with a community's grief and sorrow, celebrating cultural strength, and marking a community's joys and accomplishments. See Coates 2015, 62–3.

4 Michael Morden points out that a notable exception to Canadian state intransigence occurred in the 1990s case of the Stoney Point First Nation and its occupation of Camp Ipperwash and Ipperwash Provincial Park. In this "deviant" case, a land transfer settlement was reached, but only because it provoked a broad-based judicial inquiry that had the effect of establishing the legitimacy of the Stoney Point Nation's claim. See Morden 2013.

5 For an exploration of the issues that lie at the heart of each of these and other disputes, see Hedican 2013, 87–154; Belanger and Lackenbauer 2014. The latter in particular is an important study for the contribution it makes to setting out the circumstances under which Indigenous peoples feel compelled to resort to sit-ins and blockades and conditions under which they either succeed or fail.

6 A White Paper is a generic term used to describe a government policy document that describes and explains intended government policy on an issue. White Papers are intended to be persuasive, often describing major shifts in government policy in advance of enacting actual legislation. White Papers can be used to test public opinion, but when released it is usually the case that the proposed policy is already well into the planning stages.

7 Indigenous activist and writer Arthur Manuel identifies the White Paper's "fee simple" proposal as particularly destructive. He writes, "they proposed that our land, after some 'intermediate states,' be reduced to 'fee simple' ownership. That is to say, turn our homelands into real estate that is bought and sold on the open market with property taxes collected by the provinces, as with all other mortgage lots. Aboriginal title lands would be struck out of existence and reserve lands would cease to exist under the fee simple arrangement." See Manuel 2015, 31.

8 What follows draws heavily from material found in Schouls 2002, 20.

9 Two notable persons very much in favour of an individualistic approach to Indigenous policy are Thomas Flanagan and Gordon Gibson, the former a political scientist at the University of Calgary, the latter a former leader of the Liberal Party of British Columbia. See Flanagan 2000 and Gibson 2009.

10 The seven agreements with BC Indigenous nations are with the Tsawwassen First Nation (2009), the five Maa-nulth First Nations (2011), and the Tla'amin First Nation (2014).

11 There can be no doubt that it was the resolute advocacy of Indigenous leaders, coupled with support from non-Indigenous Canadians, that compelled federal and provincial leaders to include Aboriginal rights in the patriated Constitution. So important was this constitutional episode to Indigenous leaders that they supplemented their advocacy with highly charged symbolic action in what came to be known as the "Constitutional Express." Indigenous leaders, led by George Manuel, then president of the Union of BC Indian chiefs, chartered two trains for a four-day journey from Vancouver to Ottawa with more than a thousand grassroots protesters on board, their objective being to ensure "that recognition of Aboriginal and treaty rights be explicitly written into the constitution" (Manuel 2015, 67). Despite large-scale demonstrations as well as forceful presentations arguing the Indigenous case at various Ottawa venues, the federal government chose to drag its heels, prompting the organizers of the Constitutional Express to expand their reach by sending delegations to the United Nations in New York and then to Europe with a particular focus on the British Parliament. After months of effort, the federal government of Pierre Trudeau finally relented, agreeing that Aboriginal and treaty rights would receive recognition and protection within the patriated Canadian Constitution.

12 Chelsea Vowel, a Métis writer and educator, expresses her deep appreciation and gratitude toward Arthur Manuel for his accessible and vivid descriptions of events surrounding Indigenous activism, including the White and Red Papers and the Constitutional Express. She suggests that his book, *Unsettling Canada*, "is one of the most important resources available to people living in Canada for understanding Indigenous activism and federal policy toward Indigenous people over the past half century." I would suggest that Arthur Manuel's more recent book, *The Reconciliation Manifesto*, stands in the same category. See Vowel 2016, 271.

13 A lively and engaging personal account of the political dynamic at work in the pre-1983 conference preparations and the 1983 conference is provided by Indigenous leader Bill Wilson (Hemas Kla-Lee-Lee-Kla) who served as the vice-president of the Native Council of Canada at that time. See Sellars 2016, 117–26.

14 Though J. Rick Ponting notes that the four constitutional conferences did serve as an important political platform for both sides to educate the other about their respective positions. He also notes that the fact that four constitutional conferences on Aboriginal rights were held at all should be seen as a major symbolic victory for Indigenous peoples at the time. See Ponting 1997, 38.

15 I thank one of the anonymous reviewers of this book for offering this important observation.

16 What follows in this paragraph relies heavily on material found in Schouls 2003, 72–3.

17 I shall examine examples of negotiated self-government agreements settled within each of these policy frameworks in forthcoming chapters.

18 These five organizations included the Assembly of First Nations, the Inuit Tapiriit Kanatami, the Metis National Council, the Native Women's Association of Canada, and the Congress of Aboriginal Peoples.

19 It is worth noting, however, that the Trudeau government's decision to split the Department of Indigenous and Northern Affairs into two came as a complete surprise. Jody Wilson-Raybould, Hayden King, and Shiri Pasternak write that Indigenous leadership was neither consulted nor informed about this major structural change to the relationship. See Wilson-Raybould 2021, 163–4; King and Pasternak 2018, 9.

20 The formal titles of these acts were *The Jobs and Growth Act 2012* (Bill C-45) and *The Jobs, Growth, and Long-Term Prosperity Act* (Bill C-38).

21 See Government of Canada 2017b.

22 The framework engagement process ran between February and June 2018. The Government of Canada reported that 89 engagement sessions were conducted across the country with input from 1,300 participants. See AFN 2018b, 2.

23 Integral and parallel to this process of establishing an Indigenous Rights Recognition and Implementation Framework was the Liberal government's commitment to immediately engage in negotiations with all those Indigenous nations that wished to do so on issues of concern to them. By December 2020, 80 exploratory tables operating under the name "Recognition of Indigenous Rights and Self-Determination Discussion Tables," representing 390 Indigenous communities, had been struck. Priority items to be discussed at each table were to be set by the Indigenous group in partnership with the federal government, though most discussions were dedicated to resolving land title issues and establishing self-government rights.

24 The two pieces of legislation are entitled Bill C-91, *An Act Respecting Indigenous Languages*, which received Royal Assent on June 21, 2019, and Bill C-92, *An Act Respecting First Nations, Inuit and Métis Children, Youth and Families*, which also received Royal Assent on June 21, 2019.

25 While the National Inquiry into Missing and Murdered Indigenous Women and Girls was launched with considerable fanfare, it was soon preoccupied with several significant challenges. For example, fairly quickly upon taking up its work, the inquiry was accused of being terribly organized and of making very little progress on its mandate. In response, its chief commissioner, Marion Buller, argued that the inquiry had been granted an insufficient period of time to complete its work as well as insufficient funding. The Liberal government responded by granting the inquiry a six-month extension.

26 For a summary of these and other initiatives undertaken by the Liberal government from 2015 to 2021, see the Liberal Party of Canada's 2021 election campaign booklet, particularly "Chapter Six: Moving Forward on Reconciliation with Indigenous Peoples."

27 By September 2021, 109 long-term water advisories had been lifted in Indigenous communities, a number that included all advisories in British Columbia, Alberta, Quebec, and Atlantic Canada.

28 By September 2021, the Liberal government claimed that 80 per cent of the Calls to Action falling directly under its purview were either completed or well underway.

29 Initiatives to implement UNDRIP in Canada had been previously pursued by several private members. For example, Romeo Saganash spear-headed a private member's bill (Bill C-262) that failed to pass in the Senate before Parliament was dissolved in advance of the national federal election in October 2019. Commitments to develop new legislation were made by the Liberal government in the 2019 and 2020 Speeches from the Throne. Bill-C-15 (*The United Nations Declaration on the Rights of Indigenous Peoples Act*), which built substantially on the content of Bill C-262, was eventually passed by Parliament on June 16, 2021, and immediately came into force upon receiving Royal Assent on June 21, 2021.

30 The federal government's portion of the 2021 national action plan is called *The Federal Pathway to Address Missing and Murdered Indigenous Women, Girls and 2SLGBTQQIA+ People.*

31 The Trudeau government purchased the Trans Mountain Pipeline for $4.5 billion in 2018 when Kinder Morgan threatened to halt investment in the pipeline expansion in the face of persistent legal challenges levelled against the project. The intended expansion aims to twin the existing 1,150-kilometre pipeline between Edmonton, Alberta, and Burnaby, BC, serving mainly to export diluted bitumen to foreign markets.

CHAPTER 5

The Courts: Colonialism's Constraints and Sovereignty's Opportunities

LEARNING OBJECTIVES

1 To distinguish between the Supreme Court of Canada's definitions of Aboriginal rights, Aboriginal title, treaty rights, and the Crown's duty to consult and accommodate.
2 To explain why Indigenous peoples are entitled to a category of distinctive, constitutionally protected rights that are not available to other Canadians.
3 To explain why the Supreme Court of Canada uses the "integral to a distinctive culture" test to define Aboriginal rights and why critics refer to this test as a "frozen rights" approach.
4 To assess the Supreme Court of Canada's test for establishing Aboriginal title.
5 To describe how the Supreme Court of Canada identifies what qualifies as a treaty right.
6 To explain the nature of the governmental obligations attached to the "duty to consult and accommodate" and to describe the steps that must be taken to fulfill these obligations.
7 To assess in what ways the Supreme Court of Canada serves as a state tool to protect Canadian sovereignty from Indigenous challenges and in what ways it has also strengthened Indigenous peoples' bargaining position when they assert their sovereignty.

Over the past number of decades, Indigenous peoples have pursued legal action alongside that of political negotiations as one additional way to secure recognition for their Aboriginal rights, fulfillment of treaty rights, and title to their traditional territories (Sellars 2016, 150).[1] This chapter focuses on the Supreme Court of Canada with a view to identifying whether the legal scope of the Court's definition of Aboriginal rights, title, treaty rights, and duty to consult and accommodate have assisted in creating room for the exercise of Indigenous sovereignty.[2] While the Supreme Court does not question the proposition that the sovereignty of the Canadian state is inviolable, it also insists that the Aboriginal rights, title, and treaty rights recognized and affirmed in Section 35 of the *Constitution Act, 1982* carry substantive weight and that each must be appropriately implemented if there is to be reconciliation between Indigenous peoples and the Canadian state. Indeed, so substantive is this responsibility, in the Supreme Court's view, that for it the very honour of the Canadian state is at stake in the successful carrying out of this duty.

The objective of this chapter, therefore, is to identify the substantive content of key Supreme Court of Canada decisions on Aboriginal rights, title, treaty rights, and on the Crown's duty to consult and accommodate to illustrate how each serve to put constraints on the exercise of Canadian sovereignty over Indigenous peoples. As we shall see, tentative legal beginnings have, over time, matured into more robust legal rulings such that legal and political space for the expression of Indigenous sovereignty has expanded, though I would hasten to add, generally not as fully or completely as many Indigenous peoples would like or expect. For example, greater opportunities for the expression of Indigenous sovereignty are afforded by the Supreme Court's interpretation of Aboriginal title than is the case with its interpretation of Aboriginal rights. Also, the Supreme Court's articulation of the legal duty to consult and accommodate carries greater opportunity for rekindling genuine nation-to-nation relationships than does its articulation of the kinds of obligations the Canadian state is obliged to uphold in its treaty relations with Indigenous nations. Nevertheless, the Supreme Court has been responsive to the legal arguments of Indigenous peoples and, by extension, has compelled the Canadian state to roll back its jurisdiction in targeted areas to create meaningful space for the exercise of Indigenous sovereignty within Canada, though again, as we shall see, this space is also regularly subject to significant legal (or what might be termed colonial) constraints.

To advance my argument, this chapter is divided into six sections. To get a flavour for how court decisions can shape Indigenous opportunities for enhanced political autonomy, the first part provides a brief overview of what some term the "historic" and "game-changing" 2014 Supreme Court decision in *Tsilhqot'in Nation v. British Columbia* (Sellars 2016, 155; Courchene 2018, 154–5). The next four parts then address a select number of seminal decisions of the Supreme Court. In these sections I describe how the Supreme Court has defined Aboriginal rights, Aboriginal title, treaty rights, and the duty to consult and accommodate, respectively. Here the main objective will be to identify the nature of the political relationship that the Supreme Court believes is possible when the Canadian state grants recognition and protection to this bundle of Aboriginal rights in the form that the Court itself instructs.

In the last section I ask whether the Supreme Court has actually played a substantive role in carving out genuine political space in between the exercise of Canadian sovereignty for the expression of Indigenous sovereignty. The answer I offer is a qualified "yes." While the Supreme Court does not impose an explicit obligation on the Canadian state to recognize Indigenous sovereignty, the cumulative effect of its decisions has been to substantially increase Indigenous power. To be sure, Indigenous peoples have also suffered losses in the Canadian courts. For this reason, going to court is always a high-risk strategy and one often pursued by Indigenous peoples only as a last resort. But at the same time, Indigenous peoples would not go to court if they had no reasonable expectations of success. And success has been achieved, so much so that some argue Indigenous peoples are on a bit of a Supreme Court "winning streak" (Grant 2018, 111; see also Courchene 2018, 141; Sellars 2016, 150).[3] I refer to this promising "winning" legal environment as one that affords to Indigenous peoples an expanded space for the advancement of sovereignty's opportunities.

CASE STUDY: LANDMARK RULING AFFIRMS TŜILHQOT'IN NATION HOLDS ABORIGINAL TITLE

On June 26, 2014, a unanimous Supreme Court of Canada delivered its *Tsilhqot'in Nation v. British Columbia* decision in which it declared that the Tŝilhqot'in Nation possessed Aboriginal title to 1,750 square kilometres of land in British Columbia's interior (Sellars 2016, 155). This decision constituted a remarkable judicial development because it marked the first time in Canadian history that specific lands were declared by the Supreme Court to be the title lands of an Indigenous nation (Courchene 2018, 154). The case, advanced by Roger William on behalf of the Xeni Gwet'in First Nation's government and all Tŝilhqot'in people, sought confirmation from the Supreme Court that the Tŝilhqot'in possessed title to two tracts of land within the Tŝilhqot'in Nation's traditional territory.[4]

This litigation process started in the early 1980s in response to the province of British Columbia issuing a licence to Carrier Lumber to cut trees on lands claimed by the Xeni Gwet'in Tŝilhqot'in community as part of its traditional territory. The Xeni Gwet'in blockaded the area and then went to court. They filed a suit seeking a court declaration that would prohibit Carrier Lumber from logging as set out in the terms of their licence because title to the land belonged to them. The lands subject to logging were the ancestral lands of the Xeni Gwet'in and, as such, it should be up to the Xeni Gwet'in to decide how the lands would be put to use, or so they argued.

In November 2007, after five years at trial, the British Columbia Supreme Court ruled in favour of the Xeni Gwet'in of the Tŝilhqot'in Nation, declaring Aboriginal title to approximately 40 per cent of the claimed area. In his analysis, Judge Vickers applied the test for Aboriginal title that had been established by the Supreme Court of Canada in its 1997 decision *Delgamuukw v. British Columbia*.[5] It was the view of Judge Vickers that the Tŝilhqot'in had proven beyond any doubt that they had controlled the land awarded to Carrier Lumber when the Crown asserted sovereignty in

1846, that they had continued to occupy and use the land between the assertion of Crown sovereignty up to the present, and that their occupation and use of the land was exclusive to all other Indigenous groups. Having met the test of exclusive and continuous occupancy and use, Judge Vickers found that the Tŝilhqot'in Nation's title did exist. However, despite proving their Aboriginal title, Judge Vickers ultimately ruled against the Tŝilhqot'in on a legal technicality, stating that "they had not properly defined the claim area" (Coates and Newman 2014, 11).

Further litigation followed in 2012. The British Columbia Court of Appeal rejected the BC Supreme Court's declaration on Aboriginal title, stating that while the Tŝilhqot'in possessed Aboriginal rights to hunt, fish, and trap in their traditional territories, they had no title because, as a historically nomadic people, they could not demonstrate that they had continuously and intensively occupied the land apart from their residency at a few village sites. Tŝilhqot'in reaction was swift, charging the BC Court of Appeal with having made a mockery of their Aboriginal title. According to the Tŝilhqot'in, the court of appeal had denigrated and disregarded their Indigenous way of life, "and in particular, their distinctive systems of law and land use" (Tŝilhqot'in National Government n.d.). The Tŝilhqot'in Nation, therefore, sought leave to appeal to the Supreme Court of Canada, which was granted.

The Supreme Court found that Judge Vickers had been correct in his interpretation and application of the *Delgamuukw* test for Aboriginal title and so declared that the Tŝilhqot'in had full title to 40 per cent (or 1,700 square kilometres) of their claimed area. According to the Supreme Court, Aboriginal title is not to be restricted to small, intensely used geographic sites like villages or fishing spots. Instead, Aboriginal title includes all territory within a claimed area that an Indigenous nation has used exclusively and continuously since the Crown asserted sovereignty. All that is needed to establish Aboriginal title, said the Court, is that an Indigenous group be able to demonstrate its regular use of the land by way of hunting, fishing, and otherwise using its resources. The Court ruled that the Tŝilhqot'in Nation had clearly met this test.

Furthermore, within the title area established, the Supreme Court also declared that the Tŝilhqot'in Nation has an Aboriginal right to control the land. This legal right extends to a number of activities. As put by the Supreme Court, the Tŝilhqot'in have the right to choose how the lands will be used (whether for traditional or modern purposes), they have the right to the economic benefits of the lands and its resources, and they have the right to manage the land according to Tŝilhqot'in laws and governance practices (*Tsilhqot'in Nation v. British Columbia* 2014, para. 73). The only restriction the Supreme Court insisted on is that Aboriginal title land cannot be used in ways that would prevent future generations from also using and enjoying the benefits of that same land (*Tsilhqot'in Nation v. British Columbia* 2014, para. 74). The Supreme Court therefore concluded that if Canadian governments or others wish to use Aboriginal title land, they must secure the consent of the Aboriginal title holder first. If consent is not granted, the only recourse left to governments "is to establish that the proposed incursion on the land is justified under s.35 of the *Constitution*

Act, 1982," a justification that the Court added will be exceedingly difficult for governments to meet given that they will be held to a very high standard (*Tsilhqot'in Nation v. British Columbia* 2014, para. 76; see also paras. 92 and 97).

This Supreme Court decision would seem to be a good result for the Tŝilhqot'in Nation. With respect to the issue in dispute, the Supreme Court held that the *BC Forest Act* does not apply because the timber on Tŝilhqot'in title lands belongs to the Tŝilhqot'in Nation and not the BC Crown. The BC government, therefore, cannot issue licences to timber companies to harvest trees on Tŝilhqot'in title lands. Any attempt to do so outside of Tŝilhqot'in consent falls beyond the provincial government's jurisdiction. But beyond this single significant matter of jurisdictional clarification, the Supreme Court also established a far more important matter of legal principle from the perspective of Indigenous sovereignty. Subject to some justifiable infringements, the Supreme Court ruled that the Tŝilhqot'in Nation has an indisputable right to exclusive occupancy and independent use of their Aboriginal title lands. The BC government's claim to title over Tŝilqot'in lands had been dismissed. In short, the Supreme Court placed the Tŝilhqot'in people in a position to re-assume control over what was always rightfully theirs – their ancestral lands and its many rich and varied resources, including its forests (Palmer 2021, A7). The hard work of implementing the decision soon followed. As of 2022 (the time of writing), the Tŝilhqot'in Nation was still in negotiations with a variety of tenure-holders and property owners to transfer ownership of land and resources to the Tŝilhqot'in Nation with commitments that it would provide fair compensation at market value rates in return.

THE SUPREME COURT OF CANADA SPEAKS

As discussed in the previous chapter, in response to the intense lobbying efforts of Indigenous leaders, Canada's newly patriated *Constitution Act, 1982* included Section 35, a clause explicitly dedicated to offering recognition and affirmation to "existing aboriginal and treaty rights." Importantly, these rights are both "recognized and affirmed," lending support to the Indigenous position that their rights pre-date the Canadian Constitution and therefore are not created by it (Mainville 2001, 25). Less clear from the perspective of the Indigenous and non-Indigenous constitutional participants at the time, however, was how to secure agreement on what those Aboriginal and treaty rights amounted to in practice. While the exercise of pouring meaning into the Aboriginal and treaty rights offered protection through Section 35 has since been occurring on multiple political and legal fronts, the Supreme Court has certainly played a prominent role, particularly so in the last two decades of the twentieth century and the first decade of the twenty-first. What follows, therefore, focuses on a number of seminal cases with a view to identifying whether, and to what degree, the Supreme Court's decisions have carved out space within the Canadian constitutional order for the exercise of Indigenous sovereignty.

ABORIGINAL RIGHTS

R. v. SPARROW (1990)

The 1990 case of *R. v. Sparrow* was the first to address the meaning of the existing Aboriginal rights recognized and affirmed in Section 35. Ronald Sparrow, a member of the Musqueam Nation in British Columbia, was charged under the federal *Fisheries Act* with the offence of fishing in the Fraser River with a drift-net longer than the one permitted by the Indian food-fishing licence issued to his band (*R. v. Sparrow* 1990, 1083). Mr. Sparrow did not dispute the charge but argued instead that he had an Aboriginal right to fish, that the federal imposition of a net-length restriction violated his Section 35 rights, and that therefore the offending prohibition should be struck down as invalid. The Supreme Court of Canada chose not make a final decision about the guilt or innocence of Mr. Sparrow, but instead ordered a new trial to allow for a legal process that would follow the tests for establishing Aboriginal rights that the Court set out in the *Sparrow* case.

In overturning Mr. Sparrow's conviction, the Supreme Court ruled that despite modification due to federal and provincial regulations over time, the Musqueam peoples' right to fish had never been extinguished. Consequently, their right to fish constituted an Aboriginal right entitled to constitutional protection under Section 35. As for what the right entailed, the Supreme Court noted by way of context that Aboriginal rights must be allowed to evolve over time and should always be interpreted in a generous and liberal manner (Sellars 2016, 153). But, said the Court, the substantive core of the Aboriginal right in this case was restricted. According to the Court, Aboriginal rights exist to sustain Indigenous identity and culture and salmon clearly play such a role in sustaining the identity of the Musqueam people (*R. v. Sparrow* 1990, 1078).[6] On those grounds, the Court ruled that the Aboriginal right in this case did not extend to a commercial fishery because the Musqueam could not establish that commercial fishing existed as a practice that had pre-contact origins and was integral to their identity. Consequently, the Court concluded that the Musqueam peoples' practice of fishing was deserving of constitutional protection as a Section 35 Aboriginal right, but within the limitations of a food, social, and ceremonial framework (Macklem 2001, 248).[7]

In addition to setting out what qualifies as an Aboriginal right to fish in the Musqueam people and Mr. Sparrow's case, the Supreme Court also considered whether Aboriginal rights are absolute or whether they can be justifiably infringed upon or regulated. Known as the "Sparrow test," the Supreme Court answered this question in a qualified way. It said that because Aboriginal rights enjoy constitutional protection they can no longer be overridden or extinguished but that this does not mean that those rights cannot be regulated or infringed upon should circumstances warrant. But at the same time the Supreme Court signalled that the Canadian government has a fiduciary duty to Indigenous peoples, which means that it must always act in ways to protect and promote Indigenous interests when it seeks to reconcile those interests with that of the larger Canadian society (*R. v. Sparrow* 1990, 1114). Consequently, if the Canadian government wishes to pursue a legislative objective that might infringe on or impair an Aboriginal right, it is under a constitutional obligation to impair that right as little as possible, provide appropriate compensation, and always offer substantive justification for doing so (*R. v. Sparrow* 1990, 1109, 1113). When applied to the Musqueam right to fish, for example, the Supreme Court suggested that this right could justifiably be infringed if the government found it necessary to enact measures for the purpose of fish conservation or resource management.[8] The Court quickly added, however, that once overriding objectives like conservation are taken care of, the restoration of the infringed Aboriginal right must be given top priority (*R. v. Sparrow* 1990, 1115). Put otherwise, while the Supreme Court ruled that Aboriginal rights are not absolute, it did impose a significant duty of non-interference on the Canadian state where the exercise of its sovereign power over Indigenous peoples is concerned.

R. v. VAN DER PEET (1996)

The scope of the *Sparrow* case was fairly narrow in that all it did was identify that the Musqueam band had an Aboriginal right to fish for food, social, and ceremonial purposes. The general method developed by the Supreme Court to identify what qualifies as an Aboriginal right was set out in the 1996 cases of *R. v. Van der Peet*, *R. v. Gladstone*, and *R. v. Pamajewon*.

At issue in the *Van der Peet* case was the action of Dorothy Van der Peet, a member of the Stó:lō Nation in British Columbia, who was "charged with selling 10 salmon caught under the authority of an Indian food fish license, contrary to a section of *British Columbia Fishery Regulations*, which prohibited the sale of fish caught under the authority of this license" (*R. v. Van der Peet*, 1996, 507). In order to decide whether the sale of salmon constituted a constitutionally protected Aboriginal right for the Stó:lō Nation as Van der Peet claimed, the Supreme Court had to decide what kinds of activities qualify as Aboriginal rights under the terms of Section 35. In doing so, the Court created what became known as the "integral to a distinctive culture" test.

For an Aboriginal right to exist, the Supreme Court ruled that an Indigenous claimant must demonstrate that the activity is "an element of a practice, custom, or tradition integral to the distinctive culture of the aboriginal group" (*R. v. Van der Peet* 1996, para. 46). The test further stipulates that the activity must have been an integral and distinctive characteristic of the Indigenous group's identity prior to contact with Europeans and that it has remained so, in some continuous form, up to the present day (*R. v. Van der Peet* 1996, paras. 59, 60). Framed as questions, the Indigenous claimant must be able to answer affirmatively in response to the following: Does the practice, custom, or tradition so significantly define the Indigenous nation concerned such that without it the nation's identity would be fundamentally altered? And is the practice, custom, or tradition one of the features that marked the Indigenous nation as truly distinctive prior to contact with Europeans (*R. v. Van der Peet* 1996, para. 44)? In sum, when the Supreme Court asks what "is the basis for the special status that aboriginal peoples have within Canadian society as a whole," its answer is both very specific and narrowly construed: Aboriginal rights are attached to only those Indigenous practices that originated within the pre-contact period and that constitute unique expressions of distinctive culture into the present.

When measured against this "integral to a distinctive culture" test, the Supreme Court ruled that Dorothy Van der Peet's case failed to meet the standard. The Court agreed that fishing for food, social, and ceremonial purposes was an integral and defining feature of Stó:lō cultural identity and was therefore worthy of constitutional protection as an Aboriginal right (Macklem 2001, 58). However, because the Stó:lō could not demonstrate to the satisfaction of the Court that the trading or bartering in salmon constituted an integral and defining feature of their nation's identity prior to European contact (it was, at best, an incidental activity), the Court concluded that they possessed no constitutionally protected Aboriginal right to fish for commercial purposes. In the Court's estimation, the Stó:lō Nation's commercial sale of salmon was generated by a market economy established in the post-contact period in response to European demand (*R. v. Van der Peet* 1996, para. 84). Consequently, Dorothy Van der Peet was convicted of the charge of selling salmon illegally.

R. v. GLADSTONE (1996)

A more favourable outcome was issued by the Supreme Court in the case of *R. v. Gladstone.* When Donald and William Gladstone, members of the Heiltsuk Nation of British Columbia, were charged with illegally attempting to sell herring spawn on kelp, they too argued (like Dorothy Van der Peet) that they had a Section 35 Aboriginal right to trade in seafood commercially, but in their case herring spawn. Extensive evidence was marshalled to convince the Supreme Court that the Heiltsuk had indeed traded herring spawn on kelp extensively with other Indigenous nations prior to European contact. The evidence further showed that this trade in herring spawn was "a central and defining feature of Heiltsuk society" (*R. v. Gladstone* 1996, para. 29). The ruling of the Court, therefore, was that the Heiltsuk Nation did indeed have a constitutionally protected Aboriginal right to sell herring spawn on kelp. The question left unresolved was whether the limitations imposed on the Heiltsuk's allowable catch of herring spawn by the BC government were justified when measured against the priority that ought to be given to their Aboriginal right. Finding that there was insufficient evidence to determine if the *British Columbia Fishery Regulations* were unreasonable, the Court ordered a new trial (*R. v. Gladstone* 1996, para. 83).

R. v. PAMAJEWON (1996)

When the Supreme Court next considered the merits of the Shawanaga and Eagle Lake First Nations of Ontario's case in *R. v. Pamajewon* that they had a Section 35 Aboriginal right to operate casinos and regulate high-stakes gambling on reserve contrary to the Criminal Code, they were met with a firm rebuke. The Supreme Court concluded that a right to high-stakes gambling on reserve did not constitute an Aboriginal right because gambling was in no way an integral feature of the distinctive cultures of the First Nations in question (*R. v. Pamajewon* 1996, para. 28). Importantly, the Shawanaga and Eagle Lake First Nations had advanced their case under the argument that jurisdiction over gambling fell under their constitutionally protected Aboriginal right to self-government and their corresponding "broad right to manage the use of their reserve lands" (*R. v. Pamajewon* 1996, para. 27). The Supreme Court countered that the object of its legal analysis could not be directed at the Aboriginal claim to self-government because it was framed in far too general a way (*R. v. Pamajewon* 1996, para. 27).[9] Consequently, the convictions of the appellants for violating the gaming provisions of the Criminal Code were upheld (*R. v. Pamajewon* 1996, para. 31).

R. v. POWLEY (2003)

Not only are the Aboriginal rights of First Nations (or Indians) recognized and affirmed by Section 35 of the *Constitution Act, 1982*, but so too are the Aboriginal rights of the Inuit and Métis. One of the first major Aboriginal rights cases concerning the Métis was decided in *R. v Powley* by the Supreme Court of Canada in 2003. In this case, Steve and Roddy Powley, members of a Métis community in the area of Sault Ste. Marie, were charged with the illegal hunting of moose. They argued that they had an Aboriginal right to hunt for moose and that, as such, Ontario regulations prohibiting the Métis from hunting without a licence constituted a violation of their Section 35 Aboriginal rights. The Supreme Court agreed, reasoning that a site-specific Aboriginal right to hunt for food (including moose) exists. As far as the Court was concerned, the Métis community in the Sault Ste. Marie area provided sufficient evidence to demonstrate that they had hunted for moose (and other food) prior to the assertion of European control (around 1850), and that the hunt remained an integral part of their Métis culture. Consequently, the Supreme Court ruled that the Métis community had a traditional right to hunt for moose under Section 35.

In arriving at its decision, the Supreme Court relied on the *Van der Peet* test, though a modified version to deal with the fact that the Métis did not exist until after European contact. As the inclusion of the Métis in Section 35 cannot originate in their pre-contact occupation of Canadian territory, the Court chose to modify the pre-contact focus of the *Van der Peet* test to one that focuses instead on "the protection of those customs and traditions that were historically important features of Métis communities prior to the time of effective European control" (*R. v. Powley* 2003, para. 18). The Court was clear that the Métis are distinctive peoples. In its words, "the term Métis in s.35 … refers to distinctive peoples who, in addition to their mixed ancestry, developed their own customs, way of life, and recognizable group identity separate from their Indian or Inuit and European forbears" (*R. v. Powley* 2003, para. 9). Given their status as distinctive peoples, therefore, the Court ruled that those Métis customs, practices, and traditions originating prior to the assertion of European control would be eligible for Section 35 protection. In keeping with the *Van der Peet* template, however, Métis litigants would also have to show that those customs, practices, and traditions are integral and distinctive features of their Métis culture and that they have persisted in some continuous form to the present day (*R. v. Powley* 2003, para. 17).[10]

IMPLICATIONS AND ANALYSIS

In its extensive consideration of Indigenous issues, it is the Supreme Court's definition of Aboriginal rights that has received the most widespread critical commentary (Borrows 2002, 58–76; Lawrence 2012, 55–9; Macklem 2001, 162–80; Monture-Angus 1999, 100–11). The Supreme Court has determined that for an Aboriginal right to be recognized under Section 35 of the *Constitution Act, 1982*, it must be an element of a practice, custom, or tradition that existed prior to European contact and that was distinctive (though not necessarily unique) to the Indigenous group claiming the right. In addition, the practice must still constitute a distinctive feature of the culture of the Indigenous group today. While the practice, custom, or tradition, can evolve into modern expressions, the essential point from the perspective of the Supreme Court is that the practice itself must have its origins in pre-contact times. According to the Court, it is this pre-contact characteristic that gives the practice associated with the right its Indigenous distinctiveness. If, for example, the practice was created in response to interaction with Europeans, it does not qualify as an Aboriginal right. And why is this? Because once mixed with European influences, the practice is no longer uniquely Indigenous in character.

In response, critics argue that this constitutes what they call a "frozen rights" approach to Aboriginal rights, one that Hamish Telford observes effectively chains Indigenous peoples to their pre-contact distinctive histories (Telford 2015, 201). What is missing in this definition is any attempt to capture the inherent flexibility, fluidity, and adaptive capacity of Indigenous cultures and ways of life through time (Olthuis, Kleer, Townshend 2012, 33). As put by John Borrows, "the courts will only protect what once was integral to Aboriginal cultures, not necessarily what is significant to them today" (Borrows 2017b, 120). Surely, adds Kent McNeil, there is "a false dichotomy here between aboriginal aspects of aboriginal societies and non-aboriginal aspects that have been acquired through contact with Europeans" (McNeil 2002, 34).

While the Supreme Court's restrictive approach to Aboriginal rights is troubling enough on its own merits, critics have expressed particular concern about the implication of this "frozen rights" approach for the Indigenous right to self-government. As Thomas Isaac argues, if the right to self-government exists at all for the Court, it seems predisposed to limit that right to specific activities of governance. Furthermore, those activities must be ones that took place before the arrival of Europeans and remain an integral and defining feature of the culture of Indigenous nations (Isaac 2012, 50). But numerous critics have observed that this approach is highly restrictive, particularly so for the modern context where the exercise of self-governing powers now applies to circumstances and policy areas that extend far beyond the reach of what would have concerned Indigenous nations prior to European contact (Lawrence 2012, 58). To require that claims to self-government be measured against the same standard as the right to enjoy an activity-based Aboriginal right, therefore, simply makes no sense. Kent McNeil points out, for example, that there is a huge difference between an Aboriginal right to a natural resource like fish and an Aboriginal right to have jurisdiction over those resources by way of policy management (McNeil 2007, 13). Understandably, it is the latter right, much more so than the former, that is of greater interest to Indigenous nations as it is one required to rebuild the Indigenous capacity to enjoy the right to self-government in the first place.

In addition, the standard of proof demanded by the *Van der Peet* Aboriginal rights test means that when Indigenous nations go to court, they will have to establish their right to self-government incrementally, on an issue-by-issue basis (e.g., gambling, fishing, forestry). But, says McNeil, if Indigenous nations have "to prove every aspect of their jurisdiction separately" this will place "an impractical burden of proof and unreasonable costs upon them" (McNeil 2007, 14). Taken together, says Isaac, this "integral to a distinctive culture" test effectively guarantees one more outcome: "the reality of Canadian sovereignty is not being questioned by the courts with respect to its overarching supremacy, vis-à-vis s.35" (Isaac 2012, 50). One might therefore justifiably ask, as John Borrows does, whether this test is fair. As he puts it, the Supreme Court is "quite willing to frame Crown rights to self-government in the most excessive and general of terms," yet it does "not extend to Aboriginal people's equivalent treatment." Borrows therefore concludes that the "contrast in the court's treatment of Crown and Aboriginal sovereignty could not be more striking." Where, in this treatment, he asks, "is equality before the law?" (Borrows 2002, 104).

Critics maintain in response that Indigenous peoples would be far better served by an Aboriginal rights regime based on universal principles such as a recognition of their ongoing right to political autonomy over their peoples and over the territories they have occupied and used since time immemorial (Tully 2008, 271).[11] In essence, say the critics, to ground an Aboriginal right in an activity that is an element of a practice, custom, or tradition, integral to a distinctive Indigenous culture is simply far too restrictive to capture what Indigenous peoples are entitled to and need by way of rights to serve their modern needs (Slattery 2016, 102). Critics are quick to conclude, therefore, that placing the power to decide what counts as an Aboriginal right in the hands of the Supreme Court has resulted in those rights being given an excessively narrow scope and a culturally static meaning (Mainville 2001, 28). As we shall see in forthcoming chapters, Indigenous peoples have enjoyed far more success in defining the substance and scope of their Aboriginal rights, including their inherent right to self-government, in political negotiations with federal and provincial governments.

ABORIGINAL TITLE

One of the most important Aboriginal rights is Aboriginal title. Title is a right to the land itself that belongs to Indigenous peoples because of their occupation and use of their ancestral lands since time immemorial. Recent decisions by the Supreme Court of Canada now accept the proposition that the source of Aboriginal title lies outside legislative or other grants from the Canadian state. The Supreme Court is also increasingly predisposed to offer a more generous interpretation of what Indigenous peoples are entitled to do where occupancy and use of their ancestral lands is concerned.

While Aboriginal title in Canadian common law includes the right to exclusive occupation and use of the land, the Supreme Court has also ruled that the Canadian state (or Crown) holds what is referred to as "underlying" title to the land. The Supreme Court, therefore, continues to accept the highly questionable proposition that the Canadian state holds underlying title simply by virtue of its assertion to sovereignty over Canadian territories. How then does the Supreme Court define the relationship between Aboriginal and Crown title? The Court uses the following language. It describes Aboriginal title as a "burden" on the Crown's underlying title, which essentially means that the Canadian state has special responsibilities with respect to Indigenous peoples' use of their lands. These responsibilities can essentially be distilled to two. First, the Court has ruled that the Canadian state must protect the Indigenous right to ongoing occupation and use of their lands. And second, if the Canadian state wishes to secure what the Court calls unencumbered (or unburdened) Crown title to Indigenous-occupied land, it must do so by means of a negotiated settlement with the Indigenous nation to whom the title belongs.

As for the status of Aboriginal title land itself, it is often described in law as *sui generis*, or unique in character. This uniqueness is a product of several legal conditions that distinguish Aboriginal title from standard property rights. For example, the Supreme Court has ruled that while Aboriginal title lands can be put to multiple uses, the land may not be used in ways that are incompatible with traditional Indigenous activities (like hunting, trapping, or gathering). In addition, Aboriginal title land cannot be sold directly to any buyer but can only be transferred to the Crown. Aboriginal title land's uniqueness is also derived from the fact that it is a communal property right held by Indigenous nations, not by their individual members. Consequently, when decisions concerning the management of Indigenous land need to be made, those decisions must be ones that involve all members of the community. These and other principles have evolved over the course of the last 100 or so years as reflected in major Aboriginal title cases that have come before the Supreme Court of Canada. What follows reviews a few of the most important precedent-setting ones.

ST. CATHERINE'S MILLING AND LUMBER CO. v. THE QUEEN (1888)

The legal precedent set in the 1888 case *St. Catherine's Milling and Lumber Co. v. The Queen* defined the political landscape on Indigenous land questions for close to 100 years. The ruling was entirely in keeping with the highly regulated and tightly controlled environment in which Indigenous peoples were forced to live at that time because it established highly unfavourable terms for the legal development of Aboriginal title. The decision, rendered by the British Judicial Committee of the Privy Council (JCPC),[12] was generated in response to a land dispute that occurred at the time between Ontario and Canada over who had the right to issue timber licences on land "surrendered" by the Ojibway under the terms of Treaty 3 in 1873 (Coates 2000, 82). The JCPC eventually decided in favour of Ontario on the grounds that surrendered Indigenous lands go to the provinces and not the federal government. As part of its decision, the JCPC also offered its legal opinion on the status of Indigenous land rights.

Essentially, the JCPC ruled that in as much as Indigenous peoples had any rights to land or resources, those rights flowed exclusively from imperial grants like those identified in the Royal Proclamation of 1763. Furthermore, it was the JCPC's position that the Royal Proclamation offered no explicit recognition of Indigenous sovereignty over their lands, but instead referred exclusively to the sovereignty of the British Crown. The JCPC therefore concluded that insofar as Indigenous peoples had any rights, they were at best "personal and usufructuary." That is, while Indigenous peoples might well have a right to use and benefit from the resources of the land, they certainly had no rights to the land itself. In the JCPC's opinion, the land belonged to the Crown, and because this was so, any Indigenous right to use the resources of the land was entirely "dependent upon the good will of the Sovereign" (Isaac 2012, 71; Hedican 2013, 70). In short, the

St. Catherine's Milling case entrenched three highly restrictive conditions: Indigenous land rights were determined not to originate from Indigenous peoples' prior occupation but from imperial grant; Indigenous rights were limited to use of the resources of the land and not to the land itself; and Indigenous rights could be terminated by the Canadian government at any time (Scholtz 2006, 40). It is this view that would monopolize legal opinion for close to a century.

Given the precedent set by *St. Catherine's Milling*, it is not surprising that Indigenous peoples did not petition the Canadian courts to advance the case for their rights for many years. In fact, for a long period of time Indigenous peoples could not advance a legal challenge even if they had wanted to as the Canadian government amended the *Indian Act* in 1927 to prohibit Indians from hiring lawyers to contest federal policy. Remarkably, this amendment would not be repealed until 1951.

CALDER ET AL. v. THE ATTORNEY GENERAL OF BRITISH COLUMBIA (1973)

It was not until 1973, in the landmark case of *Calder et al. v. the Attorney General of British Columbia*, that Aboriginal title, understood as a "personal and usufructuary right," was successfully challenged. As this case is discussed extensively in Chapter 4, I will not review its details here. Suffice it to say, however, that the ability of the Nisga'a to get three of the seven Supreme Court judges to agree that "their aboriginal title to their ancient tribal territory … has never been extinguished" was enough to lend legal weight to the political argument that Indigenous peoples had been asserting for years, namely, Aboriginal title exists as a result of Indigenous prior occupancy and extends well beyond "personal and usufructuary" rights to actual ownership (or stewardship) of the land itself (*Calder et al. v. the Attorney General of British Columbia* 1973, 313).[13] The importance of this judicial reframing of the origins of Aboriginal title cannot be overstated. As Thomas Courchene (quoting from the Indigenous Foundation website) observes: "The Supreme Court's 1973 decision was the first time that the Canadian legal system acknowledged the existence of Aboriginal title to land and that such title existed outside of, and was not simply derived from, colonial law" (Courchene 2018, 146).[14] By means of *Calder*, in other words, Indigenous peoples were given a substantive legal tool within Canadian law itself to lend further justification to the legitimacy of their political assertions to sovereignty over their own lands.

GUERIN v. THE QUEEN (1984)

Another important Supreme Court case addressing Aboriginal title was the 1984 decision in *Guerin v. The Queen*. What the Supreme Court did here was establish that the Canadian government is duty-bound (indeed, the honour of the Crown depends on it) to protect Aboriginal title interests when the land is surrendered to the Crown for the purpose of securing some benefit for an Indigenous nation (Hedican 2013, 73).

At issue in this particular case were the circumstances surrounding a lease that the Canadian government had negotiated on the Musqueam Nation's behalf. In 1956, the Musqueam Nation in Vancouver surrendered 162 acres of prime reserve land to the Canadian government expecting that it would receive a highly favourable return on a lease negotiated with the Shaughnessy Heights

Golf Club. The Musqueam were informed that they would enjoy considerable profits from a 75-year lease that would be adjusted every decade in response to market rates. It was only much later that the Musqueam learned that the terms of the lease were set at a much lower rate (about 10 per cent of fair market value) than they had been led to believe. The Musqueam, led by their chief Delbert Guerin, sued the Canadian government all the way to the Supreme Court, the result being that the Court ruled in the Musqueam's favour, awarding $10 million in damages to the nation as compensation for lost revenue (Grant 2018, 130; Sellars 2016, 152).

As Ken Coates points out, on its surface the *Guerin* decision appears to be little more than a case "that set right a historical injustice" (Coates 2000, 86). But the Supreme Court also used the circumstances of the case to offer precedent-setting commentary on the status of Aboriginal title in relation to reserve lands as well as on the nature of the fiduciary obligations that the Canadian government has toward Indigenous peoples (Sellars 2016, 152). Herein lies the importance of the *Guerin* case.

With respect to the former, the Supreme Court confirmed the precedent established earlier in the *Calder* case: Aboriginal title is "a legal right derived from the Indians' historic occupation and possession of their tribal lands" (*Guerin v. The Queen* 1984, 376). The Court stated further that "the Indians' interest in their land is a pre-existing legal right not created by the Royal Proclamation of 1763, … the Indian Act, or by any other executive order or legislative provision" (*Guerin v. The Queen* 1984, 336; see also Coates 2000, 86; Courchene 2018, 148; Hedican 2013, 74). The Court then added that in Canadian law, the Musqueam Nation's interests in their reserve lands is the same as it would be for title lands, as the one (a reserve) is derived from the other (title) (Coates 2000, 86; Olthuis, Kleer, Townshend 2012, 99). As with title lands, the nature of that interest is one that entitles the Musqueam to enjoy the use and benefits of their reserve lands (*Guerin v. The Queen* 1984, 382). Thus, according to the Supreme Court, the standing of reserve lands and title lands is equal under Canadian law; the rights attached to each are a product of their status as lands occupied and used by Indigenous nations prior to European settlement.

And with respect to the nature of the Canadian state's fiduciary obligations to Indigenous peoples, the Supreme Court had the following to say. Under the terms of the *Indian Act,* Indigenous peoples cannot sell or lease their lands to "third parties" but must release the land to the Canadian government, who will then sell or lease it on their behalf (*Guerin v. The Queen* 1984, 376; Grant 2018, 130; Hedican 2013, 73).[15] It was here that the Supreme Court determined the Canadian government had been remiss. In securing the terms of the lease with the Shaughnessy Heights Golf Club, the government had failed to adequately consult with the Musqueam or provide them with enough information to make an informed decision (Coates 2000, 86; Courchene 2018, 148). Based on the evidence, the Court surmised that the Canadian government had failed to faithfully carry out its fiduciary obligation to secure a lease that was in the best interests of the Musqueam.

As a general principle, the Court explained that the Canadian government has a fiduciary duty to always act in a way that promotes Indigenous peoples' best interest, particularly so when it involves reserve lands. As for where the fiduciary duty comes from, the Court wrote that it is a product of Aboriginal title itself and the fact that title is inalienable to anyone other than the Crown (Hoehn 2012, 24). The Court, therefore, awarded damages to the Musqueam Nation. It is this concept of fiduciary duty, as clarified in *Guerin*, that has gone on to play such a pivotal role in other Aboriginal rights cases, particularly so with respect to the Supreme Court's expectations concerning what constitutes proper (or honourable) conduct by the Canadian government when fulfilling its legal obligations to Indigenous peoples (Courchene 2018, 148). As for defining the actual content and scope of Aboriginal title, however, the *Calder* and *Guerin* decisions had little to offer. These two matters were dealt with extensively by the Supreme Court of Canada for the first time in its seminal 1997 *Delgamuukw* decision.

DELGAMUUKW v. BRITISH COLUMBIA (1997)

In the *Delgamuukw v. British Columbia* case, the Supreme Court addressed the nature and extent of Aboriginal title, including what the Court determined to be the proof needed to establish title, the uses to which title land can be put, the circumstances in which title can be infringed, and the kind of justification required for infringements to be deemed acceptable. The case itself was a product of claims by the Gitksan and Wet'suwet'en hereditary chiefs to 58,000 square kilometres in British Columbia, divided into 133 territories claimed by 71 houses. The chiefs argued that the governments of Canada and British Columbia had no right to pass laws and regulate activities on the nations' ancestral lands without first securing their consent. They pointed to the fact that their societies had their own histories, cultures, laws, and rules of governance transmitted through their oral traditions, the *adaawk* for the Gitskan and the *kungax* for the Wet'suwet'en (Courchene 2018, 151; Lawrence 2012, 61; Olthuis, Kleer, Townshend 2012, 100).

While the BC Supreme Court rejected the chiefs' oral traditions as unreliable for legal purposes, the Supreme Court of Canada thought otherwise. In its view, oral evidence is acceptable because, as Indigenous peoples rely so heavily on oral traditions to transmit their history, it is these that they must also rely on to establish the credentials of their title claims in court (Hedican 2013, 80). If they could not rely on oral traditions as evidence, they would be at a considerable legal disadvantage. Therefore, because insufficient weight had been granted to legal evidence that had a substantial bearing on the facts at trial, the Supreme Court ruled that errors had been committed in the earlier trial judgment. The Court subsequently ordered a new trial without rendering a decision on the merits of the Gitksan and Wet'suwet'en hereditary chiefs' Aboriginal title case (Coates 2000, 91; Courchene 2018, 151; Sellars 2016, 154).[16] However, what the Court did do was provide legal guidelines to a future judge should the Gitskan and Wet'suwet'en wish to return to court for a definitive ruling.

With the matter of the legal status of the hereditary chiefs' oral evidence behind it, the Supreme Court next turned to setting out legal guidelines to establish Aboriginal title. While the Court had already established that Aboriginal title is a concept that exists in law, it was not clear how an Indigenous group ought to go about proving that it had title. The Court proceeded to answer this question by crafting a test. An Indigenous group asserting title must be able to prove that (1) it occupied the land prior to the assertion of Crown sovereignty;[17] (2) its occupation was exclusive; and (3) its occupation has been continuous up to the present day *(Delgamuukw v. British Columbia* 1997, para. 143; see also Sellars 2016, 154). The Court further established that proof of "occupancy" can be met in one of two ways: the Indigenous group must be able to demonstrate that they actually occupied the land, or that they employed Aboriginal laws to assert some form of control over the land (*Delgamuukw v. British Columbia* 1997, para. 147). With respect to the latter requirement, for example, the Court determined that it would be enough if the Indigenous group could show that other Indigenous users of the land had sought and received their permission to do so (*Delgamuukw v. British Columbia* 1997, para. 156; Courchene 2018, 151).

Once an Indigenous group has proven that it has Aboriginal title to an area, the next question the Supreme Court took up was "What may Indigenous peoples do with their lands?" The Court answered that an Aboriginal title holder is entitled to exclusive use of its title land for both traditional and modern purposes. As described by Bonita Lawrence, the Court's "findings were that Aboriginal title was a right to land, conferring the right to use the land for a variety of practices, not all of which need be integral to the distinctive culture of Aboriginal societies" (Lawrence 2012, 61; see also Hedican 2013, 80). Note the important interpretative shift here between what the Court decided Aboriginal rights and Aboriginal title entail. Aboriginal rights call for recognition and protection of only those Indigenous practices, customs, and traditions that, because of their pre-contact origins, are integral and distinctive to the culture of the Indigenous group. Aboriginal title, however, is much broader in scope. The Court ruled that once Aboriginal title is established, the Indigenous group may use the land in all manner of ways including for modern (e.g., residential, commercial, industrial) purposes that are unrelated to traditional or distinctive practices (*Delgamuukw v. British Columbia* 1997, para. 117). For example, the Court pointed specifically to Aboriginal title including a right to develop and profit from natural resources found on or in the land, such as minerals, oil, and gas (*Delgamuukw v. British Columbia* 1997, para. 122).

The Supreme Court did, however, impose two important restrictions on the uses to which Aboriginal title land can be put. First, as with reserve lands, title lands are inalienable in the sense that they "cannot be transferred, sold, or surrendered to anyone other than the Crown" (Sellars 2016, 154; Hedican 2013, 80). Second, given the significance of the attachment that Indigenous peoples have to their traditional lands, the Supreme Court instructed that title lands must not be used in ways that would jeopardize future generations from also using and enjoying it. While the principle is a general one, the Court justified this limitation by drawing on cultural examples. If, for example, an Indigenous group uses a portion of its title land for hunting, that land must be preserved for hunting and not strip-mined. Or, if an Indigenous group has a special bond with a portion of land for cultural or ceremonial reasons, that land must be preserved for that purpose and not, for example, turned into a parking lot (*Delgamuukw v. British Columbia* 1997, para. 128; Coates 2000, 91). The broader point the Court intended to make is that possession of Aboriginal title land does not translate into an authorization for an Indigenous group to engage in activities that would jeopardize Indigenous peoples' original attachment to it (Lawrence 2012, 61; Olthuis, Kleer, Townshend 2012, 101).

As Aboriginal title carries with it an Aboriginal right to control the land, an important implication follows. According to the Supreme Court, governments and commercial interests must seek the permission of the Aboriginal title holder if they wish to use it. However, the Court also ruled that Indigenous control of title land is not absolute. If, for example, an Aboriginal title holder refuses to grant permission to an external party to use its land, the government may proceed to authorize the incursion but only with proper justification that is framed explicitly to advance the broader public good and then still subject to limitations. In the Court's view, Aboriginal title rights cannot be absolute because Indigenous peoples are "distinctive aboriginal societies [that] exist within, and are part of, a broader social, political and economic community" (*Delgamuukw v. British Columbia* 1997, para. 165). In light of this fact, the Court said that Aboriginal rights and title are designed to reconcile the fact of Indigenous prior occupancy with the assertion to sovereignty by the Canadian state. And in the conflict that occasionally ensues between Canadian state and Indigenous interests, it is the Court's view that state interests must sometimes be allowed to prevail.

At the same time, the Court did insist that Aboriginal rights and title must never be infringed on for frivolous or negligible reasons but rather only in response to what it terms compelling and substantive public objectives. Quite controversially, however, the Court readily admitted that as far as it is concerned, the range of potentially justifiable infringements can be quite broad, including "the development of agriculture, forestry, mining, and hydroelectric power, the general economic development of the interior of British Columbia, the protection of the environment or endangered species, the building of infrastructure and the settlement of foreign populations to support those aims" (*Delgamuukw v. British Columbia* 1997, para. 165; see also Lawrence 2012, 61–2, and McCrossan and Ladner 2016, 417–18). The Court did add, however, that infringements of Aboriginal title must occur with the utmost of attention to Canada's fiduciary obligations. This means doing only what is absolutely necessary to achieve the legislative objective, paying special care to infringe the Aboriginal title in question as minimally as possible, and providing fair compensation to the Indigenous group for land that has been infringed and thus is no longer available to them (*Delgamuukw v. British Columbia* 1997, paras. 162–4; Coates 2000, 91; Grant 2018, 134–5).[18]

TSILHQOT'IN v. BRITISH COLUMBIA (2014)

One final Aboriginal title case warrants a brief revisit, namely, the 2014 *Tsilhqot'in v. British Columbia* decision. As the circumstances arising from this case received extensive coverage earlier in this chapter, I will not review those details here. However, the *Tsilhqot'in* decision did introduce a number of legal innovations into the judicial landscape following from the guidelines concerning the definition, content, and extent of Aboriginal title established in the *Delgamuukw* case. It is to these legal innovations that I briefly turn.

In the first place, the Supreme Court's *Tsilhqot'in* decision demonstrated that Indigenous people can succeed in proving their title in court.[19] The Supreme Court applied the *Delgamuukw* test and concluded that "the Tsilhqot'in occupation was both sufficient and exclusive at the time of sovereignty" (*Tsilhqot'in Nation v. British Columbia* 2014, para. 66; see also Courchene 2018, 154).[20] As a result, the Tŝilhqot'in were recognized as having ownership rights to a substantial portion of their traditional territories.[21]

Second, the Supreme Court introduced an important modification concerning the kind of "occupation and use" to which land can be put for Indigenous groups to be able to prove an Aboriginal title claim. While the BC Court of Appeal recognized that the Tŝilhqot'in had sweeping Aboriginal rights to hunt, trap, and trade in its traditional territories, it was less generous with respect to the Tŝilhqot'in's claim to title. Its test for occupancy required that Aboriginal title apply only to specific tracts of land with reasonably established boundaries that were subject to regular and intensive use, such as village sites or hunting and fishing camps. As a historically "semi-nomadic" nation, this was a test that the Tŝilhqot'in were hard-pressed to meet. The Supreme Court rejected what has been referred to as this "postage-stamp" approach to title, insisting instead that title could also be established through demonstration of intermittent but regular or seasonal use of land for traditional practices or activities like hunting, trapping, or fishing (Mackey 2016, 58; Sellars 2016, 155). The Tŝilhqot'in Nation succeeded by these more generous criteria and subsequently obtained a significant declaration of Aboriginal title.

And third, the Supreme Court used more precise language than it had provided in *Delgamuukw* to describe the kinds of use to which Aboriginal title land could be put. In the words of the Court: "Aboriginal title confers ownership rights similar to those associated with fee simple, including: the right to decide how the land will be used; the right of enjoyment and occupancy of the land; the right to possess the land; the right to the economic benefits of the land; and the right to pro-actively use and manage the land" (*Tsilhqot'in Nation v. British Columbia* 2014, para. 73). This description suggests that Aboriginal title rights can include all forms of economic use of the land, though still subject to the *Delgamuukw* proviso that those uses cannot jeopardize future generations from also using and enjoying it (*Tsilhqot'in Nation v. British Columbia* 2014, para. 74; see also Grant 2018, 137).

IMPLICATIONS AND ANALYSIS

On its surface, the Supreme Court's interpretation of Aboriginal title could well be construed as a welcome legal device to assist Indigenous peoples in their quest to assert and re-establish sovereignty over their lands. For instance, the Court has determined that Aboriginal title, where established, is a right to the land, conferring upon the rightholder a "right to use the land for a variety of activities, not all of which need to be aspects of the practices, customs, and traditions which are integral to the distinctive culture of Aboriginal societies" (*Delgamuukw v. British Columbia* 1997, para. 111). But where recognition of sovereignty has seemingly been extended with one hand, the Supreme Court has taken it away with the other. Here critics point to the fact that the Supreme Court has unilaterally placed limitations on the uses to which Indigenous peoples may put their land. It has, for example, declared that title land may not be used in ways "that would prevent future generations of the group from using and enjoying it" (*Tsilhqot'in Nation v. British Columbia* 2014, para. 74). The Court has also decided that provided a right to occupation and use of land has not been explicitly surrendered or extinguished, the onus of proof for establishing Aboriginal title lies with the Indigenous peoples themselves. They must be able to prove that they occupied the land prior to European settlement and the assertion of Crown sovereignty and that they have continued to do so exclusive to all others to the present day (*Delgamuukw v. British Columbia* 1997, para. 143).

In response, John Borrows is one critic who argues that establishing Indigenous rights to land would be more promising if Indigenous sovereignty was explicitly recognized as the standard against which British assertions to sovereignty had to be measured (Borrows 2002, 97). It is Indigenous peoples, after all, who occupied and used the lands first, and therefore original or underlying title to the land ought to rest in their hands. Yet, as he explains, the Supreme Court has simply decreed that Aboriginal title crystallized, as if for the very first time, when British sovereignty was asserted over Indigenous lands (Borrows 2002, 93–4). Likewise, Michael McCrossan and Kiera Ladner remark that the Supreme Court "seemingly appears to be operating under the assumption that Indigenous legal and political orders could not have existed, and cannot exist today, without first being 'recognized and affirmed' by the state" (McCrossan and Ladner 2016, 422). Indeed, the Court simply asserts, as though it were a matter of fact, that the Crown possesses underlying title to all lands in Canada and Indigenous title is now subservient to it. Consequently, as the Court puts it, Aboriginal title now exists as a burden upon the Crown's underlying title. But surely, argues Borrows, this is to get matters the wrong way around. "How can lands possessed by Indigenous peoples for centuries be undermined by another nation's assertion of sovereignty?" he asks (Borrows 2002, 94). For Borrows as well as McCrossan and Ladner, this position is morally and politically indefensible, yet it is the position that the Supreme Court has taken (Borrows 2002, 96; McCrossan and Ladner 2016, 422).[22] Aboriginal title lands are now subordinate to Crown control "on grounds none other than self-assertion!" (Borrows 2002, 97; see also Grant 2018, 130).

Borrows then goes on to say that it is this built-in assumption about the priority of Crown sovereignty that structures the Supreme Court's approach to Aboriginal title. The onus of proving Aboriginal title is on Indigenous peoples and not the Crown, yet it is Indigenous peoples who were here first. As Borrows puts it, "why should the Aboriginal groups bear the burden of proving their title while the Crown is presumed to possess it through mere words?" (Borrows 2002, 101). The fact that this is deeply discriminatory and unjust is only reinforced when we realize that it is also the Supreme Court who ultimately decides whether an Indigenous nation has been successful (or not) in proving its title claim. To rely on decisions of the Supreme Court, therefore, carries with it considerable risk. Furthermore, as noted by Edward Hedican, "the proof of Aboriginal title had to be made in British terms, had to be reconciled to an alien crown sovereignty, and even then, was subject to the economic and social needs of the state" (Hedican 2013, 80) As a review of the cases in this chapter illustrate, against these rather self-serving criteria, Indigenous groups are as likely to lose as they are to win, making reliance on the generosity of the Supreme Court at best a double-edged sword.

The Supreme Court has also unilaterally decided that Aboriginal title lands can only be used in ways that do not deprive future generations of similar benefits of the land. But, critics ask, what does this restriction mean, and perhaps more importantly, who decides? The fact that the Court feels compelled to place this restriction upon Indigenous land use choices at all could be perceived as the ultimate form of paternalism. Yet, as Kenneth Coates and Dwight Newman point out, the kinds of development that might be precluded to safeguard the interests of future generations have been left ill-defined by the Court (Coates and Newman 2014, 16). The problem identified by some critics is that Indigenous groups might eventually feel compelled to go to the Canadian courts for clarification when, in fact, this is a matter best handled by Indigenous nations themselves.

What some critics stress, in other words, is that Indigenous peoples do not need the Supreme Court to tell them that they have an obligation to use their lands in ways that also preserves it for the use of future generations. They would naturally be inclined to do so anyway as part of their commitment to responsible stewardship of the land and care for their citizens. The larger point to be reinforced here, say critics such as Kent McNeil, Bonita Lawrence, and Patricia Monture-Angus, is that where limitations on the use of Aboriginal title lands are imposed they should be put in place by Indigenous nations themselves "through the exercise of their right to self-government" (McNeil 2002, 36; see also Lawrence 2012, 62; Monture-Angus 1999, 126; Sellars 2016, 155).[23] It is certainly not the place of the Canadian state to do so. Indeed, as so powerfully put in their evaluation of *Tsilqot'in*, Michael McCrossan and Kiera Ladner conclude that when all is said and done, "the decision provided federal and provincial governments with greater licence to *invade* Indigenous territories through the violent elimination of alternative legal orders and Indigenous jurisdictions" (McCrossan and Ladner 2016, 412).

ABORIGINAL TREATY RIGHTS

Treaty rights also play an important role in protecting the interests of Indigenous peoples, particularly so since they received constitutional protection as a Section 35 Aboriginal right in 1982. Treaty rights are those rights identified within the provisions of the treaties that were negotiated first between the French and British Crowns and later the Canadian state (or Crown) from the seventeenth to early twentieth centuries. Essentially, treaties reflect official agreements or solemn promises that specify both the nature of and limitations on Aboriginal rights and title. The earliest treaties of the seventeenth and eighteenth centuries are often referred to as "peace and friendship" treaties, which guaranteed Indigenous nations access to hunting and fishing, for example, but generally did not include the surrender of Indigenous lands. With the expansion of European settlement westward, treaty-making began to take on a different character as the issue of land surrenders began to play a more prominent role. In 1850, the Robinson treaties were signed in Ontario, and between 1871 and 1921, 11 treaties identified with a number (the so-called "Numbered Treaties") were negotiated across the west and north of Canada. By 1920 the last of the Numbered Treaties had been signed, leaving vast stretches of Canada not covered by treaty. These areas included portions of Newfoundland and Labrador, northern Quebec, most of British Columbia, and much of Yukon and the Northwest Territories.

The written text of many of the treaties in Ontario and across the prairies contain provisions stating that Indigenous nations agreed to give up (cede, release, or surrender) their lands. In exchange, the written text guarantees Indigenous nations access to reserves; some initial payments and subsequent small annual payments; the right to hunt, fish, and gather on and off reserve; and in some cases provisions for health care and schools. Crown representatives in the negotiations essentially believed that treaties were legal tools designed to extinguish Aboriginal rights and title in exchange for a limited set of treaty rights. Indigenous negotiators, however, did not see treaties as limiting or extinguishing their rights, but rather as a means to validate and protect them. They were of the view that treaties constituted solemn promises to share land, resources, and political power with their Euro-Canadian counterparts, developing a relationship of mutual respect and a duty of political non-interference in the affairs of the other along the way (Starblanket 2020, 15, 23, 26; King, H. 2018, 116). As explained by Gina Starblanket, treaties represented "a way of agreeing to live together [in a shared space] rather than an exchange of objects or terms" (Starblanket 2020, 25).

The problem, however, is that the written terms of the treaties were composed entirely by representatives of the French, British, or Canadian Crowns and therefore often differed from or failed to capture the Indigenous nations' interpretation of what they believed had been agreed to.[24] Yet it is the written terms of the treaties that have generally been regarded by Canadian state actors as authoritative. Still, for as long as non-Indigenous peoples did not compete for the same resources, Indigenous peoples' access to treaty-protected rights such as hunting, fishing, and trapping remained relatively secure (Coates 2000, 83). However, by the 1950s and 1960s Indigenous resource use came into increasing conflict with non-Indigenous users, in turn compounded by rising concerns for conservation. The outcome, says Ken Coates, was that more and more Indigenous hunters and fishers were being arrested. Indigenous individuals were charged with violating the terms of provincial hunting and fishing regulations, while in their defence Indigenous individuals argued that they were simply exercising their harvesting rights as protected under the terms of their treaties. It is in this context, says Coates, that "the legal tide began to turn, slowly, in favour of First Nations rights" (Coates 2000, 83).

By the mid-1960s, the Supreme Court of Canada began to intervene on Indigenous peoples' behalf, arguing that treaties must be understood with Indigenous peoples' interests in mind. To take Indigenous perspectives into account, the Supreme Court developed a more sophisticated approach to identifying the content and scope of the Aboriginal rights protected in treaties. As Olthuis, Kleer, and Townshend explain, "the process involves trying to figure out what each of the parties to the treaties agreed to … at the time of the formation of the treaty" (Olthuis, Kleer, Townshend 2012, 38, 35). According to the Supreme Court, an accurate interpretation of treaty provisions requires a judicial process of several steps: judges must examine the wording of the treaty; they must reconstruct the intentions of the parties from oral history; they must study documents written at the time the treaty was negotiated; and they must attempt to look back and decipher "what the interests of the parties would have been" (Olthuis, Kleer, Townshend 2012, 36).

At this point, two other important interpretative principles come into play. The Supreme Court has established that because there was often an imbalance in the bargaining power of Indigenous and Crown negotiators, it is essential that Indigenous understandings of their treaties be given close scrutiny in legal proceedings. To that end, the Supreme Court has ruled in the first place that in all treaty disputes, any ambiguous terms in treaties are to be interpreted generously and in ways that are favourable to Aboriginal interests. And second, treaties must be construed not according to the technical meaning of their words but in a sense that they would have naturally been understood by the Indigenous parties at the time (Isaac 2012, 111). Naturally, the operation of these principles in treaty jurisprudence does not always deliver the results that Indigenous claimants hope for, the outcome being judicial losses from time to time. But there have been several judicial outcomes that have tilted significantly in the direction of Indigenous peoples' treaty interests. What follows identifies a few of the more notable cases on both sides of the judicial ledger.

WHITE AND BOB (1965), *SIMON* (1985), AND *SIOUI* (1990)

In the three cases of *White and Bob* (1965), *Simon* (1985), and *Sioui* (1990), the Supreme Court of Canada acted to protect the treaty rights of Indigenous persons against provincial governments that had levelled charges against them on the grounds that they actually had no treaty rights at all. In each case, the province in question (British Columbia, Nova Scotia, and Quebec) claimed that the documents the Indigenous plaintiffs had relied on to authorize their hunting or gathering activities were not treaties because those who had entered into them were not authorized to do so under the historical rules of treaty-making. Consequently, each of the provinces argued that their laws applied against the actions of those accused and each was therefore justifiably subject to conviction.

The Supreme Court came to the defence of the accused in all three cases, arguing that while the documents on which the accused had relied to authorize their hunting and gathering activities may well be ambiguous with respect to following the standard format of treaties, there was no doubt that the documents were, in fact, treaties. The Court ruled that those who had entered into them were authorized to do so according to the rules of the day and so, with respect to the hunting and gathering issues at trial, no conviction was warranted. This meant that in the 1965 case of *R. v. White and Bob*, the two men from the Saalequun Tribe (now part of the Snuneymuxw First Nation) near Nanaimo on Vancouver Island who were arrested for hunting deer out of season were subsequently vindicated by the Supreme Court on the grounds that they had a treaty right to hunt as provided for under the conditions of the Douglas Treaty signed by James Douglas and the Saalequun Tribe in 1854 (Coates 2000, 84). Similarly, in the 1985 case of *Simon v. The Queen*, the conviction of James Simon, a member of the Shubenacadie band of the Mi'kmaq Nation, was overturned on the grounds that he had a right to hunt (and thus carry a hunting rifle and ammunition in a safe manner) under the terms of a "peace and friendship" treaty negotiated with Governor P.T. Hobson in 1752 (Coates 2000, 87). And finally, in the 1990 case *R. v. Sioui*, the Supreme Court agreed that a group of Huron-Wendat persons had been wrongfully convicted of "illegally" camping, cutting down trees, and making fire in Quebec's Jacques-Cartier Park (outside the boundaries of the Lorette reserve, where they lived), because such activities were consistent with their treaty rights that authorized them to take up practices consistent with their "ancestral customs and religious rites" (*R. v. Sioui* 1990, 1025; see also Coates 2000, 87–8; Courchene 2018, 148–9). In short, said the Supreme Court, in all three cases the Indigenous plaintiffs' treaty rights clearly existed, and as such they could continue to hunt, gather, and practise ancestral customs and religious rites as they had before.

The three Supreme Court cases identified in the above paragraph draw into particularly sharp focus the Court's commitment to an important new principle in Canadian jurisprudence, namely, the need to resolve treaty ambiguities in favour of Indigenous interests to take into account historical imbalances in political power (Courchene 2018, 149). Other decisions draw attention to the Supreme Court's no less important commitment to interpret treaties in ways that would have been naturally understood by the Indigenous partners.[25] A particularly well-known example of the latter is the 1999 case of *R. v. Marshall.*

R. v. MARSHALL (1999)

The *Marshall* case involved a Mi'kmaq man, Donald Marshall Jr., who had been charged with fishing and selling eels without a licence and fishing during season closures with illegal nets. Marshall argued that under a 1760 Mi'kmaq "peace and friendship" treaty entered into between the British governor of Nova Scotia and a Mi'kmaq chief, he had a treaty right to catch and sell eels and therefore was exempt from federal fishery regulations (*R. v. Marshall* 1999, 456). The treaty to which Marshall was referring made no provision for the protection of Mi'kmaq hunting or fishing rights, and with respect to trade said only that the Mi'kmaq agreed to "Traffic, Barter, or Exchange any Commodities" that they might have to offer with the British only.

The Supreme Court readily accepted the fact that the text of the treaty was silent on the matter of Mi'kmaq hunting, fishing, and trading rights. However, the Court added that even though there may be no ambiguity in the words of the treaty itself, "the written document does not include all the terms of the agreement" (*R. v. Marshall* 1999, 457). In fact, said the Court, if the honour and integrity of the Crown is to be upheld, extrinsic oral evidence reflecting Mi'kmaq understandings of the negotiations must also be given appropriate weight alongside that of the written text. It is this crucial legal requirement that the lower courts had failed to consider.

When reframed against this broader criterion, the Supreme Court was convinced that the written terms of the treaty had to change. The Court pointed out, for example, that during the negotiations leading to the 1760 treaty, Indigenous leaders asked for truck-houses (trading posts) "for the furnishing them with necessaries, in Exchange for their Peltry" (*R. v. Marshall* 1999, 456). This "trade clause" could be construed narrowly to mean that the Mi'kmaq agreed to trade with no one other than the British. But when interpreted in terms that incorporate both Mi'kmaq oral evidence "and British-drafted minutes of the negotiating sessions," a more favourable treaty outcome becomes evident. As put by the Court, "the trade clause would not have advanced British objectives (peaceful relations with a self-sufficient Mi'kmaq people) or Mi'kmaq objectives (access to the European 'necessaries' on which they had come to rely) unless the Mi'kmaq were assured at the same time of continuing access, implicitly or explicitly, to a harvest of wildlife to trade" (*R. v. Marshall* 1999, 458). Put otherwise, it would simply have made no sense for the British to respond to Mi'kmaq trading demands by providing a trading facility but then offer no treaty protection to the very resources that the Mi'kmaq intended to trade.

As for how these more generous interpretive terms ought to apply to the present, the Supreme Court decided that it was the right to trade that constituted the core feature of the treaty. Consequently, although truck-houses disappeared (which the Court characterized as no more than the "mechanism created to facilitate the right"), the Court determined that the actual treaty right itself to trade had survived and persists to the present day. When situated in the contemporary context, therefore, the Supreme Court concluded that the Mi'kmaq have an ongoing treaty right to trade for a moderate livelihood. In the words of the Court, the treaty's trading clause confers upon the Mi'kmaq the right to "obtain necessaries through hunting and fishing by trading the products of those traditional activities," though subject to justifiable restrictions that may be imposed by government (*R. v. Marshall* 1999, 501). In essence, what the Court did was take the old language of "necessaries" and substitute it with a contemporary alternative – "a moderate livelihood." The Court then concluded that it was this treaty right to make "a moderate livelihood' that enjoys constitutional protection under Section 35 and as such takes priority over the Nova Scotia licensing system that Donald Marshall Jr. had purportedly violated. As Marshall's fishing was protected by his treaty right to pursue "a moderate livelihood," he was acquitted of all charges.

Interestingly, the Supreme Court seemed entirely unprepared for the political firestorm of protest in Nova Scotia and New Brunswick that was set off by its *Marshall* decision. Non-Indigenous fishers were outraged, believing that the Mi'kmaq would have unlimited and unregulated access to the Atlantic fishery, thereby effectively shutting them out of the industry. Concerns were also expressed in response to Mi'kmaq arguments that the *Marshall* decision implied they also had a treaty right to commercial logging and mineral extraction as well as fishing. As protests escalated, threatening violence, the Supreme Court was prompted to act.

In an attempt to ease political tensions, the Supreme Court took the unusual legal move of elaborating on its *Marshall* decision (referred to as *Marshall No. 2*) in the form of a clarification. Essentially, the Court said that while the Mi'kmaq had a treaty right to fish for a moderate livelihood, that right does "not extend to the open-ended accumulation of wealth" (*R. v. Marshall* 1999, 459). In addition, the Court reminded federal and provincial governments that they may impose limitations on the exercise of the treaty right if doing so advances "compelling and substantial public objectives." By way of examples, the Court identified potentially justifiable limitations to include resource management, conservation, and restrictions imposed on the Indigenous fishery for the sake of ensuring economic and regional fairness to non-Indigenous fishers. In the end, this important clarification did not fundamentally change the substance of the Supreme Court's 1999 *Marshall* decision. But what it did do is demonstrate the many ways in which the Court believed governments could "legitimately" subject the right to restrictions just short of extinguishment (Manfredi 2004, 195). Under no circumstances, said the Court, is the Mi'kmaq treaty right to hunt, fish, gather, and trade to be construed as absolute.

The *Marshall* decisions did eventually result in a series of interim fishing agreements between the federal government and Indigenous nations (Mi'kmaq, Maliseet, and Passamaquoddy) in Atlantic Canada and Quebec. But Ottawa's insistence that the Indigenous "moderate livelihood fishery" must be subject to federal regulations, including concerns for conservation, has been an ongoing source of simmering tension and dispute. It is the position of a number of the affected Indigenous nations, for example, that their right to fish for a moderate livelihood entitles them to fish in their ancestral waters when and where they like, with the proviso that those rights ought not to be subject to federal regulations, but rather to those set out within their own nation's management plans.

R. v. MARSHALL; *R. v.* BERNARD (2005)

Building on the momentum of the *Marshall* decision, the Mi'kmaq decided to harvest timber on Crown lands in New Brunswick for commercial purposes, claiming that they were exercising their rights under the terms of the same 1760 "peace and friendship" treaty. They therefore sought no authorization from the government of New Brunswick and were subsequently charged with illegal logging (Hedican 2013, 83).

On appeal in 2005, the Supreme Court of Canada dealt with two logging cases together, one against 35 Mi'kmaq individuals charged with cutting timber on Crown land without proper provincial authorization (*R. v. Marshall*) and one against a single Mi'kmaq individual in possession of spruce logs intended for sale at a local mill (*R. v. Bernard*). The Supreme Court upheld their convictions on the grounds that in its judgment, the Treaty of 1760 did "not confer on modern Mi'kmaq a right to log contrary to provincial regulation" (*R. v. Marshall; R. v. Bernard* 2005, 222). In these cases, the Court was not willing to accept the Mi'kmaq argument that commercial logging constituted a natural evolution in the trading practices for which their ancestors had received treaty protection in 1760.

In keeping with its earlier 1999 *Marshall* decision, the Court certainly did go along with the idea that Mi'kmaq "ancestral trading activities … are not frozen in time" (*R. v. Marshall; R. v. Bernard* 2005, 223). But, argued the Court, unlike trading in eels, commercial logging cannot be construed as a logical extension of the kind of trading activity that was protected by the Treaty of 1760. To be sure, the Mi'kmaq gathered and used forest products in 1760 (and before) for making canoes, baskets, snowshoes, toboggans, and wigwams. However, logging itself was not a traditional Mi'kmaq activity. Therefore, the Court concluded, the evidence does not support a treaty right to commercial logging (*R. v. Marshall; R. v. Bernard* 2005, paras. 32, 34). As a result, the Mi'kmaq lost their cases, the implication of the Court's ruling being that outside of a verifiable treaty or Aboriginal title right, the Mi'kmaq had no Aboriginal right to log for commercial purposes.[26]

IMPLICATIONS AND ANALYSIS

The inclination of the Supreme Court of Canada is to see treaties as guaranteeing a set of rights, like that of a contract (Starblanket 2020, 15). The essential issue for the Supreme Court then becomes whether those rights should be given a literal or liberal interpretation. The cases we have reviewed indicate that of late, the Court has been prepared to give the treaties a larger, more liberal interpretation, often resolving ambiguities in favour of the understanding of the Indigenous party. Now, generous and liberal interpretations are fine, but critics point out that these judicial interpretations are still rooted almost entirely in a textual analysis of the treaty. For example, the Court simply takes it as given that the treaties constituted land surrenders in which Indigenous nations agreed to "cede, release and surrender" their traditional territories in exchange for reserves, small payments, and limited rights to hunt and fish off reserve. The question that the Court then presumes it is called on to resolve is how these limited treaty rights that were negotiated in the past are to be carried through and practised in the present day.

It is at this point in the proceedings that the Supreme Court activates its generous and liberal interpretive framework. A liberal interpretation means that guaranteed access to "truck-houses" translates into a modern treaty right to fish for a moderate livelihood (*R. v. Marshall* 1999). Or a right to hunt for deer on unoccupied lands translates into a modern treaty right to hunt with guns on Crown lands even in the face of prohibiting provincial regulations (*Simon v. The Queen* 1985). From the perspective of several critics, however, this supposedly liberal approach to treaty interpretation makes a fundamental interpretive mistake because it chooses to resolve disputes on a narrow issue-by-issue and case-by-case basis. What it fails to take into consideration is the underlying relational dimension that constituted the primary reason for Indigenous peoples originally wanting to enter into treaty arrangements in the first place (Coyle 2017, 47; Starblanket 2020, 22–7). As put by Mark Walters, what the Supreme Court has done is enforce eighteenth-century treaties but only "in relation to specific activities like hunting and fishing or engaging in trade or in a particular customary practice" (Walters 2017, 191).

Rather than reduce the essential character of treaties to a set of contractual obligations, Indigenous commentators argue that treaties should be seen in much broader terms. For example, Gina Starblanket argues that as far as Indigenous peoples are concerned, treaties were designed to establish nation-to-nation relations of peaceful coexistence and mutual sharing of land and resources (Starblanket 2020, 16). A.C. Hamilton and C.M. Sinclair further explain that the treaties established permanent relationships between Indigenous nations and the Crown, in which it was understood that both took up solemn promises with respect to the other. They further argue that Indigenous signatories regarded treaties as vehicles through which, they believed, the Crown offered its recognition of Indigenous sovereignty. Through treaties, Indigenous nations promised to be allies of the Crown forever, and the "Crown was seen as committing itself to promote the well-being of its Indian allies" (Hamilton and Sinclair 1991, 148).

As for the promises contained within the text of the treaties themselves, commentators argue that they should be read comprehensively, establishing relationships designed to guarantee ongoing Indigenous rights to political autonomy. Treaty references to reserves; to hunting, fishing, and trapping rights; to ploughs and seed; to medicine chests and schools should all be read in light of this long-term comprehensive objective. Each, in its own way and in its own time, was intended to contribute to the Crown's longer-term commitment to protect and promote Indigenous ways of life. As captured by Gina Starblanket, "far from a 'sale' of land, treaties are regarded by Indigenous peoples as land use frameworks, which generally involve the establishment of separate governments and jurisdictions in distinct spaces, and dual governance and jurisdiction in shared spaces and matters of mutual concern" (Starblanket 2020, 20). When measured against this interpretive framework, say critics, the Supreme Court's approach to treaty rights is far too literalistic and disturbingly narrow.

DUTY TO CONSULT AND ACCOMMODATE

Aboriginal title claims to traditional lands and the full scope and application of historic treaty rights can take a very long time to sort out, whether it be in the political arena or in the courts. In response, the Supreme Court of Canada has developed a new doctrine that imposes a formal duty on federal and provincial governments to consult Indigenous peoples and accommodate their interests whenever their asserted (but as yet unresolved) or established Aboriginal and treaty rights might be adversely affected by government decisions. Clearly, it would be blatantly unfair if, in advance of the settlement of title claims or clarification of treaty rights, lands subject to Indigenous claims were sold off or traditional resources compromised through natural resource development. It is circumstances such as these that the Supreme Court has sought to head off.

The basis for this duty to consult and accommodate, says the Supreme Court, is the principle of the honour of the Crown, which flows from Section 35 of the *Constitution Act, 1982*. This principle requires that the Crown act honourably in its treatment of potential but as yet unproven Indigenous interests. In the words of the Court, Canadian governments have a constitutional obligation to never "cavalierly run roughshod over Aboriginal interests," but rather to treat those interests with utmost respect even if only potential and as yet unproven (*Haida Nation v. British Columbia* 2004, para. 27). In as much as special protection is afforded to Aboriginal and treaty rights when faced with potential or actual threats, then, says the Court, the duty of the Crown has been fulfilled.

The Crown's duty to consult and accommodate was first established by the Supreme Court in its *Sparrow* and *Delgamuukw* decisions, though here the duty was construed in more limited terms as part of the process required to justify infringements of Aboriginal and treaty rights (Isaac 2012, 302). Three seminal Supreme Court cases fundamentally transformed the nature of the governmental obligations that are attached to the duty to consult and accommodate while also establishing "the steps that government agencies must take prior to making various decisions" (Newman 2014, 12). The 2004 decisions of *Haida Nation v. British Columbia* and *Taku River Tlingit First Nation v. British Columbia* extended the government's duty to consult to apply to governmental decisions and regulations that might adversely affect Indigenous interests, including asserted but as yet unproven Aboriginal rights and title. The 2005 case of *Mikisew Cree First Nation v. Canada* established that the government's duty to consult must also include treaty rights (Isaac 2012, 302–3). In what follows I briefly summarize the circumstances surrounding each case and then address the political significance of the three cases together.

HAIDA NATION v. BRITISH COLUMBIA (2004)

The *Haida Nation* case originated in objections that the Haida levelled at the British Columbia Ministry of Forests over its 1999 decision to transfer a tree farm licence from MacMillan Bloedel Ltd. to Weyerhaeuser Company Limited on Haida Gwaii, land the Haida claimed (but had not yet proven) as their traditional territory. The Haida challenged the legality of the transfer, arguing that as the land was subject to a title claim, the provincial government had a duty to consult them about the transfer as part of a larger effort to seek their consent (*Haida Nation v. British Columbia* 2004, 512). The Haida were quite understandably fearful that without adequate consultation and accommodation they could very well lose access to forests of vital importance to them (Hoehn 2012, 38). The Supreme Court of Canada ruled in favour of the Haida Nation, arguing that the provincial government's obligation to consult the Haida was engaged. Given that consultation had not occurred, the Court concluded that the provincial government had breached its duties. Furthermore, said the Court, because the stakes in this case were huge given the importance of forestry to the Haida Nation, significant accommodation of Haida interests would be required (*Haida Nation v. British Columbia* 2004, para. 76).

TAKU RIVER TLINGIT FIRST NATION v. BRITISH COLUMBIA (2004)

The *Taku River* case was motivated by the Taku River Tlingit Nation's desire to overturn a plan to build a 160-kilometre road from the Tulsequah Chief Mine to the town of Atlin in northwest British Columbia. A portion of the proposed road was to pass through the Taku River Tlinglit Nation's traditional territory. The nation went to court in an attempt to get the approval certificate for the road quashed on the grounds that it would jeopardize their Aboriginal rights and title in the area, including their domestic economy and practices associated with their social and cultural life (*Taku River Tlingit First Nation v. British Columbia* 2004, para. 31). The Supreme Court was certainly receptive to the Taku River Tlingit Nation's concerns, stating, for example, that the proposed road construction carried with it the potential for negative derivative impacts upon their title claims. It was therefore clear to the Court that the nation was legally entitled to deep consultation that would result in some form of meaningful accommodation of their interests (*Taku River Tlingit First Nation v. British Columbia* 2004, para. 32). Upon weighing the evidence, however, the Court ultimately decided that the Government of British Columbia had met its duty to consult. According to the Court, a rigorous and inclusive environmental assessment process had been provided. The Court was of the view that because they had participated fully in the environmental assessment process, the Taku River Tlingit Nation had been adequately consulted and appropriate measures had been taken to accommodate their interests.[27]

MIKISEW CREE FIRST NATION v. CANADA (MINISTER OF CANADIAN HERITAGE) (2005)

In the case of *Mikisew Cree*, the doctrine of the duty to consult and accommodate was extended by the Supreme Court to treaty rights. This case involved a proposal to build a winter road in Wood Buffalo National Park in northern Alberta, also the location of the Mikisew Cree First Nation's reserve. The proposed road was originally designed to run through the Mikisew Cree's reserve, but after they protested the road design was modified to track around the boundary of the reserve instead (*Mikisew Cree First Nation v. Canada* 2005, 389). Even with the relocation, the Mikisew Cree argued that the proposed road would still substantially disrupt their hunting and trapping in the area and in doing so jeopardize their Treaty 8 rights to hunt, trap, and fish on unoccupied Crown land. The Supreme Court accepted the Government of Alberta's argument that the provincial Crown had a treaty right "to take up surrendered lands for regional transportation purposes," but it nevertheless held that the Crown still has an obligation to consult with the Mikisew Cree "in good faith." As the impacts of the proposed winter road "were clear, established, and demonstrably adverse to the continued exercise of the Mikisew hunting and trapping rights over the lands in question," the Court concluded that the duty to consult had been triggered (*Mikisew Cree First Nation v. Canada* 2005, para. 55). Given that the Government of Alberta had failed in its duty to consult the Mikisew Cree based on its mistaken belief that no consultation was required, the Court quashed the minister's approval order with instructions to begin the process again.[28]

REQUIRED STEPS IN THE DUTY TO CONSULT

In its consideration of the preceding three cases, the Supreme Court of Canada clearly laid out the political steps required of federal and provincial governments if they are to successfully meet their constitutional obligations to consult and, if circumstances warrant, accommodate Indigenous interests. In sum, these steps involve a number of interlocking components.

First, the duty to consult itself arises when proposed governmental action might infringe upon a not yet proven Aboriginal right or title claim or when it is unclear what effects a proposed governmental initiative might have on an Aboriginal or treaty right. Second, it is the Crown that owes the duty to consult, not third parties. Normally the duty falls to federal or provincial governments, but both may delegate procedural aspects of the duty to municipalities or tribunals if they wish (Olthuis, Kleer, Townshend 2012, 55). Third, the duty to consult is triggered relatively easily. Consultation is required when there are established or asserted Aboriginal or treaty rights that the Crown knows about or ought to know about and that may be affected by proposed governmental decisions or actions (Isaac 2012, 334). Fourth, the level of consultation required varies on a case-by-case basis "depending on the strength of the asserted claims to rights or land title, and on the extent to which the proposed decision or activity will potentially harm those existing or asserted rights" (Olthuis, Kleer, Townshend 2012, 58). Consultation options can range from simple notification and discussions with the affected party in the case of weak claims or minor impacts all the way up to providing guarantees to avoid, minimize, or compensate for harm done in the case of stronger claims or major impacts (*Haida Nation v. British Columbia* 2004, paras. 43–5). And fifth, court-ordered remedies in the face of governmental failure to meet its duty to consult can include injunctions against governmental action, suspension of a sale or permit, and the awarding of damages. The more typical response, however, involves the courts issuing an order to conduct deeper consultations in keeping with the seriousness of the purported impact anticipated (Newman 2014, 26).

One further matter that the Supreme Court of Canada has addressed is whether the end point of the consultation process must result in an agreement between governments and the Indigenous party. The language employed by the Supreme Court to date suggests that while desirable, as far is it is concerned there is no such requirement. In addition, the Court has also ruled that the process does not give Indigenous parties a veto, even in cases where substantial harm to Indigenous interests is anticipated. What is required, in the words of the Court, "is a process of balancing interests, of give and take" (*Haida Nation v. British Columbia* 2004, para. 48). As a general technique, the Court urges governments to begin consultations early in the planning process and that they make every effort to address Indigenous peoples' concerns.

The Court specifies that consultation should entail opportunities for Indigenous peoples to make submissions, to formally participate in the decision-making process, and to be provided with written reasons at the end of the process to show that Indigenous concerns were considered (*Haida Nation v. British Columbia* 2004, para. 44). As accommodations, the Court suggests that these could reasonably range from changes to the parameters of proposed plans to integrate Indigenous interests, all the way to abandoning plans should it become clear that Indigenous interests cannot be accommodated.

It is also worth mentioning that the Supreme Court's approach to the question of consultation and accommodation may well be evolving with the passage of time. Kenneth Coates and Dwight Newman observe in their evaluation of the 2014 *Tsilhqot'in* case, for example, that "although the Court does not make consent a generalized legal requirement, it goes out of its way to reflect upon its desirability" (Coates and Newman 2014, 17). Quoting then Chief Justice Beverly McLaughlin on this matter: "I add this. Governments and individuals proposing to use or exploit land, whether before or after a declaration of Aboriginal title, can avoid a charge of infringement or failure to adequately consult by obtaining the consent of the interested Aboriginal group" (*Tsilhqot'in Nation v. British Columbia* 2014, para. 44). Based on these statements, it would seem that in cases of potentially significant and far-reaching infringements on Aboriginal rights and title, the Supreme Court would now rule that the consent of the Indigenous nation affected is required. If this is indeed the position of the Supreme Court, it is an important development because it would signal that there is now consistency between Canadian jurisprudence on Indigenous rights and international human rights standards as found in Article 32 of the UNDRIP, which states that the free and informed consent of Indigenous peoples must be obtained "prior to the approval of any project affecting their lands or territories and other resources."

CHIPPEWAS OF THE THAMES FIRST NATION v. ENBRIDGE PIPELINES INC. (2017)

Two more recent Supreme Court cases, decided in 2017, serve as telling illustrations of how these rules have been engaged and thus are worthy of brief review. The first case, *Chippewas of the Thames First Nation v. Enbridge Pipelines Inc.*, involved a dispute over a pipeline that crossed the Chippewas' traditional territory in southwestern Ontario. The Supreme Court rejected the Chippewas claim that they had been inadequately consulted after approval was granted by the National Energy Board (NEB) authorizing Enbridge Pipelines to increase the capacity of its Line 9 oil pipeline. The Chippewas concerns were motivated by fears that the enhanced capacity of the pipeline would increase the risk of pipeline ruptures and spills, "which could adversely impact their use of the land and the Thames River for traditional purposes." They also argued that the NEB had no jurisdiction to approve the Line 9 modifications outside of Crown consultation (*Chippewas of the Thames First Nation v. Enbridge Pipelines Inc.* 2017, paras. 17, 18).

The Supreme Court rejected the Chippewas' appeal on two grounds. First, the Court determined that as a federal administrative tribunal and regulatory agency, the NEB can be authorized through federal statutory power to fulfill the Crown's duty to consult and accommodate Indigenous nations. In the Court's view, the NEB had been so authorized by the federal government and so could serve as its delegate in conducting consultations. And second, the Supreme Court concluded that the Crown's duty to consult had been adequately fulfilled by the NEB review process. The Chippewas had been granted funding to participate as an intervenor, they had filed evidence, and they had delivered oral arguments outlining their concerns (*Chippewas of the Thames First Nation v. Enbridge Pipelines Inc.* 2017, para. 18). The NEB, in turn, had assessed the potential negative impacts of the project on the Aboriginal rights of the Chippewas deciding, correctly in the Court's view, that the impacts would be minimal and, where present, could be reasonably mitigated.[29] The Court concluded, therefore, that while the strength of the Chippewas' claim was strong and thus a vigorous consultation process was required, "the consultation undertaken in this case was manifestly adequate" (*Chippewas of the Thames First Nation v. Enbridge Pipelines Inc.* 2017, 1101).

CLYDE RIVER (HAMLET) v. PETROLEUM GEO-SERVICES INC. (2017)

The second case, *Clyde River (Hamlet) v. Petroleum Geo-Services Inc.*, concerned the application by three companies to the NEB for authorization to conduct offshore seismic testing for oil and gas in the Baffin Bay and Davis Straight areas of Nunavut. The Inuit at Clyde River feared that the seismic testing would adversely affect the migratory patterns of the marine mammals they relied on for food and for their economic, cultural, and spiritual well-being. The Inuit also pointed out that their treaty rights, protected under the 1993 *Nunavut Land Claims Agreement*, included the right to harvest marine mammals (*Clyde River (Hamlet) v. Petroleum Geo-Services Inc.* 2017, para. 2). The Inuit petitioned the NEB, expressing their opposition to the proposed seismic testing.

The NEB launched an environmental assessment of the project, which included hearings conducted in the Inuit communities close to the proposed seismic testing area. On the grounds that the environmental assessment process conducted had met the required elements of the Crown's duty to consult, including, among other things, promises to develop mitigation measures, the NEB granted the requested authorization. The Inuit immediately challenged the decision on two grounds: first, the NEB had no legal authority to approve the project apart from formal Crown involvement; and second, the consultation process itself was grossly inadequate when measured against the consultation standards required.

As with the *Chippewas* case, the Supreme Court disagreed with the Inuit's first objection on the grounds that the Crown may rely on an independent regulatory agency such as the NEB to fulfill the Crown's duty to consult. Consequently, this portion of the Inuit's legal challenge was dismissed. With respect to the second objection, however, the Supreme Court agreed with the Inuit that the NEB had not properly discharged the Crown's duty to consult as the consultation process was flawed in almost every respect (*Clyde River (Hamlet) v. Petroleum Geo-Services Inc.* 2017, para. 4). For example, the Inuit had not been told that the Crown intended to rely on the NEB process to fulfill its duty to consult. The Inuit had also received no participant funding nor was there a formal hearing process. Furthermore, said the Court, the inquiry itself was misdirected. What it did was focus on the likely environmental effects of the proposed seismic testing rather than on the potential impact of that testing on Inuit treaty rights and their ability to exercise them (*Clyde River (Hamlet) v. Petroleum Geo-Services Inc.* 2017, paras. 45–7). As it was clear to the Court that the possible impacts of the proposed testing could significantly impair Inuit treaty rights, a deep level of consultation was called for. Yet, in the Court's view, this had not happened. For these reasons, the Court concluded that the Crown had breached its duty to consult, and so the NEB's authorization was overturned.

IMPLICATIONS AND ANALYSIS

As the preceding analysis indicates, when Indigenous peoples choose to advance arguments about the definition and scope of their Aboriginal and treaty rights in the Canadian court system, they take on a significant amount of risk. Canadian courts are tasked with the responsibility to uphold a constitutional order that guarantees the ongoing integrity and sovereignty of the Canadian state. Yet the Indigenous assertion to rights throws into question the very credentials of Canada. Aboriginal rights seek, on some level, to undermine the proposition that the Canadian state has the right to assert sovereignty over Indigenous peoples and their lands. But, as Patricia Monture-Angus points out, the courts cannot question Canadian sovereignty because they owe their existence to this very fact. Indeed, as she explains, if the Canadian courts were to find the sovereignty of the Canadian state to be wanting, this "would in fact disestablish their own legitimacy" (Monture-Angus 1999, 65).

Consequently, the Canadian courts, including the Supreme Court of Canada, operate under the assumption they have no authority to call into question the sovereignty of Canada as a political order. Indeed, the Supreme Court has been clear and uncompromising on this point. While the Supreme Court insists that Aboriginal rights must be both recognized and affirmed as part of the Crown's duty to deal honourably with Indigenous peoples, it is no less insistent that those rights must be exercised in a manner that is "compatible with the sovereignty of the Crown" (Panagos 2016, 86; see also McCrossan and Ladner 2016, 414–19). But critics then point out that this is to get things exactly the wrong way around. If there is to be a hierarchy of sovereignties, then surely it should be Aboriginal and treaty rights that are given priority over broader (secondary) non-Indigenous community interests.

A good case in point is illustrated by the duty to consult and accommodate. A number of critics have observed that in the context of the relatively recent introduction of the doctrine of the duty to consult in Canadian jurisprudence (*Haida Nation v. British Columbia* 2004), an important opportunity was missed. Critics readily accept that the doctrine does impose more rigorous standards about the kinds of procedures that must now be followed by governments when they want to authorize development projects on traditional Indigenous territories. This is a good thing. However, Indigenous consent is still not one of the requirements. Shin Imai observes, for example, that the requirement to consult is a far lower standard than the international human rights standard of "free, prior, and informed consent." Provided governments can show that they have engaged in adequate consultation by the standards of the Supreme Court, development projects can proceed even if Indigenous peoples say "no." In the face of such power imbalances, Imai is convinced that Indigenous peoples may be reluctant to engage in negotiations because, at the end of the day, it is still the Canadian state that holds all the power. The relationship of inferiority versus superiority is allowed to persist because the Canadian state is still authorized to reach into Indigenous peoples' areas of jurisdiction and override their decisions (Imai 2017).

Why is the higher threshold of consent or agreement to resource projects on Indigenous traditional territories justified in Imai's view? Because consent is an important principle of justice in keeping with international human rights standards as documented in UNDRIP, for example. According to international standards, consent establishes a relationship more in keeping with that of two sovereigns. If the Canadian state wishes to pursue ventures on Indigenous lands, they must secure the agreement of the affected Indigenous nations first and "would have no grounds to override any Indigenous refusal" (Grant 2018, 136). As explained by Imai, in other words, consent is the standard that can serve to balance Indigenous interests with the "superior political power of government" (Imai 2017, 386). It is through recognition of the necessity of consent that true consensus-building efforts are possible, because the negotiation process itself will have built-in protections for the position of Indigenous parties. As put by John Grant, "this is what a sovereign-to-sovereign relationship demands" (Grant 2018, 136).

In short, while the Aboriginal and treaty rights recognized and affirmed in Section 35 of the *Constitution Act, 1982* have been given substantive meaning within Canadian law by the Supreme Court of Canada, they have also been subjected to important limitations. Edward Hedican astutely observes, for example, that because Supreme Court judges have subjected Aboriginal rights and title to various narrow legal tests as a precondition to their existence, those rights are not in fact being respected in full but rather are subject to significant structural limitations (Hedican 2013, 86).[30] The Supreme Court's move to limit Aboriginal and treaty rights simultaneously with their recognition is therefore interpreted by some critics as a strategy to subject Indigenous sovereignty "to the sovereignty of the larger Canadian society" (Tully 2008, 273).[31] Far from empowering Indigenous peoples, Aboriginal and treaty rights can be seen as legal tools that the Supreme Court has employed in the service of colonialism's constraints.

SOVEREIGNTY'S OPPORTUNITIES

While it is indeed the case that the Supreme Court has refused to question the credentials of the Canadian state's assertion to sovereignty over Indigenous peoples and their territories, this does not mean that the overall political effects of its decisions have created no room for the exercise of Indigenous sovereignty within Canada. Indeed, Thomas Courchene is far more sanguine in his assessment, arguing that "by any definition, the results, as they relate to Aboriginal rights and land title claims, have been truly remarkable" (Courchene 2018, 161). He recognizes that "these achievements are in the first instance due to the perseverance and creativity of First Nations themselves" but then adds "the key player behind the achievement of the dramatic evolution of Aboriginal rights and title was the Supreme Court of Canada and its series of path-breaking decisions" (Courchene 2018 161).

Julie Jai is no less complimentary in her assessment of Supreme Court decisions. She notes that "the availability and use of court challenges has significantly improved First Nations' bargaining positions," while later she observes that "while Indigenous people are still subject to a bargaining power disadvantage as compared with governments, the playing field is more level than in the past" (Jai 2017, 116). In short, these commentators conclude that at the end of the day the Canadian court system has provided Indigenous peoples with substantive leverage in Canadian law to recapture their powers of self-determination and to reassert their position as landlords over their own traditional territories, albeit through legal processes that often proceed very slowly and incrementally. Recognizing, therefore, that Indigenous rights and title are not respected in full and in some cases are still being denied, the following paragraphs nevertheless seek to identify several important ways in which Supreme Court decisions have created room for the expression of Indigenous sovereignty. I refer to these as "sovereignty's opportunities."

While perhaps an obvious point, it is worth noting that Aboriginal rights and title now exist in Canadian law. No less important, however, are the changes set in motion by Supreme Court decisions concerning the legal origins and standing of those rights. Whereas it was once assumed that Aboriginal rights and title existed at the pleasure of the Crown, since the *Calder* decision of 1973 it is accepted in Canadian law that Aboriginal rights and title existed prior to the colonization of North America (Hedican 2013, 85–6). As put by Justice Lamer in *Van Der Peet,* "when Europeans arrived in North America, aboriginal peoples were already living here, living in communities on the land, and participating in distinctive cultures, as they had done for centuries" (*R. v. Van Der Peet* 1996, para. 30). Consequently, Aboriginal rights are now understood to be inherent in the sense that the Supreme Court recognizes them to be free-standing and independent rights rooted in original Indigenous occupation of North America. It is for this reason that Aboriginal rights are distinct from the rights enjoyed by other Canadians (Panagos 2016, 23; Sellars 2016, 156).[32]

Because Aboriginal and treat rights now enjoy constitutional protection, the Supreme Court has also forbidden their unilateral extinguishment. The fact that the Canadian government could do so before 1982 verifies that Indigenous peoples did indeed live within a system of internal colonization. The fact that the Canadian government can no longer do so, however, speaks to the profoundly important status that Aboriginal rights now enjoy in constitutional law. The Supreme Court has indicated that these rights exist beyond the purview of the Canadian state because they originate from within Indigenous nations themselves. This constitutional elevation carries with it important legal consequences. Among other things, the Supreme Court has instructed that any federal, provincial, or territorial law that infringes on an Aboriginal right may now be subject to repeal, at least to the extent of the infringement (Isaac 2012, 16). The task at hand, therefore, is not to infringe upon Aboriginal and treaty rights, but rather to find the political means to recognize and affirm them.

As for content, the Supreme Court has harnessed Aboriginal rights to ongoing Indigenous interests in lands, resources, and practices that pre-date European settlement and that were never surrendered. The Supreme Court has established that Aboriginal rights include the right to carry on any and all practices that are integral to the expression of Indigenous cultural distinctiveness. The Court has also ruled that as a subcategory of Aboriginal rights, Aboriginal title is rooted in Indigenous prior occupancy and entitles the Indigenous rights-holder to "exclusive use and occupancy of the land" in keeping with the aspirations of the Aboriginal group, whether for traditional or modern purposes (*Delgamuukw v. British Columbia* 1997, para. 155).[33] In addition, the Supreme Court has set out as a general interpretive principle that the terms of the historical treaties must be read in broad and liberal terms, with textual ambiguities resolved in favour of the Indigenous party's interpretation. In general, the Supreme Court has determined that treaty rights typically include guaranteed access to resources related to fishing, hunting, trapping, and gathering (e.g., timber).

Supreme Court judgments have likewise established that governments have a duty to consult and make every effort to accommodate Indigenous interests in the face of proposed resource development initiatives on land where Aboriginal title has not yet been proven or where treaty rights might be adversely affected. Though not a legal requirement, Indigenous consent is strongly urged.[34] The Court has further ruled that Aboriginal and treaty rights cannot be infringed by federal or provincial governments unless absolutely necessary, and even then governments must demonstrate that the infringement does not put the Indigenous peoples in question in a position of undue hardship. Justification for infringing Aboriginal rights, in other words, must meet a high legal standard, putting a significant constraint upon the exercise of Canadian sovereignty. The Court adds by way of moral reinforcement that the honour of the Crown depends on such fair dealings.

An additional opportunity for the insertion of Indigenous sovereignty into Canadian political space is provided by the fact that the Supreme Court's interpretation of Aboriginal rights and title does not stand still but rather has evolved and developed over time. Indigenous scholar Joyce Green observes that these incremental developments constitute real opportunities for the rupture and replacement of colonial practices "with a radically new relationship premised on decolonizing protocols" (Green 2005, 340). For example, the Supreme Court has until recently upheld the doctrine that the Canadian state is sovereign in a way that makes Indigenous sovereignty impossible. The standard Supreme Court formulation for many years, as expressed in *Sparrow*, was as follows: "there was from the outset never any doubt that sovereignty and legislative power, and indeed the underlying title, to such lands vested in the Crown" (*R. v. Sparrow* 1990, 1103). But a number of scholars have observed that of late, the Supreme Court's position on the sovereignty of the Crown seems to be softening. The language of the Supreme Court in cases like *Van der Peet* and *Delgamuukw*, for example, speak of the need to reconcile the "pre-existence of Aboriginal societies" with the sovereignty of the Crown (*Delgamuukw v. British Columbia* 1997, para. 186). Phrases such as these suggest that the Supreme Court recognizes the Crown's assertion to sovereignty exists in considerable tension with the pre-existence of Indigenous nations (Panagos 2016, 100). Therefore, if reconciliation between the two political orders is to materialize, the Supreme Court now seems more predisposed to the view that Aboriginal rights and title should serve, at the very least, as a constraint on the exercise of Crown sovereignty.

But even more recently the Supreme Court has taken one further step, this time actually acknowledging the existence of Aboriginal sovereignty. In the cases of *Haida Nation* and *Taku River*, the Supreme Court explains that the intention of treaties is to "reconcile pre-existing Aboriginal sovereignty with presumed Crown sovereignty" (*Haida Nation v. British Columbia* 2004, para. 20). The Supreme Court then goes on to say that the purpose of Section 35 "is to facilitate the ultimate reconciliation of prior Aboriginal occupation with *de facto* Crown sovereignty" (*Taku River*

Tlingit First Nation v. British Columbia 2004, para. 42). Legal scholar Felix Hoehn is inclined to regard these statements as signs of a remarkable development in the Court's thinking. He believes that the Supreme Court now understands that it is not just distinctive Aboriginal societies that must be reconciled with Crown sovereignty, but rather Indigenous sovereignty itself (Hoehn 2012, 35).[35] Hoehn's hopeful interpretation leads him to identify two implications that naturally follow. First, the Supreme Court's recognition of pre-existing Aboriginal sovereignty implies that Indigenous peoples have a right "to self-determination and to jurisdiction over the territory to which that sovereignty applies" (Hoehn 2012, 35). And second, the Supreme Court's qualification on Crown sovereignty promotes an ideal that would see Indigenous and settler peoples treat one another as equals tasked with negotiating "how they will share sovereignty in Canada" (Hoehn 2012, 1).[36]

CONCLUSION

Upon weighing the political implications of this extensive body of legal work, Thomas Courchene concludes that these "recent Supreme Court decisions are creating a new legal/constitutional reality for Ottawa," one that has arguably precipitated "a huge tilting of the negotiating table in favour of First Nations" (Courchene 2018, 155). Kenneth Coates and Dwight Newman similarly remark, "with each major Supreme Court decision, the legal framework for Aboriginal title, Indigenous rights, and Aboriginal claims becomes clearer." When taken as a package, they too conclude that these Supreme Court decisions constitute a remarkable advancement given that 40 years ago, "almost none of this legal framework existed" (Coates and Newman 2014, 23). In short, what the Court has done is guarantee to Indigenous peoples that they will have constitutionally protected space within the Canadian state for the expression of their Aboriginal rights.

Yet despite the contribution of the Supreme Court to expanding and clarifying the meaning of Aboriginal rights in Canadian law, it has largely left to Canadian and Indigenous political leaders the task of creating political policies and frameworks "to accommodate or incorporate" those rights (Courchene, 2018, 163). For the Supreme Court, the broad and complex issues of Indigenous rights to land, resources, and self-government are far better handled through meaningful negotiations motivated by a desire on both sides to achieve genuine reconciliation. While the Supreme Court may recognize of itself that it is not in the best position to resolve the conflicts generated by Indigenous assertions to rights, it nevertheless can and does have an important role to play. Indeed, in *Delgamuukw*, the Supreme Court itself identified what this role should be. While Canadian governments and Indigenous leaders work toward reconciliation through negotiated settlements, the Court will facilitate those settlements by means of reinforcement through its judgments (*Delgamuukw v. British Columbia* 1997, para. 186). What the Supreme Court can do and has done, in other words, is impose constraints upon the exercise of Canadian sovereignty to create protected space within the Canadian constitutional order for the expression of Indigenous sovereignty. Supreme Court interventions defining Aboriginal rights, Aboriginal title, treaty rights, and the duty to consult and accommodate all represent its mandatory legal minimums that Canadian governments are now obliged to uphold if "the honour of the Crown" is to be upheld (*Haida Nation v. British Columbia* 2004, para. 20).

Building on the Supreme Court's judgments, it now becomes the task of Canadian and Indigenous leaders to work together to further expand the spaces for Indigenous sovereignty that the Court has already established. Taken together, the reinforcement that the Supreme Court provides should, at the very least, increase pressure on Canadian governments to come in a spirit of good faith to the negotiation table.

DISCUSSION QUESTIONS

1. Is the Supreme Court of Canada, and the Canadian state more generally, justified in limiting the sovereignty of Indigenous peoples? If so, informed by what principles?
2. Is the "integral to a distinctive culture" test a good one for identifying Aboriginal rights? Why or why not?
3. Is the concept of "Aboriginal title" as defined by the Supreme Court of Canada too limiting to capture the nature of Indigenous peoples' rights to their lands?
4. What should historical treaty rights be understood to entail? Has the Supreme Court of Canada's declaration that treaties must be interpreted in a generous and liberal manner significantly expanded their meaning? Why or why not?
5. What must governments do to satisfy their obligations to Indigenous peoples under the duty to consult and accommodate? Are those duties sufficient to uphold the honour of the Crown?
6. Have the decisions of the Supreme Court of Canada created genuine opportunities for the coexistence of Indigenous and Canadian sovereignty? Is the Supreme Court a genuine ally in this regard?

SUGGESTED READINGS

Borrows, John. 2002. "Chapter 3. Frozen Rights in Canada: Constitutional Interpretation and the Trickster," and "Chapter 4. Nanabush Goes West: Title, Treaties, and Trickster in British Columbia." In *Recovering Canada: The Resurgence of Indigenous Law.* Toronto: University of Toronto Press.

Borrows, John J., and Leonard I. Rotman. 2018. *Aboriginal Legal Issues: Cases, Materials & Commentary*, 5th ed. Markham: LexisNexis Canada.

Coates, Ken. 2000. "Chapter 4. Prelude to Marshall: Aboriginal and Treaty Rights in Canada." In *The Marshall Decision and Native Rights.* Montreal: McGill-Queen's University Press.

Courchene, Thomas J. 2018. "Chapter 6. The Supreme Court and the Evolution of Aboriginal Rights and Title." In *Indigenous Nationals, Canadian Citizens: From First Contact to Canada 150 and Beyond.* Montreal: McGill-Queen's University Press.

Grant, John. 2018. "Chapter 4. The Crown and the Aboriginal: Imaginaries of Sovereignty and Control." In *Lived Fictions: Unity and Exclusion in Canadian Politics.* Vancouver: UBC Press.

Henderson, James (Sákéj) Youngblood. 2004. "Aboriginal Jurisprudence and Rights." In *Advancing Aboriginal Claims: Visions/Strategies/Directions*, edited by Kerry Wilkins. Saskatoon, SK: Purich Publishing.

Lawrence, Bonita. 2012. "Chapter 3. Aboriginal Title and the Comprehensive Claims Process." In *Fractured Homeland: Federal Recognition and Algonquin Identity in Ontario.* Vancouver: UBC Press.

McCrossan, Michael, and Kiera L. Ladner. 2016. "Eliminating Indigenous Jurisdictions: Federalism, the Supreme Court of Canada, and Territorial Rationalities of Power." *Canadian Journal of Political Science* 49 (3).

Newman, Dwight. 2014. *Revisiting the Duty to Consult Aboriginal Peoples.* Saskatoon, SK: Purich Publishing.

Olthuis, Kleer, Townshend, LLP. 2018. *Aboriginal Law Handbook*, 5th ed. Toronto: Carswell.

Panagos, Dimitrios. 2016. *Uncertain Accommodation: Aboriginal Identity and Group Rights in the Supreme Court of Canada.* Vancouver: UBC Press.

Pasternack, Shiri. 2014. "Jurisdiction and Settler Colonialism: Where Do Laws Meet?" *Canadian Journal of Law and Society* 29 (2).

Sellars, Bev. 2016. "Chapter 9. Re-establishing Aboriginal Rights: Supreme Court of Canada Decisions from Calder to Tsilhqot'in." In *Price Paid: The Fight for First Nations Survival.* Vancouver: Talonbooks.

Slattery, Brian. 2016. "The Generative Structure of Aboriginal Rights." In *From Recognition to Reconciliation: Essays on Constitutional Entrenchment of Aboriginal and Treaty Rights*, edited by Patrick Macklem and Douglas Sanderson. Toronto: University of Toronto Press.

NOTES

1 As both previous and subsequent chapters show, Indigenous rights are also defined through explicitly political processes like negotiations, through the creation of political institutions and agreements, and through direct political action like protest movements. As one of the anonymous reviewers of this book pointed out to me, while the Supreme Court of Canada has certainly had an important role to play in legally defining the substance of Aboriginal rights, the source and interpretation of Aboriginal rights within the Canadian constitutional framework is multifaceted and occurs in several political and legal arenas. For example, as pointed out in the previous chapter, the inherent right to self-government was not established by the Supreme Court but by Parliament. Indeed, as I point out later in this chapter, the Supreme Court itself is often reticent to define the content and scope of Aboriginal rights, urging that Canadian and Indigenous governments take up this matter together through political negotiations.

2 I shall refer to Indigenous rights as Aboriginal rights throughout this chapter. I do so because Indigenous rights are referred to as Aboriginal rights in Section 35 of the *Constitution Act, 1982* and because the jurisprudence of the Canadian courts employs this concept in decisions concerning the definition and scope of the Aboriginal rights recognized and affirmed in Section 35.

3 Upon reflecting on the role that the Supreme Court has had in advancing the understanding and substance of Aboriginal rights and title, Thomas Courchene argues that it has been and continues to be "path-breaking." Indeed, he goes so far as to say that "it is increasingly the courts, not our parliaments, that are now defining (actually redefining) the rights of Aboriginal peoples within the Canadian constitutional framework." See Courchene 2018, 141 and 145.

4 Kenneth Coates and Dwight Newman observe that while some characterized the Supreme Court of Canada's decision in *Tsilhqot'in* to have been a real "game changer," the sobering reality is that the land awarded to the Tŝilhqot'in Nation constituted only 2 per cent of their total traditional territory. Coates and Newman write that while the Tŝilhqot'in have a claim to a large area, they focused their legal efforts on smaller tracts of land over which, they believed, they could demonstrate clear ownership to the satisfaction of the Supreme Court. As it turns out, in its final decision, the Supreme Court awarded the Tŝilhqot'in Nation about 40 per cent of the 5 per cent of their traditional territory advanced in their legal claim. See Coates and Newman 2014, 6, 7, 27.

5 The components of this test will be explained in the forthcoming section on Aboriginal title.

6 The fact that the Musqueam people could also trace their fishing practices back to the pre-contact period, and that those practices had continued in an uninterrupted fashion to the present day, only served to reinforce the credentials of their claim. See *R. v. Sparrow* 1990, 1094.

7 The Supreme Court further ruled that because salmon is so central to the Musqueam people's sense of identity, their right to fish for food, social, and ceremonial purposes must be made paramount and given high priority. For example, while the right could perhaps be justifiably limited by concerns for conservation, it should certainly come before allowances are made for commercial and sport fishing, or so the Court ruled. See *R. v. Sparrow* 1990, 1101, 1116.

8 Another circumstance that the Supreme Court identified as a potentially justifiable reason to infringe Aboriginal rights would be the exercise of "rights that would cause harm to the general populace or to aboriginal peoples themselves." See *R. v. Sparrow* 1990, 1113.

9 As put by the Supreme Court, "Aboriginal rights, including any asserted right to self-government, must be looked at in light of the circumstances of each case and, in particular, in light of the specific history and culture of the aboriginal group claiming the right." See *R v. Pamajewon* 1996, para. 27.

10 Interestingly, the Supreme Court also weighed in on the matter of Métis community membership. As Aboriginal rights are collective in nature, the Supreme Court asked itself who exactly is eligible to exercise Métis rights? For the Court, mixed ancestry is not enough. Instead, the Court ruled that the Métis right to hunt is available only to those who are established members of the relevant Métis community. And what is required to assert such membership?

According to the Court, an individual must self-identify as a member of a Métis community, must present evidence of an ancestral connection to that community, and must enjoy acceptance by that community (*R. v. Powley* 2003, paras. 31, 32, 33). Steve and Roddy Powley certainly had no trouble establishing their membership by these criteria. Consequently, they were entitled to enjoy the Section 35 Métis right to hunt for food.

11 Bonita Lawrence formulates the problem as follows: "According to *Van der Peet*, Aboriginal rights exist not to ensure the physical and cultural survival of contemporary Indigenous people but to preserve the distinctive elements of their pre-contact culture." See Lawrence 2012, 57.

12 At this time the Judicial Committee of the Privy Council was the highest court hearing appeals from Canadian courts, a role it continued to exercise until 1949.

13 It is important to note that where the judges were divided on the Nisga'a claim was not with respect to whether they had title to their "ancient tribal territory" at one time. On this fact they all agreed. Where they disagreed was whether that title had since been extinguished by "properly constituted authorities." See Coates 2000, 85 and Courchene 2018, 145–7.

14 Thomas Courchene argues that the impact of the 1973 *Calder* decision was also immediate and far-reaching for political reasons because "it paved the way for the federal government's comprehensive land claims process," a policy in which Canada agreed to "negotiate settlements with Aboriginal groups where rights of traditional use and occupancy had neither been extinguished by treaty or superseded by law" (Courchene 2018, 147). However, as one of the anonymous reviewers of this book pointed out to me, this popular view of events is likely false. Using comparative methods and archival material, the work of Christa Scholtz, for example, demonstrates that the comprehensive claims process in Canada was not launched in response to the *Calder* decision but rather in response to intense Indigenous mobilization and lobbying efforts that were underway well before the *Calder* decision was released. Indeed, Scholtz goes so far as to argue that had Indigenous mobilization and lobbying not occurred, then *Calder*, in and of itself, would likely not have led to a comprehensive claims policy. After all, while the Supreme Court ruled that Aboriginal title could exist as a result of Indigenous prior occupancy, in the specific case of the Nisga'a, three of the seven judges also ruled that their Aboriginal title had since been extinguished. See Scholtz 2006, 68–72.

15 This old and paternalistic measure was first enacted under the terms of the *Indian Act* on the purported grounds that Indians needed to be protected from the unscrupulous dealings of land speculators who were only interested in their own profit.

16 Rather than decide where the Aboriginal title lands of the Gitskan and Wet'suwet'en are, the Supreme Court urged the parties to settle this question themselves through negotiation. In the Supreme Court's view, a political settlement through negotiation is a better route than litigation, as the latter often carries with it a sense of bitterness, acrimony, and division. It is therefore better to try to settle differences through negotiation because, as the Court put it: "Let's face it. We're all here to stay." See *Delgamuukw v. British Columbia* 1997, para. 186.

17 According to the Supreme Court, in the case of British Columbia, the date that British sovereignty was conclusively asserted would have been with the Oregon Boundary Treaty of 1846. See *Delgamukkw v. British Columbia* 1997, para. 145.

18 The requirement of fair compensation serves as an acknowledgement that Aboriginal title lands normally carry an economic component that is lost to the Indigenous group should their land be infringed for public purposes. See Isaac 2012, 86.

19 While the Tŝilhqot'in Nation was successful in proving its claim to Aboriginal title, the standard of proof set down in the *Delgamuukw* case is an onerous one. As Ken Coates observes, "given overlapping territorial and resource claims, and disputes between Aboriginal groups about specific lands, specific groups might find it difficult to achieve the level of proof required by the Supreme Court." See Coates, 2000, 91. In addition, an Indigenous nation may also fail to meet the standard of proof concerning regular and exclusive pre-sovereignty occupation, control, and use of the land. Indeed, the failure of the New Brunswick Mi'kmaq to establish their Aboriginal right to harvest timber on their ancestral territories in the 2005 case of *Marshall and Bernard* illustrates how difficult meeting this standard of proof can be.

20 The Supreme Court further added: "There is ample direct evidence of occupation at sovereignty, which was additionally buttressed by evidence of more recent continuous occupation." See *Tsilhqot'in Nation v. British Columbia* 2014, para. 66.

21 The total amount of land to which the Tsilhqot'in were recognized as having Aboriginal title was 1,750 square kilometres (675 square miles).

22 As John Grant explains, the assertion of Canadian state sovereignty over Indigenous land is morally and politically indefensible for a whole set of reasons, including racist ones that justify "the original assertions of British and French sovereignty [on] the presumed inferiority of Indigenous peoples, deemed unworthy of being recognized as sovereign." See Grant 2018, 137.

23 Concerning her evaluation of the *Delgamuukw* decision, Bev Sellars had this to say: "Court cases, still, without the consent of Aboriginal people, make rules that Aboriginal people may very well disagree with. I am not saying that I disagree with this; I am saying that law such as this will continue to restrict Aboriginal people by letting others dictate what we can or cannot do with our lands. That should be an individual nation decision, not an imposed foreign court decision." See Sellars 2016, 154–5.

24 I shall have a good deal more to say about the differences between Indigenous and Canadian state interpretations of what had been agreed to in treaty negotiations in the next chapter.

25 Recognizing, of course, that these two interpretive principles are mutually reinforcing and are usually advanced by the Supreme Court together.

26 The Mi'kmaq also advanced an Aboriginal title argument, claiming that the Crown land on which they had been logging was in fact Mi'kmaq title lands. They further claimed that as Mi'kmaq title lands, they were entitled to use the resources on those lands as they saw fit, including cutting trees for commercial purposes. However, the Supreme Court concluded

that the evidence did not support their title claim. By the criteria of the *Delgamuukw* test, the Supreme Court was of the view that the Mi'kmaq were not able to prove regular and exclusive pre-sovereignty occupation, control, and use of the lands they logged. Consequently, the Supreme Court ruled that their title claim also failed.

27 The Supreme Court further added that it fully expected "that, throughout the permitting, approval, and licensing process, as well as in the development of a land use strategy, the Crown will continue to fulfil its honourable duty to consult and, if appropriate, accommodate the Taku River Tlingit Nation." See *Taku River Tlingit First Nation v. British Columbia* 2004, 552–3.

28 In its defence, the Government of Alberta made reference to a clause in Treaty 8 to justify its actions. It claimed that Alberta had a treaty-authorized right to "take up" surrendered land "as may be required … from time to time for settlement, mining, lumbering, trading, or other purposes" (*Mikisew Cree First Nation v. Canada* 2005, 389). The Government of Alberta argued that because Treaty 8 contained no requirement that consent be secured from the Mikisew Cree in advance of "taking up" the land required for the winter road, it was under no legal obligation to do so.

29 By way of example, the Supreme Court pointed to the fact that no new land would be required to advance the project, as "most work would take place within existing Enbridge facilities and its existing right of way" (*Chippewas of the Thames First Nation v. Enbridge Pipelines Inc.* 2017, para. 22). In addition, the NEB had imposed conditions on the project, including a requirement that the Chippewas have access to ongoing consultations throughout the life of the project's development (*Chippewas of the Thames First Nation v. Enbridge Pipelines Inc.* 2017, paras. 51, 57).

30 One of the anonymous reviewers of this book takes an additional step by observing that if Indigenous rights are not respected in full (which the reviewer believes they are not) then they are, in fact, still being actively denied.

31 The position of John Borrows echoes that of James Tully when he writes: "The court's approach to reconciliation thus forcibly includes non-treaty Aboriginal peoples within Canadian society and subjects them to an alien sovereignty, even though most have never consented to such an arrangement." See Borrows 2002, 97.

32 It is worth pointing out that Aboriginal rights are collective rights, held communally by members of an Indigenous group, and therefore do not belong independently to any one particular person. Individual Indigenous persons are entitled to exercise Aboriginal rights if and only if they are members of the Indigenous community to which the right belongs. On this point see Olthuis, Kleer, Townshend, 2012, 8.

33 Though, as previously discussed, the Supreme Court qualifies its endorsement of full discretionary Indigenous use with the proviso that the use to which the land is put must not be incompatible with the nature of the Aboriginal group's attachment to the land. See *Delgamuukw v. British Columbia*, 1997, para. 155.

34 For example, in *Haida Nation* the Supreme Court consistently drew attention to the importance of balancing interests and a give-and-take approach in which both Crown and Indigenous nations employ good faith efforts to understand one another's positions and seek to address them. When cast in this light, the language of the Court would seem to more closely resemble an expectation that Canadian governments and Indigenous nations work together as partners in resolving their disputes. According to the Supreme Court, legal infringements of Aboriginal and treaty rights are still possible, but in a spirit of accommodation the Court instructs Canadian governments to be prepared to adjust, adapt, and possibly abandon their legislative objectives to leave potentially threatened Aboriginal or treaty rights undisturbed and intact. See *Haida Nation v. British Columbia* 2004, paras. 48–9.

35 Furthermore, the fact that the Crown's sovereignty is characterized by the Supreme Court as *de facto* (it exists in fact but not in law) suggests to Hoehn that the Court now also accepts that the standing of Indigenous sovereignty is *de jure* (it is rightful or in compliance with the law). See Hoehn 2012, 34.

36 Mark D. Walters wonders if the Supreme Court actually meant to say this, suggesting that Hoehn's hopeful interpretation of the Court's intent is open to debate. See Walters 2016, 39.

CHAPTER 6

Treaties Old: Sharing Lands and Resources

LEARNING OBJECTIVES

1. To outline what factors led the Canadian government to abandon its policy of treaty-making with Indigenous nations between 1921 and 1973.
2. To identify Indigenous perspectives on treaties and explain why Indigenous peoples regard treaties as foundational to their relationship with the Canadian state.
3. To compare and contrast Canadian and Indigenous motivations for negotiating the Numbered Treaties and to identify the substance of what each party thought had been agreed to.
4. To evaluate the degree to which Canadian court decisions and recent Indigenous policy on specific claims and the treaty land entitlement process contribute to the fulfillment of Canada's treaty obligations and serve to advance the Indigenous right to self-determination within Canada.

The political relationship between Indigenous nations and the Canadian state has often been described as one between treaty peoples (Poelzer and Coates 2015). Treaties are foundational agreements that regulate relationships between Indigenous nations and the Canadian state and have long roots stretching back through time. This and the next chapter discuss treaties, both old (pre-1921) and new (post-1975), to identify the spirit that animates the treaty relationship and more particularly in the modern context, the spirit that animates the negotiation and implementation of contemporary treaties. This spirit is contested, often breaking down quite distinctly when comparing the interpretations offered by the Indigenous and non-Indigenous partners to the relationship. Indigenous critics often advance the view that both the old and new treaties were intended to formalize and guarantee nation-to-nation relationships into perpetuity. What actually transpired in both past and present, however, is that they perpetuate Indigenous loss of power, land, and resources relative to what they are entitled to and enjoyed pre-contact. Indeed, from the perspective of some critics, whether old or new, treaties are identified as being deliberately designed and then used by the Canadian state as tools for Indigenous subjugation.

While Indigenous peoples have undoubtedly incurred significant loss through the interpretation and implementation of treaties, it is my contention that treaties can serve as facilitative instruments to enhance prospects for Indigenous political and economic autonomy within Canada. Treaties originated as acts of diplomacy, constituting sacred agreements to formalize relations of peace and friendship and to share land, resources, and political power between European powers and Indigenous nations. Treaties are, therefore, premised on formal government-to-government relationships, and if cast in the right spirit, can serve to recognize the sovereignty of Indigenous nations, at least to the extent spelled out in the treaty. As such, treaties have the capacity to carve out and protect key areas of control over identity, community, territory, and resources. This and the next chapter demonstrate where and to what extent Indigenous autonomy through treaties is both possible and can be measured. Both chapters also consider, by implication, the degree to which treaty-making can serve to promote the goals of reconciliation and justice. It stands to reason that if longstanding disputes concerning Indigenous rights to proprietorship over land and self-governance could be resolved successfully through treaty-making and treaty implementation, this would go some considerable distance in facilitating the restoration of trust and respect between non-Indigenous and Indigenous peoples in Canada.

This chapter develops its case for treaties as instruments to safeguard Indigenous sovereignty in a number of steps. The first part describes Indigenous perspectives on treaties, focusing on their expectations about the intent of the agreements that they entered into, both historically and in the present day, and their disappointments when the terms of many of these treaties were left unfulfilled. This part of the chapter will serve to outline the evaluative criteria that can be employed to decide whether historical and contemporary treaties have the capacity to fulfill Indigenous ambitions for self-determination into the present day.

The second part provides a brief overview of the historical treaty-making era with particular attention paid to the post-Confederation land or Numbered Treaties. I will use Treaty 1 and Treaty 4 here to illustrate the contested nature of the spirit and intent of the Numbered Treaties from Indigenous and Canadian governmental perspectives. As we shall see, the troubled legacy of perceived Canadian duplicity and deceit in the historical treaty period does much to colour prospects for the successful resolution of treaties in the contemporary era.

The third and final part of the chapter considers the merits of the Canadian government's specific claims and treaty land entitlement policies. Both were developed in response to the demand of Indigenous peoples that the Canadian government take its treaty obligations seriously and fulfill the terms of their long-neglected treaty rights. There can be no doubt that there is a significant gap between what the Indigenous right to self-determination requires and what the historical treaties have actually delivered by way of rights and benefits. The question we will consider is whether the specific claims policy and the treaty land entitlement process have contributed anything of substance to close that gap.

The chapter begins, however, with a brief description of the period between 1921 and 1973 (52 years) in which no treaties were negotiated. The point in launching the chapter with this exploration is to demonstrate that for the clear majority of Canadian history, Indigenous nations and the Canadian state have chosen, for the most part, to mediate their relations through treaties negotiated in two distinct stages, 1867–1921 (54 years) and 1975 to the present. Although fraught with challenges and difficulties associated with interpretation and design, it would nevertheless be accurate to say that Canadians and their Indigenous partners have predominantly been, and remain to this day, treaty peoples (Poelzer and Coates 2015).

CASE STUDY: TREATIES ABSENT, 1921–73

Historically, treaties negotiated between Indigenous nations, European powers, and later Canadian governments were understood to constitute codified agreements that set out the terms and conditions for their mutual coexistence on the same territory. Michael Coyle and John Borrows describe treaties as the "favoured tool" by which "colonial and later, Canadian governments secured the legal basis of settlement within its borders" (Borrows and Coyle 2017, 3). Patrick Macklem characterizes treaties as constitutional accords that guarantee Indigenous peoples treaty rights "in exchange for allowing European nations to exercise a measure of sovereign authority in North America" (Macklem 2001, 155). And for Gina Starblanket, treaties "can represent relations of generative, non-hierarchical, dialogical coexistence when they are inhabited in accordance with the laws and intentions of all the parties who signed them" (Starblanket 2020, 14). A common feature of these understandings of treaty is that they are taken up by political equals, both intent on guaranteeing one another favourable and mutually beneficial conditions for their ongoing coexistence.

A cursory look at Canadian history reveals that treaty-making has featured prominently in Indigenous–Crown relations since the eighteenth century. The "historic" treaties were negotiated before 1921, while the "modern" treaties were negotiated after 1973. The historic treaties can be further subdivided into two stages: the earliest treaties designed to promote military alliances, establish peace, and facilitate commerce and trade, culminating in the Royal Proclamation of 1763 and Treaty of Niagara of 1764, and the later "land" treaties, negotiated between the mid-nineteenth to early twentieth centuries, designed to set out the terms and conditions for settlers' access to and use of Indigenous lands (Miller 2009, 5; Belanger 2018, 86; Frideres 2020, 151–2; Vowel 2016, 244). Canada's commitment to pursue treaties ended in 1921, leaving substantial portions of the country not covered by treaty, including parts of Quebec, Labrador, Ontario, Yukon, the Northwest Territories, and most of British Columbia (Belanger 2018, 88).

Indigenous leaders contend that their status as treaty peoples is fundamental to the history of Canada. They are alone among Canadian citizens in having secured treaties with first the British and then Canadian governments. From this perspective, treaty-making represents a form of political engagement founded on the presupposition that Indigenous peoples constituted political entities that were sovereign, possessing status capable of establishing nation-to-nation relationships with Britain and later Canada. Furthermore, as John Borrows points out, in the context of present circumstances where Indigenous peoples are subject to considerable power imbalances in relation to their Canadian governmental counterparts, "invoking higher treaty principles, which are potentially constitutionally protected, provides a strong protective shield for resisting Canada's diminishment of First Nations' political power" (Borrows 2017a, 21–2). It is treaties, and the considerable political status they carry for their Indigenous signatories, that have and continue to serve as powerful tools to repel Canadian governmental policy initiatives designed to assimilate Indigenous peoples into the fabric of the Canadian state (Papillon 2020, 218).

It is against this background that the historical episode in which Canadian governments refused to engage in treaty-making with Indigenous nations should be understood. As the power balance began to shift in favour of British and then Canadian governments, colonial policy also began to shift. British and later Canadian governments moved from recognizing Indigenous peoples as autonomous political nations to treating them as colonial subjects best served by being assimilated into Canadian society. From the time of Canada's founding in 1867 to 1921, treaty-making between the Canadian government and Indigenous nations did continue, but this commitment was gradually overtaken by an assimilative policy initiative. Indigenous peoples were increasingly seen as liabilities, standing in the way of territorial development by settlers and, with the coming into being of the Canadian state, as hampering prospects for westward expansion and settlement (Belanger 2018, 87; Frideres 2020, 152; Vowel 2016, 247). Against the imperative of these territorial ambitions, Canadian state actors unilaterally decided that the political standing of Indigenous peoples was to be fundamentally altered. They were to be transformed from members of free-standing and independent Indigenous nations to subjects or "wards" of the Canadian state. The treaty order was to be abandoned, clearing the way for the unilateral assertion of sovereignty by the Canadian state over Indigenous peoples and the lands traditionally occupied, used, and governed by them (Gehl 2014, 55; Hedican 2013, 62; King, H. 2018, 113; Papillon 2020, 220–1; Starblanket 2020, 19).

In addition to territorial ambitions, historian J.R. Miller explains that the formal end to the treaty-making process was set in motion by a number of other factors. The first factor Miller identifies is that by 1921, Canada had acquired access to vast stretches of Indigenous land in the west and north that would take some time to settle and develop. As Canada had more than enough land to contend with, it simply saw no need to pursue treaties in areas like northern Quebec and Ontario or the vast domain of the north where no non-Indigenous expressions of interest in acquiring Indigenous-occupied land had yet occurred (Miller 2009, 198, 229–30).

Another factor Miller identifies was the perception at the time that Indigenous peoples were a "**vanishing race**." Indigenous peoples had been decimated by diseases as a result of contact with European settlers, while those who remained were thought to be too weak and vulnerable to long sustain a distinctive Indigenous way of life. So, observes Miller, if Indigenous peoples were going to disappear anyway, why pay any heed to their request for treaties (Miller 2009, 231)?

The final factor Miller identifies is the distraction brought on by the presence of overwhelming **world events**. The Great Depression of the 1930s constituted an economic and social crisis that severely taxed all available resources of Canadian governments, while World War II required that the Canadian government focus its attention on fighting an external enemy. Crises of this magnitude meant that the Canadian government was not particularly inclined to devote a lot of time, attention, or resources to the well-being of its minority Indigenous population (Miller 2004, 150). And underlying and motivating all of these factors was also an undeniable spirit of racism and corresponding paternalism. Indigenous peoples were identified as being uncivilized or as "savage" and therefore in desperate need of those measures that the Canadian state deemed good or best for them. By this time, for example, the Department of Indian Affairs was fully committed to a set of interlocking policies designed to eliminate the cultural identity of Indigenous peoples.

Treaty 11 was signed in 1921, the last of the treaties to be negotiated in the historical treaty period. While already well established by 1921, it is this period that constitutes the darkest days of Canadian colonialism and assimilation. Policies designed in the previous century had, by the early and middle years of the twentieth century, become so robust that they now infiltrated virtually every aspect of Indigenous life. As discussed in Chapter 3, this was the age of enfranchisement policy, which would have had all male Indians deemed eligible and ready reject their Indian status and identity in favour of Canadian citizenship. Those opting to remain "Indian" were subject to the provisions of the 1876 ***Indian Act***, a compendium of stifling legislation that determined their "status," the powers associated with their elected system of "band" governance, and the extent to which they were authorized to manage their own "reserve" lands. The taking of Indigenous children to residential schools, the appropriation of reserve lands, and the outlawing of the Potlatch in the Pacific northwest and Sun Dance ceremonies in the prairies all served to further undermine distinctive sources of Indigenous identity and community well-being. In short, the Canadian government was determined to break up Indigenous nations and assimilate Indigenous individuals into the Canadian way of life (Bruyneel 2007, 94; King, H. 2018, 112–14, 116–17; Vowel, 2016, 254). As summarized by Miller: "by the early twentieth century, Canada was more interested in changing Indians than in negotiating with them" (Miller 2009, 297).[1]

Following the devastation of World War II, the global community began to develop an international concern for the status of human rights, a concern that would also lead to questions about the racist assumptions and intentions of Canadian Indigenous policy. As a staunch advocate of human rights, then Prime Minister Pierre Trudeau released his **1969 White Paper** on Indian Policy, a policy that proposed to eliminate Indian status on the grounds that such status was inherently discriminatory. Informed by a strong commitment to individualism, Trudeau was convinced that all the problems experienced by Indigenous peoples were a product of having been kept apart from the broader Canadian society by artificial distinctions, Indian status and residency on reserves chief among them. He was also convinced that it simply made no sense within the setting of a single country for one group of citizens to have treaty relations with another as treaties are a product of foreign relations taken up between states. It was therefore Trudeau's intention to explore every avenue available to see how treaties between Indigenous nations and the Canadian state could be equitably ended (Miller 2009, 248; Papillon 2020, 223).

But as we know from previous chapters, the White Paper was met with vigorous opposition from Indigenous organizations and so, in response, the White Paper was eventually retracted. The Canadian government was even contrite in its retraction, going so far as to say that it had simply failed to comprehend the nature of Indigenous human rights, including treaty rights, that were so central to their sense of identity and prospects for well-being within Canada. Indigenous leaders were quick to mobilize into the policy vacuum with proposals of their own. They increasingly began to assert in both the political arena and at the Supreme Court of Canada that they had unextinguished Indigenous rights to their lands. When the Supreme Court agreed in the 1973 ***Calder*** decision that Aboriginal title based on original occupancy and use of the land did exist, the Canadian government was compelled to act. The comprehensive land claims policy was the Canadian government's response.

Canada re-established its policy of treaty-making in 1973. Called the comprehensive land claims process, this policy was designed by the Canadian government to establish certainty and predictability over who owns land and resources. In effect, comprehensive claims are intended to culminate in final agreements between Indigenous nations and Canadian governments (federal, provincial, territorial) that clarify the ownership and jurisdiction of all parties over lands and resources located in Indigenous peoples' traditional territories. As we shall see in the next chapter, land rights can vary in important ways, leading to different categories of land that provide different levels, types, and mixes of jurisdiction for each of the Indigenous and non-Indigenous signatories.[2] When legal title to land and resources is clarified in this way, it is the Canadian government's hope that a "more stable, competitive, and predictable environment for economic and resource development" is established, a condition that the Canadian government believes is in the best interest of industry on the one side and all Canadians, including Indigenous peoples, on the other (Eyford 2015, 37; see also Papillon 2020, 226–7).

TREATY PEOPLES AND TREATY NATIONS: DIFFERING PERSPECTIVES

Indigenous peoples in North America were well versed in the art of diplomacy and treaty-making long before the arrival of Europeans. Indigenous peoples point out that they had highly sophisticated protocols or treaties in place as part of a network of diplomatic relations that covered North America, all developed for the purpose of governing the use of land and resources and to set up peaceful relations between Indigenous nations. Julie Jai describes ancient treaty protocols that involved elaborate "ceremonies, feasts, speeches, storytelling, and exchange of ceremonial gifts such as wampum belts, which symbolically described the relationship" (Jai 2014, 2; see also Gespe'gewa'gi Mi'gmawei Mawiomi 2016, 91–2; Lawrence 2012, 73; Papillon 2020, 219; Vowel 2016, 244).

For example, in his testimony to the 1996 Royal Commission on Aboriginal Peoples, Les Healy of the Blood Tribe of Alberta explains that "the concept of treaty, *inaistisinni*, … is an ancient principle of law invoked many times by the Bloods to settle conflict, make peace, establish alliances, or trade relations with other nations such as the Crow, the Gros Ventre, the Sioux, the Americans in 1855, and the British in 1877." Healy further explains that for his nation, treaty-making was an act to establish "a sacred covenant, a solemn agreement, that is truly the highest form of agreement, binding for the lifetime of the parties" (RCAP 1996c, 39). Chelsea Vowel similarly identifies the Great Law of Peace, forged between the Oneida, Mohawk, Cayuga, Onondaga, and Seneca to bind the five nations into the Haudenosaunee Confederacy, as an exemplary illustration of pre-contact Indigenous treaty-making. By means of its 117 articles, the five nations have been bound together in a political alliance that goes back at least a thousand years (Vowel 2016, 244; see also Belanger 2018, 81–3; Gehl 2014, 54).

The point that Healy, Vowel, and so many other Indigenous people make is that Indigenous nations possessed highly sophisticated legal systems and political protocols for negotiating and concluding treaties amongst one another. Furthermore, it is these legal systems and political protocols that they also brought forward in their encounters with European settlers (Bird, Land, and MacAdam 2002, 44–5; Gehl 2014, 54; King, H. 2018, 110–11; Starblanket 2019b, 444; Vowel 2016, 244–5). In other words, Indigenous peoples fully expected that their European partners would accept them as their political equals. They believed that the treaties forged between them would carry exactly the same element of sacredness as well as mutual respect and understanding that informed the ancient treaties conducted between Indigenous nations.

In the context of their early encounters, especially during the fur trade, Europeans did conduct treaty negotiations with Indigenous nations in a way that had the protocols of each party play a prominent role (Lawrence 2012, 73; Vowel 2016, 245). As John Borrows and Michael Coyle explain, a central feature of these treaty protocols from the Indigenous perspective was that they set out the terms and conditions for a mutually beneficial and enduring relationship more so than reciprocal sets of rights (Borrows and Coyle 2017, 13). The early "peace and friendship" treaties with the Dutch, French, and English, in particular, were marked by this kind of relationship. Here we witness

European and Indigenous emissaries exchanging promises that in return for hunting, fishing, trading, and other rights, Indigenous peoples would offer Europeans peaceful relations or military alliances against their French or British adversaries.[3] In this early stage of treaty relations it is clear that European motivations were driven by survival instincts and commercial interests, circumstances that dictated need of Indigenous allies. It was Indigenous peoples, after all, who both outnumbered Europeans during this period and who possessed the knowledge and technical means to survive on and harvest the resources of the land.

The **Royal Proclamation of 1763** and the **Treaty of Niagara of 1764** are often identified as important legal precedents for treaty-making that carry political weight into the present. According to Indigenous commentators, the Royal Proclamation formalized relations between the British Crown and Indigenous nations in which it was understood that all Indigenous lands "would be reserved for them, unless or until they ceded that land to the Crown" (Erasmus and Sanders 2002, 6). There would be no settlement on or purchasing of Indigenous land except through agreements negotiated by duly constituted representatives of Indigenous nations and the British Crown. In short, the Royal Proclamation provided reassurances to Indigenous peoples that they would not be molested or interfered with in the occupation and use of their traditional territories. Peaceful coexistence was the ambition of both parties (Asch 2014, 73–5; Papillon 2020, 220).

The Treaty of Niagara, which followed the Royal Proclamation by one year, constituted an assembly of over 2,000 chiefs representing 22 Indigenous nations. According to Indigenous accounts, this treaty produced agreements between the 22 Indigenous nations and the British Crown that relations between them would be conducted according to high diplomatic standards of peace, friendship, and mutual respect (Belanger 2018, 86; Borrows 2017a, 22; Craft 2013, 32). The underlying motivation for the treaty was to reinforce a commitment that Indigenous nations believed was already operative in their relationship with the British Crown – each would practise a duty of non-interference with respect to the other, settlement of Indigenous lands would only occur with Indigenous consent, and each would continue to recognize and treat the other as sovereigns (Craft 2013, 33; Borrows and Coyle 2017, 3; King, H. 2018, 114; Papillon 2020, 220). Treaty promises were reinforced through the exchange of gifts like Two-Row Wampum belts[4] and through regular references to Indigenous protocols like the Covenant Chain.[5] Both were intended to signify that the nature of the relationship entered into was to be a deep and abiding one, enduring throughout the course of time (Gehl 2014, 54–5; King, H. 2018, 110–11).

It is to these kinds of principles that Indigenous peoples regularly refer when they explain their approach to treaty-making, whether in the historical era or under the auspices of the modern comprehensive land claims negotiation process. From their point of view, treaties have always been about establishing formal relationships of coexistence between the Indigenous peoples of North America and settler-newcomers (Papillon 2020, 221; Starblanket 2019a, 15). To that end, Indigenous understandings of their treaties all across Canada generally share the following key features.

First, Indigenous peoples tend to see their treaties as a covenant to which the Creator, the Crown, and the Indigenous nation are all party (Belanger 2018, 86; Gehl 2014, 86–7; Miller 2004, 160).[6] Treaties take on a sacred and solemn character. They are forged between "kin" and the Creator, and they establish insoluble bonds of reciprocity, care, and respect that are meant to last forever. In a spirit of good relations, it is understood that each party to the treaty takes on a sacred obligation before the Creator to guarantee conditions that contribute to one another's well-being based on an ethic of mutual sharing. As such, both parties are entitled to hold one another to a high standard of responsibility to fulfill all of the obligations they have entered into under the terms of their agreement (Gehl 2014, 54; King, H. 2018, 112; Mainville 2001, 35).

Second, and closely related, Indigenous peoples generally regard treaties as consensual agreements that set out the terms and conditions under which Indigenous peoples would share their territories and resources with settlers (Henderson 2008, 27; Craft 2013, 16, 60–1; Starblanket 2019b, 444). It is worth noting, however, that while Indigenous peoples did have a system of traditional territories attached to their nations in the sense that some lands were reserved for their exclusive use while other lands were shared with neighbouring nations, what they did not have was a concept of land ownership (King, H. 2018, 109).[7] Consequently, it would have been simply inconceivable to them that absolute title to the land could be transferred to the Crown (Mackey 2016, 65). Instead, land was regarded as a gift from the Creator, to be used responsibly and to be shared with the plants, animals, future Indigenous generations, and in the context of treaty-making, with European settlers (King, H. 2018, 109: RCAP 1995, 17; Starblanket 2019b, 453). Thus, while Indigenous partners recognized that treaties authorized Europeans to settle in their traditional territories, treaties were also understood to protect their ongoing right to occupy and use the resources of their territories much as they had done before (Ladner 2006, 5). RCAP notes, for example, that "in most, if not all treaties, the Crown promised not to interfere with their way of life, including their hunting, fishing, trapping and gathering practices" (RCAP 1996b, 174; Craft 2013, 63–4).

Furthermore, in exchange for agreeing to share the resources of their territories with settlers, treaty agreements also guaranteed Indigenous peoples various forms of compensation. These included lands reserved for exclusive Indigenous use, annual annuities, agricultural equipment, schools, and medicine to name but a few examples. Indigenous signatories took these measures as remedies, designed to help them remain self-sufficient in the context of the changing economic and other circumstances brought on by European settlement (Office of the Treaty Commissioner 2007, 20).

Third, Indigenous peoples generally maintain that in the process of negotiating their treaties they did not give up their political sovereignty (Belanger 2018, 81, 85, 88; Vowel 2016, 255). Indeed, the fact that Indigenous nations entered into treaty arrangements with sovereigns such as Britain and then Canada indicates that they too were sovereign entities, possessing similar political standing (Courchene 2018, 270; Henderson 2008, 20; Starblanket 2019b, 445). For Indigenous peoples, then, the historical treaties were understood to formalize their already existing nation-to-nation relationships because they set out terms and conditions for a peaceful and mutually beneficial coexistence between sovereigns located on the same territory (Ladner 2006, 5). Each was to enjoy a right to self-determination on traditional Indigenous territories. Each was to remain distinct sovereigns bound together as allies under treaty (Belanger 2018, 85; Henderson 2008, 20). Each was bound to the other by a duty of non-interference. Indigenous systems of law and rights and Indigenous ways of life and relationships would continue as before. Indigenous peoples understood that their own way of life would be protected and that they would not be subject to the laws of the Canadian state (RCAP 1996b, 174; Papillon 2020, 221). Or, as put by James Youngblood Henderson, "treaties extended Aboriginal governance, they did not reduce it" (Henderson 2008, 21).

Taken together, Indigenous peoples "regarded the treaty process as enabling the sharing of land and authority with non-Aboriginal people while at the same time protecting their territories, economies, and forms of government from non-Aboriginal incursion" (Macklem 2001, 153; see also Belanger 2018, 92; Starblanket 2019a, 15). Indigenous peoples genuinely believed that by signing treaties and by agreeing to share their lands and resources they would be put in a position to maintain their distinct social and cultural ways of life much as they had done for centuries.

British and later Canadian governments viewed what was agreed to in the historic treaties in quite different terms. As explained by J.R. Miller, the British and Canadian governments took treaties to be legal contracts, "limited to specific rights and obligations and restricted to the letter of the government version" (Miller 2004, 160). Martin Papillon refers to this transactional approach as distinct from the Indigenous approach, which was relational (Papillon 2020, 219; see also King, H. 2018, 113; Starblanket 2019b; 445). There can be no doubt that the officials who negotiated on behalf of the British and Canadian governments were interested in securing peaceful relations with their Indigenous counterparts. Both parties also knew full well that their treaties concerned the sharing of territory and resources as well as the exchange of benefits, all for the purpose of establishing a permanent relationship that would advance the political and economic interests of both Indigenous peoples and the Crown (Miller 2004, 160). However, beginning in the nineteenth century the objectives and tactics of Crown representatives in treaty negotiations began to change. This change was brought on by a number of factors, including a dramatic increase in a settler population requiring access to agricultural land; a dramatic shift in the balance of military and economic power in favour of the Crown; and an emerging compulsion on the part of European settlers to help advance peoples they deemed culturally "backward" (Jai 2017, 107; King, H. 2018, 108; RCAP 1995, 26–7). The focus for Crown negotiators, therefore, became acquisition of legal title to Indigenous land for the purpose of opening up the land for settlement (Belanger 2018, 87; Starblanket 2019b, 445).

The written terms of the treaties spelled out a process in which Indigenous peoples purportedly agreed to cede (or give up) all of their ancestral territories to the Crown in exchange for access to specific parcels of lands reserved for their exclusive use (reserve lands) and certain other benefits like gifts and annuities. With Indigenous title to their traditional territories thereby extinguished, the way was cleared for the land to be settled for agricultural purposes and for the harvesting of resources like minerals and timber. Essential from the Crown's perspective, in other words, was that treaties provide guarantees that no future legal claim could be made for the land by Indigenous peoples beyond the limits of their reserve boundaries (Williamson and Roberts 2004, 78). For the Crown, treaties were the means by which Indigenous peoples surrendered their rights.

In keeping with the preceding analysis, there are some scholars who point to what they see as the presence of fundamental misunderstandings and dramatic differences in perspectives concerning what Crown and Indigenous negotiators thought was being agreed to in treaty negotiations. For example, Aimée Craft and Michael Asch argue that with respect to Treaty 1 (Craft) and Treaties 4 and 6 (Asch), there are good grounds to believe that there were discrepancies between what was agreed to orally in the negotiations and what actually made it into the written text (Craft 2013; Asch 2014; see also Belanger 2018, 85, 91; Starblanket 2019b, 445–6, 455; Starblanket 2019a, 16). For example, the written text of the treaties was drafted in English and consistently used paternalistic language to describe situations in which Indigenous peoples purportedly agreed to submit themselves to the authority and care of a benevolent British and later Canadian Crown (Hedican 2013, 61–5). But, says Yale Belanger, according to Indigenous oral accounts, far from agreeing to submit to the authority of the Crown, Indigenous signatories believed that treaties guaranteed their peoples "certain rights that were to be enjoyed by the First Nations signatories in perpetuity" including "sovereignty over their own people, lands, and resources, subject to some shared jurisdiction over the lands known as 'unoccupied Crown lands'" (Belanger 2018, 93). Asch further shows that under the terms of Treaty 4, Indigenous signatories pledged their willingness to share their lands and resources with settlers, but the written text indicated that Indigenous peoples had agreed to cede, release, and surrender their lands to the Crown (Asch 2014, 88–91). But, says Asch, it was simply not possible that Indigenous peoples would have agreed to surrender their lands. Oral testimony verifies that Indigenous peoples regarded the land as a gift from the Creator, granted to them as a means for their survival. Under these terms, land simply could not be given away, though it could certainly be (and was regularly) shared (Asch 2014, 92–3; see also Belanger 2018, 92; Starblanket 2019b, 453).

This problem of differing interpretations was compounded by another. Over the ensuing years, the Canadian government has tended to view the written version of treaties to be the authoritative version while Indigenous peoples generally rely on the oral promises that were made as forming the core of each agreement (Asch 2014, 96–9; Craft 2013, 107–14). Between these two positions it is difficult to find a middle ground. Indigenous peoples argue vociferously that they did not surrender their land rights or their rights to political sovereignty when they entered into treaty, nor did they understand that from the perspective of Crown negotiators, this was the intended outcome of the treaty process. Indeed, it is the position of Indigenous peoples that their oral history clearly states "that treaty commissioners promised them continued land rights, governed by principles of sharing, mutual benefit, and friendship – without any notion of surrender" (Kleer and Rae 2014, 2). It has, therefore, been the consistent position of Indigenous peoples that the historic treaties ought now (finally) to be implemented in conformity with their true spirit and intent, that is, in a manner that accurately reflects what they had agreed to in the verbal negotiations.

It is worth noting at this point that the circumstances under which many Indigenous peoples negotiated the historical treaties were extremely difficult ones. Concerning the situation of the Plains Indigenous peoples, for example, Thomas Courchene writes that because they "had been decimated by disease outbreaks, by the near-extinction of the Plains bison, and by whisky traders, many First Nations were eager to receive food aid and other assistance from government. When government asked for the land in return, they were hardly in a position to refuse" (Courchene 2018, 270).[8] But even for those Indigenous negotiators who found themselves in severely weakened bargaining positions like the Plains nations, it is still highly unlikely that they would have agreed to treaty conditions that demanded the complete subservience of their people to the Crown. It is almost certainly the case, for example, that the Indigenous partners to the treaty relationship would not have been willing to submit themselves to terms and conditions that essentially stripped them of access to their traditional territories and its resources and also virtually guaranteed that they would suffer an immediate cultural, political, and economic demise. As put by Michael Coyle, "to adopt such an interpretative approach to the treaty arrangement would be to assume that the Indigenous partners in each of these treaties was utterly irrational" (Coyle 2017, 57).

We are therefore left with the following question: must we accept the proposition that a deal is a deal and therefore Indigenous peoples must now accept the fact that they signed written legal documents that fundamentally undermined their interests? In my view, this would be an entirely unfair approach and also totally out of step with the Supreme Court of Canada's reminder that the Crown has a duty to conduct itself honourably in its treaty relationships with Indigenous peoples. It is worth remembering that Indigenous peoples regularly signed treaties under conditions of profound duress, conditions furthermore that often led Canadian governments to take additional liberties such as choosing not to fulfill the terms of some of their treaty obligations at all (Hedican 2013, 65). So, in the words of Edward Hedican, we might now ask: "how can we instill a sense of fairness in interpreting what took place so long ago?" (Hedican 2013, 68). In response, I suggest the following. What if we take the Indigenous interpretive approach as authoritative, namely, that treaty arrangements can be just only when framed in terms that are beneficial to both parties? Can the historical treaties be construed in ways that both reinforce the Indigenous right to self-determination while also preserving the integrity of Canada? And are there any signs that such incremental steps have been taken? To address these questions the next section examines features of the historic land treaties with particular attention to the details of Treaty 1 and Treaty 4.

THE NUMBERED TREATIES

After Confederation, 11 treaties were negotiated with Indigenous nations across portions of Canada's vast land mass. Often referred to as the **Numbered Treaties**, these treaties were negotiated over a 50-year period beginning with Treaty 1 in 1871 and ending with Treaty 11 in 1921. The territory covered by these treaties includes the entire provinces of Manitoba, Saskatchewan, and Alberta, as well as portions of Ontario, British Columbia, Yukon, and the Northwest Territories. All 11 treaties were preoccupied with one essential topic, namely, establishing terms and conditions under which Canadians would be permitted to settle on Indigenous lands. It was clear to all involved in the treaty negotiations that settlement of non-Indigenous peoples on Indigenous lands could not occur without the consent of Indigenous peoples. Indeed, the terms of the Royal Proclamation of 1763 required it (Courchene 2018, 54–5, 269–70; Frideres 2020, 152).

The Canadian government's primary motivation for negotiating the Numbered Treaties was twofold: secure access to Indigenous-held territories so as to build a transcontinental railway connecting British Columbia with the eastern provinces, and establish conditions favourable for western Canadian agricultural settlement (King, H. 2018, 113; Starblanket 2019b, 445; Vowel 2016, 247). Canada had recently acquired the vast territory of Rupert's Land from the British Crown (previously acquired by the Crown from the Hudson's Bay Company) for the modest fee of 300,000 pounds. Contained within the conditions of transfer was a requirement that Canada protect the interests of Indigenous peoples, including their interests in the land (Craft 2013, 40). At the same time, the British sale of Rupert's Land to Canada generated considerable alarm among Indigenous peoples because they had never regarded the Hudson's Bay Company "as having any jurisdiction over them or their lands" (Albers 2015, 2). Consequently, the Indigenous peoples occupying these territories had made it perfectly clear that any attempts by settlers to occupy their lands or to otherwise use their resources without their permission would be met with resistance (Asch 2014, 86–7; RCAP 1995, 31).

Indigenous resistance to immigrant settlement could have been met with Canadian military force, much as had occurred between the United States and the Indigenous nations to the south. However, the Canadian government, led by John A. Macdonald at that time, looked on a military approach with disfavour. In his view, hostilities would only further entrench fractious relations and create ongoing instability and uncertainty, conditions that would pose a significant threat to prospects for successful immigrant settlement and economic development of the northwest. In addition, the Red River resistance of 1869–70 and subsequent Métis formation of a provisional government was ample proof to Canada that proceeding with a nation-building exercise without Indigenous involvement could jeopardize the entire project. The clear solution to establishing peaceful relations for all involved, therefore, was to pursue a diplomatic route with Indigenous nations by means of negotiating treaties (Miller 2009, 155–7).

For their part, Indigenous peoples' motivation for negotiating treaties was due to a number of factors. For one, Indigenous peoples wished to establish that because of their status as autonomous nations, they would not tolerate Canadian incursions into their territories without their agreement. There was an important matter of political principle at stake. But beyond this, Indigenous peoples at that time were also in a considerably weakened position. Julie Jai documents that at the time the Numbered Treaties were negotiated, Indigenous populations had been significantly depleted due to

European diseases, wars, loss of critical resources like bison, and settler pressure for agricultural land (Jai 2014, 5).[9] In the face of a succession of epidemics, food security issues, declining trading relations, and an increasing influx of settlers, Indigenous peoples found themselves in an extremely vulnerable position (Courchene 2018, 55, 270; King, H. 2018, 114–15; Miller 2009, 150–2). They were anxious about the status of their lands and their ability to secure a livelihood.

Against the uncertainties set in motion by these changing conditions, Indigenous peoples became increasingly interested in negotiating treaties. As Aimée Craft points out, Indigenous leaders at the time were motivated by "the need to secure a future for their children and grandchildren" (Craft 2013, 23; see also Belanger 2018, 90). Forging treaty alliances between Indigenous nations and the Canadian state represented the best option for a more secure future. It was expected that through treaties Indigenous peoples would retain control over their territories while also agreeing to share it with settlers, and they would attain guarantees of assistance from the Canadian government to better enable themselves to adapt to changing economic circumstances (Starblanket 2019a, 16).

The terms and conditions of each of the Numbered Treaties follows the same general pattern with some variations to take into account the unique circumstances of different treaty nations. The primary objective of the Canadian government was to open up Indigenous lands for settlement. To that end, the written text of treaties purports to clear Indigenous title to the land in exchange for certain benefits (Hedican 2013, 63; King, H. 2018, 115). Reserves were established for the exclusive use of Indigenous peoples. Indigenous peoples were provided with guarantees that they could continue to hunt, fish, and trap on their traditional territories as they had done before. For those Indigenous persons who wished to take up agricultural pursuits, assistance would be provided through the provision of farming equipment and livestock (Hedican 2013, 65). All Indigenous persons would receive an annual annuity as well as access to education and health care. From the perspective of the Indigenous signatories, these treaty terms also met their objectives. By means of these promises, Indigenous peoples believed they had gained the security they needed and to which they were entitled. Settlers could now occupy Indigenous land with Indigenous consent and under peaceful conditions while, in exchange, Indigenous peoples would have the means to live independent lives in the context of changing economic conditions (Courchene 2018, 270).

TREATY 1 (1871)

The first of the Numbered Treaties was negotiated in 1871 between Canada and the Anishinabek and Swampy Cree in what is now southern Manitoba. It was signed on August 3, 1871, after nine days of negotiations. Under its written terms, each Indigenous nation was to receive a reserve based on 160 acres per family of five.[10] The government promised that a school would be built on each reserve. Each Indigenous man, woman, and child would receive an initial gift of $3 and a yearly annuity of $3 to be paid out in goods or cash at the government's discretion.[11] The treaty made explicit reference to prohibiting the introduction and sale of alcohol on reserves.

While there was no provision for hunting or fishing recorded in its written provisions,

Lieutenant-Governor Archibald did make a verbal promise to guarantee Indigenous hunting and fishing rights on the unoccupied territories covered by the treaty. Also, the written text of the treaty made no provision for agricultural implements, animals, or articles of clothing, all of which had been promised in the later stages of the negotiations. The Indigenous nations covered by Treaty 1 petitioned hard for the fulfillment of these verbal treaty promises, an effort that eventually met with success in 1875. In exchange, the Anishinabek and Swampy Cree were required by the terms laid out in the written text to "cede, release, surrender, and yield up to her Majesty the Queen and successors forever" the lands described by the treaty, which essentially included much of present-day southeast and southcentral Manitoba. They also agreed to maintain "perpetual peace" and not interfere with the property or in any way molest any of Her Majesty's subjects (INAC, n.d.c).

TREATY 4 (1874)

The written text of all subsequent Numbered Treaties followed a similar pattern to that established in Treaty 1. However, in several cases the written terms provided were more "generous" in scope in large part because, as Julie Jai observes, Canada wished to avoid the difficulties associated with resolving conflicts over disagreements about unfulfilled oral promises (Jai 2017, 123). Treaty 4, negotiated in 1874 between Canada and the Cree and Saulteaux nations in the Qu'Appelle Lakes region of present-day southern Saskatchewan, is one such example. Under the written terms of Treaty 4, each Indigenous nation was to receive a reserve based on 640 acres per family of five, a considerable increase in acreage over the terms provided in Treaty 1. Each year, every man, woman, and child were to receive an annuity of $5, every chief $25, and every headman $15. Suits of clothing were also to be provided every three years to every chief and headman. The treaty also made explicit provision for farming tools, seed, and animals to assist those Indigenous persons who wished to take up farming.

As with Treaty 1, written provision was made for schools and prohibitions included those against making alcohol available on reserves. But in addition, Treaty 4 guaranteed annual provision of shot, ball, and twine to assist with hunting, trapping, and fishing activities. The treaty further specified that the Cree and Saulteaux could continue to hunt, trap, and fish on their traditional territories unless the land was to be "taken up" (used) "for settlement, mining, or other purposes." Finally, as with the written terms of Treaty 1, the Cree and Saulteaux were required to "cede, release, surrender, and yield up" forever "all rights, titles, and privileges" to their lands covering present-day southern Saskatchewan and portions of western Manitoba and southeastern Alberta (INAC n.d.d).[12] They also purportedly agreed to be the Queen's loyal subjects by obeying Canadian law, keeping the peace, and not disturbing settlers or others travelling through their now "ceded" territories.

CONFLICTING VERSIONS AND INTENTIONS

The verbal promises made by the Canadian treaty commissioners in the negotiations, coupled with Indigenous understandings of what they thought they had agreed to, lead to quite different versions of what treaties are said to have provided when compared to what was recorded in written form (King, H. 2018, 116). A.C Hamilton and C.M.

Sinclair, for example, summarize the significance of specific treaty promises for Indigenous peoples as follows.[13]

They write that Indigenous peoples regarded the promise of reserves as a guarantee that they would have an adequate land base "on which to flourish without external influence or control" (Hamilton and Sinclair 1991, 149; see also Courchene 2018, 55). Protection of their right to hunt, fish, and trap meant that they would be empowered to pursue their traditional economies and lifestyles across the entire range of their traditional territories. These economic rights, in turn, were premised on an ethic of sharing with settlers such that the resources of the land would remain plentiful. The promise of agricultural seed, animals, and farming tools served as an investment on the part of Canada to assist Indigenous nations with the economic development and diversification of their communities. The promise of schools served as the Canadian government's guarantee to provide Indigenous children with the knowledge and skills they would need to adapt and flourish in a rapidly changing world. A promise of disaster relief and a "medicine chest" provided Indigenous peoples with reassurance that their basic needs would be taken care of, including health care, particularly when confronted with disease, epidemics, famine, or otherwise challenging circumstances (Hamilton and Sinclair 1991, 149). And as Gina Starblanket writes, treaty "commitments from Indigenous peoples to maintain 'peace and good order between each other, and between Indigenous peoples and newcomers'" served to signal Indigenous intentions that they would use their political authority to maintain "good relations in agreeing to share the land with them" (Starblanket 2019a, 16). In short, argues Aimée Craft, assurances were repeatedly made by treaty commissioners that Indigenous ways of life would be sustained (Craft 2013, 51).

And as for the "cede, release, and surrender" provisions of the written versions of the treaties, several scholars have argued that these terms were seldom, if ever, raised or discussed in the actual negotiations (see Asch 2014, 77, 90; Borrows and Rotman 2003, 103; Craft 2013, 64; King, H. 2018, 116). Instead, they suggest that what was raised and agreed to was that the land would be shared. Through oral promises, Indigenous peoples agreed to allow settlers to occupy their lands to enable them to make a livelihood, principally by means of agriculture.[14] Indigenous peoples also agreed that "custodial responsibility" for the land would be shared with the Crown. But, according to Michael Asch, as far as he could make out from Indigenous oral history concerning the Numbered Treaties, there is no record of Indigenous peoples agreeing to release and surrender their lands to the Crown (Asch 2014, 109).

From the Canadian government's side, however, treaties were devised primarily to serve as policy instruments for Indigenous assimilation. J.R. Miller notes, for example, "that as western First Nations declined numerically and proportionally because of losses to epidemic diseases and in-migration of non-Native settlers, Ottawa came increasingly to deal with treaty matters in a narrowly legalistic manner" (Miller 2004, 142; see also King, H. 2018, 108–9). Moreover, in many cases the Canadian government also simply chose not to fulfill its treaty obligations at all. It was not unusual, for example, for some of the reserve lands promised in treaties not to be surveyed and subsequently allocated to Indigenous nations. In addition, reserve lands that had been allocated were also regularly subject to appropriation. These lands were taken up on the grounds that doing so served the greater Canadian interest, supporting initiatives like the expansion of urban centres, the building of highways and railroads, or expansion of agricultural initiatives (Erasmus and Sanders 2002, 5; see also Courchene 2018, 55, 268). In addition, when reserve lands were replaced, the land granted was often of marginal quality (Courchene 2018, 284).

Treaty rights to hunt, trap, and fish were also regularly subject to erosion, sacrificed to federal and provincial legislative regimes that restricted Indigenous access to animals that had been central to their ways of life for centuries. Other examples of broken and narrowly interpreted treaty promises are easy to identify. A treaty provision for a "medicine chest" was limited to precisely that. The federal government refused to see in this guarantee a broader treaty commitment to "government-funded hospitalization and medical care" (Miller 2004, 142). The treaty promises to provide schools on reserves was shortly thereafter replaced by a federal policy of constructing residential schools off reserve, institutions that Indigenous children were then later forced to attend. And as Miller notes, an annuity originally set at $5 for every Indigenous man, woman, and child under treaty, while still distributed today, has never been adjusted to take into account 140 years of inflation (Miller 2004, 143; see also Asch 2014, 140–9; Belanger 2018, 94).[15] In short, as put by Edward Hedican, both the wording of treaties and the practices associated with their implementation "hardly suggests an agreement between sovereign nations or some other measure of equal standing, but rather that of a subject people – forced to abide by terms more or less imposed by a more powerful party" (Hedican 2013, 63).

HISTORICAL TREATIES AND OPTIONS FOR INDIGENOUS SOVEREIGNTY

The question we are left with, then, is whether the historic treaties provide Indigenous nations with any genuine opportunities for the exercise of political sovereignty. When Indigenous peoples today speak of Canada's obligation to live up to "the spirit and intent" of their original treaty agreements, it is this element of political sovereignty that is often the focal point of their attention. Historically, Indigenous peoples gave up their right to exclusive use of their traditional territories and therefore, in a spirit of reciprocity and respect, they expected that in exchange the Canadian government would provide guarantees that they could continue to live as they had, self-sufficiently and in freedom. In addition, from an Indigenous perspective, the spirit and intent of treaties carried with it guarantees that the Canadian government would provide Indigenous nations with assistance as they strove to adapt to a rapidly changing world.

By these measures, commentators regularly judge the Canadian government's performance to be woefully inept. For example, Nancy Kleer and Judith Rae remark that with respect to the historic treaty areas, they "remain completely stuck" (Kleer and Rae 2014, 3). They and others point to the fact that Indigenous peoples' original disadvantage in power relations during treaty negotiation exercises in the late nineteenth and early twentieth centuries is still perpetrated within the treaty relations that exist today. It is simply taken as given by Canadian governments, for example, that treaties served to divest Indigenous people of all rights to their traditional territories and that jurisdiction over these lands and resources now resides exclusively with the provinces. From the Indigenous point of view, the original spirit of reciprocity, sharing, and mutual respect is entirely absent from this governmental position.

When measured against the Indigenous right to self-determination, there can be no doubt that the kind of comprehensive redress required to bring the historic treaties into conformity with what many Indigenous leaders assert was originally agreed to is an enormous task. Indeed, from the perspective of many Indigenous peoples and their supporters, given the extent of the historical damage done, redress in this area of treaty relations constitutes, above all others, Canada's greatest and most intractable of challenges (Pasternak, Collis, and Dafnos 2013, 66).[16] But here too there is reason for hope, again in large part because of the considerable efforts expended by Indigenous peoples to get their understanding of their treaty rights and the Canadian governmental obligations that flow from them on public record. Incremental steps have been taken in the larger quest to restore Indigenous sovereignty by redressing neglected treaty rights, though I hasten to add, on the Canadian government's part, these steps are often small and reluctantly taken. Nevertheless, progress is being made, and by means of it genuine space is being created in between the exercise of Canadian sovereignty for the implementation and enjoyment of Indigenous treaty rights. What follows provides a number of examples taken from the Canadian courts and federal Indigenous policy.

THE COURTS AND TREATY RIGHTS

Debate over the appropriate approach to treaty interpretation has regularly come to the Canadian courts. In this process, the Supreme Court of Canada has attempted to clarify what obligations flow from the historic treaty arrangements and, perhaps more importantly, how treaties ought to be implemented to satisfy the aspirations of both Indigenous and Canadian governmental partners.

As discussed in Chapter 5, the Supreme Court of Canada has ruled that technical, contractual, and literal interpretations of treaties should always be avoided. Instead, when coming to terms with the treaty obligations that bind Indigenous and Canadian governmental partners together, the Supreme Court instructs that the following principles must be employed.[17] First, treaties must be given large, liberal, and generous interpretations that favour Indigenous peoples. Second, where there are ambiguities in treaties, they must be resolved in favour of Indigenous peoples. Third, treaties ought also to be construed as their Indigenous signatories understood them, taking into account both the written and oral versions. Fourth, treaties must always be interpreted in a flexible manner, making sure that along the way extrinsic evidence has a role to play in deciding the meaning and intent of treaties. And finally, in the process of defining treaty obligations, Canadian governments must act in a way that preserves the honour and integrity of the Crown. What this means, according to the Supreme Court, is that that are to be no "sharp dealings" with Indigenous peoples, but rather Canadian governments must fulfill their treaty obligations in ways that protect and advance Indigenous interests (Vowel 2016, 249).[18]

While Supreme Court victories remain modest, several significant treaty rights have been recognized as a result of these principles and are now subject to protection. As reviewed in Chapter 5, these victories include the right to a commercial fishery to secure a moderate livelihood and the right to hunt off reserve on unoccupied lands that fall within the traditional territories of treaty nations.

SPECIFIC CLAIMS POLICY

While the Canadian courts have played a significant role in advancing Indigenous understandings of their treaty rights, ultimately, implementation of treaty rights is a matter of public policy. The nature of Indigenous grievances varies, but for the most part they relate to allegations that historically agreed to land entitlements under treaty have remained unfulfilled or that land was taken and then sold without Indigenous consent. Indigenous peoples also seek to gain compensation for the loss of Indigenous assets and natural resources that have been improperly administered by the Canadian government (Pasternak, Collis, and Dafnos 2013, 69).

The Canadian government's response has come by way of its specific claims policy. Developed in 1973, the policy's objective is to fulfill legal obligations following from alleged breaches in the terms of treaties, particularly with respect to unfulfilled land entitlements or alleged mishandling of Indigenous funds or assets. Compensation normally comes in the form of money or the return of land if and where possible. The fact that the Canadian government was willing to admit to its culpability signalled that an important policy shift had occurred. It was less prepared, however, for the magnitude of the Indigenous response. Since 1973, over 2,000 specific claims have been advanced by Indigenous nations (INAC n.d.a). A serious violation of treaty rights right across the country appears to have been the norm rather than the exception. The Canadian government has been emphatic in its position, though, that the specific claims process is not intended to serve as an invitation for Indigenous nations to open up the historical treaties themselves for renegotiation.

A specific claims process begins when an Indigenous group formally registers its claim with the Government of Canada. The Canadian government then reviews the claim, putting itself in a position to decide whether an outstanding legal obligation is owed to the Indigenous claimant. If the Canadian government determines that damages are owed, then negotiations begin between Canada and the Indigenous nation, the objective being to reach a mutually satisfactory settlement. If a settlement is reached, it is then ratified by each party and implemented. Should negotiations fail, or should the Canadian government reject an Indigenous claim, the Indigenous nation can choose to litigate through the courts or appeal to the independent Specific Claims Tribunal. This tribunal consists of superior court judges and is authorized to make binding decisions and to award monetary compensation to a maximum of $150 million (Frideres 2020, 157; Pasternak, Collis, and Dafnos 2013, 69). Of the approximately 2,000 specific claims advanced since 1973, 1,027 have been concluded, 555 are in progress, and 432 are either closed, in active litigation, or before the Specific Claims Tribunal

(INAC n.d.a). James Frideres reports that for those claims that have been settled, "Indigenous people have received $2.2 billion and 1.9 million acres of land that had been wrongfully ceded or taken by the government" (Frideres 2020, 158). Given the sheer number of unresolved claims still demanding attention, however, it is clear that there is much work yet to be done and much injustice yet to be remedied.

While the remedies secured are not always to the Indigenous party's satisfaction, they are nevertheless consistently attained. Compensation for treaty violations usually comes in the form of cash, which Indigenous nations can then use for investment purposes or to purchase land. Both the cash component and additional land can contribute to enhanced Indigenous well-being and self-sufficiency, and equally importantly, can lead to fulfilled treaty obligations. Two recent cases are highly illustrative.

In 2016, the **Snuneymuxw First Nation** in British Columbia received $50 million as compensation for a 32-hectare piece of land, now part of downtown Nanaimo, unlawfully taken from the First Nation in the 1880s. Negotiations with the federal government began in 2003, culminating in the cash settlement as well as an agreement to secure a replacement parcel of land, likely to come from a former military camp near Nanaimo. The Snuneymuxw First Nation's stated intention was to place the cash settlement in a trust to be used for creating economic opportunities for the members of the nation.

In 2016, the **Beardy's and Okemasis First Nation** in Saskatchewan received $4.5 million in compensation as a result of a Specific Claims Tribunal decision that found the federal government to be in breach of its lawful obligation to provide treaty annuities to each of the members of the nation. The federal government had decided in 1885 that all persons who were members of Indigenous nations that had participated in the Northwest Rebellion (13 in total, including the Beardy's and Okemasis First Nation) would be denied their treaty annuities on the grounds that they were "rebel Indians." The federal government upheld this position until 1888, also imposing a pass system on the reserves of the "rebel" nations that was strictly enforced. Finding no justification for the federal government's breach of treaty terms, the Specific Claims Tribunal awarded the Beardy's and Okemasis First Nation financial compensation commensurate with the loss of three years of annuities in modern terms. Like the Snuneymuxw First Nation, the Beardy's and Okemasis First Nation intended to put the cash in a trust to be used for housing, education, and other community priorities.

Of course, resolution of specific claims that satisfy both Indigenous nations and the Government of Canada, while commendable, is not equivalent to restored standing as politically self-governing Indigenous nations. At best, successful specific claims are but incremental steps taken to restore to Indigenous nations part of what "a large, liberal, and generous interpretation" of their historical treaties would provide. Compensations granted by way of cash or land, therefore, should be seen for the modest contribution that they are: building blocks in the larger Indigenous quest to reconstruct lives consistent with their right to self-determination.

Despite success in delivering modest results, the specific claims process itself is beset by considerable difficulties. Specific claims can take years to complete, they can be tremendously costly to Indigenous nations,[19] and they are often taxing on the limited resources of Indigenous claimants as it is they who must prepare all documentation that spells out the substance of their claim. Furthermore, while the impartial Specific Claims Tribunal now exists to step in when the Canadian government and Indigenous nation cannot agree to a settlement, it is still the case that the government acts as both judge and jury because it decides at the outset of the process whether an outstanding lawful obligation exists. The certainty of backlogs, coupled with settlement offers that often fall well short of Indigenous expectations, only act as further obstacles to discourage Indigenous nations from advancing claims within the Canadian government's specific claims policy process. For example, while Indigenous nations may desire the return of lost lands, the system seems geared toward presenting offers of monetary compensation as its preferred option instead (Auditor General of Canada 2016, 13; see also Pasternack, Collis, and Dafnos 2013, 69–70).

THE TREATY LAND ENTITLEMENT PROCESS

If Indigenous nations are not interested in rebuilding their sovereignty through the specific claims process, is there an alternative? One option, which technically falls within the specific claims process, is the **treaty land entitlement** mechanism pursued in the provinces of Saskatchewan and Manitoba. Settlement agreements typically identify an amount of land that an Indigenous nation may either buy from a willing seller or select from unoccupied Crown land, or both, within a mutually agreed upon land-selection area. The provision of cash for the land purchase to settle the land debt owed is provided to the Indigenous nation by the federal and provincial governments.[20] Once the land is either purchased or selected, the Indigenous nation can then apply to the Canadian government to have that land converted to reserve status and added to the bank of reserve lands already in the possession of the Indigenous nation. The overall effect of the treaty land entitlement program has been to significantly add to the land base of numerous Indigenous nations located in the prairie provinces.

The expansion of the Indigenous land base through the treaty land entitlement program has overall received strong support from Indigenous peoples. The essential difference between the reserves created under treaty historically and the treaty lands selected now is that the former were established by the Canadian government in order to "segregate, isolate, marginalize, and subordinate" Indigenous nations as well as to limit the size of Indigenous land allocations based on an underreporting of Indigenous populations (Garcea 2008, 287; Poelzer and Coates 2015, 152). Under the treaty land entitlement program, however, Indigenous leaders are able to select lands in locations that have significant economic and social developmental potential. Selecting lands in urban or resource-rich rural areas, for example, has done much to enhance Indigenous nations' prospects for economic development and growth. In many cases, these new reserves provide opportunities for Indigenous nations to build partnerships with businesses and local governments through investment and revenue-generating initiatives as well as employment. In short, as captured by Joseph Garcea, Indigenous leaders "are intent on adapting what, for the most part, has been a negative and counterproductive legacy in order to create a positive and productive one" (Garcea 2008, 287).

The province of Saskatchewan has led the way in using the treaty land entitlement process to enhance Indigenous political power and to create economic opportunities. In 1992, the Governments of Canada and Saskatchewan signed the *Saskatchewan Treaty Entitlement Framework Agreement* with the chiefs of 25 entitlement Indigenous nations. Since then, of the 74 Indigenous nations in Saskatchewan, 33 have signed on to the agreement (Courchene 2018, 238). Each of the three partners have responsibilities in the process. The Indigenous nation is responsible for selecting and purchasing their desired parcels of land. Importantly, the land purchased does not need to be physically connected (or contiguous) to the reserve lands already in the Indigenous nation's possession. The responsibility of the province of Saskatchewan is to make Crown land available for Indigenous nations to purchase. This stipulation is in keeping the 1930 *Natural Resources Transfer Agreement*, which required that the province transfer Crown lands to the Government of Canada so that it can fulfill its treaty obligations. And finally, the responsibility of the Government of Canada is to transfer the purchased land to reserve status once the previous two steps in the process have been taken (City of Saskatoon 2016).

As for monetary compensation, the Indigenous nation receives an amount based on an agreed upon formula. The formula itself is devised to provide compensation to the Indigenous nation consistent with the shortfall of land that was guaranteed when the surveys for the historical treaties were originally conducted. Additional "equity" compensation is also provided to take into account population growth and the fact that the entitled Indigenous nation has suffered lost opportunities over time as a result of having a much smaller reserve than they originally should have (Flanagan and Harding 2017, 6). Since 2017, more than 860,000 acres of reserve lands have been added to Indigenous nations' territories in Saskatchewan (Adam 2017, 2; Kessler 2017, 2).

Many of the lands purchased in Saskatchewan by Indigenous nations have been in small and large urban centres. The Federation of Sovereign Indigenous Nations reports that there are currently 54 urban reserves in Saskatchewan with a further 55 that have been initiated by Indigenous nations (Federation of Sovereign Indigenous Nations n.d., 1).[21] In all cases, the urban land purchases must be on a "willing buyer, willing seller" basis and are sold to Indigenous nations either by private owners or by any level of government that designates specified public lands to be "surplus" and thus expendable.[22]

Also, where urban reserves are established, several preconditions must be met before a land transfer can take place. For example, Indigenous nations and local municipalities must ensure that the Indigenous nation's land use and zoning plans are compatible with those of the municipality and that by-laws concerning matters such as building standards, business licensing and operation, and provision of local services are aimed at achieving shared goals. In addition, because urban reserves are exempt from local taxation (just like all Indian reserves), Indigenous nations must agree to provide local municipalities with payment of a service fee. The service fee plays the dual function of payment for municipal services provided on reserve, such as police and fire protection, snow removal, garbage pickup, and water and sewer services as well as compensation for lost tax revenue (Flanagan and Harding 2017, 8).[23] As for status, by far the majority of these urban reserves have been granted commercial standing and serve as locations for the establishment of businesses ranging from the relatively modest like gas stations and convenience stores all the way up to casinos, shopping centres, and business parks (Flanagan and Harding 2017, 8).

On one level, it could be argued that the treaty land entitlement process is as inept at delivering justice to Indigenous nations as was the larger historical treaty process of which it is a part. For example, the fact that Indigenous nations must purchase land that they would argue is already theirs by historic right borders on the offensive. And even with money in hand, Indigenous nations may only purchase land equivalent to "shortfall" and "equity" levels consistent with their original land allocations under the terms of the historical treaties. But, as a good number of Indigenous leaders point out, the lands actually reserved to their nations under the terms of the historical treaties were far smaller in scale than they believe was originally agreed upon. According to Indigenous memories of the oral terms of treaty agreements, Indigenous and Canadian authorities had agreed to share the land and resources in ways that would contribute to the well-being of both partners. What the treaty land entitlement process does, in other words, is restore to Indigenous nations no more than land equivalent to the quantum prescribed by Canadian authorities in the written version of the treaties, a quantum to which not all Indigenous signatories had lent their consent. On these grounds, therefore, the treaty land entitlement initiative ought not to be seen as a form of restorative justice, but rather as a further perpetuation of colonialism.

On another level, however, the treaty land entitlement process has contributed, albeit in a small way, to Indigenous self-sufficiency. Urban reserves in particular secure for Indigenous people a range of economic opportunities that are more difficult to deliver on rural reserves. Urban reserves have served as a setting for the establishment of Indigenous and non-Indigenous businesses, for example, or for lucrative tax-generating industrial and commercial activities as well as employment opportunities for Indigenous persons. With increased self-generating revenue in hand, Indigenous nations can reduce their dependency on federal government transfers. Increased employment, in turn, raises the standard of living for members as well as generates revenue for Indigenous nations to independently finance their own social, cultural, and political programs and services (Western Economic Diversification Canada 2016, 11–15). The Muskeg Lake Cree First Nation, for example, operates about a dozen Indigenous businesses on its urban reserve in Saskatoon, which provides more than 300 jobs for Indigenous people (Western Economic Diversification Canada 2016, 5). As noted by Greg Poelzer and Ken Coates, the fact that half of Saskatchewan's Indigenous peoples live off reserve means that "the creation of commercial centres and employment opportunities in the cities has been a real boon for them" (Poelzer and Coates 2015, 152). With an expanded land base and enhanced economic opportunities, in other words, comes greater economic and political self-sufficiency for Indigenous nations and their governments. And while increased self-sufficiency is not equivalent to political sovereignty, it does constitute a step in that direction.

In addition to stimulating the internal development of Indigenous nations, the treaty land entitlement initiative has also generated mutually beneficial intergovernmental partnerships. This is particularly evident at the municipal level. The success of urban reserves, for example, depends on regular meetings being held between the leadership of the Indigenous nations and the municipalities. Among other things, they have to secure intergovernmental agreements on such items as municipal tax loss compensation, provision of municipal services to the reserve, harmonization of by-laws, and protocols on enforcement mechanisms (Gibbons and Sully 2014, 4). It is also not unusual for Indigenous nations and municipalities to create a dispute resolution mechanism as part of their commitment to building a long-term relationship. In the city of Saskatoon, for example, a protocol agreement is signed before any urban reserve is created. The stated purposes of these agreements "is to establish an ongoing communication forum for information sharing, identifying common issues, and developing common resolution approaches" (City of Saskatoon 2016, 2).

And as for benefits, it is not just Indigenous peoples who enjoy prospects for enhanced well-being through the creation of urban reserves. Neighbouring municipalities also benefit as a result of economic stimulus provided through service agreements, job creation, and new taxation revenue generated by the off-reserve spin-off effects of Indigenous businesses (Courchene 2018, 259). In short, the partnerships generated between municipalities and Indigenous nations have been ones that have served to consolidate the status of Indigenous nations as distinct, self-governing bodies within Canada. And again, while the existence of intergovernmental partnerships between Indigenous nations and municipalities do not, in and of themselves, signal the return of Indigenous sovereignty, what they do signal is that Indigenous governments are being taken seriously as free-standing governments in their own right.

CONCLUSION

As for the larger project of rebuilding their sovereignty consistent with their understandings of their historical treaty agreements with the Crown, Indigenous peoples and their allies have not been short of ideas. The starting point for many is the 1764 Treaty of Niagara, an agreement that they say sets out all the appropriate protocols and rules for a genuine sharing of political power and a corresponding sharing of the lands and resources upon which both Indigenous and non-Indigenous peoples rely. Building on these historical protocols, Indigenous leaders then argue that if understood as political compacts, treaties can "rebalance their relationship with the state, based on the recognition of their rights on the land and their status as inherently self-governing nations" (Papillon 2020, 219).

The Canadian government has been significantly knocked off course because of its choice to pursue racist policies of assimilation. But this injustice need not prove devastating from the point of view of trying to get the original treaty relationship back on track. A number of commentators have offered the following suggestions: establish a fair and equitable distribution of decision-making power on all treaty subjects between Canadian and Indigenous governments; uphold a commitment to fair dealings in deciding what changing circumstances over time should mean when it comes to implementing historical treaty obligations in the present; and set up a fair process for resolving treaty disputes (Asch 2014, 96–9; Coyle 2017, 65; Jai 2017, 138, 141, 143; Macklem 2001, 183). As Michael Asch observes, had we honoured the treaties according to these principles when they were first negotiated, and had we continued to do so right up to the present, "we may have well long passed the point where the legitimacy of our (that is, non-Indigenous) settlement on these lands might be in question" (Asch 2014, 99).

DISCUSSION QUESTIONS

1 Why is the art of treaty-making so central to mediating relationships between Indigenous nations and the Canadian state?
2 Why did Canada abandon its policy of treaty-making with Indigenous nations between 1921 and 1973? What factors compelled it to do so? Were any of these factors justifiable?
3 Can the historical treaties be interpreted today in ways to support the Indigenous assertion to sovereignty while also preserving the integrity of Canada? In what ways would the Canadian political order have to be transformed to accommodate such a vision?
4 Are the specific claims and treaty land entitlement policies sufficiently robust to meet Canada's obligations under the terms of the historical treaties?

SUGGESTED READINGS

Asch, Michael. 2014. *On Being Here to Stay: Treaties and Aboriginal Rights in Canada.* Toronto: University of Toronto Press.

Belanger, Yale D. 2018. "Chapter 4: Treaties." In *Ways of Knowing: An Introduction to Native Studies in Canada.* Toronto: Nelson.

Borrows, John and Michael Coyle, eds. 2017. *The Right Relationship: Reimagining the Implementation of the Historical Treaties.* Toronto: University of Toronto Press.

Courchene, Thomas J. 2018. "Appendix A: The Numbered Treaties: Making Way for the White Man." In *Indigenous Nationals, Canadian Citizens: From First Contact to Canada and Beyond.* Montreal: McGill-Queen's University Press.

Craft, Aimée. 2013. *Breathing Life into the Stone Fort Treaty: An Anishinabe Understanding of Treaty One.* Saskatoon, SK: Purich Publishing.

King, Hayden. 2018. "Treaty Making and Breaking in Settler Colonial Canada." In *Contemporary Inequalities and Social Justice in Canada*, edited by Janine Brodie. Toronto: University of Toronto Press.

Miller, J.R. 2009. *Compact, Contract, Covenant: Aboriginal Treaty-Making in Canada.* Toronto: University of Toronto Press.

Pasternak, Shiri, Sue Collis, and Tia Dafnos. 2013. "Criminalization at Tyendinaga: Securing Canada's Colonial Property Regime through Specific Land Claims." *Canadian Journal of Law and Society* 28 (1).

Starblanket, Gina. 2020. "Crises of Relationship: The Role of Treaties in Contemporary Indigenous–Settler Relations." In *Visions of the Heart: Issues Involving Indigenous Peoples in Canada,* 5th ed., edited by Gina Starblanket and David Long. Toronto: Oxford University Press.

———. 2019. "The Numbered Treaties and the Politics of Incoherency." *Canadian Journal of Political Science* 52.

Vowel, Chelsea. 2016. "Chapter 27: Treaty Talk: The Evolution of Treaty-Making in Canada." In *Indigenous Writes: A Guide to First Nations, Métis & Inuit Issues in Canada.* Winnipeg: Highwater Press.

NOTES

1 The historical events described in this paragraph are covered at length in Chapter 3.

2 I thank one of the anonymous reviewers of this book for providing this important characterization of the comprehensive land claims policy's objective.

3 For example, between 1713 and 1763, the British made a series of "peace and friendship" treaties between themselves and the Mi'kmaq and Maliseet peoples in present-day New Brunswick and Nova Scotia. These treaties solidified peaceful relations between Mi'kmaq and Maliseet and the British, with the Crown guaranteeing both nations access to hunting, fishing, and trading rights in return. See Isaac 2012, 144.

4 The Two-Row Wampum belt signified two parallel paths on the same river, each nation occupying a different vessel, both enjoying and sharing the resources from the same waters but neither attempting to steer the other's craft, nor get in the way of the other's path. Both were to travel in peace, side-by-side, in friendship and mutual respect.

5 The Covenant Chain refers to a complex set of treaties between the Haudenosaunee (or Six Nations) and the British Crown originating in the early seventeenth century. These early treaties were referred to symbolically as "chains" because they bound the treaty partners together as allies in military and trading pursuits. It was understood that the treaties required periodic revisiting and a refreshing of terms accompanied by the exchange of gifts and aid. This process of treaty renewal became known as "polishing the silver chain."

6 J.R. Miller observes that many treaties included a pipe ceremony, significant in that the smoking of the sacred pipe signified that the Creator was brought into the proceedings and that all those party to the agreement would speak only the truth. See Miller 2004, 139.

7 I thank one of the anonymous reviewers of this book for providing this helpful observation.

8 Concerning the same point, one of the anonymous reviewers of this book commented, "if your group is in severe decline, struggling to survive (food, shelter, medicine), and you have lost many of your healthy adults to war, disease, and poverty, and the Crown says we will give you food, money, shelter, and medicine to help you survive in exchange for land, is it still irrational in those circumstances to accept? So, yes, this is indeed a 'deal with the devil' or a 'poisoned pill' but it could be that you felt you had no choice but to take the deal because the alternatives were worse." See also my remarks on the weakened negotiating position of Indigenous peoples in the next section on "The Numbered Treaties."

9 Jai further points out that the Indigenous share of the Canadian population had dropped from an estimated 67 per cent in 1763 to just 1.3 per cent in 1921. See Jai 2017, 112.

10 Less for smaller families and more for larger families.

11 Or a yearly annuity of $15 per family of five.

12 Several chiefs who were not present during Treaty 4 negotiations later signed what are called "adhesions," which meant they became party to the treaty but had to accept the terms of the treaty without opportunity for further negotiations. That is, they had to accept the treaty on the basis of a "take-it or leave-it" proposition. See Jai 2017, 124; Miller 2009, 173.

13 What follows draws substantially from Hamilton and Sinclair 1991, 149.

14 With respect to Treaty 1, for example, Aimée Craft argues that the land and its resources would be shared as follows: "plots of agricultural land for the White settlers and continued use of the land by the Anishinabe." See Craft 2013, 61.

15 Michael Asch also identifies a litany of broken treaty promises, including a reluctance on the part of the federal government to assist Indigenous nations in transitioning to an agricultural economy, federal neglect in the face of Indigenous famine and starvation, and federal abuse of Indigenous children by way of residential schools. See Asch 2014, 140–9.

16 See, for example, the 2017 book edited by John Borrows and Michael Coyle, *The Right Relationship: Reimagining the Implementation of Historical Treaties* (Toronto: University of Toronto Press). In this volume both Indigenous and non-Indigenous scholars grapple with the question concerning what it would take, at the level of both principle and practice, to implement the historical treaties today in a way that is in keeping with their original spirit and intent.

17 The following draws in large part from Chelsea Vowel's summary as found in her book, *Indigenous Writes: A Guide to First Nations, Metis, and Inuit Issues in Canada* (Vowel 2016, 249). See also Asch 2014, 83, 84; Belanger 2018, 94–5.

18 One of the anonymous reviewers of this book notes that the aforementioned principles of treaty interpretation extend beyond Canada to other settler colonial countries as well.

19 As of April 1, 2021, the Canadian government adapted the specific claims policy to allow for a reasonable portion of the costs of negotiation, including research, development, and submission of a claim, to be added to the final financial settlement.

20 The Government of Canada contributes 70 per cent of the costs while the province of Saskatchewan contributes 30 per cent.

21 The Federation of Sovereign Indigenous Nations reports that the total value of treaty land entitlement settlements to date is $595,505,684.83. Under the terms of the agreement, the 33 entitled Indigenous nations are eligible to acquire 2,277,325 acres. Of that amount, 547,667 are shortfall acres and 1,729,658 are equity acres. See Federation of Sovereign Indigenous Nations n.d.

22 In Saskatchewan, urban reserves can be found in Saskatoon, Prince Albert, Fort Qu'Appelle, Yorkton, Meadow Lake, Regina, and North Battleford. See Poelzer and Coates 2015, 152.

23 Generally, the fee-for-service on urban reserves is calculated in the same way as property taxes and is more-or-less equal to the amount that would otherwise be collected for municipal taxes.

CHAPTER 7

Treaties New: Landed Citizenship

LEARNING OBJECTIVES

1 To describe the comprehensive land claims and BC treaty processes and to identify the differences between them.
2 To assess whether the modern treaty process has been deliberately designed by the Canadian government to safeguard its monopoly on state power.
3 To explain how the modern treaty process can contribute to the exercise of restoring the Indigenous right to self-determination.
4 To identify why modern treaties are so difficult to complete and to explain how these difficulties might be overcome.
5 To compare and contrast the various features of the Inuit (Nunavut) and Algonquin (Ontario) land claim settlements to assess their relative strengths and weaknesses.

This chapter examines the contemporary treaty-making process launched by Canada in 1973. My focus will be on the Canadian government's comprehensive land claims policy as well as the parallel British Columbia treaty process. The intent of the chapter is to provide a cost-benefit analysis of contemporary treaty-making from the perspective of Indigenous sovereignty. And as we shall see, the ledger is one that contains mixed entries.

There are critics, particularly among some Indigenous observers and participants, who are convinced that contemporary treaties do little more than serve to further consolidate Canadian state control over Indigenous peoples through a series of measures that I will identify. But there are also those who see in modern treaties real opportunities for restored and enhanced Indigenous self-determination. Indeed, it is in the very act of treaty-making itself, qualified as it is by negotiations undertaken by governments leading to agreements and solemn obligations, that we witness the principle of sovereignty in action. Just how this is so and in what ways will be documented. Specifically, I will draw from examples provided by the 1993 *Nunavut Land Claims Agreement* and the Algonquin Land Claims negotiations currently underway.[1] While each is uniquely crafted to meet the particular circumstances of the two Indigenous groups, both, in their own way, lend some recognition and support to elements of the Indigenous assertion to sovereignty. In short, though fragile and often tempered by an atmosphere of cautious optimism, comprehensive land claims and self-government agreements do have the capacity to establish mutually beneficial relationships of both self-rule and shared rule between the Canadian state and Indigenous nations.

INTO THE CONTEMPORARY ERA

As discussed in previous chapters, retraction of the 1969 White Paper created a policy opening for Indigenous leaders to once again assert their rights to lands and resources within their traditional territories. The presence of increasingly sophisticated instances of Indigenous organization and activism, coupled with the Supreme Court of Canada's clear recognition of Aboriginal title in its 1973 *Calder* decision, paved the way for the comprehensive land claims process, but only in areas where Indigenous rights and title had not been dealt with through historical treaties or other legal means (Alcantara 2017, 330; Frideres 2020, 153; Pendakur and Pendakur 2017, 141). The comprehensive land claims process was designed to complete the unfinished business of treaty-making in Canada in such areas as Atlantic Canada, northern Quebec and Ontario, parts of Nunavut, the Northwest Territories, Yukon, and British Columbia (Alcantara 2017, 329).[2] Essentially, the objective of the process is to "establish new land tenure regimes as well as co-governance and self-governance arrangements for their Indigenous signatories" (Papillon 2020, 218). Canada's primary motivation for engagement is to achieve greater legal certainty over rights to lands and resources (Aragón 2015, 43). The patterns of the past understandably complicate prospects for the successful initiation, resolution, and implementation of modern treaties in the present.[3] Indigenous peoples often express distrust and suspicion of Canadian governmental motives given their experience of over a century and a half of unfair and unjust dealings where the interpretation and implementation of their historic treaties are concerned (Irlbacher-Fox 2009, 26).

Nevertheless, since 1973 Canadian and Indigenous negotiators have managed to ratify 27 comprehensive claims agreements, 18 of which include self-government provisions (Alcantara

2017, 329–31; Belanger 2018, 99–103; Courchene 2018, 181–200, 221–32; Eyford 2015, 23; Frideres 2020, 153–7; King, H. 2018, 118–19; Papillon 2020, 223–4).[4] Beginning with the ***James Bay and Northern Quebec Agreement*** in 1975, each is now protected under Section 35 of the *Constitution Act, 1982*, thereby insulating them against potentially unilateral changes that might otherwise be pursued by federal, provincial, or territorial governments. Taken together, these modern treaties cover approximately 40 per cent of Canada's land mass. As explained by Hayden King, in exchange for either surrendering or agreeing not to assert title to most of their traditional territories, Indigenous signatories receive "financial compensation distributed over a number of years, 'ownership' to a fraction of their traditional territories, and some degree of management authority over both Indigenous-owned lands and newly created categories of Crown lands" (King 2015, 84).[5]

While not without their problems, these comprehensive claims agreements are far more reflective of Indigenous peoples' aspirations and intentions than are the written versions of the historic treaties. Indigenous negotiators who enter the process are generally well organized, knowledgeable, articulate, and clear about what would constitute a meaningful settlement for their peoples. To be sure, where power at the negotiation tables is concerned, Indigenous participants are often at a distinct disadvantage given the wealth of resources in time, expertise, and money available to their federal, provincial, and territorial counterparts (Alcantara 2013, 7, 21; Belanger 2018, 96; Gehl 2014, 63; Irlbacher-Fox 2009, 19). Indeed, the existence of these significant asymmetries in power leads some commentators to conclude that the inevitable outcome of comprehensive land claims negotiations is that they draw Indigenous nations into institutional "straightjackets," confining their expression of self-determination to "within the strict boundaries of the Canadian federal regime" (Papillon 2020, 219; see also Alcantara 2013, 9; Irlbacher-Fox 2009, 10–12). These commentators further add that this is precisely the outcome that Canadian state political actors intend.

Despite these very real structural constraints, it is nevertheless my contention that the processes associated with the negotiation and implementation of modern treaties do provide Indigenous peoples with both real and meaningful opportunities for enhancing their right to political self-determination within Canada. Naturally, each comprehensive land claims agreement is customized to address the unique history, circumstances, and interests of each Indigenous signatory (Courchene 2018, 181). But despite variation, the overall design and structure of each "is broadly similar from one agreement to another" (Papillon 2020, 224). By virtue of their shared attention to land tenure and self-government issues, Martin Papillon points out that modern treaties have generally served to "enhance Indigenous identities as distinct polities, boost their institutional capacity, and establish their position as central actors in the governance of their traditional lands" (Papillon 2020, 218; see also Alcantara and Wilson 2014, 47). In the pages to follow I shall describe a number of ways in which the benefits set out in the agreements through transfer of political powers, lands, and resources do make a real contribution to both the enhancement of Indigenous well-being in Canada and to "a significant shift in indigenous–state relations" (Nadasdy 2017, 5).

THE COMPREHENSIVE CLAIMS PROCESS

Reaching modern treaty agreements is a lengthy and drawn-out process in large part because of the complexity of the negotiations and because of the difficulties associated with reaching agreements (Alcantara 2013, 31, 130–1; Frideres 2020, 154). The historic treaties were completed in a matter of a few days and usually were no more than a few pages in length. In contrast, modern treaties are tremendously complex, running on for hundreds of pages and taking years to complete (Jai 2017, 136). For example, the ***Tla'amin Final Agreement***, which was completed in 2014, is 260 pages in length, contains 26 chapters, and took 20 years to complete.

The process of treaty agreement, from inception through to implementation, is a highly complex affair made up of several stages. The process begins when the federal government accepts a statement of claim from an Indigenous group along with supporting materials. These supporting materials must establish that the Indigenous claimant is justified in advancing a claim. The justification provided must include, among other things, proof that the Indigenous claimant is, and was, an organized society and has occupied the specific territory over which it asserts title from time immemorial, and proof that the nature of its occupation has been both continuous and largely to the exclusion of all others (Alcantara 2013, 15, 31; Belanger 2018, 99–100). The Indigenous claimant must also show that it has not entered into or adhered to a treaty and it must identify exactly which bands, tribes, or communities are to be the intended beneficiaries of the claim (Gehl 2014, 64; Lawrence 2012, 69).

If the Indigenous nation successfully completes this stage, the parties then enter into negotiations, which contain a number of steps. The first step requires negotiation of a framework agreement that addresses "the scope, topics, and parameters for negotiation" (Eyford 2015, 21; see also Alcantara 2013, 15). The framework agreement then becomes the foundation upon which an agreement-in-principle (AIP) is built. The AIP stage is where all the heavy lifting takes place, as this is when the parties seek to reach detailed agreements on all the subject matters identified in the framework agreement, including political jurisdiction, land, resources, and cash. Once an AIP is completed, federal and provincial (or territorial) Cabinet approval is required, as is ratification by the members of the Indigenous nation (Jai 2017, 134). During the final agreement stage, the parties seek to finalize all components of the treaty, after which the Indigenous negotiators return to their nations for a ratification vote and federal and provincial (or territorial) governments pass enabling legislation through their legislatures (Eyford 2015, 56; see also Alcantara 2013, 14–17). The final stage involves implementation of the agreement, a process that can also take several years.

As the name suggests, the provisions of modern treaties are comprehensive in nature, touching on virtually every aspect of the lives of those Indigenous peoples who fall under a treaty's terms. In all cases, the Indigenous nations subject to treaty step out from under the provisions of the *Indian Act*. In its replacement, Indigenous nations secure a set of specific and clearly defined rights and benefits recognized and guaranteed within their final agreement. With the introduction of the federal government's inherent right to self-government policy in 1995, comprehensive claims settlements negotiated since have also contained self-government agreements.[6] Consequently, as noted by Lianne Maria Leda Charlie, as part of the implementation process, Indigenous signatories are provided with mechanisms to transition from "Indian bands" to "political entities that are, in theory, organized and managed by First Nations themselves" (Charlie 2020, 86; see also Papillon 2020, 225).

As for the actual content of settlements, each includes detailed and meticulously negotiated chapters that outline "the rights, powers, and jurisdiction of each party and how they relate to each other" (Charlie 2020, 86). Topics addressed usually include the following:

- fiscal arrangements and cash settlements;
- provisions for land ownership, land use planning, and control of natural resources;
- water management;
- rights to harvest fish and wildlife;
- rights of Indigenous governments to make laws across numerous jurisdictions and to provide many public services (including culture, heritage, recreation, housing, education, social programming, health care, and policing);
- resource revenue-sharing arrangements;
- procedures for conducting environmental assessments;
- guarantees concerning Indigenous control over Indigenous citizenship;
- economic development opportunities; and
- arrangements concerning tax matters (Alcantara 2013, 3, 16; Charlie 2020, 86).

All modern treaties negotiated to date also stipulate that Indigenous governments are to be subject to the Canadian *Charter of Rights and Freedoms*. In addition, final agreements receive protection as "treaty rights" under Section 35 of the Canadian Constitution.

Concerning the issue of land more specifically, all Indigenous signatories have, to date, been required to give up Aboriginal title to their traditional territories in the sense that they agree to either release, cede, suspend, modify, or no longer assert it (Papillon 2020, 224).[7] In exchange, they get clearly defined and specific rights to certain portions of those same territories in the form of what are usually called "settlement" lands. These "settlement" lands, in turn, are often divided up into different categories. Some lands are reserved for the exclusive use of the Indigenous signatories and carry with them ownership rights to both the land itself and to its surface and subsurface resources (Charlie 2020, 88). Other settlement lands carry with them exclusive Indigenous rights to hunt, fish, or trap, but jurisdiction over policy areas like forestry, mining, tourism, land use planning, and environmental regulation is shared with provincial or territorial governments (Papillon 2020, 224). To facilitate this process of shared jurisdiction, most comprehensive land claims agreements also provide for the creation of co-management boards. These boards are designed to bring together representatives from Indigenous and provincial or territorial governments "to provide advice on environmental and resource management issues" (Jai 2017, 130). While often able only to put forward recommendations, co-management boards can and do provide an important collaborative forum for government and Indigenous participants to articulate their respective interests and to work out the manner of their shared jurisdiction over lands and resources in a treaty settlement area (King 2015, 84; see also Charlie 2020, 90).[8] Whatever the category, however, it is important to underscore that settlement lands usually constitute only a small portion of the traditional territories that were historically occupied, used, and cared for by Indigenous nations (Papillon 2020, 224).

Nonetheless, the substantive content of modern treaties does go some considerable way "in meeting the underlying interests of both Indigenous and non-Indigenous parties to the agreement" (Jai 2017, 135–6). Canadian governmental actors "achieve clarity about rights to lands and resources in order to facilitate investment and economic development" (Jai, 2017, 132). Indigenous signatories, meanwhile, achieve enhanced opportunities for socioeconomic development and greater political capacity for self-determination. To take but one example, Douglas R. Eyford observes that in all cases where modern treaties have been completed, they "have improved socio-economic outcomes for Aboriginal beneficiaries" (Eyford 2015, 3; see also Jai 2017, 136). Recent studies by Fernando M. Aragón as well as Krishna Pendakur and Ravi Pendakur verify this point. These authors show that comprehensive land claims agreements (both with and without corresponding self-government agreements), contribute substantially to income gains for Indigenous households "primarily through increased labor income" (Pendakur and Pendakur 2017, 139; see also Aragón 2015, 43–4). As they explain it, because modern treaties clarify ownership over land and natural resources on traditional Indigenous lands, they "reduce transaction costs, especially for extractive activities," which, in turn, facilitates economic development and contributes to local Indigenous economies (Aragón 2015, 44). In my view, modern treaty benefits that contribute in such dramatic ways to Indigenous community well-being ought not to be minimized.

THE BRITISH COLUMBIA TREATY PROCESS

The modern treaty-making process in British Columbia is characterized by a number of unique features that distinguish it from the larger Canada-wide comprehensive claims process. With the exception of the very limited number of **Douglas Treaties** on Vancouver Island and **Treaty 8** covering a portion of northeastern BC, no historical treaties were negotiated in the province (Eyford 2015, 52). When BC joined Confederation in 1871 it took the position that the Royal Proclamation of 1763, which made provision for the recognition of Indigenous title and the negotiation of treaties in exchange for the right to settle on Indigenous lands, did not apply to it. Consequently, when the Canadian government established the comprehensive land claims process in 1973, BC simply refused to accept the proposition that most of the province was subject to Indigenous title. As far as the Government of BC was concerned, colonial legislation had extinguished all Indigenous rights and, therefore, the land belonged to the provincial Crown. This was the position that the province would obstinately hold to until 1990 (Miller 2009, 251).

Naturally, the Indigenous nations of BC refused to accept the position of the BC government. They waged a long and hard-fought campaign, turning to the Canadian courts, the federal government, the public, and the international community for support in forcing the BC government to take the matter of their outstanding Indigenous rights and title seriously. Regrettably, Indigenous peoples were compelled to take drastic measures to get the BC government's attention. Throughout the 1980s, blockades of highways, railroads, and forestry access roads by Indigenous peoples and their supporters were a common occurrence. Finally, in 1990, the **British Columbia Claims Task Force** was established. It recommended that BC enter into treaty negotiations with Indigenous nations using 19 recommendations authored by the task force to guide the process.[9] Two years later the ***British Columbia Treaty Commission Agreement*** was signed between the governments of Canada and BC, as well as the First Nations Summit, a body representing the political interests of those Indigenous nations that had agreed to enter the treaty process (Lawrence 2012, 75, Isaac 2012, 165). This agreement set out the principles and procedures for negotiating treaties within BC, a process that began in earnest in 1993.

While the scope, organization, and process for negotiating treaties in BC closely resembles the federal comprehensive claims model, the BC approach is marked by two unique features. First, the British Columbia Claims Task Force recommended that a **BC Treaty Commission** be established to serve as "keeper of the process" of treaty negotiations. It is the only legally established, arm's-length, independent tripartite body in Canada whose mandate is to monitor and facilitate treaty negotiations. More specifically, the BC Treaty Commission's mandate requires that it assess the readiness of Canada, BC, and Indigenous nations to begin negotiations; it assists the parties (when asked) to resolve disputes; it allocates negotiation support funding to Indigenous nations; and it serves as an educational clearinghouse, informing British Columbians about the status of treaty negotiations in the province (INAC n.d.b). Second, unlike the federal comprehensive claim process, there is no preliminary legal assessment by Canada or BC about the strength of an Indigenous nation's claim prior to entering treaty negotiations. All that the BC Treaty Commission requires of Indigenous nations is that its governing body file a "short and succinct description of the general geographic area of the claimed traditional territory as well as proof it has a mandate from its constituents to enter the process" (Eyford 2015, 66). In short, an Indigenous nation does not have to prove it has Indigenous title or rights as a precondition to entering negotiations. Instead, under the BC treaty process, it is understood that negotiations are the setting within which the existence and the extent of the Indigenous rights that belong to each nation are to be established.

Broadly speaking, the BC treaty process involves land, resources, and cash components as well as self-government provisions. The process is also entirely voluntary. No Indigenous nation is required to participate. The process itself is composed of six stages and is launched when a **statement of intent** is filed by the Indigenous nation with the BC Treaty Commission. Within 45 days of receiving the statement, the commission convenes a meeting with assigned negotiators from the Canadian, BC, and Indigenous governments to decide whether the parties are ready to negotiate. With the commission's approval in hand and ever-present offer of support at their disposal, the parties then move on to negotiate a framework agreement. The framework agreement serves as the foundation for the next stage in building the detailed agreement-in-principle, then fine-tuning occurs by way of the eventual final agreement. The process concludes with ratification votes, leading to the ultimate goal, treaty implementation.

This six-stage negotiation process took 16 years to produce its first treaty (with the **Tsawwassen First Nation** in 2009) and since then just two more have reached the implementation stage (**Maa-nulth First Nations** in 2011 and Tla'amin First Nation in 2014). The BC Treaty Commission's annual report states that as of 2021,

- 15 Indigenous nations were in final agreement negotiations (stage 5);
- 16 were in active negotiations (stage 4, 3, or 2); and
- 27 that had entered the process at one time or another had chosen for various reasons to suspend negotiations (BC Treaty Commission 2021, 14–38).

The commission notes that, altogether, 39 Indigenous nations, representing 72 former or current Indian bands in BC, are either participating in or have completed treaties through the BC treaty negotiation process (BC Treaty Commission 2021, 15).

In January 2018 the governments of Canada, BC, and the First Nations Summit significantly expanded the mandate of the BC Treaty Commission. Going forward, the commission will facilitate treaty negotiations to include implementation of the UNDRIP and the TRC's 94 Calls to Action (BC Treaty Commission 2018, 11). In addition, treaty negotiations will now be conducted on the premise that Indigenous nations already possess Indigenous rights and title. From here on in, rights and title will simply be taken as given, with efforts focused instead on how to develop strategies to secure their implementation through agreements (BC Treaty Commission 2018, 10; see also BC Treaty Commission 2019, 10–20). In keeping with this initiative, the governments of Canada and BC announced that former reliance on certainty techniques associated with the language of "extinguishment," "modification," or "suspension" of rights would be abandoned in favour of an approach that regards treaties as flexible and living partnerships capable of evolution over time (BC Treaty Commission 2018, 10; see also BC Treaty Commission 2019, 11). In its 2019 budget, the Government of Canada further committed itself to forgiving all negotiation loan debts held by Indigenous nations across Canada. It also guaranteed that as of April 2018, all negotiation funding granted to Indigenous nations would be fully paid for as a 100 per cent contribution (BC Treaty Commission 2018, 12; see also BC Treaty Commission 2019, 18). These changes in mandate and policy, moreover, were to apply not only to BC but also to wherever comprehensive land claims negotiations were being conducted across Canada.

CONFLICTING OBJECTIVES

The overriding objective of the federal and provincial governments in the comprehensive claims (and BC treaty) process has been to achieve what they call "**certainty**" about who owns and therefore is entitled to use and manage Canada's land and resources (Belanger 2018, 96; see also Jai 2017, 132). Since the Canadian courts have established that Aboriginal title exists as a "burden" on Crown title, Canadian governments can no longer proceed on the assumption that all land is Crown land and therefore available for federal or provincial governments to do with as they please. It is in the face of this legal uncertainty that Canadian governments are compelled to negotiate Indigenous land claims. What governments seek to do is transform undefined Indigenous rights and title into a set of rights that are clearly defined and explicitly set out within the terms of a modern treaty (Alcantara 2013, 3–4; Charlie 2020, 87).

Until recently, Canadian governments have insisted that for the sake of certainty, the settlement of Indigenous claims must also constitute a full and final settlement of all Indigenous rights (Papillon 2020, 227; see also Mackey 2016, 60–2). On this score, however, governmental intentions seem to be softening. Canadian governments now seem more content to use language aligned with the Indigenous view that their rights and title are implemented and then "continue" through treaties rather than constitute a full and final settlement of those rights. Still, on the larger question of land ownership, Canadian governmental objectives remain resolute. Treaties are to clarify and then assign to Indigenous nations and the Canadian state ownership over certain parcels of land to provide more stable and reliable conditions for economic development (Papillon 2020, 219). As put by Yale Belanger, Canadian governments are particularly keen to negotiate modern treaties because they see them as a way to relieve Indigenous dependency on the Canadian state by providing enhanced "economic development and socio-economic opportunities for Native communities" (Belanger 2018, 96–7; see also Alcantara 2013, 21; Papillon 2020, 226).

Indigenous peoples, on the other hand, tend to see comprehensive land claims as a process that ought to confirm and formalize their standing as full and equal partners with the Canadian and provincial governments in nation-to-nation relationships (Jai 2017, 132, 136–7; see also Starblanket 2019b, 451). For them, the terms and conditions of modern treaties should set out all those areas in which Indigenous peoples are to exercise powers independently from Canadian governments on the one hand, and all those areas in which power is to be shared on the other (Papillon 2020, 218, 221). As a general principle, therefore, modern treaties ought ideally to extend recognition and respect to Indigenous sovereignty through guaranteed protection of the Indigenous right to control their lands and resources and through validation of their political right to self-determination (Alcantara 2013, 4; Papillon 2020, 219).

When evaluated against these rigorous criteria, Indigenous disappointment may well be justified. Some Indigenous commentators argue that the modern treaty process is just another colonial tool employed by Canadian governments to deprive Indigenous peoples of much of their land, resources, and political power. For example, Hayden King argues that land claims and self-government negotiations are little more than "termination tables" because what happens there is that "Indigenous peoples forfeit pre-existing sovereign status for modified rights that take the shape of municipality-like stakeholder status" (King 2015, 85) Consequently, King urges Indigenous political leaders to give the modern treaty process an emphatic pass (Papillon 2020, 218–19, 222, 226; see also Alcantara 2013, 7–9; Mackey 2016, 66).

Other Indigenous commentators, however, insist that the modern treaty process remains worthy of their time and effort. They certainly do not minimize the frustrations associated with differences in principle or the "institutional barriers" and "process inefficiencies" that so often obstruct negotiation and implementation exercises (Eyford 2015, 3) Despite structural constraints, they nevertheless see within the treaty negotiation and implementation process significant openings for the empowerment and development of their nations (Jai 2017, 135). Indeed, there are Indigenous leaders who have used the modern treaty process to provide their nations with important opportunities for re-established political sovereignty. The Liberal government's 2018 policy declaration that henceforth comprehensive land claims negotiations would be designed to recognize and implement Indigenous rights as opposed to extinguishing, modifying, or forcing their surrender would seem to lend further credibility to this possibility. What follows provides an overview of these two conflicting perspectives.

MODERN TREATIES AS A MEANS TO CANADIAN STATE CONTROL

In their assessment of the comprehensive land claims negotiation process as conducted from 1973 to present, there are critics who conclude that the structure itself and its associated rules and procedures have, for the most part, been designed to provide the Canadian state with all the significant advantages (Miller 2009, 264). In his book-length study on comprehensive land claims negotiations conducted in Labrador and Yukon, for example, Christopher Alcantara demonstrates that treaty settlements were possible only if Indigenous peoples were willing to adopt goals that are compatible with those asserted by Canadian governments (Alcantara 2013, 9). He describes at length a negotiation process in which Indigenous participants are compelled to become claimants, forced to prove the validity of their claims to their federal, provincial, and territorial counterparts who then unilaterally put themselves in the position of granting rights to land, resources, or self-government powers based on their assessment of the strength of Indigenous claims (Alcantara 2013, 26–7, 30; see also Gehl 2014, 62; Papillon 2020, 227). While the process has evolved somewhat since Alcantara's study in 2013, Indigenous activist Arthur Manuel is nevertheless also led to conclude "the way the policy works, Canada concedes nothing but gains everything before the negotiations even start" (Manuel 2015, 203; see also King 2015, 83).

It stands to reason, therefore, that Indigenous peoples would be suspicious of a process that so many say has been designed unilaterally and for the sole purpose of safeguarding the integrity of Canadian state power (Gehl 2014, 63). Some critics take an additional step by arguing that the comprehensive claims process is structured in exactly the opposite way to what it should be. Eva Mackey, for example, points out that "it would make more sense that the settler state be required to prove the basis of its right to land and be required to prove it based on Indigenous legal traditions" than that Indigenous peoples be forced to establish the credentials of their claims to their long-occupied lands through use of Euro-Canadian rules (Mackey 2016, 66; see also Gehl 2014, 62; Irlbacher-Fox 2009, 64). Because Euro-Canadian rules are privileged, Taiaiake Alfred believes that modern treaties reinforce Canadian sovereignty at the expense of Indigenous sovereignty (Alfred 2009, 144). Hayden King makes exactly the same point. He argues, "the threats posed by modern treaties" include "a truncation of sovereignty, which dramatically reduces the power of Indigenous peoples to affect decisions on lands and resources in their territories" (King 2015, 85). What follows itemizes several of the most egregious examples regularly referred to as a verification of this trend.

EXTINGUISHED, MODIFIED, OR NON-ASSERTED RIGHTS

At the Canadian government's insistence, all modern treaties contain provisions of one kind or another that require of Indigenous nations a fundamental exchange. In the early modern treaties negotiated in the 1970s and 1980s the government required that Indigenous nations **surrender** or **extinguish** all their future or potential Aboriginal rights and title in exchange for the clearly defined package of rights and benefits set out in their treaty settlement (Miller 2009, 256, 265; Gehl 2014, 66; Mackey 2016, 61). When Indigenous peoples objected to this requirement with the result that the comprehensive claims process ground to a virtual halt, the government chose to adapt its approach. In the treaties since negotiated throughout the 1990s and early 2000s, the language of extinguishment disappeared, replaced by two purportedly better options: **modified rights** and **non-asserted rights** (Lawrence 2012, 71; Papillon 2020, 227).

In the modified version, Indigenous nations were compelled to accept the proposition that their Aboriginal rights, including all previously undefined rights and title, were not to be extinguished but instead fully and completely laid out, as modified, in their treaty. In this approach, Aboriginal rights were understood to be exhaustively accounted for in the terms of the treaty, and so there was no need for their extinguishment (Eyford 2015, 73; King, H. 2018, 118; Mackey 2016, 63–4; Papillon 2020, 227). In the non-assertion version, the Indigenous nation committed itself to refrain from asserting any Aboriginal rights it may have other than those rights set out in its treaty. Here, Aboriginal rights remained unextinguished and unmodified but Indigenous nations took on a legal obligation not to exercise them (Gehl 2014, 66; Lawrence 2012, 71; Miller 2009, 266). The ***Nisga'a Final Agreement*** of 1998 is an example of the modification approach, while the ***Tlicho Agreement*** of 2003 is an example of the non-assertion approach.

Critics responded by arguing that there is really no appreciable difference between the modification, non-assertion, and extinguishment approaches. Douglas Eyford, for example, points out that the legal effect of all three is essentially the same. Under all three approaches Indigenous nations are restricted to exercising only those rights that are set out in their treaty (Eyford 2015; see also Tully 2008, 275; Lawrence 2012, 72; Vowel 2016, 257). The consequences could not be any clearer. According to Arthur Manuel, any additional rights that Indigenous nations may have by way of Aboriginal title, "or rights not specifically described in the agreement," are effectively extinguished anyway because they cannot be exercised (Manuel 2015, 196; see also Manuel 2017, 100–8; King, H. 2018, 119; Mackey 2016, 61). In essence, say critics, the Canadian government's approach to extinguishment simply became subtler and more nuanced; while the language shifted in the direction of more benign terminology, there was no fundamental change to its policy. Once again, says Indigenous scholar Aaron Mills, the interests of settler peoples were purchased at considerable cost to Indigenous peoples. Modern treaties merely serve "as a means to empower the ends of settler certainty" (Mills 2017, 222; see also Gehl 2014, 65–7).

Indigenous opposition to the Canadian government's extinguishment policy has been unrelenting. Certainty about the existence of Aboriginal rights and title is certainly welcome to both Indigenous and non-Indigenous peoples. But the idea that certain rights can be secured only on the condition that other rights be extinguished (or modified or not asserted) has simply been an impossible step for most Indigenous peoples to take (Mackey 2016, 65). This is because rights constitute an important feature of their identity. As Sharon Venne explains it, "for most Indigenous peoples, severing links with their lands and territories means relinquishing an integral part of themselves. If Indigenous peoples give up their lands, what will happen to future generations?" (Venne 2002, 47). Stephanie Irlbacher-Fox shows that for the Dehcho Dene First Nations of the Northwest Territories, for example, extinguishment is impossible "because the responsibilities of stewardship are a central part of being Dehcho Dene" (Irlbacher-Fox 2009, 64). Arthur Manuel similarly insists that "no nation on earth should be forced to enter a negotiation that is destined to end with its own extinguishment" (Manuel 2015, 59). To do so would be to diminish Indigenous peoples as nations.

What Indigenous peoples seek, therefore, is not extinguishment of their rights but the means to exercise them. As put by RCAP, "treaties should serve as solemn acts of mutual recognition of aspects of Aboriginal and Canadian ways of structuring relationships with the land" (RCAP 1995, 47; see also Mackey 2016, 65). When Manuel asks himself rhetorically whether sovereign peoples should be allowed to do whatever deal they like through treaties even if it means extinguishing their sovereign rights, he answers as follows: "The problem is that the birthrights they are selling are not theirs alone, they are those of their children and grandchildren and great-grandchildren. And those we do not have a right to sell" (Manuel 2015, 59; see also Manuel 2017, 104).[10]

In the face of such strong opposition, the Canadian government finally seems to be relenting. All 26 land claims agreements signed to date contain some kind of extinguishment, modification, or non-assertion clauses. However, as of 2018 the Canadian government has said that the extinguishment, modification, or surrender of Indigenous rights will no longer factor into any future agreements. Instead, land claims agreements will henceforth be based on the recognition and implementation of Indigenous rights. It is too early to say what effect this change in policy will have on the goals and outcomes of future land claims agreements. Martin Papillon does point out, however, that "the federal government still insists that the exercise of Indigenous rights must be harmonized with the objectives of certainty and stability" (Papillon 2020, 227–8). In Arthur Manuel's estimation, therefore, this "new" approach remains a narrow one because governments continue to speak "about reconciling Aboriginal rights with broader Canadian economic purposes" (Manuel 2017, 104–5). In short, as far as these critics are concerned, the federal government still insists that Indigenous rights be made to conform with the primary economic ambitions of the Canadian state. When judged against Indigenous standards that would have modern treaties serve as "political covenants that reset their relationship with the settler state on a more equal footing," it would appear that this "new" approach also falls well short of the mark (Papillon 2020, 226).

LAND

The extinguishment (modification, or non-assertion) of Indigenous rights is but one example critics point to as proof that comprehensive claims are used to keep Indigenous nations subject to the Canadian state. Another example is provided by the status given to Indigenous land. Critics argue that when it comes to the land, Canadian and Indigenous negotiators ought to approach the issue from the vantage point of how it is to be shared. Furthermore, the discussion concerning the status of the land ought to begin from the premise that original title to the land belongs to Indigenous peoples by virtue of their prior occupation and use of it. What is to be decided in treaty negotiations, in other words, are the terms and conditions under which Indigenous people will agree to share their unsurrendered lands with non-Indigenous settlers.

The problem from the perspective of these critics, however, is that the comprehensive land claims policy subverts this moral and legal requirement. As explained by Felix Hoehn, rather than accepting Aboriginal title as "original title" that is both "paramount and to which Crown title is subject," Canadian governments take the position that "Aboriginal title is merely a burden on the Crown's underlying title" (Hoehn 2012, 109). Then, on the basis of this legal fiction (Canada possesses underlying title simply by willing it to be so), comprehensive land claims negotiations put Indigenous peoples in the position of having to "make a claim against the state to gain ownership of lands that they have always possessed" (Alfred 2009, 145). Taiaiake Alfred identifies this Canadian presumption of sovereignty over Indigenous land as a "prime example of co-optation," Eva Mackey calls it "a fantasy of entitlement," while Bonita Lawrence argues "that it reveals the ongoing colonialism at the heart of Canadian society" (Alfred 2009, 144; Mackey 2016, 66; Lawrence 2012, 74).

From this illegitimately claimed position of superior legal strength, Canada then enters into comprehensive land claims negotiations. And as critics point out, the results are generally not good for Indigenous nations. In every modern treaty negotiated to date, Indigenous nations are required to surrender their ancestral lands to the Canadian state. In exchange, and by way of compensation, Indigenous nations get a few benefits (including cash) and the right to retain ownership of a small portion of their traditional territories (Irlbacher-Fox 2009, 6; Charlie 2020, 89). The *Nisga'a Final Agreement* is often identified as highly illustrative of this problem. As James Tully describes it, "the Nisga'a voluntarily gave up to the Crown in the negotiations 93 percent of their traditional territory. Over the remaining 7 percent (approximately 2,000 square kilometres), they are allotted Aboriginal title in the form of an estate in fee simple proprietary right under the Constitution" (Tully 2008, 274–5; see also Miller 2004, 158). This pattern of land surrender within Indigenous traditional territories is repeated over and over again in each of the 26 modern treaties signed to date

(Irlbacher-Fox 2009, 6). The result, say the critics, is that the full extent of the territorial rights of Indigenous nations is left unacknowledged and, as such, Canada is enabled "to retain the land base that is the foundation of its power" (Lawrence 2012, 79).

RESOURCES

For Indigenous nations, the modern treaty process should serve as a way for them to reacquire control over a territorial land base and with it the resources of their ancestral lands. Critics point out, however, that because federal and provincial governments are unwilling to put much land on the negotiating table, Indigenous control over natural resources (often critical to the rejuvenation of their economies) is also put out of reach. Generally, modern treaties do provide some resource rights on settlement lands. These include rights to traditional economic ventures such as hunting, fishing, and trapping as well as rights to more contemporary economic activities such as forestry, mining, and oil and gas development. But again, because treaty settlement lands generally constitute a small fraction of their traditional territories, treaty negotiations are often seen by Indigenous peoples as exercises in which they are compelled to give up resources that were (and ought to remain) originally theirs (Charlie 2020, 87–90).

The experience of the Hul'qumi'num First Nations in the BC treaty process provides an instructive example. Sarah Morales notes with considerable concern that "small commercial forestry and fisheries opportunities are on the table for negotiation but they are narrowly defined" (Morales 2017, 281). Equally distressing is that federal and provincial negotiators simply declared from the outset that land (and water) already subject to private or public interests, including forestry licences, highway rights of way, mining tenures, and commercial fisheries, could not be put forward as potential settlement lands. This means that in the heavily non-Indigenous populated area of Vancouver Island where the Hul'qumi'num First Nations live, 85 per cent of their traditional territories was unilaterally taken off the negotiation table (Morales 2017, 301). Under such restricted terms, Taiaiake Alfred concludes that federal and provincial governments conduct treaty negotiations as though it is "business as usual" (Alfred 2009, 149). Arthur Manuel adds: "We want to be decision makers regarding access to our lands and resources, precisely what the province (British Columbia) is trying to avoid under these agreements" (Manuel 2015, 207).

CASH

Every modern treaty contains a cash component, but critics point to this as inadequate (Irlbacher-Fox 2009, 6). Here, two distinct problems have been identified. Concerning the first, critics note that federal and provincial governments have simply decided that there is little land that can be returned through treaty negotiations and so cash is offered by way of an alternative. However, as Alfred observes, "what Indigenous want is to get their land back" (Alfred 2009, 150). Consequently, when Indigenous peoples accept a cash settlement in lieu of land, this simply must be seen for what it is: a profound compromise of their primary objective in the negotiations. Cash for land is not the fulfillment of an Indigenous right but rather a cheap substitute for it.

But second, when it comes to the status of the cash settlement itself and what that cash ought to represent, critics suggest that government and Indigenous negotiators come to the table with very different objectives. For the federal and provincial governments, the cash components of treaty settlements are intended to address Indigenous poverty and serve as a stimulant for economic prosperity. But as Bonita Lawrence points out, Indigenous poverty "exists precisely because their wealth has been expropriated via the colonial process" (Lawrence 2012, 70). According to her, therefore, what really ought to be on the table are cash payments offered as compensation "for centuries of occupying people's land and usurping their resources" (Lawrence 2012, 70; see also Irlbacher-Fox 2009, 6).

Government negotiators, on the other hand, insist on de-linking the cash value of settlement offers from the matter of historical damages and decades-long lost economic opportunities. They prefer instead to award cash based on the "here and now" immediacy of social and economic development opportunities. But when framed this way, Lawrence contends, cash payments can "be kept abysmally low" (Lawrence 2012, 70). The Nisga'a treaty settlement provides a good illustration. Citing a recent study, Lawrence suggests that if the Nisga'a had been awarded a cash settlement commensurate with the "damages they had sustained in over a century of occupation and resource theft," they would have received $4.3 billion. According to the terms of their treaty, however, all that the Nisga'a were awarded was a paltry $240 million (Lawrence 2012, 70). In short, when understood for what it is, Arthur Manuel is convinced that with respect to the BC treaty process at least, "treaty negotiations are continually teetering on collapse because the people do not want to extinguish their title for a tiny piece of land and a tiny amount of cash" (Manuel 2015, 206).

SELF-GOVERNMENT

Like land, resources, and cash compensation, self-government is a central issue in modern treaty negotiations. Critics argue that the kind of self-government Indigenous nations are able to negotiate into their treaties is typically cast in a Western mode, usually encompassing more powers than a municipality but also less than a province, and always within the confines of the Canadian state (Tully 2008, 275). The result, say some, is that the Canadian state "co-opts Indigenous resistance into legal discourses that reinforces Canadian sovereignty at the expense of (authentic) Indigenous alternatives" (King 2015, 85).

Under treaty, an Indigenous nation typically acquires power over governmental structures, citizenship, cultural matters, language, lands, public infrastructure, social services, education, and nation-based assets. What concerns critics, however, is that if there are conflicts between federal or provincial laws and Indigenous laws, the treaties stipulate that in most cases, federal or provincial law will prevail to the extent of the conflict. As we shall see in the next section of the chapter, there are also a number of areas in which Indigenous laws are paramount over federal and provincial laws. As a result, critics do concede that modern treaties guarantee to Indigenous peoples some authority over their own political decision making. The source of the problem that critics identify, however, lies elsewhere. They argue that "what is recognized does not nearly approximate the freedom Indigenous peoples enjoyed prior to the settler government asserting sovereignty" (Irlbacher-Fox 2009, 6). Indigenous law, in other words, is to give way to Canadian law in far too many instances. Critics are therefore led to conclude that there is no recognition of Indigenous sovereignty reflected within modern treaties. Martin Papillon writes that despite promising language to the contrary, ultimately the federal government sees "land claims settlements as political matters internal to the Canadian state rather than as instruments to regulate relations between co-existing sovereignties" (Papillon 2020, 229).[11]

The junior status of Indigenous governments is reinforced by one additional political reality. Federal and provincial governments receive their powers directly from the Canadian Constitution. Indigenous nations, however, must rely on a treaty negotiation process for their powers, a process, moreover, in which the powers they acquire are subject to authorization by the Canadian state. Under these terms Felix Hoehn wonders whether the comprehensive claims process can possess legitimacy. As he puts it: "a treaty that does not express a genuine mutual recognition of sovereignty is likely to leave lingering questions about its fairness and this will compromise its capacity to foster reconciliation" (Hoehn 2012, 109). Taiaiake Alfred puts the matter more directly: "behind its progressive façade, the BC treaty process represents an advanced form of control, manipulation, and assimilation" (Alfred 2009, 144.) I expect that Alfred's judgment would apply no less vigorously to the federal comprehensive claims process. Stephanie Irlbacher-Fox, meanwhile, argues that from the vantage point of optics, modern treaties are far more about symbols than they are about substance. She concludes "they are settlements that return small fractions of lands, resources, and authorities to Indigenous peoples, and in that sense the settlements to a great extent cement rather than change the fundamental dominant-subordinate relationship between state and Indigenous peoples" (Irlbacher-Fox 2009, 6–7).

MODERN TREATIES AS A MEANS TO RESTORED INDIGENOUS SOVEREIGNTY

The Supreme Court of Canada has said to Canadian governments that "where treaties remain to be concluded, the honour of the Crown requires negotiations leading to a just settlement of Aboriginal claims" (*Haida Nation v. British Columbia* 2004, para. 20). But what exactly do such "just settlements" entail? The Supreme Court has decided to leave this matter to the creative ingenuity of Indigenous and Canadian governmental actors, expecting that the parties will work together in a spirit of compromise in which, it says, there is to be give and take on all sides.

So if there is to be give and take on all sides, this suggests that the Supreme Court did not expect Canadian governments to simply comply with every claim made by Indigenous nations. Certainly, the task at hand is to do justice to the constitutionally protected Aboriginal rights, Aboriginal title, and treaty rights of the Indigenous peoples of Canada. But at the same time, those rights must be drawn into a meaningful relationship with the presence of a large and diverse non-Indigenous Canadian society and with a complex economic environment driven by a range of interests. Historical wrongs and power imbalances must be corrected to be sure, but not at the cost of jeopardizing prospects for real balance, cooperative coexistence, and genuine reconciliation between Indigenous and non-Indigenous partners, or so I would argue.

The discussion of the previous section suggests that when it negotiates modern treaties, Canada's approach is still essentially colonial in orientation because it operates from the starting point that Indigenous nations are not sovereign and therefore do not possess a political status equal to that of the Canadian state (Hoehn 2012, 109). Consequently, Arthur Manuel regards treaty tables as little more than "termination tables" that "have as their stated goal the reduction or elimination of our (Indigenous) rights" (Manuel 2015, 208; see also Manuel 2017, 115). In what follows I advance a different perspective. While not without its structural constraints, it is my view that the modern treaty process does possess positive features and does contain important entitlements that, if read sympathetically, can be seen as constituting incremental steps in the larger project of re-establishing Indigenous sovereignty.

The point I want to emphasize is that while Indigenous peoples are entitled to political sovereignty, the reacquisition of that sovereignty is unlikely to occur all at once. In cases where modern treaties have been successfully negotiated, what those agreements have done in the first instance is provide the means for resolving many (though not all) longstanding Indigenous grievances. This fact is worth noting. But perhaps even more important, modern treaties have also assisted Indigenous peoples in gathering the jurisdictional powers, territorial land holdings, and resources they need to the develop their nations in ways that are more consistent with their own ambitions (Alcantara 2013, 24). Furthermore, a good number of those powers and resources have been placed beyond the purview of the Canadian state, thereby setting limits on the exercise of Canada's power over Indigenous nations. Taken together, these measures constitute a form of sovereignty because what they do is provide the means for Indigenous nations to operate as self-determining, self-sufficient peoples (Papillon 2020, 229). The cumulative effect is that the political and legal standing of Indigenous nations within Canada is considerably enhanced. What modern treaty agreements can do, in other words, is recalibrate the relationship between Indigenous nations and the Canadian state in a far more nation-to-nation-like direction (Coates and McHugh 1998, 132; Jai 2017, 136–7).

In summary, I suggest that the objective of modern treaty-making can be captured as follows: treaty negotiation must strive to develop models of Indigenous governance over Indigenous citizens, lands, and resources that can coexist with Canadian sovereignty (Papillon 2020, 229). Both Indigenous and Canadian sovereignty will undoubtedly be subjected to modification and constraint in the process of coming to acceptable treaty terms, but the important point from the perspectives of the treaty partners is that in coming to terms with one another, neither partner loses their autonomy. Put slightly differently, it is the task of treaties to find ways to reconcile two orders of sovereignty to bind them more closely together (Office of the Treaty Commissioner 2007, 105, 106).

Modern treaties are hundreds of pages long, describing in great detail the context, range, and scope of Indigenous power as it relates to a considerable number of jurisdictions and resources. The issue of concern to us, however, is to decide in what ways the underlying principles that inform modern treaties are able to breathe life into the Indigenous right to self-determination. What follows describes in general terms sovereignty's opportunities as provided by each of (1) constitutional protection, (2) recognition of Aboriginal title, (3) access to resources, and (4) enhanced political power, all of which are prominently featured in the text of modern treaties.

CONSTITUTIONAL PROTECTION

The rights that are typically contained within a modern treaty are brought into force by legislation enacted by federal and provincial or territorial levels of government as well as by a ratification vote held within an Indigenous nation. Through this process, modern treaties acquire the force of law. They are placed in the legal position of prevailing over any other legislation that may be inconsistent with the terms of the treaty (Jai 2014, 11).

In addition, modern treaties acquire constitutional protection by virtue of the recognition afforded to them through Sections 35(1) and (3) of the *Constitution Act, 1982*. Section 35(1) offers explicit recognition and affirmation of treaty rights, while subsection (3) establishes that this recognition and affirmation is also to be extended to "rights that now exist by way of land claims agreements or may be so acquired." Section 25 of the *Constitution Act* further states that the *Charter* shall not be "construed so as to abrogate or derogate from any aboriginal, treaty, or other freedoms that pertain to aboriginal peoples." What Section 25 effectively does is offer modern treaties an additional layer of legal protection because it guarantees that one set of constitutionally protected rights (*Charter* rights) cannot be used to compromise or undermine another set of constitutional rights (treaty rights). In short, these three provisions – Section 35 (1), (3), and Section 25 – are extremely important because they extend to treaties a guarantee that "any rights or powers emerging from the treaty are sheathed with constitutional protection" (Scott 2012, 98).

There has been some debate over the kind of status that the Section 35(1) and (3) constitutional provisions actually confer on treaty rights. For example, James Tully argues that what Section 35 actually does is incorporate Indigenous peoples into Canada because it subjects the validation of Aboriginal and treaty rights to Canadian constitutional affirmation. For him, colonialism thereby remains effectively intact. Canadian constitutional law is set out as paramount and Indigenous rights are subsequently made reliant on it for both recognition and protection (Tully 2008, 269–70; see also Alfred 2009, 144–54).

An alternative perspective likely more in keeping with the intentions of Canadian and Indigenous treaty negotiators is also available, however. According to this view, by including Aboriginal and treaty rights within its Constitution, Canada effectively declared its recognition of Indigenous peoples as free-standing political actors. Section 35, therefore, does not "create" Aboriginal and treaty rights, but rather offers already (pre)existing Aboriginal and treaty rights constitutional recognition and affirmation. The process of modern treaty-making, therefore, should be seen as the technique that

Indigenous and Canadian state negotiators employ to find ways to give contemporary expression to the already existing Aboriginal rights that the Canadian state now recognizes in its Constitution. Patrick Macklem puts the matter as follows: "treaties thus represent constitutional accords between aboriginal people and the Canadian state," which articulate the basic terms and conditions for their social coexistence (Macklem 2001, 150, 154). In short, the Canadian constitutional declaration of recognition can more helpfully be read as Canada's admission that it regards itself to be positioned in a nation-to-nation relationship with its Indigenous counterparts.

On balance, I believe there is sufficient justification to accept this alternative perspective as more consistent with political reality. In the first place, Indigenous leaders approach modern treaty negotiations expecting that treaty agreements will result in a meaningful distribution of political power that meets all parties' interests. If the starting point for treaty negotiations was that Indigenous peoples should expect little more than delegated powers from Canada, they likely would not be interested in treaty talks at all. From what has been established to date, treaties have legitimacy in the eyes of their Indigenous beneficiaries because they do set out in some substantive way their right to exercise meaningful political power.[12]

Second, when Aboriginal and treaty rights assumed the form of constitutional rights in 1982, the Canadian state accepted a formal legal obligation to constrain its use of legislative authority over Indigenous peoples (Macklem 2001, 150). Constitutions exist to set limitations on the use of state power. Where constitutional rights begin, it is precisely at that point that the jurisdictional authority of the state ought to end. Insofar as protection of treaty rights go, therefore, the Canadian state has committed itself to a fundamental duty of legislative non-interference in the lives of its Indigenous treaty partners. Where treaty rights begin, the jurisdictional authority of the Canadian state ends unless the terms of the treaty itself indicate otherwise.

And third, the constitutional protection of treaty rights means that those rights are now immunized against arbitrary and unilateral changes or extinguishment by Canadian governments. Any proposal to change the terms and conditions of treaties now requires the consent of all signatories, Indigenous peoples included. The fact that Indigenous peoples must be included speaks to their enhanced political status. Where control over their treaties is concerned, Indigenous nations now stand in a political relationship of equality with their federal and provincial counterparts. One partner cannot change the terms of treaty agreements that bind them all. Each must offer one another their consent. In short, the Section 35 constitutional protection that Indigenous treaty rights now enjoy translates into significant opportunities for enhanced Indigenous self-determination. Treaty agreements that reflect a distribution of political powers consistent with Canadian and Indigenous interests, and which are then coupled with self-imposed obligations to honour duties of non-interference in the affairs of one another and then reinforced by commitments to change the terms and conditions of treaties only when all parties agree, reflect the kind of behaviour one would expect of a nation-to-nation relationship.[13]

RECOGNITION OF ABORIGINAL TITLE

While constitutional recognition and affirmation of treaty rights create conditions ripe for the re-emergence of Indigenous nations, so too do many of the provisions of the modern treaties themselves. Particularly noteworthy in this regard are treaty provisions relating to the Indigenous reacquisition of land. Indigenous negotiators generally start from the position that settling the land question does not mean that Canada must "give up" land to Indigenous peoples, but rather, that Indigenous peoples' ongoing right to occupy and exercise sovereignty over significant portions of their traditional territories is restored. The question that needs to be settled in negotiations is how much traditional territory Indigenous nations are prepared to give up to Canada in exchange for treaty settlements that include compensation.

If treaties are to advance the project of Indigenous sovereignty, land provisions must perform two tasks. First, treaties must provide for exclusive Indigenous occupation and use of ancestral lands for any purpose deemed appropriate by Indigenous nations. And second, treaties must guarantee that the lands reacquired are extensive enough to make the exercise of Indigenous authority and jurisdiction over those lands meaningful. No treaty to date has performed these two tasks perfectly. Indigenous negotiators always seek a larger land quantum, more power over land and resource use decisions, and a larger proportion of resource revenues than the terms of their treaties allow (Eyford 2015, 45). Nevertheless, progress has been made on both fronts – progress, moreover, that from the perspective of those Indigenous peoples who have chosen to ratify treaties is sufficient to justify their endorsement.

In all cases, modern treaties convert reserve lands into treaty lands and also return additional lands to Indigenous nations drawn from the nation's traditional territories. While the extent of lands returned varies depending on location (i.e., urban density and whether land is already designated as private property), the quantum of land Indigenous nations get back can be considerable, sometimes ranging in the tens of thousands of hectares. Treaties also generally make provision for Indigenous nations to add more lands to their base over time, usually through purchase, often from preselected areas identified in the treaty. Treaty settlement lands are designated for the exclusive use and occupancy of the Indigenous nation and are also designated to fall under its exclusive jurisdiction. Treaties also stipulate that Indigenous nations have full ownership of or title to the lands covered by the agreement. Over treaty settlement lands, therefore, it would appear that Indigenous nations are restored to a position of enjoying considerable sovereignty.

Treaty settlement lands usually constitute a small proportion of most Indigenous nations' traditional territories. Consequently, treaties often identify a second category of land over which Indigenous nations retain an interest (but not ownership) because those lands fall within their traditional territories. In this case, the lands fall under the primary jurisdiction of the federal or provincial governments, but important participatory roles are reserved to Indigenous nations, typically through co-management boards (Papillon 2020, 225). Where co-management boards exist, one could say that sovereignty is shared between

Indigenous and Canadian governments, or perhaps more accurately, Indigenous nations are invited to wield some influence over the exercise of Canadian sovereignty. Martin Papillon observes, for example, that "modern treaties have changed the governance landscape for their Indigenous signatories" because, especially in the northern territories, "Indigenous governments and management boards now have a key role in most aspects of local and regional governance." He characterizes this state of affairs as a form of "nested" federalism (Papillon 2020, 225; see also Wilson, Alcantara, and Rodon 2020).

ACCESS TO RESOURCES

While it is often said that federal and provincial governments pursue treaties with Indigenous nations because they want to attain certainty over the status of lands and resources, the same could also be said of Indigenous nations. Treaty settlements provide Indigenous nations with certainty about the status of their right to control lands and resources so that they are able, in turn, to use those rights confidently to pursue their own social and economic development.

A critical feature of any Indigenous nation's ability to exercise its right to self-determination is having access to the resources necessary for Indigenous nation-building. Modern treaties typically assist in this task because they guarantee to Indigenous peoples control over a broad range of resources that can serve as a reliable foundation upon which to build a sound economy for both present and future generations. Some of these treaty-guaranteed resources speak to the more traditional components of Indigenous economic activity while others are more contemporary in nature. For example, treaties regularly provide a guarantee of rights to harvest fish, wildlife, plants, and migratory birds for food, social, and ceremonial purposes. But in addition to these more traditional pursuits, treaties can also provide the means to cultivate a profitable contemporary economy. Entire chapters of treaties are dedicated to setting out terms and conditions for Indigenous ownership and control over commercial fishing, forestry, water resources, tourism and recreation, and subsurface resources (e.g., oil, natural gas, minerals).

Where resources fall within core treaty land settlement areas, Indigenous ownership and control is often exclusive. Where resources are located in traditional territories but outside core treaty areas, these tend to be subject to power-sharing arrangements through co-management boards as set out in co-management agreements with either federal or provincial governments. As mentioned earlier in this chapter, the impact of modern treaties on socio-economic outcomes for Indigenous peoples has been considerable. Empirical studies conducted by Fernando Aragón and Krishna Pendakur and Ravi Pendakur, for example, show that comprehensive land claims agreements (both with and without self-government agreements) "are associated with income gains for Aboriginal households, primarily through increased labour income" (Pendakur and Pendakur 2018, 139; see also Aragón 2015).

As a further stimulant to Indigenous economies, treaties also provide benefits of millions of dollars through significant capital transfers. These capital transfers come in several forms. Treaties normally provide direct cash payments to Indigenous nations. They also often make provisions for revenue-sharing agreements for resources removed from Indigenous traditional territories. Cash benefit payments may also be made directly to individuals or come in the form of cash assistance so that members of Indigenous nations can purchase commercial licences in industries such as fishing. Capital transfers are often seen by Indigenous signatories as compensation for lost economic opportunities and revenues suffered as a result of the theft of their lands and resources. But capital transfer can also be seen in a more utilitarian light as they often serve to jumpstart viable, sustainable, and diverse local Indigenous economies. In sum, if sovereignty carries with it the notion that those who have it must be in control of the resources that constitute the foundation of their economy, then it is my belief that Indigenous nations under treaty have an increasingly reasonable basis on which to make the claim that their sovereignty is making a recovery.

ENHANCED POLITICAL POWER

The fact that Indigenous nations possess an inherent right to self-determination under international law means they are also entitled to enjoy political sovereignty. However, because treaties are intended, in part, to reconcile Indigenous and Canadian political orders to one another, it would not be realistic to expect treaties to sanction an unlimited use of Indigenous political power. Treaty approaches to political power are far more subtle. On the one hand, treaties identify all those areas of jurisdiction where Indigenous nations will exercise political power independently from the Canadian state. But on the other, treaties also identify those areas where Indigenous nations either choose to share jurisdiction with federal and provincial governments or defer to the power of the Canadian state altogether. The essential point from the perspective of sovereignty is that the power arrangements eventually agreed to are ones to which Indigenous peoples can offer their full consent. They must, in other words, see the treaty as a fulfillment of their Indigenous rights and as a means to their communal well-being.

In the first place, then, Indigenous sovereignty is realized to the degree that Indigenous nations reacquire the jurisdictional powers they need to flourish as autonomous and self-sustaining political communities. And generally speaking, modern treaties do facilitate this objective. As a first step, treaties provide passage for Indigenous peoples to come out from under the stultifying paternalism of the *Indian Act*, putting the sweeping authority of the Canadian government over Indigenous nations to an end. Treaties also verify the Indigenous right to self-government and with it the right "to govern according to Aboriginal values, culture, traditions and laws" (Jai 2014, 10). Accordingly, modern treaties set out detailed provisions for both the structure and operation of Indigenous political powers (Papillon 2020, 225). Take, for example, the *Nisga'a Final Agreement*. It identifies the Nisga'a Lisims Government as the government for the entire Nisga'a Nation and the Nisga'a Village Governments as the governments for the four Nisga'a villages. The duties, composition, and membership of each level are further spelled out in a separate and free-standing constitution. As for responsibilities, the agreement states that the Nisga'a Lisims Government and Nisga'a Village Governments have principal authority over such matters as "Nisga'a Government, Nisga'a citizenship, Nisga'a culture, Nisga'a language, Nisga'a

Lands, and Nisga'a assets" (*Nisga'a Final Agreement* 2000, 165; see also Scott 2012, 101–3).[14]

The kinds of powers reserved for exclusive Indigenous use generally focus on matters of the highest priority to the internal affairs of Indigenous nations and are regularly compared to those exercised by provinces (Jai 2014, 9). These powers usually include jurisdiction over governmental structures and elections; citizenship; lands and resources (including regulation of property rights); assets; public order, peace, safety, and administration of justice; public works; culture; language; child and family services (including adoption); social services (including health care); marriage; education; and taxation (Miller 2009, 267). For those Indigenous nations under treaty, this list captures the powers they believe they need to fulfill their right to self-determination. What these powers do not do, however, is authorize full Indigenous independence from the Canadian state.

And in the second place, Indigenous sovereignty is realized to the degree that Indigenous nations are drawn into a meaningful relationship of coexistence with Canadian sovereignty. Here again, modern treaties do provide some assistance in meeting this objective. A notable feature of modern treaties is that in key jurisdictional areas the operation of federal and provincial sovereignty is carefully woven into that of Indigenous sovereignty. A good illustration is provided by the rules of **paramountcy**. The legal doctrine of paramountcy establishes that where there is a conflict between federal or provincial law and Indigenous law, either Canadian law or Indigenous law will prevail, rendering the other two inoperative to the extent of the conflict. This legal doctrine of paramountcy makes a regular appearance in the text of modern treaties. While treaties specify that both Indigenous and Canadian laws are to apply to Indigenous peoples, they also establish that when those laws conflict, the laws of one treaty partner must be allowed to prevail over the laws of the other. The fact that in a good number of cases Indigenous laws are set out to prevail illustrates yet again that Indigenous sovereignty does play an important role in establishing rules to regulate relations between Canadian and Indigenous treaty partners.

Take the *Nisga'a Final Agreement* as an example. The treaty carefully itemizes all the political powers that are to fall under Nisga'a governmental authority (largely in keeping with the list of powers identified above). It then moves on to establish in each jurisdictional area where Nisga'a laws will prevail over those of federal and provincial governments. This list includes most matters relating to Nisga'a government, citizenship, lands and resources, culture, language, education, adoption, and assets (Hoehn 2012, 54; Scott 2012, 104). If, for instance, the federal government were to enact a law that specified who among the Nisga'a had voting rights (citizenship) and how elections on Nisga'a lands were to be conducted (governance), and that law subsequently conflicted with a Nisga'a law that addressed the same matters, the Nisga'a law would prevail to the extent of the conflict (Scott 2012, 104). But, of course, the rules of paramountcy cut both ways. There are also cases identified in the treaty where federal or provincial law will have priority. Felix Hoehn notes, for example, that in some areas, like child welfare or education, Nisga'a laws can "only prevail if they are consistent with comparable standards established by Parliament, the Legislative Assembly, or administrative tribunals, as applicable" (Hoehn 2012, 54). Nevertheless, the fact that Indigenous law is to prevail over federal or provincial law in key jurisdictional areas is important because it signals that Indigenous nations under treaty do exercise sovereignty. And where Indigenous sovereignty is exercised, Canadian sovereignty is thereby constrained.

ONGOING CHALLENGES

Of course, no treaty is perfect, nor have any of the modern treaties negotiated to date fully met the aspirations of their Indigenous signatories. Treaties are beset with problems that are an unsurprising by-product of the complex environment in which they are negotiated and the challenging circumstances in which they are implemented. Some of these problems are practical in nature while others exist more at the level of principle.

On the practical side, Douglas R. Eyford argues that one of the main reasons why only 26 comprehensive claims have been finalized in 42 years is because the treaty negotiation process has been profoundly inefficient.[15] Focusing specifically on the performance of the federal government, Eyford argues that Canada's claims procedures are cumbersome, bureaucratic, and poorly organized; federal negotiators have limited authority to make commitments at treaty tables; Canada's approach to treaty negotiations is often uncreative; and, due to its limited capacity across so many treaty tables, Canada is also regularly unable "to promptly respond to issues when they arise" (Eyford 2015, 50; see also Papillon 2020, 218, 228). In 2015, the Liberal government of Justin Trudeau adopted what it calls "a whole of government" approach to modern treaty negotiations as part of a larger effort to address a number of these practical problems. As noted by Martin Papillon, by 2020 it was still "too early to assess the impact of these measures" but it seems reasonable to expect that policy measures designed to promote greater coordination across all federal departments involved can only help to lend greater efficiency to the process (Papillon 2020, 228).

Eyford also observes that Canada has a less than stellar track record when it comes to faithfully implementing its treaty obligations in the post-ratification period (Eyford 2015, 76–8). This concern has been echoed by several others. Papillon notes, for example, that "those who have agreed to a modern treaty" often struggle "to have their agreements properly implemented," a struggle that Hayden King attributes to a general resistance on the part of the federal government to fulfill the "costly" terms of its treaty obligations (Papillon 2020, 218; King 2015, 86; see also Aragón 2015, 45). J.R. Miller documents the difficulties experienced by Cree and Inuit leaders not long after the *James Bay and Northern Quebec Agreement* (1975) was ratified. Cree leader Billy Diamond "observed that implementation was one fight after another," leading him to conclude in frustration that "negotiation of a claim settlement is only half the battle and implementation is the other half" (Miller 2009, 281; see also Jai 2017, 131). The experience of the Cree and Inuit is not isolated. As I shall point out in the next section, the more recent *Nunavut Land Claims Agreement* (1993) was beset by similar implementation challenges. The intractable nature of some of these disputes has occasionally compelled Indigenous signatories to resort to litigation, demanding compensation for treaty rights that they claim Canadian governments have consistently failed to implement (Miller 2009, 281; Papillon 2020, 218).

At the same time, however, culpability for inefficiencies does not belong exclusively to the Canadian government. Eyford points out that some Indigenous groups are hesitant to close negotiations because they do not want to lock in their rights when other rights not yet contemplated may, with time, be identified and defined by the courts (Eyford 2015, 50). Papillon also notes that after decades of negotiations it is not uncommon for Indigenous community members to reject the agreement in a referendum (Papillon 2020, 218). Negotiators on all sides must then face the daunting question: should any further negotiations be abandoned or should the process be started all over again? The problem concerning the requirement that Indigenous nations take on crippling debt to finance their treaty negotiations has since been resolved. In 2018 the Liberal government implemented a federal loan "forgiveness" and grant financing program so that Indigenous nations would no longer have to repay their loans from the cash settlement component of their eventual final agreement. And finally, Indigenous groups regularly find it difficult to resolve disputes about how to share traditional territories and resolve overlapping claims (Eyford 2015, 61–3, 65–7).

As for obstacles rooted in principle, these originate primarily with Indigenous peoples and are in the order of what has been discussed earlier. Rather than regarding modern treaties as an opportunity to breathe life into Indigenous sovereignty, some Indigenous leaders see treaties as structurally designed to suck the life out of Indigenous sovereignty. Where federal and provincial negotiators offer terms of "coexistence," for example, they see only limitations designed to further consolidate Canadian control over Indigenous peoples' lands and resources.

Treaties, in other words, are seen by some as structural devices designed to draw Indigenous peoples deeply into the fabric of the Canadian state. These Indigenous leaders concede that treaty rights may entitle Indigenous peoples to follow some of their own customs and traditions. But they are also of the view that these rights are never granted at the expense of the dominant position that Canada now holds over Indigenous nations. Indeed, from the perspective of these Indigenous leaders, what treaties offer at best is an opportunity for Indigenous peoples "to accommodate their interests within the political and legal regime imposed by the Settlers" (Asch 2014, 106; see also Irlbacher-Fox 2009, 6–7). Recognition of Indigenous sovereignty is glaringly absent according to this interpretation of events.

Even so, modern treaties constitute a worthwhile option for many Indigenous nations to pursue. As we shall see in the next section, for the Inuit in Nunavut and the Algonquin in Ontario, modern treaties can provide a means for the expression and validation of the Indigenous right to self-determination and for the implementation of self-government. Modern treaty negotiations do change relations of power, not just for Indigenous peoples but for non-Indigenous peoples too. As Indigenous peoples assert political, social, cultural, and economic autonomy from the Canadian state, the Canadian state in turn is compelled to release it. The result is not only improvements in Indigenous community well-being but also a realignment in the distribution of political power between the Canadian state and Indigenous nations. Despite limitations, therefore, it is my view that treaties do provide genuine opportunities for the exercise of Indigenous sovereignty in the spaces in between Canadian sovereignty, and in the process Canadian sovereignty is both challenged and pulled back.

CASE STUDY: TWO MODERN TREATIES IN ACTION

Modern treaty negotiations are intense processes, each marked by unique steps and corresponding provisions in keeping with the distinctive histories, circumstances, interests, and rights of each Indigenous nation. Books could be (and in some cases have been) written about the unique characteristics of each of the negotiation processes and agreements undertaken to date.[16] What unites all modern treaties, however, is the fact that each does serve in some important way to recalibrate power relationships between Indigenous nations and the Canadian state. Indigenous signatories act as Indigenous governments in their own right and, as such, the agreements that form the outcome of negotiations are ones settled between nations on a government-to-government basis. As for outcomes, all treaties are characterized by measures intended to improve the social and cultural well-being as well as the economic prosperity of Indigenous peoples. Treaties also regularly provide the means for enhanced Indigenous political power and independence.

THE *NUNAVUT LAND CLAIMS AGREEMENT*

The ***Nunavut Land Claims Agreement*** (NLCA) was signed in May 1993 and enacted through federal enabling legislation in the Parliament of Canada in June 1993. It is the largest land claim negotiated in Canada to date. It also led to the creation of Canada's third territory, Nunavut. The eastern Arctic Inuit entered the comprehensive land claims process in 1976 while also working on a campaign to split the Northwest Territories into two, a campaign that was overwhelmingly supported in a plebiscite held in 1982 (Belanger 2018, 184–94; Courchene 2018, 224–7; Hicks and White 2015, 35–57; Isaac 2012, 177).[17] On April 1, 1999, Nunavut came into being, a new territory comprising a land mass of 1,994 square kilometres with a population of 34,028, of which 86 per cent self-identify as Inuit, most living in 26 Inuit communities.[18] It was decided that the territorial capital would be Iqaluit, formerly known as Frobisher Bay.

The NLCA has several distinctive features that make it unlike any other modern treaty negotiated in Canada. As J.R. Miller observes, the Inuit of the eastern Arctic were a highly cohesive social group who framed their political interests and advanced a political strategy quite distinct from those of the Inuit to the west. He also notes that the eastern Inuit pursued a less confrontational style than that of the westerners, "who, for example, joined with the Dene in 1975 in *The Dene Declaration*, which proclaimed they were 'a nation' and evinced a sense of alienation from southern Canada" (Miller 2009, 268; see also Alcantara 2013, 14–32). Rather than emphasize political separation, the eastern Inuit focused on their desire to join Canada through a land settlement that would emphasize their integration into Canada's larger social and economic fabric. But in addition, by splitting the Northwest Territories into two, the Inuit also assured themselves a position of considerable political power as they would form the numerical majority and thereby exercise political control in the newly constituted Canadian territory.

That said, the process of creating a new territory through a land claims settlement and a related political agreement took considerable effort and patience. Jack Hicks and Graham White describe how the Inuit had to bargain long and hard with federal officials, largely because Ottawa was reluctant "to accede to the fundamental Inuit goal of establishing a new territory in the Eastern Arctic, controlled – de facto if not de jure – by Inuit" (Hicks and White 2015, 43). Yale Belanger further explains that the Inuit ran into difficult boundary disputes with other Indigenous groups, particularly so in the west, that were not easy to resolve (Belanger 2018, 185; see also Miller 2009, 271). Deciding on the powers of the new territorial government as well as financial arrangements to keep the new government afloat also proved exceedingly difficult. But eventually agreements were reached and then passed through two separate pieces of federal legislation: the ***Nunavut Land Claims Agreement Act***, setting out the terms of the land and resources agreement, and the ***Nunavut Act***, creating Nunavut as a territory with its own public form of government (Belanger 2018, 186; Courchene 2018, 224–7).

Under the terms and conditions of the NLCA, the Inuit agreed to "cede, release and surrender to Her Majesty in Right of Canada, all of their aboriginal claims, rights, title, and interests, if any, in and to lands and waters anywhere within Canada and adjacent offshore areas within the sovereignty or jurisdiction of Canada" (RCAP 1995, 42). By agreeing to surrender all rights and title in their traditional territories, the Inuit also agreed that they would never assert any further claims based on future interests that might be later discovered or defined in law. In return for agreeing to the "blanket extinguishment" of all their undefined rights and title, the Inuit gained recognition and protection of a specified package of rights, title, and governance provisions as set out in the terms of their treaty. As part of the package, the Inuit gained the territory of Nunavut, joint membership on several management boards to manage land and water resources and wildlife, money by way of compensation, and substantial federal contributions to the development of targeted Inuit programming (Belanger 2018, 186–9; Courchene 2018, 226; Isaac 2012, 177).

Regarding lands and resources, the NLCA guaranteed the Inuit title to 356,000 square kilometres of land, 38,000 square kilometres of which included subsurface rights (about 18 per cent of the land in Nunavut). In addition to these Inuit title lands, the treaty guarantees the Inuit rights to hunt, trap, and fish on Crown lands as well as the right to participate in the management of these Crown lands. The entire Nunavut settlement area constitutes close to 2 million square kilometres contained within an area stretching from James Bay to the North Pole, from Labrador and Quebec to the east and from a western boundary heading roughly north from Saskatchewan and Alberta (Isaac 2012, 177, 178). The NLCA also provided the Inuit with $1.148 billion in compensation to be paid out over 14 years as well as a share of the government's royalties from oil, gas, and mineral development conducted on Crown lands (RCAP 1995, 42). Finally, the NLCA ensured Inuit participation in political decision-making committees and co-management boards mandated with the task to regulate wildlife, land use planning, the screening and review of environmental impact assessments, and water use (Jai 2017, 131–2). Through these provisions, the Inuit were guaranteed an integral role in resource management throughout Nunavut. In short, when taken together, the stated objective of the land and resources provisions of the NLCA was to ensure the "economic self-sufficiency of the Inuit throughout time" (RCAP 1995, 42).

As for governance, the NLCA set in motion processes that culminated in the creation of a new territory with an elected legislature mandated to govern all residents of Nunavut. Given that the Inuit make up 86 per cent of the territory's population, the expectation was that an elected public government would essentially be a form of Inuit self-government. The federal enabling legislation, the *Nunavut Act* of 1993, established a legislature with a wide range of powers, including control over governance structures, the administration of justice, municipal and local institutions, education, language, health, direct taxation, property and civil rights, incorporation, agriculture, preservation of game, and environmental matters (Government of Canada 1993, 5–6; see also Hicks and White 2015, 50–2). Made up of 19 elected representatives, Nunavut's political culture is one in which partisan politics and party-led governments are avoided on the grounds that the kind of political divisions that are encouraged by partisanship only serve to break down territorial cohesiveness. So once the 19 members of the legislative assembly are elected, they in turn elect a premier, a speaker, and a Cabinet, all by secret ballot. Those members left over once all these positions are filled form the political opposition.

In addition, the governmental administration of Nunavut is highly decentralized to ensure that civil servants are in close geographical proximity and thus better able to respond to the distinct needs of the territory's scattered communities. Decentralization of governmental services was also pursued to create new jobs in as many of Nunavut's communities as possible (Belanger 2018, 189; Hicks and White 2015, 53–6). While the public government model chosen by the Inuit fits within the constitutional model of Canada, the fact that the Inuit form the majority in Nunavut means that the territorial legislature can be used by the Inuit to protect and develop their culture and distinctive ways of life. It has sufficient jurisdiction over a range of territory and resources, in other words, that the legislature can assist in building the kind of life that the Inuit of Nunavut desire.

The establishment of Nunavut constitutes a creative approach on the part of the Inuit of the eastern Arctic to realize their right to self-determination within Canada. The rights, benefits, and governing institutions guaranteed within the NLCA provide the Inuit with a mutually reinforcing and supportive set of resources that can and do contribute to their social, cultural, spiritual, political, and economic well-being. While a route to political sovereignty through significant detachment from the Canadian state was never on offer, the prospect of achieving greater political autonomy by becoming a new territory within Canada certainly was. The Inuit of Nunavut exercise the powers of a Canadian territory, powers that enable them to determine their own political future, to set their own economic priorities, to invest in jobs and training for Inuit, and to protect and nurture their distinct cultural and social institutions.

There have certainly been challenges along the way. The difficulties associated with governing a territory and a people in desperate need of education and training, employment, health services, improved housing, and social programs are not easily met under the terms of any treaty (Belanger 2018, 189–94). In addition, the implementation of the treaty has not always gone according to plan. For example, the Inuit did issue Canada with a claim for damages of $1 billion in 2006 on the grounds that Canada had not upheld its side of the bargain in implementing several treaty provisions for which it was responsible (Hicks and White 2015, 48–50). In short, the relationship between the Canadian government and Inuit has been fragile. Furthermore, the carrying capacity of treaty rights, benefits, and institutions to solve all the Inuit peoples' problems is far from assured. Nevertheless, despite limitations, the NLCA has gone some considerable distance in restoring the confidence of the Inuit of the eastern Arctic in being a part of Canada. As put by Nunavut Tunngavik Inc.: "the Nunavut Land Claims Agreement will be a living document. It will grow with time. It is a foundation upon which Inuit can build their future" (Nunavut Tunngavik Inc. 2004, 6).

THE ALGONQUINS OF ONTARIO AGREEMENT-IN-PRINCIPLE

In October 2016, the Algonquins of Ontario signed an agreement-in-principle (AIP) with the governments of Ontario and Canada. All three parties declared that the AIP constituted an important step forward in settling the status of the Algonquin peoples' rights to lands and resources within their traditional territories. The proposed settlement would have the Algonquin receive $300 million in capital transfers from Canada and Ontario and retake ownership of 47,550 hectares of land in eastern Ontario. The proposed beneficiaries are some 10 Algonquin communities constituting in aggregate about 8,000 people.

The treaty settlement proposed would be the first modern-day treaty to be ratified in Ontario. It is also one of the largest land claims in Canadian history, covering 34,000 square kilometres falling roughly between Ottawa, Kingston, and North Bay, including the national capital, the Ottawa Valley, and Algonquin Provincial Park. The lands themselves are occupied by 1.2 million people and include 86 municipalities. The current round of negotiations began in 1991, finally producing a ratified AIP in October 2016, a time span of 25 years. As an AIP is both non-binding and no more than a framework that sets out the basic elements for a final settlement (though it is highly detailed), several years of work remain, including another stage of negotiations, consultations, Algonquin ratification votes, and settlement legislation at both the provincial and federal levels. Only once these steps are successfully concluded will a final agreement be reached. The stated objective of the Algonquin in treaty negotiations is to achieve certainty about ownership, use, and management of their lands and natural resources, both for themselves and for everyone else in the eventual treaty settlement area.[19]

The Algonquins have had to defend their right to occupy and use their traditional territories for 250 years, dating as far back as the Royal Proclamation of 1763. Over the course of this lengthy period, the

Algonquins maintain that they never surrendered their rights to their land nor did they ever sign a treaty (Steckley and Cummins 2008, 145; Gehl 2014, 12–13). With no treaty to provide them with protection, the Algonquins were forced to act in defence of their rights, petitioning the Crown in 1772 for formal recognition of their land rights with several more petitions to follow over the course of the next two centuries. But all Algonquin efforts fell on deaf ears. Even though the Algonquins had fought on the side of the British in the War of 1812, they were granted no formal recognition of their rights as faithful allies and friends. Instead, the British actively recruited immigrants to come from Britain, and an immigrant onslaught quickly ensued. Over time, settlers gradually but inexorably crowded out the Algonquins from their own territories (Steckley and Cummins 2008, 146; Gehl 2014, 26–36).

In September 1988, the Algonquins and their supporters set up a protest camp on a road leading into Algonquin Park, arguing that their claim to 34,000 square kilometres had to be addressed. Importantly, the Algonquins conceded that a return of all their traditional territories was not their objective. They were not interested in reacquiring private, corporate, or municipal lands, for example. What they did want, however, was acknowledgement of their right to own and use unoccupied Crown lands. Central to the Algonquin claim were four priority areas they insisted be addressed: their right to land, to resources, to self-government, and to compensation for the loss of their way of life (Steckley and Cummins 2008, 148; Lawrence 2012, 87).

Negotiations have been complicated by several factors, almost all of which are a product of a protracted history of colonial pressures that fragmented the Algonquins as a unified nation. These difficulties can be distilled to three: the provincial boundary between Ontario and Quebec, which arbitrarily cuts through the centre of Algonquin territory; the *Indian Act*, which places tremendous obstacles in the way of who can and who cannot legitimately claim to be a beneficiary under the proposed treaty (Lawrence 2012, 83); and the fact that there is such a high concentration of non-Indigenous peoples residing in Algonquin traditional territories. As all parties to the negotiations have agreed that no privately owned land will be taken to settle the claim, the original land settlement offer turned out to be rather paltry, particularly so when compared to what the Inuit in Nunavut were able to acquire in their treaty, to name but one example.

Perhaps the most protracted difficulty for the Algonquins in treaty negotiations has been the issue of representation and who is entitled to claim Algonquin identity. Treaty negotiations between Canada, Ontario, and the Pikwakanagan First Nation began in 1991 but fell apart by 2001. The primary problem was that while the Pikwakanagan First Nation is a recognized band under the *Indian Act*, the band was not seen by many Algonquins in Ontario as able to represent their interests. The Pikwakanagan Band Council, speaking on behalf of the interests of the status Indians of their band, maintained that to be a beneficiary of the treaty, an individual should have at least one-eighth Algonquin blood quantum (Lawrence 2012, 88–104; Gehl 2014, 22–6). But nine other Algonquin communities in eastern Ontario also came forward demanding representation at the negotiation table. These nine communities are largely made up of non-status Algonquins. So, after protracted discussions, the decision was made to include all status, non-status, on-reserve and off-reserve Algonquins, represented by these 10 communities, in treaty negotiations (Steckley and Cummins 2008, 152). From 2005 on, these 10 communities sent 16 treaty negotiators (elected for three-year terms) to the treaty negotiation table. The composition of this recalibrated treaty negotiation team, however, still favours the status Indians of the Pikwakanagan First Nation, as it sends the chief and six councillors. The remaining nine communities can send only one representative each.[20]

Political unity among the Algonquin has also proven elusive. When held to a ratification vote across the 10 communities in 2016, the Algonquins offered overwhelming support for the proposed AIP.[21] But the Piwakanagan First Nation held a separate vote and its members voted decisively against the deal, 74 per cent rejecting it with only 26 per cent in favour (Tabachnick 2017, 1). At stake for the Piwakanagan First Nation were the Indigenous credentials of non-status Indians who stood to gain from cash payouts and other benefits set out in the treaty. Some within the nation argued that a good number of those without Indian status were not Algonquin at all and therefore should not be treaty beneficiaries. Others argued in response that many non-status Algonquins have simply made the journey back into their Indigenous identity. Furthermore, they do so not for personal gain but because it is now possible to rekindle Algonquin family ties in an environment that is less hostile to Indigenous identity. Basically, Canadians are not so overtly racist as they were before (Lawrence 2012, 95). Thus, while these individuals may be landless and without status under the *Indian Act*, this does not mean that they lack an Algonquin identity. According to Bonita Lawrence, therefore, treaty negotiations should be explicitly dedicated to a nation-building exercise designed to draw status and non-status Algonquin alike back into the Algonquin community fold (Lawrence 2012, 95–6).

Other issues and disputes have also threatened the treaty negotiation process. Some members of the Pikwakanagan First Nation, for example, have expressed concerns about the self-government provisions, which appear to them at this stage in the negotiations as consistent with those of a municipality rather than with those of a nation exercising a right to self-determination (Tabachnick 2017, 1). Concerns about overlapping traditional territories with other Indigenous nations have also been raised. As noted by Julius Melnitzer, four separate Algonquin First Nations have challenged the Algonquins of Ontario on the grounds that their claims "overlap with more than 364,000 hectares they claim for themselves" (Melnitzer 2017, C3). And as for the Algonquin nations in Quebec, they too assert that they are entitled to treaty compensation for lands subject to negotiation in Ontario. They ground the strength of their claim in the obvious fact that pre-colonial Algonquin lands were not divided by provincial borders (Tabachnick 2017, 3). Because they are forging ahead with a separate claim, however, Bonita Lawrence worries that the Algonquins of Ontario have given very little thought to the possibility that doing so will result in the permanent severing of the Algonquin nation (Lawrence 2012, 85).

As for substance, the AIP follows the standard approach that eventually forms the core of all final agreements. The four key elements that the

Algonquins have insisted upon are all present in the AIP. Each element constitutes a starting point for further negotiations.

Concerning land, the AIP states that approximately, but certainly not less than, 117,500 acres of provincial Crown land, including mineral rights, will be transferred to Algonquin ownership. The proposed package of lands includes over 200 parcels ranging in size from just a few acres to over 30,000 acres (Algonquins of Ontario 2016, 28–30). Resources identified include provisions for Algonquin rights to harvest wildlife, fish, migratory birds, and plants as well as rights to participate in and benefit from the forestry industry in the treaty settlement area (Algonquins of Ontario 2016, Chapters 7 and 8). In a separate chapter on parks, the AIP provides details about how the Algonquins will share management of provincial parks and conservation areas with the Government of Ontario (Algonquins of Ontario 2016, Chapter 9)

As for self-government, the AIP offers little detail except to say that a final agreement will address self-government arrangements for the Algonquins of the Pikwakanagan First Nation. The political aspirations of the other nine Algonquin communities receive no attention (Algonquins of Ontario 2016, Chapter 11). By way of contrast, heritage and culture receive a good deal more attention. An entire chapter is dedicated to identifying, among other things, measures designed to guarantee that Algonquin institutions will have stewardship and powers of conservation over heritage resources such as archaeological sites, artifacts, and burial sites (Algonquins of Ontario 2016, Chapter 10). The language of compensation for loss of their way of life does not enter into the text of the treaty, but the language of capital transfers does. The AIP identifies a transfer from Canada and Ontario in the amount of $300 million, based on December 2011 values and adjusted for inflation, to be paid out in three instalments over two years, the first one occurring on the effective date of the final agreement (Algonquins of Ontario 2016, Chapter 6).

Despite rejection by the Pikwakanagan First Nation, Algonquin negotiators, including those from Pikwakanagan, have forged ahead into the next stage of treaty negotiations. The mixed results of the AIP ratification vote certainly signal that the divisions within the Algonquin nation are real and cannot be easily papered over. But the nature of an AIP is that it is non-binding and forms no more than a basis on which to negotiate a final agreement. Many of the details identified within the AIP have yet to be fleshed out, and other changes not yet negotiated may still appear. The question, of course, is whether the AIP is a solid enough foundation upon which to rebuild the Algonquin nation. Further time and considerable effort will be needed to come to an agreement on certain matters, chief among them the nature of the Algonquins' right to self-government. There are also festering issues associated with criteria for enrolment as a beneficiary, acceptable compensation for irretrievably lost traditional territories, and the fact that the Algonquins of Ontario and Quebec will be permanently severed once a ratified treaty takes effect. In the case of the Algonquins of Ontario's AIP, therefore, perhaps all that can be said with certainty is best put by Kirby Whiteduck, the chief of Pikwakanagan: "the agreement-in-principle is more of a weight off our shoulders, not so much a celebration" (Tasker 2016, 3).

IMPLICATIONS AND ANALYSIS

In both of these cases, the Inuit of Nunavut and the Algonquins of Ontario, we see to varying degrees how the exercise of modern treaty-making can draw the Indigenous right to self-determination back out from the shadows. In particular, the final agreement of the Inuit of Nunavut is having positive effects. Lands and resources more consistent with the Inuit peoples' needs are now under their ownership and jurisdiction. They also have access to political power more in keeping with their right to build Indigenous institutions that are meaningful to them. Their peoples' capacity for political, social, cultural, and economic autonomy is being advanced as a result. In short, the Inuit of Nunavut have taken incremental steps forward in their quest to revive the practice of their political sovereignty within Canada.

Whether the Algonquins of Ontario will succeed in their quest for restored sovereignty is still very much an open question. Significant components concerning land allocation, resources, and political jurisdiction have yet to be assembled. There is also the important matter of community fragmentation and the presence of deep fissures between those Algonquin persons who have Indian status and those who do not. Despite these challenges, however, some measurable progress is being made. For one thing, treaty negotiations have assisted the Algonquins in gaining clarity about the challenges they face and what it will take to get them to the point where the can more fully enjoy their political, social, cultural, and economic rights.[22] It is worth remembering that while treaties are intended to carry sacred status as covenantal understandings between nations, they also represent pragmatic agreements about how Indigenous and non-Indigenous peoples are to live together in Canada as we now find it. The key, of course, is that in all cases Indigenous peoples must offer their consent. They must be convinced that proposed treaty settlements will serve as a facilitative instrument for the enhancement of their communities' well-being and for the empowerment of their nations. If they are not so convinced, as the Algonquins of Ontario may not be, then they are entirely justified in refusing to submit to the terms of any proposed treaty settlement.

CONCLUSION

Treaties are foundational to Canada because they establish the basis for the political relationship that exists between Indigenous nations and the Canadian state. The relationship that treaties should embody is often characterized as nation-to-nation in design. They formalize a relationship in which the treaty partners agree to distribute benefits and to undertake obligations with respect to one another so that both are guaranteed the right to self-determination within a framework of peaceful coexistence. The fact that Canada has consistently failed its Indigenous partners in fulfilling the promises it made calls into question the very legitimacy of the Canadian state itself. The question we now face is whether reconciliation is possible based on a practice that restores Indigenous nations to their rightful place as political partners with Canada. The very reputation of Canada as a country committed to fairness depends on it.

Guidance concerning the best way forward to achieve reconciliation is readily available within the oral and written accounts of the historical treaties themselves. Herein we find reliable evidence that what was agreed to was a sharing, in a fair and equitable way, of land, resources, and political power between sovereign nations. Only through a genuine commitment to sharing, in other words, could the foundations of a new Canadian state be laid that would be able to withstand the test of legitimacy. Treaties are intended to reconcile the pre-existing sovereignty of Indigenous nations with the asserted sovereignty of the Crown, and this is possible only if the treaty partners' respective rights to self-determination are protected. It is this right that the historical treaties sought to protect and now must be restored. And it is this right that modern treaty-making also seeks to advance and must be fulfilled.

While it may sound contradictory, treaty partners also do not proceed on this venture of self-determination alone. The whole point of a treaty is to establish a covenantal relationship in which lands, resources, and political power are shared according to terms and conditions that all treaty partners agree will facilitate their independent and interdependent coexistence. It is essential, therefore, both for the future well-being of Canada and for the legitimacy of Canada as a state, that all those who reside within its borders come to see themselves as "treaty peoples" (Poelzer and Coates 2015). The next step in this process falls to Canada. While the results have been slow in coming, recent exercises in treaty-making suggest that a shifting of the power imbalance in favour of Indigenous peoples is underway. Modern treaties in particular have restored to Indigenous peoples a good measure of the lands, resources, and political powers they need for the survival of their nations. In short, Indigenous sovereignty can and already does exist within the fabric of the Canadian state.

DISCUSSION QUESTIONS

1. Should treaties constitute the full and final settlement of an Indigenous nation's rights and title? Or does such insistence on settled and unalterable terms fundamentally misconstrue what treaties are meant to represent? Are there good grounds to believe that Canada has abandoned this requirement because it now says that all agreements with Indigenous nations are to constitute a recognition and implementation of their rights rather than their extinguishment, modification, or surrender?
2. What are some of the challenges associated with completing treaties, and how might those challenges be addressed?
3. Some critics argue that modern treaties merely serve as yet another "advanced form of control, manipulation, and assimilation" over Indigenous peoples by the Canadian state (Alfred 2009, 144). Do you find these arguments convincing? Why or why not?
4. Can the modern treaty process establish beneficial relationships of independence and interdependence between the Canadian state and Indigenous nations? If yes, how so? If no, why not?

SUGGESTED READINGS

Alcantara, Christopher. 2013. *Negotiating the Deal: Comprehensive Land Claims Agreements in Canada.* Toronto: University of Toronto Press.

———. 2017. "Implementing Comprehensive Land Claims Agreements in Canada: Towards an Analytical Framework." *Canadian Public Administration* 60 (3).

Alfred, Taiaiake. 2009. "Modern Treaties: A Path to Assimilation?" In *Peace, Power, Righteousness: An Indigenous Manifesto,* 2nd ed. Toronto: Oxford University Press.

Aragón, Fernando M. 2015. "Do Better Property Rights Improve Local Income? Evidence from First Nations' Treaties." *Journal of Developmental Economics* 116.

Belanger, Yale D. 2018. "Chapter 4: Treaties." In *Ways of Knowing: An Introduction to Native Studies in Canada,* 3rd ed. Toronto: Nelson.

Charlie, Lianne Marie Leda. 2020. "Piecing Together Modern Treaty Politics in the Yukon." In *Visions of the Heart: Issues Involving Indigenous Peoples in Canada,* 5th ed., edited by Gina Starblanket and David Long. Toronto: Oxford University Press.

Courchene, Thomas J. 2018. "Chapter 8: First Nations Land Claims Agreements," and Chapter 9: Inuit Land Claims Agreements." In *Indigenous Nationals, Canadian Citizens: from First Contact to Canada 150 and Beyond.* Montreal: McGill-Queen's University Press.

Gehl, Lynn. 2014. *The Truth that Wampum Tells: My Debwewin on the Algonquin Land Claims Process.* Halifax: Fernwood Publishing.

Hicks, Jack, and Graham White. 2015. *Made in Nunavut: An Experiment in Decentralized Government.* Vancouver: UBC Press.

Jai, Julie. 2017. "Bargains Made in Bad Times: How Principles from Modern Treaties Can Reinvigorate Historic Treaties." In *The Right Relationship: Reimagining the Implementation of Historical Treaties,* edited by John Borrows and Michael Coyne. Toronto: University of Toronto Press.

King, Hayden. 2015. "New Treaties, Same Old Dispossession: A Critical Assessment of Land and Resource Management Regimes in the North." In, *Canada: The State of the Federation 2013, Aboriginal Multilevel Governance*, edited by Martin Papillon and André Juneau. Montreal: McGill-Queen's University Press.

Lawrence, Bonita. 2012. *Fractured Homeland: Federal Recognition and Algonquin Identity in Ontario.* Vancouver: UBC Press.

Mackey, Eva. 2016. *Unsettled Expectations: Uncertainty, Land and Settler Decolonization.* Halifax: Fernwood Publishing.

McKee, Christopher. 2009. *Treaty Talks in British Columbia: Building a New Relationship,* 3rd ed. Vancouver: UBC Press.

Papillon, Martin. 2020. "The Two Faces of Treaty Federalism." In *Canadian Politics,* 7th ed., edited by James Bickerton and Alain-G. Gagnon. Toronto: University of Toronto Press.

Pendakur, Krishna, and Ravi Pendakur. 2018. "The Effects of Modern Treaties and Opt-In Legislation on Household Incomes in Aboriginal Communities." *Social Indicators Research* 137 (1).

Scott, Tracie Lee. 2012. *Postcolonial Sovereignty? The Nisga'a Final Agreement.* Saskatoon, SK: Purich Publishing.

NOTES

1 I have selected these two land claims settlements for a variety of reasons. I wanted to showcase an Inuit settlement (Nunavut) to draw the Inuit into the land claims discussion and the Algonquin agreement-in-principle because it illustrates in a particularly instructive way many of the complexities associated with resolving a modern land claim. I investigate the Algonquin also at the urging of one of the anonymous reviewers of this book. Another of the anonymous reviewers asks why I chose not to include a land claim settlement from Yukon, given these are particularly notable for recognizing and advancing the Indigenous right to self-determination. While I do not deal with any Yukon comprehensive land claim and self-government agreements in this chapter, I do so in the next when investigating the settlement of the Kluane First Nation. Here, the self-government provisions are highlighted specifically.

2 While much of Atlantic Canada is covered by historic "peace and friendship" treaties, these agreements made no mention of how land and resources were to be shared. Therefore, there are outstanding treaty matters yet to be negotiated between the Indigenous nations of Atlantic Canada and the federal and provincial governments.

3 Indeed, one of the anonymous reviewers of this book suggests that equating the contemporary comprehensive land claims process with treaties is highly contestable. The term "treaty" suggests a process of negotiation leading to recognition of obligations between treaty partners possessing some form of equitable sovereign status. As we shall see in this chapter, however, no such equitable standing between Indigenous negotiators and their federal, provincial, and territorial counterparts exists. In the face of clear asymmetries in power, there are those who conclude that the outcome of comprehensive land and self-government agreements generally lean in the direction of a clear capitulation to the interests of the Canadian state.

4 The treaties concluded since 1973 under the comprehensive claims policy include the following: *James Bay and Northern Quebec Agreement*, 1975; *Northeastern Quebec Agreement*, 1978; *Inuvialuit Final Agreement*, 1984; *Gwich'in Comprehensive Land Claim Agreement*, 1992; *Council of Yukon Indians Umbrella Final Agreement*, 1993 (in turn containing 11 separate treaties with individual Yukon nations); *Nunavut Land Claims Agreement*, 1993; *Sahtu Dene and Métis Comprehensive Land Claim Agreement*, 1994; *Nisga'a Final Agreement*, 1998; *Tlicho Agreement*, 2003; *Labrador Inuit Land Claims Agreement*, 2005; *Nunavik Inuit Land Claims Agreement*, 2006;

Tsawwassen First Nation Final Agreement, 2007; *Maa-nulth First Nations Final Agreement*, 2011; *Eeyou Marine Region Land Claims Agreement*, 2010; *Yale First Nation Final Agreement*, 2013; *Tla'amin Final Agreement*, 2014.

5 Krishna Pendakur and Ravi Pendakur use less critical language to describe the accomplishments of the comprehensive land claims process when they write "to date, comprehensive land claims agreements have incorporated (among other things) 600 thousand square kilometres of land, capital transfers of $3.2 billion, access to resource development opportunities and participation in resource management decision-making." See Pendakur and Pendakur 2017, 144.

6 Before 1995, the federal government refused to negotiate self-government under the comprehensive land claims process, demanding instead that self-government form side agreements under federal legislation, thereby ensuring that they would not receive constitutional protection. See Papillon 2020, 224.

7 In 2017 the Government of Canada released 10 principles that it declared would henceforth guide Canada's relationship with Indigenous peoples. Among them, the government stated that the presence of Indigenous rights is not dependent on agreements such as comprehensive land claims settlements. Instead, those rights pre-exist agreements and so "where agreements are formed, they should be based upon the recognition and implementation of rights and not on their extinguishment, modification, or surrender." I shall have more to say about the implications of this shift in policy later in this chapter. See Government of Canada 2017b, 4.

8 I say no more than consultative because in most cases the decisions of co-management boards are subject to provincial or territorial ministerial vetoes. Thus, as put by Hayden King, despite often enjoying 50 per cent representation, Indigenous participation is reduced to mere consultation because there is no guarantee that the plans presented will actually be used to guide decisions about land and resource use in the traditional territories of Indigenous peoples. I shall have much more to say about the role of co-management boards in relation to Indigenous sovereignty in Chapter 9. See King 2015, 84–5.

9 The report of the British Columbia Claims Task Force was released on June 28, 1991. Its membership was composed of representatives from the First Nations of British Columbia, the Government of British Columbia, and the Government of Canada.

10 It is also worth noting that Indigenous rights are in a constant state of flux and development. Indigenous peoples, therefore, resist the language of extinguishment or the limitations imposed by the language of modification or non-assertion because it is entirely likely that through the courts or political negotiations the meaning and scope of their rights may become more extensive. Why, then, agree to give them up or limit them by means of modification or agreements of non-assertion when their value as unspecified rights may only increase with time?

11 One of the anonymous reviewers of this book offers a similar assessment of modern treaties in the following remarks: "I'm not sure that modern treaties have established a

nation-to-nation relationship. Existing research on shared rule finds very few opportunities for intergovernmental relations or executive federalism that occurs between federal and provincial governments." The reviewer then cites the edited volume by Martin Papillon and André Juneau that is dedicated to examining the theme of "Aboriginal multilevel governance" as evidence. See Papillon and Juneau 2015.

12 One of the anonymous reviewers interjects at this point with this astute observation: "But Taiaiake Alfred's counter would be that those Indigenous peoples are so co-opted that they cannot see how co-opted they actually are." To follow this line of argument, see Alfred 2009, 97–104.

13 Of course, significant asymmetries in power may well continue to exist where implementation of comprehensive land claims agreements are concerned. The preponderance of responsibility for turning over land, resources, and political power lies with federal, provincial, and territorial governments who may well choose to be recalcitrant or negligent in these treaty duties. Indeed, as Martin Papillon points out, "many treaty signatories end up in court defending their treaty rights against government agencies unwilling to fulfil their part of the deal." See Papillon 2020, 218. I shall have more to say about the problem of treaty implementation in forthcoming sections of this chapter.

14 I will have much more to say about the actual design and structure of several Indigenous governments in the next chapter on self-government. Suffice it to say for now that the machinery of Indigenous governments under treaty, like that of the Nisga'a Nation, is considerably larger and more complex than that of the typical *Indian Act* band government.

15 Douglas R. Eyford was appointed ministerial special representative by Bernard Valcourt, minister of Aboriginal and Northern Affairs in the Conservative Government of Stephen Harper. Mr. Eyford was mandated to review the comprehensive land claims policy as part of the Conservative government's larger initiative to develop a new framework to address Aboriginal and treaty rights. Mr. Eyford delivered his report and recommendations to the minister on February 20, 2015. See Eyford 2015, 48–54.

16 See, for example, Alcantara 2013, Hicks and White 2015, and Scott 2012.

17 The eastern Arctic Inuit were represented in land claim and governmental negotiations by the Tunngavik Federation of Nunavut, since renamed Nunavut Tunngavik Inc.

18 These communities are Arctic Bay, Arviat, Baker Lake, Bathurst Inlet, Cambridge Bay, Cape Dorset, Chesterfield Inlet, Clyde River, Gjoa Haven, Grise Fiord, Hall Beach, Igloolik, Iqaluit, Kimmirut, Kugluktuk, Pangnirtung, Kugaaruk, Pond Inlet, Qikiqtarjuaq, Rankin Inlet, Repulse Bay, Resolute, Sanikiluaq, Taloyoak, Coral Harbour, and Whale Cove.

19 See Algonquins of Ontario website, www.tanakiwin.com.

20 These Algonquin communities are Antoine, Bonnechere, Greater Golden Lake, Kijicho Manito Madaouskarini (Bancroft), Mattawa/North Bay, Ottawa, Shabot Obaadjiwan (Sharbot Lake), Snimikobi (Ardoch), and Whitney and Area.

21 The ratification vote was held in March 2016. A total of 3,575 ballots were cast, out of 7,540 eligible Algonquin voters – a participation rate of 47 per cent. Of those ballots cast, 3,341, or over 90 per cent, voted in favour of the agreement-in-principle and for continuation of negotiations moving toward a final agreement. See "Proposed Agreement in Principle" on the Algonquins of Ontario website: www.tanakiwin.com.

22 Bonita Lawrence is less optimistic, believing that the deep fracturing of the Algonquin nation brought on by the imposition of provincial boundaries that divides the Algonquin homeland and *Indian Act* policies that divide Algonquins from one another as status and non-status Indians cannot be overcome through a modern treaty. Lawrence also points to the structural limitations of the comprehensive land claims process itself, with its delegated form of "self-government that permits no real Indigenous control" and its approach to negotiations that are so tightly controlled that it disallows for any expression of real Indigenous nationhood, as largely to blame. See Lawrence 2012, 287–301.

CHAPTER 8

Self-Government: Incremental Sovereignty

LEARNING OBJECTIVES

1 To describe the four approaches to self-government and explain how each can contribute to the Indigenous right to self-determination.
2 To assess whether band councils qualify as governments and whether they can perform tasks consistent with the Indigenous right to self-determination.
3 To evaluate the merits of legislated self-government agreements as tools to enhance Indigenous political power.
4 To identify typical modern treaty self-government provisions and describe both the opportunities and limitations presented by this option.
5 To assess whether there are good grounds to prefer treaty federalism over other self-government models on the grounds that it is the most consistent with Indigenous rights.
6 To show that the individual rights of Indigenous women are integral to and a necessary feature of the Indigenous collective right to self-determination.

A sovereign people are those who are in a position to make political decisions about the direction of their collective lives free of external interference. It is this kind of political autonomy that has been at the heart of the Indigenous quest for self-determination in Canada for over half a century. Moreover, this Indigenous quest has not just been advanced as a response to a desire but also as an entitlement flowing from an international human right. Indigenous peoples were once politically autonomous and assert that they are entitled to be so again. The question for Canada is whether it is willing to recognize and protect this international human right. As is typical of states, Canada has guarded its sovereignty jealously on the grounds that it is justified in holding a monopoly on state power. The issue before us, therefore, is whether the Canadian state is flexible enough to move over and create political and legal space conducive to the re-emergence of an Indigenous right to self-determination consistent with Indigenous ambitions.

While Indigenous peoples in Canada are universally committed to the principle of self-determination, what this means in practical terms will likely vary from Indigenous nation to nation. What all do seem to agree on, however, is that their right to self-determination ought to be put in the service of ending Canadian governmental paternalism. As put by Joanne Barker, when Indigenous peoples "claim an identity as sovereign," they do so for the purpose of "reasserting a politically empowered self-identity within, besides, and against colonization" (Barker 2005, 20). In short, Indigenous sovereignty amounts to "Aboriginal rather than external authority over jurisdictions and institutions of relevance to Aboriginal peoples" (Fleras and Elliott 1992, 24; see also Scott 2012, 90–1). What Indigenous peoples seek is to decolonize their lives by bringing them into conformity with their own distinctive perspectives and priorities.

It is my contention that how Indigenous peoples take up this task of decolonization is entirely up to them, including approaches to self-government. Two implications immediately follow. First, ahead of all other criteria, Indigenous self-government is about choice (Hunter 2006, 30; Scott 2012, 95). What matters from the perspective of sovereignty is that the choices Indigenous nations make about how to express their right to self-government must be ones they make in freedom, as judged by them, according to their own interests. For some Indigenous nations, the range of self-government power they will wish to exercise may be modest, while for others it may be far more wide-ranging. The important point from the perspective of Indigenous sovereignty is that the Canadian state must not set arbitrary limits on the extent of Indigenous power permitted as a precondition for exercising the right in the first place.

Second, as noted by Greg Poelzer and Ken Coates, the "attainment of self-government is a process, not a single event," a process, moreover, in which Indigenous nations will invariably rebuild their political sovereignty incrementally, "moving at their own pace to assume responsibilities currently managed by the Government of Canada" (Poelzer and Coates 2015, 223; see also Coates 2008, 19; Warry 1998, 47–51). There is simply no single self-government template for all Indigenous nations, in other words, nor is there a required pace that Indigenous nations must follow to achieve full decolonization. All that is required from the perspective of sovereignty is that Indigenous self-government be structured to strengthen Indigenous identity and match the particular circumstances and needs of each Indigenous nation (Coates and McHugh 1998, 143). In short, self-government must facilitate appropriate mechanisms for decolonization and the re-emergence of Indigenous nations in all their diversity.

What follows examines how current self-government arrangements contribute to Indigenous community capacity and, by extension, to Indigenous self-determination. As we shall see, while all Indigenous nations enjoy the same political right to self-determination, the institutional terms through which this right is being realized varies from nation to nation. Indigenous nations differ significantly from one another in terms of their number of citizens, socioeconomic conditions, access to resources, and relationships with the Canadian state. As Indigenous peoples are not homogenous, it stands to reason that there is no single Indigenous viewpoint on what Indigenous governance ought to accomplish. Self-government invariably means different things to different Indigenous nations.

The analysis to follow draws extensively on the four models or approaches to self-government discussed at length in Chapter 1. In revisiting the four models, I arrange the practice of self-government along a continuum. The continuum illustrates that Indigenous governance is, in fact, in active operation across Canada in a variety of institutional forms. Many Indigenous nations have chosen to activate their right to self-government within the framework of one or another of the identified models. The chapter advances the proposition that while the level of Indigenous sovereignty exercised across most of these models is framed within and contained by Canadian sovereignty, this need not mean that the power exercised by Indigenous nations amounts to little or nothing when measured against the standard of their right to self-determination. Instead, self-government arrangements across the entire continuum, whether relatively modest or more robust in scope, can be seen as important tools for the incremental growth and redevelopment of Indigenous sovereignty. Each, in other words, can and often does contribute in some small or greater measure to the larger project of enhancing Indigenous self-reliance and autonomy. I begin with an examination of Indian band governance.

BAND GOVERNANCE

Most Indigenous nations exercise political authority as **band councils** under the *Indian Act.* Band councillors are elected to office by the members of Indian bands which, under **Section 74** of the *Indian Act*, determines that there will be one chief and one councillor for every 100 members of a band. Councillors must number no less than two and no more than 12. While many Indigenous nations follow the *Indian Act* procedures for electing chief and council, others choose to appoint their councils according to what are called "band customs." Band customs can include elements of traditional Indigenous governance, but they also often amount to little more than a variation on *Indian Act* election procedures. For example, "custom" may mean electing more councillors than called for by *Indian Act* electoral rules or electing councillors to terms longer than the two-year period specified by the Act.

Band council governance under the *Indian Act* is deliberately designed to provide limited jurisdiction over members and territories to Indigenous nations. Indigenous government is limited to local government on reserves and band council powers are, at best, often characterized as municipal in nature (Abele and Prince 2006, 573). Generally speaking, bands are authorized to serve three functions: they pass by-laws, administer programs for their members, and raise taxes on reserve. As a general rule, band councils do not pass laws. Instead, they make by-laws, which are laws made under the auspices of delegated authority granted to the band under the terms of the *Indian Act* and which are subject to the discretionary power of disallowance held by the minister of Indigenous Affairs.

As for areas of jurisdiction, bands can make by-laws in the following subject areas:

- public health;
- regulation of traffic;
- observance of law and order;
- prevention of disorderly conduct;
- control of trespass of cattle and other domestic animals;
- construction of roads and other local works;
- zoning for land use;
- regulation of construction;
- surveying and allocating reserve lands to individuals;
- control of public games;
- regulation of salespersons;
- management of fish and game;
- residence of band members and other persons on reserve; and
- application of by-laws to spouses, common-law partners, and children (*Indian Act*, Section 81(1)).

In addition, bands are authorized to exercise powers over the surrender of reserve lands, the control of band membership, and the regulation of alcohol consumption. However, on these matters, jurisdiction does not fall to chief and council alone but must include band members as a whole, usually by majority support through a vote. Responsibility for the design, delivery, and administration of services and programs also falls to band councils, particularly so in the areas of health care, education, social services (including family and child care), and community and economic development (Abele and Prince 2006, 573; Williamson and Roberts 2004, 128). Finally, band taxation powers extend to taxation of reserve lands; sales taxes; the licensing of businesses, trades, and occupation; and raising money from band members to support local projects (*Indian Act*, Section 83(1)).

On one level, band councils do not even classify as governments given their limited range of delegated powers. Indeed, Indigenous leaders regularly identify band councils as a manifestation of colonialism given that their powers are delegated to them by the federal government located in Ottawa (Green 2020, 248). Band councils do not enjoy constitutional protection as sovereign Indigenous governments, nor do they participate in the constitutional division and distribution of powers granted to the federal and provincial governments. Instead, the minister responsible for Indigenous Affairs claims the right to veto band council by-laws and resolutions and, more alarming still, assumes the right to "replace a band council with an appointed administrator if it is felt that the affairs of the band are not well managed" (Whittington 2000, 113). One could well conclude, therefore, that band councils serve largely as the administrative arm of the federal government, delivering programs and services to Indigenous peoples on reserve according to criteria largely set by Ottawa (Ladner 2006, 6; Wilson-Raybould 2019, 32, 103).

Critics of band councils, therefore, seem justified in arguing that this form of Indigenous governance is little more than a way for Canada to maintain firm control over the affairs of Indigenous nations (Papillon 2014, 117; Green 2020, 248). They are, after all, entirely subject to federal authority. The circumstances of the band council model dictate that Indigenous nations are to have access to restricted law-making powers as determined by federal statute and that those powers are only to be exercised within the limited setting of Indian reserves. In addition, prospects for improvements to reserve-based programs and services are subject to the financial whims and wishes of the federal government alone. In effect, Indigenous nations remain firmly locked within an institutional system of colonialism where prospects for enhanced Indigenous sovereignty are slim at best. In fact, it is precisely this system of *Indian Act* band council governance that so many Indigenous leaders seek to replace because its underlying principle rests on a firm rejection of self-determination as a pre-existing and inherent Indigenous right. In short, it seems reasonable to conclude that band councils are subordinate governments by virtue of their very structure and design (Green 2020, 248; Papillon 2014, 117; Wilson-Raybould 2019, 22).

Despite significant structural limitations, however, I would suggest that band councils can still be seen as governments, or at least from the perspective of self-determination as governments in development (Abele and Prince 2006, 574). They do perform tasks that are consistent with the kinds of responsibilities exercised by governments, tasks moreover that their members typically regard to be appropriate. Under the *Indian Act*, band councils are able to exercise some degree of self-government through use of by-law-making powers. They also enjoy some discretionary autonomy over the administration and management of programs associated with reserve lands, education, social and health services, and local taxation, to name a few examples (Papillon 2014, 117). Indigenous leaders will be first to say that while they do not accept delegated jurisdiction to be a legitimate source of Indigenous governmental power, they nevertheless have to meet the expectations of their members for governmental services in the here and now and in immediate and practical ways. Consequently, as pointed out by Frank Cassidy and Robert L. Bish, Indigenous leaders will regularly assert that they have an inherent right to self-determination but at the same time will make the fullest use "of the powers delegated to them under the *Indian Act*" (Cassidy and Bish 1989, 42). Having to live in a world of such confounding political contradictions is quite simply an integral and inescapable feature of Indigenous lived experience.

Cassidy and Bish also point out that Indigenous leaders who assert their inherent right to self-government but who nevertheless choose to exercise *Indian Act* band powers do so not because they accept the legitimacy of federal authority. Instead, they do so because they see this approach to be one way to take pragmatic and incremental steps toward greater control over their lands, resources, governance, and citizens on traditional territories. For example, making fullest use of delegated powers under the *Indian Act* and even going beyond those powers whenever and wherever opportunities arise can serve to assist Indigenous nations to develop policy capacity, political and administrative expertise, and democratic accountability. It may simply be the case, therefore, that some Indigenous leaders choose to use the *Indian Act* because it is an expedient tool to expand Indigenous government in practice (Cassidy and Bish 1989, 46). Expanded capacity acquired over time, in turn, can serve as a foundation upon which to build the kind of jurisdictional authority that normally comes with political sovereignty. I would suggest, therefore, that in many instances Indian band councils can appropriately be regarded as political platforms repurposed to serve a distinct objective: assist Indigenous peoples to assert their presence as nations in (re)development. The following describes the circumstances of one such Indigenous nation committed to precisely such an ambition.

THE SQUAMISH NATION (BC)

The Squamish of southwestern British Columbia is one nation that has both used the *Indian Act* powers and moved beyond them in targeted areas to achieve substantial progress in practising a form of a self-government that reflects at least some aspects of a sovereignty paradigm. The total area of the Squamish Nation's traditional territories is 6,732 square kilometres (673,200 hectares). The Squamish people occupied 23 village sites scattered across 24 reserves that encompass 28.28 square kilometres (2,828 hectares). Their main reserves are located in North Vancouver on the Burrard Inlet and near the town of Squamish on Howe Sound. The nation's population numbers about 4,080, with 51 per cent of members residing on reserve (Squamish Nation 2021, 11). The Squamish Nation itself is the product of a political amalgamation that was signed by 16 Coast Salish chiefs in 1923. Their band council consists of 16 elected councillors who serve four-year terms alongside an elected band manager. The 16 elected councillors are intended to reflect the 16 chiefs who signed the original amalgamation agreement. The Squamish Nation has a close relationship with and family ties to the neighbouring Tsleil-Waututh Nation as well as the Musqueam Nation peoples who live on the southern edge of Vancouver (Squamish Nation 2016, 1).

The parcels of reserve land that the Squamish Nation hold are limited (approximately 0.42 per cent of their traditional territories), but they are also extremely valuable given their proximity to the cities of Vancouver and North Vancouver. Accordingly, the Squamish Band Council has adopted a business plan that seeks to generate as much "own-source revenue" (as opposed to government-provided revenue) from those lands as possible. The rationale here is a straightforward one – the greater the revenue-generating capacity of the Squamish Nation, the more independent it will be with respect to its ability to define and set the direction of the nation's political, economic, and cultural programs and services. The origin of the Squamish Nation's own-source revenue (OSR) come from leases, taxation, and Squamish-owned businesses. Particularly lucrative here are leases with tenants like the Park Royal Shopping Centre,

Superstore, Capilano River RV Park, International Plaza, and Greater Vancouver Storage Sewage Plant, which, when taken together, generate close to half of the OSR secured annually by the nation. In 2020/21, the nation's OSR accounted for 62 per cent (or $63.6 million) of its $102.5 million in total revenues, a percentage that the band council expects will only increase over the coming years (Squamish Nation 2021, 7).

Financial stability of this sort has put the Squamish Nation in a good position to invest in economic development and enhanced employment opportunities for its members. The nation is also committed to expanding existing and creating new programs and services consistent with the nation's needs and priorities.[1] Notably, a good number of these programs are either entirely or almost entirely self-financed. These include recreational services, elder programs, membership services and communication, and programs dedicated to the preservation of the Squamish language and culture (Squamish Nation 2014, 7). Federal funding to the order of approximately 40 per cent per year still constitutes a significant level of financial dependency on outside sources. But the Squamish Nation is nevertheless taking deliberate steps in the direction of restoring its own autonomy. The nation is providing a firm, though limited, foundation for the expression of Indigenous self-government by financing its own programs and services to the greatest extent possible (Cassidy and Bish 1989, 45).

The Squamish Nation supplements its increasing internal autonomy with an approach to intergovernmental relations that takes its political sovereignty as a given. For example, since 2006 the Squamish Nation has been working collaboratively with the Tsleil-Waututh and Musqueam nations through a protocol agreement to jointly share economic benefits and business opportunities that arise from Crown land dispositions or sales in their shared traditional territories. The operative assumption of all three nations is that each is entitled to a full measure of rights and title attached to traditional territories that may overlap with one another. Consequently, when the federal or BC government decides that properties under their control are surplus, the three nations mobilize to do everything in their power to have those properties brought back under their joint jurisdiction.

To date, these efforts have met with some success. Within the city of Vancouver, the three nations have acquired joint ownership as equal partners over such "surplus" properties as a Canada Post facility, a Liquor Distribution Branch warehouse, and most significantly given its size, the Jericho Lands property formerly owned by the Department of National Defence (Squamish Nation 2014, 12; 2015, 6). Each acquisition is highly strategic, both because of the revenue it will generate and because the three nations collectively have limited reserve lands that they can use for development initiatives. But there is also an important matter of principle at stake. The federal and BC governments now accept the proposition that as formerly autonomous Indigenous nations with rights to their traditional territories, the three nations are entitled to a joint stake in Crown lands whenever and wherever those lands become available.

The Squamish Nation has asserted rights in a manner consistent with sovereignty in one other significant way. Fortis BC has proposed to build a natural gas pipeline through the Squamish Nation's traditional territory, terminating at Woodfibre's proposed $1.6 billion LNG plant at the Squamish village site of Swiyat on Howe Sound (Squamish Nation 2015, 6). As with all such projects, this proposal was subjected to both a federal and provincial environmental assessment. However, the Squamish Nation found both assessments to be inadequate on the grounds that neither paid adequate attention to the Squamish Nation's Aboriginal title and rights interests. For one thing, both assessments failed to consider the impact of the proposed project on "culturally significant and sacred areas as well as environmentally sensitive lands and aquatic habitats." Both assessments also failed to register the adverse impact the proposed project might have on the Squamish Nation's ability to govern its own lands and waters (Squamish Nation 2016, 6).

In response, the Squamish Nation unilaterally decided to run its own environmental assessment, issuing its own list of criteria to be used to assess the risks and benefits of the project. At the end of the day, the nation advanced 25 conditions that Woodfibre LNG had to meet if the project was to earn the Squamish people's consent. Remarkably, the company agreed to all 25 conditions (Hunter 2017, 7). With the Squamish Nation thus reassured, the band council proceeded to offer its support to the project, though not without significant opposition from some members of the nation.[2]

Important for our purposes, however, is the principle that guided this outcome. On the basis of its right to self-determination, the Squamish Nation simply asserted its right to conduct an environmental assessment alongside those of its federal and provincial counterparts. The fact that Woodfibre LNG agreed to comply, coupled with the fact that the federal and BC governments did not rule the Squamish Nation's actions out of order, indicates that the Squamish Nation's political authority over its traditional territories is being recognized. At the very least, those non-Indigenous interests and Canadian governments invested in the project now seem to understand that without endorsement by the Squamish Nation, both the pipeline and LNG plant ought not to be built.

LEGISLATED SELF-GOVERNMENT AGREEMENTS

A small number of Indigenous nations are empowering their governments through legislated **self-government agreements.** Recent examples include the Sechelt Nation on the Sunshine Coast of BC, the Westbank Nation of BC's central Okanagan, the Métis Settlements of Alberta, and the Sioux Valley Dakota Nation of southwestern Manitoba.[3] In each case, the Indigenous government exercises its power through federal or provincial enabling legislation that places the Indigenous nation outside the *Indian Act.* In all cases, the Indigenous nation acquires legislative authority on reserve lands through a process of negotiation that transfers power from federal or provincial governments to the nation (Abele and Prince 2006, 578). While not without their problems, legislated self-government agreements do have the advantage of removing Indigenous nations out from under the *Indian Act*, thereby enhancing their political autonomy.

Legislated self-government agreements authorize Indigenous nations to exercise a greater range of powers than those permitted under the *Indian Act.*

Furthermore, the political decisions made under the terms of the agreement are no longer subject to the approval or veto powers of the minister of Indigenous Affairs. In practical terms, therefore, Indigenous governments that operate governments under the authority of federal or provincial legislation generally do enjoy political power that far exceeds that of Indigenous nations existing under the *Indian Act*.

For example, agreements generally make provision for new governance models designed by Indigenous nations under terms established by their own constitutions. Agreements also provide for enhanced Indigenous control over programs and services, guaranteed fiscal support, and new and expanded law-making powers. Typical powers authorized include the right to legislate on lands, including all matters relating to zoning, land use planning, and local taxation. Indigenous governments can also pass laws on important internal matters like education, language, culture, adoption, training, social services, and the administration of justice. In addition, agreements confer legal standing on Indigenous nations so that they can enter into contracts and acquire and hold property. As a rule, there are no changes to the tax exemption status that Indigenous peoples now enjoy under the *Indian Act*. And finally, as the agreements are designed to be non-prejudicial, it is understood that Aboriginal rights and title remain undisturbed by the terms of the legislation. Indigenous peoples do not lose their Aboriginal rights simply because they seek to enhance their governing capacity through parliamentary legislation.

Importantly, however, because legislated self-government agreements are detached from the land claims process, the powers secured through them can only be exercised within the limited confines of reserve lands.

From the vantage point of Indigenous sovereignty, a fundamental problem with the legislated self-government approach is that the jurisdiction of these governments flows from parliamentary legislation. Critics are therefore quick to point out that nowhere within this model is there recognition that the origin of Indigenous political power resides within Indigenous peoples themselves (Grant 2018, 127; Tully 2008, 286). If the claim to Indigenous sovereignty is to be taken seriously, then it is Indigenous peoples, not Canadian governments, that must be in the position to define the range and scope of Indigenous governmental powers. Critics also worry about the reliability of self-government agreements. Because they are granted through federal legislation, they can be unilaterally altered or repealed through acts of Parliament (Murphy 2005, 12). Self-government agreements are also said to be structurally deficient because they do not provide Indigenous peoples with the additional lands or natural resources needed to build a sound fiscal base or an expanded economy. Taken together, critics conclude that far from promoting Indigenous sovereignty, what self-government agreements actually do is promote further Indigenous dependency on the Canadian state (Starblanket 2019a, 19). For these reasons, it is not uncommon to find that some Indigenous peoples who enter into self-government negotiations choose to abandon the process after a period of time.[4]

The structural limitations presented by legislated self-government arrangements are both real and pressing. But this does not mean that they cannot contribute something of value to the overall

Indigenous quest for self-determination within Canada. For example, self-government agreements do contribute to the partial elimination of the *Indian Act* in the lives of Indigenous peoples. They also provide for the orderly and expedient transfer of powers to Indigenous governments. And they validate the long-held Indigenous position that Indigenous peoples have both the right and capacity to govern themselves under political institutions of their own design.

One way to cast legislated self-government agreements in a more positive light is to characterize them as incremental steps taken in the long-haul journey to restore Indigenous sovereignty. Framed this way, self-government agreements can be seen as an encouraging sign of political relationships in transformation. For those Indigenous peoples who choose them, legislated self-government agreements are tools designed to assist them in the practical task of governing themselves. They are, in short, choosing to operate under Canadian statutes because they grant them a greater degree of political agency and autonomy (Poelzer and Coates 2015, 224; Olthuis, Kleer, Townshend 2012, 171). As such, I suggest that legislated self-government agreements constitute an expedient opportunity for Indigenous nations to operationalize certain key aspects of their broader Indigenous right to self-determination.

THE SIOUX VALLEY DAKOTA NATION (MANITOBA)

Characterizing legislative self-government agreements as incremental steps taken in the larger project to restore Indigenous sovereignty is well represented by the Sioux Valley Dakota Nation. After 20 years of negotiation, a self-government agreement between the Sioux Valley Dakota Nation, Canada, and Manitoba came into effect on July 1, 2014. This agreement is the first of its kind in both Manitoba and on the Canadian prairies.[5] The Sioux Valley Dakota Nation is located on the banks of the Assiniboine River in southwestern Manitoba. Its reserve is 38.2 square kilometres (9,439 acres) in size, created by an order in council of the Canadian government in 1876. It has a membership of approximately 2,500, just over half living on reserve (Sioux Valley Dakota Nation 2016c, 1). Members both on and off reserve vote for a chief and four councillors in elections held every three years. Unlike its surrounding Indigenous neighbours, the Sioux Valley Dakota Nation was not a signatory to Treaty 2 of 1871. Because they stand outside the historical treaty process, the Sioux Valley Dakota insist that their Aboriginal rights and title remain intact.

The Sioux Valley Dakota pursued a self-government agreement with Canada and Manitoba because they wanted to come out from under the debilitating interference of the *Indian Act*. In the words of the nation, it is determined to once again "be a Dakota Nation which is self-governing by the Dakota Oyate under Sioux Valley Dakota Nation Law" (Sioux Valley Dakota Nation 2016b, 2). The nation has been firm in its resolve that it has an inherent right to create its own governance model based on Dakota traditions (Sioux Valley Dakota Nation 2016a, 2). Not surprisingly, therefore, the self-government agreement falls well short of these lofty ambitions, a reality of which the Sioux Valley Dakota are fully aware. For starters, the agreement does not address the nation's land title claim nor does it possess the status of a treaty. The agreement is thus limited by design because its reach extends only to activities conducted by Sioux Valley Dakota members on reserve. In addition, the agreement contains provisions that put significant constraints on the use of the Sioux Valley Dakota's political power. For example, the nation is prohibited from passing laws in certain jurisdictions where the federal government has decided it has key interests, among them criminal law. The agreement also requires that the *Charter of Rights and Freedoms* must apply to all actions undertaken by the nation's government.

Given these structural constraints, the Sioux Valley Dakota Nation decided it could proceed with a self-government agreement only if the governments of Canada and Manitoba agreed to the following condition: the agreement itself must not be allowed to negatively prejudice the legal standing of the nation's Aboriginal or treaty rights. Practically speaking, this meant that there must be no corresponding requirement that the nation give up its Aboriginal rights and title in exchange for the provisions found within the self-government agreement itself. Instead, those Aboriginal rights and title must remain intact both as a guarantee of the Sioux Valley Dakota's ongoing sovereignty and as resources against which to negotiate a fuller expression of self-determination in the future should they wish to do so. The text of their self-government agreement provides the Sioux Valley Dakota Nation with precisely such a guarantee (INAC 2014, 9–10).

With the above guarantee in place, the Sioux Valley Dakota were prepared to move on to the more practical matter of removing themselves from *Indian Act* policy. The self-government agreement provides no recognition of sovereignty, but it does advance the nation's ambition to pass its own laws and to be recognized as a government by Canada and Manitoba. What the agreement does do, in other words, is "open new doors" for the development and empowerment of Sioux Valley Dakota people (Sioux Valley Dakota Nation 2018, 3). On these grounds, the agreement can be seen as a significant practical step in the larger quest of the Sioux Valley Dakota people to once again become a self-determining Indigenous nation. In its essentials, the agreement contains the following two defining elements.

First, much of the agreement is dedicated to establishing principles and practices for good governance. There are provisions for the recognition of the Sioux Valley Dakota Oyate Government as a legal entity and for the establishment of a government-to-government relationship between it and the governments of Canada and Manitoba. There are also provisions describing the nation's constitution, including details about the structures (including powers, authority, and duties), composition and membership, means of selection, conflict of interest rules, and accountability measures for its government. Taken together, the agreement provides guarantees that the self-governing institutions of the Sioux Valley Dakota Nation are to be free-standing, independent, and accountable in the first instance to its own members, all in accordance with the principles of democratic transparency and fairness.

Second, the agreement recognizes the right of the Sioux Valley Dakota Nation to exercise law-making power in over 50 subject areas (Sioux Valley Dakota Nation 2018, 2). These 50 areas of jurisdiction are all concerned with the internal affairs of the nation and contribute to its capacity for self-development and prospects for economic well-being. Some of the most important subject areas are citizenship, management of reserve lands, agriculture, natural resources (including water, forests, fish, and wildlife), the environment, culture, education, health, child and family matters, social development, regulation of business, taxation, traffic and transportation, public works, and justice. In each area of jurisdiction, when the Sioux Valley Dakota Nation chooses to pass a law, that law must be harmonized with existing federal or provincial laws and must also be exercised within the framework of the Canadian Constitution (Sioux Valley Dakota Nation 2016b, 6). While this requirement appears designed to constrain the nation's power in favour of Canada, for the most part it does not. According to the terms of the agreement, "harmonization" means that if there were to be a conflict between a Sioux Valley Dakota Nation law and either federal or provincial laws, in most subject areas relating to the internal life of the Sioux Valley Dakota the nation's law would prevail to the extent of the conflict.

The Sioux Valley Dakota Nation mobilized quickly to put their powers of self-government to work. Five subjects were initially identified priority areas in which to draft laws: health, child and family services, education, economic development, and lands (Clarke 2017, 4). The nation has since passed a number of laws relating to commercial development and land management, elections, and recreation and gaming (Sioux Valley Dakota Nation 2016d, 5–6). It has also acquired 80 acres of additional reserve land on which it has constructed a Petro-Canada station with plans to add a restaurant, hotel, commercial space for businesses, and a gaming and entertainment facility (Sioux Valley Dakota Nation 2016d, 4, 13). On the child welfare front, the nation established its own Child and Family Services Agency, in part to protect Sioux Valley Dakota children from being apprehended by outside authorities (Sioux Valley Dakota Nation 2016d, 7). Well-advanced plans are also underway to develop a traditional healing centre on the site of the former Brandon Residential School as well as to build a new school and educational facility (Sioux Valley Dakota Nation 2016d, 8,10).

In summary, because the Sioux Valley Dakota Nation exercises political power as a product of Canadian state authorization, its self-government agreement cannot be construed as accurately reflecting Indigenous sovereignty in action. However, the agreement does establish room for the Sioux Valley Dakota people to take greater control of their own destiny. And to the degree that the nation now has some tools to build a stronger, more accountable, self-sufficient, and prosperous community, it could also be said that the nation is rebuilding the foundations of its own sovereignty.

THE MÉTIS NATION OF ALBERTA

The Métis have long argued that they also have a right to self-determination as distinct peoples (Saunders and Dubois 2019, 3–8). They too have a distinct political history and were once in control of their political destinies. The Métis therefore insist "that they retain the right to govern themselves and, more generally, to control their social, cultural, and economic development" (RCAP 1996c, 113). The fact that the Métis have held on so tenaciously to their right to self-determination is verified by the historical record. In what is now called the province of Saskatchewan, for example, the Métis' historical claim to political autonomy on lands they long occupied resulted in disputes between the Métis and European settlers, escalating into the Métis resistance of 1885. The Métis point out that while their military resistance was short-lived, "the political struggle to protect Métis economic, social, and cultural values and goals has persisted" into the present (RCAP 1996c, 114; Saunders and Dubois 2019, 8–11).

In the mid-1800s, many Métis individuals settled in present-day Manitoba, particularly so in the Red River community. It is this historical community that is so often referred to as the birthplace of the Métis nation (Saunders and Dubois 2019, 8, 18–36). Unlike Indians, when the province of Manitoba came into existence in 1870, the Métis were granted no treaties or reserves. Instead, a scrip system was adopted in which Métis individuals were issued a certificate that could be redeemed for money or land. Importantly, however, scrip failed to provide the Métis with a land base or with the resources necessary to sustain their collective existence. Instead, more commonly, scrip passed into the hands of speculators and land was lost. These problems were magnified by a diminished food supply brought on by the extinction of the bison and by a climate of resentment directed against the Métis by Canadians for their role in the resistance (or as Canadians prefer to call it, the rebellion) of 1885. The Métis soon found themselves alienated and ostracized from Canadian society (Métis Settlements General Council 2017, 7). Finding themselves alone and destitute, some Métis "migrated west to join other Métis communities in central and northern Saskatchewan and Alberta" (Bell and Robinson 2008, 263).

Today, Alberta is the only province in Canada to have set aside land for the exclusive occupation and use by the Métis. In 1935, the Ewing Commission was established to look into Métis health, education, homelessness, and land issues in the province (Bell and Robinson 2008, 264; Saunders and Dubois 2019, 31). Among its recommendations was that 12 Métis Settlements be established to address the dire conditions of poverty and lack of economic opportunities suffered by the Métis. From the perspective of the commission, the Métis needed to make the transition to farming, and for that they needed land (Renke 2014, 6). The Métis, in turn, saw provision of a land base to be essential to protect their culture, distinctive lifestyle, and traditions, including hunting and trapping (Métis Settlements General Council 2017, 9). Of the 12 original settlements, eight still exist today.[6]

In 1990, the Métis and Alberta government signed the **Alberta–Métis Settlements Accord**. This Accord is dedicated to the pursuit of three goals: the protection of Métis land, the establishment of local self-government, and the provision of adequate financing through governmental transfers and access to resource revenues. Concerning land, the Accord provided for the legal transfer of land title from the province to the Métis, the land in turn to be controlled by a Métis General Council. The settlement lands comprise 1.25 million acres, all located in the north and central parts of Alberta. Approximately 8,000 Métis are members of the eight settlements.[7] Concerning governance, the Accord established that the basic institutions of governance would include eight Settlement Councils, a General Council, a Métis Settlements Appeal Tribunal, and the minister. And concerning finance, the Accord provided for provincial transfers, revenues from surface and subsurface resources, and own-source revenue generated through such measures as local taxation.

The Accord stands together with a co-management agreement in which the Métis Settlements and province jointly manage and receive royalties from oil, gas, and other subsurface resources located on settlement lands. The constitution of Alberta was also amended to lend specific recognition and protection to the Métis Settlements, including their rights to lands and resources (Gadacz 2006, 3). Importantly, as noted by Saunders and Dubois, "the Métis Settlements in Alberta remain the only governing entity to have powers recognized in provincial statute" (Saunders and Dubois 2019, 88).

The Accord is described by the Métis of Alberta as a pragmatic, results-oriented tool that they have used strategically to secure a land base for future generations, get local autonomy, and acquire the means for economic self-sufficiency (Métis Settlements General Council 2017, 16). But it is not the fulfillment of their ideal, nor, say Métis leaders, does the Accord represent the full realization of their Aboriginal rights. Indeed, the fact that the Accord is a product of delegated provincial legislation and that it does not enjoy constitutional protection at the national level speaks to its incompleteness. Métis leaders were therefore adamant that the Accord not be construed as the fulfillment of their Aboriginal rights nor that it be allowed to impact those rights negatively. In response, a clause was included in the *Constitution of Alberta Amendment Act, 1990* stating that the Métis Settlements legislation did not abrogate or derogate in any way from the Métis peoples' Aboriginal rights (Bell and Robinson 2008, 261). Only with this reassurance in hand were the Métis prepared to negotiate the acquisition of self-government powers under the laws of Alberta (Saunders and Dubois 2019, 148–9). In short, the Accord was seen to be an incremental step in the larger Métis journey to have their right to self-determination validated and protected by the Canadian state.

The eight Métis Settlements each have local governments called **Settlement Councils** consisting of five elected members who serve three-year terms. The councils make by-laws on matters of local governance as delegated to them by the province of Alberta. The by-laws govern the activity of members, non-members, and all companies operating on settlement land. All by-laws must not contravene laws made together with the other settlements, nor can they contravene provincial laws. Furthermore, a prerequisite for enactment is that all by-laws must be approved by the settlement membership at a general meeting (Graham 2007, 2, 5). As for jurisdiction, councils are responsible for the settlement's membership lists as well as for land management and allocation decisions. They also administer and deliver programs and services to their members, including core services (water, sewer, roads, fire protection), housing, social services, training, recreation, infrastructure development and maintenance, and economic development, among other things (Graham 2007, 5). While Settlement Councils carry many of the responsibilities typical of Canadian municipalities, responsibilities directed at the level of social and cultural services as well as economic development have them operating in ways more in keeping with a province.

Hovering over the eight Settlement Councils is a **Métis Settlement General Council** tasked with the responsibility of making law and policy in areas of collective interest to all eight settlements. The General Council is the sole political representative of the eight settlements to both the Alberta and Canadian governments. It is composed of 44 members, 40 being the elected councillors of the eight settlements and the remaining four being elected executive members. As the central government for the eight Métis Settlements, the General Council holds fee simple title to Métis settlement lands and has "the power to create new interests in that land" (Graham 2007, 3). As described by the General Council, its mandate "includes law making, land stewardship, resource management, financial management, and community development" (Métis Settlements General Council 2017, 35). Among its administrative functions, the General Council has responsibility for education and training, economic development, social services, and resource development and management (Métis Settlements General Council 2017, 35). As the coordinating governing body for all eight settlements, the laws and policies developed by the General Council are equally applied and binding on all settlements. Some suggest that the political relationship between the General Council and Settlement Councils is akin to federalism, and not unlike that which exists between Canada and its provinces (Graham 2007, 2, 23; see also Saunders and Dubois 2019, 61–73).

The Métis Settlement Councils and General Council have been empowered by Alberta provincial legislation to meet many of the Métis peoples' aspirations for political power. But it is also the case that those powers are subject to several significant constraints. In the first place, all Métis laws must be consistent with provincial laws. If Métis laws are found to be inconsistent with provincial law, it is provincial law that enjoys paramountcy in the sense that Métis law will be ruled of no effect to the extent of the inconsistency.[8] And second, all Métis law must be submitted to the provincial minister, who has the power to veto the law, or a portion of it, within 90 days. To date, the minister has not used this veto power. Nevertheless, the fact that the minister has this power of review indicates that the Alberta government regards Métis governments as junior to it and thus appropriately prohibited from exercising power that could jeopardize provincial interests.

Despite structural limitations, two notable features of the Métis Settlement governance system also suggest that the Métis political power base is increasing, as is its standing as an economic partner with the Alberta government. First, on the political front, the 1990 *Métis Settlements Act* made provision for a **Métis Settlements Appeal Tribunal**. The tribunal functions as a quasi-judicial body mandated to resolve disputes in the regular life and workings of the Métis Settlements. The primary focus of its work is to address disputes arising over membership in the settlements and land allocation decisions (Métis Settlements General Council 2017, 29). It also addresses matters relating to financial interests, property rights, and resource development. In the words of the General Council, "the mission of the tribunal is to contribute to the self-sufficiency of Métis life by providing resolution of issues affecting the progress of the Métis Settlements and individuals" (Métis Settlements General Council 2017, 29). In short, the tribunal contributes to Métis self-sufficiency by providing the settlements with an independent judicial body that is empowered to resolve conflicts that arise in the setting of their own self-governance.

And second, on the economic front, the **1990 Co-Management Agreement** between Alberta, the eight Métis Settlements, and the Métis

Settlement General Council established a protocol for subsurface mineral and oil exploration and development on Métis settlement lands. While Alberta retains ownership of subsurface resource title, the agreement provides the Métis Settlement Council with the power to set terms and conditions on tenure access to resources under their lands, including a right of veto. The kinds of terms and conditions that the Métis Settlement Council usually sets address concerns over environmental protection, respect for cultural artifacts, and assurances that Métis workers will be provided employment. But in addition, the agreement "also requires that successful bidders offer participation rights of up to 25 percent to the General Council and affected Settlement and commit to negotiating overriding royalties (which range from 3 to 10 percent)" (Bell and Robinson 2008, 272). These provisions were further strengthened through amendments negotiated into the agreement in 2013. Among the most important are (1) a guarantee that a 100 per cent owned Métis Settlement Corporation could bid on public postings of mineral leases as well as secure a direct purchase from Alberta Energy of a mineral lease outside of the public posting process; and (2) a guarantee that all bids in a public posting process must describe the benefits that the company proposes to the Métis settlement as a condition for putting forward a bid (Renke 2014, 10–12).

In short, the Co-Management Agreement between Alberta, the eight Métis Settlements, and the Métis Settlements General Council has contributed significantly to enhanced Métis economic prosperity as a result of the substantial revenues generated. But perhaps more important still, in partnership with Alberta, the Métis have found a way to control the pace and development of subsurface resources on settlement lands by bringing management of those resources under local Métis governmental control.

It is legislated agreements of the kinds described here that have contributed to the political and economic autonomy of the eight Alberta Métis Settlements. And further opportunities for enhanced autonomy may well lie ahead. It has long been the position of the federal government that while the Métis are an Aboriginal people under the Canadian Constitution and therefore possess Aboriginal rights, actual legislative responsibility for the Métis falls to the provincial governments. But the 2016 *Daniels* decision of the Supreme Court of Canada has likely changed all that (*Daniels v. Canada* 2016). In this decision, the Supreme Court determined that the Métis and non-status Indians are "Indians" for the purposes of Section 91(24) of the *Constitution Act, 1867*, and therefore a fiduciary duty is owed to them by the federal government just as it is owed to status Indians (Saunders and Dubois 2019, 132–4).

What fiduciary duty is owed to the Métis and non-status Indians by the federal government, however, is not yet clear. At minimum, the Supreme Court has said the duty requires that the federal government consult and negotiate with the Métis and non-status Indians in good faith. The duty may also include a right to enhanced programs and services. More promising yet, however, is the likelihood that this duty requires the federal government to negotiate in good faith the substantive meaning and content of the Aboriginal rights recognized and affirmed as belonging to the Métis and non-status Indians in Section 35 of the Constitution. And here too, some tentative steps have recently been taken. Under the terms of a ***Framework Agreement*** signed in late 2017, the federal government and the Métis of Alberta have agreed to negotiate such topics as Métis self-government, lands, rights, and consultation protocols (Government of Canada 2017a, 1; Saunders and Dubois 2019, 7, 80, 124–5, 135–8).

The Métis of Alberta have decided to accept the invitation to negotiate the substance of their rights as one prong in their overall strategy to rebuild Métis political autonomy. But operating alongside that rights agenda is the ongoing Métis commitment to practicality and pragmatism (Bell and Robinson 2008, 283). In the interest of expediency and achieving results, the Métis of Alberta also continue to petition for power and resources through provincial legislative agreements. And as has been demonstrated, this step-by-step approach to building Métis autonomy in specific areas of jurisdiction has contributed significantly to the Métis' quest for land security, increased autonomy, and economic opportunity, or, in a word, Métis self-determination (Bell and Robinson 2008, 278; Dubois and Saunders 2013, 205–7).

TREATY SELF-GOVERNMENT AGREEMENTS

A significant number of Indigenous nations are rebuilding their governments within the framework of the modern treaty process. Recent examples include the Yukon First Nations; the Nisga'a, Tsawwassen, and Maa-nulth First Nations of British Columbia; and the Tlicho of the Northwest Territories. In each of these cases, the model of self-government being recognized is not a product of legislation passed by either the federal or provincial governments. **Treaty self-government agreements** are products of negotiation in which it is understood that federal and provincial governments do not possess the power to change their terms. Because they are integral to treaty agreements, the self-government provisions can be changed only if agreed to by all signatories, including, most importantly, the Indigenous nation whose political power is validated under its terms.

Worth noting also is that all modern treaties concluded prior to 1995 did not have self-government provisions protected as Section 35 treaty rights within the *Constitution Act, 1982*. With the introduction of the 1995 federal government's inherent right to self-government policy, however, the federal government's policy position changed, largely in response to the political pressure of Indigenous leaders. The federal government agreed that all subsequent self-government agreements negotiated as part of a treaty package would become treaty rights protected under the terms of Section 35. Some suggest that the constitutional protection of treaty-based Indigenous self-government effectively establishes those Indigenous nations as a third order of Canadian government, equal in status to that of the provinces and the federal government (Malcolmson, Myers, Baier, and Bateman 2021, 70; Wilson-Raybould 2019, 57, 59). Whatever their status, it is certainly the case that Indigenous governments recognized within modern treaty agreements enjoy greater political and legal security than do *Indian Act* band governments or those Indigenous governments validated through federal or provincial legislation. Indeed, it could be said that by virtue of their constitutional protection from arbitrary internal interference, these Indigenous governments do enjoy a form of political sovereignty within Canada.

Treaty self-government agreements have not only provided Indigenous nations with constitutionally protected political powers, but also with significantly enhanced political standing relative to their *Indian Act* band counterparts. In the first place, treaties establish that the terms of the agreement itself will always prevail over federal, provincial, or territorial legislation. What this means is that treaties essentially occupy the legal position of constitutional law. They stand above and serve to constrain all acts of the Canadian Parliament as well as provincial and territorial legislatures. Second, treaties establish that Indigenous governments have extensive law-making powers. These typically address matters of internal interest to the Indigenous nation and include the power to do the following:

- develop their own constitutions along with governance structures;
- develop criteria for citizenship (or membership);
- make economic, social, and cultural policy (including housing, social welfare, health, and education);
- manage land and natural resources (including forestry, fishing, wildlife, water, and surface and subsurface resources);
- pass laws;
- administer justice;
- collect taxes; and
- establish relations with other levels of government.

In addition, in cases when Indigenous law conflicts with federal or provincial laws, treaties predetermine with a fair degree of regularity that Indigenous law will prevail to the extent of the conflict. And also, while the extent of governmental powers exercised under treaty closely follow the pattern established in legislated self-government agreements (e.g., the Sioux Valley Dakota Nation), there is one very important difference. Unlike legislated self-government agreements, treaty governance is to be exercised not only on reserve lands but also on what are termed treaty settlement lands. As reserves are generally very small, all treaties contain an additional land component, usually drawn from the Indigenous nations' traditional territories. Reserves are then absorbed into the treaty settlement lands, which, in turn, become the new and much larger territorial setting on which Indigenous self-government powers are to be exercised (Abele and Prince 2006, 576–9; Olthuis, Kleer, Townshend 2012, 172).

Of course, the treaty self-government agreements negotiated to date also carry with them structural limitations when measured against the criteria of sovereignty. For one thing, the Canadian government has adopted the practice of predetermining the range and extent of political powers that are available to Indigenous nations even before they enter into treaty negotiations. Generally speaking, powers are restricted to those termed essential to the internal life of the nation. While these criteria are not strictly cultural, they have imposed significant constraints on the range of eligible powers that can be negotiated. For example, in negotiations concluded to date, the federal government has simply decided that Indigenous nations need not exercise power in areas that "have a major impact on adjacent jurisdictions," nor in areas that are "the object of transcendent federal or provincial concern" (RCAP 1996a, 215; see also Papillon 2014, 119).

The federal government has also taken the position that while Indigenous nations possess an inherent right to self-government, that right cannot be operationalized until its scope and extent has been defined through a process of negotiation (Abele and Prince 2006, 578). On its surface, this requirement would seem to be an unjustifiable infringement on the inherent nature of that right. For if the right to self-government is truly inherent, then Indigenous nations should be free to exercise the right without having to first secure negotiated agreements with federal and provincial (or territorial) governments. But the federal government has decided otherwise. Its priority is to use treaties to integrate Indigenous nations into the Canadian constitutional order. And to do that effectively, it believes negotiations are a necessity (Starblanket 2019a, 19; Tully 2008, 285–6; Wilson, Alcantara, and Rodon 2020, 10, 27).

Some Indigenous nations may be (and indeed are) uninterested in pursuing their right to self-determination through treaty agreements precisely because of the constraints and limitations attached to the process as just identified (Abele and Prince 2006, 579; Green 2020, 249; Manuel 2015, 51–65; Papillon 2020, 222; Wilson, Alcantara, and Rodon 2020, 25). For other Indigenous nations, however, the treaty self-government process is seen as a political opportunity, even if a limited and not entirely satisfying one. For example, treaty self-governance establishes an opportunity for Indigenous nations to design their own political institutions in keeping with their ancient traditions of constitution-making should they so wish. Treaty self-governance also provides Indigenous nations with a bundle of significant powers and resources that take them well beyond those available under the *Indian Act* or legislated self-government agreements. In addition, treaty self-governance offers the practice of Indigenous governance constitutional protection as an Aboriginal right and in doing so insulates it from Canadian state interference. And finally, while treaty self-governance does lock Indigenous nations into the constitutional framework of the Canadian state, it also protects the Indigenous right to enjoy autonomy across an extensive range of jurisdiction that is integral to the life, identity, and well-being of Indigenous peoples (Eyford 2015, 37). Treaty self-government agreements, in other words, effectively establish Indigenous governments as independent third orders of government in the same way that the federal and provincial orders are independent from one another.

In sum, treaty self-government agreements constitute one additional (significantly more robust) option available to Indigenous nations in their quest to push back the reach of the Canadian state into their lives. They can be seen as another incremental step that Indigenous nations can take on the road to re-establishing their sovereignty. What follows examines the treaty self-government agreement negotiated by the Kluane First Nation in Yukon by way of example.

THE KLUANE FIRST NATION (YUKON)

The Kluane First Nation is one of 14 First Nations located in Yukon. It is a small First Nation whose administrative centre is located in the community of Burwash Landing on the Alaska Highway, 285 kilometres west of Yukon's capital, Whitehorse. The nation's traditional territory is concentrated in the southwest corner of Yukon, taking in the Ruby and Nisling mountain ranges to the northeast and the St. Elias mountains to the southwest. The heart of the nation's traditional territories contains Kluane Lake as well as the Tachal Region of Kluane National Park (Yukon Government n.d., 1). There are approximately 200 Kluane First Nation members, about half of whom live on settlement lands. A chief and council constitute the governing body of the nation, elected to a three-year term. The council consists of five members: one chief, two councillors-at-large, one youth councillor, and one elders' councillor.

The Kluane First Nation is one of 11 Yukon First Nations to have ratified both a land claims agreement and a self-government agreement with the federal and territorial governments.[9] The land claims and self-government agreements came into effect in 2004 and, while structurally separate, are intended to be complementary and mutually supportive of one another. The land claims agreement enjoys the protection of the Canadian Constitution as a Section 35 treaty right while the self-government agreement does not.[10] However, both serve as constitutional documents insofar as they set out the terms of the legal relationship that now exists between the Kluane First Nation and the governments of Canada and Yukon.

The Council of Yukon First Nations (formerly known as the Council of Yukon Indians) has represented the 14 First Nations at the comprehensive claims' negotiation table since 1973.[11] From the very beginning, the objective of the council was to retain significant portions of the Yukon First Nations' traditional territories, secure a substantial economic base through access to resources, and acquire broad powers of self-government. The council was determined that the outcome of negotiations must be a settlement that would guarantee the future prosperity of all 14 First Nations as well safeguard the right of each to decide their own futures (Morse 2008, 47). After a protracted and frustrating negotiation period of 20 years, the council, Yukon government, and Canadian government signed an Umbrella Final Agreement in May 1993. The Umbrella Final Agreement sets out common provisions that apply to all 14 Yukon First Nations. These provisions, in turn, formed the backdrop against which each of the Yukon First Nations, including the Kluane First Nation, negotiated their more customized land claims settlements and self-government agreements. As a general framework, the Umbrella Final Agreement provided the Yukon First Nations with 41,596 square kilometres of settlement land, including surface and subsurface resources; a cash settlement of $242,673,000; rights to both harvest and co-manage fish and wildlife across Yukon; the right to co-manage national parks and wildlife areas; protection of cultural and heritage resources; access to resource revenue sharing; and a range of economic and employment opportunities, including access to training (INAC n.d.b, 8; Jai 2014, 9; Morse 2008, 47; Nadasdy 2017, 20–5).

After the Umbrella Final Agreement was ratified in 1993, it took the Kluane First Nation another 10 years before it signed a land claims settlement and a self-government agreement. They were determined that the land base secured must be sufficient to rebuild the nation's capacity for self-sufficiency. To that end, the settlement provided the nation with

647 square kilometres of Category A land (meaning the nation owns both the surface of the land and the resources below it), and 259 square kilometres of Category B land (meaning the nation owns the surface of the land but not what is below the surface) (Yukon Government n.d., 3). Particularly striking, however, is the self-government agreement, which is structurally designed to adapt and grow over time. This same flexibility is built into the other 10 Yukon First Nation self-government agreements, which contain the following principles.

First, the self-government agreement identifies and protects a bundle of political powers that the Kluane First Nation takes to be consistent with its Aboriginal rights. But at the same time, the nation was firm in its position that its rights, titles, and interests extend well beyond the agreement and as such must not be constrained by its terms (Minister of Indigenous Affairs and Northern Development 2003, 3).

It is this understanding that lends flexibility to the language chosen to animate a pivotal clause. The language reads that if another Yukon First Nation achieves more favourable terms in its self-government agreement than did the Kluane First Nation, then at its request, the Yukon and federal government must agree to adapt the nation's agreement to bring it into conformity with those more favourable terms (Minister of Indigenous Affairs and Northern Development 2003, 5). The political intent here is clear. While the Kluane First Nation accepts that their Aboriginal rights inform the content of their agreement, they also insist that those rights be understood as standing behind and existing independently of it.

Second, the self-government agreement establishes that the Kluane First Nation's political power will be exercised through a government structure set out in the nation's constitution. To that end, the nation's constitution outlines the structure and responsibilities of five branches of government, including a general assembly, an elected council, an advisory elders council and youth council, and the Kluane First Nation Court (Yukon Government n.d., 3).[12]

Third, the agreement identifies three distinct forms of law-making power that the Kluane First Nation may exercise: (1) powers associated with the administration and operation of the nation's internal governmental affairs; (2) powers over cultural, health, social, child and family, educational, estate related, and dispute resolution programs and services delivered to citizens wherever they reside in Yukon; and (3) powers connected to the management, administration, control, and protection of settlement land, including over natural resources; activities associated with gathering, hunting, trapping, or fishing; licensing and regulation of businesses; and control of buildings including planning, zoning, and land development (Minister of Indigenous Affairs and Northern Development 2003, 13–15). While the third set of powers applies equally to Indigenous and non-Indigenous persons residing on the Kluane First Nation's settlement lands, it is the second set of powers that is particularly unique and innovative. These powers apply to Kluane First Nation members whether they reside on or off settlement land. Given that approximately half of the nation's members live elsewhere in Yukon, this provision means that, theoretically at least, these members can still enjoy programs and services delivered to them by their nation's government.

Fourth, where Kluane First Nation law-making power exists, it is almost always given paramountcy over the law-making power of the Yukon government. The *Kluane First Nation Self-Government Agreement* says that when the Kluane First Nation passes a law, "a Yukon Law of General Application shall be inoperative to the extent that it provides for any matter for which provision is made in a law enacted by the Kluane First Nation" (Minister of Indigenous Affairs and Northern Development, 2003, 17). With respect to the federal government, however, the agreement requires that the Kluane First Nation and federal government decide in future negotiations whose laws should prevail in the event of a conflict (Minister of Indigenous Affairs and Northern Development 2003, 16). The effect of the above clause, however, is to confer significant power on the Kluane First Nation at least in its relationship with the Yukon government.

Fifth, the Kluane First Nation has the power to tax those with interests on settlement land as well as the occupants and tenants on that land. The self-government agreement also provides opportunity for the nation to enter into tax-sharing arrangements with Canada and Yukon in areas of mutual interest and joint jurisdiction. While the ultimate goal of establishing a stable tax base is to assist the Kluane First Nation to become economically self-sufficient, its relatively small size makes that unlikely in the short term. Thus, the agreement sets up a system of transfer payments through a financial transfer agreement to be negotiated every five years. The objective of the transfer agreement is to ensure that the Kluane First Nation can provide its members "with public services at levels reasonably comparable to those generally prevailing in Yukon, at reasonably comparable levels of taxation" (Minister of Indigenous Affairs and Northern Development 2003, 25). From the vantage point of political autonomy, the wording here is important. It is not enough that Kluane First Nation members have access to comparable programs and services enjoyed by those living in Yukon. Rather, as put by Sari Graben and Matthew Mehaffey, what is important is "that the First Nation, as a government, has the resources to provide those services at comparable levels" (Graben and Mehaffey 2017, 170).

Taken together, the Kluane self-government agreement establishes the right of the Kluane First Nation to exercise an extensive range of powers. Because the Kluane First Nation is small, however, the agreement is designed to allow the nation to draw down its powers bit by bit, in keeping with the evolving needs and emerging policy priorities of its members. This is a positive feature of the agreement given that the Kluane First Nation now has extensive responsibilities over a significant portion of its traditional territories (Belanger 2018, 306).

Since ratifying the agreement, the Kluane First Nation leadership has proceeded carefully. It has chosen not to exercise its powers all at once, but instead draw powers down strategically and incrementally, as they build governance capacity over time. The Kluane First Nation has opted for a more traditional governance structure, represented, for example, by its commitment to an elders' council and youth council, both of which participate in political deliberations at the council level. In addition, the nation has been selective in its law-making and program delivery initiatives. Program delivery to date has focused on public works; housing; land and resource management; employment; recreation; community health and education; culture, language, and heritage; and enrolment and citizenship management. As for law-making powers, the nation has passed the *Kluane First Nation Income Tax Act* and the *Lands and Natural Resources Act*. It has also developed a strategic plan and an integrated community sustainability plan (2015).

In short, for the Kluane First Nation, their self-government agreement provides a road map with some reliable directions pointing the way back to sovereignty. While "self-government is a long-term work in progress," it nevertheless affords them the opportunity in the here and now to live a way of life more consistent with their values, culture, traditions, and identity (Coates and Morrison 2008, 112).

SOVEREIGNTIST POSITIONS

A feature shared by the three models of Indigenous self-government discussed to this point is that each is exercised within the framework of the Canadian political system. As we have seen, it is now a matter of federal policy that the Indigenous right to self-government is both recognized to be inherent to Indigenous peoples themselves and is accepted as enjoying legal protection under Section 35 of the *Constitution Act, 1982*. However, on one matter Canadian state actors have remained firm. Whether expressed in an expanded form of *Indian Act* band governance, legislated self-government agreements, or treaty self-government arrangements, each model is premised on the stipulation that emerging Indigenous governments are not to fundamentally disrupt the constitutional distribution of powers between the federal and provincial governments. Indigenous governments are to be empowered, to be sure, and this is now seen as a matter of fulfilling an Indigenous right. But the specific powers and jurisdiction of Indigenous governments are to be a product of negotiated agreements that each Indigenous government takes up with other affected governments, most typically federal, provincial, and territorial governments. What is essential from the perspective of Canadian state actors, in other words, is that Indigenous governments be integrated into the framework of the already existing Canadian constitutional order (Wilson, Alcantara, and Rodon 2020, 25; Tully 2008, 286).

However, some Indigenous leaders take the position that a requirement to negotiate the self-government in advance of exercising the powers associated with it is a fundamental violation of their inherent right to self-determination. If you are required to negotiate the specific scope and range of your political powers as a precondition to their existence, they ask, how can those powers be inherent? As an alternative, these Indigenous leaders favour a more robust approach that they believe is more in keeping with sovereignty's intentions, namely **treaty federalism**. This model injects the right to self-determination with a significantly greater amount of cultural, economic, legal, political, and jurisdictional content than do the other three models. More so than the other models, treaty federalism is also inspired by the distinct Indigenous legal and political traditions and constitutional orders that pre-date European contact (Abele and Prince 2006, 579–83; Ladner 2003, 55).

Treaty federalism begins from the premise that Indigenous nations do not need to enter into negotiations with the Canadian state to secure self-government arrangements because they are already sovereign. All they need do is assert their political autonomy and exercise what are already their (pre)existing Indigenous rights (Hunter 2006, 32; Wilson, Alcantara, and Rodon 2020, 25). An important legal implication naturally follows. On a constitutional level, what is required is a new constitutional order in which "Indigenous–state relations are premised on the notion that treaties are the defining elements of the Canadian federation" (White 2020, 8). That is, Indigenous constitutions should exist in a parallel relationship to the Constitution of Canada and not be subsumed within it as one of three domestic orders of government. The political ambition here, in other words, is to manufacture a reality in which Indigenous and Canadian constitutions operate side by side, separate but linked in nation-to-nation relationships like those both signified and intended by the Two-Row Wampum (Tully 2008, 286; Abele and Prince 2006, 579; Papillon 2020, 222).

Most Indigenous leaders who hold to this more robust position do not necessarily advocate for an Indigenous right to secession from Canada (although they might well support such a right in principle). In general, these leaders accept the proposition that there are benefits to be had through maintaining ongoing partnerships with federal, provincial, and territorial governments. What they do not accept, however, is the Canadian state's assertion to sovereignty over their peoples. Put simply, these leaders maintain that their peoples retain the right to self-determination within international law (Green 2014b, 26–30).

In many cases, the Indigenous ability to practise their right to self-determination has been profoundly compromised by the abusive and discriminatory policies of the Canadian state. It is therefore perfectly reasonable, say advocates of treaty federalism, that Indigenous people are within their rights to seize their political power back. They certainly are under no legal obligation to secure the permission of the Canadian state as a precondition to exercising their rights (Olthuis, Kleer, Townshend 2012, 182; Papillon 2020, 230). All they need to do (and indeed, are entitled to do) is assert their inherent powers and then begin exercising them. Once those assertions have been made, it may well be expedient for an Indigenous nation and federal, provincial, or territorial governments to decide together what that assertion means for their ongoing political partnerships. The Mohawk of Kahnawà:ke (Quebec) stand as an excellent illustration of this sovereigntist position in action.

THE MOHAWK OF KAHNAWÀ:KE (QUEBEC)

The Mohawk of Kahnawà:ke are located on a reserve approximately 15 kilometres southwest of Montreal on the south shore of the St. Lawrence River. Their reserve lands total about 12,000 acres (48 square kilometres). Kahnawà:ke has a population of approximately 11,000 people, of whom approximately 8,000 live on reserve. The name "kahnawà:ke" is derived from a word originating in the Mohawk language meaning "place of the rapids." The term refers to the location of the Mohawk village, which was beside rapids on the river before the St. Lawrence Seaway Canal was built. Kahnawà:ke is one of eight communities that make up the Mohawk Nation. The Mohawk Nation, in turn, is one of the six nations that constitute the Haudenosaunee (or Six Nations) Confederacy. The traditional territory of the Mohawk Nation extends over vast portions of what is now known as Ontario, Quebec, and the northeastern United States.

It is the position of the Mohawk that their traditional territories were never surrendered, which means that as far as they are concerned their title to the land remains intact (Mohawk Council of Kahnawà:ke 2016, 10). Land was lost over time due to non-Indigenous encroachment, including seizure of land for the building of railways, highways, bridges, hydroelectric and telephone lines, and a canal. In response, the Mohawk of Kahnawà:ke have pursued land claims, enjoying modest success recently with the return of 700 acres as compensation for land the province of Quebec expropriated in 1990 to construct Highway 30. The Mohawk have developed a reputation for being fierce defenders of their land. They have made it clear that they will not tolerate further encroachment on their lands and the way of life supported by it.

The Mohawk of Kahnawà:ke hold the position that they are a sovereign people independent from both Canada and the United States. Audra Simpson, a Mohawk scholar, describes the nature of this nationalist sentiment in particularly compelling language. She describes the Mohawk as a people whose political order has been strangulated by the forces of colonialism and whose land and sense of collective identity have been assaulted by the relentless march of Euro-Canadian settlement (Simpson 2014, 3). Despite damage perpetrated by colonial aggression, however, Simpson also explains that the Mohawk are a people whose identity has survived "conquest" and who now "do all they can to live a political life robustly, with dignity *as* Nationals" (Simpson 2014, 3). According to Simpson, rather than accept Canadian or American citizenship as if this were something to be desired, the Mohawk are inclined to refuse it, opting instead to do everything within their power to care for and defend their territory, their distinctive identity, and "the integrity of Haudenosaunee governance" (Simpson 2014, 7). Thus, despite the fact that the Mohawk are regulated at every turn by the uninvited priorities of a "foreign" Canadian government (e.g., the *Indian Act*, reserves, and the band council system), Simpson characterizes the Mohawk of Kahnawà:ke as a people who remain firm in their resolve to live as "nationals with sovereign authority over their own lives and over their membership" (Simpson 2014, 16). What follows identifies several instances of this sovereignty in action.

The Mohawk of Kahnawà:ke establish their credentials as a sovereign nation through the story they tell about themselves as a people both historically and in the present. The Haudenosaunee (People of the Longhouse), or Six Nations Confederacy (of which the Mohawk of Kahnawà:ke are a part), argue that for more than three centuries they have steadfastly upheld a commitment to intergovernmental relations that would see their Confederacy exist independently from Canada and the United States.[13] They claim that their Confederacy was sovereign prior to colonization, and that with the arrival of Europeans they entered into treaties and compacts with a number of states, including the Netherlands, Great Britain, France, and the United States. The fact that their Confederacy could (and did) enter into treaties with other states verifies its standing as a sovereign nation as set out in international law. The Haudenosaunee had (and continue to have) a permanent population, a defined territory, a governing structure, and the capacity to enter into relations with other states (Haudenosaunee n.d., 2).

The Mohawk point to the Two-Row Wampum as the symbolic representation of the criteria they employed when engaged in international treaty-making with other states such as Britain (later Canada) and the United States. The two rows of purple wampum represent two vessels travelling side by side down the river of life, neither vessel crossing into the path of the other. The fact that the two vessels travel together represents that they are allies, sharing in the abundance that the river has to offer. The fact that the vessels do not cross into the path of the other and that neither crew seeks to steer the other's vessel, however, establishes a strict code of non-interference and a corresponding policy of mutual respect for the independence and sovereignty of each party to the treaty (Haudenosaunee n.d., 2).

It is this tradition of political non-interference that informs much of the Mohawk's sovereigntist position today. The Mohawk have certainly experienced a profound level of colonial interference into their way of life, a clear violation of Britain's (and then Canada's) promises not to try to steer the Mohawk's vessel. The task now, as the Mohawk of Kahnawà:ke see it, is to purge themselves of their colonial status and regain their standing as an autonomous sovereign nation (Hunter 2006, 34). Furthermore, in keeping with the Two-Row Wampum tradition, this autonomy should not come as enhanced political power within the Canadian state system, but rather as power that operates outside of it, parallel to and alongside Canada, in a nation-to-nation relationship.

Despite the best of intentions, however, the Mohawk Council of Kahnawà:ke suffers from a legitimacy crisis because it is a product of federal legislation and because the power it exercises is delegated to it by the Canadian government. This crisis is so severe that voter turnout for chief and council elections typically registers at only about 25 per cent (Curtis 2018, 2). As observed by Christopher Curtis, many among the Mohawk of Kahnawà:ke "take sovereignty so seriously they believe voting in a band council election would only legitimize Canada's authority over Kahnawà:ke" (Curtis 2018, 2). Essentially, the Mohawk Council is seen by many within the nation as little more than an administrative arm of the Canadian state because it is the instrument through which the federal government distributes funding.

In place of the *Indian Act* band council system, many prefer instead the Mohawk's original pre-contact governance processes, the Haudenosaunee Longhouse tradition. The Longhouse is an ancient form of government created by the Six Nations and was integral to the way of life promoted by the then politically sovereign Haudenosaunee Confederacy. The system was a complex one, involving Haudenosaunee governments operating at three different levels: federal via a Grand Council of Chiefs (the Haudenosaunee Confederacy); national via each member nation's Council Fire (the Mohawk); and territorial via each local Longhouse (Kahnawà:ke) (Haudenosaunee n.d., 2). Under the territorial Longhouse system, clan mothers representing the three clans of the Mohawk of Kahnawà:ke (Turtle, Wolf, and Bear) nominated chiefs from within their clan for life-long service. In close consultation with their clan members, and working by consensus, the chiefs were responsible for presiding over the political affairs of the people as well as facilitating seasonal ceremonies, all according to the Great Law of Peace (Deer 2011, 1).

While the two governance systems operate side by side today, it is the Mohawk Band Council that receives the harshest criticism given its origin in the *Indian Act* and the stigma it carries as a product of colonial imposition. In keeping with their sovereignty, the Mohawk of Kahnawà:ke are more generally inclined to support the governance structure that was the source of their autonomy in the first place – the Haudenosaunee Longhouse tradition. To it legitimacy is bestowed because it is seen as the "local custodian of the sovereignty which the Confederacy provides" (Deer 2011, 1). Consequently, primary responsibility for all political matters relating to land, citizenship, justice, and the economy ought to fall to it, or so Mohawk nationalists would argue (Deer 2011, 2).

Even so, the reality is that the Mohawk band council is the only governance structure recognized by the federal government and, as such, it is to that structure that many of the Mohawk of Kahanawà:ke must turn if they are to have their daily needs met. Band councillors are also fully aware that they operate within an environment in which their credibility as a governing body is constantly in question. As a result, band council has worked hard to acquire political legitimacy by "rejecting on principle … the legal status of the Indian Act as a sponsoring institution," choosing instead to conduct itself as though it were the government of a sovereign Indigenous nation" (Haslip 2002, para. 53). Two policy areas that provide an excellent illustration of this sovereigntist approach in action are the Kahnawà:ke Membership Law and the Mohawk Council's decision to cultivate cannabis on their territory.

The Membership Law of the Mohawk of Kahnawà:ke decrees that non-Indigenous people cannot live on their territory and that all Mohawk who marry or live common law with persons from outside of the nation lose the right to live in Kahnawà:ke (Simpson 2014, 62). The Mohawk are quick to point out that this policy is inconsistent with their traditional historical practices, which regularly had them integrating adoptees and marriage partners from outside into their nation (Simpson 2014, 48). However, those who defend the Kahnawà:ke Membership Law argue that the measures contained within it are essential to protect Mohawk culture and identity from further erosion (Alfred 1995, 164). According to this view, if non-Indigenous persons are permitted to live on Kahnawà:ke territory, Mohawk identity will eventually be "diluted" right out of existence. Community boundary maintenance, therefore, is seen as an essential defence against further assimilation. Defenders of the membership code also raise the matter of scarce resources. If all 1,200 Mohawk women who regained legal status in 1985 were permitted to return, the already strained resources of the Kahnawà:ke Mohawk would simply be overwhelmed. There is simply not enough land, housing, or programs and services to go around. So, while its Membership Law is both rigid and exclusive, its defenders argue that it can be justified on the grounds that it plays an important role in ensuring the survival of the Kahnawà:ke

Mohawk as a distinctive people and nation (Alfred 1995, 164).

Furthermore, as a sovereign people, the Mohawk of Kahnawà:ke also assert that they are perfectly within their rights to decide who is entitled to take up membership within their nation and who is not (Simpson 2014, 63). Thus, when in June 2018 a Quebec Superior Court Justice declared that the "marry out, get out" provision of the Membership Law violated the Canadian *Charter of Rights and Freedoms*, the Mohawk band council was quick to respond. In true sovereigntist fashion, Grand Chief Joe Norton said, "obviously, we maintain the position that matters so integral to our identity have no business in outside courts." At the same time, however, Norton was willing to offer some concession to the Canadian state, saying that now that a decision had been rendered, the Mohawk Council would be willing to take some time to study the decision (Hamilton 2018). And interestingly, in a corresponding concession to the political authority of the Mohawk Council, the judge admitted that the council "has a duty to govern on its reserve" and therefore "must be allowed to fix its own law" (Everett-Green 2018, 2).

As is the case for so many Indigenous nations across Canada, the Mohawk of Kahnawà:ke rely heavily on federal government funding to finance quality programs and services for their members. In an effort to secure greater self-sufficiency, the Mohawk Council is constantly in search of socio-economic opportunities that can deliver stable and reliable self-generated revenue. One such economic opportunity has come by way of the Liberal government's legalization of cannabis in the fall of 2018. The Mohawk Council has spearheaded an initiative to establish a 50,000-square-foot state-of-the-art cannabis greenhouse facility. An additional 20,000 square feet will eventually be added and will be dedicated to post-harvesting processing activities. Canadian company Canopy Growth has been contracted to purchase 100 per cent of the cannabis produced (Mohawk Council of Kahnawà:ke 2018, 1). The company will use its established brand and distribution channels to sell the product and in the process of doing so generate significant revenue for the nation. The facility will also provide significant employment to the nation by generating approximately 75 full-time jobs (Mohawk Council of Kahnawà:ke 2018, 2).

From the vantage point of sovereignty, what makes this initiative so interesting is the fact that the Mohawk Council declared it would not abide by Quebec's system of government-run and -taxed production facilities, nor would it accept outside regulation. Instead, the cannabis producer would be required to hold a local Kahnawà:ke licence and must follow Kahnawà:ke's internal licensing procedures. In short, what the Mohawk of Kahnawà:ke have done is move forward independently to capitalize on a potentially highly lucrative economic opportunity. In keeping with its assertion to sovereignty, the Mohawk Council acted unilaterally, justifying its actions as any sovereign nation would; namely, it is motivated to act to in the best interests of its people.

THE PRIORITY OF TREATY FEDERALISM?

There are some commentators who would argue that among the four models of self-government outlined, treaty federalism is the only honourable option available to Indigenous peoples. Treaty federalism is privileged because, according to this view, it is premised on the idea that the treaties establish nation-to-nation relationships in which a robust set of Indigenous rights are reserved for Indigenous nations while other specifically identified rights are delegated by Indigenous nations to the Crown. According to scholars like Kiera Ladner, for example, it is this historical approach that is the most viable one for today because it is unique among all models in giving credence to the priority of Indigenous rights (Ladner 2003, 57). Only it possesses the sophistication and depth required to ensure that the decolonization process is one in which a genuine recalibration of political power occurs between Canada and Indigenous nations. As Ladner explains it, treaty federalism provides the means for Canada to realize "that it is just one of many nations with which power and resources must be shared" (Ladner 2003, 56).

All other self-government models fall short by these standards because they are said to involve an extraordinarily high level of compromise. Traditional Indigenous territories are relinquished, political power and jurisdiction is forfeited, and Indigenous citizenship is constrained by the compulsory application of Canadian state instruments like the *Charter of Rights and Freedoms* and the Criminal Code. In essence, the other models offer Indigenous peoples little more than municipal-like self-administration framed within a consolidated Canadian state relationship that preserves the colonial dominance of federal and provincial governments over Indigenous lands, resources, and people (Murphy 2005, 12). Faced with options such as these, which are viewed as offering little of substantive depth, critics urge Indigenous leaders to await better offers containing real substance. Not to do so, argues Taiaiake Alfred, is to submit to "an advanced form of control, manipulation, and assimilation" (Alfred 2009, 144).

I believe that this type of criticism is important because it compels Indigenous and non-Indigenous political leaders alike to squarely face the question about what power and resources Indigenous nations are entitled to if their right to self-determination is to be met. In this sense, the treaty federalism model serves as an important normative reference point against which to judge the merits of the various other approaches to Indigenous self-government.

What does not follow in my view, however, is that in each and every case the Indigenous approach to self-government must possess the attributes of treaty federalism to meet the standard of self-determination. For example, Article 3 of the UNDRIP reads: "Indigenous peoples have the right to self-determination. By virtue of that right they freely determine their political status and freely pursue their economic, social, and cultural development." Noticeably absent in this formulation is any requirement that the right to self-determination must conform to some predetermined substantive outcome. Rather, what is essential is that the approach used to animate the Indigenous right to self-determination be the outcome of an equitable process in which the members of the Indigenous nation have offered their full consent. Treaty federalism, therefore, may constitute one among a range of models that Indigenous nations might wish to pursue in their quest to restore their original sovereignty. But other approaches may be no less legitimate. Where appropriate, more modest steps in keeping with an Indigenous nation's needs and priorities may also be taken. These could include enhanced band responsibilities, legislated self-government agreements, and constitutionally protected treaty arrangements, among others.

As noted by Ken Coates and P.G. McHugh, while several models are undoubtedly a product of historical imposition, "they do not necessarily negate the aboriginal right to self-government" (Coates and McHugh 1998, 139). Instead, as they explain, "especially where it can be shown that aboriginal practice has adaptively reconfigured itself about imposed forms," while also drawing legitimacy for that practice from within the Indigenous nation, the model that an Indigenous nation "may select is not necessarily a qualification upon, so much as a manifestation of, its entitlement to self-determination" (Coates and McHugh 1998, 138, 139). Understood in this way, it could be said that in those cases where a negotiated outcome between Canada and an Indigenous nation enhances Indigenous political power, in those same cases Indigenous peoples are simultaneously provided with a degree of *de facto* sovereignty because they move yet further away from Canadian state control.

THE GENDERED DYNAMICS OF POWER

One final question merits our attention. As discussed, the politics of Indigenous self-government employs the normative language of original occupancy, inherent rights to self-determination, and treaty entitlements to carve out political space within the Canadian state for the expression of Indigenous political autonomy. Here, what Indigenous leaders seek to do is challenge the monopoly of political power that the Canadian state has both unilaterally and illegitimately imposed on their peoples. No less important, however, is the matter of self-government and the standing of Indigenous citizens within their nations. Here, the voices of Indigenous minorities, including those of Indigenous women, demand our attention.

A gendered analysis reveals that the politics of Indigenous self-government is no remedy to colonial dispossession unless it is accompanied by efforts to address the destructive presence of power imbalances within Indigenous nations. To that end, Indigenous feminists compel us to confront two pressing challenges. First, the politics of self-government must confront the presence of patriarchy and the degree to which its practices have excluded Indigenous women from their home communities, political power and influence, and access to the basic social and economic resources they need, including that of personal safety. Second, the politics of self-government can succeed only to the degree that the collective Indigenous right to self-determination is held together with the individual right of Indigenous women (and other minorities) to full participatory status and equal political standing within their nations. There is no self-government, in other words, if Indigenous women are denied the means to exercise the community power and influence to which they are entitled. Indeed, I would argue that self-government is authentic only to the degree that it involves all eligible members.

Indigenous feminist analysis shows us that the forces of colonization resulted not only in the loss of Indigenous political sovereignty, lands, and resources, but also the loss of Indigenous identity due to "the imposition of Western gender roles and patriarchal social structures" on Indigenous peoples (Huhndorf and Suzack 2010, 2). The results have been nothing short of catastrophic. As Gina Starblanket and Heidi Stark explain, "the imposition of Western gender ideals … aimed to distort Indigenous notions of identity [in order] to render them legible to (and easier to regulate within) colonizing orders" (Starblanket and Stark 2018, 184). Commentators usually target the *Indian* Act for particular condemnation here given its imposition of Victorian standards of patriarchy that both displaced and devalued the traditional positions and roles of Indigenous women within their communities. Through the *Indian Act*, Indigenous women often found themselves dispossessed, relegated to positions of even greater inferiority than those that had been imposed on Indigenous men. Only women, for example, risked loss of Indian status, band membership, and their reserve home if opting to "marry out" of their Indigenous communities.

Indigenous feminists then go on to show how many of these historical patterns of exclusion became entrenched and exist into the present day. As described by Rauna Kuokkanen, "the reality in indigenous communities today is that the internalization of patriarchal colonial structures has resulted in circumstances where women often do not enjoy the same level of rights as men" (Kuokkanen 2012, 233). Put differently, while all Indigenous people are victimized by the forces of colonization, it is Indigenous women who have to bear the additional burden of oppression through patriarchy. Faced with a denial of their rights as both Indigenous persons and as women, it is women in particular who suffer the violence associated with both racism and sexism. Indigenous feminist literature features the various manifestations of this structural violence as central to much of its analysis. Much of the literature, for example, seeks to identify the root causes of and provide remedies for the physical and sexual abuse, social and political marginalization, and crushing conditions of poverty that are the daily lived experiences of so many Indigenous women (National Inquiry into MMIWG 2019; see also Green 2017b, 5).

For the purposes of this chapter, the important point I wish to underscore is that Indigenous feminist critiques also target patriarchal power and oppression as it relates to Indigenous self-government (Starblanket 2017, 24). What commentators have noticed is that contemporary Indigenous women not only struggle against patriarchal and colonial oppression within Canadian society, but also within their own communities (Green 2017b, 10). Indigenous women often say they have to contend with an entrenched male political elite and hierarchy of chief and council that often fail to put the social issues of greatest concern to women at the top of their agenda. It is as though sexual inequality and the problem of domestic and sexual abuse is not even seen by some of the Indigenous male leadership as integral to the liberation of Indigenous peoples. Instead, as noted by Kim Anderson, feminist concerns are sidestepped in favour of the purportedly bigger issues associated with decolonization, sovereignty, and nation-building (Anderson 2010, 84, 85; see also Schouls 2003, 94). But as Anderson argues, "in spite of our efforts to achieve self-determination since the middle of the twentieth century, the lives of Indigenous women continue to be plagued by violence and poverty." Consequently, she, along with many other Indigenous women, insist that "contrary to the trickle-down logic that says Indigenous women's lives will improve when we address the bigger issues," we must instead "seriously address the political, social, and economic inequities faced by Indigenous women, [or] we will never achieve full healing, decolonization, and healthy nation building" (Anderson 2010, 85; see also Borrows 2016, 188–9; Green 2017b, 12, 16; Schouls 2003, 94, 97; Starblanket 2017, 23; St. Denis 2017, 58). Arguments such as these have only been further substantiated by the analysis contained within the 2019 final report of the National Inquiry into Missing and Murdered Indigenous Women and Girls and its sweeping set of 231 recommendations, aptly named Calls to Justice. In short, Indigenous feminists insist that protecting the individual rights of Indigenous women to safety, health, and well-being is "a condition for sustainable and strong collective self-determination" (Kuokkanen 2012, 247). They conclude that one simply cannot occur in the absence of the other.

An important implication for the operation of sovereignty and the politics of Indigenous self-government naturally follows.[14] In order to be authentic, the practice of sovereignty (understood as the Indigenous right to be self-defining) must be an inclusive and broadly participatory one. Indigenous feminists instruct us that self-government simply cannot be the answer to the oppression that women face unless women have access to political power and influence equal to that of Indigenous men. They must, in other words, have equal status and influence within their nations and they must have equal rights to full participation in the decision-making processes of their lives, including that of governance structures (Borrows 2016, 187). Outside of full participatory rights, Indigenous women are justifiably fearful that the implementation of self-government may only entrench existing abuses of power, male elitism, and infringement of individual rights (Green 2017b, 15). The remedy to political exclusion is thus an accountable leadership that addresses women's issues through broadly consultative community processes and an open political process that invites the full participation of women (Borrows 2016, 187). Naturally, Indigenous women share concerns about lands, resources, self-government, and treaties with the entrenched Indigenous leadership (Starblanket 2017, 23). But what many Indigenous women insist on in addition is that all Indigenous citizens, including women, should have the same political rights within their nations, including "to vote, to run for office, to assemble, to speak freely, and most significantly, to exercise influence in the communal self-definition process" (Schouls 2003, 99; see also Kuokkanen 2012, 236–7).

It is not my intention to suggest that the exercise of self-government by the Indigenous nations described earlier in this chapter are remiss in their responsibility to include women in their power structures. Indeed, a quick review of the composition of each nation's chief and council in 2023 reveals that while men form the majority in all but one case, women are also noticeably present without exception. My point is simply to suggest that all exercises of self-government, whether through band governance, legislated or treaty self-government agreements, or direct declarations of political autonomy, must meet one further criterion to qualify as true exercises in sovereignty. Wherever inequitable internal relations exist, they must be transformed into equitable ones that extend to women (and other minorities) a genuine sharing of community political power. Indigenous nations, in other words, "must extend to their members the same power and influence of self-definition that they demand for their communities more generally within Canada" (Schouls 2003, 163). As put by Rauna Kuokkanen, "if women are not surviving as individuals in their communities due to physical or structural violence, collective survival as a people is also inevitably called into question" (Kuokkanen 2012, 247–8).

CONCLUSION

The political relationship between Indigenous nations and the Canadian state remains a troubled one. The legacy of a colonial dynamic in which Indigenous nations were refused a place in the original exercise of building Canada casts a long shadow over their relations today. So, when the Canadian government now professes to want to get rid of the *Indian Act* and restore the original pre-Confederation nation-to-nation relationship, many Indigenous leaders are naturally suspicious, believing that such overtures amount to little more than renewed attempts to modify, constrain, or extinguish their original sovereignty. What the Canadian government puts forward as a genuine overture at reconciliation, in other words, Indigenous leaders often see as just another attempt to subsume and domesticate their nations within a colonial political order. While Canadian political leaders may well be willing to negotiate the release of some political powers to Indigenous nations, they seem less than willing to initiate a radical reconfiguration of Canadian state sovereignty.

As this chapter has demonstrated, however, incremental steps have been taken in shifting power relations between Indigenous nations and the Canadian state. Moreover, while gradual, these shifts have acquired momentum over time. There can be no doubt that the Canadian state has not been enthusiastic about giving up its illegally acquired power, nor has it been quick to concede lands, resources, and jurisdictions that have belonged to Indigenous nations since time immemorial. Nevertheless, through sheer determination and hard work, the Indigenous goal of restoring their right to self-determination is gradually taking shape.

Indigenous peoples have been active in defining what their right to self-determination entails. Moreover, as we have seen, this proactive exercise in asserting their rights has been played out in multiple locations. Some Indigenous nations seek as a first step to expand their *Indian Act* powers to the maximum degree possible while simultaneously pursuing avenues to add jurisdiction that takes them beyond the parameters of the *Indian Act*. Other Indigenous nations pursue legislated self-government agreements as a way to rebuild their communities, while still others pursue self-government within the framework of modern treaties. And then there are those Indigenous nations who regard all three approaches to be too limited, so they choose to pursue more robust sovereigntist models. The point is that Indigenous self-government can take many forms, all in keeping with the distinct settings, needs, capacities, expectations, and ambitions of individual Indigenous nations as they lay claim to their inherent rights over time. And as each Indigenous nation asserts the political power that has always been theirs by right, they also take deliberate steps to reshape their relationship with the Canadian state.

In sum, Indigenous nations will not be denied political power. In many instances, Indigenous nations now have control over their own land, they now participate with Canada in the management of resources, and they now have law-making jurisdiction over many of those matters that are integral to their identity and sense of collective well-being. In short, Indigenous peoples are increasingly coming to occupy the spaces in between the exercise of Canadian state sovereignty. They now exercise powers of self-government that are, and always were, their own. Indigenous nations are rebuilding their political sovereignty within Canada, and Canada is undergoing a fundamental political transformation as a result.

DISCUSSION QUESTIONS

1 What do you make of the suggestion that band council structures can be used as tools to increase the Indigenous capacity for self-determination? Is this a fundamentally misguided notion?
2 Do legislated self-government agreements provide Indigenous nations with political powers to take them beyond the *Indian Act*? Or do such agreements represent a fundamental capitulation to the forces of colonialism?
3 Do self-government agreements as found in the Kluane First Nation's treaty represent a genuine step forward in restoring Indigenous nations to a position of sovereignty? Why might some judge these treaties to fall well short of the sovereignty standard? Do you agree?
4 Should all Indigenous nations in Canada seek to replicate the approach to self-determination taken by the Mohawk of Kahnawà:ke? Is this approach the truest and most meaningful expressions of sovereignty taken by Indigenous nations to date?
5 Is Indigenous self-determination possible only if violence against Indigenous women and girls is addressed first?

SUGGESTED READINGS

Abele, Frances, and Michael J. Prince. 2006. "Four Pathways to Aboriginal Self-Government in Canada." *American Review of Canadian Studies* 6 (4).

Belanger, Yale D. ed. 2008. *Aboriginal Self-Government in Canada: Current Trends and Issues*, 3rd ed. Saskatoon, SK: Purich Publishing.

———. 2018. "Self-Government." In *Ways of Knowing: An Introduction to Native Studies in Canada*, 3rd ed. Toronto: Nelson Education.

Borrows, John. 2016. "Chapter 5. Legislation and Indigenous Self-Determination in Canada and the United States." In *Freedom and Indigenous Constitutionalism.* Toronto: University of Toronto Press.

Cassidy, Frank, and Robert L. Bish. 1989. *Indian Government: Its Meaning in Practice.* Lantzville and Halifax: Oolichan Books and The Institute for Research on Public Policy.

Frideres, James S. 2020. "Chapter 10. Aboriginal Rights, Self-Government, and the Inherent Rights of Indigenous Peoples." In *First Nations in the Twenty-First Century,* 3rd ed. Toronto: Oxford University Press.

Irlbacher-Fox, Stephanie. 2009. *Finding Dahshaa: Self-Government, Social Suffering, and Aboriginal Policy in Canada.* Vancouver: UBC Press.

Ladner, Kiera. 2003. "Rethinking Aboriginal Governance." In *Reinventing Canada: Politics of the 21st Century,* edited by Janine Brodie and Linda Trimble. Toronto: Prentice Hall.

Papillon, Martin. 2014. "The Rise (and Fall?) of Aboriginal Self-Government." In *Canadian Politics,* 6th ed., edited by James Bickerton and Alain-G. Gagnon. Toronto: University of Toronto Press.

Papillon, Martin, and André Juneau, eds. 2015. *Canada: The State of the Federation 2013, Aboriginal Multilevel Governance.* Montreal: McGill-Queen's University Press.

Poelzer Greg and Ken S. Coates. 2015. "Chapter 12. Aboriginal Self-Government." In *From Treaty Peoples to Treaty Nation: A Road Map for All Canadians.* Vancouver: UBC Press.

Saunders, Kelly, and Janique Dubois. 2019. *Métis Politics and Governance in Canada.* Vancouver: UBC Press.

Wilson, Gary N., Christopher Alcantara, and Thierry Rodon. 2020. *Nested Federalism and Inuit Governance in the Canadian Arctic.* Vancouver: UBC Press.

NOTES

1 The programs and services the Squamish Nation provides to its members include child and family services; employment and training; human resources; communications and band member services; finance and technology; recreation; community operations; health services; Squamish Valley operations; education; housing and capital projects; and registry, membership, and lands (Squamish Nation 2015, 12).

2 In fact, the Squamish band council election of 2017 saw the return of a council that in its majority opposed the proposed Woodfibre LNG plant. That said, construction of the plant and terminal facility began in September 2023, while pipeline construction is projected for completion by the end of 2026.

3 Indigenous and Northern Affairs Canada documents that legislated self-government negotiations are also underway with the Miawpukek First Nation of Conne River (Newfoundland and Labrador); the Cree Nation of Quebec; the Anishinabek Nation of Ontario;

the Akwesasne of Ontario and Quebec; the Nishnawbe Aski Nation of Ontario; and the Whitecap Dakota Nation of Saskatchewan. See INAC n.d.b.

4 Indigenous and Northern Affairs documents that self-government negotiations that have recently either ceased or been placed in hiatus include those with the Nunavik Regional Government (Quebec); the Mi'gmaq Nation of Gespeg (Quebec); the Fort Frances Tribal Area First Nations (Ontario); the Blood Tribe (Alberta); and the Meadow Lake First Nations (Saskatchewan). See INAC n.d.b.

5 The self-government agreement was ratified by 64 per cent of the Sioux Valley Dakota Nation's membership in a referendum held in 2012.

6 In the late 1950s, four of the settlements were closed. These were Touchwood, Marlboro, Cold Lake, and Wolf Lake.

7 The eight settlements are Paddle Prairie, Peavine, Gift Lake, East Prairie, Buffalo Lake, Kikino, Elizabeth, and Fishing Lake.

8 John Graham notes that the one exception to the provincial paramountcy rule is in the area of hunting, fishing, trapping, and gathering. In these areas a General Council policy can have priority over provincial legislation, but only if the policy is approved by the provincial cabinet. See Graham 2007, 18.

9 Despite considerable efforts, three Yukon First Nations have not reached land claims or self-government agreements. They are White River First Nation, Ross River Dena Council, and the Liard First Nation.

10 The Yukon land claims negotiation process began in 1973, just as the federal government was developing its comprehensive land claims policy but well before its policy on the inherent right to self-government was introduced. Consequently, early comprehensive land claims settlements received the status of treaties and thus constitutional protection while self-government agreements did not.

11 The 14 Yukon First Nations are Carcross Tagish First Nation, Champagne and Aishihik First Nation, Kluane First Nation, Kwanlin Dun First Nation, Liard First Nation, Little Salmon Carmacks First Nation, Na-Cho Nyak Dun First Nation, Ross River Dena Council, Selkirk First Nation, Ta'ankwach'an Council, Teslin Tlingit Council, Tr'ondek Hwech'in First Nation, Vuntut Gwitchin First Nation, and White River First Nation.

12 The Kluane First Nation has also established six departments to provide programs and services to its members: Housing and Public Works; Lands, Resources, and Heritage; Wellness and Education; Executive; Governance; and Finance.

13 The Six Nations of the Haudenosaunee Confederacy include the Mohawk, Oneida, Onondaga, Cayuga, Seneca, and Tuscarora.

14 The material in this and the following paragraph draws heavily from Schouls 2003, especially Chapters 4 and 6.

CHAPTER 9

Partnerships: Shared Ventures, Shared Sovereignty

LEARNING OBJECTIVES

1. To explain how the Truth and Reconciliation's Calls to Action can serve as moral guides to heal Indigenous nations and restore Indigenous power.
2. To critically evaluate the utility of incremental treaty agreements as tools to rebuild the capacity of Indigenous nations.
3. To compare and contrast UNDRIP's principle of "free, prior, and informed consent" with the Supreme Court of Canada's principle of "duty to consult and accommodate" and to explain the differences between them.
4. To describe what impact and benefits agreements are and to discuss the degree to which they can contribute to rebuilding Indigenous sovereignty.
5. To evaluate the merit of arguments suggesting that impact and benefits agreements are designed to undervalue the participation and interests of Indigenous women.
6. To assess whether economic development and shared economic ventures with non-Indigenous partners can serve as building blocks to Indigenous autonomy.
7. To explain what co-management initiatives are and to assess whether they can contribute to a renewed political relationship between Indigenous nations and the Canadian state.

Indigenous peoples have long held the position that their political relationship with the Canadian state must be predicated on recognition of their right to self-determination. While Indigenous peoples do not insist that this right is absolute, many do insist that the right entitles them to a renewal of their treaty relationships, functional forms of government that advance genuine self-determination, and renewed nation-to-nation relationships with the Canadian state. They must, as a matter of rights, be able to determine the political direction of their own lives free of external constraint, and they must be able to negotiate the terms of their political relationships with Canada based on the premise of mutual consent. The topics taken up thus far in this book have been primarily directed at these relatively high-profile arenas, where the Indigenous right to self-determination has been most persistently advanced.

At the same time, some important changes have also been taking place at the more indirect level of local, day-to-day Indigenous governance. It is my contention that while not without their problems, these changes have had the cumulative effect of tilting the relationship between Indigenous governments and the Canadian state toward solidifying the Indigenous right to self-determination. These developments come in the form of intergovernmental partnerships and shared ventures and have emerged in response to the undeniable reality that Indigenous peoples have rights and that those rights must be accommodated. Taken together, these developments usually involve transfers of power in targeted areas from the Canadian state to Indigenous governments. The interactions that result sometimes lead directly to greater Indigenous autonomy while at other times to more collaborative decision-making approaches between Canadian and Indigenous governments (Alcantara and Morden 2019, 252). The objective of this chapter, therefore, is twofold: (1) to describe what these emerging intergovernmental partnerships, shared ventures, and experiments in what some commentators refer to as "multilevel" Indigenous governance look like; and (2) to explain what these initiatives have done to contribute to the development and practical operation of Indigenous self-determination (Papillon and Rodon 2017; Alcantara and Morden 2019; White 2020).

Before proceeding, however, an important warning is in order. Intergovernmental partnerships and shared ventures can advance the strategic interests of both Indigenous and Canadian governments, but what they generally do not do is pose a significant challenge to the configuration of power relations that inform the Canadian federal system of government (Alcantara and Morden 2019, 252, 253).[1] Alcantara and Morden astutely point out, for example, that "Indigenous and non-Indigenous actors frequently collaborate and interact in the shadow of a hierarchy" in which "relationships are shaped by the historical legacies of colonialism and specifically, the Canadian state's long history of marginalizing and disempowering Indigenous communities across Canada" (Alcantara and Morden 2019, 254). What this means, argue some, is that intergovernmental partnerships and shared ventures should be carefully scrutinized on the grounds that they may well act to further circumscribe Indigenous power within the limitations of the "Canadian legal-political order" and thus contribute little to their right to self-determination (Alcantara and Morden 2019, 253; White 2020,

320). In the pages to follow I will review a number of these important criticisms.

The variety and number of intergovernmental partnerships, shared ventures, and experiments in multilevel governance in Canada is vast, so the analysis to follow must, by necessity, be selective. This chapter, therefore, addresses four distinct themes: incremental treaty agreements as developed in British Columbia; impact and benefits agreements as shaped by the Supreme Court of Canada's duty to consult and accommodate; shared economic ventures as pursued by three First Nations: the Membertou (Nova Scotia), Muskeg Cree (Saskatchewan), and Osoyoos (British Columbia); and co-management initiatives as designed for lands and resources in Indigenous peoples' traditional territories. Following Alcantara and Morden, it will be my contention that while the "potential for power asymmetries, both between partners and within Indigenous communities" is ever present, on balance, the advantages of such agreements generally outweigh their limitations. The benefit of intergovernmental partnerships and shared ventures is quite simply that they secure for Indigenous nations "governance space not otherwise provided by the Canadian federation in the formal distribution of powers" (Alcantara and Morden 2019, 261). In so doing, they can and often do serve to replace "elements of the state system with significant aspects of the Indigenous system" and thus contribute to enhancing Indigenous people's ability to direct the course of their own lives (White 2020, 12). As a segue into the topic, the chapter begins by consulting two of the Truth and Reconciliation Commission's Calls to Action for inspiration about how to put intergovernmental partnerships and shared ventures on solid moral foundations.

SETTING THE STAGE: THE TRUTH AND RECONCILIATION COMMISSION'S CALLS TO ACTION #43 AND #45

There can be no doubt that the Indigenous right to self-determination carries clear entitlements to political autonomy. But there are also points of mutuality and interdependence between Indigenous nations and the Canadian state that ought to be both accommodated and nurtured. Indigenous and non-Indigenous peoples are now interconnected in all kinds of ways as a result of a long history of association, some an unfortunate product of coercion, but others a product of genuine choice. The issue before us is whether those more edifying experiences of interdependence should be supported as part of a restored Indigenous experience of sovereignty. While the Truth and Reconciliation Commission's report dealt primarily with the legacy of the residential schools, its **Calls to Action #43** and **#45** provide a solid moral starting point for thinking about how this could be done.

The fact that Indigenous and non-Indigenous peoples relate to each other through a wide range of intergovernmental partnerships and joint ventures demonstrates that they already share a good number of the resources and lands that make up Canada. The problem, however, is that in many instances these arrangements are disproportionately skewed in favour of non-Indigenous interests. If these arrangements are to be ones in which Indigenous and non-Indigenous peoples operate side by side in true partnership, then the Truth and Reconciliation Commission (TRC) instructs that they must be based on renewed principles of mutual respect and mutual recognition. To that end, the TRC recommends an entirely new way of conceptualizing how intergovernmental partnerships ought to operate, one founded on a "**Royal Proclamation of Reconciliation** to be issued by the Crown" (TRC 2015, Call to Action #45, 199).

The TRC's proposed proclamation would build on the Royal Proclamation of 1763 and the Treaty of Niagara of 1764. Its operating premise would be to "reaffirm the nation-to-nation relationship between Aboriginal peoples and the Crown." To that end, it would include rejection of all concepts used to justify the assertion of European sovereignty over Indigenous peoples, including the Doctrine of Discovery and *terra nullius*. In its place, the proclamation would give expression to the moral imperative that Indigenous peoples "are full partners in Confederation" and as such are entitled to have their laws and traditions included "in negotiations and implementation processes involving treaties, land claims, and other constructive agreements." These principles, in turn, could then be used to build an "action-oriented Covenant of Reconciliation," which would pave the way "toward an era of mutual respect" and, importantly for economic relations, "equal opportunity" (TRC 2015, Call to Action #45, 199–200).

As a framework to guide this proposed "action-oriented Covenant of Reconciliation," the TRC calls upon federal, provincial, territorial, and municipal governments to fully adopt and implement the UNDRIP (TRC 2015, Call to Action #43, 191). Within its provisions, the TRC sees not only the necessary "minimum standards for the survival, dignity and well-being of the indigenous peoples of the world," but also (importantly for our purposes) the standard to guarantee Indigenous peoples decision-making power over economic development on their lands and territories. Particularly noteworthy is the Declaration's inclusion of an Indigenous right to "**free, prior, and informed consent**" (UNDRIP, Article 32(2)). While interpretation of this right is subject to debate, the TRC is nevertheless convinced that the contribution it can make to reconciliation is considerable. As explained by Martin Papillon and Thierry Rodon, "free, prior, and informed consent is rooted in the recognition that Indigenous peoples, as self-determining collective actors, should be empowered to make decisions over their future and that of their traditional lands." They should, in other words, be in a position to offer or withhold consent when proposed economic development projects "may have a major impact on their lands and communities" (Papillon and Rodon 2017, 216). Such power, argues the TRC, is the moral requirement that follows from taking the Indigenous right to free, prior, and informed consent seriously.

RESOLVING CLAIMS, RESTORING RESOURCES: INCREMENTAL TREATY AGREEMENTS

As we have seen, the Indigenous right to self-determination carries with it the right to exercise control over Indigenous internal affairs, including the right to exercise jurisdiction over lands and resources within Indigenous traditional territories. It is lands and resources that have been the focus of particular attention in comprehensive and specific land claims negotiations. Here negotiations are absolutely essential because Indigenous nations and Canadian governments at all levels regularly advance claims to the same lands and resources. As argued in earlier chapters, the policies and processes the Canadian government has put in place to deal with Indigenous rights and title have resulted in a number of agreements that provide important opportunities for Indigenous sovereignty to exist within the Canadian state. Since 1973, for example, 24 modern treaties (or comprehensive land claims agreements) have been successfully concluded and are now in effect. These agreements cover approximately 40 per cent of Canada's land mass (Anaya 2014, 17).

Despite some success, the comprehensive and specific claims processes have also been beset by significant difficulties. And it is because of these difficulties that many Indigenous nations have become leery about defining their Indigenous rights within these processes. For example, negotiating a comprehensive land claim through to a ratified treaty can take a long time, typically decades. A ratified treaty depends on the negotiating parties agreeing to the location and amount of land to be restored to an Indigenous nation, the cash that is to be transferred, and the self-government powers that the Indigenous nation is to exercise. This process is exceedingly complex and can be frustrating to complete, often leaving negotiators overwhelmed, stuck, or entrenched in positions that defy easy resolution (Alcantara 2013, 123). Moreover, while negotiations are underway, the population in the claimed territory may increase and local resources may be developed and thus depleted. Consequently, some land may be taken off the negotiation table while the value of other land may diminish. Finding themselves with a land asset that is losing value, Indigenous peoples are often compelled to go to court to seek remedy through injunctions.

In the face of difficulties such as these, the province of British Columbia has taken up the practice of negotiating **incremental treaty agreements** as a way to maintain trust and build confidence in the larger treaty process. Incremental treaties are not, nor are they meant to stand in for, a modern treaty. Instead, as stated on the BC government's website, "incremental treaty agreements allow First Nations and the Province to enjoy shared benefits in advance of a Final Agreement" (Province of British Columbia 2018, 1). They are pre-treaty agreements, or "stepping stones," designed to deliver immediate results to Indigenous nations and intended to build momentum to conclude treaties. They also almost always count as a portion of BC's contribution to the eventual treaty settlement.

The underlying intent of an incremental treaty settlement is to provide immediate economic benefits to an Indigenous nation so that it can begin to rebuild its community. Under the terms of most settlements, Indigenous nations acquire title to portions of land within their traditional territories as well as cash to help build institutional capacity (e.g., educational or social services provision) and to pursue business opportunities, including resource development ventures. Agreements might also include measures that guarantee to Indigenous nations a role in local land, resource, or park planning and management initiatives (Penikett 2006, 152). In all cases, incremental treaty measures are undertaken with a long-term goal in mind, namely, that each should serve as an adjunct, perhaps by way of an eventual chapter, of a future treaty still under negotiation.

The first incremental treaty agreement was signed by the Government of BC and the Tla-o-qui-aht First Nation in 2008 (McKee 2009, 130). As of 2022, an additional 25 have been signed.

The **Lake Babine Nation** signed its incremental treaty agreement in 2013. Under its terms, the nation reacquired a total of 13 parcels of land comprising 510 hectares, each to be transferred from the province at different time intervals in keeping with milestones attained in treaty negotiations. In addition, the nation received $100,000 for capacity building – $80,000 initially with the remaining $20,000 to be provided once the nation had a business plan in place to support the operation of a tourist enterprise, the Fort Babine Lodge (Lake Babine Nation 2014). In 2015, an incremental treaty agreement was signed with the **Haisla First Nation,** whose traditional territory lies in the Kitamaat region of northern BC. Under its terms, the nation reacquired 120 hectares of land between Kitamaat Village and Walth reserve on the Douglas Channel. This transfer was secured so that the nation could establish additional housing for its members as well as create commercial opportunities for local businesses (Steel 2015). The **Kitselas First Nation** on the north coast of BC negotiated an incremental treaty agreement in 2013, which saw three parcels of land totalling 248 hectares transferred to the nation. Upon evaluating the importance of this land transfer, the Kitselas First Nation said it constituted a step in good faith negotiations by the governments of BC and Canada (Spencer 2014, 6).

From the vantage point of Indigenous sovereignty, incremental treaty agreements would appear to be, at best, rather modest initiatives. In the first place, these agreements secure benefits for an Indigenous nation that are eventually bundled into a final treaty. As Christopher Alcantara points out, they amount to little more than "treaty-related advances" In this sense, the agreements break no new ground (Alcantara 2013, 128).

Second, as Alcantara also observes, these agreements are having no appreciable effect in speeding up the six-stage BC treaty negotiation process (Alcantara 2013, 128). They are designed to serve as enticements, but in some cases incremental treaty agreements seem to have exactly the opposite effect. Treaty negotiations can become stalled because Indigenous leaders focus their attention on exploiting the new opportunities created by the agreements rather than devote precious time to the abstract exercise of chapter-by-chapter treaty discussions.

And third, the agreements are identified by some to be dangerous distractions. From the perspective of Indigenous activist Arthur Manuel, for example, incremental treaty agreements fall into a category of measures that are little more than diversions, designed by the BC government to distract Indigenous leaders from the ultimate prize: settling land, resource, and self-government questions in terms that truly build the Indigenous capacity for self-determination (Manuel 2017, 208). As Manuel sees it, the problem with incremental treaty agreements is that Indigenous leaders might be tempted to see them as ends in themselves. But, he argues, because they are so modest in scope, they do little to challenge the inequitable distribution of land, resources, and power between Canada, BC, and Indigenous nations in ways they must if all three are to exist in conditions of genuine partnership.

These are difficult objections to respond to in a satisfactory way. While incremental treaty agreements are seen by some Indigenous leaders as a way to inject some of the much-needed resources into their nations immediately, others see them as compromises that threaten to undermine their much more robust self-determination projects. It is my view, however, that if these agreements are seen to be no more, but also no less, than what they are intended to be, then it is possible to reconcile them with the spirit and intent of Indigenous rights. The important point is that these agreements must be seen not as ends in themselves, but rather as stepping stones in the much larger and more ambitious journey of rebuilding Indigenous nations.

And this is overall exactly how incremental treaty agreements are described by both Indigenous and Canadian governmental leaders. They are supposed to provide Indigenous nations immediately with title to lands and resources that have already been agreed to within their treaty negotiation process. They also provide cash by way of a down payment to assist Indigenous nations in the here and now to rebuild institutional capacity and to provide essential services to their members. They are, in other words, building blocks designed for the purpose of rebuilding Indigenous nations, piece by piece. Framed this way, incremental treaty agreements can be seen as an important part (but no more than a part) of longer-term Indigenous efforts to restore their right to self-determination. They are not a substitute meant to undermine Indigenous sovereignty, but rather can be seen as a helpful adjunct to it.

CONSULTING INDIGENOUS STAKEHOLDERS: ACCOMMODATING INDIGENOUS INTERESTS

The incremental treaty process in BC is but one example of a political instrument designed to assist Indigenous nations regain control of their collective destinies. The Supreme Court of Canada's 2004 decision in *Haida Nation* has created additional space for the expression of Indigenous sovereignty within Canada. In this decision, the Supreme Court clarified what is required of the Canadian state in its duty to consult and accommodate, and in so doing has put Indigenous nations in a position to negotiate a significant number of wide-ranging impact and benefit agreements (IBAs) with both federal and provincial governments as well as private companies. The objective in each case is to attain agreements about development projects on Indigenous traditional territories to ensure they contribute to Indigenous interests. While not without their problems, the resulting economic initiatives have created jobs, provided joint venture opportunities for Indigenous and non-Indigenous businesses, and built capacity within Indigenous nations (Alcantara and Morden 2019, 251, 259; Eyford 2015, 41).

The Supreme Court's requirement that Canadian governments must pay greater attention to Indigenous peoples' constitutionally protected rights and title when engaged in resource development projects has served as substantial legal leverage to both strengthen and enhance Indigenous political power. What follows identifies several of the legal and political implications that follow from this important shift in power. The section ends on a cautionary note, however, by identifying some asymmetries in power between Indigenous and non-Indigenous actors that IBAs also tend to leave in their wake.

UNDRIP AND THE PRINCIPLE OF "FREE, PRIOR, AND INFORMED CONSENT"

The UNDRIP establishes that states must "consult and cooperate in good faith with indigenous peoples concerned through their own representative institutions in order to obtain their free and informed consent prior to the approval of any project affecting their lands or territories or other resources" (Article 32.2). This international principle concerning "free and informed consent" has become the gold standard that Indigenous peoples around the world, including Canada, now use in their relations with extractive industries wishing to engage in resource development on their traditional territories. Building on the 46 articles contained in UNDRIP, Indigenous peoples start from the premise that along with all other peoples of the world, they "have the right to self-determination" and "in exercising their right to self-determination … have the right to lands, territories, and resources which they have traditionally owned, occupied, or otherwise used or acquired" (Articles 3, 4, 26.1). The right to free, prior, and informed consent (FPIC) is rooted in this broader right to self-determination. As self-determining actors, Indigenous peoples are entitled "to own, use, develop, and control the lands, territories, and resources that they possess by reason of traditional ownership or traditional occupation or use" (Article 26.2). Consequently, when it comes to proposed economic development projects on their lands, Indigenous peoples must be in a political position to decide whether to offer or withhold their consent. In addition, as put by Martin Papillon and Thierry Rodon, "this consent must be expressed freely and in possession of all relevant information regarding the proposed activity and its potential impact" (Papillon and Rodon 2017, 217).

It is also worth pointing out that this right to FPIC is not a uniquely Indigenous right but rather one that is possessed by all self-determining peoples throughout the world. As such, it is an international human rights standard that Indigenous peoples possess equal to all other peoples. Understood in this way, the stipulation concerning "consent" should be seen as a basic universal principle of democracy and democratic decision making that all self-determining peoples are entitled to exercise.[2]

As explained in Chapter 5, the Supreme Court of Canada has established a more limited standard that it says must be used when resource development projects are proposed on traditional Indigenous territories. Rather than requiring FPIC in all cases, the Supreme Court stipulates that Canadian state actors must first consult and then seek to accommodate Indigenous interests. Furthermore, such consultation and accommodation must occur wherever Aboriginal and treaty rights have been established and also wherever claimed but not necessarily settled either through political negotiations or decisions rendered by the Canadian courts (Coates and Newman 2014,

16). In both situations, while every effort must be made to consult Indigenous peoples and accommodate Indigenous interests, the Supreme Court has also ruled that, while desirable, Indigenous consent may not be a requirement in all cases. On the grounds that Aboriginal rights and treaty rights must always be balanced against national interest concerns, the Supreme Court has determined that Aboriginal rights can sometimes be infringed. However, if those Aboriginal or treaty rights are to be infringed, the Supreme Court further instructs that the infringement must be justified according to a very strict standard involving two steps.

In the first place, the proposed project must contribute to a compelling and substantive objective, and in the second place, the project must be designed to impair the actual (or potential) Aboriginal or treaty right as minimally as possible. As put by the Supreme Court, the contribution of the proposed project to the national interest must not be outweighed by the detrimental effects of that project on the Indigenous nation (McIvor 2014, 35). There must be a balance struck, in other words, and this balance must be characterized by an attempt on the part of both Indigenous and governmental parties to reconcile their competing interests to the best of their respective abilities (Helin 2006, 187). Both are obliged to act reasonably with each other, but ultimately the objective is to reach an agreement that guarantees the Aboriginal and treaty rights at issue will be protected to the greatest extent possible (Newman 2014, 88).

When UNDRIP was endorsed by the UN General Assembly on September 13, 2007, only four countries voted against it, among them Canada.[3] At the time Canada justified its opposition by arguing that the degree of political autonomy established as a right for Indigenous peoples under UNDRIP would effectively undercut the sovereignty of the Canadian state. Particularly worrying to Canada was the FPIC standard, which it improperly took to guarantee Indigenous peoples a veto over all natural resource extraction projects on their traditional territories. As explained by the TRC, however, the word "veto" does not appear in UNDRIP, nor does it have any basis "in the wider body of international law. Like standards of accommodation and consent set out by the Supreme Court of Canada, FPIC in international law is applied in proportion to the potential for harm to the rights of Indigenous peoples and to the strengths of these rights" (TRC 2015, 189).

Nevertheless, despite assurances from Indigenous leaders that its fears were unfounded, far more favourable from the Canadian government's perspective was the Supreme Court's "consult and accommodation" standard. This purportedly less rigorous standard left open the possibility that resource projects on Indigenous land could proceed over Indigenous objections provided that appropriate consultation and attempts at accommodation had been made. Canada preferred this more "balanced" approach because it appeared to be more flexible and designed specifically to uphold the sovereignty of the Canadian state in situations where securing the consent of Indigenous peoples proved to be impossible (Manuel 2017, 197).

In 2010 Canada reversed its position opting to endorse UNDRIP. It did so, however, on the grounds that as far as it was concerned, UNDRIP was an aspirational document. As such, UNDRIP was neither legally binding nor had the power to change Canadian laws, laws which, the government added, were already committed to protecting Indigenous rights in any case (Olthuis, Kleer, Townshend 2012, 189–90; Papillon and Rodon 2017, 218). Then in 2016, Canada took one further step, this time signalling to the world a fundamental change in position. Canada announced its unqualified support for UNDRIP, stating that it would be fully implemented in partnership with Indigenous peoples (Government of Canada 2018, 2). In June 2021, the federal government made good on its intentions by adopting Bill C-15, legislation designed to implement UNDRIP. Among its provisions were two key goals: first, to take all measures necessary to bring Canadian federal laws into conformity with the Declaration, and second, to develop and implement an action plan (within two years) to achieve the objectives of UNDRIP in consultation with Indigenous peoples.

As part of its legislated commitment to UNDRIP, Canada claimed that it was now prepared to go beyond the legal duty to consult by building processes and approaches aimed also at securing Indigenous consent. In its words: "the Government of Canada recognizes that meaningful engagement with Indigenous peoples aims to secure their free, prior, and informed consent when Canada proposes to take actions which impact them and their rights, including their lands, territories, and resources" (Government of Canada 2017b, 4; see also Papillon and Rodon 2017, 218). The question, of course, is whether these good intentions to take up such meaningful engagement will be translated into practice. At the very least, Canada's newfound enthusiasm to attain Indigenous consent in advance of resource development on Indigenous land signals a greater willingness on its part to take the Indigenous right to self-determination more seriously. Consultation without the necessity of Indigenous consent implies an uninterrupted Canadian sovereignty and an ongoing subjugation of Indigenous peoples. Consultation with the intent to secure Indigenous consent, if possible, signals a greater commitment to shared sovereignty within the political space that is Canada.

CONSENT AND PRIVATE CONSULTATION PRACTICES

While it took a considerable amount of time for the Government of Canada to accept UNDRIP's standard of "free, prior, and informed consent," it took the non-state private sector in Canada virtually no time at all (Papillon and Rodon 2017, 216). As explained by Shin Imai, for those in the business world, some version of the consent standard makes good practical and economic sense (Imai 2017, 370).[4] In principle, the duty to consult and accommodate is an obligation that the Supreme Court of Canada has determined applies only to governments. However, as a matter of expediency, private sector actors and Indigenous nations often take up the matter of consultation on their own, independently of governmental involvement. For example, many companies have adopted corporate policies that require they first identify the potential impacts of their proposed development projects on Indigenous nations and then secure the participation of Indigenous nations in deciding how they will address those impacts. In almost all cases, the standard that companies employ as a condition for proceeding with a new project on Indigenous lands is consultation leading to Indigenous consent. As Papillon and Rodon note, "the language of FPIC is increasingly integrated into the corporate social responsibility guidelines of major players in the extractive industry" (Papillon and Rodon 2017, 216).

Invariably the arrangements that are worked out, should Indigenous nations offer their consent, involves some form of IBAs. These agreements are designed to offer the Indigenous nation some form of economic accommodation or compensation through equity partnerships, skills training and employment, revenue sharing, and lump sum payments in exchange for granting licence to the company to proceed with its proposed project on Indigenous lands (Newman 2014, 134–8; Alcantara and Morden 2019, 255; Papillon and Rodon 2017, 220). As observed by Perry Bellegarde, former national chief of the Assembly of First Nations, "obtaining the consent of affected indigenous groups before starting a resource project is now considered a best practice" (Sellars 2016, 163).

While consent may be the standard most consistent with best practices and with reconciliation, why would companies not opt for the considerably lower standard of consultation and then accommodation if and where possible? Would it not be more consistent with corporate interests to pursue a strategy in which Indigenous nations do not have the option of saying no? A number of commentators have offered compelling reasons why most companies opt for consent as their preferred standard.

First, Shin Imai points out that decisions about proceeding with major resource projects on Indigenous land without Indigenous consent can incur high costs and significant risks to companies. Should Indigenous peoples choose to oppose a proposed project at the conclusion of what they identify as an inadequate consultation process, the project itself may be killed (Imai 2017, 382). Faced with the prospect of protests and blockades, a much safer course of action is to secure Indigenous consent from the outset. Consent signals that Indigenous social licence has been secured, meaning the proposed project can move forward assured that it will be insulated against potential rejection and abandonment.

Second, securing Indigenous consent makes good business sense. Consent is a form of investment in a respectful relationship. As observed by Papillon and Rodon, "the duty to consult is an evolving target with many [legal] grey areas left to the discretion of the parties involved" (Papillon and Rodon 2017, 217). For those Indigenous nations that welcome some resource development on their lands (and not all do), consent can be a route to securing equity stakes in a company or the development of an Indigenous workforce. The payoff to companies, therefore, is legal certainty about their right to be on Indigenous land and confidence that they can expect a lucrative economic return on their investment. As put by Bev Sellars, achieving consent is the route to "how you avoid delays. It's how you build lasting relationships" (Sellars 2016, 163).

A third, more normative, point ensues. Imai observes that the standard of consent plays an important role in addressing counterproductive power imbalances. The problem with the "consult and accommodate" standard, according to Imai, is that Indigenous nations may feel powerless because the more powerful party (the Canadian government) reserves for itself the right to impose a solution in the absence of an agreement (Imai 2017, 385). But if a solution is imposed, even with accommodations, Indigenous nations may not be inclined to consent to it, leaving the solution without durability. It is far better, therefore, to embrace Indigenous nations as full partners in resource development projects, a situation that the standard of consent invites. As observed by Imai, it is far more likely that Indigenous peoples will trust a process in which they know from the outset that when it comes to deciding what development is to occur on their lands, the final decision rests with them (Imai 2017, 385–6).

At the same time, while the standard of consent may rectify some power imbalances, others may still be left unattended. By what criteria do we decide, for example, that substantive Indigenous consent has indeed been secured? What if there are disagreements within an Indigenous nation about who may or may not be in a legitimate position to offer consent? And what about situations where significant dissent remains within an Indigenous nation despite an IBA having been signed?[5] It may well be the case, for example, that IBAs are good at providing some economic development and benefit opportunities to Indigenous nations but in the process neglects "more complex questions about the social acceptability of projects and their cultural, social, and economic cumulative impact" (Papillon and Rodon 2017, 217). These questions constitute a stark reminder that despite increasing commitments to the standard of consent, significant asymmetries in power relations between both Indigenous and non-Indigenous actors and within Indigenous nations may well persist. Consent, in other words, is not a panacea to cure all Indigenous ills, a point I shall return to in the next section.

One final legal point is worthy of mention. While the Canadian courts have not as yet made the standard of consent a general legal requirement in cases of unresolved Aboriginal title, its "consultation and accommodation" expectations are such that they are now not far off the "consent" mark. In the 2014 *Tsilhqot'in Nation* case, for example, then Chief Justice Beverley McLaughlin offered the following advice: "governments and individuals proposing to use or exploit land, whether before or after a declaration of Aboriginal title, can avoid a charge of infringement or failure to adequately consult by obtaining the consent of the interested Aboriginal group" (*Tsilhqot'in Nation v. British Columbia* 2014, para. 97). As Bev Sellars observes in response, "we have not arrived at the right of refusal but some believe we are close" (Sellars 2016, 157).

IMPACT AND BENEFIT AGREEMENTS

To avoid the kinds of aforementioned pitfalls attached to insufficiently rigorous consultation and accommodation processes, federal and provincial governments now routinely encourage resource companies and Indigenous nations to negotiate **impact and benefit agreements**. IBAs are usually private and confidential agreements, negotiated bilaterally in response to expectations that a proposed project will have an impact (possibly negative) on Indigenous lands and on actual or potential Aboriginal or treaty rights (e.g., harvesting) and interests (e.g., the social fabric of the community) (Papillon and Rodon 2017, 220). As bilateral partnerships between Indigenous nations and corporate actors (also sometimes Canadian governments), IBAs constitute an important political innovation. Quoting legal scholar Douglas Sanderson, for example, Alcantara and Morden observe that some believe "IBAs represent the new order – new diplomatic protocols, as it were – for a new century" (Alcantara and Morden 2019, 255).

The way an IBA typically works is as follows. The Indigenous nation promises to approve a project on condition that, in return, the company (or government) provides compensation to offset impacts on its traditional territories through a range of opportunities and benefits extended to the Indigenous nation. Industries that typically pursue IBAs with Indigenous nations come from the forestry, mining, tourism, and oil and gas sectors while governments may do so for the purpose of advancing public interest projects such as parks (Alcantara and Morden 2019, 256). The kinds of benefits provided in an IBA can include the following:

- financial compensation;
- equity partnerships in the development project;
- revenue-sharing agreements;
- preferential hiring of Indigenous workers and procurement of services from Indigenous businesses;
- education and skills training programs;
- environmental protection provisions;
- social, cultural, and community service supports;
- flexible working conditions to allow Indigenous workers to engage in periodic traditional cultural and economic activities (e.g., hunting, trapping, and fishing);
- guaranteed participation in environmental regulatory processes;
- protection of important cultural, archaeological, and sacred sites;
- joint IBA implementation and review committees;
- clear dispute resolution measures; and
- a community ratification mechanism (Alcantara and Morden 2019, 255, 256; Olthuis, Kleer, Townshend 2012, 388; Papillon and Rodon 2017, 220).[6]

The last requirement ensures that no development project can proceed on Indigenous lands until such time as the members of the Indigenous nation have provided their collective consent through a community vote.

Overall, IBAs are relatively easy to complete and have the advantage of providing a fair degree of legal and economic certainty for resource development companies because they are respectful of Aboriginal and treaty rights (Papillon and Rodon 2017, 220). They are also used by Indigenous nations to exercise greater control over resource decision making on their lands and more particularly "to facilitate project development in a way that addresses Aboriginal interests" (Eyford 2015, 35). As put by Papillon and Rodon, IBAs intend to minimize negative impacts of development projects on Indigenous lands while "maximizing its potential benefits" (Papillon and Rodon 2017, 220). Consequently, as noted by Shin Imai, "in spite of some highly publicized conflicts …, the majority of projects in Canada are able to proceed after IBAs have been signed" (Imai 2017, 405). They are deliberately designed, in other words, to provide gains for all.

CRITICISMS AND CONFLICTS

Yet the process of negotiating and then settling on the terms of an IBA is not always conflict or trouble free. As pointed out by Alcantara and Morden, the processes leading to IBAs are still regularly marked by asymmetries in power that can operate to the distinct disadvantage of certain groups within Indigenous nations (Alcantara and Morden 2019, 251, 261–2).

For example, conflict sometimes occurs within Indigenous nations in situations where some members oppose others on the grounds that the capitalist forms of development and resource exploitation being entertained will undermine traditional values and cultural practices as well as destroy the environment on which the nation has relied since time immemorial (Murphy 2005, 18). This criticism features particularly prominently in some of the interventions led by Indigenous women (Dalseg, Kuokkanen, et al. 2018). In such cases, an IBA under any conditions will be seen as insufficient to mitigate or compensate for harmful impacts against important cultural and social values as well as traditional economies (Papillon and Rodon 2017, 220). Yet over the objections of some, it is fairly common for IBAs to proceed anyway based on majority support within the nation. A capitalist economic development model is thereby privileged to the detriment of broader, possibly less tangible community perspectives and priorities (Papillon and Rodon 2017, 220).

Others, while not opposed to economic development on their lands, may not be impressed by the conduct of resource companies with whom partnerships are being proposed. As Alcantara and Morden point out, it is a fairly common practice that resource companies do not approach Indigenous nations to negotiate IBAs until they have already invested considerable resources in exploration and viability studies. With development plans well advanced, resource companies are then often reluctant to accommodate Indigenous peoples' concerns, particularly so if accommodation requires significant changes to the companies' plans (Alcantara and Morden 2019, 258, 260; see also Anaya 2014, 22). When reluctance to accommodate is compounded by "differences in capacity between negotiating partners," the problem can become even worse. As Alcantara and Morden explain, "IBAs are highly technical documents, clearly more closely catered to industry than to Indigenous approaches to issues like cultural and ecological conservation" (Alcantara and Morden 2019, 257). As Indigenous nations are likely to participate in just one IBA negotiation while a resource company "could be party to dozens of IBAs in Canada and abroad," capacity differentials may well mean that Indigenous interests are not as fully reflected in the final agreement as are those of their industry partners (Alcantara and Morden 2019, 258).

And in still other cases where IBAs have been signed, Indigenous partners are sometimes frustrated because they believe that the resource company is withholding promised benefits and also failing to meet community expectations (e.g., fulfilling employment quotas) (Bradshaw, Fidler, and Wright 2016, 2; Alcantara and Morden 2019, 258, 260). For example, Alcantara and Morden point to a study showing that where "employment training was made available," training "was seen to only provide community members with access to low-level jobs" (Alcantara and Morden 2019, 258). Other complaints identified in the study include the charge that only those who are actually employed in the resource company's extractive activity actually receive any benefit. Benefits to the larger Indigenous community in the form of education and skills training; social, cultural, and community service supports; or environmental protection initiatives are often deemed to be, at best, negligible. Furthermore, when it comes to activating dispute resolution measures in response to IBAs having "fallen short in the implementation of their stated goals," these too do not always meet Indigenous expectations (Alcantara and Morden 2019, 258). It is not uncommon, for example, for Indigenous partners to be disappointed in the financial compensation offered by resource companies as recompense for breaches in the terms of IBA agreements.

There is also the important matter of consent. As we have seen, IBAs are essentially a transaction in which Indigenous nations offer their consent to a proposed development project on their traditional lands in exchange for a range of benefits. The question that then naturally follows is: what level of Indigenous consent is required for the UNDRIP standard of FPIC to have been met? One can well imagine, for example, that there may be disagreements within an Indigenous nation about who is actually authorized to give consent to an agreement. And even when IBAs have been signed there may be lingering reservations about the terms and conditions agreed to as well as about the wisdom of proceeding with an agreement at all. Papillon and Rodon observe, for example, that most IBA negotiations occur "through elite negotiations, often with very little input from the community" (Papillon and Rodon 2017, 220). This secrecy in negotiations is a product of mandatory confidentiality clauses intended to protect agreements from visibility and thus critical scrutiny by the general public. But the cost of a lack of transparency may well be a corresponding lack of legitimacy for the agreement eventually struck. As explained by Papillon and Rodon, "the negotiators, often lawyers and consultants, and the elected leaders involved in the process can easily become divorced from the community's actual preoccupations" (Papillon and Rodon 2017, 220, 221).

This problem concerning legitimacy may, in turn, be compounded by another. Alcantara and Morden point out that in some cases, "Indigenous governments must contend with legitimacy crises within their communities, largely as a result of their association with the settler state" (Alcantara and Morden 2019, 360–1). Band councils are the governing structures that come most readily to mind. Taken together, these problems concerning legitimacy and consent suggest, therefore, that greater efforts may need to be expended to create opportunities for enhanced community involvement. As summarized by Papillon and Rodon, "substantive Indigenous decision-making, anchored both in community deliberations and the reconciliation of interests through negotiations" are the preconditions necessary to attaining successful IBA outcomes (Papillon and Rodon 2017, 217).

Finally, several Indigenous feminist scholars point to the structural limitations of IBAs because of their failure to forefront matters of gender as an economic precondition to promoting healthy Indigenous communities and nations. The litany of projected and actual harms identified is considerable. Based on their comparative scan of the literature, for example, Shenna Dalseg, Rauna Kuokkanen, and colleagues are led to conclude "that Indigenous women and children are less likely than men to benefit from large-scale resource development, and are, in turn, more likely to bear the social costs" (Dalseg, Kuokkanen, et al. 2018, 136; see also Koutouki, Lofts, and Davidian 2017, 64). We need look no further than to the recent final report of the National Inquiry into Missing and Murdered Indigenous Women and Girls (MMIWG) for a series of highly disturbing examples.

On the "economic benefits" side of the ledger, the final report shows that Indigenous women are far less likely to be employed in resource-extractive projects than are men. And when women are employed, they tend to be placed in lower-paid and less valued positions (such as housekeeping, cleaning, and food services) where they are often stuck in rotational shifts that not only place considerable strain on their families but also put them at significant risk of sexual harassment and assault (National Inquiry into MMIWG 2019, 587–90; see also Koutouki, Lofts, and Davidian 2017, 65). As for "social costs," studies show that IBAs privilege male-led capitalist economic activity over traditional or mixed economic pursuits. Yet it is the latter category that has historically done a much better job of incorporating Indigenous women as full and equal participants. The final report then identifies the social costs associated with privileging capitalist economic activity to be considerable, among them "alcohol consumption and gambling, gendered and family violence, incidences of child neglect, and gendered income inequality" (Dalseg, Kuokkanen, et al. 2018, 139; National Inquiry into MMIWG 2019, 588–9, 591–2).

The final report also describes how the influx of a largely transient and temporary male workforce who are then often placed into work camps (characterized as "hyper-masculine" man camps) on Indigenous traditional territories can lead to serious safety concerns for Indigenous women and girls. It is not uncommon, for example, for Indigenous women and children to be the targets of racial violence and sexual exploitation as these men, who have both "high salaries and little at stake in their host communities," seek ways to amuse themselves when they are not working (National Inquiry into MMIWG 2019, 586; see also Stienstra 2015, 641; Koutouki, Lofts, and Davidian 2017, 66).

The range of problems identified is formidable and as such calls for a comprehensive set of solutions. One important place to begin is at the level of resource governance. Dalseg, Kuokkanen, and colleagues argue that Indigenous women's worries "about the impact of resource development on the health of their communities and traditional territories" must be addressed as a political matter of first concern (Dalseg, Kuokkanen, et al. 2018, 158). It simply will not do to leave Indigenous women out of IBA assessment and negotiation processes because doing so risks neglecting "issues traditionally viewed as important to women, such as community development (as opposed to large-scale economic development), education, public and private safety [and] health and social issues" (Stienstra 2015, 640). To that end, commentators regularly insist that women's voices simply must be part of the IBA decision-making process. Indeed, some see this issue as a fundamental matter of human rights. Just as Indigenous women's interest in the well-being of their communities is equal to that of their male counterparts, so too are their rights to contribute to all efforts aimed at community development. Remedies consistent with this right to political participation are not difficult to find. As suggested by Konstantia Koutouki, Katherine Lofts, and Giselle Davidian, a process that "strengthens and adds legitimacy" to the IBA decision-making process would be one in which Indigenous women are included and robustly participate "in all phases of a project – from planning, funding and implementation, to monitoring and evaluation" (Koutouti, Lofts, and Davidian 2017, 73).

BENEFITS

Given the enormous scale of many resource development projects being proposed on Indigenous lands, it is not surprising that the Indigenous peoples affected would have differing perspectives and approaches about how they would like to proceed. In this respect, political conflict and the challenges associated with consent generated by it is a feature that exists within all communities, Indigenous nations included. One commitment binds all Indigenous peoples together, however, and that is their shared determination to protect their traditional territories. As observed by Wayne Warry, "however strategically Indigenous peoples have acted, their aim has always been to assert their own values about the economy and the environment and, increasingly, to participate in development projects – but on their own terms" (Warry 2008, 145). Development that is both environmentally sustainable and can provide income and security is generally welcomed by Indigenous peoples. Development that threatens the long-term health of Indigenous peoples, the continuation of Indigenous culture, or the integrity of the land is more likely to be rejected. Where to draw the line between where the benefits end and where a harm begins is clearly and regularly a matter for debate within Indigenous communities. The important matter to underscore at this point is that leaving it to Indigenous nations themselves about where to draw the line and what to decide is an important feature of their political right to self-determination.

While not all attempts to secure IBAs are successful given the formidable challenges they present to Indigenous peoples, those that are successfully concluded inevitably give rise to shared economic ventures and business partnerships between Indigenous nations and resource companies.[7] For many Indigenous peoples, participation in such development projects is seen as an avenue for their nations to develop both economically and politically (Murphy 2005, 18). And, as documented by Michael Murphy and others, many of these shared ventures and business partnership have generated encouraging levels of success (Murphy 2005, 19; Alcantara and Morden 2019, 256–7, 259, 261–2; Papillon and Rodon 2017, 220; Poelzer and Coates 2015, 260–2). From a purely economic standpoint, for example, IBAs can provide Indigenous peoples with skills training and decent, well-paying jobs. They can also provide Indigenous nations with large injections of cash by way of start-up payments as well as stable, own-source funding provided through equity partnerships and preferential contracts for local Indigenous service and support companies. Stable revenue streams can, in turn, be dedicated to supporting the pursuit of self-defined economic, social, and cultural development. In short, as summarized by Alcantara and Morden, the initial appeal of IBAs comes from "the fact that they create decision-making space that would not otherwise exist for Indigenous communities" (Alcantara and Morden 2019, 256). What follows describes a number of successful joint venture IBAs.

VOISEY'S BAY

The Voisey's Bay nickel mine is located on the traditional territories of two Indigenous nations, the Innu and Inuit of Labrador, represented by the Innu Nation and the Nunatsiavut Government, respectively. The project involved the extraction of nickel, copper, and cobalt from open pit and underground mines as well as the construction of a hydrometallurgical processing plant on the Avalon Peninsula (Warry 2008, 144). Inco successfully negotiated IBAs with the Innu Nation and the Nunatsiavut Government, resulting in a mutually beneficial relationship between the two Indigenous nations and the mining company.

While the details of the agreements are confidential, they do contain a wide range of specific benefits for both nations. During the construction phase of the mine, for example, 40 per cent of the workforce came from the Innu and Inuit nations (Poelzer and Coates 2015, 261). Further education and training were offered to local Indigenous residents in mine-related jobs once the mine was up and running. The IBAs also contain provisions for financial compensation, business opportunities, social and cultural protection, "and community consultations and partnerships concerning the use and stewardship of lands" (Warry 2008, 144). In addition, the Inuit secured guarantees that there would be limits imposed on winter shipping to and from the mine so that winter ice would be protected for travel by Inuit hunters. Also noteworthy is the fact that in the initial environmental assessment and subsequent IBA agreement processes, the issue of gender garnered significant attention. For example, in the environmental assessment phase, "a dedicated technical session to 'Women's Issues' was incorporated" as were requirements that feminist research be undertaken to show exactly how the resource extraction project would affect women as distinct from men (Dalseg, Kuokkanen, et al. 2018, 141, 146; see also Stienstra 2015, 640).

EAST WEST TIE TRANSMISSION LINE

The East West Tie Transmission Line is a $777 million, 450-kilometre-long development designed to bring a reliable source of electricity to northwestern Ontario. In this case, a consortium of six Anishinabek First Nations have formed a partnership called "Bamkushwada," which in turn partnered with NextBridge to construct the hydro line from Wawa to Thunder Bay, Ontario.[8] The IBA provides the six Indigenous nations with a 20 per cent equity stake in the project as well as an economic partnership that connects the construction manager with local Indigenous contractors and journeymen for the purposes of training and employment (Richardson and Mackay 2018, 3–4). The key benefit provided to the Anishinabek in this agreement is twofold: the equity partnership with NextBridge ensures that the six First Nations will have access to a steady source of revenue, and the opportunities that the project provides for contracting, training, and the employment of Indigenous workers will provide access to education and enhanced income leading to a more diversified local economy (Richardson and Mackay 2018, 4).

VANCOUVER INTERNATIONAL AIRPORT

The Vancouver International Airport is located on the traditional territory of the Musqueam

First Nation. In 2017, the Musqueam signed a 30-year IBA with the airport that guarantees the nation employment and educational opportunities as well as a revenue-sharing deal valued at more than $200 million (Chan 2017, A9). Under the terms of the agreement, the airport commits 1 per cent of its annual revenue each year to the Musqueam (about $5 million based on 2016 figures). It also provides an education-to-employment pathway for Musqueam members, which includes jobs, four apprenticeship positions, and up to 10 scholarships per year (Chan 2017, A9). An important additional feature of the IBA is that it establishes a formal role, by way of a protocol, for the Musqueam Nation to be involved in any future development of long-term airport-related projects. Both parties also pledge to work together on environmental protection and to safeguard Musqueam archaeological sites. The agreement also commits the airport to feature additional Musqueam art alongside the considerable collection of Musqueam work already on prominent display in its public spaces (Chan 2017, A9).

Comments exchanged at the signing ceremony testify to the importance of the IBA for all involved. The Vancouver Airport Authority president and CEO is reported as saying, "the agreement was a natural outgrowth of the idea that business should try to pursue agreements like this with their First Nation neighbours," while Wendy John, chief negotiator for the Musqueam, replied, "the agreement is a significant historical event for all Canadians. This agreement reflects YVR's acknowledgement that we are the people of this land and we have a part in the growth of the economy and employment" (Chan 2017, A9).

TRANS MOUNTAIN PIPELINE

A particularly difficult challenge is presented when a proposed development project has to pass through the traditional territories of a large number of Indigenous nations. In such cases, IBAs are possible only when the agreement of all affected Indigenous nations is secured. Just how difficult this task can be is illustrated by the 2018 Federal Court of Appeal decision that halted construction of the Trans Mountain Pipeline project for a time.

In this situation, IBA agreements were secured with 42 affected Indigenous nations along the proposed route. Just six Indigenous groups objected on the grounds that their nations had not been sufficiently consulted nor had adequate attempts been made to accommodate their pressing concerns. Consequently, these Indigenous parties were not interested in negotiating IBAs. For example, the C'eletkwmx First Nation in central British Columbia proposed an alternate route for the pipeline so that it would not pass so close to the only aquifer that provided the community with drinking water. And the Tsleil-Waututh First Nation, whose traditional territories lie long the Burrard Inlet near Vancouver, expressed concern about the increased likelihood of oil spills in the inlet with added tanker traffic (Hayward 2018, A3).

The Federal Court of Appeal decided that in its consultations with these two and the other four Indigenous nations, the Government of Canada had listened to Indigenous perspectives and tried to understand their positions, but in the end had simply not done enough to address their concerns. Because of the weighty nature of the objections raised, the court decided that construction of the Trans Mountain Pipeline be halted until such time as all concerns were addressed. Further consultations ensued until the Government of Canada believed that all its court-mandated obligations had been met. When the six Indigenous nations filed yet another legal challenge in the Federal Court of Appeal in 2019 on the grounds that Canada had still failed to fulfill its duty to consult, the court decided otherwise. In its February 2020 decision, the court stated that "reasonable and meaningful" attempts had been made to appease First Nations' concerns and, as such, the project could now go ahead (Snyder 2020, NP1).

Despite challenges, it is worth pointing out that when consent is a product of an inclusive, community-wide consultative process, IBAs are not just worthwhile because they serve as an economic stimulus to the capacity-building efforts of their nations. They can also represent "a step toward greater recognition of Aboriginal and Treaty rights and the reassertion of Aboriginal forms of governance over resource development" (Olthuis, Kleer, Townshend 2012, 401). As observed by Olthuis, Kleer, and Townshend, IBAs "have evolved as a mechanism for building respectful relationships" between Indigenous nations and resource companies (Olthuis, Kleer, Townshend 2012, 400). Papillon and Rodon further point out that "IBAs are a practical recognition, by private interests, of Indigenous peoples' right to have a say in the future of their traditional lands" (Papillon and Rodon 2017, 230). Indeed, it could be argued that as part of their corporate social responsibility guidelines, many resource companies now operate on the assumption that the local Indigenous nation is the rightful steward of the land and therefore will serve as the resource company's landlord.

While there can be no doubt that IBAs have their problems, they also have their virtues. IBAs do build in all kinds of mechanisms to ensure that Indigenous peoples are both directly and deeply involved in all aspects of the resource development planning process that takes place on their lands. Framed within the larger context of Indigenous sovereignty, these measures can constitute important steps in addressing imbalances in power. Verified status as landlord, guaranteed access to a variety of income sources, and protected participatory rights in resource project development planning all add up to a measure of restored Indigenous sovereignty. IBAs and the respectful partnerships they encourage, in other words, can and do play a meaningful role in enhancing Indigenous autonomy within the Canadian state.

INDIGENOUS NATIONS AND JOINT ECONOMIC INITIATIVES

The preceding analysis demonstrated how some Indigenous nations have used policy instruments such as incremental treaty agreements and impact and benefit agreements to solidify their hold on important aspects of their Aboriginal and treaty rights. This section examines how a number of Indigenous nations have used their powers of self-government to pursue self-determination through active and extensive participation in the economy.

Many Indigenous leaders regard economic development as a critical component to achieving healthy and more prosperous nations. Participation in the global economy, investment in Indigenous enterprises, and the development of business partnerships are regularly central building blocks in this larger nation-based reconstruction exercise. Significantly, much of this economic development work occurs largely independently of Canadian governmental support. While many of the Indigenous nations involved are *Indian Act* bands and thus subject to *Indian Act* constraints, they nevertheless use the political power they do have to build local, vibrant, and prosperous economies. Their focus, in other words, is not simply on generating income and securing jobs for Indigenous workers while leaving it to others outside of Indigenous nations to set local economic priorities (Frideres 2016, 236). Instead, what many Indigenous nations seek to do is be in control of their own economies. To that end, they design specific institutions (often corporations) and generate targeted fiscal resources that are dedicated to the longer-term strategic goal of building capacity to achieve economic self-sufficiency. As part of their right to self-determination, Indigenous leaders increasingly insist that their nation's participation in the economy will be on their own terms, for their own purposes, as informed by their own culture and values.

Those Indigenous nations in a position to take control of their economies have enjoyed a considerable measure of success. Not all Indigenous nations, of course, are well positioned for economic investment and entrepreneurship given that they may be located in isolated regions of the country or may possess lands with marginal resources. For those Indigenous nations who, through good fortune, find themselves in resource-rich areas or who are located close to major urban centres, their economic circumstances can be quite different. They have access to resources and opportunities that make the achievement of self-determination through strategic and targeted participation in the economy a possibility. What follows identifies three Indigenous nations that have been the epitome of economic development and advancement. The success stories of the Membertou First Nation of Cape Breton, Nova Scotia, the Muskeg Lake Cree Nation of Saskatchewan, and the Osoyoos Indian Band of southcentral British Columbia will be taken up in turn.

THE MEMBERTOU FIRST NATION (CAPE BRETON, NOVA SCOTIA)

The Membertou First Nation is one of the most dynamic and economically successful Indigenous nations in Canada. It is an urban Indigenous community located in Sydney on Cape Breton Island in Nova Scotia.[9] The nation has a membership of 1,400, of which approximately 80 per cent live on reserve. Named after their historic leader Grand Chief Henri Membertou (1510–1611), Membertou belongs to the greater tribal group of the Mi'kmaq Nation. It is one of five Mi'kmaq nations on Cape Breton and one of 13 in Nova Scotia. It also operates under the *Indian Act* and is governed by a chief and 12 councillors who are elected to two-year terms.

During the last number of decades, the Membertou First Nation has gone from a position of profound economic hardship to one of economic prosperity. In 1995 unemployment was at 95 per cent, most members had to leave the reserve to find work, and as many as 85 per cent of members were dependent on various social assistance programs (Helin 2006, 231). The nation was also running a massive budget deficit and was almost entirely reliant on federal funding to run its programs and services.[10] In 2000, under the visionary direction provided by Chief Terrance Paul and CEO Bernd Christmas, the nation began to reorganize its institutions of governance as well as assert full control over the planning of its economic priorities. No longer would the nation focus on the short-term benefits of creating income and jobs, but instead it would set a long-term economic development agenda that made real investments "in building and diversifying its economic base" (Frideres 2020, 224). To that end, the nation adopted a corporate mindset into their structures of governance, insisting that the band administration function as a corporation and that all band assets, including government funding, be considered investments to be used for community capacity building and commercial development projects.

As part of its corporate strategy, the Membertou First Nation built an economic foundation for itself that involved three critical steps. The first was to make the nation ISO compliant. The International Organization for Standardization (ISO) is a worldwide agency that sets standards to ensure quality and consistency in business performance around the world. In 2001, the nation achieved ISO 9001:2000 certification, the first Indigenous government in Canada to do so (Helin 2006, 231). With ISO certification, the nation put itself in the position of having a credential that verified it was a credible organization in the business world. Second, the nation worked at elevating its business profile. To increase business prospects and corresponding options for economic partnerships, the nation set up the Membertou Corporate Office at the strategically located Purdy's Wharf Towers in downtown Halifax. This downtown location put the nation in a good position to nurture business contacts and develop shared ventures with Atlantic Canada's private sector companies (Helin 2006, 233). The third was to develop education and career-related training programs for the members of the nation. With training in hand, the expectation was that members would be ready to step into the jobs produced by the new business partnerships and economic initiatives being developed on reserve.

Within the framework provided by this threefold corporate strategy, the Membertou First Nation has enjoyed tremendous economic success. In less than 10 years, the nation's operating budget grew from $4 to $65 million, and as of 2016 had reached $112 million (Tammemagi 2017, 3) The land base of its reserve has doubled, and its reliance on federal funding has decreased from 100 per cent to 10 per cent (Centre for First Nations Governance 2013, 1). The number of reserve-based employees grew from 37 to over 500. Furthermore, as noted by Calvin Helin, the nation "also contributes approximately $165 million annually to the maritime economy" (Helin 2006, 231).

The engine that drives much of the Membertou First Nation's economic success comes from the lucrative business partnerships it has established with the Canadian and international business community. In all cases where business partnerships are pursued, however, the nation insists that business must be conducted in a way that incorporates "indigenous knowledge-based principles of conservation, sustainability of resources and reverence for the land and the waters" (Membertou First Nation 2018, 3). The only forms of economic development that are considered legitimate, in other words, are those that combine a strong respect for Membertou culture and tradition with business innovation and entrepreneurship. Under these terms the nation has entered into business partnerships with such companies as Clearwater Fine Foods, SNC Lavalin, Lockheed Martin, Sodexho Canada, Anaia Global Renewable Energies, and Canadian Maritime Engineering Limited (Kayseas, Hindle, and Anderson 2006, 17–19; King, N. 2018, 2; Taylor 2013, 2). As for local, reserve-based business ventures, the nation is no less active. The nation has built and operates a trade and convention centre, a market and gas bar, an entertainment centre, a gaming building, a shopping centre, a business plaza, a fisheries enterprise, a sports plex, a restaurant, and a hotel. Taken together, the pursuit of joint ventures conducted through business partnerships and the development of a wide-ranging and targeted set of reserve-based enterprises and services has done much to contribute to the Membertou First Nation's experience of autonomy. While still an *Indian Act* band, the nation has nevertheless found economic resources to engage in an active process of rebuilding its community.

With ample business-generated revenue in hand, the Membertou First Nation has also put itself in a position to invest in community-building projects. Economic self-empowerment, in other words, is now the foundation upon which the nation also exercises its powers of self-government more effectively. For example, economic assets have been leveraged into the pursuit of a better standard of living for all members. And corporate standards concerning accountability have been translated into a governance model that ensures band council decisions are transparent and subject to the overview of members and not the Department of Indigenous Affairs. In short, the Membertou First Nation has begun to assert sovereignty over its own resources and perhaps just as importantly, over the political processes where the decisions are made about how those resources are to be used. In the words of James Frideres, the nation has moved "from short-term to long-term goals, from reactive to proactive decisions," all with a view to building momentum towards the nation's aspirations of economic independence and political self-sustainability (Frideres 2020, 225).

THE MUSKEG LAKE CREE NATION (SASKATCHEWAN)

The Muskeg Lake Cree Nation is another Indigenous nation that strives to achieve economic autonomy and political self-sufficiency through business development and political partnerships with local governments. Located 110 kilometres north of Saskatoon, Saskatchewan, the nation has approximately 2,000 members, about 400 of which live on its main reserve. It owns and manages a total of 35,123 acres of land in both rural and urban settings. The nation's lands are used for a variety of purposes, including community living, agriculture, recreation, and business (Muskeg Lake Cree Nation, n.d.a). In addition, the nation's political affairs are managed by a chief and six councillors who rely on Cree Law and the guidance of community elders to make their decisions (Muskeg Lake Cree Nation, n.d.b). The chief and council are elected under *Indian Act* rules to three-year terms.

What distinguishes the Muskeg Lake Cree as a particularly innovative Indigenous nation is that it was the first in Canada to establish an urban reserve. The reserve itself is located in Saskatoon and is often identified as the standard for other prairie Indigenous nations to follow when using their treaty land entitlements as leverage for securing economic opportunities.

The *Treaty Land Entitlement Trust Agreement* that was negotiated between the province of Saskatchewan and 20 Indigenous nations in 1992 resulted in the Muskeg Lake Cree acquiring several parcels of land, including 36 acres in the city of Saskatoon. The nation's choice to purchase land in Saskatoon was a carefully considered one. Its view was that urban land provided a particularly lucrative economic development opportunity for its members given the land could be used for leasing and commercial purposes as well as for entrepreneurial growth.

In the process of acquiring the urban land, the nation was also able to develop a closer relationship with the city of Saskatoon. For example, in 1993 the city and the nation signed a service agreement in which Saskatoon agreed to provide water, sewer, garbage pickup, and fire protection services and in return the nation agreed to collect property taxes on the reserve to pay for those services (Municipal-Aboriginal Adjacent Community Cooperation Project 2002, 14).[11] The nation also agreed that any development initiated on its urban reserve would conform to the laws of Saskatchewan and the by-laws of Saskatoon. A spin-off to these discussions and agreements followed rather naturally. The city and nation meet regularly to both discuss and pursue partnerships aimed at enhancing economic, employment, and training opportunities for Indigenous and non-Indigenous Saskatoon residents alike (Alcantara and Nelles 2016, 5)

The Muskeg Lake Cree's urban reserve in Saskatoon is dedicated entirely to business ventures. To that end, the nation has established the Muskeg Lake Cree Nation Investment Management Corporation to oversee all business investment. The corporation operates at arm's length from the nation's governance structure and reports directly to a board of governors. Under its direction, the corporation seeks out investment, partnership, and new development opportunities. It also operates within a corporate mandate that frames strategic planning and goal setting within a business model that "ensures stability and security for investors" (CTV Saskatoon 2018). Within this corporate-friendly environment, 60 businesses operate on the reserve, employing over 600 people (Muskeg Lake Cree Nation 2018, 1). The largest on-reserve employers are Indigenous organizations, including the Federation of Sovereign Indigenous Nations, the Saskatoon Tribal Council, and the Saskatchewan Indian Gaming Authority. Other businesses include a dry-cleaning plant, medical and professional services, a transportation company, a restaurant, retail stores, a gas station, and a travel agency, among others (Western Economic Diversification Canada 2016, 5; Poelzer and Coates 2015, 152).

It is generally accepted that the Muskeg Lake Cree Nation's urban reserve has become an important commercial hub in southeast Saskatoon, breathing new life into that part of the city (Courchene 2018, 259). Upon celebrating the thirtieth anniversary of the urban reserve in 2018, for example, Mayor Clark said, "for 30 years Saskatoon has benefitted from increased economic activity, job creation and a closer relationship with the Muskeg Lake Cree Nation. This is something that we can be proud of" (City of Saskatoon 2018, 1). While Saskatoon has benefited from its partnership with the Muskeg Lake Cree, the reverse is also true. Through business development projects and strategic partnerships, the nation has also generated vital economic opportunities for its members. Employment opportunities have increased, as have opportunities for Indigenous entrepreneurs to start and run successful businesses. In addition, the rental and commercial activities that occur on reserve are important sources of self-generating revenue for the nation. Taken together, these economic benefits have reduced dependence on federal government funding, increased the standard of living of members, and increased the capacity of the nation to finance its own programs and services (Poelzer and Coates 2015, 249; Garcea 2008, 303).[12] In short, the Muskeg Lake Cree Nation has been able to leverage its many urban reserve-based economic and political partnerships in the direction of diversifying its local economy and enhancing its economic self-sufficiency.

THE OSOYOOS INDIAN BAND (BRITISH COLUMBIA)

The Osoyoos Indian Band is located in British Columbia's agriculturally rich Okanagan Valley near the towns of Osoyoos and Oliver. It is a member of the Okanagan Nation Alliance and controls about 32,000 acres of reserve land. The band was formed in 1877 and has 540 members, about 400 of whom live and work on the reserve (Thom 2017, 1). It operates under the *Indian Act* governance model, electing its chief and three councillors to two-year terms. The band enjoys a particular advantage because of its prime geographical location. It is situated in a rich agricultural and tourism area that provides the band with numerous opportunities in agriculture, tourism, commercial, industrial, and residential developments. Based on these substantial economic assets, the Osoyoos Indian Band has a reputation for having built an impressive business empire. In fact, it is known to be one of the most prosperous Indigenous nations in Canada (Macdonald, J. 2014, 2).

The Osoyoos Indian Band has chosen to assert its sovereignty principally through making independent decisions about its own economic development. In the words of Band Chief Clarence Louie, "the band does not owe its membership dependency. It owes them opportunity and a chance to become independent" (Helin 2006, 233). To that end, the goal of the band has been to rebuild its political autonomy through economic initiatives like land leases, joint economic ventures, and the development of band-owned and operated businesses. All serve to inject much needed financial resources and employment opportunities into the community. Interestingly, this focus on internal economic development is entirely in keeping with the band's own perception of its historical and cultural identity, which it describes as having traditionally been focused on trade and commerce with neighbouring Indigenous nations (*Osoyoos Times* 2017, 2). In the modern economic context, the band remains fiercely independent, insisting that its Aboriginal rights include an inescapable political component that authorizes the band to develop its economy according to its own priorities without external interference. Getting its own economic affairs in order, in other words, has been identified by the band as the first vital step to social and political autonomy. As put by Chief Louie, "I became convinced that the remedy to most of our problems was economic development ... If you get people working, most of the social problems in a community fade away" (Macdonald, J. 2014, 4, 12). The key building block to political sovereignty for

Chief Louie, in other words, is to bring back the economic self-sufficiency and "working culture that we all had before the reserve system, before the takeover of this continent" (Eggertson 2011, 3).

The band's efforts to assert control over its own economy gained significant momentum with the creation of the Osoyoos Indian Band Development Corporation in 1988 (Macdonald, J. 2014, 8). The corporation was developed as an economic vehicle to pursue reserve-based business ventures and establish partnerships with outside investors. Thus, while it is the Osoyoos Indian Band that sets out the overall vision for the nation, it is the corporation that brings the economic components of that vision to life. The corporation's mandate is guided by the rigorous utilization of business principles, including commitments to sound financial practices, long-term sustainability, human resource development, and guaranteed, predetermined minimum rates of investment return (Turtle Island Native Network 2008, 63). By submitting to these principles, the band has disciplined itself to pursue business ventures on its own only when it has the knowledge, confidence, and resources to do so. When lacking such knowledge, confidence, or resources, the band has often chosen the joint venture route by collaborating with business partners it has determined do have the requisite resources, necessary expertise, and management skills.

In 2000, the Osoyoos Indian Band set itself the goal of achieving economic independence from the federal government within five years (Eggertson 2011, 2). Under the direction of the Band's Development Corporation this goal was achieved, in large part because of careful investment choices made in growth industries such as commercial leasing, tourism, and construction services (Osoyoos Indian Band Development Corporation 2018, 16). Among the band's successful economic ventures are band-owned businesses, including a golf course, vineyards, a winery (Nk'Mip Cellars), an RV park and campground, a construction company, a cement company, a gas station and convenience store, a business park, a sawmill, and a desert cultural centre. Notably, Nk'Mip Cellars was Canada's first Indigenous-owned winery and in 2016 was voted Canada's winery of the year (*Osoyoos Times* 2017, 2). Land leases are also a lucrative source of revenue, with grape production, resort development, and agricultural production initiatives by leaseholders leading the way (Turtle Island Native Network 2008, 62). The band also enjoys financial payouts generated by a number of IBAs with the province of British Columbia and with industry, through forestry production occurring on Osoyoos Indian Band land.

In addition to its own businesses, the Osoyoos Indian Band has also pursued several large-scale business opportunities through joint venture partnerships with significant industry players. Some of these partnerships include the Mt. Baldy Ski Resort, Spirit Ridge Vineyard Resort & Spa (recently leased to Hyatt Hotels), Bellstar Hotels and Resorts, and Arterra Wines Canada (Turtle Island Native Network 2008, 63). The band joined with Bellstar Hotels and Resorts, for example, to build Canyon River Resort, a year-round vacation destination with 450 residences. Recently, the band decided to sell off 49 per cent of Nk'Mip Cellars to Arterra Wines Canada, retaining a 51 per cent stake in the business for itself. While this move constituted a substantial sell off of a highly lucrative business asset, from the perspective of the financial bottom line, the sale made good economic sense. Arterra has expertise in professional wine making and marketing that far exceeds that of the band, so joining forces with it promised significant financial returns (Brijbassa 2018, 4).

The Osoyoos Indian Band has also developed a strong and mutually beneficial working relationship with the town of Osoyoos. Rather than compete with each other for the same projects or funding, the town and band have nurtured a relationship that sees them operating cooperatively to develop the local economy together. For example, the town has extended services beyond its boundaries to provide amenities on the reserve. They both undertake joint fundraising for regional projects, they pursue cooperative marketing programs promoting industries like local wine producers, and they have quarterly meetings of town and band councils to discuss local issues (Government of British Columbia 2007, 58).

For the Osoyoos Indian Band, the route to sovereignty has been through charting a course to economic independence. The band has developed long-term corporate plans and then insisted, as a matter of its own right to self-determination, that those plans not be subjected to external interference. It is they who are entitled to decide what is in the best interests of their nation and, for the most part, this has been through economic development. And, based on sound economic planning, they have prospered.[13] Economic conditions are such that the Osoyoos Indian Band now enjoys virtually no unemployment and is also almost entirely independent of federal government financial support (Thom 2017, 1–2). Indeed, the band is now faced with a situation where it has more jobs on reserve than it has members, and so it employs people from the surrounding communities to meet the shortfall.

In sum, the political dynamic that motivates Indigenous nations such as the Membertou Mi'kmaq, Muskeg Lake Cree, and Osoyoos peoples is their right to develop their lands and resources into sustainable economies as set by their own priorities. At the same time, however, there many Indigenous nations who are not so well endowed with natural resources nor so strategically placed near major population centres. That said, Chief Louie of the Osoyoos Indian Band is still of the view that every reserve in Canada has its own unique potential and opportunities. When asked about how to accelerate economic development in the Canadian north, for example, Louie argues that many Indigenous nations are well positioned to pursue shared ventures with outside companies. In his words: "You have to exploit whatever potential there is in the area. If you are on the coast, it's trees and fish. If you are up north, it's mining and fishing. For us, it's agriculture and tourism. You let your natural resources tell you what business you're in" (Macdonald, J. 2014, 15). The key, it would seem, is to find creative ways to harness Indigenous land and resource-based economic potential.

CO-MANAGEMENT INITIATIVES

Intergovernmental **co-management initiatives** have also served as an emerging and increasingly important platform for significant power-sharing between Indigenous and Canadian governments. In the process of attempting to gain greater control over the management of lands and resources in their territories, Indigenous nations have found that entering into co-management agreements with federal, provincial, and territorial governments can be very beneficial. This is because co-management initiatives are built on the premise that Indigenous peoples have rights to lands and resources and therefore are entitled to participate in deciding to what economic ends those lands and resources should be put. Indeed, co-management initiatives serve to validate the principle that because Indigenous nations have a fundamental interest in their lands that pre-dates European contact, they also have an ongoing and corresponding right to both manage and benefit from those lands in the present.

Canadian governments at all levels were compelled to pursue co-management initiatives with Indigenous nations because of principles established by the Supreme Court of Canada in decisions such as *Delgamuukw* (1997), *Haida Nation* (2004), *and Tsilhqot'in Nation* (2014). Based on the reality of existing Aboriginal title, the Supreme Court ruled that Indigenous peoples have the right to be consulted about land use development proposals on their traditional territories. Indeed, going a step further, the Supreme Court instructed that proceeding without Indigenous consultation and, in some cases, consent could put proposed development projects in jeopardy.

Most productive are those instances where there are co-management arrangements in which Indigenous nations and Canadian governments agree to work together from the start. Such arrangements are ones in which land use and resource development decisions are shared between governments but always with a view to ensuring that resource development on Indigenous lands reflect Indigenous priorities. Structurally speaking, shared management arrangements usually come in the form of co-management boards or committees. They generally provide for an equal number of Indigenous and non-Indigenous representatives and, while usually negotiated into modern treaty agreements, can also exist as interim treaty measures or as arrangements that exist entirely outside modern treaty agreements (Scott 2005, 134; see also White 2020, 20–52).

Co-management boards have been described by some scholars as a unique form of governing institution in Canada. They are identified as existing in between the institutional structures of Indigenous, federal, provincial, and territorial governments and as such are neither a form of Indigenous autonomy nor "exclusively federal or provincial institutions" (Murphy 2005, 17). Instead, these boards are said to reflect a form of shared sovereignty. As common institutions, they are designed to encourage a cooperative use of decision-making power between Indigenous and Canadian governments over land and resource management. As a collaborative exercise, they are intended to arrive at recommendations or decisions, as the case may be, that reflect a consensus position between Indigenous and non-Indigenous participants. The boards are mandated, in other words, to serve the public interest, Indigenous and non-Indigenous alike, by advancing the economic management priorities of all concerned in a given territory (Murphy 2005, 17; White 2020, 5–8).

From the vantage point of rebuilding Indigenous sovereignty, co-management initiatives can be seen as providing an incremental step forward. Co-management boards do increase Indigenous decision-making authority over their lands and resources but often within the constraints of a shared sovereignty model in which the final decision-making power still rests with federal, provincial, or territorial governments. Graham White notes, for example, that while co-management boards can "decide, advise, and recommend," their powers are ultimately constrained. He writes: "in most cases, however, certainly in almost all matters with far-reaching implications, the boards have only advisory powers" (White 2020, 7–8). In short, as put by Olthuis, Kleer, and Townshend, "achieving a degree of equality between participating Aboriginal and state government parties remains an objective" rather than an achieved result (Olthuis, Kleer, Townshend 2012, 393).

Nevertheless, as Graham White has shown in his study of the Canadian territorial north, the power Indigenous peoples exercise within this shared sovereignty model can be substantial. Within the context of co-management boards, for example, it is possible for Indigenous peoples to make sustainable land use recommendations and decisions designed specifically to enhance the socioeconomic well-being of their members. It is also possible for them to exercise influence in setting out protocols for the management and protection of wildlife, cultural heritage sites, and sensitive ecological areas. And it is possible for them to establish collaborative agreements that guarantee Indigenous nations a leadership role in managing aquatic resources and ocean habitats. Despite challenges, in other words, shared management initiatives can and do restore to Indigenous nations a measure of political control over their traditional lands and resources (White 2020, 297–323). Olthuis, Kleer, and Townshend conclude "as a consequence of the significant role that they play in the mechanics of resource management within a settlement region, these institutions have a profile and importance that goes beyond providing advice or engaging in consultations with government" (Olthuis, Kleer, Townshend 2012, 395). Advice and recommendations, in other words, are more often than not eventually reflected in policy outcomes (White 2020, 302–6). What follows describes several co-management arrangements in the areas of land use planning and parks, wildlife, fisheries, and coastal conservation.

LAND USE PLANNING AND PARKS

The federal and a number of provincial and territorial governments have negotiated agreements with Indigenous nations that have included shared decision making and consultation protocols for land use planning and parks. The four examples that follow are drawn from British Columbia, Nova Scotia, and the Northwest Territories.

Haida Gwaii

On the islands of Haida Gwaii a shared decision-making protocol has been developed between the Haida Nation and the province of BC in which both jurisdictions have delegated political authority to a joint management board. Signed in 2009 and since amended in 2015, the agreement is called the Kunst'aa Guu–Kunst'aayah Reconciliation Protocol and is composed of two representatives from both governments. This board, which goes by the name "Solutions Table," operates on a consensus model and makes joint decisions on Haida Gwaii land use and resource management issues (Haida Nation 2017, 10). While the protocol stipulates that land use decisions are to be made together, even more important from the Haida Nation's perspective is the protocol's guarantee that from here on in, all land use decisions will reflect Haida values. With Haida values now prominently featured at the outset, the Haida have been able to say with some confidence that "the Protocol is the beginning of an evolving process in which the Haida are regaining management of their land" (Haida Nation 2017, 12).

Tahltan Nation

Also, in British Columbia, the Tahltan Nation and provincial government signed an agreement in 2017 to protect what the Tahltan term their "sacred headwaters" from any resource development for an initial period of 20 years (Hoekstra 2017, A8). The vast area of 286,000 hectares is situated in the northwestern part of BC and is the source of the salmon-bearing Nass, Skeena, and Stikine rivers. For the Tahltan Nation, the agreement is important because it signals provincial acknowledgement of their right to protect a significant portion of their traditional territories from mining, forestry, and energy-related activities. While the Tahltan Nation is not opposed to development within its territories per se, the "sacred headwaters" are in a category of their own because they carry profound social, sacred, and environmental significance and because they are an important source of wildlife and fish for the nation (Hoekstra 2017, A8).

Fertile ground was prepared for the agreement as early as 2012 when the provincial government imposed a ban on oil and gas exploration in the area and then in 2015 when it bought back a number of coal licences that it had issued to several companies. Interestingly, the companies have been given an option to buy back their licences, but only if the Tahltan Nation agrees, an eventuality that seems unlikely given that the Tahltan have said they hope to protect the "sacred headwaters" permanently. As with other co-management initiatives, the implementation of the management agreement over the "sacred headwaters" region includes the creation of a board made up of Tahltan Nation and provincial representatives.

Mi'kmaq of Nova Scotia

In Nova Scotia, negotiations between the Government of Canada and the Assembly of Nova Scotia Mi'kmaq Chiefs led to the National Parks Interim Arrangement in 2012.[14] In recognition that Canada had unilaterally imposed national parks on traditional Mi'kmaq territories, the arrangement established the right of all Mi'kmaq peoples of Nova Scotia to free entry to Kejimkujik National Park/National Historic Site, Cape Breton Highlands National Park, and the Fortress of Louisberg National Historical Site. In 2014, this initial arrangement was extended to include all national parks and national historical sites managed by Parks Canada in Nova Scotia. In 2018, the arrangement was again renewed until 2022 (Mi'kmaq Rights Initiative 2018, 1). While free entry to national parks and historical sites might seem to be a rather superficial concession to Mi'kmaq Indigenous rights, it did have the effect of recognizing and verifying the strong connections that the Mi'kmaq have to their traditional lands. As expressed by Chief Gerard Julian, "gaining free access to these parks and important lands is a significant step for our people as we move forward in our government-to-government relationship" (Dorey 2012, 1).

More important from the perspective of rebuilding Mi'kmaq sovereignty, however, was the arrangement's establishment of advisory committees. Generally speaking, the powers of an advisory committee are less robust than those of a co-management board as, in this case, the committees are designed to serve only in an advisory capacity to Parks Canada. But that said, the advisory committees are a product of joint consultations between Parks Canada and the Assembly of Nova Scotia Mi'kmaq Chiefs and are intended as forums to present and integrate Mi'kmaq values into parks management (Mi'kmaq Rights Initiative 2014, 6). According to the terms of the interim arrangement, the objective of advisory committees is to, among other things, "provide a venue for Mi'kmaq involvement in processes related to the management of natural resources and Mi'kmaq cultural resources such as monitoring, ecological restoration, environmental assessment, research permits, fire management, and species at risk stewardship" (Mi'kmaq Rights Initiative 2014, 6). The advisory committee structure is not designed to put the Mi'kmaq Nations in a position to control what goes on in Nova Scotia's national park system, but what it does do is establish a partnership in cultural and natural resource management in areas of shared interest between Parks Canada and the Mi'kmaq of Nova Scotia. In this sense, the National Parks Interim Arrangement constitutes an incremental step in the direction of a co-management model.

Dehcho First Nations

The Dehcho region of the southwest corner of the Northwest Territories is vast, covering 216,000 square kilometres. It is home to 10 First Nations (primarily Dene) and three Métis locals whose numbers approximate 3,500 people and who collectively call themselves the Dehcho First Nations.[15] This group has been in modern treaty negotiations with the governments of Canada and the Northwest Territories since 1999 and, to date, has been unable to move beyond the agreement-in-principal stage. Treaty negotiations have stalled on several occasions, in large part because the parties have been unable to agree on land quantum, resource ownership, a governance model, and capital transfer issues (INAC 2015a, 28). The inability of the parties to achieve clarity on Dehcho rights to ownership and jurisdiction over lands and resources within its traditional territories became so entrenched that in 2016 the governments of Canada and the Northwest Territories announced that a ministerial special representative would be appointed to attempt to break the logjam (White 2020, 29). At their annual general assembly held in July 2019, the Dehcho instructed their leadership to set aside lands and resources negotiations for the time being and focus on negotiation of a self-government agreement instead.

While final agreement on the terms of a modern treaty have proven to be difficult to achieve, the same cannot be said for the ability of the parties to reach an interim measure agreement at an early stage of the treaty negotiation process. The point of an interim measure agreement is to protect Indigenous rights and interests in advance of a treaty settlement. In the case of the Dehcho First Nations, their Interim Measure Agreement of 2001 guaranteed them an immediate role in land use and resource management decisions on their traditional territories. This role was solidified by developing a co-management model with the governments of Canada and the Northwest Territories. In it, provisions were made for the participation of Dehcho representatives on the Mackenzie Valley Environmental Impact Review

Board and for the creation of a Dehcho advisory panel to the Mackenzie Valley Land and Water Board (INAC 2015a, 28).

In addition, the Dehcho First Nations insisted on their right to identify culturally and spiritually significant lands as well as ecologically sensitive areas for immediate protection from resource development activities. And in those areas where resource development is permitted, the Dehcho asserted rights to benefits. Accordingly, the agreement established a process for land withdrawals for conservation purposes while a parallel resource development agreement was established in 2003 to ensure that mining and oil and gas development in the Dehcho region would also generate royalties for the Dehcho peoples (Dehcho First Nations 2001; see also White 2020, Chapter 5).

Perhaps most significantly, however, is the Interim Measure Agreement's provision for a Land Use Planning Committee. Made up of one representative each from the Government of Canada and the Government of the Northwest Territories and two representatives from the Dehcho Nations, its mandate is to develop a land use plan for the entire Dehcho territory. With equal representation guaranteed in this way, the Dehcho could move forward knowing that the values and cultural concerns of their peoples would play a prominent role in shaping all future local land use planning exercises on their traditional territories.

This guarantee was not only reflected in the composition of the committee but also in the language of the agreement itself: "taking into consideration the principles of respect for the land, as understood and explained by Dehcho Elders, and sustainable development, the Plan shall provide for the conservation, development, and utilization of the land, waters and other resources in the Dehcho territory" (Dehcho First Nations 2001, 5). By implication, no future land use plans can proceed without building into it the principles and priorities of the Dehcho First Nations at its very foundations. Added to this assurance, the agreement also established significant Dehcho control over resource development. It stipulates that no sales or leases of Crown land can occur in Dehcho territory without Dehcho support, nor can mineral prospecting permits, oil and gas exploration licences, or new forest management authorizations be issued without Dehcho authorization (Dehcho First Nations 2001, 8–11).

NATIONAL INDIGENOUS GUARDIAN NETWORK

An additional step taken toward Indigenous sovereignty in the Canadian territorial north comes by way of the Canadian government's support of a National Indigenous Guardian Network program in which the Dehcho First Nations are participants. In this case, there is no joint intergovernmental management but, more significantly, just federal financial support for a program initiated and independently run by Indigenous nations. The program employs Indigenous guardians who serve as "eyes on the ground" in Indigenous traditional territories. These guardians perform a range of tasks including monitoring ecological health, maintaining cultural sites, protecting sensitive areas and species, interpreting Indigenous culture and heritage for visitors, contributing to land and marine planning and management, and promoting intergenerational sharing of Indigenous knowledge (Indigenous Leadership Initiative 2016, 1–2).

The performance of the above tasks can be interpreted as Indigenous nations peacefully asserting their sovereignty over their traditional territories. As put by Haida Nation leader Miles Richardson, "what they [the guardians] are asserting is the policies of their governments, their sovereignty, if you will, in a constructive way" (O'Neil 2016, A8). The partnership component comes in because, while Indigenous nations create the policy and legislative framework, the federal government contributes funding to support Indigenous governments in operating their programs. Currently, there are approximately 30 Indigenous Guardian programs operating across Canada, including the Dehcho guardians, "the Haida Watchmen, the Coastal Guardian Watchman Network, the Innu Environmental Guardians, and the Lutsel K'e Ni Hat'Ni Dene" (Indigenous Leadership Initiative 2016, 2). The Indigenous Leadership Initiative (along with Assembly of First Nations support) would like to see that number increased to at least 200, and to that end it requested of the federal government in its 2017–18 budget cycle an investment of $500 million over five years.[16] The Liberal government responded with an initial investment of $25 million over five years. While falling well short of the $500 million mark, the Indigenous Leadership Initiative nevertheless declared that as seed funding the amount would help in developing a national guardian network and in preparing "Indigenous Nations and communities to launch their own Indigenous Guardian programs" (Indigenous Leadership Initiative 2017, 1).

WILDLIFE MANAGEMENT, FISHERIES, AND COASTAL CONSERVATION

The federal, provincial, and territorial governments have also negotiated several shared decision-making agreements with Indigenous nations in the areas of wildlife management, fisheries, and coastal conservation. The following four examples come from Ontario, Nunavut, and British Columbia.

Haudenosaunee

The protocol agreement concluded between the Haudenosaunee Wildlife and Habitat Authority and the Hamilton Conservation Authority in 2011 is unique because it is built on specific recognition of the historic treaty rights of the Haudenosaunee as negotiated at Albany in 1701. Under the terms of the treaty, the Crown agreed to respect Haudenosaunee rights in their beaver hunting grounds, lands that now fall partially under the jurisdiction of the Hamilton Conservation Authority in the Dundas Valley region of Ontario. The protocol agreement itself is not a treaty but is crafted in a way that reflects a commitment to treaty principles that grant recognition to the political authority of both partners in the arrangement. Under the terms of the protocol, both parties acknowledge that "under the laws of their nations" they "share a responsibility to protect [their] home ecosystems," which includes a commitment to work together to manage local wildlife populations in a way that respects Haudenosaunee hunting rights, particularly their right to harvest deer (Haudenosaunee Wildlife and Habitat Authority and Hamilton Conservation Authority 2011, 1).

With the principle of shared responsibilities placed front and centre, the protocol then goes on to provide details about how it is to be operationalized. The protocol takes up such subjects as what conservation principles are to govern the terms of their relationship, expectations concerning when and how often conservation planning meetings between the parties are to take place, and what techniques will be employed to cull deer populations if and when justified for the sake of maintaining balance in the local ecosystem. Most significantly, however, the entire protocol is animated by a treaty-informed spirit of mutual "respect, trust, and friendship." At one point, for example, the protocol commits the parties to a "joint approach to reducing the deer population," while at another the Haudenosaunee treaty right to harvest deer is specifically tied to seasonal use in keeping with the Haudenosaunee's ancient traditions. As described by the protocol: "deer taken under the aegis of this protocol will be used by the Haudenosaunee for midwinter ceremonies; for food for elders; and for food for families" (Haudenosaunee Wildlife and Habitat Authority and Hamilton Conservation Authority 2011, 2).

Nunavut Wildlife Management Board

As part of the 1993 *Nunavut Land Claims Agreement*, Inuit negotiators were determined to secure enhanced political powers for the Inuit over land, wildlife, and ocean management within their territories. To that end, the Inuit were able to negotiate into the agreement the Nunavut Wildlife Management Board, among other boards and tribunals (White 2020, 59). The board is an institution of Nunavut's Public Government and is designated as its main instrument for wildlife management and the principal regulator of access to wildlife in the Nunavut Settlement Area (Nunavut Wildlife Management Board 2018, 1).

The board was designed intentionally to operate as a co-management authority, as it is composed of nine members appointed by all those parties with a direct stake in wildlife conservation and welfare in Nunavut. The board is composed of four representatives from the Designated Inuit Organizations, three representatives from the Government of Canada, one representative from the Nunavut Territorial Government, and one chairperson appointed by Canada, with board input. Under the terms of its co-management mandate, the board exercises considerable independent authority in the planning and making of decisions about wildlife management, though final approval for all policy ultimately rests with the responsible federal or territorial minister. Yet even here the unique circumstances of the Nunavut Territorial Government's composition leave the Inuit in a favourable position. The Inuit constitute a political majority in Nunavut and thus are bound not only to dominate representation on the board but also the territorial Cabinet. Consequently, the interests of the Inuit will likely predominate at both levels, particularly so should there be a tendency for the interests of Canada to conflict with those of the Inuit in co-management discussions (Scott 2005, 151; White 2020, 59–60).

Nisga'a

The *Nisga'a Final Agreement* in British Columbia combines aspects of self-rule over fisheries and wildlife within the Nisga'a traditional territories with those of co-management. The line separating where Nisga'a self-rule ends and co-management begins is determined in part by the uses to which these resources are put and in part by geography. Questions concerning jurisdiction over fish and wildlife feature prominently in the agreement because both are integral to the Nisga'a way of life (Chapters 8 and 9). They are an important source of food for the people, but they also have commercial significance, particularly so with respect to fish. But because fish and much wildlife are migratory and therefore cannot be contained and regulated within the borders of Nisga'a settlement lands, a co-management regime with federal and provincial governments is an unavoidable necessity.

There are clear provisions within the *Nisga'a Final Agreement* guaranteeing the Nisga'a people the right to designated annual fish and wildlife allocations. These guaranteed entitlements are seen as a matter of Indigenous rights. The capacity of the Nisga'a Lisims Government to regulate and tend to the internal distribution and allocation of those resources is also a response to an Indigenous right, in this case the right of the Nisga'a Nation to internal self-governance. Consequently, the Nisga'a Lisims Government can make laws to manage the nation's harvesting rights and conservation responsibilities over fish and wildlife provided that Nisga'a laws are consistent with the terms of the final agreement and with annual Nisga'a fishing and wildlife harvesting plans.

These self-governing provisions, however, are also accompanied by a co-management arrangement. This is because, as put by Tracie Lee Scott, "fisheries [and wildlife] cannot be regulated solely within national boundaries" (Scott 2012, 80). Consequently, according to the terms of the final agreement, it is the federal minister who is granted ultimate responsibility for fish and wildlife management (*Nisga'a Final Agreement* 2000, 112, 138). Importantly, however, the federal minister does not act alone, but rather works in cooperative consultation via committee with the Nisga'a on all matters relating to the regulation and conservation of fish and wildlife in the Nass area.

A Joint Fisheries Management Committee and a Wildlife Committee are provided for within the terms of the final agreement, made up in each case of Nisga'a, federal, and provincial representatives. Furthermore, while advisory only, all committee recommendations are to be presented to both the minister and the Nisga'a Lisims Government. These committees, in other words, are bodies created to promote shared decision making over fishery and wildlife resources that are valuable to Nisga'a and Canadian citizens alike. It therefore stands to reason that when it comes to making recommendations about matters such as allowable annual harvest levels, conservation requirements, short- and long-term management plans, or research strategies, these recommendations emerge as a product of intergovernmental discussions and agreements. To that end, the Joint Fisheries Management and Wildlife Committees can be seen as an exercise in which jurisdiction, and thus sovereignty, is shared between the governments of Canada, British Columbia, and the Nisga'a Nation.

Pacific North Coast of British Columbia

Under the terms of the 2018 *Reconciliation Framework Agreement for Bioregional Oceans Management and Protection*, 14 central and north coast Indigenous nations have agreed with the Government of Canada that they will share responsibility and authority for governing coastal waterways along the Pacific north coast of British Columbia.[17] The agreement commits the federal government and coastal nations to coordinate their marine governance, management, and conservation efforts over such areas as "marine ecosystems, marine resources, and marine use activities" (Prime Minister's Office, 2018, 1). Areas identified in the agreement as top priorities include "marine spatial planning and developing a network of marine protected areas" (West Coast Environmental Law 2018, 7).[18] The agreement also emphasizes the importance of shipping management, emergency preparedness, and in particular building the response capacity of local Indigenous nations. According to Marilyn Slett, this latter priority will require significant investments to make sure that Indigenous "community members have training, employment, and procurement opportunities in the industry," an eventuality that the agreement anticipates (Smart 2018, A4).

Taken together, the agreement has been heralded as an important step forward in protecting Canada's northern shelf bioregion, an extensive area that includes the four subregions of Haida Gwaii, the north coast, the central coast, and North Vancouver Island. But just as important from the perspective of Indigenous governance is the fact that the agreement represents a true commitment by Indigenous nations and the Canadian state to share jurisdiction over coastal marine areas.

IMPLICATIONS AND ANALYSIS

Evaluating the overall effectiveness of shared management initiatives from an Indigenous perspective is challenging for at least two reasons. First, many co-management committees are designed to be merely advisory and consultative in nature. Their task is to do no more than make recommendations to federal or provincial governments, governments that ultimately hold the final decision-making power. While these governments may choose to accept the recommendations of co-management committees, they may also choose to modify or reject them. The observation naturally follows that this power imbalance between Indigenous and Canadian governmental representatives on many co-management committees cannot be accidental. These factors lead Hayden King to conclude that colonialism remains very much intact because Canadian governments seem determined to maintain their stranglehold on land and resource management decision making (King 2015, 85; see also White 2020, 313–21).

Second, as observed by Olthuis, Kleer, and Townshend, while co-management committees are designed "to ensure that Aboriginal knowledge and perspectives are meaningfully incorporated," such attempts at incorporation may not fundamentally "change how problems are addressed or how knowledge is framed and incorporated into the work of a co-management board" (Olthuis, Kleer, Townshend 2012, 399). It is their view that when cultural differences are factored in alongside power imbalances, the outcomes of co-management deliberations can regularly be unsatisfactory from the perspective of Indigenous participants. They observe, for example, that more often than not it is Indigenous participants who are expected to adapt and work within frameworks (scientific and otherwise) that are "fundamentally rooted in state government perspectives" and not the other way around (Olthuis, Kleer, Townshend 2012, 400; see also White 2020, 313–21).

Nevertheless, based on the evidence reviewed in this chapter, I believe that co-management initiatives can and often do provide an important forum for political engagement between Indigenous nations and Canadian governments. As demonstrated, there is a shift in power underway based largely on the fact that Indigenous peoples will accept nothing less than that they be treated as full and equal partners at the various co-management tables. So, while many co-management initiatives may not constitute arenas within which Indigenous sovereignty is explicitly recognized or in which Indigenous knowledge and stewardship approaches are fully embraced, they can nevertheless serve as building blocks that may lead incrementally in the Indigenous sovereignty direction. Indeed, in some cases, true co-governance is gradually emerging as the new and preferred institutional reality. Some shared management initiatives are guided by nation-to-nation protocols, for example, while others are marked by a genuine sharing of policy-making powers. Consequently, while at their worst co-management initiatives may have no more than an advisory function in which Indigenous participants play a minor part, a parallel and gradually strengthening dynamic is also at play. In this scenario, federal, provincial, and territorial governments are gradually drifting closer to establishing genuine co-governance regimes with their Indigenous partners because they are making co-jurisdiction the new institutional norm (White 2020, 321–3).

CONCLUSION

Parallel to high-level negotiations about modern treaties, self-government agreements, and judicial review of Aboriginal and treaty rights are the more modest arrangements emerging between Indigenous and Canadian governments on the ground. Throughout this chapter, these arrangements have been identified as partnerships. They typically come in the form of shared ventures, sometimes political and at other times economic, and carry with them some promise of advancing Indigenous sovereignty, albeit in an incremental fashion. The advantage of these partnerships is that they are often less complex to complete than a full modern treaty or a negotiated self-government agreement. They can also be negotiated relatively quickly and can lead to immediate benefits for Indigenous nations, whether in the form of enhanced jurisdictional power or economic opportunities. They are interim arrangements, in other words, designed to enhance Indigenous capacity, power, and well-being right away while the larger issues of Indigenous title and rights, treaty rights, and the inherent right to self-determination are settled elsewhere. This chapter has cast the net rather wide in its examination of some of these partnerships and shared initiatives. When taken as a group, partnerships such as BC incremental treaties, impact and benefit agreements, and co-management initiatives reflect an increasing willingness on the part of Indigenous nations to work constructively with business enterprises and Canadian governments at all levels to advance the ambitions of their peoples.

But what is the impact of these partnerships and shared ventures on prospects for restored Indigenous sovereignty? While there can be no doubt that these partnerships and shared ventures do enhance Indigenous political power and access to economic resources, what they do not do is fundamentally challenge the legal and political standing of Indigenous nations in relation to their federal and provincial counterparts (Wilson,

Alcantara, and Rodon 2020, 6). Perhaps, therefore, these initiatives are best seen as tools primarily designed to facilitate the further integration and assimilation of Indigenous peoples into the Canadian state.

Based on their experiences of the past, Indigenous peoples have good reason to be skeptical of motivations that seek to draw them deeper into the operation of Canadian state federalism and free market capitalism. But at the same time, it is important not to underestimate the extent to which partnerships and shared ventures can establish fertile ground for the rebuilding of Indigenous sovereignty. In the first place, for the vast majority of Indigenous peoples, political sovereignty does not mean severing ties to Canada. Most assert sovereignty in the expectation that it will establish new political relationships with Canadian governments based on partnerships committed to sharing land, resources, and political power. Such partnerships need not preclude relationships that include mutually supportive interdependencies.

Second, partnerships need not relegate Indigenous nations to junior positions in a hierarchy that is manufactured by the Canadian state for its own benefit. Instead, partnerships can be deployed by Indigenous nations as a deliberate strategy in their own nation-building. Under this model, Indigenous nations reacquire land by whatever means are available to them, they secure economic benefits as the price companies must pay to extract resources from their lands, and they develop sound fiscal management and investment principles as a way to attract businesses to their territories. No less important, at every step along the way they also insist on their right to co-govern lands, waters, resources, and wildlife that they see as integral to their sense of themselves as distinct peoples and nations. Each initiative tends to build upon the others. Cumulatively, all contribute to the strengthening of Indigenous autonomy. Partnerships and shared ventures, in other words, can be seen as one of the avenues through which Indigenous nations are reasserting the presence of their sovereignty within Canada.

And third, just as partnerships and shared ventures can serve as tools to rebuild the internal capacity of Indigenous nations, they can also serve to facilitate the rebuilding of nation-to-nation relationships. Partnerships and shared ventures necessarily carry with them commitments to regular consultation and coordination of efforts between governments. Ongoing discussions are a required feature of the political landscape if Indigenous and Canadian governments are to come to land use agreements and co-management arrangements (of parks, wildlife, fish, and oceans) that can command Indigenous consent. The better the power balance in the relationship between Indigenous and Canadian governments, in other words, the more likely that those relationships will yield agreements that are reinforced on both sides by a sense of legitimacy. While it is still the case that Indigenous governments do not stand on an entirely equal footing with their federal and provincial counterparts in all their partnerships and shared ventures, there are also occasions where real power-sharing has been achieved. In this sense, enhanced Indigenous sovereignty can flow from the cooperative partnerships that Indigenous and Canadian governments take up with one another. Indigenous nations are increasingly insisting that they will have it no other way.

DISCUSSION QUESTIONS

1 How likely is it that the Government of Canada will implement all 94 of the Truth and Reconciliation Commission's Calls to Action? Are you optimistic or pessimistic, and on what grounds?
2 Can BC's strategic use of incremental treaty agreements help build confidence and trust in the larger BC treaty process? Or are they more likely to serve as a distraction from the more important objective of restoring the full extent of Indigenous rights to lands, resources, and political power?
3 Do impact and benefit agreements provide genuine opportunities for Indigenous political and economic empowerment? Or are they better seen as capitalistic arrangements that act to undermine Indigenous traditional values and cultural practices?
4 Some Indigenous feminists argue that because the gendered impacts of resource development projects can be so detrimental to the interests of women, all assessments of major development initiatives should be filtered through a gendered lens. What do you make of this argument?
5 Do co-management initiatives reflect a genuine commitment on the part of the Canadian state to share political power with Indigenous nations? Could they serve as important policy instruments to promote political reconciliation based on an equitable nation-to-nation relationship? Why or why not?

SUGGESTED READINGS

Alcantara, Christopher, and Jen Nelles. 2016. *A Quiet Evolution: The Emergence of Indigenous–Local Intergovernmental Partnerships in Canada.* Toronto: University of Toronto Press.

Alcantara, Christopher, and Michael Morden. 2019. "Indigenous Multilevel Governance and Power Relations." *Territory, Politics, Governance* 7 (2).

Belanger, Yale. 2018. "Chapter Twelve. Economic Development." In *Ways of Knowing: An Introduction to Native Studies in Canada*, 3rd ed. Toronto: Nelson.

Dalseg, Sheena Kennedy, Rauna Kuokkanen, Suzanne Mills, and Deborah Simmons. 2018. "Gendered Environmental Assessments in the Canadian North: Marginalization of Indigenous Women and Traditional Economies." *The Northern Review* 47.

Frideres, James S. 2020. "Chapter 11. The Political Economy of Indigenous Peoples." In *First Nations in the Twenty-First Century*, 3rd ed. Toronto: Oxford University Press.

Helin, Calvin. 2006. *Dances with Dependency: Indigenous Success Through Self-Reliance.* Vancouver: Orca Spirit Publishing & Communications.

King, Hayden. 2015. "New Treaties, Same Old Dispossessions: A Critical Assessment of Land and Resource Management Regimes in the North." In *Canada: The State of the Federation 2013, Aboriginal Multilevel Governance*, edited by Martin Papillon and André Juneau. Montreal: McGill-Queen's University Press.

Koutouki, Konstania, Katherine Lofts, and Giselle Davidian. 2017. "A Rights-Based Approach to Indigenous Women and Gender Inequities in Resource Development in Northern Canada." *Review of European, Comparative, and International Law* 27 (1).

Olthuis, John, Nancy Kleer, and Roger Townshend. 2012. "Chapter 20. Protection, Use and Management of Lands and Resources." In *Aboriginal Law Handbook*, 4th edition. Toronto: Thomson Reuters.

Papillon, Martin and Thierry Rodon. 2017. "Proponent–Indigenous Agreements and the Implementation of the Right to Free, Prior, and Informed Consent in Canada." *Environmental Impact Assessment Review* 62.

Poelzer, Greg, and Ken S. Coates. 2015. *From Treaty Peoples to Treaty Nation: A Road Map for All Canadians*. Vancouver: UBC Press.

Stienstra, Deborah. 2015. "Women's Relationships and Resistances to Resource Extractions." *International Feminist Journal of Politics* 17 (4).

Warry, Wayne. 2008. "Chapter 9. Sustainable Economic Development." In *Ending Denial: Understanding Aboriginal Issues*. Toronto: University of Toronto Press.

White, Graham. 2020. *Indigenous Empowerment Through Co-Management: Land Claims Boards, Wildlife Management, and Environmental Regulation*. Vancouver: UBC Press.

NOTES

1 As put by Christopher Alcantara and Michael Morden, "negotiations, cooperation and partnerships are governed by and work within the shadow of the Canadian state and the division of powers enumerated within the Canadian constitution." See Alcantara and Morden 2019, 253.

2 I thank one of the anonymous reviewers of this book for pointing out that the right to free, prior, and informed consent is one to which all the peoples of the world can lay claim, and as such constitutes an international human rights standard. Indigenous peoples therefore possess this right equal to all other peoples.

3 The other three countries to vote against the UNDRIP were the United States, Australia, and New Zealand, all countries that share similar colonial histories with Canada where relations with Indigenous peoples are concerned.

4 Shin Imai provides an instructive set of examples of international and Canadian institutions that have adopted the "free, prior, and informed consent" standard as an integral feature of their

business practices when pursuing development projects on Indigenous lands. See Imai 2017, 378–82.

5 I thank one of the anonymous reviewers of this book for providing me with this set of challenging and important questions.

6 For an exploration of the details that typically accompany each of the benefits identified, see Olthuis, Kleer, Townshend 2012, 407–14. See also Gilmour and Mellett 2013, 390–8.

7 Martin Papillon and Thierry Rodon demonstrate that not all IBAs are secured under terms that invite full community consultation and negotiation. It is for this reason (among others) that they argue IBAs are often rejected when submitted to the citizens of an Indigenous nation in a referendum. See Papillon and Rodon 2017, 220.

8 The Anishinabek First Nations involved in the Bamkushwada partnership include Fort William, Red Rock Indian Band, Pays Plat, Biigtigong Nishnaabeg, Pic Mobert, and Michipicoten. See Richardson and Mackay 2018, 3–4.

9 The Membertou First Nation was not always situated in its present location. Formerly located on what was known as the Kings Road Reserve, the then 125 Membertou members were forcibly relocated to their present reserve in 1926. The move was precipitated by a 1916 decision of the Exchequer Court of Canada on the grounds that the reserve was needed for Canadian settlement purposes. This was the first time in Canadian history that an Indigenous community was legally required by the courts to move. See Brown and Pyke 2015, 1.

10 When the Membertou First Nation reached its worst point in the mid-1990s, it received approximately $4.5 million in annual federal funding but also had a deficit to the order of $1 million. See Kayseas, Hindle, and Anderson 2006, 6–7.

11 The amount collected by the Muskeg Lake Cree Nation and turned over to the city of Saskatoon is equivalent to what the city would have received in property taxes if the land had remained under its control.

12 The specific programs and services mentioned by the Muskeg Lake Cree Nation include housing, finance, health and wellness, social development, community justice, recreation, and economic development. See Muskeg Lake Cree Nation 2018, 2.

13 The Osoyoos Indian Band Development Corporation reports that the band's business investments generated an estimated $28.2 million in revenue in 2017. See Osoyoos Indian Band Development Corporation 2018, 4, 5.

14 The Assembly of Nova Scotia Mi'kmaq Chiefs represents the interests of 12 Mi'kmaq Nations: Acadia, Annapolis Valley, Bear River, Potlotek, Eskasoni, Glooscap, Membertou, Millbrook, Paq'tnkek, Pictou Landing, Wagmatcook, and Waycobah.

15 The 13 First Nations are the Acho Dene Koe, Deh Gah Gotie, K'a'agee Tu, Katlodeeche, Liidlii Kue, N'ah Adehe, Pehdzeh Ki, Sambaa K'e, Ts'uehda, The'K'ehdeli, Fort Liard Métis, Fort Providence Métis, and Fort Simpson Métis.

16 The Indigenous Leadership Initiative is an organization that focuses on Indigenous land management and on strengthening Indigenous nationhood. It also works in partnership with the International Boreal Conservation Campaign.

17 The 14 central and northern British Columbia Indigenous nations participating in the agreement include Council of the Haida Nation, Lax Kw'alaams Band, Gitxaala Nation, Metlakatla First Nation, Gitga'at First Nation, Kitasoo/Xaixais First Nation, K'omoks First Nation, Heiltsuk Nation, Nuxalk First Nation, Wuikinuxv First Nation, Mamalilikulla Nation, Tlowitsis Nation, Da'naxda'xw Awaetlatla First Nation, and Wei Wai Kum First Nation.

18 Marine spatial planning is an internationally recognized approach to ocean planning that brings together partners from federal, provincial, and Indigenous governments and organizations to make informed decisions about balancing the increased demand for human activities on oceans with the need to protect marine ecosystems.

CONCLUSION

Occupying the Spaces In Between

Significant barriers continue to impede prospects for genuine reconciliation between Indigenous nations and the Canadian state. Perhaps the most significant of these barriers is that the Canadian state must accept responsibility for the fact that it has built its declaration of sovereignty on the unjust dispossession of Indigenous nations' right to self-determination over their lands, resources, and peoples. Throughout Canada's history, the British Crown and successor Canadian state have systematically denied the spirit and intent of the historical treaties, ignored Indigenous rights to political self-determination, dispossessed Indigenous peoples of their ancestral lands, and devalued the distinctive ways of life upon which Indigenous peoples have forged their identities. Against this background of colonial history, Canada must now accept its culpability. Justice requires that Canada examine the foundations of its own claim to sovereignty and then recalibrate the distribution of state power to restore to Indigenous nations a full measure of their inherent rights.

Fortunately, there are signs indicating a new relationship based on a more equitable distribution of power between Indigenous nations and the Canadian state is emerging. The pre-eminent responsibility for this recalibration of power falls to those who have profited from colonization. Yet, not surprisingly, it is Indigenous peoples who have taken the lead in articulating what is required by way of response from the Canadian state. Indigenous peoples have long insisted, for example, that they continue to possess their right to self-determination. While they agreed to share land, resources, and political power with settlers as documented in the oral and written terms of the historical treaties, they did not consent to British and later Canadian assertions to sovereign control over them. And because their Indigenous rights were never surrendered, Indigenous nations insist that they retain rights to political self-determination, to their lands, and to ways of life in keeping with their own distinct identities. In short, what Indigenous peoples have done is fight for their right to be free of unwarranted Canadian state interference in their lives. And what they have also done is insist on their right to enjoy political autonomy in the targeted spaces that they have claimed for themselves in between the exercise of Canadian sovereignty. While these Indigenous demands have been unsettling for Canada, they have also been necessary. Failure to meet them means that Indigenous and non-Indigenous peoples will not be reconciled.

The challenge of decolonizing the Canadian state is complex and is only made more so by the debate on the substantive meaning and practical implications of the Indigenous right to self-determination. As this book has demonstrated, the debate on Indigenous rights and what those rights demand from the Canadian state is fairly polarized. On the one side are those who argue that Indigenous self-determination is an inherent and independent class of political right that both justifies and requires maximizing Indigenous autonomy from the Canadian state. For those who hold this position, as put by Greg Poelzer and Ken Coates, "the solution is coexisting solitudes, with other Canadians recognizing full sovereign rights of Aboriginal societies" (Poelzer and Coates 2015, 267). On the other side are those who argue that Indigenous self-determination is a class of political right that originates within Canada and that both justifies and requires a division of political powers between Indigenous, federal, and provincial governments within a united Canada. For those who hold this position, Canada is the ultimate source of sovereign state power but is also a state in which Indigenous nations are entitled to their fair share of that power.

As important as these two positions may be from the perspective of principle, the approach taken in this book has been developed within a more practical and less polarizing framework. It has been my aim to demonstrate that these two positions do not adequately represent the actual progressive reacquisition of sovereignty that many Indigenous nations are already attaining, bit by bit, within the everyday settings of their collective lives. So, while there can be no doubt that Indigenous sovereignty is a class of political standing that pre-exists the Canadian state, the practicalities of the here and now demonstrate that sovereignty should be (and indeed, is being) exercised within the Canadian state with the objective of transforming the place of Indigenous nations within it. Understood this way, the standard of sovereignty is best seen as one that Indigenous peoples attain (and are often content to attain) incrementally rather than in an absolute form. The political imperatives advanced by this framework, therefore, are twofold. First, Indigenous peoples are entitled as a matter of right to reacquire political power from the Canadian state that is rightfully and already theirs; and second, they are entitled to do so according to schedules that are in keeping with their capacity for self-government and their associated priorities for community health, development, and well-being. Taken together, these imperatives form an internally integrated approach to reconciliation, namely, a commitment to rebuild the Indigenous capacity for political autonomy while also protecting Indigenous nations from external Canadian governmental interference.

Indigenous activist Arthur Manuel is convinced that Indigenous declarations of independence cannot only be "done within the Canadian space," as he puts it, but should be because doing so provides opportunity to reimagine a common future together (Manuel 2017, 196). This approach speaks to a notion of reconciliation in which the Canadian state itself is transformed because it becomes a space in which alternative forms of Indigenous sovereignty can both be expressed and serve as checks on Canadian state power. The image Manuel invokes is that of a partnership as expressed in the story of the Two-Row Wampum: "Indigenous and non-Indigenous peoples should be travelling in two canoes on the river together, but each moving under their own power and in control of their own direction" (Manuel 2015, 224). Important to emphasize from the vantage point of reconciliation is that the two canoes travel in the same river and in the same direction. They are bound together, in other words, expressing a common purpose to paddle side by side in peace, friendship, and respect, but also in mutual support of one another sharing in the bounty of the same waters and lands (Warry 2008, 184). Reconciliation in this scenario would be the attainment of such a balanced and equitable relationship.

Many Canadian citizens have also lent their voices to a movement that would see the place of Indigenous nations fundamentally transformed within the Canadian political order. In particular, the 94 Calls to Action of the Truth and Reconciliation Commission have served to galvanize Canadians' intention that Indigenous peoples receive the rights to which they are entitled. Indeed, "reconciliation" has become the new national buzz word and, in that vein, citizen groups are now applying political pressure to ensure that Canadian governments, public institutions, and private corporations embrace those Calls to Action in ways that are relevant to their respective mandates (Courchene 2018, 264).

Indigenous peoples have persisted in their refusal to submit to Canadian state assertions to sovereignty over their peoples, resources, and lands. But the consequences of their refusal to submit have often been devastating. In the face of confronting and regularly staring down the hegemonic power of the Canadian state, Indigenous peoples have lost so many of those characteristics that go into the forging of an identity of a people – land, resources, culture, spirituality, economic opportunity, political power, and most critically, life itself. And yet, throughout it all, Indigenous peoples have remained resilient and strong. They have persisted in their efforts to assert their rights to self-determination. They have insisted on their right to define what that right to self-determination means in practical terms for their nations. And they continue to expose the immorality of the Canadian state's presumption to claim totalizing sovereignty over their peoples and territories. In essence, the goal of Indigenous nations has been to create political space within Canada for their peoples to be autonomous again. Against such a compelling claim there ought to be no detractors. Indeed, reconciliation and the restoration of "right relations" between Indigenous peoples and the Canadian state depends on it.

And as the central theme of this book has repeatedly pointed out, Indigenous peoples are making significant headway in their quest. In their efforts to establish title to their ancestral lands and to their rights to self-determination, Indigenous peoples are transforming the very foundations of Canadian law and governance. Indigenous peoples now occupy many of the political spaces that exist in between the practice of Canadian sovereignty, and it can only be expected that they will expand those spaces with time. In short, Canada is already living with the presence of Indigenous sovereignty and is richer and better for it.

References

Abele, Frances. 2007. "Like an Ill-Fitting Boot: Government, Governance and Management Systems in the Contemporary Indian Act." Report prepared for National Centre for First Nations Governance. Vancouver: National Centre for First Nations Governance.

Abele, Frances, and Michael J. Prince. 2006. "Four Pathways to Aboriginal Self-Government in Canada." *American Review of Canadian Studies* 36 (4): 568–95. https://doi.org/10.1080/02722010609481408.

Adam, Betty Ann. 2017. "Treaty Land Entitlement Agreement Signed 25 Years Ago." *Star Phoenix*, October 20. https://thestarphoenix.com/news/local-news/treaty-land-entitlement-agreement-signed-25-years-ago.

Aiello, Rachel. 2021. "National MMIWG Action Plan Released with Short-Term Goals, Federal Support." *CTV News*, June 3. https://www.ctvnews.ca/politics/national-mmiwg-action-plan-released-with-short-term-goals-federal-support-1.5454751.

Albers, Gretchen. 2015. "Treaties 1 and 2." *Canadian Encyclopedia*. https://www.thecanadianencyclopedia.ca/en/article/treaties-1-and-2#:~:text=Treaty%201%20was%20signed%203,see%20Eastern%20Woodlands%20Indigenous%20Peoples.

Alcantara, Christopher. 2013. *Negotiating the Deal: Comprehensive Land Claims Agreements in Canada*. Toronto: University of Toronto Press.

———. 2017. "Implementing Comprehensive Land Claims Agreements in Canada: Towards an Analytical Framework." *Canadian Public Administration* 60 (3): 327–48. https://doi.org/10.1111/capa.12219.

Alcantara, Christopher, and Michael Morden. 2019. "Indigenous Multilevel Governance and Power Relations." *Territory, Politics, and Governance* 7 (2): 250–64. https://doi.org/10.1080/21622671.2017.1360197.

Alacantara, Christopher, and Jen Nelles. 2016. *A Quiet Evolution: The Emergence of Indigenous-Local Intergovernmental Partnerships in Canada*. Toronto: University of Toronto Press.

Alacantara, Christopher, and Zachary Spicer. 2016. "A New Model for Making Aboriginal Policy? Evaluating the Kelowna Accord and the Promise of Multilevel Governance in Canada." *Canadian Public Administration* 59 (2): 183–203. https://doi.org/10.1111/capa.12166.

Alacantara, Christopher, Zachery Spicer, and Roberto Leone. 2012. "Institutional Design and the Accountability Paradox: A Case Study of Three Aboriginal Accountability Regimes in Canada." *Canadian Public Administration* 55 (1): 69–90. https://doi.org/10.1111/j.1754-7121.2012.00206.x.

Alacantara, Christopher, and Gary N. Wilson. 2014. "The Dynamics of Intra-jurisdictional Relations in the Inuit Regions of the Canadian arctic: An Institutionalist Perspective." *Regional and Federal Studies* 24 (1): 43–61. https://doi.org/10.1080/13597566.2013.818981.

Alfred, Gerald R. 1995. *Heeding the Voices of Our Ancestors: Kahnawake Mohawk Politics and the Rise of Native Nationalism.* Toronto: Oxford University Press.

Alfred, Taiaiake. 1999. *Peace, Power, Righteousness: An Indigenous Manifesto.* Toronto: Oxford University Press.

———. 2005. "Sovereignty." In *Sovereignty Matters: Locations of Contestation and Possibility in Indigenous Struggles for Self-Determination*, edited by Joanne Barker. Lincoln: University of Nebraska Press.

———. 2009. *Peace, Power, Righteousness: An Indigenous Manifesto*, 2nd ed. Toronto: Oxford University Press.

Algonquins of Ontario. 2016. "Agreement in Principle Among: The Algonquins of Ontario and Ontario and Canada." October 26. https://files.ontario.ca/algonquins_of_ontario_agreement_in_principle.pdf.

Anaya, James. 2014. *Report of the Special Rapporteur on the Rights of Indigenous Peoples: The Situation of Indigenous Peoples in Canada.* New York: United Nations General Assembly.

Anderson, Kim. 2010. "Affirmations of an Indigenous Feminist." In *Indigenous Women and Feminism: Politics, Activism, Culture*, edited by Cheryl Suzack, Shari M. Huhndorf, Jeanne Perreault, and Jean Barman. Vancouver: UBC Press.

Aragón, Fernando M. 2015. "Do Better Property Rights Improve Local Income? Evidence from First Nations' Treaties." *Journal of Development Economics* 116: 43–56. https://doi.org/10.1016/j.jdeveco.2015.03.004.

Asch, Michael. 2014. *On Being Here to Stay: Treaties and Aboriginal Rights in Canada.* Toronto: University of Toronto Press.

———. 2018. "Confederation Treaties and Reconciliation: Stepping Back into the Future." In *Resurgence and Reconciliation: Indigenous–Settler Relations and Earth Teachings*, edited by Michael Asch, John Borrows, and James Tully. Toronto: University of Toronto Press.

Assembly of First Nations. 2012a. "National Dialogue on First Nations Citizenship: Background." Retrieved from https://www.aadnc-aandc.gc.ca [document no longer available online].

———. 2012b. "National Dialogue on First Nations Citizenship: Final Report and Recommendations for Action." Retrieved from https://www.aadnc-aandc.gc.ca [document no longer available online].

———. 2018a. "First Nations Determination of the Path to Decolonization." https://www.afn.ca/wp-content/uploads/2018/09/2018-39-First-Nations-Determination-of-the-Path-of-Decolonization.pdf.

———. 2018b. "Policy Forum: Affirming First Nations Rights, Title, and Jurisdiction." September 11 and 12. https://www.afn.ca/wp-content/uploads/2018/11/18-11-01-Affirming-FN-Rights-Title-and-Jurisdiction-Forum-Report-EN_REV.pdf.

———. 2019. "Honouring Promises: 2019 Federal Election Priorities for First Nations and Canada." https://www.afn.ca/wp-content/uploads/2019/09/Honouring-Promises_ENG_Rev.pdf.

Assembly of First Nations and Canada. 2017. "Memorandum of Understanding on Joint Priorities." June 12. https://www.afn.ca/wp-content/uploads/2020/01/06-MOU-on-Joint-Priorities.pdf.

Auditor General of Canada. 2016. "2016 Fall Reports of the Auditor General of Canada: Report 6 – First Nations Specific Claims – Indigenous and Northern Affairs Canada." November 6. https://www.oag-bvg.gc.ca/internet/English/parl_oag_201611_06_e_41835.html.

Barker, Joanne, ed. 2005. *Sovereignty Matters: Locations of Contestation and Possibility in Indigenous Struggles for Self-Determination*. Lincoln: University of Nebraska Press.

Barrera, Jorge. 2016. "Author Joseph Boyden's Shape-Shifting Indigenous Identity." *APTN National News*. December 24. https://www.aptnnews.ca/national-news/author-joseph-boydens-shape-shifting-indigenous-identity.

BC Treaty Commission. 2018. *Annual Report*. https://www.bctreaty.ca/annual-reports.

———. 2019. *Annual Report*. https://www.bctreaty.ca/annual-reports.

———. 2020. *Annual Report*. https://www.bctreaty.ca/annual-reports.

———. 2021. *Annual Report*. https://www.bctreaty.ca/annual-reports.

Belanger, Yale D. 2018. *Ways of Knowing: An Introduction to Native Studies in Canada*, 3rd ed. Toronto: Nelson Education.

Belanger, Yale D., and P. Whitney Lackenbauer, eds. 2014. *Blockades or Breakthroughs: Aboriginal Peoples Confront the Canadian State*. Montreal: McGill-Queen's University Press.

Bell, Catherine, and Harold Robinson. 2008. "Government on the Métis Settlements: Foundations and Future Directions." In *Aboriginal Self-Government in Canada: Current Trends and Issues*, 3rd ed., edited by Yale D. Belanger. Saskatoon, SK: Purich Publishing.

Bellrichard, Chantelle. 2019. "Budget 2019: $1.4B in Loans to Be Forgiven or Reimbursed to Indigenous Groups for Treaty Negotiations." *CBC News*, March 19. https://www.cbc.ca/news/indigenous/budget-2019-treaty-loans-forgiven-1.5063128#:~:text=Indigenous-,Budget%202019%3A%20%241.4B%20in%20loans%20to%20be%20forgiven%20or,negotiate%20comprehensive%20claims%20and%20treaties.

Bird, John, Lorraine Land, Murray MacAdam, eds. 2002. *Nation to Nation: Aboriginal Sovereignty and the Future of Canada*. Toronto: Irwin Publishing.

Boldt, Menno. 1993. *Surviving as Indians: The Challenge of Self-Government*. Toronto: University of Toronto Press.

Borrows, John. 1997. "Wampum at Niagara: The Royal Proclamation, Canadian Legal History, and Self-Government." In *Aboriginal and Treaty Rights in Canada: Essays on Law, Equality, and Respect for Difference*, edited by Michael Asch. Vancouver: UBC Press.

———. 2002. *Recovering Canada: The Resurgence of Indigenous Law*. Toronto: University of Toronto Press.

———. 2010. *Canada's Indigenous Constitution*. Toronto: University of Toronto Press.

———. 2016. *Freedom and Indigenous Constitutionalism*. Toronto: University of Toronto Press.

———. 2017a. "Canada's Colonial Constitution." In *The Right Relationship: Reimagining the Implementation of Historical Treaties*, edited by John Borrows and Michael Coyle. Toronto: University of Toronto Press.

———. 2017b. "Challenging Historical Frameworks: Aboriginal Rights, The Trickster, and Originalism." *Canadian Historical Review* 98: 114–35.

Borrows, John, and Michael Coyle, eds. 2017. *The Right Relationship: Reimagining the Implementation of the Historical Treaties*. Toronto: University of Toronto Press.

Borrows, John, and Leonard I. Rotman. 2003. *Aboriginal Legal Issues: Cases, Materials & Commentary*, 2nd ed. Markham, ON: LexisNexis Butterworths.

Boyden, Joseph. 2017. "My Name Is Joseph Boyden." *Maclean's*. August 2. https://www.macleans.ca/news/canada/my-name-is-joseph-boyden.

Bradshaw, Ben, Courtney Fidler, and Adam Wright. 2016. "Impact and Benefit Agreements & Northern Resource Governance: What We Know and What We Still Need to Figure Out." *Gap Analysis Report #9*. ReSDA. https://www.taylorfrancis.com/chapters/edit/10.4324/9781351019101-11/impact-benefit-agreements-northern-resource-governance-ben-bradshaw-courtney-fidler-adam-wright.

Brijbassa, Adrian. 2018. "As Osoyoos Indian Band Flourishes, so too Does Okanagan's Wine Tourism." *Youkon News*, April 23. https://www.yukon-news.com/trending-now/as-osoyoos-indian-band-flourishes-so-too-does-okanagans-wine-tourism/#:~:text=The%20efforts%20of%20the%20OIB,has%20found%20from%20its%20neighbours.

Brodsky, Gwen. 2014. "*McIvor v. Canada*: Legislated Patriarchy Meets Aboriginal Women's Equality Rights." In *Indivisible: Indigenous Human Rights*, edited by Joyce Green. Halifax: Fernwood Publishing.

Brown, Keith G., and Joanne Pyke. 2015. "Brand Membertou: Walking in Two Different Worlds." https://library2.smu.ca/handle/01/25502.

Bruyneel, Kevin. 2007. *The Third Space of Sovereignty: The Post-Colonial Politics of US–Indigenous Relations*. Minneapolis: University of Minnesota Press.

Carrigg, David. 2020. "Elected Wet'suwet'en Councils Reject Deal Made with Hereditary Chiefs." *Vancouver Sun*, May 13, A10.

Cassidy, Frank, and Robert L. Bish. 1989. *Indian Government: Its Meaning in Practice*. Lantzville and Halifax: Oolichan Books and the Institute for Research on Public Policy.

CBC News. 2017. "18,044 Applicants Eligible for Qalipu First Nation Band." February 7. https://www.cbc.ca/news/canada/newfoundland-labrador/qalipu-first-nation-numbers-1.3970137.

Centre for First Nations Governance. 2013. "Best Practices: Accountability and Reporting Membertou First Nation." https://www.askecdev.ca/directory/best-practices-accountability-and-reporting-membertou-first-nation-national-center-first.

Chan, Cheryl. 2017. "Airport, Musqueam Band Sign 30-Year Partnership." *Vancouver Sun*, June 22, A9.

Charlie, Lianne Marie. 2020. "Piecing Together Modern Treaty Politics in the Yukon." In *Visions of the Heart: Issues Involving Indigenous Peoples in Canada*, 5th ed., edited by Gina Starblanket and David Long. Toronto: Oxford University Press.

Chartrand, Larry. 2001. "Métis Identity and Citizenship." *Windsor Review of Legal and Social Issues* 5: 1–47.

Chiefs of Ontario. n.d. "Understanding First Nation Sovereignty." https://chiefs-of-ontario.org/firstnations/#:~:text=Understanding%20First%20Nations%20Sovereignty,-We%20are%20the&text=As%20the%20sovereign%20Nations%20of,economic%2C%20social%20and%20cultural%20systems.

City of Saskatoon. 2016. "Treaty Land Entitlement." https://www.saskatoon.ca/sites/default/files/documents/community-services/planning-development/future-growth/urban-reserves-treaty-land-entitlement/2019_tle_brochure.pdf.

———. 2018. "City, Muskeg Lake Cree Nation & Business, Celebrate Urban Reserve Anniversary." September 27. https://ilrtoday.ca/city-muskeg-lake-cree-nation-businesses-celebrate-urban-reserve-anniversary/.

Clarke, Tyler. 2017. "Sioux Valley Pursues Economic Growth to Take Advantage of Self-Government Powers." *The Brandon Sun*, January 4.

Clatworthy, Stewart, and Anthony Smith. 1992. *Population Implications of the 1985 Amendments to the Indian Act: Final Report*. Ottawa: Assembly of First Nations.

Coates, Ken. 2000. *The Marshall Decision and Native Rights*. Montreal: McGill-Queen's University Press.

———. 2008. "The Indian Act and the Future of Aboriginal Governance in Canada." Research Paper for the National Centre for First Nations Governance. Ottawa: National Centre for First Nations Governance. https://fngovernance.org/wp-content/uploads/2020/05/coates.pdf.

———. 2015. *#Idlenomore and the Remaking of Canada*. Regina, SK: University of Regina Press.

Coates, Ken, and P.G. McHugh. 1998. *Living Relationships: The Treaty of Waitangi in the New Millennium*. Wellington: Victoria University Press.

Coates, Ken, and W.R. Morrison. 2008. "From Panacea to Reality: The Practicalities of Canadian Self-Government Agreements." In *Aboriginal Self-Government in Canada: Current Trends and Issues*, edited by Yale D. Belanger. Saskatoon, SK: Purich Publishing.

Coates, Ken, and Dwight Newman. 2014. *The End Is Not Nigh: Reason over Alarmism in Analysing the Tsilhqot'in Decision*. Ottawa: MacDonald–Laurier Institute.

Cobo, José Martinez. 1983. *Study of the Problem of Discrimination Against Indigenous Populations*. New York: United Nations Department of Economic and Social Affairs. https://www.un.org/development/desa/indigenouspeoples/publications/martinez-cobo-study.html.

Coulthard, Glen Sean. 2014. *Red Skin, White Masks: Rejecting the Colonial Politics of Recognition*. Minneapolis: University of Minnesota Press.

Courchene, Thomas. 2018. *Indigenous Nationals, Canadian Citizens: From First Contact to Canada 150 and Beyond*. Montreal: McGill-Queen's University Press.

Coyle, Michael. 2017. "As Long as the Sun Shines: Recognizing That Treaties were Intended to Last." In *The Right Relationship: Reimagining the Implementation of Historical Treaties*, edited by John Borrows and Michael Coyle. Toronto: University of Toronto Press.

Craft, Aimée. 2013. *Breathing Life into the Stone Fort Treaty: An Anishinabe Understanding of Treaty One*. Saskatoon, SK: Purich Publishing.

CTV Saskatoon. 2018. "Muskeg Lake Cree Nation Marks 30 Years of Economic Development." https://saskatoon.ctvnews.ca/muskeg-lake-cree-nation-marks-30-years-of-economic-development-1.4112691.

Curtis, Christopher. 2018. "Kahnawake Election Uncontested, but Mohawk Politics Never Boring." *Montreal Gazette*. June 13. https://montrealgazette.com/news/local-news/politics-kahnawake.

Dalseg, Sheena Kennedy, Rauna Kuokkanen, Suzanne Mills, and Deborah Simmons. 2018. "Gendered Environmental Assessments in the Canadian North: Marginalization of Indigenous Women and Traditional Economies." *The Northern Review* 47: 135–66. https://doi.org/10.22584/nr47.2018.007.

Deer, Thomas. 2011. "Standardizing Governance in Kahnawa:ke: How Traditional Government Can Work Today – A Political Essay." *Iori:wase*. January 31. https://kahnawakenews.com/standardizing-governance-in-kahnawke-how-traditional-government-can-work-p1144-1.htm.

Dehcho First Nations. 2001. "Dehcho First Nations Interim Measures Agreement." https://reviewboard.ca/upload/project_document/EA03-005_Deh_Cho_First_Nations_Interim_Measures_Agreement.pdf.

Dorey, Crystal. 2012. "Mi'kmaq Negotiate Free Entry for Three Parks and Historic Sites in Nova Scotia." https://www.mmnn.ca/2012/06/mikmaq-negotiate-free-entry-for-three-parks-and-historic-sites-in-nova-scotia.

Dubois, Janique, and Kelly Saunders. 2013. "'Just Do It!': Carving Out a Space for the Métis in Canadian Federalism." *Canadian Journal of Political Science* 46 (1): 187–214. https://doi.org/10.1017/S0008423913000164.

Eberts, Mary. 2014. "Victoria's Secret: How to Make a Population of Prey." In *Indivisible: Indigenous Human* Rights, edited by Joyce Green. Halifax: Fernwood Publishing.

———. 2017. "Being an Indigenous Woman Is a 'High-Risk Lifestyle.'" In *Making Space for Indigenous Feminism*, 2nd ed., edited by Joyce Green. Halifax: Fernwood Publishing.

Eggertson, Laura. 2011. "Transparent, Entrepreneurial First Nations Reap Economic Success from Coast to Coast." *Toronto Star*, January 14. https://www.thestar.com/news/insight/2011/01/14/transparent_entrepreneurial_first_nations_reap_economic_success_from_coast_to_coast.html.

Elliott, Michael. 2018. "Indigenous Resurgence: The Drive for Renewed Engagement and Reciprocity in the Turn away from the State." *Canadian Journal of Political Science* 51 (1): 61–81. https://doi.org/10.1017/S0008423917001032.

Erasmus, Georges, and Joe Sanders. 2002. "Canadian History: An Aboriginal Perspective." In *Nation to Nation: Aboriginal Sovereignty and the Future of Canada*, edited by John Bird, Lorraine Land, and Murray MacAdam. Toronto: Irwin Publishing.

Everett-Green, Robert. 2018. "Court Ruling Settles Little in Continuing Dispute over Kahnawake Mohawk Membership Law." *Globe and Mail*. May 11. https://www.theglobeandmail.com/canada/article-court-ruling-settles-little-in-continuing-dispute-over-kahnawake.

Eyford, Douglas. 2015. *A New Direction: Advancing Aboriginal and Treaty Rights*. Ottawa: Indigenous and Northern Affairs Canada.

Federation of Sovereign Indigenous Nations. n.d. "Treaty Land Entitlement." Retrieved from https://www.fsin.com/ [document no longer available online].

———. 2007. "Treaty Implementation Principles." https://www.fsin.ca/tgo.

Flanagan, Tom. 2000. *First Nations? Second Thoughts*. Montreal: McGill-Queen's University Press.

———. 2019. *The Wealth of First Nations*. Vancouver: The Fraser Institute.

Flanagan, Tom, and Katrine Beauregard. 2013. *The Wealth of Nations: An Exploratory Study*. Vancouver: Fraser Institute.

Flanagan, Tom, and Lee Harding. 2017. "Treaty Land Entitlement and Urban Reserves in Saskatchewan: A Statistical Evaluation." *Frontier Centre for Public Policy*. https://fcpp.org/wp-content/uploads/FC17005_TreatyLand_F1.pdf.

Fleras, Augie, and Jean Leonard Elliott. 1992. *The Nations Within: Aboriginal–State Relations in Canada, the United States, and New Zealand*. Toronto: Oxford University Press.

Forrest, Maura. 2018. "Talk and Not a Lot of Action: Truth and Reconciliation Commission Drawing Mixed Reviews." *Vancouver Sun*, January 4.

Frideres, James S. 2016. *First Nations in the Twenty-First Century*, 2nd ed. Toronto: Oxford University Press.

———. 2020. *Indigenous Peoples in the Twenty-First Century*, 3rd ed. Toronto: Oxford University Press.

Furi, Megan, and Jill Wherrett. 2003. "Indian Status and Band Membership Issues." Revised February 2003. Parliamentary Research Branch. https://publications.gc.ca/Collection-R/LoPBdP/BP/bp410-e.htm#:~:text=Prior%20to%201985%2C%20automatic%20entitlement,be%20members%20of%20a%20band.

Gadacz, Rene R. 2006. "Métis Settlements." *Canadian Encyclopedia*. https://www.thecanadianencyclopedia.ca/en/article/Métis-settlements.

Garcea, Joseph. 2008. "First Nations Satellite Reserves: Capacity-Building and Self-Government in Saskatchewan." In *Aboriginal Self-Government in Canada: Current Trends and Issues*, 3rd ed., edited by Yale D. Belanger. Saskatoon, SK: Purich Publishing.

Gehl, Lynn. 2014. *The Truth that Wampum Tells: My Debwewin on the Algonquin Land Claims Process*. Halifax: Fernwood Publishing.

Gespe'gewa'gi Mi'gmawei Mawiomi. 2016. *Nta'tugwaqanminen: Our Story: Evolution of the Gespe'gewa'gi Mi'gmaq*. Halifax: Fernwood Publishing.

Gibbins, Roger. 1997. "Historical Overview and Background, Part I." In *First Nations in Canada: Perspectives on Opportunity, Empowerment, and Self-Determination*, edited by J. Rick Ponting. Toronto: McGraw-Hill Ryerson.

Gibbons, Lise, and Lorne Sully. 2014. "Urban Reserves: Lessons Learned from Saskatoon, Saskatchewan." Retrieved online [document no longer available].

Gibson, Gordon. 2009. *A New Look at Canadian Indian Policy: Respect the Collective – Promote the Individual*. Vancouver: Fraser Institute.

Gilmour, Brad, and Bruce Mellett. 2013. "The Role of Impact and Benefit Agreements in the Resolution of Project Issues with First Nations." *Alberta Law Review* 51 (2): 385–400. https://doi.org/10.29173/alr71.

Giokas, John, and Paul L.A.H. Chartrand. 2002. "Who Are the Métis? A Review of the Law and Policy." In *Who Are Canada's Aboriginal Peoples? Recognition, Definition, and Jurisdiction*, edited by Paul L.A.H. Chartrand. Saskatoon: Purich Publishing.

Giokas, John, and Robert K. Groves. 2002. "Collective and Individual Recognition in Canada: The *Indian Act* Regime." In *Who Are Canada's Aboriginal Peoples? Recognition, Definition, and Jurisdiction*, edited by Paul L.A.H. Chartrand. Saskatoon: Purich Publishing.

Goar, Carol. 2009. "Welcome to Sandy Lake." *The Star.com*, August 28. https://www.thestar.com/opinion/2009/08/28/welcome_to_sandy_lake.html.

Goetz, Steven. 2016. "Controversy over Canadian Author Joseph Boyden's Indigenous Roots Isn't about Blood." *Vice News*. December 30. https://www.vice.com/en/article/zmyp99/controversy-over-canadian-author-joseph-boydens-indigenous-roots-isnt-about-blood.

Government of British Columbia. 2007. "Best Practices: Creating Resort Partnerships with First Nations, 3." Victoria: Government of British Columbia. https://www2.gov.bc.ca/assets/gov/farming-natural-resources-and-industry/natural-resource-use/all-seasons-resorts/guide_to_creating_resort_partnerships.pdf.

Government of Canada. 1969. *Statement of the Government of Canada on Indian Policy, 1969*. Ottawa: Minister of Indian Affairs and Northern Development.

———. 1992. *The Charlottetown Accord, Draft Legal Text*.

———. 1993. *Nunavut Act*. SC 1993, c.28. https://laws-lois.justice.gc.ca/eng/acts/n-28.6/page-1.html.

———. 1995. *Federal Policy Guide: Aboriginal Self-Government: The Government of Canada's Approach to Implementation of the Inherent Right and Negotiation of Aboriginal Self-Government*. Ottawa: Minister of Public Works and Government Services Canada.

———. 1997. *Gathering Strength: Canada's Aboriginal Action Plan*. Ottawa: Minister of Public Works and Government Services Canada.

———. 2017a. "Canada and the Métis Nation of Alberta Advance Reconciliation with Signing of Framework Agreement." November 16. https://www.canada.ca/en/indigenous-northern-affairs/news/2017/11/canada_and_metisnationofalbertaadvancereconciliationwithsigningo.html.

———. 2017b. "Principles Respecting the Government of Canada's Relationship with Indigenous Peoples." October 4. https://www.justice.gc.ca/eng/csj-sjc/principles-principes.html.

———. 2018. "Government of Canada to Create Recognition and Implementation of Rights Framework." February 14. https://pm.gc.ca/en/news/news-releases/2018/02/14/government-canada-create-recognition-and-implementation-rights.

———. 2019. "Collaborative Process on Indian Registration, Band Membership and First Nations Citizenship: Fact Sheets." http://www.akwesasne.ca/wp-content/uploads/2019/01/Bill-S-3-Fact-Sheets.pdf.

———. 2020a. "The Final Report to Parliament on the Review of S-3: December 2020." https://www.sac-isc.gc.ca/eng/1608831631597/1608832913476.

———. 2020b. "Memorandum of Understanding Between Canada, British Columbia, and Wet'suwet'en as Agreed on February 29, 2020." https://www.rcaanc-cirnac.gc.ca/eng/1589478905863/1589478945624.

Graben, Sari, and Matthew Mehaffey. 2017. "Negotiating Self-Government Over & Over & Over Again: Interpreting Contemporary Treaties." In *The Right Relationship: Reimagining the Implementation of Historical Treaties*, edited by John Borrows and Michael Coyle. Toronto: University of Toronto Press.

Graham, John. 2007. "Advancing Governance of the Métis Settlements of Alberta: Selected Working Papers." Institute on Governance. March 31. http://www.metisportals.ca/cons/wp-content/uploads/2009/02/advancing-governance-metis-settlements-of-alberta.pdf.

Grammond, Sebastien. 2009. *Identity Captured by Law: Membership in Canada's Indigenous Peoples and Linguistic Minorities*. Montreal: McGill-Queen's University Press.

Grant, John. 2018. *Lived Fictions: Unity and Exclusion in Canadian Politics*. Vancouver: UBC Press.

Green, Joyce. 2005. "Self-Determination, Citizenship, and Federalism: Indigenous and Canadian Palimpsest." In *Canada: The State of the Federation 2003: Reconfiguring Aboriginal–State Relations*, edited by Michael Murphy. Montreal: McGill-Queen's University Press.

———. 2009. "The Complexity of Indigenous Identity Formation and Politics in Canada." *International Journal of Critical Indigenous Studies* 2 (2): 36–46. https://doi.org/10.5204/ijcis.v2i2.29.

———. 2014a. "Introduction: Honoured in Their Absence: Indigenous Human Rights." In *Indivisible: Indigenous Human Rights*, edited by Joyce Green. Halifax, NS: Fernwood Publishing.

———. 2014b. "From Colonialism to Reconciliation through Indigenous Human Rights." In *Indivisible: Indigenous Human Rights*, edited by Joyce Green. Halifax, NS: Fernwood Publishing.

———. 2017a. "Rebalancing Strategies: Aboriginal Women and Constitutional Rights in Canada." In *Making Space for Indigenous Feminism*, 2nd ed., edited by Joyce Green. Halifax: Fernwood Publishing.

———. 2017b. "Taking More Account of Indigenous Feminism: An Introduction." In *Making Space for Indigenous Feminism*, 2nd ed., edited by Joyce Green. Halifax: Fernwood Publishing.

———. 2020. "Enacting Reconciliation." In *Visions of the Heart: Issues Involving Indigenous Peoples in Canada*, 5th ed., edited by Gina Starblanket and David Long. Toronto: Oxford University Press.

Haida Nation. 2017. "Kunst'aa Guu–Kunst'aayah: Moving to a Sustainable Future Together." https://coastfunds.ca/stories/kunstaa-guu-kunstaayah-reconciliation-protocol-moving-to-a-sustainable-future-together.

Hamilton, A.C., and C.M. Sinclair. 1991. *Report of the Aboriginal Justice Inquiry of Manitoba, Volume 1: The Justice System and Aboriginal People*. Winnipeg: Queen's Printer.

Hamilton, Graeme. 2018. "Reserve's Mixed-Couple Law Unconstitutional." *Vancouver Sun*, May 1, NP7.

Haslip, Susan. 2002. "The (Re)Introduction of Restorative Justice in Kahnawake: Beyond Indigenization." *Murdoch University Electronic Journal of Law* 9 (1). http://www.murdoch.edu.au/elaw/issues/v9n1/haslip91.html.

Haudenosaunee. n.d. "Government." http://www.kahnawakelonghouse.com/index.php?mid=1#:~:text=The%20Haudenosaunee%20Grand%20Council%20of%20Chiefs%2C%20also%20know%20as%20the,Nations%20of%20the%20Iroquois%20Confederacy.

Haudenosaunee Wildlife and Habitat Authority and the Hamilton Conservation Authority. 2011. "Protocol Between the Haudenosaunee Wildlife and Habitat Authority and the Hamilton Conservation Authority." November. https://conservationhamilton.ca/wp-content/uploads/2020/11/Protocol-between-the-Haudenosaunee-Wildlife-and-Habitat-Authority-and-the-HCA.pdf.

Hayward, Jonathan. 2018. "Leak Warnings, Altered Routes among Ignored Suggestions." *Vancouver Sun*, September 8, A3.

Hedican, Edward J. 2013. *Ipperwash: The Tragic Failure of Canada's Aboriginal Policy*. Toronto: University of Toronto Press.

Helin, Calvin. 2006. *Dances with Dependency: Indigenous Success through Self-Reliance*. Vancouver: Orca Spirit Publishing & Communications.

Henderson, James (Sákéj) Youngblood. 2008. "Treaty Governance." In *Aboriginal Self-Government in Canada: Current Trends and Issues*, edited by Yale D. Belanger. Saskatoon: Purich Publishing Limited.

Hicks, Jack, and Graham White. 2015. *Made in Nunavut: An Experiment in Decentralized Government*. Vancouver: UBC Press.

Hilleary, Cecily. 2017. "Native Americans Call for Rethink of Bering Strait Theory." *Voice of America*, June 15. https://www.voanews.com/a/native-americans-call-for-rethink-of-bering-strait-theory/3901792.html.

Hoehn, Felix. 2012. Reconciling Sovereignties: Aboriginal Nations and Canada. Saskatoon: Native Law Centre.

Hoekstra, Gordon. 2017. "Plan Provides Protection for 'Sacred Headwaters': Province Strikes 20-Year Deal with Tahltan Nation." *Vancouver Sun*, May 26, A8.

Huhndorf, Shari M., and Cheryl Suzack. 2010. "Indigenous Feminism: Theorizing the Issues." In *Indigenous Women and Feminism: Politics, Activism, Culture*, edited by Cheryl Suzack, Shari M. Huhndorf, Jeanne Perreault, and Jean Barman. Vancouver: UBC Press.

Hunter, Anna. 2006. "The Politics of Aboriginal Self-Government." In *Canadian Politics: Democracy and Dissent,* edited by Joan Grace and Byron Sheldrick. Toronto: Pearson.

Hunter, Justine. 2017. "Reconciliation of a Different Kind with LNG." *Globe and Mail*, January 13. https://www.theglobeandmail.com/news/british-columbia/bc-first-nation-shapes-a-new-approach-with-lngproject/article33625413.

Imai, Shin. 2017. "Consult, Consent, and Veto: International Norms and Canadian Treaties." In *The Right Relationship: Reimagining the Implementation of Historical Treaties*, edited by John Borrows and Michael Coyle. Toronto: University of Toronto Press.

Independent Assessment Oversight Committee. 2021. *Independent Assessment Process, 2021*. http://www.iap-pei.ca/media/information/publication/pdf/FinalReport/IAP-FR-2021-03-11-eng.pdf.

Indigenous and Northern Affairs Canada. n.d.a. "National Summary on Specific Claims." https://services.aadnc-aandc.gc.ca/scbri_e/main/reportingcentre/external/externalreporting.aspx.

———. n.d.b. "General Briefing Note on Canada's Self-Government and Comprehensive Land Claims Policies and Status of Negotiations." https://www.rcaanc-cirnac.gc.ca/eng/1373385502190/1542727338550.

———. n.d.c. "Treaty Texts – Treaties No. 1 and No. 2." https://www.aadnc-aandc.gc.ca/eng/1100100028664/1100100028665.

———. n.d.d. "Treaty Texts – Treaty No. 4." https://www.aadnc-aandc.gc.ca/eng/1100100028689/1100100028690.

———. 2014. "Sioux Valley Dakota Nation Governance Agreement and Tripartite Governance Agreement." https://www.rcaanc-cirnac.gc.ca/eng/1385741084467/1551118616967.

———. 2015a. "General Briefing Note on Canada's Self-Government and Comprehensive Claims Policies and the Status of Negotiations." https://publications.gc.ca/site/eng/9.836051/publication.html.

———. 2015b. "Transfer of Control of Membership." https://www.aadnc-aandc.gc.ca/eng/1100100032466/1100100032467.

———. 2017. "Have You Applied to Join the Qalipu Mi'kmaq First Nation?" https://www.aadnc-aandc.gc.ca/eng/1319805325971/1319805372507.

Indigenous Leadership Initiative. 2016. "Towards a National Indigenous Guardians Network: Brief to the Standing Committee on Finance from the Indigenous Leadership Initiative." https://www.ourcommons.ca/Content/Committee/421/FINA/Brief/BR8398284/br-external/IndigenousLeadershipInitiative-e.pdf.

———. 2017. "Release: National Indigenous Guardians Network Receives Funding in Federal Budget." March 22. https://www.ilinationhood.ca/news/national-indigenous-guardians-network-receives-funding-in-federal-budget#:~:text=National%20Indigenous%20Guardians%20Network%20Receives%20Funding%20In%20Federal%20Budget,-Mar%2022&text=Ottawa%3A%20Wed.,the%202017%2D2018%20federal%20budget.

Irlbacher-Fox, Stephanie. 2009. *Finding Dahshaa: Self Government, Social Suffering and Aboriginal Policy in Canada*. Vancouver: UBC Press.

Isaac, Thomas. 2012. *Aboriginal Law: Commentary and Analysis*. Saskatoon, SK: Purich Publishing.

Jai, Julie. 2014. "The Journey of Reconciliation: Understanding our Treaty Past, Present, and Future." Caledon Institute of Social Policy. https://maytree.com/wp-content/uploads/1032ENG.pdf.

———. 2017. "Bargains Made in Bad Times: How Principles of Modern Treaties Can Reinvigorate Historic Treaties." In *The Right Relationship: Reimagining the Implementation of Historical Treaties*, edited by John Borrows and Michael Coyle. Toronto: University of Toronto Press.

Joint Technical Working Group, AFN–INAC. 2008. "First Nations Registration (Status) and Membership Research Report." https://fngovernance.org/wp-content/uploads/2020/06/First_Nations_Registration_and_Membership_Research_Report.pdf.

Jung, Courtney. 2016. "Walls and Bridges: Competing Agendas in Transitional Justice." In *From Recognition to Reconciliation: Essays on the Constitutional Entrenchment of Aboriginal and Treaty Rights*, edited by Patrick Macklem and Douglas Sanderson. Toronto: University of Toronto Press.

Kayseas, Bob, Kevin Hindle, and Robert B. Andersson. 2006. "Fostering Indigenous Entrepreneurship: A Case Study of the Membertou First Nation, Nova Scotia, Canada."

Kelly, Ash. 2017. "Newly Elected Squamish Nation Council May Have Implications for Future of Woodfibre LNG." *CBC News*, December 11. https://www.cbc.ca/news/canada/british-columbia/newly-elected-squamish-nation-council-may-have-implications-for-future-of-woodfibre-lng-1.4443203.

Kessler, Ryan. 2017. "Sask. Indigenous Leaders Celebrate Treaty Land Entitlement Agreement." *Global News*, October 19. https://globalnews.ca/news/3814752/saskatchewan-indigenous-treaty-land-entitlement-agreement.

King, Hayden. 2015. "New Treaties, Same Old Dispossession: A Critical Assessment of Land and Resource Management Regimes in the North." In *Canada: The State of the Federation 2013, Aboriginal Multilevel Governance*, edited by Martin Papillon and André Juneau. Montreal: McGill-Queen's University Press.

———. 2016. "Joseph Boyden, Where Are You From?" *Globe and Mail*, December 28. https://www.theglobeandmail.com/opinion/joseph-boyden-where-are-you-from/article33441604.

———. 2018. "Treaty Making and Breaking in Settler Colonial Canada." In *Contemporary Inequalities and Social Justice in Canada*, edited by Janine Brodie. Toronto: University of Toronto Press.

King, Hayden, and Shiri Pasternak. 2018. "Canada's Emerging Indigenous Rights Framework: A Critical Analysis." Yellowhead Institute. June 5. https://yellowheadinstitute.org/rightsframework.

King, Nancy. 2018. "Membertou-CME Deal Ship-Shape." *Cape Breton Post*, May 26. https://www.capebretonpost.com/business/membertou-cme-deal-ship-shape-213308.

Kleer, Nancy, and Judith Rae. 2014. "Divided We Fall: Tsilhqot'in and the Historic Treaties." https://www.oktlaw.com/divided-fall-tsilhqotin-historic-treaties/#:~:text=What%20is%20at%20stake%20is,the%20group%20and%20broader%20society.

Koutouki, Konstania, Katherine Lofts, and Giselle Davidian. 2017. "A Rights-Based Approach to Indigenous Women and Gender Inequities in Resource Development in Northern Canada." *Review of European, Comparative, and International Law* 27 (1): 63–74. https://doi.org/10.1111/reel.12240.

Kuokkanen, Rauna. 2012. "Self-Determination and Indigenous Women's Rights at the Intersection of International Human Rights." *Human Rights Quarterly* 34: 225–50. https://doi.org/10.1353/hrq.2012.0000.

———. 2014. "Confronting Violence: Indigenous Women, Self-Determination and International Human Rights." In *Indivisible: Indigenous Human Rights*, edited by Joyce Green. Halifax: Fernwood Publishing.

Ladner, Kiera L. 2003. "Rethinking Aboriginal Governance." In *Reinventing Canada: Politics in the 21st Century*, edited by Janine Brodie and Linda Trimble. Toronto: Prentice Hall.

———. 2005. "Up the Creek: Fishing for a New Constitutional Order." *Canadian Journal of Political Science* 38 (4): 923–53.

———. 2006. "Indigenous Governance: Questioning the Status and the Possibilities for Reconciliation with Canada's Commitment to Aboriginal and Treaty Rights." Research Paper for the National Centre for First Nations Governance. https://nnigovernance.arizona.edu/indigenous-governance-questioning-status-and-possibilities-reconciliation-canadas-commitment.

———. 2017. "Taking the Field: 50 Years of Indigenous Politics in the CJPS." *Canadian Journal of Political Science* 50 (1): 163–79.

———. 2018. "Proceed with Caution: Reflections on Resurgence and Reconciliation." In *Resurgence and Reconciliation: Indigenous–Settler Relations and Earth Teachings*, edited by Michael Asch, John Borrows, and James Tully. Toronto: University of Toronto Press.

Lake Babine Nation. 2014. "Lake Babine Nation Incremental Treaty Agreement – Summary and Q & A." Lake Babine Nation Treaty Office. http://www.lbntreaty.com/updates/lake-babine-nation-incremental-treaty-agreement-summary-and-qa.

Larocque, Florence, and Alain Noël. 2015. "Kelowna's Uneven Legacy: Aboriginal Poverty and Multilevel Governance in Canada." In *Canada: The State of the Federation 2013 – Aboriginal Multilevel Governance*, edited by Martin Papillon and André Juneau. Montreal: McGill-Queen's University Press.

Lawrence, Bonita. 2004. *"Real" Indians and Others: Mixed-Blood Urban Natives Peoples and Indigenous Nationhood*. Vancouver: UBC Press.

———. 2012. *Fractured Homeland: Federal Recognition and Algonquin Identity in Ontario*. Vancouver: UBC Press.

Liberal Party of Canada. 2021. *Forward for Everyone*. https://liberal.ca/our-platform.

Little Bear, Leroy. 2013. "An Elder Explains Indigenous Philosophy and Indigenous Sovereignty." In *Philosophy and Aboriginal Rights: Critical Dialogues*, edited by Sandra Tomsons and Lorraine Mayer. Toronto: Oxford University Press.

MacDonald, David B., and Graham Hudson. 2012. "The Genocide Question and Indian Residential Schools in Canada." *Canadian Journal of Political Science* 45 (2): 427–49. https://doi.org/10.1017/S000842391200039X.

Macdonald, Fiona. 2014. "Democratic Multinationalism: A Political Approach to Indigenous–State Relations." *Constellations*, September. https://www.researchgate.net/publication/266378880_Democratic_Multinationalism_A_Political_Approach_to_Indigenous-State_Relations.

Macdonald, Fiona, and Karine Levasseur. 2014. "Accountability Insights from the Devolution of Indigenous Child Welfare in Manitoba." *Canadian Public Administration* 57 (1): 97–117. https://doi.org/10.1111/capa.12052.

Macdonald, Jake. 2014. "How a BC Native Band Went from Poverty to Prosperity." *Globe and Mail*, May 29. https://www.theglobeandmail.com/report-on-business/rob-magazine/clarence-louie-feature/article18913980.

MacDonald, Moira. 2017. "Six Indigenous Scholars Share Their Views of Canada at 150: Most of Them Won't Be Celebrating." *University Affairs Newsletter*, June 7. https://www.universityaffairs.ca/features/feature-article/six-indigenous-scholars-share-views-canada-150/#:~:text=Most%20of%20them%20won't%20be%20celebrating.,-BY%20MOIRA%20MACDONALD&text=Confederation%20has%20been%20described%20as,1763%20recognized%20certain%20Indigenous%20rights.

Mackey, Eva. 2016. *Unsettled Expectations: Uncertainty, Land, and Settler Decolonization*. Halifax, NS: Fernwood Publishing.

Macklem, Patrick. 2001. *Indigenous Difference and the Constitution of Canada*. Toronto: University of Toronto Press.

Macyshon, Jill. 2021. "Long-Awaited National Action Plan on MMIWG Falls Short, Critics Say." *CTV News*, June 3. https://www.ctvnews.ca/politics/long-awaited-national-action-plan-on-mmiwg-falls-short-critics-say-1.5454171.

Mainville, Robert. 2001. *An Overview of Aboriginal and Treaty Rights and Compensation for their Breach*. Saskatoon, SK: Purich Publishing.

Malcolmson, Patrick, Richard Myers, Gerald Baier, and Thomas Bateman. 2021. *The Canadian Regime: An Introduction to Parliamentary Government in Canada*, 7th ed. Toronto: University of Toronto Press.

Manfredi, Christopher P. 2004. "Fear, Hope, and Misunderstanding: Unintended Consequences and the Marshall Decision." In *Advancing Aboriginal Claims: Visions/Strategies/Directions*, edited by Kerry Wilkins. Saskatoon, SK: Purich Publishing.

Manuel, Arthur. 2015. *Unsettling Canada: A National Wake-Up Call*. Toronto: Between the Lines.

———. 2017. *The Reconciliation Manifesto: Recovering the Land, Rebuilding the Economy*. Toronto: James Lorimer and Company.

Maracle, Lee. 2003. "The Operation Was Successful, but the Patient Died." In *Box of Treasures or Empty Box? Twenty Years of Section 35*, edited by Ardith Walkem and Halie Bruce. Penticton, BC: Theytus Books.

McCrossan, Michael, and Kiera L. Ladner. 2016. "Eliminating Indigenous Jurisdictions: Federalism, the Supreme Court of Canada, and Territorial Rationalies of Power." *Canadian Journal of Political Science* 49 (3): 411–31. doi:10.1017/S0008423916000822.

McGregor, Deborah. 2020. "All Our Relations: Indigenous Perspectives on Environmental Issues in Canada." In *Visions of the Heart: Issues Involving Indigenous Peoples in Canada*, 5th ed., edited by Gina Starblanket and David Long. Toronto: Oxford University Press.

McIvor, Bruce. 2014. "How to Fulfil the Duty to Consult." In *First Peoples Law, 2014*. Vancouver: First Peoples Law Corporation.

McKee, Christopher. 2009. *Treaty Talks in British Columbia: Building a New Relationship*, 3rd ed. Vancouver: UBC Press.

McNeil, Kent. 2002. "Aboriginal Rights: The Legal Landscape in Canada." In *Speaking Truth to Power III: Self-Government: Options and Opportunities*. Vancouver: BC Treaty Commission.

———. 2007. "The Jurisdiction of Inherent Right Aboriginal Governments." Research Paper for the National Centre for First Nations Governance. https://digitalcommons.osgoode.yorku.ca/all_papers/261.

———. 2016. "Sovereignty and Indigenous Peoples in North America." *University of California Davis Journal of International Law and Policy* 22 (2): 81–104. https://digitalcommons.osgoode.yorku.ca/cgi/viewcontent.cgi?article=3639&context=scholarly_works.

———. 2018. "Indigenous and Crown Sovereignty in Canada." In *Resurgence and Reconciliation: Indigenous–Settler Relations and Earth Teachings*, edited by Michael Asch, John Borrows, and James Tully. Toronto: University of Toronto Press.

Melnitzer, Julius. 2017. "Ontario, Algonquins Move Closer to Signing Major Land-Claims Treaty." *Vancouver Sun*, November 23.

Membertou First Nation. 2018. "About Us." https://membertou.ca/community.

Metallic, Naiomi Walqwan. 2020. "The Relationship between Canada and Indigenous Peoples: Who Are We?" In *Canadian Politics*, 7th ed., edited by James Bickerton and Alain-G. Gagnon. Toronto: University of Toronto Press.

Métis Settlements General Council. 2017. "Making History: Our Land. Our Culture. Our Future." https://metissettlements.files.wordpress.com/2017/01/msgc_centennial_book.pdf.

Mi'kmaq Rights Initiative. 2014. "National Parks Interim Arrangement between Mi'kmaq of Nova Scotia as Represented by the Assembly of Nova Scotia Mi'kmaq Chiefs and Parks Canada Agency." https://novascotia.ca/abor/docs/Framework-Agreement.pdf.

———. 2018. "Parks Canada Interim Arrangement." https://www.pc.gc.ca/en/pn-np/ns/cbreton/visit/permis-permit/mikmaq.

Miller, J.R. 1989. *Skyscrapers Hide the Heavens: A History of Indian-White Relations in Canada*. Toronto: University of Toronto Press.

———. 2004. *Lethal Legacy: Current Native Controversies in Canada*. Toronto: McClelland & Stewart.

———. 2009. *Compact, Contract, and Covenant: Aboriginal Treaty-Making in Canada*. Toronto: University of Toronto Press.

Milloy, John. 2008. "Indian Act Colonialism: A Century of Dishonour, 1869–1969." Research Paper for the National Centre for First Nations Governance. https://nnigovernance.arizona.edu/indian-act-colonialism-century-dishonour-1869-1969#:~:text=In%201867%2C%20with%20the%20passage,nation%20from%20sea%20to%20sea.

Mills, Aaron/Waabishki Ma'iingan. 2017. "What Is a Treaty? On Contract and Mutual Aid." In *The Right Relationship: Reimagining the Implementation of Historical Treaties*, edited by John Borrows and Michael Coyle. Toronto: University of Toronto Press.

Minister of Indigenous Affairs and Northern Development. 2003. *Kluane First Nation Self-Government Agreement*. Ottawa: Minister of Public Works and Government Services, Canada.

Mintz, Eric, Livianna Tossutti, and Christopher Dunn. 2017. *Canada's Politics: Democracy, Diversity, and Good Government*, 3rd ed. Toronto: Pearson.

Mohawk Council of Kahnawá:ke. 2016. "Strategic Plan 2017/2018–2021/2022." http://www.kahnawake.com/org/docs/MCK-StrategicPlan(2017-2022).pdf.

———. 2018. "Kahnawá:ke Economic Opportunity Fact Sheet." Septembr 13. http://www.kahnawake.com/legalcannabis/attachments/Cannabis-KahnawakeEconomicDevelopmentFactSheet-Sept13-2018.pdf.

Monture-Angus, Patricia. 1999. *Journeying Forward: Dreaming First Nations' Independence*. Halifax: Fernwood Publishing.

Morales, Sarah. 2017. "(Re)Defining 'Good Faith' through *Snuw'uyulh*." In *The Right Relationship: Reimagining the Implementation of Historical Treaties*, edited by John Borrows and Michael Coyle. Toronto: University of Toronto Press.

Morden, Michael. 2013. "Telling Stories about Conflict: Symbolic Politics and the Iperwash Land Transfer Agreement." *Canadian Journal of Political Science* 46 (3): 505–24. https://doi.org/10.1017/S0008423913000668.

Morse, Bradford W. 2008. "Regaining Recognition of the Inherent Right of Aboriginal Governance." In *Aboriginal Self-Government in Canada: Current Trends and Issues*, 3rd ed., edited by Yale D. Belanger. Saskatoon, SK: Purich Publishing.

Municipal-Aboriginal Adjacent Community Cooperation Project. 2002. *Partnerships in Practice: Case Studies in Municipal and First Nations' Economic Development Co-operation*. Ottawa: Federation of Canadian Municipalities, Indian Taxation Advisory Board, Indian and Northern Affairs Canada.

Murphy, Michael. 2005. "Relational Self-Determination and Federal Reform." In *Canada: The State of the Federation 2003: Reconfiguring Aboriginal–State Relations*, edited by Michael Murphy. Montreal: McGill-Queen's University Press.

Muskeg Lake Cree Nation. n.d.a. "About Muskeg Lake." https://muskeglake.com/about-muskeg-lake/#:~:text=Muskeg%20Lake%20Cree%20Nation%20is,and%20informed%20by%20Cree%20Law.

———. n.d.b. "Leadership & Governance." https://muskeglake.com/leadership.

———. 2018. "First Nation Community Profile: Muskeg Lake Cree Nation." https://www.saskatoon.ca/sites/default/files/documents/community-services/planning-development/future-growth/urban-reserves-treaty-land-entitlement/fnp_muskeglake.pdf.

Nadasdy, Paul. 2017. *Sovereignty's Entailments: First Nation State Formation in the Yukon*. Toronto: University of Toronto Press.

National Inquiry into Missing and Murdered Indigenous Women and Girls. 2019. *Reclaiming Power and Place: The Final Report of the National Inquiry into Missing and Murdered Indigenous Women and Girls*. June 3. https://www.mmiwg-ffada.ca/final-report.

Newhouse, David, and Yale Belanger. 2020. "The 'Canada Problem' in Indigenous Politics." In *Visions of the Heart: Issues Involving Indigenous Peoples in Canada*, 5th ed. Toronto: Oxford University Press.

Newman, Dwight, G. 2014. *Revisiting the Duty to Consult Aboriginal Peoples*. Saskatoon, SK: Purich Publishing.

Nisga'a Final Agreement. 2000. Ottawa: Federal Treaty Negotiation Office.

NunatuKavut Nation. 2015a. "Constitution of NunatuKavut." Revised October 16, 2015. https://nunatukavut.ca/site/uploads/2019/05/constitution_oct_2015_f.pdf.

———. 2015b. "Governance Policies of NunatuKavut." January 2015. https://nunatukavut.ca/documents/governance-documents.

Nunavut Tunngavik Inc. 2004. "A Plain Language Guide to the Nunavut Land Claims Agreement." https://www.tunngavik.com/documents/publications/2004-00-00-A-Plain-Language-Guide-to-the-Nunavut-Land-Claims-Agreement-English.pdf.

Nunavut Wildlife Management Board. 2018. "Introduction, Mandate, Vision." https://www.nwmb.com/en.

Office of the Parliamentary Budget Officer. 2017. "Bill S-3: Addressing Sex-Based Inequalities in Indian Registration." December 5. https://www.pbo-dpb.gc.ca/web/default/files/Documents/Reports/2017/Bill%20S-3/Bill%20S-3_EN.pdf.

Office of the Prime Minister. 2017a. "Minister of Crown–Indigenous Relations and Northern Affairs Mandate Letter." October 4. https://www.pm.gc.ca/en/mandate-letters/2017/10/04/archived-minister-crown-indigenous-relations-and-northern-affairs.

———. 2017b. "Minister of Indigenous Services Mandate Letter." October 4. https://www.pm.gc.ca/en/mandate-letters/2017/10/04/archived-minister-indigenous-services-mandate-letter.

Office of the Treaty Commissioner. 2007. *Treaty Implementation: Fulfilling the Covenant*. Saskatoon, SK: Office of the Treaty Commissioner.

Olthuis, Kleer, Townshend, LLP. 2012. *Aboriginal Law Handbook*, 4th ed. Toronto: Carswell.

O'Neil, Peter. 2016. "Guardians Need $500M to Patrol Aboriginal Lands." *Vancouver Sun*, October 4, A8.

Osoyoos Indian Band Development Corporation. 2018. "Preserving the Past by Strengthening Our Future: Corporate Plan 2018–2022." https://www.readkong.com/page/corporate-plan-2018-2022-preserving-the-past-by-6208266.

Osoyoos Times. 2017. "Chief Louie Says First Nations Open for Business during Order of Canada Luncheon." April 4. https://www.timeschronicle.ca/chief-louie-says-first-nations-open-for-business-during-order-of-canada-luncheon.

Palmater, Pamela D. 2011. *Beyond Blood: Rethinking Indigenous Identity*. Saskatoon: Purich Publishing.

———. 2015. *Indigenous Nationhood: Empowering Grassroots Citizens*. Halifax: Fernwood Publishing.

Palmer, Vaughn. 2020. "Wet'suwet'en Deal May Sow further Disputes." *Vancouver Sun*, May 16, A16.

———. 2021. "Winds of Change A-stir for BC Crown Land." *Vancouver Sun*, April 27, A7.

Panagos, Dimitrios. 2016. *Uncertain Accommodation: Aboriginal Identity and Group Rights in the Supreme Court of Canada*. Vancouver: UBC Press.

Papillon, Martin. 2014. "The Rise (and Fall?) of Aboriginal Self-Government." In *Canadian Politics*, 6th ed., edited by James Bickerton and Alain-G. Gagnon. Toronto: University of Toronto Press.

———. 2020. "The Two Faces of Treaty Federalism." In *Canadian Politics*, 7th ed., edited by James Bickerton and Alain-G. Gagnon. Toronto: University of Toronto Press.

Papillon, Martin, and André Juneau, eds. 2015. *Canada: The State of the Federation 2013, Aboriginal Multilevel Governance*. Montreal: McGill-Queen's University Press.

Papillon, Martin, and Thierry Rodon. 2017. "Proponent–Indigenous Agreements and the Implementation of the Right to Free, Prior, and Informed Consent in Canada." *Environmental Impact Assessment Review* 62: 216–24. https://doi.org/10.1016/j.eiar.2016.06.009.

Parliament of Canada. 2008. "Statement of Apology – To Former Students of Indian Residential Schools." https://www.rcaanc-cirnac.gc.ca/eng/1100100015644/1571589171655.

Pasternak, Shiri, Sue Collis, and Tia Dafnos. 2013. "Criminalization at Tyendinaga: Securing Canada's Colonial Property Regime through Specific Land Claims." *Canadian Journal of Law and Society* 28 (1): 65–82. https://doi.org/10.1017/cls.2013.4.

Patterson, Lisa L. 2006. *Aboriginal Roundtable to Kelowna Accord: Aboriginal Policy Negotiations, 2004–2005*. Ottawa: Parliamentary Information and Research Service. https://caid.ca/AboPolNeg2006.pdf.

Pendakur, Krishna, and Ravi Pendakur. 2017. "The Effects of Modern Treaties and Opt-In Legislation on Household Incomes in Aboriginal Communities." *Social Indicators Research* 137 (1): 139–66. https://doi.org/10.1007/s11205-017-1593-5.

Penikett, Tony. 2006. *Reconciliation: First Nations Treaty Making in British Columbia*. Vancouver: Douglas & McIntyre.

Penner, Derrick. 2019. "Wet'suwet'en Dispute over Pipeline Deal Highlights Complexity of Indigenous Law." *Vancouver Sun*, January 12, A6.

Poelzer, Greg, and Ken S. Coates. 2015. *From Treaty Peoples to Treaty Nation: A Road Map for All Canadians*. Vancouver: UBC Press.

Ponting, J. Rick. 1997. "Historical Overview and Background: Part II 1970–96." In *First Nations in Canada: Perspectives on Opportunity, Empowerment, and Self-Determination*, edited by J. Rick Ponting. Toronto: McGraw-Hill Ryerson.

Prime Minister's Office. 2018. "Reconciliation Framework Agreement for Bioregional Oceans Management and Protection." June 21. https://pm.gc.ca/en/news/backgrounders/2018/06/21/reconciliation-framework-agreement-bioregional-oceans-management-and.

Province of Alberta. 2000. *Métis Settlements Act*. RSA 2000, c. M-14. Edmonton: Alberta Queen's Printer.

Province of British Columbia. 2018. "Incremental Treaty Agreements." https://www2.gov.bc.ca/gov/content/environment/natural-resource-stewardship/consulting-with-first-nations/first-nations-negotiations/incremental-treaty-agreements.

Qalipu First Nation. n.d. "Background." https://qalipu.ca/about/background.

Renke, Wayne. 2014. "Alberta's Métis Settlements and the Co-Management Agreement." *Constitutional Forum* 23 (2): 5–18. https://doi.org/10.21991/C9Z393.

Richardson, Don, and Scott Mackay. 2018. "Indigenous Impact Benefit Agreements that Broke New Ground in 2017." Shared Value Solutions, January 26. Retrieved from https://info.sharedvaluesolutions.com/ [document no longer available online].

Royal Commission on Aboriginal Peoples. 1993. *Partners in Confederation: Aboriginal Peoples, Self-Government, and the Constitution*. Ottawa: Minister of Supply and Services Canada.

———. 1995. *Treaty Making in the Spirit of Co-Existence*. Ottawa: Minister of Supply and Services Canada.

———. 1996a. *People to People, Nation to Nation: Highlights from the Report of the Royal Commission on Aboriginal Peoples*. Ottawa: Minister of Supply and Services Canada.

———. 1996b. *Report of the Royal Commission on Aboriginal Peoples, Volume 1: Looking Forward, Looking Back*. Ottawa: Minister of Supply and Services Canada.

———. 1996c. *Report of the Royal Commission on Aboriginal Peoples, Volume 2: Restructuring the Relationship*. Ottawa: Minister of Supply and Services Canada.

———. 1996d. *Report of the Royal Commission on Aboriginal Peoples, Volume 3: Gathering Strength*. Ottawa: Minister of Supply and Services Canada.

———. 1996e. *Report of the Royal Commission on Aboriginal Peoples, Volume 5: Renewal: A Twenty-Year Commitment*. Ottawa: Minister of Supply and Services Canada.

Saltman, Jennifer. 2019. "Police Break Up Northern BC First Nation's Pipeline Checkpoint." *Vancouver Sun*, January 8, A8.

Sandy Lake First Nation. 2015. "Sandy Lake First Nation Membership Code." Revised May 2015. http://sandylake.firstnation.ca/sites/default/files/SLFN%20Membership%20Code%20May%202015.pdf.

Saunders, Kelly, and Janique Dubois. 2019. *Métis Politics and Governance in Canada*. Vancouver: UBC Press.

Scholtz, Christa. 2006. *Negotiating Claims: The Emergence of Indigenous Land Claims Negotiations Policies in Australia, Canada, New Zealand, and the United States*. New York: Routledge.

Schouls, Tim. 2002. "The Basic Dilemma: Sovereignty or Assimilation." In *Nation to Nation: Aboriginal Sovereignty and the Future of Canada*, edited by John Bird, Lorraine Land, and Murray MacAdam. Toronto: Irwin Publishing.

———. 2003. *Shifting Boundaries: Aboriginal Identity, Pluralist Theory, and the Politics of Self-Government.* Vancouver: UBC Press.

Scott, Colin H. 2005. "Co-Management and the Politics of Aboriginal Consent to Resource Development: The Agreement Concerning a New Relationship between Le Gouvernement du Quebec and the Crees of Quebec (2002)." In *Canada: The State of the Federation 2003. Reconfiguring Aboriginal–State Relations*, edited by Michael Murphy. Montreal: McGill-Queen's University Press.

Scott, Tracie Lea. 2012. *Postcolonial Sovereignty? The Nisga'a Final Agreement*. Saskatoon, SK: Purich Publishing.

Sellars, Bev. 2013. *They Called Me Number One: Secrets and Survival at an Indian Residential School.* Vancouver: Talonbooks.

———. 2016. *Price Paid: The Fight for First Nations Survival.* Vancouver: Talonbooks.

Simpson, Audra. 2011. "Settlement's Secrets." *Cultural Anthropology* 26 (2): 205–217. https://doi.org/10.1111/j.1548-1360.2011.01095.x.

———. 2014. *Mohawk Interruptus (Political Life across the Borders of Settler States).* Durham, NC: Duke University Press.

———. 2016. "Consent's Revenge." Cultural Anthropology 31 (3): 326–33.

Simpson, Leanne Betasamosake. 2017. *As We Have Always Done: Indigenous Freedom through Radical Resistance*. Minnesota: University of Minnesota Press.

Sioux Valley Dakota Nation. 2016a. "Mission Statement." https://svdngovernance.com/governance/mission-statement.

———. 2016b. "A Self-Governing Dakota Nation." https://svdngovernance.com/governance/a-self-governing-dakota-nation.

———. 2016c. "Stats Sheet." https://svdngovernance.com/governance/svdn_facts_sheet.

———. 2016d. "Sioux Valley Dakota Nation: A Year in Review, 2015–2016." https://svdngovernance.com/media/svdn_YearInReview_2015-2016.pdf.

———. 2018. "Welcome to Sioux Valley Dakota Nation." https://svdngovernance.com.

Slattery, Brian. 2016. "The Generative Structure of Aboriginal Rights." In *From Recognition to Reconciliation: Essays on the Constitutional Entrenchment of Aboriginal and Treaty Rights*, edited by Patrick Macklem and Douglas Sanderson. Toronto: University of Toronto Press.

Smart, Amy. 2018. "First Nations and Federal Government Collaborate: Trudeau Announces Plan to Partner with Indigenous Communities to Protect Coast." *Vancouver Sun*. June 22, A4.

———. 2019a. "AFN Urges Liberals to Keep Going on Indigenous Issues." *Vancouver Sun*, October 24. A4.

———. 2019b. "Hereditary Claims Paramount, BC Chief Says." *Vancouver Sun*, January 17, A5.

Snyder, Jesse. 2020. "Trans Mountain Pipeline Gets 'Historic' Go-Ahead." *Vancouver Sun*, February 5, NP1.

Special Committee on Indian Self-Government. 1983. *Indian Self-Government in Canada*. Ottawa: Queen's Printer for Canada.

Spencer, Clarisa. 2014. "Negotiations Update: What's Happening at the Treaty Negotiation Table?" *Canyon Current* 5 (9).

Squamish Nation. 2014. *Annual Report 2013/2014*. North Vancouver: Squamish Nation.

———. 2015. *Annual Report 2014/2015*. North Vancouver: Squamish Nation.

———. 2016. *2015/16 Annual Report: Supporting and Sustaining Our Community and Culture*. North Vancouver: Squamish Nation.

———. 2021. *Annual Report 2020/2021: Supporting and Sustaining Our Community and Culture*. North Vancouver: Squamish Nation.

Standing Senate Committee on Aboriginal Peoples. 2010. *First Nations Elections: The Choice Is Inherently Theirs*. https://sencanada.ca/content/sen/Committee/403/abor/rep/rep03may10-e.pdf.

Starblanket, Gina. 2017. "Being Indigenous Feminists: Resurgence Against Contemporary Patriarchy." In *Making Space for Indigenous Feminism*, 2nd ed., edited by Joyce Green. Halifax: Fernwood Publishing.

———. 2019a. "Constitutionalizing (In)justice: Treaty Interpretation and the Containment of Indigenous Governance." *Constitutional Forum* 28 (2): 13–24. https://doi.org/10.21991/cf29383.

———. 2019b. "The Numbered Treaties and the Politics of Incoherency." *Canadian Journal of Political Science* 52 (3): 443–59. https://doi.org/10.1017/S0008423919000027.

———. 2020. "Crisis of Relationship: The Role of Treaties in Contemporary Indigenous–Settler Relations." In *Visions of the Heart: Issues Involving Indigenous Peoples in Canada*, 5th ed., edited by Gina Starblanket and David Long. Toronto: Oxford University Press.

Starblanket, Gina, and David Long. 2020. "Introduction." In *Visions of the Heart: Issues Involving Indigenous Peoples in Canada*, 5th ed., edited by Gina Starblanket and David Long. Toronto: Oxford University Press.

Starblanket, Gina, and H.K. Stark. 2018. "Towards a Relational Paradigm – Four Points for Consideration: Knowledge, Gender, Land, and Modernity." In *Resurgence and Reconciliation*, edited by Michael Asch, John Borrows, and James Tully. Toronto: University of Toronto Press.

Stark, Heidi Kiiwetinepinesiik. 2020. "Colonialism, Gender Violence, and the Making of the Canadian State." In *Visions of the Heart: Issues Involving Indigenous Peoples in Canada*, 5th ed., edited by Gina Starblanket and David Long. Toronto: Oxford University Press.

Statistics Canada. 2017. "Aboriginal Peoples in Canada: Key Results from the 2016 Census." https://www150.statcan.gc.ca/n1/daily-quotidien/171025/dq171025a-eng.htm.

St. Denis, Verna. 2017. "Feminism Is for Everybody: Aboriginal Women, Feminism and Diversity." In *Making Space for Indigenous Feminism*, 2nd ed., edited by Joyce Green. Halifax: Fernwood Publishing.

Steckley, John L. and Bryan D. Cummins. 2008. *Full Circle: Canada's First Nations*, 2nd ed. Toronto: Pearson/Prentice Hall.

Steel, Debora. 2015. "A Land Transfer Agreement through an Incremental Treaty with British Columbia." *Ammsa.com* 33 (8). https://www.ammsa.com/publications/ravens-eye/land-transfer-agreement-through-incremental-treaty-british-columbia.

Stienstra, Deborah. 2015. "Women's Relationships and Resistances to Resource Extractions." *International Feminist Journal of Politics* 17 (4): 630–51. https://doi.org/10.1080/14616742.2015.1060695.

Tabachnick, David. 2017. "Who Has the Right to Ontario's Algonquin Lands?" *TVO*, November 21. https://www.tvo.org/article/who-has-the-right-to-ontarios-algonquin-lands.

Talaga, Tanya. 2017. "Joseph Boyden's Identity Crisis Opens Up Questions on Who Is Part of a Community." *TheStar.com*, January 14. https://www.thestar.com/news/canada/2017/01/14/joseph-boydens-identity-crisis-opens-up-questions-on-who-is-part-of-a-community.html.

Tammemagi, Hans. 2017. "Membertou First Nations Band Leads the Way." *Road Stories*. May 3. https://roadstories.ca/membertou-first-nations-band-leads-way.

Tasker, John Paul. 2016. "Historic Land Deal with Algonquin Peoples Signed by Federal, Ontario Governments." *CBC News*, October 18. https://www.cbc.ca/news/politics/ottawa-ontario-algonquin-agreement-in-principle-1.3809876.

Taylor, Mark. 2013. "First Nations Boosts Partnerships with Business Community." *Globe and Mail*, April 26. https://www.theglobeandmail.com/report-on-business/small-business/sb-growth/first-nations-boost-partnerships-with-business-community/article11555856.

Telford, Hamish. 2015. *Rules of the Game: An Introduction to Canadian Politics*. Toronto: Pearson Canada.

Temper, Leah. 2018. "Is Next Standing Rock Looming in BC's North?" *Vancouver Sun*, December 22, A15.

Thom, Shelby. 2017. "Osoyoos Indian Band Generates More Revenue Than It Receives from the Federal Government." *Global News*, November 24. https://globalnews.ca/news/3880509/osoyoos-indian-band-generates-more-revenue-than-it-receives-from-federal-government/#:~:text=A%20recent%20study%20by%20the,for%20building%20a%20business%20empire.

Tomsons, Sandra and Lorraine Mayer. 2013. "General Introduction." In *Philosophy and Aboriginal Rights: Critical Dialogues*, edited by Sandra Tomsons and Lorraine Mayer. Toronto: Oxford University Press.

Townshend, Roger. 2015. "The Case for Native Sovereignty." In *Crosscurrents: Reader's Choice*, edited by Mark Charlton and Paul Barker. Toronto: Nelson Education.

Tremonti, Anna Maria. 2017. "Indigenous Identity and the Case of Joseph Boyden." *The Current*, January 5. https://www.cbc.ca/radio/thecurrent/the-current-for-january-5-2017-1.3921340/indigenous-identity-and-the-case-of-joseph-boyden-1.3922327#:~:text=A%20report%20by%20the%20Aboriginal,ways%2C%20raising%20suspicion%20among%20many.

Trudeau, Justin. 2017. "Prime Minister Justin Trudeau's Address to the 72th Session of the United Nations General Assembly." September 21. https://pm.gc.ca/en/news/speeches/2017/09/21/prime-minister-justin-trudeaus-address-72th-session-united-nations-general.

Truth and Reconciliation Commission of Canada. 2015. *Honouring the Truth, Reconciling for the Future: Summary of the Final Report of the Truth and Reconciliation Commission of Canada*. Ottawa: Truth and Reconciliation Commission of Canada.

Tŝilhqot'in National Government. n.d. "Tŝilhqot'in Rights and Title." https://www.tsilhqotin.ca/tsilhqotin-rights-title.

Tully, James. 2008. *Public Philosophy in a New Key. Volume I: Democracy and Civic Freedom.* Cambridge: Cambridge University Press.

Tumilty, Ryan. 2021. "Calls to Action Find Slow Response." *Vancouver Sun*, June 5.

Turtle Island Native Network. 2008. "Osoyoos First Nation." *Journey to Economic Independence*, February 13. https://nnigovernance.arizona.edu/journey-economic-independence-bc-first-nations-perspectives.

United Nations. 2007. *United Nations Declaration on the Rights of Indigenous Peoples*. New York: United Nations.

Venne, Sharon. 2002. "Treaty-Making with the Crown." In *Nation to Nation: Aboriginal Sovereignty and the Future of Canada*, edited by John Bird, Lorraine Land, and Murray MacAdam. Toronto: Irwin Publishing.

Vowel, Chelsea. 2016. *Indigenous Writes: A Guide to First Nations, Métis & Inuit Issues in Canada*. Winnipeg: Highwater Press.

Walters, Mark. 2016. "'Looking for a Knot in the Bulrush': Reflections on Law, Sovereignty, and Aboriginal Rights." In *From Recognition to Reconciliation: Essays on the Constitutional Entrenchment of Aboriginal and Treaty Rights*, edited by Patrick Macklem and Douglas Sanderson. Toronto: University of Toronto Press.

———. 2017. "Rights and Remedies within Common Law and Indigenous Legal Traditions: Can the Covenant Chain be Judicially Enforced Today?" In *The Right Relationship: Reimagining the Implementation of Historic Treaties*, edited by John Borrows and Michael Coyle. Toronto: University of Toronto Press.

Warry, Wayne. 1998. *Unfinished Dreams: Community Healing and the Reality of Aboriginal Self-Government*. Toronto: University of Toronto Press.

———. 2008. *Ending Denial: Understanding Aboriginal Issues*. Toronto: University of Toronto Press.

Webber, Jeremy. 2016. "We Are Still in the Age of Encounter: Section 35 and a Canada Beyond Sovereignty." In *From Recognition to Reconciliation: Essays on the Constitutional Entrenchment of Aboriginal and Treaty Rights*, edited by Patrick Macklem and Douglas Sanderson. Toronto: University of Toronto Press.

West Coast Environmental Law. 2018. "Tide Turning on Marine Co-governance in Canada." https://www.wcel.org/blog/tide-turning-marine-co-governance-in-canada#:~:text=Perhaps%20the%20best%2Dknown%20examples,Pacific%20Seamounts%20Expedition%20just%20concluded.

Western Economic Diversification Canada. 2016. "Urban Reserves in Saskatchewan." https://publications.gc.ca/collections/collection_2016/deo-wd/Iu92-4-36-2005-eng.pdf.

White, Graham. 2020. *Indigenous Empowerment Through Co-Management: Land Claims Boards, Wildlife Management, and Environmental Regulation*. Vancouver: UBC Press.

Whitt, Laurelynn. 2013. "Transforming Sovereignties." In *Philosophy and Aboriginal Rights: Critical Dialogues*, edited by Sandra Tomsons and Lorraine Mayer. Toronto: Oxford University Press.

Whittington, Michael S. 2000. "Aboriginal Self-Government in Canada." In *Canadian Politics in the 21st Century*, edited by Michael Whittington and Glen Williams. Toronto: Nelson.
Williamson, Pamela, and John Roberts. 2004. *First Nations Peoples*, 2nd ed. Toronto: Emond Montgomery.
Wilson, Gary N., Christopher Alcantara, and Thierry Rodon. 2020. *Nested Federalism and Inuit Governance in the Canadian Arctic*. Vancouver: UBC Press.
Wilson-Raybould, Jody. 2019. *From Where I Stand: Rebuilding Indigenous Nations for a Stronger Canada*. Vancouver: Purich Books.
———. 2021. *Indian in the Cabinet: Speaking Truth to Power*. Toronto: HarperCollins Publishers.
Yukon Government. n.d. "Kluane First Nation – Communities of Burwash Landing & Destruction Bay." *First Nation Community Profiles*. https://yukon.ca/sites/yukon.ca/files/ybs/ybs-forms/fin-kluane-first-nation-census-2006.pdf.

COURT CASES

Calder et al. v. Attorney General of British Columbia, [1973] SCR 313
Chippewas of the Thames First Nation v. Enbridge Pipelines Inc., [2017] 1 SCR 1099
Clyde River (Hamlet) v. Petroleum Geo-Services Inc., [2017] 1 SCR 1069
Daniels v. Canada, [2016] 1 SCR 99
Delgamuukw v. British Columbia, [1997] 3 SCR 1010
Descheneaux c. Canada (Procureur Général), [2015] QCCS 3555
Guerin v. The Queen, [1984] 2 SCR 335
Haida Nation v. British Columbia (Minister of Forests), [2004] 3 SCR 511
Mikisew Cree First Nation v. Canada (Minister of Canadian Heritage), [2005] 3 SCR 388
R. v. Gladstone, [1996] 2 SCR 723
R. v. Marshall, [1999] 3 SCR 456
R. v. Marshall; R. v. Bernard, [2005] 2 SCR 220
R. v. Pamajewon [1996] 2 SCR 821
R. v. Powley, [2003] 2 SCR 207
R. v. Sioui, [1990] 1 SCR 1025
R. v. Sparrow, [1990] 1 SCR 1075
R. v. Van der Peet, [1996] 2 SCR 507
R. v. White and Bob (1965) 52 DLR (2d) 481
Simon v. The Queen [1985] 2 SCR 387
St. Catharines Milling and Lumber Company v. The Queen, (1888) 13 SCR 577
Taku River Tlingit First Nation v. British Columbia (Project Assessment Director), [2004] 3 SCR 550
Tsilhqot'in Nation v. British Columbia, [2014] 2 SCR 256

Index

Abele, Frances, 42, 117
Aboriginal peoples, use of term, 8, 9, 23n13, 62–3. *See also* Indigenous peoples
Aboriginal rights
about, 218n1, 222n32
Canadian government acceptance of, 166–7, 173
in *Constitution Act* (1982), 39, 63, 152–4, 177n11, 181, 184–5, 186, 187, 188, 219n2, 269
constitutional conferences on, 153, 177nn13–14
court cases (*see* Aboriginal rights, court cases)
extinguished, modified, or non-asserted rights, and land claims, 150–1, 262–4, 288n10
land base and, 89
Métis and, 66, 188
prior occupancy and, 31
Supreme Court and, 181, 188–90, 211–12, 213, 214, 218n1, 219nn8–9, 223n34
use of term, 219n2
Aboriginal rights, court cases
R. v. Gladstone (1996), 187
R. v. Pamajewon (1996), 187
R. v. Powley (2003), 188
R. v. Sparrow (1990), 184–6, 207, 219nn6–7
R. v. Van der Peet (1996), 31, 186–7, 188, 189, 214, 220n11
Aboriginal title
about, 146, 190–1
comprehensive land claims and, 264–5, 271–2 (*see also* comprehensive land claims)
court cases (*see* Aboriginal title, court cases)
Delgamuukw test (standard of proof), 194–5, 221n19
fair compensation and, 196, 221n18
Supreme Court and, 181, 190–1, 197–9, 214, 221n22, 222n33
Aboriginal title, court cases
Calder et al. v. Attorney General of British Columbia (1973), 146–8, 192, 193, 194, 214, 220nn13–14, 229
Delgamuukw v. British Columbia (1997), 182, 183, 194–6, 196–7, 214, 220n16, 221n17, 221n19, 221n26
Guerin v. The Queen (1984), 192–4
St. Catherine's Milling and Lumber Co. v. The Queen (1888), 191–2
Tsilhqot'in Nation v. British Columbia (2014), 182–4, 196–7, 221nn20–1, 338, 354
accommodation. *See* duty to consult and accommodate
Akwesasne, 140, 326n3
Alberta, Métis Settlements, 61, 66, 298, 303–7, 326nn6–7
Alcantara, Christopher
on Canadian state, 16
on comprehensive land claims, 261
on impact and benefit agreements (IBAs), 338–9, 339–40, 341, 343
on nested federalism, 24n19
on partnerships, 328, 332, 366n1

Alfred, Taiaiake
on comprehensive land claims, 261–2, 264, 265, 267, 289n12
Indigenus resurgence and, 56n7
on sovereignty, 22n5, 32–3, 34
on treaty federalism, 319
Algonquins
comprehensive land claims, 253, 280–3, 284, 287n1, 289n20, 290nn21–2
land claims in Ontario, 253, 280–3, 284, 287n1, 289n20, 290nn21–2
pre-contact sovereignty, 103
Allied Tribes of British Columbia, 140
Anaya, James, 123, 149, 160
Anderson, Kim, 130, 321–2
Anishinabek First Nations, 344, 367n8
Anishinabek Nation of Ontario, 325n3
Anishinabek people, 237–8
Aragón, Fernando M., 257, 272
Asch, Michael, 31, 32, 55n4, 234, 239, 248, 250n15
Assembly of First Nations (AFN)
on Bill C-3 (2011), 95n27
on citizenship and membership, 68, 82, 94n19
establishment of, 141
on *Indian Act*, 83
Indigenous guardians and, 359
Kelowna Accord and, 160, 177n18
on Recognition and Implementation of Indigenous Rights Framework (2018), 171–2
residential schools lawsuit, 126
on sovereignty, 32
Trudeau government legislation and, 168
Assembly of Nova Scotia Mi'kmaq Chiefs, 367n14
assimilation
band council system (delegated sovereignty model) and, 36–7, 50, 120
colonial policies for, 15, 113, 114, 131, 140, 227, 228–9
enfranchisement and, 75–6, 77, 116, 128, 228
Indian Act and, 73, 74, 114–15, 127–8
reserves and, 117, 119
residential schools and, 123–7
treaties and, 239
White Paper (1969) and, 143–5
See also colonialism and colonial policies
Atleo, Shawn, 162–3
Australia, 133n1, 154, 366n3
autonomy, 12. *See also* treaty federalism

band councils, 119–23, 293–6
council selection and custom codes, 120, 121, 293–4
criticisms of, 10, 24n15, 37–8, 122–3, 135n14, 294–5
as delegated sovereignty, 36–8
vs. hereditary chiefs, 5, 6–7, 22n9
hostility towards, 135n13
as imposed, colonial system, 68, 116, 119–21, 135n11
jurisdiction and responsibilities, 121–2, 294
self-government and, 123, 295–6
Squamish Nation and, 296–8
Barker, Joanne, 3–4, 22n5, 292
Barrera, Jorge, 84
Beardy's and Okemasis First Nation, 243
Bedard, Yvonne, 76
Belanger, Yale, 82, 110, 113, 134n9, 234, 260, 278
Bellegarde, Perry, 165, 337
Bennett, Carolyn, 151, 166–7
Bernard, R. v. (2005), 204–5, 221n19, 221n26
Bill C-3 (*Gender Equity in Indian Registration Act*, 2011), 72, 79, 82, 83, 95n27
Bill C-5 (2021), 170
Bill C-8 (2021), 170
Bill C-15 (*United Nations Declaration on the Rights of Indigenous Peoples Act,* 2021), 21n1, 170, 179n29, 336

Bill C-31 (1985), 76–83
background, 76–7
on descent and Indian status, 77–8, 95n25
gender discrimination and reform attempts, 72, 78–81, 83, 95n27
reinstated status Indians, challenges rejoining nations, 82–3
sovereignty over membership codes and, 69, 70
two-generation cut-off rule, 64–5, 77, 78, 79, 81–2
Bill C-38 (*Jobs, Growth, and Long-Term Prosperity Act*, 2012), 165, 178n20
Bill C-45 (*Jobs and Growth Act,* 2012), 142, 165, 178n20
Bill C-91 (*An Act Respecting Indigenous Languages*, 2019), 168, 178n24
Bill C-92 (*An Act Respecting First Nations, Inuit and Métis Children, Youth and Families*, 2019), 168, 178n24
Bill S-3 (2017), 72, 80, 82, 83, 95n27
Bish, Robet L., 295–6
blood quantum, 71, 78, 81–2, 281
Blood Tribe, 230, 326n4
Borrows, John
on *Constitution Act,* Section 35, 154
on Great Law of Peace, 103
on Indigenous political empowerment, 17, 138
pre-contact Indigenous sovereignty and, 133n2
The Right Relationship (with Coyle), 250n16
on Royal Proclamation and Treaty of Niagara, 111, 112
on Supreme Court's approach to Aboriginal rights and Aboriginal title, 189, 190, 198, 222n31
on treaties, 226, 227, 230
on treaty federalism, 42
Boyden, Joseph, 84–6
British Columbia
co-management of Pacific north coast, 361–2, 368n17
incremental treaty agreements, 331–2
modern treaty process, 148, 159, 176n10, 257–9, 266
British Columbia Claims Task Force, 258, 288n9
British Columbia Treaty Commission, 258–9
British North America (BNA) Act (1867), 113–14
Bruyneel, Kevin, 8, 17–18, 38
Buller, Marion, 178n25

Calder et al. v. Attorney General of British Columbia (1973), 146–8, 192, 193, 194, 214, 220nn13–14, 229, 253
Canada
fiduciary duty to Indigenous peoples, 67, 114, 117, 185, 193–4, 306
150th anniversary, 2–3
postcolonial period, contested, 1–2
reconciliation, 19–20, 25n20, 48, 53, 330, 369, 370–1
UNDRIP and, 2, 133n1, 335–6
See also Chrétien, Jean; colonialism and colonial policies; *Constitution Act*; Harper, Stephen; Indigenous peoples; Martin, Paul; Mulroney, Brian; Supreme Court of Canada; Trudeau, Justin; Trudeau, Pierre; Truth and Reconciliation Commission of Canada
Carcross Tagish First Nation, 326n11
Caron, Fred, 90
cash, and comprehensive land claims, 265–6, 272–3
Cassidy, Frank, 295–6
C'eletkwmx First Nation, 345
certainty, 259–60
Champagne and Aishihik First Nation, 326n11
Charlie, Lianne Marie Leda, 256
Charlottetown Accord (1992), 155, 173

Charter of Rights and Freedoms, 39, 77, 95n26, 152, 156, 256, 301, 318, 319
chiefs, hereditary, vs. band councils, 5, 6–7, 22n9
Chiefs of Ontario
  Understanding First Nations Sovereignty, 28–9, 52–3
Chippewas of the Thames First Nation v. Enbridge Pipelines Inc. (2017), 210, 222n29
Chrétien, Jean (Chrétien government), 148, 155–6, 158
Christmas, Bernd, 348
citizenship, 67–72, 91, 128–9, 315. *See also* identity; membership
Citizens Plus, 145
civil rights movement, 76, 141, 144
claims process
  background, 147–8
  criticisms of, 149–51
  positive developments, 151–2
  specific claims, 148–9, 151, 242–4, 251n19, 331
  See also Aboriginal title; comprehensive land claims
Clatworthy, Stewart, 81
Clyde River (Hamlet) v. Petroleum Geo-Services Inc. (2017), 211
coastal conservation, 361–2
Coastal Gaslink pipeline, 4–7, 22n7, 23nn10–11
Coates, Ken
  on Aboriginal title, 221n19
  on duty to consult and accommodate, 209
  on *Guerin v. The Queen* (1984), 193
  on Indigenous sovereignty ambitions, 139
  on Round Dance, 176n3
  on self-determination and self-government, 292, 320, 370
  on Supreme Court, 199, 216
  on treaty rights, 200
  on *Tsilhqot'in Nation v. British Columbia* (2014), 219n4
  on urban reserves, 246
Cobo, Jose R. Martinez, 23n12, 62
colonialism and colonial policies
  about, 14–16, 98, 105, 131–2, 138
  assimilation (*see* assimilation)
  band councils (*see* band councils)
  British North America Act (1867) and, 113–14
  Doctrine of Discovery, 14, 107, 108, 134nn5–6, 164, 330
  early contact between Indigenous peoples and settlers, 104–5
  early pre-Confederation period, 105–6, 108–9, 112
  gendered dynamics of, 15, 62, 72, 129–30, 320–1
  impacts of, 139, 323
  imperialism and, 24n16
  Indian Act (see *Indian Act*)
  Indigenous activism against, 51, 138, 140–2, 152, 173, 175n1, 253, 369–70
  Inherent Right Policy (1995), 154, 155–7, 159
  later pre-Confederation and post-Confederation periods, 112–14, 134n9
  reserves (*see* reserves)
  residential schools, 123–7, 128, 130, 135n15, 135n18, 136nn20–1
  Royal Proclamation (1763) (*see* Royal Proclamation)
  Sixties Scoop, 126, 135n17
  terra nullius, 107–8, 134n6, 164, 330
  treaties (*see* treaties)
  Treaty of Niagara (1764), 108, 111–12, 131, 134n8, 164, 231, 247
  White Paper on Indian Policy (1969), 52, 140, 143–6, 147–8, 176n7, 229, 253
co-management initiatives
  about, 353–5

co-management boards, 256–7, 271–2, 279, 288n8, 354–5
Dehcho First Nations, 357–8
Haida Gwaii, 355–6
Haudenosaunee, 359–60
implications and analysis, 362–3
land use planning and parks, 355–8
Mi'kmaq in Nova Scotia, 356–7
National Indigenous Guardian Network, 358–9
Nisga'a, 360–1
Nunavut Wildlife Management Board, 360
Pacific north coast, 361–2, 368n17
Tahltan Nation, 356
wildlife management, fisheries, and coastal conservation, 359–62
comprehensive land claims (modern treaties)
about, 148, 226, 229, 252–3, 253–4, 277, 285
Aboriginal title and, 264–5, 271–2
Algonquins' agreement-in-principle, 253, 280–3, 284, 287n1, 289n20, 290nn21–2
BC's process, 148, 159, 176n10, 257–9, 266
Calder decision (1973) and, 220n14
as Canadian state control, 254, 261–2, 287n3, 289n13
cash and, 265–6, 272–3
certainty and, 259–60
challenges and criticisms, 149–51, 275–6, 331
concluded treaties, 253–4, 287n4
conflicting objectives, 259–61
constitutional protection and, 269–70
extinguished, modified, or non-asserted rights, 150–1, 262–4, 288n10
Kluane First Nation, 287n1, 309–13, 326nn11–12
land and, 264–5, 271
nation-to-nation relations and, 288n11
Nisga'a Final Agreement (1998), 24n17, 262, 264, 266, 273–4, 287n4, 307, 360–1
Nunavut Land Claims Agreement (1993), 211, 253, 275–6, 277–80, 284, 287n1, 287n4, 360
paramountcy and, 274–5, 326n8
political power and, 273–5
positive developments, 151–2, 159, 288n5
process of, 255–7
resources and, 265, 272–3
as restored Indigenous sovereignty, 267–9, 276–7
self-government and, 266–7, 288n6, 289n14
socio-economic benefits, 257
Tlicho Agreement (2003), 262, 287n4, 307
treaty self-government agreements, 307–9
Trudeau government and, 275, 288n7
Yukon First Nations, 287n1, 307, 310, 311, 326nn9–11
See also treaties
conceptual framework, 115
Congress of Aboriginal Peoples (formerly Native Council of Canada), 141–2, 177n18
consent
about, 330, 334, 366n2, 366n4
Canadian commitment to, 336
vs. duty to consult and accommodate, 212–13, 334–5, 338 (*see also* duty to consult and accommodate)
impact and benefit agreements (IBAs) and, 341
private sector and, 336–8
Constitution Act (1982)
Métis, Inuit, and non-status Indians and, 66, 188, 306–7
Section 25, 110, 152, 269
Section 35 (see *Constitution Act* (1982), Section 35)
Section 37, 153
Constitution Act (1982), Section 35
Aboriginal rights and, 39, 63, 152–4, 177n11, 181, 184–5, 186, 187, 188, 219n2, 269
"Aboriginal" term and, 9, 23n13, 63

Constitution Act (1982), Section 35 (*continued*)
comprehensive claims agreements and, 148, 254, 256, 269–70
duty to consult and accommodate and, 206
Indigenous sovereignty and, 215
self-government and, 154, 155, 307, 313
Constitutional Express, 177n11
consultation. *See* duty to consult and accommodate
Corntassel, Jeff, 56n7
Coulthard, Glen, 45–6, 56n7
Council of Yukon First Nations (formerly Council of Yukon Indians), 310
Council of Yukon Indians Umbrella Final Agreement (1993), 287n4, 310
Courchene, Thomas
on *Calder* decision (1973), 220n14
on Haudenosaunee's influence on US, 134n4
on Royal Proclamation (1763), 110
on Supreme Court, 213, 216, 219n3
on TRC's Calls to Action, 163
on treaties, 235
on Treaty of Niagara (1764), 134n8
Covenant Chain of Friendship, 111, 231, 249n5
Coyle, Michael, 226, 230, 235
The Right Relationship (with Borrows), 250n16
Craft, Aimée, 234, 237, 239, 250n14
Cree, 238. See also *Mikisew Cree First Nation v. Canada* (2005); Muskeg Lake Cree First Nation; Swampy Cree
Cree Nation of Quebec, 325n3
Crown, honour of the, 151, 192, 206, 215, 216–17, 267
Cullen, Nathan, 23n10
cultural genocide, 125, 164
Curtis, Christopher, 316

Dalseg, Shenna, 341, 342
Da'naxda'xw Awaetlatla First Nation, 368n17
Daniels v. Canada (2016), 66–7, 73, 94n10, 306
Davidian, Giselle, 342–3
decolonization, 292–3. *See also* self-determination; self-government; sovereignty
Dehcho First Nations, 263, 357–8, 367n15
delegated (municipality) model, 36–8, 50, 51
Delgamuukw v. British Columbia (1997)
Aboriginal title and, 194–6, 214, 220n16, 221n17, 221n19
co-management initiatives and, 354
duty to consult and accommodate and, 207
R. v. Marshall and *R. v. Bernard* (2005) and, 221n26
Sellars on, 221n23
on sovereignty and Supreme Court's role supporting, 215, 216
Tsilhqot'in v. British Columbia (2014) and, 182, 183, 196–7
Dene Declaration (1975), 277
Department of Crown–Indigenous Relations and Northern Affairs, 99, 164–5, 171
Department of Indian Affairs, 114, 118, 228
Department of Indigenous and Northern Affairs (INAC), 68, 70, 94n15, 99–100, 164–5, 178n19
Department of Indigenous Services, 99, 165, 167–8
Descheneaux at al. v. Canada (Attorney General) (2015), 80
Diamond, Billy, 275
Doctrine of Discovery, 14, 107, 108, 134nn5–6, 164, 330
Douglas Treaties, 202, 257
Drybones, R. v. (1970), 128
Dubois, Janique, 304
duty to consult and accommodate, 206–13
about, 181, 206–7, 222n30
vs. consent, 212–13, 334–5, 338 (*see also* consent)
court cases (*see* duty to consult and accommodate, court cases)

impact and benefit agreements (IBAs) and, 333–4
required steps, 208–10
Supreme Court and, 206–7, 212–13, 215, 334–5
duty to consult and accommodate, court cases
Chippewas of the Thames First Nation v. Enbridge Pipelines Inc. (2017), 210, 222n29
Clyde River (Hamlet) v. Petroleum Geo-Services Inc. (2017), 211
Haida Nation v. British Columbia (2004), 206, 207, 209, 212, 223n34, 333, 354
Mikisew Cree First Nation v. British Columbia (2005), 207, 208, 222n28
Taku River Tlingit First Nation v. British Columbia (2004), 207–8, 222n27

Eagle Lake First Nation, 187
East West Tie Transmission Line, 344
economic development
about, 346–7, 353
Membertou First Nation, 347–9
Muskeg Lake Cree First Nation, 346, 349–51, 367nn11–12
Osoyoos Indian Band, 351–3, 367n13
Eeyou Marine Region Land Claims Agreement (2010), 287n4
Elliott, Jean, 144
Elliott, Michael, 48
enfranchisement, 75–6, 77, 116, 128, 228
Ewing Commission, 303
extinguishment, 150–1, 262–3, 288n10
Eyford, Douglas R., 257, 262, 275, 276, 289n15

federalism. *See* nested federalism; treaty federalism
Federation of Sovereign Indigenous Nations (FSIN), 28, 52–3, 245, 251n21, 350
fiduciary duty, 67, 114, 117, 185, 193–4, 306
First Nations, use of term, 9, 93n7. *See also* Indigenous peoples
First Nations Financial Transparency Act, 165
First Nations Lands Management Act (1999), 118, 123
First Nations Summit, 258, 259
fisheries, 360–2
Flanagan, Thomas, 176n9
Fleras, Augie, 144
Fort Frances Tribal Area First Nations, 326n4
free, prior, and informed consent. *See* consent
Frideres, James, 52, 130, 243, 349
Furi, Megan, 81, 82

Garcea, Joseph, 244–5
gender
band elections and, 128
colonialism and, 15, 62, 72, 129–30, 320–1
decolonization (self-government) and, 130–1, 320, 321–3
impact and benefit agreements (IBAs) and, 341–3
Indian Act and Bill C-31, discrimination and reform attempts, 15, 72, 74–5, 78–81, 83, 95n23, 95n27, 130
pre-contact Indigenous nations and, 101
Voisey's Bay nickel mine and, 344
See also National Inquiry into Missing and Murdered Indigenous Women and Girls
genocide (cultural genocide), 125, 164, 168–9
Gibson, Gordon, 176n9
Gitga'at First Nation, 368n17
Gitskan Nation, 194, 220n16
Gitxaala Nation, 368n17
Gladstone, R. v. (1996), 187
Graben, Sari, 312
Gradual Civilization Act (1857), 73–4
Gradual Enfranchisement Act (1869), 74
Graham, John, 326n8

Grammond, Sebastian, 94n11
Grant, John, 29, 213, 221n22
Great Law of Peace, 103, 230, 317
Green, Joyce, 8, 10, 15, 16, 24n16, 44, 73, 130, 215
guardians, Indigenous, 358–9
Guerin v. The Queen (1984), 192–4
Gustafsen Lake standoff, 142
Gwich'in Comprehensive Land Claim Agreement (1992), 287n4

Haida Gwaii, 355–6
Haida Nation, 355–6, 361–2, 368n17
Haida Nation v. British Columbia (2004)
  on duty to consult and accommodate, 206, 207, 209, 212, 223n34, 333, 354
  on just settlements, 216–17, 267
  on sovereignty, 215
Haisla First Nation, 332
Hamilton, A.C., 151, 152, 205–6, 238–9
Hamilton Conservation Authority, 359–60
Harper, Stephen (Harper government), 127, 142, 161–2, 165
Haudenosaunee
  Covenant Chain of Friendship, 111, 231, 249n5
  Great Law of Peace, 103, 230, 317
  influence on US government, 134n4
  Longhouse tradition, 316–17
  pre-contact sovereignty of, 102–3, 315–16
  Six Nations of, 102, 134n3, 326n13
  wildlife co-management agreement, 359–60
  See also Mohawk; Six Nations
Healy, Les, 230
Hedican, Edward, 93n9, 198, 213, 235, 240
Heiltsuk Nation, 187, 368n17
Helin, Calvin, 103, 127, 348
Hemas Kla-Lee-Lee-Kla (Bill Wilson), 177n13
Henderson, James (Sákéj) Youngblood, 42–3, 233
hereditary chiefs, vs. band councils, 5, 6–7, 22n9
Hicks, Jack, 278
Hoehn, Felix, 108, 216, 223nn35–6, 264, 267
honour of the Crown, 151, 192, 206, 215, 216–17, 267
Hudson, Graham, 125
Huhndorf, Shari, 72, 130
Hul'qumi'num First Nations, 265
human rights, 32, 55n3, 108, 141, 169, 229, 334
Huron-Wendat people, 202

identity, 58–9, 81–2, 83–6, 90–1. *See also* citizenship; membership
Idle No More movement, 142, 165
Imai, Shin, 212, 213, 336, 337–8, 339, 366n4
impact and benefit agreements (IBAs)
  about, 333–4, 337, 338–9
  benefits of, 343, 346
  criticisms and conflicts, 338, 339–43, 367n7
  East West Tie Transmission Line, 344
  Osoyoos Indian Band, 352
  Trans Mountain Pipeline, 345–6
  Vancouver International Airport, 344–5
  Voisey's Bay nickel mine, 344
imperialism, 24n16
Inco, 344
incremental treaty agreements, 331–3
independent model (Indigenous resurgence), 36, 44–50, 51, 56nn7–8
Indian
  status vs. non-status, 64–5, 68, 74–5, 77–8 (*see also* non-status Indians)
  use of term, 8, 9
  See also Indigenous peoples
Indian Act
  about, 73–4, 114, 131, 228
  amendments, 127–9 (*see also* Bill C-3; Bill C-31; Bill S-3)

assimilationist and paternalistic goals, 73, 74, 114–15, 127–8
band councils (*see* band councils)
ban on legal representation and political organization, 116, 128, 192, 220n15
ban on Potlatch and Sun Dance, 127, 128
on citizenship, identity, and membership, 58–9, 62, 68–70, 73, 74–5, 83, 87, 128–9
comprehensive land claims and, 255, 273, 281
on enfranchisement, 75–6, 77, 116, 128
federal control, continued, 95n30
gender-based discrimination, 15, 74–5, 83, 95n23, 130, 321
impacts and legacy, 86, 115–16
Inuit and, 66, 94n12
legislated self-government agreements and, 298–9, 300
Métis and, 66, 94n12
reserves (*see* reserves)
on residential schools, 124, 128
on status vs. non-status Indians, 64–5, 68, 74–5, 77–8
Indian agents, 115, 120
Indian Association of Alberta, 141
Indian Residential Schools Settlement Agreement, 126–7
Indigenous Leadership Initiative, 359, 368n16
Indigenous peoples
about and approach to, 18–19, 62
Aboriginal peoples, use of term, 8, 9, 23n13, 62–3
activism against colonialism, 51, 138, 140–2, 152, 173, 175n1, 253, 369–70
ancestral origins, 100–1
ancestry vs. identity, 63
author's positionality, 20
decolonization, differing views on, 1–3
early contact with European settlers, 104–5
fiduciary duty towards, 67, 114, 117, 185, 193–4, 306
First Nations, use of term, 9, 93n7
geographic distribution, 63–4
growth rate, 64
Indian, use of term, 8, 9
languages, 64, 126, 168
as nations, 10, 23n14, 158
Native, use of term, 9
new bands, establishment, 135n12
political activism, 16–17, 139
pre-contact sovereign nations, 30–1, 55n4, 101–4, 133n2
reconciliation, 19–20, 25n20, 48, 53, 330, 369, 370–1
socio-economic inequalities, 159–60, 176n2
spaces in between and, 4
use of term, 8–9, 23n13
See also Aboriginal rights; Aboriginal title; colonialism and colonial policies; Inuit; Métis; partnerships; self-determination; self-government; sovereignty; treaty rights
Indigenous resurgence (independent model), 36, 44–50, 51, 56nn7–8
inherency, 13, 38–9
inherent model (third order of government), 36, 38–41, 50, 51
Inherent Right Policy (1995), 154, 155–7, 159
Innu Nation, 142, 344
"integral to a distinctive culture" test, 186
intergovernmental partnerships. *See* partnerships
international law, 32, 55n3, 106. *See also* human rights; United Nations Declaration on the Rights of Indigenous People
International Organization for Standardization (ISO), 348
Inuit
about, 63, 66

Inuit (*continued*)
  Aboriginal rights and, 63, 188
  Clyde River (Hamlet) v. Petroleum Geo-Services Inc. (2017) and, 211
  Indian Act and, 66, 94n12
  NunatuKavut Nation of Labrador, 60–1
  Nunavut Land Claims Agreement (1993), 211, 253, 275–6, 277–80, 284, 287n1, 287n4, 360
  Nunavut Wildlife Management Board and, 360
  Voisey's Bay nickel mine and, 344
Inuit Tapiriit Kanatami (formerly Inuit Tapirisat of Canada), 142, 160, 168, 177n18
Inuvialuit Final Agreement (1984), 287n4
Irlbacher-Fox, Stephanie, 263, 267
Iroquois. *See* Haudenosaunee
Isaac, Thomas, 189–90

Jago, Robert, 86
Jai, Julie, 109, 153, 213, 230, 236–7, 238, 250n9
James Bay and Northern Quebec Agreement (1975), 148, 254, 275, 287n4
John, Wendy, 345
Judicial Committee of the Privy Council (JCPC), 191–2, 220n12
Julian, Gerard, 356

Kayseas, Bob, 2–3, 22n4
Kelowna Accord (2005), 160–2
King, Hayden
  on co-management initiatives, 288n8, 362
  on comprehensive land claims, 254, 260, 262, 275
  on Joseph Boyden, 86
  on settler colonialism, 14
  on Trudeau government, 170, 178n19
Kitasoo/Xaixais First Nation, 368n17
Kitselas First Nation, 332
Kleer, Nancy, 240
Kluane First Nation, 287n1, 309–13, 326nn11–12
K'omoks First Nation, 368n17
Koutouki, Konstantia, 342–3
Kunst'aa Guu–Kunst'aayah Reconciliation Protocol, 355–6
Kuokkanen, Rauna, 15, 32, 55n3, 83, 131, 321, 323, 341, 342
Kwanlin Dun First Nation, 326n11

Labrador Inuit Land Claims Agreement (2005), 287n4
Ladner, Kiera
  on band councils, 37, 120, 122, 123, 135n14
  on *Constitution Act,* Section 35, 154
  on Inherent Right Policy (1995), 154, 157
  pre-contact Indigenous sovereignty and, 133n2
  on Supreme Court's approach to Aboriginal title, 198, 199
  on third order of government, 41
  on treaty federalism, 43–4, 319
Lake Babine Nation, 332
land
  land use planning and parks, 355–8
  sovereignty and, 22n6
  See also Aboriginal title; comprehensive land claims; reserves
languages, Indigenous, 64, 126, 168
Larocque, Florence, 162
Lavell, Jeannette, 76
Lawrence, Bonita
  on Aboriginal rights, 220n11
  on Aboriginal title, 199
  on Algonquins, 103, 282, 290n22
  on band councils, 36, 120
  on comprehensive land claims, 150, 264, 266
  on *Delgamuukw* decision (1997), 195
  on *Indian Act,* 115
  on Inherent Right Policy (1995), 157
  on nationhood, 29

Lax Kw'alaams Band, 368n17
League of Indians of Canada, 141
League of Western Indians, 141
legislated self-government agreements
about, 298–300, 325–6n3, 326n4
comparison to treaty self-government agreements, 308
Sioux Valley Dakota Nation, 298, 300–2, 326n5
Liard First Nation, 326n9, 326n11
Little Bear, Leroy, 29, 38
Little Salmon Carmacks First Nation, 326n11
Lofts, Katherine, 342–3
Longhouse, Haudenosaunee, 316–17
Louie, Clarence, 351–2, 353
Lovelace, Sandra, 76–7
Lubicon Lake Cree, 142

Maa-nulth First Nations Final Agreement (2011), 176n10, 259, 287n4, 307
MacDonald, David B., 125
Macdonald, John A., 236
Mackey, Eva, 8, 261, 264
Macklem, Patrick, 226, 270
Maliseet, 204, 249n3
Mamalilikulla Nation, 368n17
Manitoba
Red River community, 65, 303
Sioux Valley Dakota Nation legislated self-government agree, 298, 300–2, 326n5
Manuel, Arthur
on comprehensive land claims, 150, 261, 265, 266, 268
on constitutional conferences, 153
Constitutional Express and, 177n11
on extinguished, modified, or non-asserted rights, 262, 263
on incremental treaty agreements, 332–3
on Indigenous declarations of independence, 371
The Reconciliation Manifesto, 177n12
on Trudeau government, 163, 170
on UNDRIP, 163
Unsettling Canada, 177n12
Vowel on, 177n12
on White Paper (1969), 143, 146, 176n7
Maracle, Lee, 153
marine spatial planning, 362, 368n18
Marshall, R. v. (1999), 202–4, 205
Marshall, R. v. (2005), 204–5, 221n19, 221n26
Martin, Paul (Martin government), 160, 162
McCrossan, Michael, 198, 199
McGregor, Deborah, 31–2
McHugh, P.G., 320
McIvor v. Canada (2007), 79, 95n26
McLaughlin, Beverly, 209–10, 338
McNeil, Kent, 189, 199
Meadow Lake First Nations, 326n4
Mehaffey, Matthew, 312
Melnitzer, Julius, 282
membership
about, 58–9, 90–1
Bill C-31 and other amendments, 69, 72, 77–8, 78–83
blood quantum and, 71, 78, 81–2, 281
vs. citizenship, 67
federal control, 71, 73, 74, 81, 95n30
gender discrimination, 72, 74–5
Indian Act and, 58–9, 62, 68–70, 73, 74–5, 83, 87, 128–9
Indigenous control, importance of, 67, 83, 94n11
Indigenous understanding of, 71, 94n19
Joseph Boyden and authentic Indigenous identity, 83–6
membership codes, Indigenous-designed, 61–2, 70–1, 87, 90, 91
Métis Settlements of Alberta, 61

membership (*continued*)
Mohawk of Kahnawà:ke, 317–18
NunatuKavut Nation, 60–1
Qalipu Mi'kmaq First Nation, 87–90, 91, 96n31
reinstated status Indians, challenges rejoining nations, 82–3, 91
Sandy Lake First Nation, 60
self-government negotiations and, 94n15
sovereignty (self-determination) and, 59–60, 62, 67, 71, 72–3, 83, 90, 93n2
status vs. non-status Indians, 64–5, 68, 74–5, 77–8
two-generation cut-off rule, 64–5, 77, 78, 79, 81–2
See also citizenship; identity
Membertou First Nation, 347–9, 367nn9–10
Metallic, Naiomi Walqwan, 2–3, 21n4, 149, 158
Métis
about, 65–6, 93nn8–9, 303
Aboriginal rights and, 66, 188
Congress of Aboriginal Peoples and, 141–2
Daniels v. Canada (2016) and, 66–7, 94n10, 306
geographic distribution, 63–4
Indian Act and, 66, 94n12
Métis Settlements of Alberta, 61, 66, 298, 303–7, 326nn6–7
political autonomy claims, 302–3
Red River resistance (1869-70), 236
R. v. Powley (2003) and, 66, 188, 219n10
specific claims and, 151
Métis National Council, 168, 177n18
Metlakatla First Nation, 368n17
Miawpukek First Nation, 325n3
Migizi ow-kwe (Shirley Williams), 2–3, 21n4
Mi'gmaq Nation of Gespeg, 326n4
Mikisew Cree First Nation v. Canada (Minister of Canadian Heritage) (2005), 207, 208, 222n28
Mi'kmaq
Burnt Church fishing dispute, 142, 176n5
co-management in Nova Scotia, 356–7, 367n14
fragmentation into bands, 94n13
Membertou First Nation, 347–9, 367nn9–10
"peace and friendship" treaties with, 249n3
as pre-contact sovereign nation, 101–2
Qalipu Mi'kmaq First Nation, 87–90, 91, 96n31, 135n12
R. v. Marshall (1999), 202–4, 205
R. v. Marshall and *R. v. Bernard* (2005), 204–5, 221n19, 221n26
Miller, J.R.
on Indigenous activism, 140–1, 176n2
on *James Bay and Northern Quebec Agreement* (1975), 275
on Mi'kmaq, 102
on *Nunavut Land Claims Agreement* (1993), 277
pre-contact Indigenous sovereignty and, 133n2
on treaties, 227–8, 228–9, 233, 239, 240, 250n6
on White Paper (1969), 144
Mills, Aaron, 263
missing and murdered Indigenous women. *See* National Inquiry into Missing and Murdered Indigenous Women and Girls
modern treaties. *See* comprehensive land claims
modified rights, 262
Mohawk Nation, 23n11, 140, 315. *See also* Akwesasne; Haudenosaunee
Mohawk of Kahnawà:ke, 314–18
Mohawk Warrior Society of Oka, 142
Monture-Angus, Patricia, 52, 199, 212
Morales, Sarah, 265
Morden, Michael, 142, 176n4, 328, 338–9, 339–40, 341, 343, 366n1
Mulroney, Brian (Mulroney government), 40, 157
multilevel governance. *See* partnerships
municipality (delegated) model, 36–8, 50, 51
Murphy, Michael, 343

Muskeg Lake Cree First Nation, 246, 349–51, 367nn11–12
Musqueam Nation, 185, 192–4, 219nn6–7, 297, 344–5
Myers, Lorraine, 28

Na-Cho Nyak Dun First Nation, 326n11
Nadasdy, Paul, 24n18, 27–8, 33, 34, 47–8, 55n1
Napoleon, Val, 22n9
National Council for Reconciliation, 170
National Day for Truth and Reconciliation, 170
National Energy Board (NEB), 210, 211, 222n29
National Indian Brotherhood, 141
National Indian Council, 141
National Indigenous Guardian Network, 358–9
National Inquiry into Missing and Murdered Indigenous Women and Girls (MMIWG)
  about, 168–9, 178n25
  federal response and national action plan, 21n2, 170, 172–3, 179n30
  on Indigenous women and children, 322, 342
  Trudeau government commitment to, 2, 162–3
nations, Indigenous peoples as, 10, 23n14, 158
nation-to-nation relationships, 2, 14, 40, 98, 323, 330, 364. *See also* partnerships; treaties; treaty federalism
Native, use of term, 9. *See also* Indigenous peoples
Native Council of Canada (now Congress of Aboriginal Peoples), 141–2, 177n18
Native Women's Association of Canada, 173, 177n18
Natural Resources Transfer Agreement (1930), 245
nested federalism, 24n19, 272
nested sovereignty, 17
Newfoundland
  Qalipu Mi'kmaq First Nation, 87–90, 91, 96n31, 135n12
Newman, Dwight, 199, 209, 216, 219n4
New Zealand, 133n1, 154, 366n3
Nisga'a Nation
  Calder et al. v. Attorney General of British Columbia (1973), 146–8, 192, 193, 194, 214, 220nn13–14, 229, 253
  Nisga'a Final Agreement (1998), 24n17, 262, 264, 266, 273–4, 287n4, 307, 360–1
Nishnawbe Aski Nation, 60, 326n3
Noël, Alain, 162
non-asserted rights, 262
non-Indigenous peoples, use of term, 11
non-status Indians
  Algonquin treaty negotiations and, 281–2, 290n22
  Congress of Aboriginal Peoples and, 141–2
  Daniels v. Canada (2016) and, 66–7, 306
  vs. status Indians, 64–5, 68, 74–5, 77–8
North American Indian Brotherhood, 141
Northeastern Quebec Agreement (1978), 287n4
northwest coast, BC, 103–4. *See also* Pacific north coast
Northwest Rebellion, 65, 243
Northwest Territories, 64
Norton, Joe, 318
Nova Scotia
  Mi'kmaq co-management, 356–7, 367n14
Numbered Treaties, 200, 235–7, 239. *See also specific treaties*
Nunatsiavut Government, 344
NunatuKavut Nation, 60–1
Nunavik Inuit Land Claims Agreement (2006), 287n4
Nunavik Regional Government, 326n4
Nunavut, 63–4, 123, 167, 277–9, 289n18
Nunavut Act (1993), 278, 279
Nunavut Land Claims Agreement (1993), 211, 253, 275–6, 277–80, 284, 287n1, 287n4, 360
Nunavut Tunngavik Inc. (formerly Tunngavik Federation of Nunavut), 280, 289n17

Nunavut Wildlife Management Board, 360
Nuxalk First Nation, 368n17

Olthuis, Kleer, and Townshend, LLP, 135n13, 200–1, 346, 355, 362
O-Pipon-Na-Piwin Cree Nation, 135n12
oral traditions, 126, 194, 202–3, 234
Oregon Boundary Treaty (1846), 221n17
Osoyoos (BC), 353
Osoyoos Indian Band, 351–3, 367n13

Pacific north coast, 361–2, 368n17. *See also* northwest coast, BC
Palmater, Pamela, 68, 71, 73, 79, 86, 94n13, 101, 129
Pamajewon, R. v. (1996), 187
Papillon, Martin
  on activism against colonialism, 142
  on comprehensive land claims, 254, 263, 267, 272, 275, 276, 289n13
  on consent, 330, 334, 336–7
  on impact and benefit agreements (IBAs), 339, 341, 346, 367n7
  on third order of government, 41
  on treaties, 233
  on treaty federalism, 43
Paquette, Aaron, 85
paramountcy, 274–5, 326n8
parks and land use planning, 355–8
partnerships, 328–9, 363–4, 366n1. *See also* co-management initiatives; consent; economic development; impact and benefit agreements; incremental treaty agreements
Passamaquoddy, 204
pass system, 115, 243
Pasternak, Shiri, 170, 178n19
paternalism, 74, 118, 199, 228, 273
patriarchy, 15, 72, 76, 129–31, 320–1
Paul, Terrance, 348
Pendakur, Krishna, 257, 272, 288n5
Pendakur, Ravi, 257, 272, 288n5
Penner Committee (Penner Report), 155
Pikwakanagan First Nation, 281–2, 283
pipe ceremony, 250n6
pipelines
  Coastal Gaslink pipeline, 4–7, 22n7, 23nn10–11
  Trans Mountain Pipeline, 172, 179n31, 345–6
Poelzer, Greg, 139, 246, 292, 370
Ponting, J. Rick, 177n14
Potlatch, 104, 127, 128, 140
Powley, R. v. (2003), 66, 188, 219n10
Prince, Michael, 42
prior occupancy, 31–2
private sector, 336–8. *See also* impact and benefit agreements

Qalipu Mi'kmaq First Nation, 87–90, 91, 96n31, 135n12
Qwul'sih'yah'maht (Robina Thomas), 2–3, 22n4

racism, 144, 168, 228, 321
Rae, Judith, 240
recognition, politics of, 45–6, 47–8
Recognition and Implementation of Indigenous Rights Framework (2018), 162, 167, 171–2, 178n22
Recognition of Indigenous Rights and Self-Determination Discussion Tables, 178n23
reconciliation, 19–20, 25n20, 48, 53, 330, 369, 370–1. *See also* Truth and Reconciliation Commission of Canada
Reconciliation Framework Agreement for Bioregional Oceans Management and Protection (2018), 361–2
Redbird, Elsie, 131

Red River resistance (1869-70), 236
reserves
about, 116–19, 135n10
Numbered Treaties and, 237, 239–40
opting out of, 118, 123
treaty land entitlement process, 244–7, 251nn20–1, 350
treaty self-government agreements and, 308
urban reserves, 245–7, 251nn22–3, 349–51
residential schools, 123–7, 128, 130, 135n15, 135n18, 136nn20–1
resurgence, Indigenous (independent model), 36, 44–50, 51, 56nn7–8
Richardson, Miles, 359
rights. *See* Aboriginal rights
Robinson treaties (1850), 200
Rodon, Thierry, 16, 24n19, 330, 334, 336–7, 339, 341, 346, 367n7
Ross River Dena Council, 326n9, 326n11
Round Dance, 142, 176n3
Royal Commission on Aboriginal Peoples (RCAP)
about, 40, 157–8
on Doctrine of Discovery and *terra nullius*, 108, 134n6
on early contact period, 105
Gathering Strength (report), 159
on gendered dynamics of colonialism, 130
on Indigenous nations, use of term, 10, 23n14, 158
on northwest coast nations, 104
pre-contact Indigenous sovereignty and, 133n2
on self-government, 13, 158–9
on sovereignty, 34, 39–41
on treaties, 232, 263
Royal Proclamation (1763), 108–12
about, 108, 231
British Columbia and, 257
colonial ambitions, 110–11
Indigenous sovereignty and, 28, 30, 109–10, 111–12, 131, 134n7, 236
proposals for new Royal Proclamation, 158, 164, 330
St. Catherine's Milling and Lumber Co. v. The Queen (1888) and, 191
R. v. Bernard (2005), 204–5, 221n19, 221n26
R. v. Drybones (1970), 128
R. v. Gladstone (1996), 187
R. v. Marshall (1999), 202–4, 205
R. v. Marshall (2005), 204–5, 221n19, 221n26
R. v. Pamajewon (1996), 187
R. v. Powley (2003), 66, 188, 219n10
R. v. Sioui (1990), 201, 202
R. v. Sparrow (1990), 184–6, 207, 215, 219nn6–7
R. v. Van der Peet (1996), 31, 186–7, 188, 189, 214, 215, 220n11
R. v. White and Bob (1965), 201–2

Saganash, Romeo, 179n29
Sahtu Dene and Métis Comprehensive Land Claim Agreement (1994), 287n4
Sanderson, Douglas, 338
Sandy Lake First Nation, 60
Saskatchewan, and treaty land entitlement, 244–5, 251n20, 251n22, 350
Saskatchewan Indian Gaming Authority, 350
Saskatoon, 246, 247, 349–50, 367n11
Saskatoon Tribal Council, 350
Saulteaux, 238
Saunders, Kelly, 304
Scholtz, Christa, 220n14
Scott, Tracie Lee, 361
scrip system, 303
Sechelt Nation, 298
second generation cut-off rule, 64–5, 77, 78, 79, 81–2

self-determination
about, 11, 12–13, 13–14
Aboriginal rights and, 63
and citizenship and membership, 59–60, 62, 67, 91, 93n2
Indigenous insistence on, 292, 328
polarized views of, 370
right to, 1–2, 32
Trudeau government on, 166
UNDRIP on, 12, 32, 319
See also self-government; sovereignty
self-government
about, 11, 13, 159, 293, 313, 323–4
band councils (*see* band councils)
Charlottetown Accord (1992) and, 155
choice and, 292
comprehensive land claims and, 266–7, 288n6, 289n14
constitutional conferences on, 153
diversity of approaches, 292–3
gender and, 320, 321–3
inherency and, 13, 38–9
Inherent Right Policy (1995), 154, 155–7, 159
Kluane First Nation, 309–13, 326n12
legislated self-government agreements, 298–300, 308, 325–6n3, 326n4
legitimacy of models, 319–20
membership control and, 94n15
Métis Settlements of Alberta, 303–7
Mohawk of Kahnawà:ke, 314–18
Penner Committee on, 155
Royal Commission on Aboriginal Peoples on, 13, 158–9
Sioux Valley Dakota Nation, 300–2, 326n5
Squamish Nation, 296–8, 325nn1–2
treaty federalism and, 313–14, 318–19
treaty self-government agreements, 307–9
See also self-determination; sovereignty
Selkirk First Nation, 326n11
Sellars, Bev
on activism against colonialism, 175n1
on Allied Tribes of British Columbia, 140
on consent, 338
on *Delgamuukw* decision (1997), 221n23
on *Indian Act*, 116, 127, 128, 129
on Potlatch, 104
on Songhees First Nation and reserves, 118
settler colonialism. *See* colonialism and colonial policies
shared ventures. *See* partnerships
Shawanaga First Nation, 187
Simon v. The Queen (1985), 201, 202, 205
Simpson, Audra, 3, 17, 30, 46, 56n7, 72, 315
Simpson, Leanne Betasamsosake, 15, 31, 46–7, 48, 49, 56nn7–8, 75
Sinclair, C.M., 151, 152, 205–6, 239
Sioui, R. v. (1990), 201, 202
Sioux Valley Dakota Nation, 298, 300–2, 326n5
Six Nations, 135n13, 140. *See also* Haudenosaunee
Sixties Scoop, 126, 135n17
Slett, Marilyn, 362
Smith, Anthony, 81
Smith's Landing First Nation, 135n12
Smylie, Janet, 2–3, 22n4
Snuneymuxw First Nation, 201–2, 243
Songhees First Nation, 118
sovereignty
about, 3, 8, 11–12, 27
autonomous model (treaty federalism), 36, 40, 41–4, 49, 50, 51, 53, 174, 313–14, 318–19
autonomy and, 12
boundaries and, 24n18
challenges facing, 7–8

comprehensive land claims and, 267–9, 276–7
within context of Canadian state, 29–30, 51–2
delegated (municipality) model, 36–8, 50, 51
as freedom from colonialism, 50–1
historic treaties and, 28, 29, 30–1, 240–1, 247–8, 250n16
incremental change, 52, 53, 370
independent model (Indigenous resurgence), 36, 44–50, 51, 56nn7–8
Indigenous nations, pre-contact sovereignty, 30–1, 55n4, 101–4, 133n2
Indigenous peoples, applicability to, 33–5
Indigenous peoples, views and efforts, 3–4, 12, 16–17, 22n5, 27–9, 52–3, 292, 370–2
inherent model (third order of government), 36, 38–41, 50, 51
internal vs. external, 11–12
international law and, 32, 55n3
land and, 22n6
membership codes and, 62, 71, 72–3, 83, 90
models of, 35–6, 50, 51
nested sovereignty, 17
partnerships and, 364
principal unit for, 10–11
prior occupancy and, 31–2
vs. statehood, 29, 55n1
Supreme Court and, 215–16, 223n35
treaties and, 24n17, 53
Western state sovereignty, critique of, 32–3
Wet'suwet'en protests of Coastal Gaslink pipeline and, 4–7
See also self-determination; self-government
spaces in between, 3, 4, 17–18, 51
Sparrow, R. v. (1990), 184–6, 207, 215, 219nn6–7
Sparrow test, 185
specific claims, 148–9, 151, 242–4, 251n19, 331
Specific Claims Tribunal, 149, 242, 244
Squamish Nation, 296–8, 325nn1–2
Standing Senate Committee on Aboriginal Peoples, 121
Starblanket, Gina, 31, 200, 205, 206, 226, 239, 321
Stark, Heidi, 321
statehood, 29, 55n1
state sovereignty, 32–3. *See also* sovereignty
status
benefits of, 93n6
status cards, 95n22
status vs. non-status Indians, 64–5, 68, 74–5, 77–8
St. Catherine's Milling and Lumber Co. v. The Queen (1888), 191–2
Stó:lō Nation, 186–7
Stoney Point First Nation, 176n4
Sun Dance, 127, 128
Supreme Court of Canada
about, 181–2, 184, 216–17
Aboriginal rights and, 181, 188–90, 211–12, 213, 214, 218n1, 219nn8–9, 223n34
Aboriginal title and, 181, 190–1, 197–9, 214, 221n22, 222n33
assessment of, 213–16, 219n3
court cases (*see* Supreme Court of Canada, court cases)
on duty to consult and accommodate, 206–7, 208–10, 212–13, 215, 334–5
Indigenous sovereignty and, 215–16, 223n35
on treaties, 267
treaty rights and, 200–1, 205–6, 211–12, 213, 214–15, 223n34, 241–2
Supreme Court of Canada, court cases
Calder et al. v. Attorney General of British Columbia (1973), 146–8, 192, 193, 194, 214, 220nn13–14, 229, 253
Chippewas of the Thames First Nation v. Enbridge Pipelines Inc. (2017), 210, 222n29

Supreme Court of Canada, court cases (*continued*)
Clyde River (Hamlet) v. Petroleum Geo-Services Inc. (2017), 211
Daniels v. Canada (2016), 66–7, 73, 94n10, 306
Delgamuukw v. British Columbia (1997), 182, 183, 194–6, 196–7, 207, 214, 215, 216, 220n16, 221n17, 221n19, 221n23, 221n26, 354
Guerin v. The Queen (1984), 192–4
Haida Nation v. British Columbia (2004), 206, 207, 209, 212, 215, 217, 223n34, 267, 333, 354
Mikisew Cree First Nation v. Canada (Minister of Canadian Heritage) (2005), 207, 208, 222n28
R. v. Bernard (2005), 204–5, 221n19, 221n26
R. v. Drybones (1970), 128
R. v. Gladstone (1996), 187
R. v. Marshall (1999), 202–4, 205
R. v. Marshall (2005), 204–5, 221n19, 221n26
R. v. Pamajewon (1996), 187
R. v. Powley (2003), 66, 188, 219n10
R. v. Sioui (1990), 201, 202
R. v. Sparrow (1990), 184–6, 207, 215, 219nn6–7
R. v. Van der Peet (1996), 31, 186–7, 188, 189, 214, 215, 220n11
R. v. White and Bob (1965), 201–2
Simon v. The Queen (1985), 201, 202, 205
St. Catherine's Milling and Lumber Co. v. The Queen (1888), 191–2
Taku River Tlingit First Nation v. British Columbia (2004), 207–8, 215–16, 222n27
Tsilhqot'in Nation v. British Columbia (2014), 182–4, 196–7, 219n4, 221nn20–1, 338, 354
Suzack, Cheryl, 72, 130
Swampy Cree, 237–8

Ta'ankwach'an Council, 326n11
Tahltan Nation, 356
Taku River Tlingit First Nation v. British Columbia (2004), 207–8, 215–16, 222n27
Tall Bear, Kim, 85
TC Energy (formerly TransCanada Corporation), 5, 22n8. *See also* Coastal Gaslink pipeline
Telford, Hamish, 189
Teme-Augama Anishnabai, 142
terra nullius, 107–8, 134n6, 164, 330
Teslin Tlingit Council, 326n11
third order of government (inherent model), 36, 38–41, 50, 51
Thomas, Robina (Qwul'sih'yah'maht), 2–3, 22n4
title. *See* Aboriginal title
Tla'amin Final Agreement (2014), 176n10, 255, 259, 287n4
Tla-o-qui-aht First Nation, 332
Tlicho Agreement (2003), 262, 287n4, 307
Tlowitsis Nation, 368n17
Tomsons, Sandra, 28
Townshend, Roger, 30, 106
TransCanada Corporation (now TC Energy), 5, 22n8. *See also* Coastal Gaslink pipeline
Trans Mountain Pipeline, 172, 179n31, 345–6
treaties
about, 224–6, 284–5
incremental treaty agreements, 331–3
in other settler colonial countries, 251n18
significance for Indigenous peoples, 227
sovereignty and, 24n17, 53
specific claims and, 151, 242–4, 251n19
treaty land entitlement process, 244–7, 251nn20–1, 350
See also comprehensive land claims; treaty federalism; treaty rights; treaty self-government agreements
treaties, historic
about, 109, 199–200, 226–7, 250n8

Covenant Chain of Friendship, 111, 231, 249n5
Douglas Treaties, 202, 257
end of and absence of new treaties, 146, 227–9
Indigenous vs. colonial views, 230–5, 238–40, 250n15
Numbered Treaties, 200, 235–7, 239
"peace and friendship" treaties, 109, 199, 202, 204, 225, 230–1, 249n3, 287n2
pipe ceremony and, 250n6
Royal Proclamation (1763) (*see* Royal Proclamation)
sovereignty and, 28, 29, 30–1, 240–1, 247–8, 250n16
Treaty of Niagara (1764), 108, 111–12, 131, 134n8, 164, 231, 247
Two-Row Wampum, 40, 111, 112, 132, 146, 231, 249n4, 314, 316, 371
Treaty 1 (1871), 234, 237–8, 250n14, 250nn10–11
Treaty 2 (1871), 300
Treaty 4 (1874), 234, 238, 250n12
Treaty 6 (1876), 234
Treaty 8 (1899), 208, 222n28, 257
Treaty 11 (1921), 228
treaty federalism (autonomous model)
about, 36, 40, 41–4, 50, 51, 53, 313–14, 318–19
comparison to Indigenous resurgence, 49
Trudeau government and, 174
treaty land entitlement process, 244–7, 251nn20–1, 350
Treaty of Niagara (1764), 108, 111–12, 131, 134n8, 164, 231, 247
treaty rights
about, 199–200
court cases (*see* treaty rights, court cases)
Supreme Court and, 200–1, 205–6, 211–12, 213, 214–15, 223n34, 241–2
treaty rights, court cases
R. v. Bernard (2005), 204–5, 221n19, 221n26
R. v. Marshall (1999), 202–4, 205
R. v. Marshall (2005), 204–5, 221n19, 221n26
R. v. Sioui (1990), 201, 202
R. v. White and Bob (1965), 201–2
Simon v. The Queen (1985), 201, 202, 205
treaty self-government agreements
about, 307–9
Kluane First Nation, 287n1, 309–13, 326nn11–12
See also comprehensive land claims
Tr'ondek Hwech'in First Nation, 326n11
Trudeau, Justin (Trudeau government)
assessment of, 169–73, 173–4
commitment to UNDRIP and TRC's Calls to Action, 21n1, 99, 133n1, 162, 163–4, 167, 170, 172, 178n28, 179n29
comparison to Harper government, 165
comprehensive land claims and, 151, 275, 276, 288n7
on delivery of services, 167–8, 172
Indigenous and Northern Affairs Canada, split by, 164–5, 178n19
Indigenous policy objectives, 164–5
Indigenous rights, recognition of, 166–7
National Inquiry into Missing and Murdered Indigenous Women and Girls and, 2, 168–9, 170, 172–3, 178n25, 179n30
principles for Indigenous relations, 166, 288n7
promises to Indigenous peoples, 2, 21n3, 162–3
Recognition and Implementation of Indigenous Rights Framework (2018), 162, 167, 171–2, 178n22
Recognition of Indigenous Rights and Self-Determination Discussion Tables, 178n23
UN speech on Canada-Indigenous relations, 98–100

Trudeau, Pierre (Trudeau government), 143–4, 145, 177n11, 229
Truth and Reconciliation Commission of Canada
  Calls to Action, 2, 162, 163–4, 167, 172, 178n28, 259, 371
  on cultural genocide, 125, 164
  on Doctrine of Discovery and *terra nullius*, 108, 134n6
  establishment, 127
  on reconciliation, 25n20
  on residential schools, 125
  on Royal Proclamation of Reconciliation (Call to Action #45), 330
  on UNDRIP (Call to Action #43), 330, 335
Tsawwassen First Nation Final Agreement (2007), 24n17, 176n10, 259, 287n4, 307
Tŝilhqot'in Nation
  federal apology to, 170
  Tsilhqot'in Nation v. British Columbia (2014), 182–4, 196–7, 219n4, 221nn20–1, 338, 354
Tsleil-Waututh Nation, 297, 345
Tully, James, 42, 51, 153, 222n31, 264, 269
two-generation cut-off rule, 64–5, 77, 78, 79, 81–2
Two-Row Wampum, 40, 111, 112, 132, 146, 231, 249n4, 314, 316, 371
2SLGBTQQIA+ people, 168–9, 170, 172–3

Union of Saskatchewan Indians, 141
United Nations
  on Indigenous identity, 84
  Trudeau speech at, 98–100
United Nations Declaration on Decolonization, 32
United Nations Declaration on the Rights of Indigenous People (UNDRIP)
  about, 163
  BC Treaty Commission and, 259
  Canada and, 2, 133n1, 335–6
  on citizenship and membership, 67
  on consent, 330, 334–6
  countries against, 133n1, 366n3
  "Indigenous" term and, 9
  on self-determination, 12, 32, 319
  Trudeau government's commitment to, 21n1, 99, 133n1, 162, 163, 167, 170, 179n29
  Truth and Reconciliation Commission on, 330
United Nations International Covenant on Civil and Political Rights, 76–7
United States of America, 133n1, 134n4, 154, 366n3
Universal Declaration of Human Rights, 128
University Affairs Newsletter, 2–3
urban reserves, 245–7, 251nn22–3, 349–51

Vancouver International Airport, 344–5
Van der Peet, R. v. (1996), 31, 186–7, 188, 189, 214, 215, 220n11
"vanishing race" trope, 113, 228
Venne, Sharon, 263
Vitoria, Francisco de, 134n5
Voisey's Bay nickel mine, 344
voting rights, 128–9
Vowel, Chelsea, 76, 81, 119, 125, 135n18, 177n12, 230
Vuntut Gwitchin First Nation, 326n11

Walters, Mark D., 205, 223n36
War of 1812, 106, 113, 134n8, 281
Warry, Wayne, 343
water advisories, long-term, 167, 172, 178n27
Wei Wai Kum First Nation, 368n17
Westbank Nation, 298
Wet'suwet'en Nation
  Coastal Gaslink pipeline protests, 4–7, 22n7, 23nn10–11
  Delgamuukw decision (1997) and, 194, 220n16

Wherett, Jill, 81, 82
White, Graham, 278, 355
White and Bob, R. v. (1965), 201–2
Whitecap Dakota Nation, 326n3
Whiteduck, Kirby, 283
White Paper on Indian Policy (1969), 52, 140, 143–6, 147–8, 176n7, 229, 253
White Papers, definition, 176n6
White River First Nation, 326n9, 326n11
Whitt, Laurelyn, 31
wildlife management, 359–62
William, Roger, 182
Williams, Shirley (Migizi ow-kwe), 2–3, 21n4
Williamson, Karla Jessen, 2–3, 22n4
Wilson, Bill (Hemas Kla-Lee-Lee-Kla), 177n13
Wilson, Gary, 16, 24n19
Wilson-Raybould, Jody
  on band councils, 10, 24n15, 120, 122, 123
  on Canadian denial of Indigenous rights, 2
  on *Constitution Act,* Section 35, 153
  on "Indian" definition, 74
  on Indigenous citizenship, 69, 71
  on Indigenous sovereignty and nation-building, 10, 27, 169
  on land management, 118
  on Potlatch, 104
  on Recognition and Implementation of Indigenous Rights Framework, 167
  on reconciliation, 19
  on reserves, 117
  on Trudeau government's approach to Indigenous relations, 21n3, 170–1
  on Trudeau's split of Indigenous and Northern Affairs Canada, 165, 178n19
women. *See* gender; National Inquiry into Missing and Murdered Indigenous Women and Girls
Woodfibre LNG, 297–8, 325n2
Wuikinuxv First Nation, 368n17

Xeni Gwet'in First Nation, 182

Yale First Nation Final Agreement (2013), 287n4
Yukon First Nations, 287n1, 307, 310, 311, 326nn9–11. *See also* Kluane First Nation

Milton Keynes UK
Ingram Content Group UK Ltd.
UKHW050624030824
446392UK00002B/12

9 781487 587413